YUCATAN &
MAYAN MEXICO

'an overwhelmingly green
landscape of giant leaves in which
even the trees seem to sweat'

CADOGANguides

Contents

About the author

Nick Rider was born in Coventry, England, where there are no pyramids, although there may be portals to the Otherworld that nobody has quite noticed yet. He lived in Spain for several years and wrote a Ph.D on Spanish history before first travelling in Mexico. He has edited and written for various editions of the Time Out Guides to Madrid and Barcelona, and for Cadogan he has also written *Short Breaks in Northern France*. In preparing the current book he reached the top of Mount Tzontehuitz, nearly foundered on the Xcalak ferry, and took many wrong turnings down Yucatán country roads. He does not know Subcomandante Marcos personally, but he has met a man who drove him in the back of his van once.

Acknowledgements can be found after the Index.

Cadogan Guides
Highlands House, 165 The Broadway, London
SW19 1NE
info@cadoganguides.co.uk
www.cadoganguides.com

The Globe Pequot Press
246 Goose Lane, PO Box 480, Guilford,
Connecticut 06437–0480

Copyright © Nick Rider 1999, 2002
Updated by Nick Rider 2002

Cover and photo essay design by Kicca Tommasi
Book design by Andrew Barker
Cover photographs: Alex Robinson
Maps © Cadogan Guides,
    drawn by Map Creation Ltd
Editorial Director: Vicki Ingle
Series Editor: Christine Stroyan
Editor: Justine Montgomery
Editorial Assistant: Tori Perrot
Design: Jodi Louw, Sarah Lyon, Tracey Ridgewell
Site Plans: Jon Workman
Proofreading: Alison Mills
Indexing: Isobel McLean
Production: Book Production Services

Printed in Italy by Legoprint
A catalogue record for this book is available
    from the British Library
ISBN 1-86011-821-6
Reprinted 2004

The author and publishers have made every effort to ensure the accuracy of the information in this book at the time of going to press. However, they cannot accept any responsibility for any loss, injury or inconvenience resulting from the use of information contained in this guide.

Please help us to keep this guide up to date. We have done our best to ensure that the information in this guide is correct at the time of going to press. But places and facilities are constantly changing, and standards and prices in hotels and restaurants fluctuate. We would be delighted to receive any comments concerning existing entries or omissions. Authors of the best letters will receive a copy of the Cadogan Guide of their choice.

Yucatán &
Mayan Mexico
a photo essay

by Alex Robinson

01

cathedral, Campeche

monastery of San Antonio
de Padua, Izamal

Structure II, Chicanná

murals, Bonampak

relief carvings, Yaxchilán

Temple of the Count,
Palenque

Tulum ruins

birthday party, Xcalak

Campeche

San Cristóbal de Las Casas

cathedral, Mérida

terrace, Hacienda
Katanchel

San Cristóbal de Las Casas

cathedral, San Cristóbal
de Las Casas

coast, Quintana Roo

chilis

mats, Zinacantán

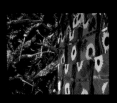

Akumal

cabaña, Tulum

terns, Sian Ka'an

iguana, Tulum

cenote, Quintana Roo

temple excavations,
Toniná

Temple of Inscriptions,
Palenque

The Arch of Labná

Photographers
Alex Robinson © pp.2–20, 22–7.
Tim Street Porter © p.21, reproduced courtesy of
Hacienda Katanchel.
Alex Robinson has taken pictures for various broadsheets
and broadcasters, travelling in Asia, Latin America, Europe
and Australia. He now lives between the UK and Rio.

Introduction

Every country has its stereotypes. Mexico conjures up more than most. Big *sombreros*. Cactus. *Mariachis*. Men sitting against walls half asleep. Tequila. *Enchiladas*. Tropical colour. Romance. At other times and in another, more negative stereotype it's seen, especially by many Americans, as somewhere vaguely threatening, that place down there where they don't behave rationally and you don't know what they're going to do next.

Yet there is much more to Mexico than any of these images. The variety of scenery is tremendous, a whole continent of different terrains and climates. Another feature of Mexico is what can only be called 'density of culture'. What does this mean? It means that Mexico is a world of its own, a world in which patterns of behaviour are distinctive and highly developed, quite often downright cranky, strongly defined by tradition and culture. In its history as an independent country Mexico has never been seriously swayed by any foreign theory or political movement; although Mexicans have often looked over their shoulders to see what the rest of the world thought of them, the nation's triumphs and disasters have always been home-grown. It has its own music, its own food, its own religious cults. And within this self-sufficiency, the human diversity from place to place is immense, an extraordinary richness. This is a place where every new town, every new area, brings a sense of discovery and its own surprises. It is not bland, and it is not a place you can second-guess. And amid all this there are 'Mexican moments' to be treasured, as when you come upon a Scottish theme bar in a small town in Chiapas, or a chapel to the Virgin of Guadalupe right next to a swimming pool.

Modern Mexico is also a world in itself in other ways. Some people still think of it as a 'Third World' country. Several times during the 1990s the country's ruling circles got very excited when US magazines began to discuss whether booming Mexico could be awarded the accolade of permanent 'First World' membership. It is in fact both, or neither. You can find the highest levels of modern technology, and people who farm as their ancestors did centuries before the Spaniards came, existing alongside each other. Every major feature of the 21st-century world can be found in Mexico – ecological problems, luxury, ancient tradition, the presence of the poor – not as discussion topics but as tangible realities, and all together at the same time. With this eclectic mish-mash the country could be a true laboratory of the future, more realistic than any polished-up, hi-tech research facility.

If this can be said of the entire country, it is even more the case in the south. Big *sombreros* have scarcely ever been worn here, except perhaps to please the tourists. Mexico's five southernmost states have always been distinct from the rest of the country. Here 'density of culture' is multiplied 100 times by the presence of the Maya, in the past and very much in the present. They bring a special element into play, with reactions and ways of doing things that easily challenge the preconceptions and habits of industrialized visitors. Rather than any threat, in the Yucatán you encounter an almost gracious courtesy and kindliness now hard to find anywhere else, a rare, seductive atmosphere that needs to be experienced. Few people transmit tranquillity as well as Yucatecans. There are still many twists and paradoxes in the ways of local people, which only adds to the fascination. And as a setting there is a unique set of

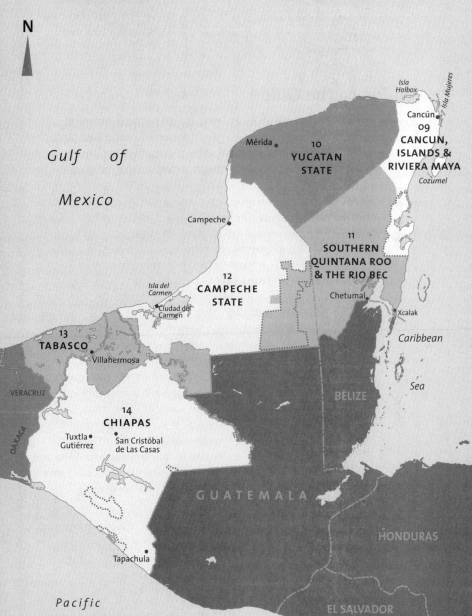

Chapter Divisions

200 kms
100 miles

N

Gulf   of

Mexico

Isla Holbox

Isla Mujeres

Cancún

**09
CANCUN,
ISLANDS &
RIVIERA MAYA**

Mérida

**10
YUCATAN
STATE**

Cozumel

Campeche

**11
SOUTHERN
QUINTANA ROO
& THE RIO BEC**

Isla del Carmen

**12
CAMPECHE
STATE**

Chetumal

Ciudad del Carmen

Xcalak

**13
TABASCO**

Caribbean

Villahermosa

Sea

VERACRUZ

BELIZE

**14
CHIAPAS**

Tuxtla Gutiérrez

San Cristóbal de Las Casas

OAXACA

GUATEMALA

HONDURAS

Tapachula

Pacific

EL SALVADOR

Ocean

landscapes, from dazzling coral reefs, pure-white beaches and turquoise seas, through the cave-riddled limestone brush of the Yucatán to rainforest, swamps and spectacular high, Alpine mountains in Chiapas. Wherever in the five states you choose to sling your hammock, you can easily sway gently for a long, long time without tiring of the view.

A Guide to the Guide

After the photo essay has inspired you, the early chapters of the guide aim to provide all the background information you need to make the most of your trip. Chapters entitled **The Maya** and **History** offer an insight into the turbulent history of Mexico's southern states, throwing light on the great civilization of the Maya and the years of Spanish colonial rule right up to the political issues of the present day. This is followed by **Topics**, a collection of essays drawing out some of the special features of the region. **Food and Drink** introduces the essential flavours of the southern Mexican kitchen, highlighting local customs and regional specialities. Here, too, you'll find a Menu Decoder, including descriptions of some of the most common items on the menu. After this, the comprehensive **Travel** chapter details everything you need to Zget where you're going, while the **Practical A–Z** is packed with useful information and contact addresses, covering a whole range of areas from climate and currency to health, accommodation and leisure activities.

The regional chapters are ordered roughly following the itinerary of a traveller entering the Yucatán through Cancún, its main airport, beginning with **Cancún and the Riviera Maya**, then moving west into **Yucatán State** or south down the Quintana Roo coast (**Quintana Roo and the Río Bec**) and into **Campeche State**, ending with the states of **Tabasco** and **Chiapas**. You could of course follow many alternative routes, especially if you approach from Mexico City and the north. As a rule, chapter divisions follow Mexican state boundaries, with the exception of the Río Bec area of southern Campeche, which is most quickly reached from Chetumal in southern Quintana Roo.

The book concludes with a brief reference section, including a chapter on **Language**, supplying essential vocabulary and a guide to the pronunciation of Mexican Spanish, a **Glossary** of local terms and, finally, some suggestions for **Further Reading**.

The Maya

When the first Spanish expeditions reached the Yucatán peninsula, they thought it was another isolated Caribbean island. Mexico's tropical south has always followed its own history, its own dramas. Fundamentally, the peninsula and Chiapas to the south were the home of the Mayas, very distinct from the cultures of 'Mexico' proper across the isthmus of Tehuantepec, but extending east into modern Guatemala, Belize and Honduras. In art, architecture and trade, in their knowledge of astronomy, the Maya were the most sophisticated of the cultures of ancient America; they were also the only really literate American culture, with a complete writing system, and thanks to the huge progress made in deciphering Mayan hieroglyphs since the 1970s they are now the only pre-Columbian people with a history of names, dates and individuals rather than just an anonymous archaeological record. After the Conquest, while Indian communities were decimated or driven to extinction throughout central Mexico, the Maya and their culture survived more strongly than any other indigenous group in Mexico and Central America. They continue very much alive today.

One of the most remarkable things about the Maya is that our image of them is not some fixed, established text, all set down except for a few details, but has been transformed over the last 30 years, and is still developing. More has been learnt about the ancient Maya in the past two decades than during the previous century and a half, and a great many of what were once accepted facts about them have been put up for grabs. This shifting image only reflects the variety and complexity of Mayan communities themselves. Mayan cities were not all of the same size and style, but changed and developed over centuries. Nor were there only a few giant – and now famous – sites like Palenque or Chichén Itzá; rather, they made up an extraordinary patchwork of communities of different scales and histories, forming a complete civilization. This density and richness give the Maya a very special fascination.

The Land

A very distinctive – sometimes unique – physical setting has provided the background to all human habitation in the region. The whole Yucatán peninsula is one giant slab of very ancient limestone, jutting out into the Caribbean. This Yucatán shelf retains scarcely any surface water. In its northern half it is almost completely flat, and there is not a single surface river north of Champotón, on the Gulf of Mexico, and the Río Hondo, now the frontier with Belize to the east. In contrast to this surface flatness the whole of the slab is riddled with cave systems and underground rivers, access to which is sometimes possible through natural sinkholes called *cenotes* (see **Topics**, p.84). The soil on top of the limestone is very thin: the Spanish Friar Diego de Landa marvelled that 'Yucatán is the land with least land that I have ever seen', and that in many places it was not possible to dig even a shallow trench without hitting bedrock. The natural vegetation this land supports, often called jungle, is more like a huge, dry, brushlike wood, with trees 5 or 6 metres high. This landscape is full of strange phenomena, with many species of trees and plants that are unique to the Yucatán.

For an agricultural people this land imposed special demands, as well as being imbued with a sense of mystery. The whole of the Yucatán and Chiapas has a similar tropical seasonal pattern of a long dry season (roughly November to May) followed by a shorter rainy season, but in the peninsula the rains are less reliable than in many tropical regions, and at times there have been catastrophic droughts. For the lowland Maya water was a divine substance, and awaiting the rains and then keeping or maintaining access to their waters before they ran into the rock – through *cenotes* or ingenious artificial cisterns and watercourses – was a constant obsession.

In the southern half of the peninsula the land is more uneven, with thicker soil and better watered, as it runs into the great plain of the Petén, which extends across

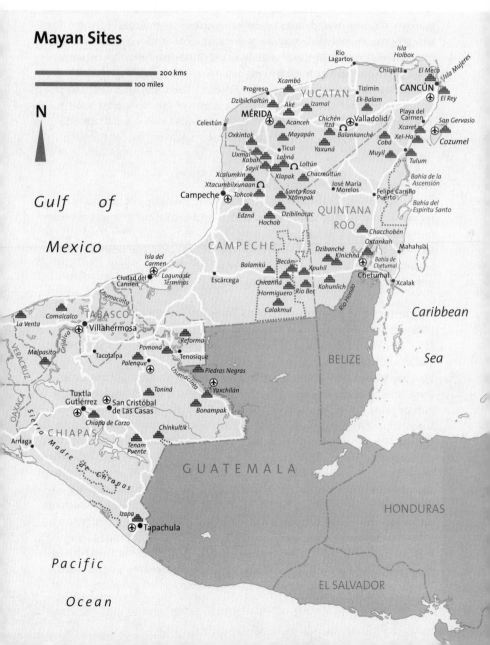

Mayan Sites

northern Guatemala and into Chiapas to the west. Rainfall here is heavier and more consistent, and the Yucatán brush gives way to denser and denser forest, and real rainforest in the Chiapas lowlands and southern Campeche (although today vast areas have been deforested). The most important Classic Maya cities – Palenque, Calakmul, Tikal – grew up in this forest region, although it is likely that at that time (around 1500 years ago) the area had more of a savannah climate than it has now, more amenable to agriculture. To the west it is also crossed by giant rivers running off the mountains to the south, the Grijalva and the Usumacinta. These rivers come together in a wide, swampy delta which makes up most of the state of Tabasco. The radical contrast in the whole Mayan region comes south of Palenque, as the terrain rises abruptly into the Highlands of Chiapas and Guatemala. Temperatures are far lower, pine woods replace tropical forest, and the soil, if thin, is often very rich, in cool, green valleys between massive mountain ridges. Further south again comes an abrupt descent to the narrow plain of the Soconusco on the Pacific coast, another area that's hot, low, lush and very tropical. The Maya have lived in and adapted to every part of the region – the dry Yucatán plain, the rainforest, the delta, and the mountain valleys.

The Eras of Mesoamerican Civilization

Since the 19th century experts have used a common division into historical periods for all the cultures of Mesoamerica (modern Mexico and Central America), as shown on the facing page. This has been challenged in points of detail (some Mayanists call the first era 'Formative' instead of Preclassic, or add a 'Protoclassic' period before the Classic, and boundaries between periods are always up for argument), but in outline remains a universal shorthand when referring to pre-Conquest cultures.

Academics and Adventurers: the Changing Image of the Maya

The story of the rediscovery of the ancient Maya is as remarkable as the actual ruins. Once the different territories had been conquered, Spanish authorities and resident *criollos* lost interest in the ruined cities except as sources of building stone, and most were abandoned to the forest. Reports from the time of the Conquest connecting these cities to local people were forgotten, and they were entirely unknown to the outside world. Among local whites, it became an established truth that *Indios* were too primitive ever to have built such things as cities. Things only began to change in the late 18th century, when King Charles III tried to inject the intellectual curiosity of the Enlightenment into Spain's colonial administration. The king wanted knowledge of every part of his empire, and instructions went out that reports of ancient ruins in Chiapas were to be investigated. In 1787 a captain of dragoons, **Antonio del Río**, was duly sent to survey the utterly remote site of Palenque, hacking his way through the jungle. He compiled the first modern report on a Mayan ruin, with drawings by his artist Ricardo Almendáriz. Copies were sent to Guatemala, Mexico and Spain, along with several artefacts which are now in Madrid's Museo de América. Then nothing happened, for one of the features of this story is the number of times documents were deposited in imperial archives in Spain or Mexico and left completely unread.

Eras of Mesoamerican Civilization

Archaic	prior to 1800 BC	Hunter-gatherers begin settled agriculture and ceramics-making in about 2000 BC
Early Preclassic	1800–900 BC	Olmecs create the first city-civilization, centred on San Lorenzo (Veracruz)
Middle Preclassic	900–300 BC	La Venta takes over as main Olmec city First settled Mayan communities on the Pacific coast, in the Guatemalan highlands, the Petén and in Belize.
Late Preclassic	300 BC–AD 250	The first era of a distinctive Mayan civilization. Mayan writing system and Long Count calendar developed.
Early Classic	AD 250–600	Great flourishing of Mayan civilization. Period of greatest influence of Tikal in the Petén, prior to 562.
Late Classic	600–950	Apogee of Mayan civilization. 562–695, ascendancy of Calakmul in the Petén; 650–800, intensified warfare between southern cities. After 700, in the 'Terminal Classic', rapid growth of cities in northern Yucatán In the 9th century, the 'Maya Collapse' leads to rapid abandonment of the southern cities, but Mayan civilization flourishes for another 100 years in the north. Long Count calendar abandoned. 850-950, ascendancy of Chichén Itzá in northern Yucatán.
Early Postclassic	950–1200	Mayan culture fails to revive in the south.
Late Postclassic	1200–1530	After final collapse of Chichén, Mayapán becomes last 'capital' of Yucatán Maya cities. Trading communities expand on east coast. Some city states form in southern highlands.

The next significant stage came in 1822, when an edition of Del Río's report was published in English in London. It had been prepared by the most extraordinary figure in Mayan exploration, **Count Jean-Frédéric de Waldeck**, from an original bought from a traveller who had picked it up in Mexico. Waldeck was most probably born into a Jewish family in Vienna, in 1766, but for most of his life he was a French citizen, and claimed that his title of 'Count' (never confirmed) had been given him by Napoleon. Nothing about him is certain, for he was a teller of tales about himself of Baron Münchhausen proportions, creating clouds of mystery wherever he went. However, by publishing Del Río's text and illustrations he did reveal the existence of Mayan cities for the first time to a world beyond the Mayan regions themselves or the Spanish bureaucracy. To pursue his new interest in 1825 he moved to Mexico, and after more adventures tried to get its government to pay him to study the ruins at Palenque. Aged 67, he spent a year there in 1832–3, holed up in great discomfort with his Indian mistress in the building now known as the 'Temple of the Count'. Returning to Europe, he published a series of drawings and an account of his travels in 1838.

It has been the fate of the Maya to be the object of other people's fantasies. Waldeck and other early travellers to Palenque shared the colonials' assumption that the local Indians were incapable of building the temples themselves, certainly not without help. Captain del Río suggested Greeks or Romans could have reached this far. Waldeck himself developed a complicated theory according to which the now-extinct American civilization was the work of wandering Greeks, Egyptians, Jews and Indians

Mr Stephens and Mr Catherwood

John Lloyd Stephens and Frederick Catherwood are inseparable from any account of the Mayan lands and Mayan cities. Stephens' books, *Incidents of Travel in Central America, Chiapas and Yucatán* (1841) and *Incidents of Travel in Yucatán* (1843), superbly illustrated with Catherwood's engravings, revolutionized knowledge of ancient American ruins and first made them known to a wide public.

They were an odd pair. Stephens was born in 1805, the son of a wealthy New York merchant. After qualifying as a lawyer at Columbia he became something of a man about town, and dabbled in politics. Campaigning in support of Andrew Jackson in 1834 he caught a throat infection, and it was suggested he travel for his health. Like most men of the Romantic era he was eager to visit Rome and Greece, but unlike others he kept on going to Egypt, Syria and Palestine, becoming the first American ever to visit Petra, before returning via Turkey and Russia. He had not intended to be a writer, but unknown to him some of his letters to a friend had been shown to a publisher, who at once declared them worthy of a wider public. At a time when few Americans could travel so far, Stephens' first book, *Incidents of Travel in Arabia Petraea*, already with his easygoing style, made him an immediate celebrity.

In London on his way home two more things happened that would change his life forever. First, he met Frederick Catherwood. Reserved, intense and fanatically precise, he had none of Stephens' social connections nor his social graces. Born in Hoxton in east London in 1799, he early showed great drawing ability and was apprenticed as an architectural draftsman. After working around Britain he spent ten years travelling in Greece and the Middle East, drawing cities and ancient sites. Back home without money, he exhibited his drawings at 'Burford's Rotunda' in Leicester Square, a display of pictures of exotic places which in those pre-photographic days was a big attraction, and it was at one such show that he met Stephens. Secondly, Catherwood showed Stephens Waldeck's edition of Del Río, bringing to his attention the existence of unexplored pyramids and temples in Mexico. These two dissimilar personalities shared a passion for ruins and an awareness of the thousand questions left unanswered in Del Río's report, and a new double act was born.

On their first trip, from 1839 to 1840, they travelled through British Honduras, Honduras and Guatemala, up through Chiapas to Palenque and then by ship to Mérida and Uxmal. Stephens had with him credentials as US Ambassador to the from India. He was a trained artist (he said he had been taught by David in Paris), but in his drawings shamelessly distorted his material to fit his theories, adding in classical details and even elephants. To publish his book, Waldeck in turn wangled finance out of another eccentric, Lord Kingsborough, who was obsessed with an idea that the ancient American cities were built by the Lost Tribes of Israel. In the meantime another traveller, '**Juan Galindo**', an Irish adventurer (real name unknown) serving as a soldier with the Central American Confederation, visited Copán and Palenque and made the radical suggestion that local Indians and the builders of the cities were the same people, but he died fighting in 1840. This was the state of knowledge before John Lloyd Stephens' first book on the region appeared in 1841 (*see* below).

Confederation of Central America – a job of exploration in itself, since no one was sure such a government still existed, or where it could be found – and conscientiously made side-trips to Nicaragua and Costa Rica. Their first book was an extraordinary success, selling as much as best-selling novels of the time in America and Europe. On the strength of it they thoroughly explored the Yucatán peninsula in 1841–2, this time with no diplomatic responsibilities, for their still more successful second book. After that it was suggested they try Peru, but Stephens had to attend to family business and went back to politics, before getting wrapped up in a scheme to build a railway across Panama and dying there of one bout of malaria too many in 1852. Catherwood published a beautiful separate edition of his engravings in London in 1844, and worked as a surveyor on a railway in British Guyana and with Stephens in Panama before he also died when his ship sank crossing the Atlantic in 1854.

One of the great attractions of the books is Stephens himself: endlessly good-natured, endlessly curious, perceptive, enthusiastic, full of a rather preppy charm and always willing to be distracted by a fiesta or 'charming young ladies'. In the background there is the obsessive figure of Catherwood, making his infinitely detailed drawings in atrocious conditions and through recurrent attacks of 'fever'. A great many passages begin 'Leaving Mr Catherwood at the ruins…', where he stayed alone for days and weeks with his hammock and *camera obscura* while Stephens explored the surrounding villages and their village characters. On several occasions he nearly died, but would not give up, and their first journey only ended when Stephens found Catherwood collapsed by his drawing-board at Uxmal. The result was images of an extraordinary precision that stand up well against modern photographs.

Stephens' greatest achievement stemmed from his generosity of spirit, aided – as he characteristically acknowledged – by the research of Yucatecan scholars such as Juan Pío Pérez: leaving aside the prevailing racism, he and Catherwood were able to see what was in front of their noses, that the builders of the ancient cities had been the region's native people. They effectively 'discovered' the Maya for the outside world: when they set out in 1839, they had only vague references to ruins in Copán, Palenque and Uxmal. They provided the first detailed descriptions of these cities and Chichén Itzá, and brought the first news of scores of other unknown sites. Not the least compliment paid to them is that of all the gringo books on Mexico Stephens' rate consistently among those best-regarded by Mexicans themselves.

After Stephens the next great figure in Mayanology was the **Abbé Charles Brasseur de Beaubourg**, a French priest who worked in Mexico and Guatemala in the 1850s. He discovered and published the manuscript of the *Popol Vuh* (*see* p.47), and then in 1862 found Bishop Landa's *Relación* (*see* p.68) in a library in Madrid, where it had been lying ignored for three centuries. When published it became impossible to deny the connections suggested by Stephens. The information in Landa also made it possible to begin understanding what was then the only known Mayan manuscript, the *Dresden Codex*, believed to have been sent to Charles V by Cortés, and which had reached Germany via Vienna. With the rapid growth of interest in the subject, two more, the *Paris* and *Madrid* codices, came to light in Europe in the 1860s (a fourth, the *Grolier*, appeared in a private collection in the 1970s and is now in the Anthropology Museum in Mexico City). From the 1860s to the 1880s three explorers, **Desiré Charnay**, **Alfred Maudslay** and **Teobert Maler**, French, English and German, took the first photographs of Mayan ruins. At around the same time academic Mayanism began with the work of the great German scholars **Ernst Förstemann**, Keeper of the Royal Saxon Library and so of the *Dresden Codex*, and **Eduard Seler**. Working patiently away many thousands of miles from the heat of Central America, Förstemann worked out the basics of the Mayan calendar and the Mayas' astronomical knowledge.

Archaeological excavations of Mayan sites began with the first expeditions from the Peabody Museum in Harvard in the 1890s. During the 1900s **Edward Thompson**, US Consul in Mérida, bought the site and *hacienda* of Chichén Itzá, and began his amateur excavations by crudely dredging the great *cenote*. Then, in 1914 a young Harvard academic called **Sylvanus Morley** persuaded the Carnegie Institution to fund ongoing research into the Maya. For the next 40 years, led by Morley and his British deputy and friend **Eric** (later Sir Eric) **Thompson**, the Carnegie dominated the field, particularly with their excavation of Chichén Itzá in the 1920s. Their discoveries were enthusiastically publicized by Morley, which is one reason why 'Mayan' features became so prominent in kitsch Art Deco around the same time. They were not the only people working on the Maya, though, for excavations were also undertaken by the Dane **Frans Blom**, who worked for Tulane University in Louisiana and went on to found Na Bolom in San Cristóbal de Las Casas, and the extravagant and unscrupulous British explorer **Thomas Gann**, supposedly one of the models for Indiana Jones. By the 1930s the nationalist culture of the Revolution also led Mexicans to take an interest in their own past at last – and sparked a strong desire to end its appropriation by foreigners – resulting in the foundation of the **INAH**, the National Institute of Anthropology and History. One of its great early successes was the excavations at Palenque led by **Alberto Ruz Lhuillier**, and the discovery of the tomb of Pakal in 1952.

By this time a certain image of the Maya had become established. The early studies were all based on the major buildings of the largest Mayan cities and the codices, and the first great achievements of Mayanism were all to do with deciphering numbers and the complexities of the calendar. The rest of the Mayan inscriptions remained impenetrable. On this basis eminent figures such as Morley presented a picture of the Maya that had considerable appeal to their scholarly minds: in contrast to the Aztecs, who, as the Spaniards had chronicled, were bloodthirsty and militaristic, the Maya appeared as the cultured Greeks of ancient America, a rather ethereal, pacific people ruled by astronomer-priests who spent their time in abstruse calculations and observations of the stars. Morley also put forward the existence of an 'Old Empire' (roughly the area around the Classic cities in the Petén and Chiapas) and a later 'New Empire' (northern Yucatán), terms which still turn up in some books, although it is well established that neither empire ever existed. Another broadly accepted idea was that the Mayan cities were not real cities at all, but only 'ceremonial centres', temple complexes with a permanent population of only a few hundred priests and nobles, to which scattered villagers came only for special ceremonies and rituals.

Simultaneously a belligerent debate had gone on in both institutes and academic journals (beautifully described in Professor Michael Coe's *Breaking the Maya Code*) over whether Mayan glyphs could ever be read as text in any language, in the way Egyptian hieroglyphs had been. Several writers claimed to have found a key to the glyphs – Brasseur, Cyrus Thomas – only to be shot down by eminent figures such as Seler or Eric Thompson, who maintained that Mayan inscriptions were purely ideographic symbols, without any relation to spoken language, and referred only to the calendar, numbers and astronomical calculations. This was a central assumption underlying the idealized, other-wordly vision of the Maya.

This image, however, would be eaten away at from the 1940s, and has been turned on its head since the 1970s. In 1952 a Russian named **Yuri Knorosov** published an article saying that by studying the codices he had worked out a viable system for reading Mayan glyphs, based on the idea that they were neither purely ideographic nor phonetic symbols, but a combination of both, rooted in actual Mayan languages. Thompson, who dominated Mayan studies after the death of Morley in 1948, had spent years in the dust of archaeological sites, and was a ferocious anti-Communist; the idea that a Russian who had never set foot in Central America could see something he didn't appalled him, and for the next 20 years anyone who suggested that Knorosov had a point was battered with all the capacity for sarcastic malice that a Cambridge education can give you.

Nevertheless, the 'abstract' vision of the Maya would also be undermined by evidence harder to dismiss. Belief in Mayan pacifism was shattered by discoveries such as the murals at Bonampak in Chiapas (*see* p.461), which show bloody battles and human sacrifices, and in the 1960s **Heinrich Berlin** and a member of Thompson's own Carnegie team, **Tatiana Proskouriakoff** (born in Russia, but American), demonstrated that many Mayan monuments referred to historical events and not simply the calendar. What has been called the 'great decipherment' really began, however, in 1973, with the first Palenque *mesa redonda* (round table) organized by what could be called the hippy generation of Mayanists. These informal gatherings brought together academics such as **Floyd Lounsbury**, **Peter Mathews** and **David Stuart** with others who were not professionals in the field, like artist **Merle Green Robertson** and art teacher **Linda Schele**. Starting from Knorosov's basic idea and an assumption that the language of the glyphs was related to modern Yucatec or Chol, they began the laborious process of actually reading Mayan inscriptions. One of their first successes was to make out the name of the greatest king of Palenque, Pakal. The decoding of

Mayan Spelling, or the Lack of it

Mayan names and terms are regularly being reinterpreted, so there are different forms and spellings to choose from (for example, it was long thought that the first king of Palenque was Balam-Kuk, 'Jaguar-Quetzal', but experts now tend to think he was the other way round, K'uk-Balam or 'Quetzal-Jaguar'). Some writers also use a set of standard spellings for all Mayan languages developed in Guatemala (with which Campeche becomes Kampeche). However, this is scarcely ever seen in Mexico. For convenience, this book uses the most common current archaeologists' interpretations of historic names, while sticking with the most widely used (if inconsistent) Mexican spellings for places and terms, but you will often see alternatives.

Mayan inscriptions has accelerated ever since: far from being purely abstract statements, inscriptions and carved *stelae* have revealed a complex interplay of dynastic history and religious beliefs, providing an incomparably fuller image of Mayan society.

For years this approach continued to meet with resistance, but since the 1980s not only Palenque but other cities have been given substantial 'histories'. Simultaneously with the 'decipherment' has come a major acceleration in archaeological investigations using modern techniques – such as satellite mapping – which have opened up lesser-known, smaller sites alongside those that have been famous for decades, and focussed on the material minutiae of Mayan life as much as major buildings. These studies have revealed, firstly, a far higher number of substantial settlements than was ever previously recognized, and secondly that the 'ceremonial centres' were actually sprawling agglomerations with complex systems of drained-field agriculture, living cities supporting populations of thousands.

Much of what has been considered 'enigmatic' about the Maya stems from the fact that they do not fit into any of the habitual stages of history invented to describe Europe or Asia. Their sophistication in some areas seems belied by an apparent primitiveness in others. Strictly speaking the Maya lived in the Stone Age. They began to work metals very late, when gold and silver reached them from South America, and then only on a small scale. Like all the pre-Columbian American cultures they did not use the wheel, although in the Anthropology Museum in Villahermosa there are some ancient wheeled trolleys – as children's toys. To know about the wheel but not use it seems deliberately perverse. However, many of the most basic advances in Old World civilization came about due to continual intercommunication between Europe, Asia and Africa: the domestication of the horse, for example, began in Central Asia and spread towards Europe, and metals, crops and foods moved in similar ways. In ancient America, on the other hand, there were only two great centres of civilization, Mesoamerica and the Andean region, with relatively limited contact between them. Left largely to its own resources, Mesoamerica is rich in some things but surprisingly poor in others. In the Mayan region, there are no useful metals, nor a single native animal that could be used as a beast of burden – without which wheeled carts give only a limited advantage. The most intriguing 'enigma' about the Maya is that they developed amid very special circumstances. They 'progressed' less by technical innovation than by complex social organization and the mobilization of collective labour.

Origins and the Olmecs

The earliest human inhabitants of the Mayan region were primitive hunters and gatherers who moved across from Asia and south through North America in the Ice Age, spreading to every part of the American continent by about 14000 BC. Exactly where and when agriculture began in the Americas is still hotly debated, but it seems likely that it started in central Mexico in around 5000–4000 BC with the domestication of maize (corn), always the staff of life on the continent. It would be joined by other staples: beans, squashes, chilis. The next fundamental advance came in around 2000 BC with the invention of *nixtamal* flour, a mixture of maize and white lime powder, boiled together and ground on a *metate* grinding stone. By itself, maize is deficient in some nutritional values, especially amino acids; the creation of this minerally enhanced flour was essential for settled agriculture to be able to support an expanding population. Whether in *tamales* or *tortillas*, *nixtamal* has been consubstantial with civilization in Mesoamerica throughout its history.

Just as inseparable a part of the region's life over millennia is the *milpa* slash-and-burn cultivation system of the maize farmer. A *milpa* is a corn patch. With a new *milpa*, the vegetation is cut down around January, and then burnt off in the spring months to prepare the soil for planting, which has to be timed to the arrival of the rains. Each *milpa* can only be planted for a few seasons, after which the farmer moves on to a new patch, leaving the old one to regenerate. The time this takes varies: in good soils some *milpas* can be used for ten years and left for only five, but in the dry Yucatán plots can often be planted for only three years and then must be left for an equal time or even more. *Milpa* cultivation imposes an unavoidable schedule – to miss the rains is suicidal – which has always set the rhythm for Mayan village life.

These elements of village life were in place by about 1800 BC. The first great civilization to build cities in Mesomerica, ruled by a powerful élite, were the Olmecs. They are a mysterious people, discovered only in the 1920s; they left no writing system that has been decoded, and much about them is still unknown. They emerged in apparently unpropitious territory, the river deltas and swamplands around the base of the Gulf of Mexico, which in later centuries were avoided by other cultures as disease-ridden; however, the delta region provided easy river communications, and abundant food, in fish and the produce of its rich soils. The first great Olmec city was **San Lorenzo** in southern Veracruz, which grew up around 1600–1500 BC and disintegrated for reasons unknown some 500 years later. It was surpassed by **La Venta** in western Tabasco, flourishing from about 900 to 400 BC, the greatest monuments from which are now in the Parque La Venta in Villahermosa.

Straddling – unlike later pre-Conquest civilizations – central Mexico and the Mayan region, the Olmecs were the 'mother culture' of the whole of Mesoamerica. Many traits of Mayan civilization are already visible in the Olmec: a polytheistic religion involving astronomical observations and a cosmos divided between the heavens, this world and the underworld, with constant contact between them; a ritual ballgame played in two-sided courts; and cities built around temple-mountains as a sacred 'base' for the community, for these were Mesoamerica's first pyramid builders. For the Maya and nearly all the region's later cultures civilization was always seen as 'centred' at the foot of a mountain, and, like the Olmec, they sought to recreate this cosmic pattern in symbolic, stylized form with their own pyramid-mountains. Parts of the Mayan calendar may also have been of Olmec origin, and another recurrent image in all Olmec cities is the jaguar, as a god-like, awesome symbol of cosmic forces.

The Olmecs had a unique, dynamic style of sculpture, seen at its best in the giant heads from La Venta now in Villahermosa. They also began the tradition of mobilizing huge collective efforts in the creation of monuments. These heads are all made of giant blocks of basalt, which is nowhere to be found in the delta around the city. The rock had to be brought from the Tuxtlas mountains in Veracruz, over 200 kilometres to the west, on wooden rafts or dragged on rollers over the ground. Major buildings, similarly, must have required the work of thousands for decades to be completed. On a smaller scale, the Olmec were also Mesoamerica's first skilled workers in jade, seen in small figurines left as tomb offerings. Nevertheless, their civilization disintegrated, in a collapse more mysterious than that of the Classic Maya a thousand years later, and their cities were abandoned in about 400 BC.

Classic Maya Society: A World of City States

It is a curious feature of Mayan history that most people see it backwards. The most-visited Mayan sites – Chichén Itzá, Tulum, San Gervasio on Cozumel – all date from the last centuries of Mayan civilization. Very few people visit the oldest proto-Mayan cities, **Izapa**, outside Tapachula near the Pacific coast, from about 300–200 BC, or **Kaminaljuyú**, now mostly buried beneath Guatemala City. From there Mayan culture moved northwards: **El Mirador** and Tikal in the Petén were already monumental cities during the 1st century AD, and early buildings have even been found in the north, at **Acanceh** and **Yaxuná**. The early Maya evidently took a great deal from the Olmecs, whose influence spread south along the Pacific plain – a communications channel throughout history – but among the 'unknowns' of Mesomerica is when a clear division can be drawn between them, and when a full-blown Mayan culture can be said to exist. The defining elements of Classic Mayan civilization – the Long Count calendar, the glyph writing system, the *ahau* system of kingship, styles of architecture – were all established by around AD 250. Recent studies, though, have traced them further and further back, and stress the continuities between the Preclassic and Early Classic eras. The oldest known Long Count date inscription – from **Chiapa de Corzo**, outside the main Mayan area, and predating most Mayan inscriptions – is from 36 BC.

In their inscriptions the Maya showed an awareness of themselves as distinct from other, non-Mayan peoples. However, they were never politically united, but divided, like Ancient Greece, into a mass of city-states, over 60 of them by the Late Classic. They varied greatly in size and power, and a few dominated whole webs of smaller communities as 'overkings', via a range of relationships from loose alliances to direct subordination. The greatest of all these 'superpowers' of the Mayan world were **Tikal** and **Calakmul**, whose rivalry over centuries is one of the central conflicts of Classic Mayan history. Far from being peace-loving, city states of all sizes were continually warring and forming alliances with each other. A fractious disunity can almost be said to have been the Achilles heel of the Maya throughout their history.

The earliest Mayan agricultural communities were made up of groupings of extended families or patriarchal lineages. Within each community, there was little inequality. One reason for the belief that Mayan sites were only 'ceremonial centres' was that it was never understood how this simple society could have grown and how *milpa* agriculture alone could have supported large populations. However, modern aerial and ground surveys have shown that many Mayan cities were surrounded by a web of man-made raised fields, ringed by drainage ditches. Although slash-and-burn continued to be basic to Mayan agriculture, the Maya also developed a range of more intensive farming techniques. With more sophisticated and productive agriculture went a growth in trade, between the Mayan communities and with other non-Mayan peoples in central Mexico and to the south.

As they developed into cities, each of the Mayan centres came under the rule of a single king or lord, called an *ahau* (also spelt *ahaw*), assisted by warrior-nobles called *sahalob* (singular *sahal*; in Yucatec, the ending -*ob* indicates a plural). The institution of the *ahau* served to justify inequality to a society that had traditionally rejected it, by setting up a web of mutual obligation. The *ahau* was far more than just a ruler or the representative of God on earth: he was the actual centre of the religious life of the community, an awesome figure whose survival, together with that of his lineage, and the performance by them of spectacular rituals were essential for the well-being of everyone. In return for this service the *ahau* and *sahalob* called on the populace for massive efforts in building and other labours – which, as far as anyone knows, were made voluntarily. The *ahau* and his lineage 'became' in effect the community. Few societies have ever glorified power and their rulers more than the Classic Maya.

The lords and nobles were, naturally, men, but the enormous emphasis placed on lineage meant that women of royal blood were also accorded great respect, especially if they married into neighbouring royal houses. The most complete surviving image of Classic-era court life we have, the murals of **Bonampak**, show sacrifices, rituals and celebrations in which royal women play a prominent and honoured part. They could also sometimes exercise great power, when a dynasty found itself short of a male heir or a matriarch had to keep control for a young son.

The ritual accession of a new *ahau* was an event of enormous importance in the life of a city, nearly always commemorated in monuments. When a city had some kind of alliance or subordinate relationship with a larger patron this would be mentioned too, and it is through these inscriptions that the intricate network of 'overkingship' has been traced. Calakmul was for many years better known for the extraordinary geographical range and number of its vassals than for the city itself. This system was highly intricate, since there were many degrees of alliances, and an *ahau* who had vassal-cities could in turn be subordinate to someone else. It was also inherently unstable, since a city could renounce its established alliances and seek the support of a new 'overking', risking fierce retribution from its former patron.

Although this was an aristocratic society, the greatest source of wealth, unlike in medieval Europe, was not land but control of and access to trade. Like most Native American peoples the Maya did not have much of an idea of the individual ownership of land, but only of its products. Most land was theoretically held by the community, which allocated it to individual farmers. They were obliged to pay tribute to the élite, who would trade with the excess. Father Landa wrote of the Conquest-era Maya that 'the occupation to which they are most inclined' was that of merchant. From the Guatemalan highlands came jade, amber and obsidian, the natural black glass that was in high demand for jewellery, weapons and sacrificial knives. The Petén produced cotton and cacao, and the Yucatán honey and salt, from salt-beds in the lagoons around the northwest coast. Feathers and flowers were given enormous value among the Maya, as symbols of wealth and natural abundance. All areas produced ceramics, and there was a regular trade in slaves, using captives taken in war.

Festivals in different cities were opportunities for 'fairs', where trading went on. The amounts traded were limited to what could be carried in canoes or on men's backs, but these were luxury commodities and their value was high. Most transactions were matters of simple exchange or barter, but cacao beans or types of seashell may also have been used as money. An important element in this commerce was the Chontal Maya of Tabasco, also known as the **Putunes**. Taking their canoes around the coasts or up the Usumacinta river, they were the greatest traders and transporters of the Mayan world, even though other Maya regarded them as primitive. Trade also led to considerable contact between the Maya and central Mexico, much more than was once thought, beginning in the 4th century AD when **Teotihuacán** in the Valley of Mexico – then the largest city in Mesoamerica – had great influence over Tikal.

A city that was subordinate to another also had to pay tribute to its *ahau*, so that a city with many vassals – like Calakmul – could grow enormously rich. Many images on ceramic vases show reclining lords accepting bundles of cloth or baskets of foods from lesser lords. The *ahauob* and *sahalob* lived well; examination of their remains has shown that they tended to be significantly taller and more robust than the peasants around them. Together with these noble lineages – which must have spread into families of several hundred – other privileged groups included the scribes. Mayan glyph writing was, naturally, a means of communication, but it was never a general system of literacy. Instead, writing was the work of a prestigious specialized caste, forming, like the nobility, hereditary lineages. Some may have been related to royal houses. Each scribe was expected to make personal touches to his inscriptions, as a magical work of art – which is another reason why they are so enormously difficult to decipher. Among the Postclassic Maya there was also a caste of priests alongside the nobility, but it seems that in earlier eras these roles were absorbed into each other.

The opulent way of life of the élite included ornate jewellery, finely-worked clothing and rich foods. The condition of the rest of the population is harder to determine, but in good years, at least, they too seem to have enjoyed a fairly benevolent standard of living. Knowledge of daily life among the Maya gleaned from archaeological remains is supplemented by observations made by the Spaniards among the Postclassic Maya. Father Landa – a generous observer when he saw things among the Maya that he approved of – praised greatly the hospitality shown to all strangers (outside of war), and the way in which Mayan farmers helped each other at planting time. He also noted that all the Maya washed frequently – unlike any *conquistador* – and loved fine scents, decorating their houses with 'very curious and well-worked' bouquets of flowers and herbs. In many palace complexes there are sweat baths (*temazcal*), a Mayan tradition that survives today. All the Maya had a tradition of lavish celebrations, at which men, above all the élite, drank themselves into infinity on fermented chocolate, a kind of mead called *balché* or *pulque*, made from the maguey cactus. This relentless drinking was an inseparable part of celebration, but also had mystical significance; stranger still, among the élite intoxicants were also taken in the form of enemas. They were among the world's first smokers, using raw tobacco that made a much stronger drug than modern tobacco. Ideas of beauty were distinctive: a high, sloping forehead was a mark of aristocracy, and babies' heads were placed inside a kind of wooden clamp during the first months of life to induce it. Teeth filed to points were attractive in women, as were cross-eyes, to encourage which small balls were tied to girls' heads, dangling over their noses. Warriors were elaborately tattooed.

Despite its endless wars Mayan society continued expanding through the Classic era, and the 8th century saw a whole new wave of city-building in central and northern Yucatán. Estimates of the population of Mayan cities have been continually revised upwards: now widely accepted are figures of the scale of 70,000 for Palenque or Calakmul, 60,000–100,000 for Tikal, and 25,000 for Uxmal. The full total may have been over ten million, much more than the same land has supported since then.

Religion, Mythology and the Stars

The Maya had a great many gods and complex beliefs, but they were all based in one mythology and vision. An essential source on all Mayan myths is the *Popul Vuh*, the 'council book' of the Quiché Maya of Guatemala, written down after the Conquest in Quiché but with the Latin alphabet, and discovered by a Spanish priest, Francisco Ximénez, in the 18th century. There are many differences of detail, but the basic elements of the *Popol Vuh* stories have been traced in every area of Mayan culture.

The Maya believed there are three levels of existence, the heavens, the middleworld that we inhabit, and the dark underworld, **Xibalba**. The central creation myth begins with 'everything in suspension, everything in calm, in silence' in the featureless primordial sea, and only the two creator-gods, called Tepeu and Gucumatz in the *Popol Vuh* but translated as **First Mother** and **First Father** from Classic inscriptions (an example of Mayan myths' preference for pairs or groups over single figures, and their tendency to include a female and a male principle). They (sometimes with other gods) create the universe several times, normally four. In the first creation the gods create the animals, but find that they do not praise or nurture them. They next create men out of mud, but they are too soft and dissolve in water. They then make men of wood, but they are too stupid and forget to nurture their creators. In their anger the gods send in a great flood, and the wood-men run into the trees, becoming the monkeys. In the fourth creation, this one, the gods make men of maize, which satisfy them.

The beginning of this final creation is the central era of Mayan myth, when the story of the **Hero Twins** (*see* p.49) takes place. In Classic-era versions of the myth, once the Maize Gods have been resurrected at the Ball Court by their own sons, they grow to adulthood and awaken three sleeping old gods, two of whom are known as the **Paddler Gods** because they take the Maize Gods in a canoe across the primordial sea to the place of creation. There, the Maize Gods rise up out of a crack in the back of a Cosmic Turtle, and direct the old gods to set down three stones as the first 'Hearth of Creation' at the centre of the new universe; 542 days after that they finish their work by sending different gods to set up the four sides of the new creation and raising up the great world-tree, the **wakah-kan** (**yaxché** in Yucatec), between them, to separate the heavens from the earth and form the central axis of the universe. The cosmos having thus been centred, creation could begin.

In the Long Count calendar the laying-down of the stones was held to have taken place on a date corresponding to 3114 BC, on 13 August, and the raising of the tree in 3112 on 5 February, two dates (give or take a few days) which always had tremendous significance for the Maya. In their book *Maya Cosmos* the late Linda Schele and David Freidel argue convincingly that this image of the world-tree corresponds to the shape of the Milky Way as it moves through the night sky, as seen from Mayan territory in mid-August and early February. The three setting-stones represent three stars of Orion, and are still represented in the three hearthstones that are an obligatory part of the cooking fires in many Mayan homes – a typical Mayan transition in scale from the intimately domestic to cosmic vastness in one leap. Obviously, these observations were not actually made in 3114–12 BC, but they could be confirmed each year in the Classic era.

As the prime axis of existence the world-tree is the principal conduit between this world, the heavens and *Xibalba*, and the centre of the four cardinal points (*bacab*, *bacabob* in Yucatec), each one of which is associated with a specific colour and different cosmic forces: east (red), south (yellow), west (black) and north (white). In all Mayan regions the *ceiba* (silk-cotton tree) was held to symbolize the *wakah-kan* and represent spiritual powers. At the same time, the idea of the world-tree, often shown crossed by a bar or a vision serpent representing the Paddler Gods' canoe, means that the cross is as much a Mayan as a Christian symbol, something that disconcerted the Spanish missionaries greatly and has caused great confusion ever since.

The movement of the stars is of course cyclical, and this was only one of many endlessly repeated cycles that the Maya saw in the universe. With a certain sense of ecological insecurity characteristic of Native American religions, they conceived creation not as stable but as requiring regular human intervention to sustain it and guarantee the cycle of regeneration. The gods were not just almighty beings, for gods and men were mutually dependent: the gods created humans to praise 'and nurture them' because they needed to as well as wanted to. Hence the importance of sacrifice. The gods sent humanity life-giving rain; humans gave sustenance to the gods in offerings of food and, above all, blood. Mayan religion was very physical, and fluids – semen, spit, blood – were considered to have great power.

Contact between men and supernatural beings and forces was also possible, and unavoidable, at all kinds of levels. The three elements of existence, if often seen as separate 'levels', sometimes appear more like parallel planes, with only thin barriers between them. In the Mayan conception, the whole world is alive: every part of the environment, animate or inanimate, was possessed of some degree of 'soul' or spiritual energy, although there are certain places, such as caves or mountains, that were particularly important as points of contact with the Otherworld. The world was believed to be full of such power points, and places such as the giant caverns of the Yucatán were naturally seen as the very gates of *Xibalba*.

Mayan religion was essentially shamanistic, focussed around making mystical contact with the gods and conjuring up supernatural forces to the community's aid via these power points. Hence the enormous importance of the *ahau*, effectively the great shaman of the city and in his own person the community's very link to the Otherworld, who became, in ritual, a form of the world-tree itself. It was essential for

Playing Ball with the Lords of Death

The era of myth at the dawn of the current creation is the realm of the 'Hero Twins', another Mayan pair, called Hunahpu and Xbalanqué in the *Popol Vuh* but probably Hun-Ahau and Yax-Balam in the Classic era. They have many adventures, but their central story begins with an earlier set of twins, Hun-Hunahpu and Vucub-Hunahpu. They are great ballgame-players, and play so continuously that they disturb the Lords of Death below the ground. The Lords summon these elder twins down to Xibalba, where they defeat them in a ballgame and kill them. The decapitated head of Hun-Hunahpu is hung in a tree, until a daughter of one of the Lords of Death, defying her father, goes to look at it. The skull spits in her hand and impregnates her. Fleeing from her father's rage the princess, Ixquic, runs from Xibalba into the Middleworld and takes refuge with the first twins' mother, in turn giving birth to the Hero Twins.

As they grow up, their grandmother, mindful of the elder twins' fate, hides their ballgame equipment, but Hunahpu and Xbalanqué make a deal with a rat to show it to them, and become dedicated ballplayers. Like their father and uncle they disturb the Lords of Xibalba, who summon them downstairs. The twins play the ballgame continually with the Lords of Death for days, while each night the Lords submit them to a series of tests. To their fury, the fearless twins outwit them every time, until the Lords decide to burn them. Hunahpu and Xbalanqué, though, are two steps ahead, and instruct two seers to tell the Lords to dispose of the twins' remains in a special way. The twins then go along with the Lords' next trick and jump into a flaming pit.

The Lords of Xibalba, following the seers' instructions, grind the twins' bones into dust and cast them into a river. A few days later, the twins revive with the faces of fish. They return to Xibalba disguised as wild carnival dancers, and perform all kinds of extraordinary feats, including decapitating and reviving each other. So excited are the Lords by this dance they beg to be killed and revived themselves. The twins naturally oblige with the killing, but then do not revive them – thus triumphing over the Lords of Death. They then revive their own father and uncle, Hun-Hunahpu and Vucub-Hunahpu, who are buried beneath the Ball Court of Xibalba. In the *Popol Vuh* Hunahpu and Xbalanqué leave them beside the Ball Court to be honoured for ever after, but in the Classic myth they are reborn as the Maize Gods, who go on to create our universe (*see* p.47).

The story of the Twins is full of archetypically Mayan ideas of regeneration after death, and of a son regenerating his own father. Another striking feature of the myth is that the twins defeat their enemies by wit and cunning, never brute force.

the very continuity of the city that the *ahau* and his lineage performed the central religious rituals, and above all gave their own blood, for royal blood was the most powerful sacrifice of all. In bloodletting rituals, royal women passed cords spiked with thorns through their tongues, while the *ahau* – and sometimes other members of his family and *sahalob* nobles – made cuts in his penis and other parts of the body. Strips of bark paper were inserted into the cuts to soak up the blood, and with them attached the *ahau* danced in an ecstatic trance during which he made contact with his ancestors – another instance of the son regenerating the father – and the gods. Apparently, as in mystical rites elsewhere in the world, they felt no pain (and there doesn't seem to be any record of what was done to bind wounds and prevent infection). At the end of the dance, the paper strips were burnt amid clouds of incense to carry the sustaining blood to the gods. The same rituals also included the sacrifice of prisoners, who, again, ideally needed to be of royal blood, captives from other cities.

Closely associated with these beliefs is the image of the **Vision Serpent**, a two-headed creature that is shown held by or at the feet of an *ahau* in many Classic-era *stelae*, and is an obsessive image in cities such as Uxmal. This was a conduit from this world to the Otherworld and the gods, which the *ahau* 'opened up' through his trance. In some cases it appears that men actually danced with live snakes. Another aspect of the Mayan conception of the soul is the idea that everyone has a 'spirit companion', called a *way*. In ritual dancing, it was believed that people could actually become their *way*, often seen as an animal or mythological beast.

These shamanistic rituals required a suitable space, and in fact the creation of such spaces was one of the Mayas' central activities. As Octavio Paz noted, pre-Columbian traditions were informed by a strong formal sense of order. Underlying much of religion was a desire to maintain order in the universe and so keep it safe for human habitation, against a tendency for it to sink back into primeval chaos. If the gods were regarded as having 'centred' the universe at the moment of creation, Mayan builders sought to repeat the same act time and again, in structures that mirrored directly, and therefore intersected with, the cosmic order. Hence the sometimes astonishingly intricate alignments of major buildings with the movements of stars and planets, and the often rigid, rhythmic geometry of Mayan cities. Mesoamericans – and the Maya above all – were obsessive city-builders because the 'centring' of a community around a ceremonial core was seen as essential for settled life. Mayan temples were built as mountain-like pyramids or with entrances like mythical monsters not simply as symbols but because they actually took on the powers of their natural models, as sacred objects in themselves. In the same way that caves or trees could be points of contact with the Otherworld, so too could power points be created, and the dedication rituals of a temple – bringing it 'alive' with spiritual forces – were vital moments in sustaining a community and linking it to the general pattern of creation.

Within this overall religious scheme there was room for a very varied pantheon of gods, for gods were often seen as divine energies with more than one earthly manifestation rather than fixed beings. In the Postclassic Yucatán **Itzamná**, inventor of writing and god of medicine, was the paramount god, while his wife **Ixchel** was the most important female deity, goddess of fertility, childbirth and weaving. Another god prominent in the dry north was the long-nosed **Chac**, god of rain and lightning. Palenque had its own set of patron-gods, the '**Palenque Triad**'. As good polytheists, the Maya had no problem in absorbing alien gods into their system. In the Early Classic the central Mexican war god **Tlaloc** was imported from Teotihuacán, and in the Postclassic the Mexican feathered-serpent god **Quetzalcoatl** was introduced into the Yucatán with the name **Kukulcán**. Legends across the Mayan lands referred to Kukulcán as a historical figure, but the image of the god also blended in with the older Mayan concept of the Vision Serpent. As a god Kukulcán became the centre of a major cult in Postclassic Yucatán, and the focus of a hereditary caste of priests.

The Calendar and Numbers

If the Maya marked out space, they also marked out time. Seen as a series of repetitive cycles, for the Maya it was a dimension almost as solid as physical space, just as much a part of the structure of the universe. They observed and recorded the passage of time and the movements of the sun and stars obsessively, and their calendrical, astronomical and mathematical knowledge, gained through enormous collective effort – the Mayan records of the movement of Venus were based on observations made over 384 years, all with the naked eye or only primitive instruments – is one of the most remarkable features of Mayan civilization. Each phase within the calendar was associated with different omens and auguries, and the periods at the end of the main cycles of the calendar and the beginning of a new one were considered unstable, and marked by ceremonies as important as those to dedicate a temple.

The calendar was expressed in the simple Mayan bar-and-dot numbering system. It uses only three symbols, a dot for one, a bar for five and a shell-symbol, often more like a bean, for zero, the Maya being, with the Arabs, one of two peoples to have invented the concept of zero. Larger numbers were calculated on a vigesimal basis, in multiples of 20. Whereas our numbers increase in value by a factor of ten from right to left (as in 1,234), Mayan numbers were written in vertical columns, increasing in value by a factor of 20 from bottom to top. So, in a column of numbers (*see* p.53), if the bottom row is two dots above a bar this means seven, in the next row up three dots indicates 3 x 20 = 60, a five bar in the next row means 5 x 400 = 2,000, and two dots in the next line means 2 x 8,000 = 16,000. The total corresponds to 18,067. Taking 20 and not 10 as a base means this system moves rapidly into very large numbers.

The Maya had three different calendar cycles. The simplest was the 260-day **Short Count** or *tzolkin*, believed to be of Olmec origin and the oldest of Mesoamerican calendars. This combines numbers from one to 13 (seven, nine and 13 were special numbers for the Maya) with a sequence of 20 day-names, as in *1-Imix*, *2-Ik* and so on. Once the first 13 is completed the sequences are out of step, and it takes 260 days for the same number-day combination to come round again. The *tzolkin* cycle intermeshes with the **haab** cycle or 365-day year. It is also called the 'vague year', because it does not allow for the fact that the solar year does not correspond to 365 days (the reason we have leap years); Mayan astronomers were aware of this inaccuracy, but seem to have disregarded it. The *haab* year is divided into 18 months of 20 days each. This left five 'loose' days at the end of the year, called the *uayeb*, a time considered

Glyphs for the 18 months in the 365-day count, and the **uayeb**,
the 'unstable' five days at the end of a year

unlucky and full of potential dangers. Hence, if a day in our calendar has three identi-
fiers within a year (Thursday, 14 May), a Mayan day has four, such as *5 cauac 11 yax*
(*tzolkin* number, *tzolkin* name, number in the *haab* month, name of the *haab* month).
It takes 52 vague years or 18,980 days for any one combination of all four elements
to come round again. This 52-year cycle is known as the **Calendar Round**, and was
common to all the Mesoamerican cultures. To this day elements of it, especially the
tzolkin, are still used by the Highland Maya and other indigenous communities.

   The limitation of the Calendar Round was that, with only a 52-year cycle, it had no
way of differentiating between events in successive cycles, making dating events
through the centuries impossible. The Maya compensated with their most awesome
exercise in mathematics, the **Long Count** calendar. Since the oldest known Long Count
date is from non-Mayan Chiapa de Corzo, it seems likely it was first invented by an
earlier culture, but it was only the Maya who fully used and developed it, and then
only in the Classic era. In the Long Count (sometimes called the Initial Series), 20 *kins*

(days) make up one *uinal* (month). Eighteen *uinals* make a 360-day *tun* or year. The system then goes back to 20: so 20 *tuns* make a *katun*, and 20 *katuns* a *baktun*, or close to 400 conventional years. The *baktun* is the largest multiple usually written, but there are plenty more available, into infinity. A period of 13 *baktuns* (around 5,200 years) represents a **Great Cycle**, of enormous importance in the movement of time. According to the 'Thompson Correlation', established by Sir Eric Thompson and now almost universally accepted, the current Great Cycle began on or near 13 August 3114 BC, also the date of the current creation of the earth. All dates in historical time therefore fall within it. This is what makes it possible to date Classic-era monuments with such precision, since so many were rigorously inscribed with Long Count dates. The ending of a *katun* was particularly important, an occasion for ceremonies and blood-letting rituals to ensure the well-being of the city in the new era.

With their several multiples, Long Count dates were written in columns of five numbers or more. The day on which the great Lord Pakal of Palenque was born was 9.8.9.13.0 into the Great Cycle, or 26 March AD 603 (*see* below). The calendar also made it possible for Mayan scribes to place mythological events and prophecies within unimaginable caverns of time, with calculations of baroque intricacy. A *stela* at Cobá recording the creation places it in a cycle that amounts to some 41 thousand, million, million, million, million years. How much the Maya believed in these immense wheels within wheels is uncertain, but they served to express the vastness of the universe. Another feature of the Long Count is that the present Great Cycle is due to end on 23 December 2012. New Agers with an interest in the Maya predict something drastic for that day. It could be a whole new cycle of creation. Optimists can draw consolation from the fact that the combination of calendrical elements is so complex (since the Long Count was always used in association with the Calendar Round, and there are other factors such as the movements of Venus to be taken into account) that establishing one set of omens for the date seems near impossible.

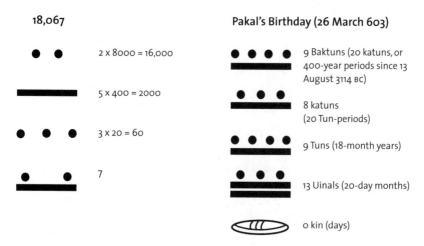

The Mayan numbering system, using columns of bars and dots to represent large numbers and dates.

Mayan Warfare

Ideas of Mayan warfare are another area where accepted notions have been revised several times over. For Mayan cities warfare was a religious imperative. Waging war was an essential proof of the continuing power, physical and supernatural, of an *ahau* and his followers, and was vital to secure royal captives to use as sacrifices. However, it is clear that the Maya also went to war for more conventional reasons – to grab their neighbour's markets, lands and sources of tribute. A successful warrior-state gained in vassals and allies, and grew rich from the inflow of tribute. Conversely, a defeat like those of Calakmul in 695 or Palenque in 711 could lead to a collapse in prestige and a falling away of support, so that a city could became rapidly impoverished.

It appears that these wars were initially quite ritualized, and tended to end once one side felt it had taken enough captives to be considered the winner, prestige being more important than conquering territory. Over time, though, they became more bitter and more destructive. Associated with this change was the introduction of the Mexican war-god Tlaloc from Teotihuacán, in the 4th century AD. Wars intensified in number and their consequences particularly in the Late Classic, especially with the struggle between **Tikal** and **Calakmul** and their many allies, almost as titanic a conflict in the Classic Mayan world as that between Rome and Carthage in the ancient Mediterranean. In 562 a massive defeat of Tikal by an alliance of Calakmul, Caracol and Naranjo established Calakmul as the most powerful state in the Petén; then, from about 650 a resurgent Tikal challenged this ascendancy with a see-saw series of wars that culminated in the victory of 695, which left Calakmul's prestige mortally wounded. The 8th century saw no let-up in more localized conflicts, and it has been suggested that this intensification of warfare was a major factor in causing aristocratic groups from defeated cities to migrate northwards to new cities such as Uxmal and Chichén Itzá, and, equally, a major cause of the general Mayan Collapse.

All these wars took place within the overall context of Mayan belief, and attacks, for example, were often timed to coincide with movements of Venus, closely associated with Tlaloc. The intensification of warfare led to 'revenge wars', as a lineage struggled to avenge the humiliation of an ancestor, and placed strains on Classic kingship, causing some *ahauob* to relinquish considerable power to their nobles. What has been reconstructed of the history of the Classic Mayan cities reveals a web of conflict, intrigue, alliances and betrayal as intricate as anything in Renaissance Italy.

The Ballgame

Centuries before the invention of professional soccer, the Maya already knew all about spectator sport as a representation of broader dramas. The Mesoamerican ballgame was played by the Olmecs and has even been traced in Archaic-era settlements in Oaxaca, making it older than pyramids or temples. It is found in every one of the region's ancient cultures. As the story of the Hero Twins shows (*see* p.49), it was charged with symbolic meaning: in a world where everything was laced with omens and cosmic powers, it represented a chance to defy the forces of destiny. In Mayan cities, ball courts were at the heart of the network of power points that formed the ceremonial core of the city.

No one knows exactly how it was played. In general, there were two main types of ball court in Mesoamerica. The most normal Classic-era Mayan ball court is relatively small, with sloping parallel banks either side of a flat central channel. It was probably played by only two opposing players, or perhaps in doubles or threes. Scoring was probably a matter of getting the ball out of the opponent's end of the court, and it was also essential not to let the ball touch ground in the central channel, although it could be bounced off the sides. In all forms of the ballgame players could not touch the ball directly with hands or feet: instead, they had to use shoulders, backs, buttocks and especially hips. They wore thick leather helmets, pads and belts to protect them as they threw themselves around the court, and injuries must have been common. In the later, central-Mexican variant of the game the ball court is much bigger, with flat sides and large stone rings jutting out from the middle of each side. It was probably played between teams of seven, with scoring a matter of getting the ball through one of the rings (which means it must have been a very low scoring game). This version of the game was introduced into the Mayan area in the Terminal Classic, and is represented by the greatest court of them all, the Great Ball Court of **Chichén Itzá**.

Yet another endless subject for debate is whether defeat always meant death for the loser. It seems possible the game was played both as sport and in solemn ritual. It is certain, though, that ball courts were also places of sacrifice. Held to represent the crack in the Cosmic Turtle through which the Maize Gods emerged to begin creation, they were also gateways to Xibalba. Several Classic-era images, such as the hieroglyphic stairs at Yaxchilán, show an *ahau* playing the game with the heads of captives. Royal prisoners were possibly brought to the ball court for one last combat. Whether they could go free if they won is unknown.

Art and Architecture

Mayan large-scale architecture is intensely theatrical. The role of major buildings as symbolic, sacred spaces, continually reproducing cosmic structures and 'mimicking' natural features, meant that they were often more than anything giant stages for the performance of public ritual. As hot weather architecture, too, the spaces they enclosed – plazas, patios – could be as important as the buildings themselves. Behind the awe-inspiring façades, they could be surprisingly plain.

The veneration of the *ahau* also meant that large parts of Mayan cities were giant monuments to their rulers, against which the populace could appear tiny by comparison. One consequence of this cult was the practice of building on top of existing buildings. Most *ahauob* felt it necessary to continue the work of their forefathers and demonstrate their own sacred powers by commissioning and dedicating their own monuments. Temples were built next to other temples, and pyramids built over existing ones, sometimes when they had only been completed a few decades.

Mayan building techniques were a mixture of the simple and the sophisticated. Most structures were built up by amassing together crude rubble work with a simple form of concrete, which was then clad in smooth or elaborately carved facings in stone or stucco. Characteristic of all Mayan architecture was the 'Mayan arch', a flat-sided upturned V topped by a flat coping stone. The Maya never discovered the true arch, and the rooms that could be built with the Mayan arch, if sometimes long, were narrow. The builders of Chichén Itzá created larger spaces by placing Mayan arches on top of pillars, but these structures were unstable, and have all collapsed. Also, the Mayan arch could only support a certain amount of weight, which is why the Maya were never able to build true buildings of more than one storey. The apparently multi-storey buildings they did produce were created by building up solid masses at the back to support the upper floors, slightly pyramid-style. Mayan-arch roofs could support a 'roof comb', seen in most Classic cities, monumental stone screens that rose out of the top of buildings and were clad in intricately carved and decorated stucco. One prime feature that has been lost is that buildings were brightly coloured: walls were mostly painted red, and carvings were picked out in brilliant blues and yellows.

Temples and pyramids are the most famous Mayan buildings, but large élite residential complexes have been identified. The **Palacio** at **Palenque** is the most famous and complete Mayan palace, but there are many others, especially at **Sayil**, **Kohunlich** and **Comalcalco**. Most follow a similar pattern, with small rooms around connecting patios. Much of court life went on in the open air in these patios, and remains of food preparation have been found in some and not in others, suggesting that the former were the domain of servants. Again, a major feature that can no longer be appreciated is their colour and paintings: the irreplaceable Bonampak murals are the only substantial surviving wall paintings (except, maybe, for the murals recently found at Palenque), and can only leave you breathless when you think what might have been.

What most homes of humbler people were like can be deduced without any archaeological knowledge. Look in any Yucatán village and you can see examples of the *na*, the stick and palm-leaf hut that has housed ordinary Mayan people throughout history, surrounded by a *jacal*, a family enclosure with space for cooking, keeping animals and other daily tasks. Mayan cities were not orderly urbanizations: instead, most were mixtures of clusters of *nas*, stone buildings, raised fields, fruit gardens, open spaces and *milpas* straggling into the forest. Nor were they all uniform, for there were some that were concentrated within a perimeter wall, like **Becán**, and others spread over a wide area, like **Cobá** and **Dzibanché**. Some – notably **Kohunlich** and **Dzibanché** – have a high number of small stone buildings, suggesting, surprisingly, that even non-aristocrats may have lived in them. Mayan builders deployed their techniques with great ingenuity and variety, and could build in brick (**Comalcalco**) or out of a massive mountainside (**Toniná**). Within the overall repertoire of Mayan architecture, some of the most distinctive styles (which ran into each other) have been identified and named (*see* 'Distinctive Styles of Mayan Architecture', facing page).

As well as buildings, another feature of Mayan cities was the ***stela*** or standing-stone. Elaborately carved with reliefs and inscriptions, they formed the ceremonial and historical record of the city. *Stelae* are common in the great southern cities, but much less so in the north. If much Mayan architecture has a geometrical simplicity, Mayan carving often abhors a vacuum, covering surfaces with entangled shapes.

Mayan public art and architecture stresses the awesome, but another element in Mayan art is that 'genres' are not separated, and it is possible to find details of ordinary life portrayed alongside imposing cosmic rituals (this is a striking feature of

Distinctive Styles of Mayan Architecture

Petén: The 'root style' of Mayan architecture, out of which later styles developed. Centrepieces of Petén cities are pyramid-platforms built up in horizontal layers of rublework or plain stone, often with rounded corners, to which ornamentation is added in the shape of elaborately carved stucco masks, stelae, roof combs, panels and so on. Pyramids are often grouped in 'acropolises', with a 'triad' of one huge and two smaller pyramids forming a square plaza open on one side.

Puuc: Uxmal and the Puuc cities have the most refined of all Mayan architectural styles, with an elegant, very 'modern' sense of geometry and a dynamic contrast between plain walls and carved friezes. Buildings that appear completely abstract in form 'mimic' humbler structures: the small drum pillars or 'colonnettes' at the base of walls represent the stick walls of a basic na, and roof friezes often have a line of moulding (an atadura or binding) that represents the ropes around a thatched roof.

Chenes: In the Chenes region of Campeche extravagant carved decoration takes over entire façades of buildings. Temple entrances, especially, are made into the mouths of giant gods and cosmic beasts.

Río Bec: The most theatrical of Mayan styles. The Río Bec cities of southern Campeche have tower-like pyramids with near-vertical false staircases on their main façades. They were never actually meant to be climbed (there was an easier access at the back) but they increased the temples' awesomeness for the crowds below.

Bonampak). Images of daily life, though, are most often seen on smaller objects, especially ceramics. Vases were painted with scenes of Maya eating, smoking, writing and receiving guests, as well as mythology and ceremony. Separate mention is owed to the **Jaina figurines**, clay figures that were placed in graves on **Isla Jaina** off the coast of Campeche. Superbly vivid and naturalistic, they depict every part of Mayan society, and include a wider range of images of women than any other type of Mayan art.

The Terminal Classic and Chichén Itzá

The greatest Classic Mayan cities – Palenque, Calakmul, Tikal – were all in the Petén lowlands and the Usumacinta valley. It used to be thought that the northern Yucatán was scarcely inhabited before around 800, when migrants from the south supposedly arrived to found Morley's 'New Empire'. Modern research has indicated that in fact there was a high level of settlement in the north throughout the Classic era, with major cities such as **Dzibilchaltún** and especially **Cobá**, which was linked to Calakmul. It is true, though, that the 200 years after 700 witnessed an extraordinary effervescence of Mayan culture in the north, perhaps influenced by southern migrants, in what is known as the 'Terminal Classic', with the rapid growth of cities from **Uxmal** and the **Puuc** hills – where most settlements did not exist before 750 – through the **Chenes** to the **Río Bec** and **Dzibanché**. This remarkable burst of activity produced some of the greatest creations of Mayan architecture, especially at Uxmal.

At around the same time, there also appeared a new interloper community among the Yucatán cities: **Chichén Itzá**. Chichén's Mayan-ness is one of the longest-running debates among Mayanists. The first visitors to the site immediately noted the architectural differences between it and other Mayan cities, and its similarities with central Mexican styles. It used to be more or less accepted that the larger, 'new' part of Chichén was founded by an alien people called the Toltecs, who invaded the Yucatán after their capital of Tula, north of Mexico City, was overthrown in about the year 1000. They were said to have created a hybrid 'Toltec-Maya' culture, and in idealistic visions of the Maya were held responsible for introducing bloodthirsty Mexican practices such as mass sacrifice into the Yucatán. By the time of the Conquest it was widely told that the founders of Chichén Itzá had been led by a great king called Kukulcán; however, the same figure also turns up as coming to lead the Quiché Maya, hundreds of kilometres to the south, in the *Popol Vuh*, and Kukulcán-the-mythical-king obviously blended in with the Mexican serpent-god of the same name. Later, most theories went, another alien people called the Itzá followed after the Toltecs, and took over the city in its last years of power.

This image has been comprehensively challenged. The argument is still not over, but investigations have traced 'Mexican' influences at Chichén further and further back in time and stressed the continuity in its history, and it now appears to have always been an unusually mixed, polyglot community, in which central Mexicans and a range of Mayan groups lived side by side (*see* p.240).

This does not mean that Chichén was not very different from earlier Mayan cities. Instead of a single *ahau* it had a collective form of government called a *multepal*, with power rotated between the heads of several lineages. This structure enabled it to mobilize far greater resources and gave it much greater flexibility than its neighbours and rivals. After it defeated Cobá in about 860, Chichén dominated the Yucatán with few major challengers for nearly a century, becoming one of few Mayan cities semi-acknowledged as a regional 'capital'.

The Mayan Collapse

Classic Mayan civilization was still flourishing in the 8th century, at the same time that the great late flowering of the Terminal Classic was developing in the Yucatán. Then, over the next 150 years, city after city ceased to build, gave up marking the major ceremonies, and was abandoned to be reclaimed by the trees. Archaeologists trace the irregular fall of the Classic Maya by the last dates recorded in the Long Count calendar: 795 at Bonampak, 799 at Palenque, 810 at Calakmul, 879 at Tikal.

The 'Mayan Collapse' is one of the great enigmas of history, and there are theories to explain it for all tastes (including extraterrestrials). Some stress the effects of warfare, others climate change and overpopulation, others rebellion by the Mayan masses. Much evidence suggests the Maya fell victim to a spiralling combination of disasters.

With their thin soils and irregular water supplies, the Mayan lands are an ecologically delicate and not naturally highly productive area, and their productivity had been stretched to the maximum. Population had grown continually, and area studies indicate that by the 8th century it had reached – or exceeded – the limit the land could support. Forensic-archaeological excavations undertaken at Copán in Honduras show strong evidence of malnutrition among the lower classes and even the élite at the end of the Classic era. As food ran short, overused land became less and less productive, and farmers extended slash-and-burn *milpas* further and further into the forest. Strong recent evidence also suggests that from the early 9th century there were long periods of drought of unprecedented intensity, which may well have detonated all these crises-in-waiting and pushed Mayan civilization over the edge.

As hardship grew, the peoples of the cities looked to their *ahauob* lords to provide answers and regain the favour of the gods. With the stakes higher, wars became more bitter and more destructive. The Maya were also threatened, like the empires of Rome or China, by barbarians on the fringes, like the Putún Maya, who were raiding up the Usumacinta and into the Petén. A decisive point may have come with a generalized crisis of confidence in each city's rulers. For a society that had always tried to nurture and sustain a balance with the universe, to be hit by incomprehensible disasters to which the sacred *ahau* and his nobles had no response was profoundly undermining, tearing at the bonds of obligation that bound a community together. Revolts spread, and the fall in prestige of the *ahau* is visible in many Late Classic carvings.

Classic Maya civilization, with so much done by collective organization and through the structure of power, was very top-centred, and once the state crumbled a whole city could disintegrate. The collective management of land and the raised-field farming system were dependent on city organization, for it was impossible for individual peasants to maintain the drainage channels by themselves. Most of the caste of scribes, scholars and keepers of the calendar disappeared with the city-states, and with them a great part of Mayan written culture: later communities still used glyph writing, but in a much more limited fashion. Classic-era vases frequently show scribes with bark books, of which there must have been hundreds, but none have survived.

None of this can be stated with absolute certainty, but it appears very likely that the Maya were destroyed by an early, partly self-induced eco-political catastrophe, a demonstration that such things actually can happen. This did not happen in a flash, but over a century and a half. Millions died through drought, famine, wars and revolts. Among the survivors, some *sahalob* founded small-scale, short-lived states, while many peasants just wandered off to find watered land and continue village farming. Huge areas were left nearly empty. The last known Long Count dates come from opposite ends of the Mayan world, Uxmal (907) and Toniná in Chiapas (909).

The Postclassic Maya

The great collapse did not affect every area at the same time, and through the 9th century, while city after city was disintegrating in the south, the cities of the northern Yucatán continued to trade, build and fight each other. From about 900–950, though, the Collapse arrived there too, with a still more intense drought to accentuate the effects of overpopulation. The Puuc cities, always environmentally fragile, were among the first to be abandoned, from around 920 onwards. Decline was never as drastic in the Yucatán as it was in the southern lowlands, and some cities, Chichén Itzá especially, lingered on, but even Chichén was partially abandoned in 948.

Mayan culture remained semi-silent for some 200 years, until the minor revival of the Postclassic began around 1150. Limited to the north – in the south the Collapse was terminal – Postclassic culture appears less sophisticated than that of the Classic Maya. Agriculture regressed, with greater dependence on the *milpa* and less of the complex range of farming methods of the Classic era. In the calendar only the 52-year round was used. The northern cities had never had as many written inscriptions as those in the south, and after the collapse there were scarcely any, although Mayan glyphs continued to be used in bark books. Relative illiteracy has made it much harder to reconstruct the history of the Postclassic than that of the earlier era. However, trade continued, and it was during the Postclassic that the Maya began to work gold, copper and other metals, brought from Mexico or modern-day Colombia and Panama. From around 1350 there was an impressive growth in coastal trade in both directions centred on trading settlements on the East Coast such as **Tulum**, and one theory goes that had the Spaniards arrived 50 years later they would have found the Maya much further advanced in a commercial-cultural renaissance, and much harder to conquer.

Chichén Itzá seems to have survived as some kind of political entity through the collapse, for according to the Mayan chronicles, written after the Spanish Conquest, it was not finally overthrown until the 1190s, by the lords of the newly-founded city of **Mayapán**, last 'capital' of the Yucatán Maya and the last major Mayan city. In style Mayapán was visibly based on Chichén, as if its builders deliberately sought to evoke former glories. It again had a type of *multepal* government, as the lords of Mayapán, the lineage of the *Cocom*, were only first among equals among several *halach uinicob* or 'first men'. Here the Mayan past enters conventional history, as events in the downfall of Mayapán were sufficiently recent to be recounted to the Spaniards. In around 1440 the lineage of the High Priests, the *Xiu*, led a revolt against the Cocom, and the city fell apart. The Cocom withdrew to their lordship at Sotuta, the Xiu to theirs at Maní, and the Yucatán broke up into a patchwork of small, bickering chieftaincies.

History: Conquest and After

04

The Mayan south of Mexico has remained very distinct from the rest of the country since the arrival of the Spaniards. Under Spanish rule the region was outside the Viceroyalty of 'New Spain' ruled from Mexico City: the Yucatán (meaning the whole of the peninsula, before its division into three states under Mexico) under its own administration; Chiapas as part of Guatemala. Both became part of an independent Mexican Republic out of economic convenience and as a result of a series of what were more-or-less accidents, while the Yucatán flirted with complete independence for years. Mexican history is full of statements that could end 'except in the south'. In the 20th century the Mexican Revolution, economic development and modern communications increasingly integrated the Yucatán states and Chiapas with the rest of the country, but the south remains in many ways a world apart.

First Contact

In February 1517 **Francisco Hernández de Córdoba** sailed with three ships and 110 men from Cuba, conquered by the Spaniards a few years earlier, to explore the unknown lands to the west. Driven south by a storm, they made the first Spanish landfall on or near the Mexican mainland at Isla Mujeres, where they saw statues that they took to be female figures – leading them to give it the name 'Island of Women' – and some gold ornaments. From there they followed the Yucatán coast to Kin Pech (Campeche) and, looking for water, put into the bay at Champotón, by the first river they had found. While on shore they were attacked by the armies of the lord of Kin Pech, Moch-Cuouh. Many Spaniards were killed, Hernández de Córdoba himself was wounded, and they were forced to turn back. Nevertheless, this first news of the existence of monumental buildings, real cities and gold in the Americas was electrifying, both in Cuba and in Spain. The following year a second expedition set out under **Juan de Grijalva**, who landed on Cozumel and continued down the east coast to the Bahía de la Ascensión, passing, awestruck, the cliff-top temples of Tulum. Turning back, they retraced the coast westwards: after another clash with Moch-Cuouh at Champotón, they discovered the Laguna de Términos – which led them to think the Yucatán was an island – and the mouth of the river that now has Grijalva's name, before reaching the Panuco river in modern Veracruz. There they first encountered the Aztec Empire, which then dominated all of central Mexico, and saw a rich range of goods including precious stones, fine fabrics and, most magnetic of all, gold and silver.

In February 1519 a third expedition left Cuba under **Hernán Cortés**, with 11 ships, cannon, 400 men and some 50 horses. They too landed on Cozumel, where they were approached by a group of Indians in canoes, from which a solitary figure ran toward them yelling *'Dios, Santa María y Sevilla'* ('God, Saint Mary and Seville'), to avoid being shot. This was **Jerónimo de Aguilar**, a Spanish priest who had been shipwrecked on the Yucatán coast in 1511, and who immediately became invaluable to Cortés as an interpreter. Ignoring the Yucatán and drawn west by tales of gold, Cortés sailed round the peninsula, avoiding Champotón, to land at Xicalango on the Laguna de Términos. The Spaniards defeated a local chieftain, and as part of the booty Cortés was given **La Malinche** (*see* pp.64–5), the former princess who was to prove still more important than Aguilar in the events that followed. In April Cortés founded the first Spanish settlement on the mainland at Veracruz, from where within two years his pocket army would destroy the Aztec Empire and set in stone Spanish rule in the New World.

When the Apollo astronauts landed on the moon, they knew vastly more about where they were going, and had incomparably more back-up from home, than the first Spanish *conquistador* columns as they wandered into the Americas. The wild, greedy bravery involved in their epic journeys at times seems incomprehensible. Small bands of only a few hundred men – down-at-heel aristocrats or soldiers ready to gamble everything for wealth and glory – marching across completely unknown territories, they were frequently terrified. This atmosphere of panic was one element in the savage violence often used against native peoples who resisted.

The Conquest took place differently in the two main areas of Mayan Mexico, Chiapas and the Yucatán, a pattern that has continued ever since.

The Conquest of the South

The first part of the south conquered by the Spaniards was the Pacific plain of the Soconusco, the only part of the Mayan lands dominated by the Aztecs, who used it as a trade route to Guatemala. In 1523, Cortés' troublesome and brutal lieutenant **Pedro de Alvarado** passed through on his way to conquer Guatemala. The following year another column, led by **Luis Marín** – and which included the great chronicler of the Conquest, Bernal Díaz – headed into Chiapas from Veracruz, and after skirmishes at Zinacantán and Chamula discovered the Valley of Jovel, where San Cristóbal de Las Casas now stands. They were entranced by the valley, pronouncing it an ideal site for a Spanish colony. The true conquest of Chiapas would be undertaken in 1528 by **Diego de Mazariegos**, who defeated the Chiapa, a non-Mayan people who then inhabited the western valleys around modern Tuxtla Gutiérrez, and whose warriors supposedly flung themselves into the great gorge of the Sumidero rather than accept defeat. Mazariegos founded the first Spanish town in Chiapas, Chiapa de Indios (now Chiapa de Corzo) on the site of their former capital, and then Ciudad Real de Chiapa (San Cristóbal), a lonely outpost surrounded by Tzotzil Maya villages.

The Yucatán, by contrast, was strangely neglected for several years, while most *conquistadores* headed for the wealth of central Mexico. The Spanish Conquest functioned on a high-risk, semi-private enterprise basis. A noble or commander would secure a royal warrant to explore and conquer some uncharted territory. He himself, though (perhaps with other 'investors'), had to bring together the men and ships necessary and meet all their costs, with only the prospect of first pick of the spoils of conquest and an eventual title and salary as Governor-for-Life as recompense. No one showed much interest in the Yucatán, until at the end of 1526 **Francisco de Montejo** secured from Emperor Charles V the title of Governor and ***Adelantado*** (literally 'he who goes before', or 'first promoter') of the territory. Montejo was a minor noble from Salamanca in Castile, who had made himself rich in Cuba and Santo Domingo, and then served on the expeditions of Grijalva and Cortés before returning to Spain for some years. His 'fleet' reached Cozumel in September 1527 and landed on the Yucatán mainland at Xel-Ha – where tourists now snorkel in the lagoon – to found the first Spanish settlement next to the Mayan town, calling it 'Salamanca de Xel-Ha' in honour of the Adelantado's birthplace. Leaving 50 men there, he then made a six-month expedition into the peninsula, meeting continual resistance and conquering no territory. Returning to Salamanca he found only ten men alive, the rest having gone down with disease, but met up with reinforcements sent from Santo Domingo. With them he sailed to Chetumal, where he was again defeated by the Maya, this time probably led by **Gonzalo Guerrero**, and from there down the coast to Honduras, establishing that the Yucatán was not an island. Then, accepting failure, he withdrew his surviving men and sailed back to more profitable service under Cortés in Tabasco.

At the end of 1531 the Adelantado Montejo, who still held 'exclusive rights' to the Yucatán, decided to try again, taking with him his illegitimate son, a tough young soldier also called **Francisco de Montejo**, *El Mozo* ('the boy'). They landed by the Champotón river – an essential source of water – and again met strong resistance, taking Campeche only after fierce battles during which the Adelantado himself was wounded. Montejo el Mozo then made one of the reckless marches that so often brought results for the Spaniards, leading a small detachment right across the peninsula to the ruins of Chichén Itzá, where he tried to found a Spanish 'capital'. However, the Yucatán Maya lords, completely against the grain of their usual quarrelsomeness, offered concerted resistance, and the divide-and-rule tactics that had been so fruitful for Cortés failed to function. The Montejos were bottled up in Campeche and Chichén,

Guerrero and La Malinche: Two Sides of a Coin

Gonzalo Guerrero and Cortés' aide and mistress Malinche are two emblematic figures in the Conquest of Mexico. Guerrero was an ordinary seaman and soldier who was one of 13 Spaniards shipwrecked on the coast of Yucatán, probably somewhere near Tulum, in 1511. Most soon died as sacrifices, but two, Guerrero and the priest Jerónimo de Aguilar, were kept alive as slaves. Their luck began to improve when they came into the hands of Nacanchán, lord of Chetumal. Aguilar was only given fieldwork, but Guerrero made himself useful to his new lord, using his knowledge of European war to advise on tactics in inter-Mayan conflicts. From a slave he became a trusted warrior, and married one of Nacanchán's own family, possibly his daughter. When Spanish ships were seen off the coast in 1519 and Aguilar urged that they should escape to find them, Guerrero refused to go, no matter how much the priest argued with him and warned he could lose his eternal soul. Condemned by Cortés as a traitor, he is thought to have played a decisive part in later Spanish defeats at Chetumal, Champotón and other battles in the Yucatán. He is believed to have died in about 1536, fighting the Spaniards in Honduras.

La Malinche, on the other hand (real name probably *Malintzín*), was a princess from Jalisco in west-central Mexico. Captured in war, she was made a slave and passed between owners in Yucatán and Tabasco before she was given to Cortés. She spoke Nahuatl and Yucatec, while Aguilar spoke Yucatec. Between them they gave Cortés a key to the Aztec Empire. Malinche's role went well beyond that of an interpreter, learning Spanish and being credited with advising Cortés on how to trick and defeat the Aztecs at decisive moments. She also had several children with the commander.

their men began to desert them, and in 1534 they gave up, and withdrew. Once again, the Adelantado had gained no return from a very large investment, and he went back to serve elsewhere as Governor of Honduras and, later, Chiapas.

In 1540 the Adelantado delegated his powers to El Mozo to have one more try. This time he had with him yet another **Francisco de Montejo,** *El Sobrino* ('the nephew', as the Adelantado was his uncle). In the interim the Maya had been weakened by disease – the Spaniards' most effective advance guard – and drought, and had fallen back into fighting against each other, with a bitter dispute between the Cocom and the Xiu. Nevertheless, initially they still gave effective joint resistance to the invaders. The Montejos again landed at Champotón and Campeche, fortunately finding that the belligerent old lord Moch-Cuouh had died, although they still had to fight off repeated attacks. From there Montejo el Sobrino struggled north to establish himself in the ruined Mayan city of Ti'ho, where he was joined by El Mozo. They and their 200 men were then surrounded in a months-long siege, which reached its climax in June 1541 with frontal attacks by thousands of Maya, slashed down in ranks by gunfire, until one murderous day when Mayan morale seemed to collapse, and their force began to break up. The Spaniards had thought themselves doomed, and took their survival as clear evidence of divine intervention. Shortly afterwards **Tutul Xiu**, Lord of Maní, came to the Spanish camp to accept Catholicism and the rule of the kings of

As symbols Guerrero and Malinche are regarded very differently in modern Mexico, *machismo* playing an obvious part in the interpretations. A giant statue of Guerrero and his Mayan family stands outside modern Chetumal, proclaiming the town as the *Cuna del Mestizaje* or 'cradle of racial mixing'. His decision to stay with his family is presented as a manly choice, a noble gesture of early multi-culturalism. There are no monuments to La Malinche, although she does figure in one of the most powerful images by the great mural painter José Clemente Orozco, *Cortés y La Malinche*. Traditionally she is Cortés' whore, selling herself for Spanish baubles. As the ultimate humiliation, she was discarded by Cortés when he went back to Spain to be made a *marqués* and marry a high-born Spanish woman. *Malinchismo* is part of the special terminology of Mexican nationalism, a contemptuous word used to condemn a supposedly uncritical acceptance of anything foreign.

In the motivations of the original individuals, though, there seems to have been plenty of ambiguity. According to Bernal Díaz, when Aguilar argued that they should go to meet Cortés, Guerrero answered, 'I have a wife and three children, and they consider me a lord...you go with God, for I have tattoos on my face and holes in my ears [the marks of a Mayan warrior]; what will the Spaniards say about me when they see me like this?', suggesting a fear of the consequences of returning, and a sense that he had just gone too far to go back. Malinche, for her part, was already a slave, and it appears that, baptized as 'Doña Marina' and accorded considerable respect, she was treated better by the Spaniards than she had been at many times in her life, certainly until Cortés left her. Either way, as figures of myth these two represent different sides of *mestizo* Mexico's very complex attitudes towards its origins.

Castile, thus breaking the Maya front. As so often, disunity let the Maya down, and the local lords could be picked off one by one. Mérida was founded in the ruins of Ti'ho in January 1542 and, over the following year, Montejo el Mozo defeated the most important of the Mayan lords, **Nachi Cocom** of Sotuta. By 1546 the Yucatán was considered sufficiently subdued for the Adelantado Montejo to return to take up his governorship – only to meet a major Mayan revolt, which took months to overcome.

The Yucatán Maya had resisted the Conquest longer and more effectively than any other major pre-Columbian culture. Moreover, some Maya remained outside Spanish control for years to come. The Itzá kingdom on Lake Tayasal in the Guatemalan Petén – near modern Flores – had been visited by Cortés himself in 1525, when he passed through on his way to Honduras, but resisted all attempts to conquer it until 1697.

The *Encomienda* and the Cross: Colonial Society

Once a territory was under Spanish control *conquistadores* were rewarded through the *encomienda* system, under which they were given lands and 'entrusted' (*encomendado*) with authority over all the Indians in an area, with the right to demand labour from them. In practice this gave near-absolute power, and there were many instances of Indians being worked to death. At the same time, churchmen were arriving in the colonies to carry out the 'spiritual conquest' of the American population. Different regions were allotted to different Catholic orders: the Yucatán to the Franciscans, Chiapas to the Dominicans. They began by building missionary monasteries – Maní, Izamal and Sisal in the Yucatán, San Francisco de Campeche, Santo Domingo in San Cristóbal in Chiapas – from which to spread out into the countryside.

Conflicts arose between the two 'arms' of the Conquest. Monks complained that *encomenderos* even begrudged their Indians the time to go to Mass. The new landed gentry argued back that all the priests wanted was for the Indians to work for them, on building churches and keeping them comfortable, although some priests – above all the remarkable Bishop of Chiapas, **Bartolomé de Las Casas** (*see* p.485) – defended Indians with intense dedication. *Encomenderos* defied the Church and royal governors with violence. Neither the Spanish crown, nor even the Church hierarchy, necessarily sided with humanitarian priests, but Charles V had already decided more order was needed in his empire. *Encomiendas* were stripped of most of their political powers, and their owners compensated with hereditary estates. However, this still left them with immense power, and in backward areas – such as Yucatán and Chiapas – parts of the *encomienda* system persisted till the end of the colonial era. The Yucatán was to be governed as a separate *Audiencia*, only vaguely linked to the Viceroyalty of New Spain in Mexico, while Chiapas was to be a province of the Audiencia of Guatemala; in practice, each region was largely self-contained under the crown.

In most of Mexico these conflicts took place against a dramatic backdrop: the disappearance of the Indian. According to one widely accepted estimate, there was an indigenous population of 25 million in Mexico, not including the Mayan region, before the Spaniards arrived, while one of the lowest calculations gives 12 million. By the 1630s, there were only some 750,000 Indians left, a staggering decline of at least 93 per cent. Bishop Las Casas claimed that huge numbers were simply massacred or worked to death by the *conquistadores*, but few believe that even at their most brutal they could have been responsible for such a fall in population. As with the Maya Collapse centuries earlier, a complex of disasters built up. Agriculture throughout Mexico rested on a delicate balance: when Spaniards grabbed much of the best land for stock-raising or growing cash crops, this had a catastrophic effect on food production. Food itself was requisitioned by the new masters, and men were marched off to work in building or gold and silver mines, robbing the fields of hands. The dwindling of the labour force was noted and laws issued against overexploitation, but numbers continued to fall. Black African slaves were brought in to make up for it. Of fundamental importance was disease. In its isolation, America had had few diseases. With the Europeans came measles, typhus, flu and above all smallpox, to all of which indigenous people had no resistance. One viceroy of Peru said that Indians stopped having children out of pure depression. The shrinking of indigenous America took place at different rates in each place, but together amounted to the greatest population collapse in world history. In Mexico, many Indian communities were confined to remote pockets, while great areas were taken over by an increasingly *mestizo* society.

Except in the south. Once again, no one knows precisely why, but in the Yucatán and Highland Chiapas population loss, if significant, was far less acute, between 25 and 50 per cent. Diseases seem to have had less of an effect in the Yucatán woods and the Highlands. Of the greatest importance was the fact that in the south there was, as local *conquistadores* soon came to rue, 'no other wealth than the Indian'. To their immense frustration they realized they had drawn the short straw in the Conquest, and that in the Yucatán and Chiapas there were neither precious metals nor other great riches. After a while they accepted that their best source of wealth was simply to extract tribute in food and labour from the Indians. For this to be provided Mayan village farming had to continue, and with it much of the traditional way of life.

This had profound cultural consequences. Across Mexico, even many surviving Indian communities were gradually obliged to learn Spanish. In the south, many Maya had little contact with the colonizers much of the time, and the opposite happened: as Spaniards and 'Mexicans' continually complained, outside the towns even *mestizos* spoke Mayan languages to get by. Some Yucatán communities kept up their traditional chronicles, the books of *Chilam Balam*, in Yucatec but in Latin script, and sometimes the old Mayan aristocracy continued to lead their communities, as *batabob* or headmen. Deprived of trade, the great Mayan source of wealth, they became little richer than other villagers, but were still accorded great respect. In religion, there were severe penalties for lapses into 'idolatry', but the Church never had enough manpower to keep a constant control over the religious life of the rural Maya. This left plenty of room for the development of 'syncretic religion', the often bizarre mix of Catholic and Mayan belief and ritual so characteristic of the south.

The Spanish Empire operated on a caste system, in which political status depended on both race and birth. In central Mexico, this tended to develop into something of a class society, with an important division between élite *criollos* (Mexican-born whites) and a lower class of *mestizos* and Indians. The south remained more colonial, with a major gulf – ironically, given the widespread use of Indian languages – between

Father Landa's Bonfire

Father Diego de Landa (1524–79), first head of the Franciscans in Yucatán and second bishop of the province, is responsible for a great deal of what we know and do not know about the Maya. In 1566 he wrote a 'report' for his religious superiors entitled *Relación de las Cosas de Yucatán* ('Relation of the Affairs of Yucatán'), a painstaking account of every aspect of Mayan life before the Conquest, based on his own acute observations and long conversations with (or interrogations of) Mayan aristocrats. Rediscovered in the 19th century, it also contained information that provided the basis for any understanding of the Mayan calendar and, later, the unravelling of the Mayan glyphs. He also defended the Maya against *encomendero* abuses. However, it was the same Landa who as Provincial of the Franciscans learnt in 1562 that large numbers of the Maya, including many he had instructed in religion himself, were continuing 'idolatrous practices' in secret. Enraged, he organized a giant *auto-da-fé* in front of the monastery at Maní, at which 'idolaters' were beaten, humiliated and tortured to the point of death. He also brought together every Mayan idol, pot or other artefact he could find and destroyed them all, and, as he wrote, 'we found a great number of books [written] in their letters, and because there was nothing in them but superstition and falsehoods of the devil we burnt them all, which had an extraordinary effect on [the people] and caused them great sorrow'.

Today, there are only four Mayan manuscripts in existence. Mayanists never know whether to thank or curse the man in the same breath.

There is a modern Church version of Landa's actions, given on leaflets available near his great monastery of Izamal, which claims that he deeply regretted the cruelty and cultural genocide of Maní, and this was why he was moved to write his *Relación*. All very neat and multicultural, but there is no sign of any such regret in his writings. Landa was a believer. He believed that he was right and they were wrong. His paternalistic concern for the Maya against the *encomenderos* was in no way incompatible with a belief that their religion was the work of the devil, to be beaten out of them if necessary. He did undergo one crisis of faith, in the extraordinary 43rd chapter of the *Relación*, in which he meditates on the sufferings and sacrifices – literally – the Maya were prepared to undergo for their religion, and wonders with anguish whether Christians would be ready to suffer as much for the true faith.

ladinos (all Spanish-speakers, white or *mestizo*, a term used only in southern Mexico and Guatemala) and a surviving Maya world with many traditions intact.

The great hubs of the *ladino* world and Spanish administration were the colonial cities: wherever the Spaniards founded a colony, they founded a city. These followed a set plan, laid down in the *Leyes de Indias* of 1523: a rectangular grid running out from a central plaza, with a cathedral on the east side and a government palace next to it around the corner. This appealed to the methodical mind of Charles V. In the first two centuries after the Conquest, only whites were allowed to live in the central streets. Outside of them were *barrios* reserved for black ex-slaves or *mestizos*, and beyond them were Indian settlements. A sharp division between Spanish-speaking towns and a Mayan countryside appeared by both accident and design.

Colonial Backwaters

As the Conquest faded into memory, the Yucatán and Chiapas settled into their places among the less prominent parts of Spain's empire. A constant problem for the governors of the Yucatán was the continuing independence of the Itzá Maya in the Petén. Spanish authority was even pushed back, for in 1636 a revolt forced the evacuation of Franciscan missions along the rivers of modern Belize, leaving a space later occupied by British pirates. Not until 1697 was Governor Martín de Urzúa able finally to conquer Tayasal. Other thorns in governors' sides were the pirates who had lodged themselves in Belize and the renowned buccaneer haunt of Tris, the Isla de Carmen on the Laguna de Términos. To resist them a 'castle' was built at Bacalar, and Campeche, attacked time and again, was given massive fortifications. Indians were still obliged to offer services to landowners and contributions to the Church, and were held subject to *ladinos* in a hundred other ways. When this pressure became too great there were sporadic revolts, the largest in Chiapas in 1712 and Yucatán in 1761.

The pace of life accelerated a fraction in the 1760s after Charles III ascended the Spanish throne. New-broom governors were sent to distant provinces to modernize the administration. In colonial capitals like Mexico City wealthy *criollos* chafed at being subordinate to Spanish economic controls, and in towns like Mérida groups met to discuss 'advanced' ideas. Ironically, Charles III's reforms probably acted as a spur to opposition, irritating the *criollos* by interfering in their affairs while also giving them more awareness of the possibilities of independence.

Independence

Nationalist sentiments were only tentatively expressed until Napoleon conveniently kidnapped the Spanish royal family in 1808. This had a huge impact in central Mexico. *Criollos* demanded they be represented in the regency that took over government, but were resisted by Spanish-born *peninsulares*, who had monopolized power in the old colonial system. This argument among the wealthy was thrown into sharp focus in 1810 when **Father Miguel Hidalgo**, a free-thinking *criollo* priest in the town of Dolores, launched his *grito* ('cry'), calling on all Mexicans to throw off the inequalities of Spanish rule. It's unlikely he intended to launch a social upheaval, but a ragged army of poor *mestizos* and Indians flocked to join him, and massacred whites irrespective of origin in Guanajuato and Guadalajara. Faced with the awful prospect of a rebellion of the dispossessed, *criollos* and Spaniards drew together to resist the revolt, with equally bloody reprisals. Hidalgo was executed, and after King Ferdinand VII was restored to his throne in 1814 the rebels were worn down in a fierce guerrilla war.

Then, the situation was stood on its head once again. In 1820 radical army officers in Spain took over the government and issued a series of liberal decrees, against slavery and the power of the Church. Revolution was now coming from the centre of the Empire, so Mexican conservatives had a whole new motive for independence. In an extraordinary about-face the Mexican-born commander of the royal army, **Agustín de Iturbide**, made contact with the surviving guerrilla leaders and called on them as patriots to accept his authority in an independent Mexico. Quite naïvely, they accepted. Mexican independence, like that of much of Latin America, thus arrived branded with a profound ambiguity, a combination of mass revolt from below and a movement by a colonial élite aimed precisely at defending their privileges. Many still held on to the idea of a monarchy as a bulwark of social order, and in 1822 Iturbide proclaimed himself Mexico's first 'Emperor'.

The south stood on the margins of these dramatic conflicts. In Chiapas politics were all but nonexistent until the Spanish Empire began to crumble around it. When they heard of Iturbide's new monarchy, the deeply conservative élite of San Cristóbal (then still Ciudad Real, the 'Royal City' of Chiapas) declared their intention to renounce the authority of Spain and Guatemala, and take Chiapas into Mexico. Their predominance in local affairs was opposed by the *ladinos* of the Soconusco and the growing town of San Marcos Tuxtla, who took up the cause of Guatemala or Chiapan independence. After ragged fighting, an equally disorderly referendum in 1824 decided that Chiapas was to be part of Mexico. In the Yucatán educated *ladinos* were more self-aware. When the vacuum appeared in government after 1808 a group of liberals called the **Sanjuanistas** (because they met in Mérida's church of San Juan) emerged to demand reform; then, after Ferdinand VII's restoration local conservatives reasserted themselves through repression, although with nothing like the violence seen in Mexico. As elsewhere, the situation was confused by the liberal coup in Spain in 1820. In late 1821, as news arrived of Iturbide's conversion to independence and it became clear Spanish power was collapsing, the Governor Marshal Echéverri himself called a meeting of important local citizens to discuss the Yucatán's response. It was decided to declare the Yucatán's sovereignty, with a grudging 'conditional' adhesion to Mexico. Then the last Spanish governor departed amid declarations of affection from all the leading figures in the country, in one of the most peaceful transfers of power ever seen.

This was very atypical of the next 50 years in the peninsula and Mexico. Iturbide's 'Empire' lasted less than a year before it went down in the first of many coups. The political argument was generally described as being between Centralists, in favour of a strong Mexican state (frequently led by **General Antonio López de Santa Anna**), and Federalists. The former were normally seen as more conservative, and linked to the Catholic church. Some brave souls evoked the principles of the French Revolution, but many of these revolts and uprisings revolved just as much around crude power conflicts between generals, local bosses and the élites of different cities. The political system was rudimentary, and in whole areas of rural Mexico the real system of power was *caciquismo*, the domination of administration, law and much else by leading landowners. The mass of the population had only walk-on parts in their disputes.

For most of the next century politics in Chiapas consisted of little more than squabbles between the leading families of San Cristóbal and Tuxtla, each of them looking for allies outside the state. The Yucatán had a much more spectacular history. Since many white Yucatecans regarded Mexico as almost as foreign as Spain, there was naturally strong opposition to Centralism, but bickering also arose between Mérida and Campeche. Uprisings, coups and smaller incidents sparked up all around the peninsula, and in 1838 a Federalist revolt against Mexican interference (and taxes) in Tizimín led to the Yucatán declaring its independence. This was the situation when John Lloyd Stephens (*see* pp.38–9) arrived in 1840, finding it led by men who were aware of the Yucatán's limited prospects as an independent state but didn't know what else to do with it. In 1842 Santa Anna sent an army to bring the unruly province back under control, but after several battles and a siege of Campeche, the Yucatecan forces covered themselves in glory and were victorious. The dictator was obliged to accept a peace which left the Yucatán only very loosely linked to Mexico, which was soon fully occupied with the national calamity of the Mexican-American War.

If political life was chaotic, things also changed in other areas after independence. Most *ladinos* could agree that now the country was theirs it was necessary to modernize and develop it, and the obvious way to do this was by extending into the countryside the principles of the market and *laissez-faire* economics they had heard about from Europe and the USA. An argument developed that has resounded ever since, as modernizers identified one special feature of Mexico – the village system of collective landholding, which had survived, even among *mestizo* peasants, from pre-Columbian times – as a specific obstruction to progress. Landowners increasingly took over common lands for their own plantations. At the same time, since Indians had theoretically become equal citizens, they could also be taxed more heavily than ever before. For Indians, then, conditions could get worse with independence.

The Caste War and the Talking Cross, 1847–1901

In 1841 John Lloyd Stephens wrote that he had never seen a people as accepting of 'the most abject submission' as the Yucatán Maya. This only shows how difficult it is to interpret Mayan quietness. A few years later the Maya burst out of their placidity in the most organized, most far-reaching indigenous revolt anywhere in the Americas since the Conquest, and came within an inch of retaking their land for themselves.

Under Spanish rule Indians had never been allowed to have military weapons or serve as soldiers. The post-independence faction-fights, however, required cannon fodder, and some of the Yucatán's generals began recruiting among the Maya, in particular for the revolt of 1838 and the war against Santa Anna. They were promised remission of taxes and the money contributions paid to the Church, and guaranteed rights to common lands. Such was the contempt with which *ladinos* regarded Indians that they clearly felt they could say anything to them without any concern for delivering on their pledges. The Maya, though, felt they had been lied to too many times.

In January 1847, after one more political squabble, Mayan troops in Valladolid ignored their officers and rioted, killing over 80 people and sending shock waves throughout the peninsula. It was noticed that Indian soldiers had not handed in their weapons after the wars, and rumours were heard of meetings between local *batabs*, especially **Cecilio Chi** of Ichmul and the highly respected **Jacinto Pat** of Tihosuco, and that the Maya had acquired more arms from traders in Belize, then British Honduras. One of the conspirators was executed, which, however, only provided the final provocation to action. On 30 July Chi and his men descended on Tepich, south of Valladolid, and murdered the entire *ladino* population, and more attacks followed immediately.

With the news that a *Guerra de Castas*, a 'Caste War' or race war, had begun, a wave of terror ran through *ladino* Yucatán. Vicious reprisals were taken even against the still-peaceful western Maya. The Yucatecan militias, however, were unable to hold back the growing revolt. Columns sent off into the woods to find the rebels were ambushed, their paths were blocked, and they were picked off in the forest with machetes. Town after town was surrounded and besieged. *Ladino* Tihosuco was taken in October 1847, and Peto in February 1848. A peace was briefly negotiated with Pat that would potentially have freed the Maya from the most hated *ladino* impositions, but it collapsed amid distrust on both sides. In March the order was given to evacuate Valladolid, colonial capital of eastern Yucatán, after a two-month siege. Some 10,000 people were left in the town – whites, *mestizos*, loyal Maya, troops and civilians of all ages – and it took them three days to reach safe territory, in desperate panic, as militia units collapsed and Mayan guerrillas slaughtered a third or more of the column. Appalled, **Santiago Méndez**, Governor of the Yucatán, sent identical letters to Spain, Britain and the United States, offering sovereignty over the Yucatán to whichever country would save its civilized population from its fate. The USA, then still at war with Mexico proper, briefly showed interest, but decided against further involvement. Towns closer and closer to the capital fell to the Maya, and even Campeche was attacked, as *ladino* morale fell apart. Mérida was crowded with refugees, who were strung out along the road to the port of Sisal, looking for any boat willing to take them to Cuba, Veracruz or anywhere else. At the end of May 1848 the new State Governor **Miguel Barbachano** wrote a proclamation ordering Mérida to be evacuated, but was unable to distribute it because the printers had already left.

Then the Maya went away. In one of the most extraordinary episodes in this whole drama, winged ants appeared, indicating the early arrival of rain. To the village Maya this meant that it was time to begin their year's planting, without which they could not eat, and so they went home. Some *batabob* argued with their followers to stay, but the general opinion was that they could just as easily come back at the end of the year. Saved at the eleventh hour, however, the Yucatecan militias regained confidence, and set off in pursuit. In order to plant, the Maya had to come out into the fields, where they were vulnerable. Outside aid finally came for the *ladinos*: if there had been no takers among the major powers, there was one country ready to send troops and arms: Mexico – if only the Yucatán would come back into the national fold. There was still savage fighting, but gradually the Maya were pushed back, from Peto in October and Valladolid in December 1848. As so often, the Mayans' chronic inability to act together played its part in their defeat: Cecilio Chi was killed by one of his lieutenants, apparently in an argument over the *batab's* wife, and Jacinto Pat, ablest of the Mayan leaders, was murdered by a fellow chieftain in September 1849. The rebel Maya lost any sense of political direction, and retreated into the forests south of Valladolid.

The Yucatán Caste War was of a totally different order from the political skirmishes of the era, an explosion of the tensions and hatreds of three centuries. The Maya massacred *ladinos*, while Yucatecan troops exterminated and burnt out entire Indian communities. After the war, imprisoned Maya were sold to Cuba as slaves to restore the Yucatán state finances. The effect of the war can still be seen on the map of Yucatán: the eastern 'frontier', an area of growing *ladino* settlement before 1847, was to remain depopulated for the next 100 years. The system of independent village leadership by *batabob* that had survived since the Conquest was fatally undermined.

The war also knocked the swagger out of white Yucatecan nationalism: there were no more serious attempts at independence, and a few years later the old Audiencia was divided as Campeche became a separate Mexican state.

Moreover, the war was still not over. Many of the Maya had accepted defeat, but there were still thousands of rebels in the woods, and they were soon to regain a sense of purpose. The rebel Maya had not abandoned Christianity as they understood it; rather, they denounced the Church and the whites as bad Catholics. Their defeat caused profound confusion, as if God and the spirits had turned against them. Then, in late 1850, one of the Mayan bands, led by a renegade *mestizo* called **José María Barrera**, declared that they had found a 'Talking Cross' by a remote forest *cenote*, a traditional shrine. The Cross told the Maya that God had not abandoned them, that if they followed the instructions of the Cross they would be invulnerable to bullets, and that one day the Cross would lead them to victory. *Ladinos* who heard of this immediately said it was a ventriloquist's act masterminded by Barrera, but within traditional Mayan beliefs the idea that a sacred object should 'speak' was perfectly admissible. The scattered rebel bands became a messianic cult. They founded a town of their own around the shrine of the Cross, **Chan Santa Cruz** – 'Little Holy Cross', a typical combination of Maya (*chan*) and Spanish – which is now Felipe Carrillo Puerto.

Every year, columns of soldiers were sent south into the territory of the **Cruzob** (the followers of the Cross) without achieving any significant victory. On several occasions they took Chan Santa Cruz, but the Maya just fell back, closed the paths behind the troops and cut away at them bit by bit. At other times the Maya emerged to attack and take Tihosuco, the Yucatecan army's main forward base, or make raids deep into pacified territory. The only Spanish town in the southeast, Bacalar, had been taken by the Maya in 1848, and then retaken by the army. In 1857 the Cruzob seized it for good, so that they had the whole Belize frontier to themselves. In Mérida the idea gained ground that, if it was impossible and too expensive to destroy the Cruz Maya, it might be safe just to ignore them in the wilderness. After one last major campaign under Maximilian's empire in 1866, when Tihosuco was besieged by the Cruzob, the frontier town itself was abandoned, and the Maya were left to themselves for years at a time.

The area the Cruz Maya carved out for themselves extended from the Belize border to Tulum. At Chan Santa Cruz they built their 'church', the **Balam Na** ('Jaguar House'), and developed a comprehensive religion and system of authority: a combination of Mayan tradition, Catholicism and 19th-century military organization. They enjoyed an on-off relationship with the authorities of British Honduras, whose traders (entirely unofficially) continued to sell them arms. On more than one occasion they applied to join the British Empire. The passage of time, though, together with epidemics and internal disputes, brought a fall in both Cruzob numbers and morale. Things turned against them in 1895, when the regime of Porfirio Díaz decided it was intolerable that this part of the national territory should be outside government control, and signed a treaty with Britain recognizing its ownership of British Honduras in return for a serious attempt to prevent gun-running across the border. Perhaps just as important as patriotic concerns was a major change that had come about in the background thanks to the soaring demand in the USA for newly invented chewing gum, the natural ingredient of which, *chicle*, is found in huge amounts in the *sapodilla* trees of Quintana Roo. For the first time, the Cruzob's wilderness was potentially valuable, and *chicle*-tappers were pushing at the Cross's frontiers.

In 1901 General Ignacio Bravo and a large army marched into Chan Santa Cruz to reassert Mexican sovereignty. The Cruzob fled to the forest, but no longer had the resources to resist. The story did not end there, though, for in 1915 Salvador Alvarado, Revolutionary Governor of the Yucatán, decided that the Mexican Revolution had no interest in imposing itself on the Maya and, with remarkable magnanimity, withdrew troops from the area. It did not come definitively under government control – by negotiation – until 1930, and even then some die-hard Cruzob retreated to villages north of Felipe Carrillo Puerto, from where they still reject Mexican authority today.

The Empire and the Porfiriato

While the Yucatán was paralyzed by its Caste War, in Mexico history had moved on. In 1854 there was an uprising of more substance than those of other years, bringing to power a group of liberals led by **Benito Juárez**. He was the first Indian to govern Mexico since Moctezuma, although ironically some parts of his great programme, the *Reforma*, were profoundly destructive of traditional Indian life. Juárez's government was the first to give Mexico some of the institutions of a modern state, and in the Constitution of 1857 set out to remake the country in line with the doctrines of 19th-century liberalism, changing, they hoped, a nation of élites and peasants into one of independent farmers. The mass of legal privileges and inequalities left from Spanish times was abolished. In the countryside, village lands were to be divided up and sold off as private plots. Freedom of speech and education, and separation of Church and state, were guaranteed. The intensely conservative Catholic Church, accused of having meddled in politics and held the country back ever since independence, lost its lands, much of its wealth and its special legal powers.

This provoked a violent Catholic-conservative revolt, and another bitter civil war. Juárez was victorious, but in 1861 he announced a suspension of payments on Mexico's massive foreign debts. As there was no IMF around to impose terms in such circumstances, a combined Spanish, British and French fleet appeared off Veracruz to demand payment. The Spaniards and British withdrew after an agreement had been reached, but the French stayed, and against dogged resistance installed the Austrian **Archduke Maximilian** as Mexico's second emperor. In Mexican patriotic rhetoric this episode has always been presented as a foreign invasion, but in fact the idea had been put into Napoleon III's head by Mexican conservatives, whose belief in the value of a monarchy had been intensified by 40 years of chaos, and who had just lost the civil war. In the Yucatán the Empire was actually very popular among the battered white and *mestizo* population, who seemed genuinely taken by its promise of stability. In 1865 Maximilian's Belgian Empress María Carlota was lavishly welcomed in Mérida. In the same year, however, the American Civil War ended, and it was made clear to Napoleon III that the USA would not tolerate permanent interference in Mexico. French troops were withdrawn, and without them the Empire, which had never won control of the whole country, crumbled. Nevertheless the Yucatán stayed loyal, and it was even suggested that if Maximilian could escape there Mérida could become a new capital of the Empire. In May 1867 news arrived that the Emperor himself had been captured by the Republicans in Querétaro, but even then Mérida fought on for another month, as the last redoubt of an empire that no longer existed.

Reinstated, Juárez remained president until his death in 1872. Mexico briefly fell back into a round of rebellions and minor incidents, until in 1876 power was seized by one of Juárez' generals, **Porfirio Díaz**. His reign, the Porfiriato, would last 34 years.

Porfirio Díaz is remembered for the one statement all Mexicans can agree with, '*Pobre México, tan lejos de Dios, y tan cerca de Estados Unidos*' – 'Poor Mexico, so far from God, and so close to the United States'. In his lifetime he also enjoyed an excellent press internationally, as a model leader of a 'backward' nation ('third world' not having been invented). To the financial markets, he was a man you could do business with. First, he imposed order, establishing his authority over local bosses and ending Mexico's reputation for chaos. Secondly, Díaz, himself a tough soldier, surrounded himself with highly educated young men known as the *científicos*, 'scientists', who set out to bring rational progress to the country in line with the spirit of the age. All kinds of commercial development were encouraged, and foreign investment welcomed. That Díaz' authoritarian regime might conflict with the spirit of democracy was openly acknowledged: the great problem of Mexico, it was officially stated, was its ordinary people, who were lazy, stupid and lacking in enterprise. For the nation to move forward, the Mexican masses had to be dragged into the 19th century.

In the countryside, it became clear that the laws of Juárez' *Reforma*, intended to fill the country with small farmers, could also allow big landowners to amass even larger estates. The abolition of legal inequalities had not altered the real balance between rich and poor, while the freeing up of land made it easier for it to be bought and sold. As commercial agriculture boomed, whole villages might find their lands had been sold from under them without them ever being aware of it. Whole states came into the hands of a few dozen families. This was quite right, in the *científico* view, since big landowners would make the land productive, whereas villagers would only misuse it.

The Díaz regime had some phenomenal successes, in its own terms. Its time in power coincided with the great expansion in the world economy at the end of the 19th century. By 1910 Mexico's foreign trade reached ten times its level of 1876, with a huge expansion of cattle ranching, cash crop production and mining. Mexico acquired a rail network, built by European investors, who were favoured by Díaz in order to take the country a little further away from the United States. Oil was discovered and industry appeared, including textiles, iron and cement works. Debts were paid off, and the Mexican government was treated with respect abroad. At times Mexico had one of the highest rates of growth in the world.

However, this, and the acquisition of truly astronomical wealth by some individuals, was not incompatible with a worsening of poverty among the mass of the population. This is a trick Mexico has pulled off more than once, a rebuttal of trickle-down economics. The boom in cash farming led to disruption of food production, and rising prices. Industry was limited to a few places – Mexico City, Monterrey – and wages were pitifully low. Statistics of impoverishment during the Porfiriato are astonishing:

in one estimate, the standard of living of the Mexican poor in 1910 was under half what it had been at the time of Hidalgo's revolt a century earlier. Since then Mexico's booms have regularly failed to touch the depths of poverty in the country.

No part of Mexico witnessed a greater transformation in the Díaz era than Yucatán. It was at last discovered that the peninsula could produce something valuable: *henequen*, a type of cactus used to make sisal rope. The world's ships and factories needed millions of feet of rope, and before the invention of synthetics Yucatán sisal made the best in the world. From the 1850s the value of *henequen* exports increased continually, and the crop, *el oro verde* ('green gold'), dominated the life of the State. This was Yucatán's 'gilded age' when, from a backwater, it became the wealthiest state in Mexico. As elsewhere, *haciendas* were extended by grabbing village lands. Many Mayan estate workers were kept in debt slavery, the system in which a sum of money was advanced to the worker that it was impossible for him to pay off, so that he was as bound to the estate as he had been under the old tribute system.

Modernization also came to Chiapas during the Porfiriato. A *científico* governor, Emilio Rabasa, sought to set progress in motion with roads, schools and telegraph lines. Commercial agriculture began with coffee- and sugar-growing in the north and the Soconusco, and many destitute Maya from the Highlands were lured to work on lowland estates, where debt bondage was even more common than in the Yucatán.

The Revolution, 1910–40

Mexico has had many revolutions but only one Revolution. The great upheaval that began in 1910 is the founding moment of the modern country. Entire books are written, though, attempting to define what it was about. As in 1810, leaders set movements in motion without any real awareness of the forces they were dealing with, events slipped out of anyone's control, and the final outcome was a strange composite that emerged out of the contributions of different elements, some of whom were in outright conflict with each other. No single group came forward to dominate it. The Revolution was intended to bring democracy to Mexico, to create a state that responded to and did not despise its people. It was nationalistic, in politics and culture, an intense reaction to the denigration of everything uniquely Mexican under Díaz. It was expected to modernize the country, in the interests of the whole nation and not just an élite. It was to bring agrarian reform, to give land and security to the country's millions of peasants. International -isms – anarchism, communism – had a little influence, but the Revolution's major tendencies – *Maderismo*, *Zapatismo*, *Villismo*, *Carrancismo* – were home-grown and derived from different leaders' names. They did not issue theoretical statements. At times it could seem like an elevated debate, at others a brawl in a *cantina*. As so often in Mexico, power struggles, egos and personal loyalties could be as prominent as political agreements or differences.

It began very modestly in 1910, as Díaz, then nearly 80, was getting ready for one more rigged election and his seventh presidential term. A mild, wealthy liberal called **Francisco Madero** began a campaign of opposition around the simple constitutional demands of clean elections and a ban on re-election to office. Díaz swatted him aside, but Madero didn't give up. The context of the campaign changed utterly, and the

Revolution began, when all sorts of groups previously ignored by politics revolted in support of Madero: tough cowboys in the northern border states, among them a former bandit, **Pancho Villa**, and village Indians in the southern state of Morelos, led by **Emiliano Zapata**, who had been dispossessed of their lands by sugar planters. In May 1911 Díaz gave up and retired to Paris, and Madero was elected president. This was only the end of the beginning, for the next months saw an explosion of political activity. Zapata's movement issued their *Plan de Ayala*, demanding the immediate return of land to the villages. Madero did not comply, and they continued their rebellion. He increasingly relied on the army to keep order, but the generals despised him. In February 1913 he sent the army commander **Victoriano Huerta** to suppress a coup by the old dictator's nephew, Félix Díaz. Huerta changed sides, had Madero arrested and murdered, and made himself president with a government of old Díaz *científicos*.

In former times, that would have been that, but in the new situation Huerta's brutal act brought forth a wave of opposition. As the country descended into chaos, there were two main centres of resistance: the north, where **Venustiano Carranza**, Governor of Coahuila, led a 'Constitutionalist' alliance with Villa and generals **Alvaro Obregón** and **Plutarco Elías Calles**, and Zapata's growing 'Army of the South'. There were major differences between all the Revolutionary armies, but especially between these two main groups. Zapata's movement was an irregular army of Indians and peasants, led by an Indian who acquired an aura of absolute, unbreakable honesty. Joined by some anarchists and urban revolutionaries they took over *haciendas* and attempted a peasant revolution in Morelos, Guerrero, Oaxaca and Puebla. The northern chiefs and *comandantes* (except for Villa, a strange amalgam) were mostly middle-class ranchers and soldiers, enemies of 'privilege' but no socialists. They had no set views on land redistribution, but seized the estates of anyone who opposed them. Another characteristic of the Revolution emerged: that Revolutionary power could be a very quick way of getting rich. High idealism, brutality and staggering corruption often combined in the same people. One thing most of the northern leaders could agree on was an intense opposition to the Catholic Church, which had supported Huerta and was regarded as an arm of the élite that had consistently held the country down.

By mid-1914 Huerta's counter-revolution was defeated, but fighting broke out almost immediately between Carranza and an alliance of Villa and Zapata. After another year Villa's forces had been broken, but the Zapatistas fought on in the south.

Since chaos was in the essence of the Mexican Revolution, each state had its own story. In the Yucatán, so powerful were the *henequen* barons that they were able to resist the influence of the Revolution for all of five years after 1910. The Revolution finally arrived in March 1915 in the shape of an army sent by Carranza under **General Salvador Alvarado**. A stern radical moralist who imposed the Revolution by decree, Alvarado closed all churches in the state. He also ended debt slavery and imposed on the *hacendados* a single, state-run authority to buy and market *henequen*, and with the profits proposed to build a thousand schools. In all of the southeast the main bridgehead of the Revolution was the less tradition-bound state of Tabasco. In Chiapas the cause of Madero was first taken up by some of the most conservative sectors in the state, who had felt excluded under Díaz, and who, still more bizarrely, incited the Maya of Chamula to revolt for them by insincerely promising land and the abolition of taxes, as in the Yucatán in the 1840s. Led by a Chamula known as *Pajarito* ('bow-tie'), the Indians advanced on Tuxtla Gutiérrez in July 1911, but were beaten back as all the *ladino* factions agreed it was better not to allow the Maya an independent role in political disputes. In 1914 a Carrancista army arrived in Chiapas and attempted to impose Revolutionary control, the opening to years of violence and abuse of power.

At the end of 1916 Carranza, as president, called a national convention in Querétaro to agree a new constitution and give the Revolution some shape. Zapata's followers were not represented, but their persistence meant that peasant demands had to be acknowledged. In **Article 27**, on land, it was declared that there was to be a limit to individual landholdings in each state, and that land would be redistributed to be worked as smallholdings or collectively. The thrust of the reforms of the 19th century, which had tried to destroy the old communal system of village landholding, was reversed. Article 27 was completely vague as to what this might mean in practice, but the Indians' most basic demand was enshrined in law. The 1917 Constitution's most radical provision was profoundly conservative, an appeal to pre-Conquest tradition.

By 1919 the Zapatistas were virtually defeated, and Zapata himself was lured into a trap and murdered by followers of Carranza. Then, since Revolutionary *caudillos* could never stand each other for long, a rift grew between Carranza and Obregón, when the former seemed to be planning to prolong his reign in power in contravention of one of the central principles of the Revolution, the prohibition of presidential re-election. Forced out of Mexico City, Carranza was assassinated by yet another chieftain in 1920. It was under Obregón (President 1920–24), and Calles (1924–8), both from Sonora near the Arizona border, that the consolidation of the Revolution really began. They made overtures to Villistas and Zapatistas. Many labour unions had been formed around the country, and Obregón began the practice of granting favours to some and not to others, in return for their loyalty as political power bases. The Mexican Revolutionary state adopted a belligerently radical style, especially in its clash with the Church. This diverted attention from the absence of any clear position on the country's property system, for the Sonorans were supporters of 'national capitalism', not communists.

Within the archipelago of states all sorts of experiments were still possible. The Revolution had made little use of political parties, but the Yucatán after 1917 saw the rise of the **Partido Socialista del Sureste** (Socialist Party of the Southeast), led by a former railwayman who had fought with Zapata, **Felipe Carrillo Puerto**. In 1922 he was elected state governor and, himself a *mestizo*, caused astonishment by giving his inaugural address in Yucatec. He also required that all official documents be signed in red ink. Beyond these rhetorical flourishes, Carrillo Puerto distributed land to 35,000 families, expanded roads and schools, founded the Yucatán's university and even introduced family planning, although further plans were limited by the declining profitability of the *henequen* trade as the world found other sources of rope. Carrillo Puerto was assassinated in one more factional putsch in 1924, but his work meant that the Revolution brought tangible benefits in the Yucatán sooner than in many parts of the country. Tabasco, meanwhile, became the fiefdom of the Partido Socialista Radical under **Tomás Garrido Canabal**, who sought to eradicate religion, drawing down worldwide condemnation from Catholics such as Graham Greene. In Chiapas, on the other hand, events were still dominated by power squabbles, and many of the Revolutionary reforms went unnoticed in large parts of the state.

In 1928, as his term came to an end and the question of the presidential succession reared its head again, Plutarco Elías Calles decided more institutions were needed to demilitarize the Revolution, give it final stability and prevent the same old crises every four years. He proposed that all the many elements identified with the Revolution – regional parties like that in Yucatán, local bosses – should come together in one single party, the **Partido Nacional Revolucionario**. Together they formed what was called the *familia revolucionaria*, irrespective of their differences. If the PNR was sufficiently inclusive its election would be guaranteed, and for additional continuity presidential terms would be extended to six years, a *sexenio*. Instead of presidential succession being fought over in chaos in the streets, it would be sorted out in smoke-filled rooms. The official party, one of the Mexican Revolution's abiding features, was born.

The high-water mark of the radical Revolution came in the term of the most revered of Mexico's modern presidents, **Lázaro Cárdenas**, 1934–40. He was originally a protégé of Calles, but unlike his old boss had a genuine commitment to land reform. Over 17 million hectares were distributed, and an elaborate structure of state bodies was set up to help communally-owned villages, called *ejidos*, farm successfully. Cárdenas took special interest in the Yucatán, where 25 per cent of estate lands were divided up. Against furious opposition in the USA and Britain he also nationalized the railways and, in March 1938, oil, winning the admiration of all Mexican patriots. The Cárdenas years were also the high point of the cultural transformation of the Revolution, one of its most lasting consequences, as reflected in the paintings and murals of Rivera, Siqueiros, Orozco and Frida Kahlo. Previously, Mexico had turned its back on its American and pre-Columbian heritage, but now it gloried in it, and made it the base of a new national mythology. It was at this time that official interest was first shown in pre-Columbian relics. While Cárdenas was a radical In many of his policies, though, he also built up the PNR, renamed **Partido de la Revolución Mexicana**, as a centralized, professional party of power. In 1946 the PRM in turn became the **PRI**, the strangely titled **Partido Revolucionario Institucional** or 'Institutional Revolutionary Party'.

The Príato

Under its different names the PRI remained in power for 71 years, from 1929 to 2000, one of the longest political reigns in history. Many Mexicans thought that it would never end. The PRI regime was a peculiar institution, which liked to describe itself as 'expressing' the Mexican Revolution and, like the event itself, requires interpretation. Mario Vargas Llosa described the rule of the PRI as 'the perfect dictatorship', because it was never quite perceived as one. Dissidents were rarely prevented from decrying the party in print, and in any case the PRI realized that rather than create martyrs it was much better to flood out criticism with positive adulation from its own friendly media. If more active opposition arose the PRI acted like a sponge, acknowledging some complaints and ignoring others, and suggesting a movement's leaders be found some place in the labyrinth of party organizations, where they would gradually shut up. If this failed, election rigging or the iron fist were still available as last resorts.

Straddling the centre ground, the PRI was able to be all things to all men, maintaining a bizarre pseudo-Marxist-nationalist style and rhetoric in its labour unions, while simultaneously helping some of its other friends to amass some of the largest private fortunes on the planet. With a divided opposition to its right and left, for decades it could present itself as the only viable option for government.

The PRI became a giant octopus, extending into every part of the country. Ever since Obregón, the primary role of the great web of Mexican 'official' unions – run in a rigidly authoritarian, top-down manner – had been that of ensuring support for the party ahead of winning benefits for their members, which were limited apart from the job itself. All kinds of jobs were organized through them, and for millions there was the unspoken fear they might be out on the street if they lost the favour of the local PRI boss who had got them the job, or if the PRI itself lost its leverage. The union membership, in turn, was required to turn out at election time. This system supported a huge party and union bureaucracy, with a pervasive atmosphere of corruption.

Like the Revolution the PRI did not have a set ideology, but its dominant attitudes changed over time. Of the four impulses behind the Mexican Revolution – democracy, nationalism, modernization and land reform – the last of them was the first priority only in the Cárdenas years. If Cárdenas was the most celebrated of modern Mexican Presidents, more influential in creating the present-day country was **Miguel Alemán**, in power from 1946 until 1952. Mexico did very well out of the Second World War, producing goods for the Allies. At the same time PRI tariff policies kept out imports, and Mexican industry expanded into a growing market. Under Alemán it was made clear that nationalism and modernization, through industrialization, were the main objectives, and that growth was more important than any social programme. Giant state enterprises played a major part in industrial development, in cooperation with 'national', Mexican, business. Politicians and PRI officials were also constantly involved in granting concessions, awarding contracts and so on. All this gave hugely expanded scope for corruption. Nevertheless, for a long while this programme seemed very successful: the Mexican economy grew consistently from the 1940s to the mid-1960s, and for once this was reflected in better living standards for many ordinary people.

In the countryside, the great estates of the Díaz era had been swept away, but the *ejido* system failed to satisfy the great hopes pinned on it at the time of Cárdenas. The over-complex structure of credit banks and organizations, intended to help *ejidos* work as modern farms, was underfunded and infected with the same corrosive corruption as the rest of the administration. Without proper support it has been ever more difficult for *ejido* farmers to keep up with changes in agriculture; moreover, in the interests of modernization (or their own interests) state and national governments have consistently favoured private commercial farmers over *ejidos*, when they've had the choice. Article 27 has remained in the Constitution and with it the *ejido*, as venerated institutions, but as something of a nostalgic anomaly within an aggressively expanding commercial agriculture. In addition, where there have been conflicts over land – as in Chiapas – abuses of power have still been common.

In the late 1960s, Mexico's long post-World War summer ended as the economy stagnated, production failed to keep up with accelerating population growth and social tensions became evident. In the 1970s respite came with the sudden rise in the oil price, and another brief boom. Then, in 1982, an oil glut set off a massive economic crisis. Political opposition grew, and the PRI's ability to control elections started to slip. For decades it had held every major elected office in the country, but in the mid-'80s for the first time it began to lose state governorships, to the conservative, free-market **Partido de Acción Nacional (PAN)**. In the 1988 Presidential election opposition centred around the left-wing **Cuauhtémoc Cárdenas**, the son of the great president. Most independent observers consider that he actually won the election, but against huge protests the victor was declared to be the PRI candidate, **Carlos Salinas de Gortari**.

Salinas enjoyed a better press in the USA than any Mexican leader since Porfirio Díaz. For years, US economists and business figures had battered at Mexico's self-sufficient, crypto-Soviet economy of state enterprises, arguing it formed a block to growth. Salinas agreed, and reversed the traditional economic policies of the PRI, privatizing industries, including the banks, ending state subsidies and opening the country to foreign investment. Though his admirers didn't make much of it, this did not mean a total departure from PRI traditions, for many privatization beneficiaries were close friends of the president. Foreign business flowed in, and Mexico once more had one of the highest growth rates in the world. The pinnacle of Salinas' achievement was the NAFTA agreement, binding Mexico into the US economy, for which it was necessary to amend the sacred Article 27 on the inalienable status of *ejido* land. Then, on New Year's Day 1994, the **Zapatista** rebels appeared in Chiapas (*see* p.467). Once again, it was suddenly noticed, a Mexican boom had failed to make more than a dent in overall poverty.

These events were only a prelude to the complete disintegration of Salinas' personal world. In March 1994 his choice to succeed him as president, **Luís Donaldo Colosio**, was assassinated in still-unexplained circumstances in Tijuana, and in January 1995 his own brother, **Raul Salinas**, was accused of contracting the murder of a former Secretary General of the PRI. Scandals emerged one after another, revealing a level of corruption that could astonish even a cynical Mexican public. That guarantee of stability, the monolithic PRI, was falling apart.

An Uncertain New Era

Having been cut adrift from their old state-based policies by Salinas, the mutually bickering elements of the PRI had little to unite them except a desire to stay in power. The new President elected in 1994, **Ernesto Zedillo**, was a compromise candidate who promised to find a negotiated solution to the Chiapas conflict, but then played for time while permitting a massive military build-up in the state. In 1997 the PRI lost its majority in the federal congress, and Cuauhtémoc Cárdenas was elected mayor of Mexico City for the left-wing **Partido de la Revolución Democrática (PRD)**, an unprecedented situation in a system centred on one-party rule. Zedillo, perhaps concerned for his place in history, resisted pressures from the shadowy old PRI bosses and business figures known as the *dinosaurios* (dinosaurs) to deploy the full range of dirty tricks against their opponents, and undertook to ensure that the 2000 presidential election would be the cleanest in Mexico's history. The PRI's best ally was the division of the opposition: much of the middle class had despaired of the PRI and gone over to the PAN, but leftists supported the PRD. The PRI hung on, hoping to survive in the middle.

Before the election the opposition again failed to agree, but the candidate for the PAN, **Vicente Fox**, won support far beyond his own party with his call for change, liberalization, a clean break with the old system and a fresh approach to Chiapas and Mexico's other long-stagnating problems. He won the elections on 2 July 2000, and so finally brought the one-party rule of the PRI to an end. Many commentators observed that only with this changeover of power, 90 years after the Revolution, could Mexico really be called a democracy. The PRI by no means disappeared, but, shorn of support from the top, its different parts have fended for themselves, unsure whether they're still a power structure or a real political party, and riven by factional hatreds.

What has happened in some of the southern states is illustrative. A still greater shock than the presidential election was that at the end of 2000 the notoriously hard-line local PRI lost the governorship of Chiapas to a liberal lawyer, **Pablo Salazar**, supported by a multi-party opposition alliance including the PAN and PRD. In Yucatán a businesslike PAN candidate was elected governor in place of a PRI 'dinosaur' in 2001. In Quintana Roo, meanwhile, a state awash with money from tourism and more dubious business, and where the system of PRI kick-backs had been most pervasive, events took a pulp-fiction turn in 1999 when long-serving governor **Mario Villanueva** went into hiding after the US DEA demanded his extradition for drugs trafficking. He was replaced with a less embarrassing, more 'respectable' PRI figure, and in May 2001 the inimitable Don Mario was arrested outside Cancún, and is currently awaiting trial.

Time has now gone by since the July election, but exactly what the new Mexico will be remains strangely vague. President Fox continues to make optimistic statements about the country having embarked on a new era, but with a distinct lack of definition, and disillusion threatens as people wonder when the substance will arrive. Behind Fox's impeccably liberal personal image there are more traditionally right-wing figures in his party – notably **Diego Fernández de Cevallos**, PAN leader in the Senate – who sometimes seem to play as big a part in the details of government. The biggest disappointment has come in the Fox administration's handling of the Chiapas conflict, which Fox had said he could sort out 'in 15 minutes'. After optimistic months in which it seemed the government had abandoned further confrontation, a new hard-line Law on Indigenous Rights appeared, which did not meet the central demands of the Zapatistas nor of other indigenous groups, nor did it make any progress toward a real settlement. One thing that is clear about Mexico's new, open politics is that things are much more fluid, and that conflicts are visible between Fox and his own supporters, for example, of a kind that were always papered over in the monolithic structure of the PRI. In many ways, Mexico is still feeling its way.

Topics

Cenotes and Caves

The features that make the Yucatán landscape unique are usually noticed little by little: the immense flatness of the scrub, which can make it seem dull, superficially; the thinness of the dusty soil if you kick the ground, revealing that you're standing on one giant ledge of rock; the total absence of rivers, streams or other surface water. Instead, water can be found beneath the surface, in kilometres of caverns within the limestone shelf, accessible only through natural sinkholes in the rock, called *cenotes*.

The word is a Hispanicized version of the original Yucatec, *dzonot*. They can be small water holes with just room enough to pass a bucket through, or huge chasm-like pools, often because a cavern roof, eroded over centuries, has collapsed to open the *cenote* to the skies; in many cases a seemingly narrow entrance can lead into magnificent giant chambers and underground rivers. Until modern machinery allowed wells to be dug or blasted, every Yucatán village needed to be attached to a *cenote*, and the major Mayan cities were built near the largest pools. Where there were no or only inadequate *cenotes*, in the Puuc hills, artificial ones had to be created to retain water in the form of enormous man-made cisterns called *chultunes*. In the Chenes region of Campeche (*chen* means well), where the water table is much further from the surface, the Maya could only obtain water by going down into caverns hundreds of metres below ground, as at the Great Well of **Bolonchén de Rejón** (*see* p.397). As sources of life-giving water and entrances to the underworld, *cenotes* had a special place in the cosmic vision of the Maya, but this aside they are innately mysterious. Some seem like bottomless pits into the centre of the world – the most famous of all, the **Sacred Cenote** at Chichén Itzá, is a prime example – while others that look to be placid pools in fact extend far below, into chamber after unexplored chamber.

They're also magical places in which to swim, with echoing walls, shafts of sunlight and underground water that's wonderfully cool, clean and fresh in the Yucatán heat. **Dzibilchaltún** and the unmissable **Cenote Dzitnup** outside Valladolid are both superb for swimming. In addition, since the attractions of *cenotes* have become more widely appreciated, a greater number of other, formerly half-hidden village *cenotes* are gradually being made known and opened up to outside visitors, especially in Yucatán state (*see* pp.304–8). As the extent of the Yucatán's great labyrinth of subterranean watercourses has become appreciated, *cenotes* have also attracted a growing number of divers, and the area just inland from the Caribbean riviera is now one of the most important in the world for cave diving (*see* pp.206–7). **Dos Ojos** cenote near Tulum is the longest underwater cave system yet found anywhere in the world.

As well as *cenotes* filled with water, the Yucatán limestone is riddled with other cave systems. To the Maya all caves had special significance, and the earliest signs of human presence anywhere in the peninsula have been found in the astonishing caves of **Loltún** near the Puuc hills, with a record of uninterrupted human use dating back to before 3000 BC. The smaller but better-known caves of **Balankanché** near Chichén-Itzá do not have quite such a long history, but still contain extraordinary relics, while to the west, at **Calcehtok**, another huge cavern near the Mayan ruins of Oxkintok holds the added mystery that it is still scarcely visited at all.

Colonial Builders and Missionary Churches

Colonial churches and old patio houses seem as embedded into the scenery of southern Mexico as Mayan ruins, and can appear almost as ancient, a legacy in stone of Spanish rule. The churches, especially, are the product of a remarkable adaptation of European styles to the New World. The introduction of Christianity was carried out almost like a military campaign by the missionary orders entrusted with the Yucatán and Chiapas, the Franciscans and Dominicans respectively. Both had professional priest-architects, principally Friar Juan de Mérida for the Franciscans and Pedro Barrientos for the Dominicans. Each order, however, built in very different ways.

In each region the first large, permanent Spanish buildings were the monasteries, the main bases for the missionary friars. In the Yucatán, **Maní**, the Assumption in Mérida (since demolished), **Izamal** and **Sisal** in Valladolid were all built under the direction of Juan de Mérida. As well as a chapel they all included a plain, massive cloister and an equally solid well-head, built over a natural *cenote*. The first rudimentary churches built to hold services for newly converted locals were *capillas de indios*, Indian chapels, consisting effectively of only one solid wall, a kind of arch containing the altar, coming away from which was a narrow roof of wood and palm leaves to give some shade to the congregation. When these altars were free-standing they were called *capillas abiertas*, 'open chapels', of which one example remains remarkably intact, in the middle of the Mayan ruins at **Dzibilchaltún**. In the monasteries *capillas de indios* were set into the outside walls, in order to 'deal with' as large a number of Maya as possible. This can be seen very clearly at Maní. Another feature of these monasteries was the 'atrium', a great open space in front of the façade that enclosed the Maya brought together for the open-air services at the *capilla*. The best example is the huge courtyard at Izamal. One other characteristic is that they were nearly all built over old Mayan temple platforms. This was partly to take advantage of the existing stones, but it also came out of a desire to show the superiority of the new religion in 'taking over' a sacred spot. Building work was undertaken by local Maya, who had to give one day's work a week to the Church, in the same way that they had given labour services to their communities in building temples.

As far as architectural style is concerned Friar Mérida and his Franciscan colleagues, in line with the tradition of their order, seem to have been austere and practical men with little interest in visual fashions. Although they were working from the 1540s onwards, their buildings refer to a much older Spanish rustic Gothic, and some, such as the **Hospital de San Juan de Dios** in Mérida, are distinctly archaic. Superficially, the early Franciscan churches of the Yucatán bear a resemblance to late-medieval European churches; however, they have very few of the details or decorative features found in even the simplest Gothic churches. Instead, they are up-and-down, slab-sided holy blockhouses, intended to give the true religion a presence every bit as solid as Mayan pyramids. The effect is one of austerity and solidity rather than gracefulness, further increased by the grey Yucatán stone.

After the initial, post-Conquest burst of activity the resources devoted to church building fell rapidly. A more gradual wave of church construction came in the 17th century, the greatest period for colonial religious art in the Yucatán, when several churches acquired ornate altarpieces or mural paintings, as in **Teabo**, near Maní.

The architecture of the Dominicans, in Chiapas, was always more sophisticated and less puritanical. Their first major building, Pedro Barrientos' monastery of Santo Domingo in **Chiapa de Corzo**, reveals a far greater awareness of the styles of the Renaissance, with a light, elegant cloister. They also made clever use of Spanish styles such as *mudéjar* (Moorish-influenced) brickwork and Plateresque decoration, so called because it was seen as reproducing the effects of silverware (*plata*) in stone and plaster. The Chiapas Dominicans also had more contact with the extravagant colonial Baroque of Oaxaca and Guatemala. Consequently their buildings, with their ornate, often exuberant decoration, provide a radical contrast to those further north.

Several of the largest Dominican buildings have fallen into ruin, but there are plenty left in the city of churches, **San Cristóbal de Las Casas**. The summit of 'Chiapanecan Baroque' is the church of Santo Domingo itself, especially its extraordinary 17th-century façade. The Dominicans' openness to decoration also combined perfectly with the tastes and customs of the Highland Maya. The Cathedral of San Cristóbal is painted in ochre, terracotta, white and black, and Spanish heraldic motifs are coupled with traditional local flower designs. Inside, the decoration continues; San Cristóbal's churches have more Baroque altarpieces than any other city in Mexico.

Ecotourism: What Is It?

Ecotourism is one of the buzzwords of modern travel in Mexico. Everywhere you go, local authorities and private agencies are eager to signal their *proyectos ecoturísticos*. This word, though, has two distinct meanings. Sense one involves enabling people to see and experience wildlife, rainforests, lakes, reefs and other natural environments remote from the main centres of development. Sense two refers to sustainable tourism, developing facilities for travellers in such a way that they do not disturb delicate ecological balances. They are often confused, but it's actually quite possible for these two meanings to be seriously (or completely) at odds with each other, since taking tour groups into remote areas in the conditions that many people take for granted can involve the provision of infrastructure – plumbing, roads, 24-hour water – on such a scale that it amounts to a major transformation.

Sense one is the way the word is usually understood in Mexico. You can find the *ecoturístico* label attached to dinky nature parks holding a morose caged jaguar, production-line boat trips, restaurants that are not at all out of the way, just about anything, in fact, that's in any way different from lying on a beach in Cancún. Geared up for big-money beach tourism, though, Mexican private developers don't adapt at all smoothly to the low-level implications of sense two.

To avoid disappointment it's best to be aware of the potential tension between meanings one and two. Like any marketing term Ecotourism can be completely empty, or it can actually mean something, and is open to a great deal of manipulation. Also, the balance between the two sides of ecotourism is complex and shifting.

On the one hand, developers may build their supposed eco-hotel very big so as to maximize return on their investment, while still clinging to the 'eco' banner; on the other, projects with genuinely idealistic objectives may cut low-impact corners just to get going.

There is an argument that says that the most eco-friendly thing one can do for the jaguar and its threatened environment is stay at home and look at them on TV. Then again, even ecotourism projects that don't completely satisfy purist standards can contribute to remedying worse problems. In the Río Bec region of Campeche there are now hotels that enable you to visit the Mayan ruins and wildlife reserve of Calakmul in comfort, where a few years ago there were only very basic huts. Naturally, this involves a substantial change in the life of the area, but one motive behind the introduction of tourism has been a deliberate attempt to create an alternative to constant erosion of the forest. If it becomes a resource, attracting foreign visitors, then local people should have an incentive to preserve trees rather than continually cut them down. Leaving the forest alone as if the people did not exist is not an option.

One reason why rigorously low-impact sustainable tourism schemes are so thin on the ground is that they're very expensive, so that in rural Mexico 'community-based, low-impact' tourism can be a contradiction in terms. Solar energy systems, non-environmentally damaging drainage and so on require such an investment that the obvious way to recoup it is to charge luxury prices. One alternative is to stay on one of the schemes actually run by village people (*see* p.139). They may not meet every low-impact criterion, but their use of resources will necessarily be small-scale.

Ecological Problems in the Region

Any consideration of ecotourism intersects with the real problems in the ecology of southern Mexico. In tropical conditions, delicate and volatile environmental problems cease to be discussion points and become clearly apparent to the naked eye.

Foremost among these problems is **deforestation**. Until the 1960s the state of Tabasco, for example, was almost covered by swamp and forest, which spread right to the edges of Villahermosa; since then, the state has lost 95 per cent of its forest cover and now consists overwhelmingly of cattle pasture and fruit farms. A similar process has been spreading eastward and southward in Campeche and Chiapas. There are two major driving forces behind deforestation. One is the acquisition of land for cattle ranching, the so-called *ganaderización* or 'stock-ization' of the region. The other is the clearing of land by an ever-growing number of poor village farmers. There is a political relationship between the two, which is at the centre of recent events in Chiapas. As ranchers buy up, or simply grab, the good lowland terrain for their cattle, poor farmers and *ejidatarios* have been more or less officially encouraged to avoid problems by moving into supposedly 'vacant' national lands in forested areas such as the Lacandón jungle or southern Campeche. The alternatives, such as better land management in settled areas, have involved too many difficult choices for the political system to deal with. Anywhere there are new roads, such as Highway 186 in Campeche, settlements appear and forest is cleared.

Contacts and Further Information

For a select list of local ecotourism tour agencies, see p.110. The main centres of efforts to promote sustainable development of the Quintana Roo coast are Puerto Morelos and Akumal, which has a Centro Ecológico and the SAVE organization, based at the Villas de Rosa hotel (see pp.202–3).

Eco Travels in Mexico, www.planeta.com/eco travel/mexico (see p.136). A useful resource.

RARE Center for Tropical Conservation (www.rarecenter.org). An organization based in the US, specializing in the development of conservation- and community-based ecotourism, which currently operates several projects in Mexico.

Pronatura (see also p.110). The most important local conservation organization.

Amigos de Sian Ka'an, Cancún. Another good information source (see p.217).

In an effort to call a halt to the encroachment into mangroves and forests, several areas have been made into Biosphere Reserves. The 'Biosphere' concept is based on the idea of ensuring a sustainable environment that takes into account every aspect of an eco-system – fauna, the forest, the needs of local communities – rather than just setting up a 'game reserve' that ignores human use. There are four such reserves in the region: Sian Ka'an, Calakmul, and El Triunfo and Montes Azules in Chiapas.

Another problem is **reef loss** around the northeast coast and the 'Riviera Maya' itself. To some extent it's unavoidable given the huge increase in human numbers and boat traffic in the last 30 years, but it has accelerated significantly as giant-scale hotel-building has spread outside Cancún on to formerly empty beaches along the coast, and with the growth in cruise liner traffic. Campaigns have been launched to oppose the all-inclusive take over of unoccupied coastline, and there are at least some faint glimmers that the authorities may respond. Visitors themselves can minimize damage to the reef by acting sensibly when diving, swimming or snorkelling, above all by avoiding touching the coral, and by not going into the sea covered in sun lotion.

Around the Laguna de Términos in Tabasco and southern Campeche, careless exploitation of that region's greatest modern resource, oil, has led to some **oil spills**. Northwest of Mérida, the decay of mangroves in the Yucatán coastal lagoon has left an expanse of ghostly grey stumps (see p.254) dubbed the '**petrified forest**', though no one can quite decide whether it's an ecological problem or just a natural process.

One other specific problem is **lethal yellowing**, amarillamiento letal, a plague that only destroys coconut palms. In the 1990s it had a devastating effect along the coast of Yucatán state and Campeche, leaving palm groves as leafless stumps. On a positive note, new growth and replanting schemes are finally making up for some of the lost trees, especially along the coast east of Progreso.

Mayan Textiles

If the growing of corn has traditionally been a semi-sacred function for Mayan men, weaving has been the sacred role of women. Ixchel, goddess of fertility, was also the goddess of weaving, and was often shown with her loom in Classic-era images. By tradition, Mayan men in Highland Chiapas will not marry a woman who cannot weave. From the point of view of women themselves, weaving is an essential skill that enables them to supplement their income and gain some independence.

The same word, *huípil*, is used throughout Mayan Mexico for the main items of women's traditional dress, but means different things. In the hot Yucatán peninsula – where embroidery rather than weaving is the main traditional skill – it refers to the light cotton shift dress that is one of the region's identifying images. A variation for special occasions is the *terno*, which unlike the one-piece *huípil* consists of three parts, a lace-edged underskirt, the main skirt and, most richly embroidered of all, a smock-like yoke around the neck. Fine *ternos* are exquisitely worked, and always worn with bright flowers – roses, orchids – in the hair. The MACAY museum in Mérida (*see* p.284) has a permanent exhibition of fine Yucatecan embroidery.

The real repository of weaving skills in Mayan Mexico is Highland Chiapas, where, like most things, it comes with a much greater sense of tradition. The basic weaving implement is the backstrap loom, called the *telar de cintura*, as seen in ancient Jaina figurines of women weaving. It consists of two wooden end-rods, between which the main threads are stretched. One end-rod is attached, by a cord looped around both ends, to a post or tree; the other end is fixed to a strap around the woman's lower back. She works kneeling, moving backwards and forwards to alter the tension in the loom, using the only other parts of the loom, the five spacing rods, to separate and weave the threads. When it's too dark to weave, Highland women move on to embroidery or the *petet*, the wheel used for spinning.

Though all Highland women weave, not all do so to the same standard. In each village there are women known and admired for their special skills. In the last few decades, as tourist sales have become an important source of income – and given that Indian weaving is constantly undervalued in price terms – there has been a strong incentive to produce more and more simple pieces and more items purely for foreign buyers, while neglecting the more time-consuming traditional techniques. Cooperatives, the most important of them Sna Jolobil and SODAM in San Cristóbal de Las Casas, have been set up with the aim of promoting and ensuring the survival of best-quality weaving, as well as to establish the principle of a fair price for Indian women's work. Another question is the use of synthetic materials. The Maya love colour and, when cheap, bright lurex and other synthetic threads became available, they took to them with glee, often abandoning the laborious process of producing natural dyes (which would usually turn out duller). The Maya, however, have always adapted to new materials, and the wool and sheep of Chamula and Zinacantán were themselves introduced by the Spaniards.

The most traditional garment made by Highland women is also called a *huípil*, here meaning a loose blouse – essentially two pieces of cloth sewn together at the top and sides, with holes for the head and arms – with richly brocaded panels around the neck at front and back. They also produce belts, shawls, smocks for men, embroidered everyday blouses and small decorative pieces for the home. Skirts are made of heavy, plain black wool. In contrast to the styles of the Yucatán there is no arbitrariness in the designs of Highland weaving. Each community has its own, easily identifiable style, and after only a brief time in San Cristóbal recognition of people from the surrounding villages becomes immediate: the embroidered blue or white blouses of women from Chamula, the brilliantly bright shawls and flower-embroidered smocks of Zinacantán, the red and orange *huípiles* of older women from Amatenango, or the red and white *huípiles* of Chenalhó. In each community there are legends that it was the First Mother – a common way of referring to Santa Lucía, Catholic patron saint of weavers, and a modern manifestation of Ixchel – who taught the village's women their designs.

Within these set styles, though, there is considerable leeway for the individual weaver to work the pattern and display her skill, and no specific design is ever repeated. The main patterns and shapes used in each design style all have symbolic meanings: like so much in Mayan culture, they mirror the Mayan conception of the universe. Recurrent diamond patterns are the most common feature, representing creation between the four *bacabs* or cardinal points, and centred on an inner diamond symbolizing the sun, Jesus Christ and the *yaxché* or world-tree, three apparently different elements that are intertwined in the universe of the Highland Maya. Virtually the same diamond patterns can also be seen on the robe of Lady Xoc on an 8th-century lintel at Yaxchilán (*see* p.460). Some *huípiles* can almost be read as texts: sequences of diamonds and other shapes correspond to the months and days of the *haab* calendar, reproducing a whole year's planting cycle, and near-abstract, stylized shapes indicate vultures and monkeys – symbols of uncontrolled nature – and other animals. Weavers are so used to working within these patterns that they are often not fully conscious of them when starting a design, though they form a background to all their work; in addition, each woman has a personal motif with which she 'signs' her weaving, often coupled with a family motif.

The finest weaving of all is reserved for the special *huípiles* that dress the saints and the virgins in village churches. These are never discarded, but once a year they are removed and washed in special ceremonies, and new, bright *huípiles* are placed over the old ones. They therefore represent a museum of centuries of weaving. Women who wish to improve their skills pray to the saints of weaving, and it is believed that their new abilities and the inspiration for new designs then come to them in dreams. Similarly, at times when weaving skills have been lost – which has happened at times when the Maya have come under strong pressure to adopt non-Indian customs and dress – they have been revived by praying to the saints, and by studying their *huípiles*.

Wildlife and the Natural World

Birds

The abundance of birds that this land possesses is marvellous in extent, and of such diversity, that it does great honour to he who filled it with them, as a blessing.
Father Diego de Landa, *Relación de las Cosas de Yucatán*

Landa, Stephens and many other travellers have been equally impressed, even awestruck, by the exceptionally rich birdlife of the Yucatán, with some 500 species present at one time or another during the year. Many are permanent residents –

including several species unique to the peninsula – and the Yucatán's position and combination of woods and mangrove wetlands also make it a favourite wintering ground for birds from North America. Towards the south of the peninsula the dry tropical woodland blends into the rain forest that runs – or ran, until a few years ago – from southern Quintana Roo into Chiapas, the home of more exotic, brilliantly colourful birds such as toucans and parrots.

The full range of birds is extraordinary, and many can be seen simply by looking around. Throughout the region, the most universally sighted is the **great-tailed grackle** (in Mexican Spanish *zanate*), a relative of the blackbird with a long thin tail. There are a few hopping around wherever you go, and the call of the *zanate*, a long, rising whistle that seems unnervingly human, is one of the constant background sounds of the Yucatán. Another inescapable presence is the *zopilote* or **black vulture**, the great garbage-picker of Mexico. All around the coast the **brown pelican** is very common, perched on mooring posts or floating in the sky against the wind. The most famous birds in the Yucatán are its **flamingos** which, though not especially common, are easy to locate because you're taken to see them. There are two main flamingo breeding grounds, at Celestún and Río Lagartos (*see* pp.292–4 and pp.253–6).

Places To See Birds

Northern Yucatán

Under your own steam you can see plenty of water and sea birds around the Quintana Roo coast, especially near **Puerto Morelos**, on **Isla Holbox**, or from **Tulum** to **Punta Allen** and from **Mahahual** to **Xcalak**. Naturally, your best chance of seeing the region's unusual birds may be in its zoos, or aviaries like those at **Playa del Carmen** or **Xcaret** (*see* pp.200–201).

Campeche Petenes: this little-known region of northern Campeche contains huge stretches of mangrove wetlands, but visiting facilities are so far very basic (*see* p.378).

Celestún and **Río Lagartos**: most people only visit these towns to see flamingos, but their lagoons are also home to egrets, ibises, ducks, herons and other water birds. The coastal lagoon east of Progreso similarly hosts flamingos and a huge range of wetland and sea birds, especially winter migrants, and at **Uaymitún** there is a (*free*) viewing tower (*see* p.300).

Isla Contoy: this island sea bird reserve is most easily visited from Isla Mujeres. However, the tours (including snorkelling) are over-subscribed in peak season (*see* p.170).

Mayan sites: an added attraction of less-visited Mayan sites is that they're great places for walks and seeing birds. Among the best are **Dzibilchaltún**, smaller Puuc sites (**Xlapak**) and **Cobá**.

Sian Ka'an: the best single place for wetland birds, a must for birders (*see* pp.216–19).

Southern Peninsula and Chiapas

Calakmul: the biggest rainforest reserve in Mexico, and the best place of all to see forest birds and other wildlife in the southern Yucatán (*see* pp.369–70).

Lacandón Forest/Pico de Oro: the largest area of undisturbed rainforest, in the remote southeast corner of Chiapas, which still contains substantial numbers of macaws. Near Pico de Oro there are now some guest cabins, at **Las Guacamayas** (*see* pp.452–5).

Mayan Sites: great opportunities to see birds: **Dzibanché** and **Kohunlich** are spectacular for this, and among the places where you have the best chance of seeing wild toucans.

Palenque, **Bonampak** and **Yaxchilán**: parrots and hummingbirds are easily found in Palenque, but for toucans and rarer birds it's better to take the trip to the latter two sites, deep in the forest.

El Triunfo: this huge reserve in the remote southern mountains of Chiapas is now the only place to find some of the region's rarest birds: curassows, guans and quetzals. Access is difficult, but trips (with serious hiking) can be arranged (*see* pp.511–13).

In the dry Yucatán woods, frequently spotted birds include the **Yucatán jay**, the brilliant-blue **indigo bunting** (*azulito*, little blue bird, in Spanish), many colourful **woodpeckers** and vivid yellow and black **orioles**. Also still not too hard to find is the *chachalaca*, a wild relative of the turkey. Its name comes from its unmistakable clucking call, and it's more often heard than seen. Winter visitors include **tanagers**, little, luminous-red birds that you may see dart in front of your car on country roads. The wetlands and mangroves around the Yucatán coasts are home to a beautiful variety of American **herons** and, in winter, most non-Arctic species of American **duck** and **goose**. The margins of mangroves, beach and sea are the best place to see the **magnificent frigate bird**, a commanding presence that justifies its name with its fierce bill and long, crooked wings.

Further south, the true tropical forest of the southern peninsula and Chiapas is under heavy pressure from deforestation, and the birds that remain most numerous are those that adapt best to patches rather than undisturbed swathes of forest. Only when the trees are above a certain height do they provide a home for the most spectacular tropical birds, such as **toucans**, their smaller relative the **aracari** (*tucancillo*, little toucan, in Spanish) and, now confined to the Lacandón forest, scarlet and blue **macaws**. Scarcer still is the **quetzal**, the enormous tail feathers of which were greatly prized by Mayan kings. In Mexico it is now found only in the high forests of the Sierra Madre in Chiapas, and then very rarely. Small, bright green **parrots**, though, are very common, as are tiny **hummingbirds**.

Animal Life

Father Landa suggested that the Almighty had blessed the Yucatán with so many birds partly to compensate for the shortage of useful animals – no beasts of burden, no cattle – which seemed so strange it led him to ponder what the divine intention could have been. In fact, the region has pretty near as much variety of life on the ground as it does flying above it. In Tuxtla Gutiérrez there is a complete zoo, the Zoomat, with the peculiarity that its several hundred species are exclusively natives of the state of Chiapas. It's just that many of the region's animals are not very user-friendly from a human point of view. Many are also nocturnal, and go unnoticed most of the time; hence any sighting of them is particularly special.

The most frequently-seen animal by far in the northern Yucatán is the **iguana**. They are especially common at Mayan sites, where the gullies and crannies in the ancient walls provide ideal nesting-places. Some are dragons as big as sheep, but they are all completely harmless. Even more common are tiny **geckos**: very useful to have around, as they gobble up mosquitos.

Other animals are more elusive, but the Yucatán woods contain **white-tailed deer**, **collared peccaries** (the Mesoamerican wild boar), **armadillos**, **coatimundis**, **grey foxes** and an extraordinary range of rodents such as *tepezcuintles* (paca, in English), *agoutis* and *guaqueques*. All are more common the further south you go, and in Calakmul some are quite plentiful. The rarest animals, still more than birds, are likely to be found only in reserves or remote forest areas. There are **tapirs** in the remotest parts of the Calakmul reserve and Chiapas, but you will have to work very hard to find one.

Places To See Wildlife

Since it's unfortunately against the odds that you'll catch sight of a *leoncillo* in the wild, you may choose to settle for the region's zoos and animal reserves. Of these, the best are **La Venta** in Villahermosa and the **Zoomat** in Tuxtla Gutiérrez. In second rank lie **Xcaret**, **Yumká** (also near Villahermosa), and a rather cramped zoo in Mérida. There are a few small private wildlife parks, especially near Cancún.

In northern Yucatán, there is a good chance of seeing animals in the wild at **Punta Laguna** near Cobá (especially spider monkeys) and **Sian Ka'an**. Overall, **Calakmul** is by far the best place to see a wide range of animals, particularly rarer species. Crocodiles are most easily found in the **Sumidero**. All rarer species, above all the big cats, are more visible in the rainy season. This, though, is when you need to be most wary of snakes and scorpions, and when mosquitos and ticks cause most torment.

The one animal most people want to see is the **jaguar**, spotted or black, symbol of cosmic power to the Olmecs and Maya. They are still reported from Sian Ka'an to Calakmul and the Lacandón forest, but you will be very lucky to see a wild one. Jaguars are only one of an ample range of wild cats, all now as rare or rarer. The **lynx**, **ocelot** and **puma** are the most well-known big cats, but there are also engaging (or undeniably cute) smaller ones such as the *leoncillo* (jaguarundi in English) and the *tigrillo* (margay). **Monkeys** are much easier to find. There are two kinds here, spider monkeys (*mono araña*) and howler monkeys (*mono aullador* or *saraguato*). Thin, long-limbed spiders are still quite widespread; the bigger howlers are more reclusive, but can be seen and heard in Punta Laguna, Calakmul and, especially, at Yaxchilán.

The more spectacular animals of southern Mexico include three types of **crocodiles**, alligators and caymans, all of which are usually called *cocodrilos* by the locals, with their lack of interest in defining terms. Not especially numerous but wide-ranging, they sometimes turn up around Río Lagartos (the name of which, Lizard River, refers to their earlier abundance there) and even in the Cancún lagoon as well as more obvious places such as Sian Ka'an. One place where alligators are common is the Sumidero gorge, north of Tuxtla Gutiérrez. Other reptiles few people try deliberately to see are **snakes**: rattlesnakes, several more venomous species and a huge range of innocent smaller snakes. The chances of being bitten by a dangerous one, though, are minimal unless you work at it. They are most active by night, at dawn and dusk, and after rain. Walking by day in the dry season you are unlikely to come across one, and if you do it will probably slither away faster than you can run in the opposite direction. To be doubly sure, avoid walking through undergrowth where you can't see what's on the ground, don't walk into the brush at night, and keep to cleared paths.

Lastly there are **insects**, which are inescapable. Most people find them an irritation, and in forests and mangroves they make life dire if you don't have repellent, but the sheer range is astonishing, and as night falls in the forest the cacophony of bizarre sounds they produce is something no amount of description prepares you for. Most do not bite. Bugs with more serious bites are the *tábano* (horse fly) and the African killer bee, a nasty import (which cannot kill, though bites require medical attention), but even they are not very common. More dangerous than most bugs are **scorpions** (bites require medical attention, though are not immediately life-threatening), but in the dry season you're unlikely to find them by accident. Far more attractive are the 40,000 species of **butterflies**, sometimes seen in huge swarms.

Sealife and the Reefs

The 'Great Maya Reef' (or Cozumel Reefs) along the northeast coast of the Yucatán Peninsula is the second-largest coral reef system in the world after the Great Barrier Reef in Australia. It stretches over 300 kilometres, from Contoy in the north to Banco Chinchorro off southern Quintana Roo. The reefs are most concentrated, and closest to the surface, between the islands and the mainland: between Isla Mujeres and Cancún; along the west coast of Cozumel; off Puerto Morelos, Playa del Carmen and Akumal across the Cozumel channel. There is also a separate reef system in the Gulf of Mexico 100 kilometres northwest of Yucatán, Arrecife Alacranes or Scorpion Reef, an older reef that is rarely visited.

Coral reefs are perhaps the most fragile of all eco-systems, and the increase in human traffic here has led to deterioration in some of them, particularly the inshore reefs closest to Cancún. Nevertheless, huge stretches are still full of life. Off Cozumel and Puerto Morelos you can get a good idea of the sheer wealth of undersea life just by sticking your head in the water, without any need for tanks or even swimming very far; you'll see fine-veined fan coral, luminous shoals of fish like **butter hamlets** and yellow-tailed **snappers**, **queen angelfishes** or striped **sergeant-majors**. There are also several species of **sharks** and **barracudas**, though shark attacks are all but unknown in the region, and barracudas scarcely ever attack people unprovoked in clear water like that around the Maya reef. They prefer to eat other fish.

Dolphins are quite common in the deeper waters offshore, and a considerable business has built up in places like the Dolphin Discovery centres at Isla Mujeres, Cozumel and Puerto Aventuras where tourists can swim with them. They're kept in the sea, in small pools which have barriers across to stop them leaving, but these can still be sad places. Dolphins are too obliging for their own good, and can be relied on to jump about on demand even to the detriment of their own health. The best place to see dolphins un-penned is Holbox.

The Caribbean coast of Quintana Roo is also a major breeding ground for giant **sea turtles**, though they have seen an appalling reduction in numbers (to under five per cent of the figure of 40 years ago). They were long hunted by the Maya, but this is now illegal, and even poaching is now rare. Hunting has been less of a factor in their decline than the fact that the turtles' favourite egg-laying beaches are smack in the middle of the main tourist areas. Where the turtle beaches are properly protected (the largest is at Akumal) signs inform you that you should keep your distance. There are turtle breeding and repopulation programmes at Xcaret, Akumal and Isla Mujeres.

Still rarer, but not under such immediate threat, is the **manatee**, a large aquatic mammal related to the African sea-cow, a kind of mangrove seal, that's one of only three such species in the world. The north end of Chetumal Bay has been made into a reserve for these gentle animals, and trips can be made to look for them from Chetumal, but there's no guarantee they'll actually cooperate.

For a list of **bird** and **wildlife guides**, *see* **Further Reading**, p.528.

Food and Drink

06

Mexican food is familiar just about everywhere: *tacos*, *burritos*, *guacamole* and the rest. Much less well known is that the dishes served in the vast majority of Mexican restaurants across the world are from just one part of the country, along the US border (if not actually Tex-Mex). Mexico, though, is a big place, and Mexican cooking varies greatly from region to region, every one of which has its traditional dishes. Differences are especially marked in the south, and the food of the Yucatán, *la cocina yucateca*, is widely considered the finest and most distinctive of all Mexico's regional cuisines. Rich use is made of fruit, turkey, subtle and fragrant seasonings, and the excellent fish and seafood from the Gulf and the Caribbean coast. The recurrent flavours that linger on the palate and in the memory are those of lime and coriander.

Eating Out

All across Mexico, eating is a very public, social activity. Every town has its crop of restaurants: smart tourist or upscale restaurants (thin on the ground except in certain areas), comfortable places with lofty roof-fans, or plainer, rough-and-ready little eating houses with plastic seats with beer logos on the back. Even in small towns and villages (except maybe the most rural parts of Chiapas) there will nearly always be at least one basic, very cheap *lonchería* or *cocina económica* (literally 'cheap kitchen'), and some of these are open in the evening as well as for *lonch*. In towns, the market area will always offer a cluster of *cocinas económicas*, open for breakfast and lunch only, and these are invariably the cheapest places to eat. If you want immediate immersion in local life, eat there. Anywhere that calls itself a *restaurante* will usually have beers to go along with the food, while *loncherías* and *cocinas económicas* normally have no alcohol, only colas and juices. Throughout the guide, restaurants are divided into three price categories as described in the **Practical A–Z** under 'Eating Out', *see* pp.120–21.

In **restaurants** of all grades you may be presented with a menu that's surprisingly long, offering a wide choice of local and 'Mexican' dishes. In more basic restaurants, though, you'll often find that many listed dishes are not actually available, and in many cheaper or more isolated places it's a good idea to pass over the written menu and just ask *¿qué hay de bueno hoy?* ('what's good today?'), which should bring forth the freshest and best-prepared thing they have rather than forcing them to put together some more complicated dish. By the coast, you'll often get great fresh fish.

Sit-down restaurants only make up part of the range of eateries. Mexicans are among the world's greatest **snackers**. Around the *plazas* and main streets of every town there are stands and hole-in-the-wall shops selling *tacos*, *tortas* (bread rolls) and a range of *antojitos* (aptly translated as 'something you want on a whim'); nearby, women and old men sell peeled fruit, potato crisps or ice creams. On Sundays and *fiesta* days the number of food-stands trebles again. Should you get into *tortas* and *taco*-stands, this is a very cheap way of eating. On the coast and in cities, international fast-food chains are now well established. Pizza has been thoroughly adopted across all five states, often with Mexican touches such as *jalapeño* peppers.

Mexicans get up early, and **breakfast** is a main meal. As a result, most restaurants open from about 7am and people actually go out for breakfast, especially the more affluent in the more sultry cities. Get into the habit and you'll find that the powerful egg, sauce and bean-rich traditional wake-ups, with fruit on top, are a great way to get set up for the day. At **midday** many cheap restaurants offer a set menu or *comida corrida*. A full meal of this sort can be $2 or less, but the dishes are usually very basic (and the cheapest can be a reckless test of your stomach tolerance). One peculiarity of the 'best' restaurants in Yucatán state and Campeche is that they only open for lunch. Otherwise, plenty of restaurants stay open for the evening *cena*; in tourist areas and cities many will even be open quite late, but in small towns they may close soon after 9pm, or earlier. Other than that, meal times are predictably flexible. So too are meal sizes, as you are rarely obliged to eat a set number of courses.

The Food of Southern Mexico

Yucatecan cooking has several characteristic dishes that appear all across the peninsula, and many rarer specialities. Staple **meats** are pork, chicken and the most common bird in the Mayan farmyard, turkey, which is leaner and more flavoursome than the festive fare served up in the USA or Britain. Beef is common in some areas, particularly around Tizimín; it's far thinner than prime steak, but when good it's very tasty. There is also a rich variety of fragrant **soups**, taken as a first course; outstanding among them is one of the great Yucatecan classics, *sopa de lima*, actually a chicken soup sharpened with lime, which when done well has a unique, superbly delicate flavour. The most common **fish** are red snapper, grouper and grey mullet, but they are less widespread than **shellfish**, which in coastal areas are virtually the staple diet.

One feature of Yucatecan food is that it is not necessarily hot. This is because hot spices (called simply *picante*) are not added in the cooking of many dishes, but served on the side in little bowls. The red sauce is (relatively) mild, the green one is a blaster. Most locals will spoon on at least a little, for the Yucatán is actually known for having the most powerful chilis and hot spices in all Mexico (*see* 'Know Your Chilis', below).

Know your Chilis

Down here the *jalapeño*, familiar in Tex-Mex food, is considered a bit of a softy. An enormous range of chilis is available: among the most common are *chile güero* ('pale chili') or *xcatik* (its Mayan name), mild and used in the actual cooking of dishes; *chile poblano*, the most widely used medium-strength chili, used in making milder *picantes*; the hotter *serrano* and *jalapeño* chilis, which figure in a lot of central-Mexican dishes; *chipotle*, a dried, hot chili used as seasoning; and, most powerful but most beloved of all in the Yucatán, the tiny, explosive green chili *habanero*. Taken straight, simply chopped up, *habaneros* are used to make the most thermo-nuclear *picantes*, but dried, ground up and mixed with other herbs and spices they also feature in Yucatecan mixed seasonings like *achiote* powder and *recado negro*, in which case their influence is much more subtle.

Mexican Menu Decoder

Restaurant Basics

carta/menu menu

lonchería cheap, basic restaurant, which won't normally serve alcohol

menu del día/comida corrida set meal

mesero/a waiter/waitress

¿Tiene una mesa (para dos, cuatro)? Do you have a table (for two, four)?

el menu (o la carta), por favor Can I see the menu, please?

¿Qué hay? What have you got?

¿Qué hay de bueno hoy? What's good today?

¿Hay una lista de vinos? Do you have a wine list?

la cuenta/la nota bill (check)

la cuenta, por favor Can I have the bill (check), please?

¿Puedo pagar con tarjeta de crédito? Can I pay by credit card?

cambio change

propina tip

General Terminology

almuerzo lunch

cazuela large, earthenware cooking pot

cena dinner

copa glass, wine glass

cuchara spoon

cuchillo knife

desayuno breakfast

ensalada salad

hielo ice

al horno oven-baked

mantequilla butter

miel honey

pan bread

pan dulce sweet rolls

pimienta pepper

plato plate, dish

postres, dulces desserts

sal salt

servilleta napkin

sopa soup

taza cup

tenedor fork

torta sandwich made with a small roll

vaso glass

Meats

arracheras thin steak, fast-grilled in strips

asado/a roast

carnitas deep-fried pork

chicharrones deep-fried belly pork

chorizo spiced red sausage, of Spanish origin but found in most parts of Mexico, and especially Chiapas

chuleta chop

cochino/cochinita pork

Skilful **marinades** are integral to many Yucatecan classics, giving the cooking a distinctly tropical colour and tone. Lime juice features frequently, often with coriander and a touch of *achiote*, as do the peninsula's distinctive bitter oranges. Marinating is one of the prime techniques used in intricate dishes such as *poc-chuc* or *pollo oriental de Valladolid*, in which some seven to ten seasonings are combined with two fruit juices to achieve the final result. Fish and seafood are often served in the form of a *ceviche*, raw but marinated in lemon or lime juices with coriander, and usually eaten as a refreshing, simple salad with chopped onions, peppers and tomatoes. Otherwise, fish is generally served simply: either plain-grilled, in breadcrumbs or fried in garlic.

Meat or fish dishes nearly always come with a variety of **accompaniments**, such as salads, sliced onion, guacamole, skinny French-fries (especially with steaks) and one of the basics throughout Mexico, red kidney beans (*frijoles*), generally served in a refried mass. They can also be eaten in a kind of broth, usually as a starter (*frijoles charros*). Another culinary staple is, of course, the staff of life throughout Mesoamerica, **maize**. The corn *tortilla*, made fresh every day, is served either hot and soft (the most usual), or as crisp, dry chips, and a pile of them appears on the table with just about every meal, to mop up any sauce. Less celebrated are the excellent breads of the south, particularly good in Yucatán state and Chiapas.

jamón ham
lomo, lomitos loin of pork
longaniza pork sausage, not especially spicy, that was originally Spanish. There are variants in both Yucatán and Chiapas.
pavo/guajolote turkey
pollo/gallina chicken
puerco pork
res/carne de res beef, steak
tasajo dry-cured beef (common in Chiapas)
tocino bacon
venado venison, deer

Fish and Seafood
almejas clams
atún/bonito tuna
calamares squid
camarones prawns/shrimp
cangrejo large crab
caracol conch
cazón hammerhead shark/dogfish
esmedregal black snapper
huachinango/pargo red snapper
jaiba small crab
langosta spiny lobster
lenguado sole, flounder
lisa/mojarra grey mullet
mariscos shellfish (general)
mero grouper
ostiones oysters

pámpano pompano
pez espada swordfish
pulpo octopus
sierra mackerel
tiburón shark

Vegetables and Basic Ingredients
aceite (de maiz) oil (corn oil)
aceitunas olives
achiote stock-like Yucatecan seasoning made from a mixture of dried herbs and chilis
aguacate avocado
ajo garlic
alcaparras capers
arroz rice
azúcar sugar
calabaza pumpkin/courgette
canela cinnamon
cebolla onion
chaya spinach-like leaf vegetable
chía chaya in Chiapas
chipilín spinach-like vegetable, with quite a strong flavour, used in several traditional dishes of Chiapas
chícharos peas
chirmole or chilmole a traditional Mayan seasoning mix made with dried, ground and roasted chilis, dried ground pork stock and coriander, mint and other herbs. Used in *relleno negro* (black sauce) and other dishes.

While *cocina yucateca* is the best-known cuisine of the south, other areas have their own specialities. **Campeche** has perhaps the most subtle cooking, a variation on Yucatecan food but with delicious fish, together with rice and distinctive sauces that feature coconut and chilis. **Tabasco** too offers very individual cuisine, with imaginative dishes featuring native river fish such as the *pejelagarto*. **Chiapas** is home to different styles in every region: around Tuxtla and the Pacific the most prominent dishes are *tamales (see* 'Glossary of Dishes', pp.101–103) more typical of Central America than Mexico. **Highland Chiapas** shows the traces of a colonial society: the diet of the rural Maya has traditionally been a mix of *tortillas* and beans, while the food of the *coletos*, the Spanish-speaking people of San Cristóbal de Las Casas, is the closest to that of Spain, with very Iberian sausages and wonderful bread. Many menus feature a section headed *platos mexicanos*, referring to central-Mexican specialities such as *fajitas* and *enchiladas*. Even these will differ from familiar Tex-Mex variants: you're bound to come across *mole*, a wonderful, thick savoury chocolate sauce seasoned with chili and spices, which is frequently ignored in 'international' Mexican food.

Vegetarians do not fare very well with traditional dishes: nearly all include some meat or fish and if you don't eat eggs either, you could be really stuck. Soups and snacks offer more possibilities than main dishes. However, there are dedicated

cilantro coriander
clavos cloves
comino cumin
elote corn cob
frijoles red beans
frijoles refritos refried beans
guacamole avocado mashed into a purée with
    lemon/lime juice, coriander and a little chili
hongos mushrooms
huevos eggs
jicama a local gourd-like root vegetable,
    between a potato and a pumpkin
jitomate tomato
lechuga lettuce
mantequilla butter
miel honey
mole (poblano) spicy savoury chocolate sauce
nopalitos nopal cactus, similar to palm hearts
papas potatoes
    papas fritas chips/french fries
pepino cucumber
pepitas, pepita de calabaza pumpkin seeds
pimienta ground pepper
pimientos peppers
    morron red,
    verde green
queso cheese
rabanitos radishes
totopos broken-up, fried *tortilla* chips
zanahoria carrot

Fruits and *Agua* Ingredients
chicozapote/zapote the fruit of the *sapodilla*
    tree, from the sap of which comes *chicle*, the
    raw ingredient of chewing gum. Its texture
    is slightly custardy when eaten straight, but
    it is a delicate flavour in juices or ice cream
coco coconut
durazno peach
fresas strawberries
guanábana soursop, a kind of custard apple
guayaba guava
jamaica a type of hibiscus flower, dried and
    used to make *agua de jamaica*
lima lime
limón lemon
mamey a member of the mango family, but
    smaller and not as sweet
mango mango
manzana apple
melón melon
naranja orange
naranjil/naranja agria bitter orange
papaya papaya/paw paw
plátano banana
    hoja de plátano banana leaf
piña pineapple
sandía watermelon
tamarindo tamarind
toronja grapefruit
uvas grapes

vegetarian restaurants in most cities and, elsewhere, there are restaurants that offer a good choice of animal-free dishes, such as the '100% Natural' chain in Cancún and along the coast. Dishes to look out for include those containing *chaya*, a vegetable similar to spinach which is extraordinarily good for you, and also tastes good.

Desserts are not a highlight of Mexican cooking and the wide variety featured in books rarely ever turn up on menus. As everywhere in the Hispanic world, the *flan* is the standard dessert, and there's a good variety of ice creams (*helados*). A *pay* is a pie, so a *pay de queso* is cheesecake. Apart from that, it's best to go for the fruit.

Drinks and Drinking Habits

Mexico has an export in which it leads the world – **beer**. Corona is now the globe's best-selling label. Foreigners often drink this light beer near-automatically, but other lagers with more body are Superior, Dos Equis (XX) Lager, Modelo, Carta Blanca, Sol and Tecate. There are also slightly more expensive, finer quality versions, such as Corona Especial or Modelo Especial. The Yucatán's own brewery, the Cervecería Montejo, also produces a good lager (Montejo Especial). As well as lagers there are some very good Mexican dark beers: Negra Modelo, Dos Equis Negra and Yucatán

Drinks

agua mineral mineral water
  con gas/sin gas fizzy/still
  agua purificada purified water
café coffee
  agua para café water for instant coffee
cerveza beer
coca cola
jugo juice
leche milk
licuado milkshake
raspado mixture of juice and crushed ice
refresco soft drink
vino wine
  tinto red
  blanco white

Glossary of Dishes

The following are some of the dishes that you will find most frequently in this region.

Breakfasts

Chilaquiles: heavy casserole of slivers of crisp *tortilla* baked in a cheese sauce with tomato, onions, spices and strips of chicken or turkey.
Huevos estrellados/fritos: fried eggs.
Huevos mexicanos/a la mexicana: scrambled eggs with peppers, chili, onions and *chorizo*.

Huevos motuleños: *tortillas* topped by refried beans, fried eggs, a mild-chili tomato sauce, peas, ham and grated cheese; often served with pieces of fried banana on the side.
Huevos rancheros: *tortillas* topped by refried beans, fried eggs, and spicy tomato sauce.
Huevos revueltos: scrambled eggs; usually includes a little onion and sweet pepper.
Platillo de fruta: a plate of mixed fruit.

Yucatecan *Antojitos/Botanas* (Snacks)

Chalupas: crisp, boat-shaped *tortillas* with a filling of refried beans and different meat and vegetables; typical of Chiapas.
Coctel de camarones (de calamares/de langosta...): in the Yucatán, seafood cocktails are served in a light, vinaigrette-style dressing with loads of coriander.
Garnachas: small *tortilla* snacks, similar to *panuchos*, in Tabasco and Chiapas.
Panuchos: small *tortillas* with a coating of refried beans, rapidly fried, then topped with chopped tomato, onion, lettuce, avocado, medium-hot chili and strips of chicken or turkey, previously cooked with a little *achiote* and bitter orange juice.
Papadzules: chopped hard-boiled eggs in a sweet pumpkin-seed sauce, served in rolled *tortillas*, often with tomato sauce on top; meat-free, but very filling.

brown ale, Cervecería Montejo's León Negra. One thing Mexicans do not usually do is drink beer with a piece of fruit jammed in the bottle, nor do they always drink straight from the bottle. This is a Californian invention; in real Mexican bars beer is served with a glass, and if you want fruit you have to ask for it.

For some years press comments abroad have suggested that the quality of Mexican **wines** (*vinos*) is improving. This is news to wine-buyers inside the country, who generally find them a little metallic. About the best Mexican wines are those from the Cetto label from Baja California, but others still fail to impress. Good Chilean, Spanish and Californian wines are available in upscale restaurants, at relatively high prices. Mid-range restaurants will only have a limited choice of 'national' labels, if any, and except on the coast cheaper restaurants will scarcely ever have wines at all. In any case, wine doesn't go especially well with Mexican and Yucatecan food.

The most famous of Mexican drinks is, of course, **tequila**. It comes from hair-on-the-chest Jalisco, in central Mexico, but a big choice is now available in every part of the country. There are literally hundreds of tequilas available and, should you wish to embark on a tasting, most Riviera barmen will be happy to assist. Of the larger-scale producers, anything from the Hornitos label is well regarded. There are three basic 'grades' of tequila: *blanco* is clear, has not been through any ageing process, and is

Salbutes: like *panuchos*, but with a thicker, spongier base instead of standard *tortillas*. The double act of *panuchos* and *salbutes* turn up everywhere in the Yucatán, and women sell them from trays at small-town bus stations.

Mexican *Antojitos/Botanas* (Snacks)

Enchiladas: large, rolled soft *tortillas* with different fillings and sauces. Southern *enchiladas* are usually served with cheese and savoury chocolate *mole* (called *enchiladas suizas*) rather than tomato sauce.

Quesadillas: small soft *tortillas*, folded over with cheese and sometimes other fillings inside, and grilled or fried; usually served with a choice of sauces.

Tacos: rolled *tortillas* filled with meat, fish or whatever else is available; there are as many types as there are things to fill them. At *taco* stands you are given the *taco* complete rolled up in paper; in sit-down *taquerías* (where the basic order is normally three *tacos*) all the ingredients are brought to your table, and you assemble them yourself. *Tacos al pastor* feature chili-spiced pork meat, compressed into a mass similar to a Turkish doner kebab, and then charcoal-grilled (*al carbón*); cheese, guacamole, onions and other extras are usually added.

Tostadas: round *tortillas* fried crisp and served open with a great variety of toppings (like *panuchos*). *Taquerías* also serve *tostadas*; *gringas* are meat and onion *tostadas* topped by melted cheese.

Southern Soups and Main Dishes

Cochinita pibil: pork marinated in *achiote*, lime and bitter orange juices, then wrapped in banana leaves and oven-baked in an earthenware dish. Pure Mayan in origin (most traditionally baked in a hole dug into the ground, covered in hot stones), this is the Yucatán's most famous dish, served as a main course or a *taco*-ingredient. *Pollo pibil*, made with chicken, is similar.

Crepas de chaya: large soft crèpes (made with wheat flour, and so not maize *tortillas*) with a stuffing of cooked *chaya* and garlic, and a light cheese sauce.

Fríjol con puerco: a casserole of black beans, chopped pork, onion, tomato, lemon, coriander and hot chili, served with rice.

Manitas de cangrejo (Campeche only): crab claws cooked with chilis and onions, and served with salad. Campeche also has many other variations on seafood dishes.

Mondongo kabik: powerful stew of chili, fruit and offal, maybe recommended to anyone who really wants to kick sand in the face of

allowed to 'rest' in barrels for a maximum of 30 days after being distilled; *reposado* is aged for between two to 11 months in oak barrels; *añejo* is aged for one to five years. In general, as it ages a tequila gets darker in colour, stronger, but also more subtle in flavour. Some tequila drinkers consider fine *añejos* too refined and lacking in a real tequila kick, and prefer a good *reposado*. The most traditional way to take tequila is now a rather self-conscious ritual. It is served straight in a small glass (a *caballito*), and on the bar are bowls of salt and lime or lemon slices: you lick a pinch of salt from your fingers, knock the tequila down in one and suck the juice from a slice of fruit. A popular variation is to alternate shots of tequila with sips from a glass of tomato juice spiked with chili or *sangrita*. Alternatively, you can sip tequila rather than shoot it, and many people just enjoy it in margaritas. Another cactus-based drink is **mezcal**, from the state of Oaxaca, which is stronger, coarser and famously has a worm in the bottle.

The most traditional booze in the Yucatán, however, is actually rum (*ron*), still the favoured hard drink at country *fiestas*. There are many different brands of Yucatecan rum, which is cheaper than tequila (but note that really cheap non-label Yucatecan village rum is to be avoided, even by the most adventurous). There are also some drinks of pre-Conquest origin. Also Yucatatecan is **xtabentún**, a mead-like Mayan liqueur made with fermented honey, aniseed and other herbs. It's very sweet, but health warnings. Anything called *mondongo* is made with guts; the northern Mexican equivalent is *menudo*.

Pan de cazón (Campeche only): hammerhead shark, chopped up with spices, served between cooked *tortillas* with tomato sauce.

Pavo en relleno negro: boned pieces of turkey (or chicken) in a rich, thick, black sauce made with very finely minced pork, herbs, spices, chili, peppers and grated hard-boiled egg.

Pollo oriental de Valladolid: chicken (or turkey) pieces on the bone casseroled with onion, garlic, mild and hot chilis and cloves, then quickly oven-roasted in a baste of oil and bitter orange juice, and then served all together. Typical of Valladolid and the east (*oriente*) of the Yucatán, hence the name.

Poc-chuc: pork marinated in bitter orange juice and then cooked with onions, garlic and herbs, served with black *fríjoles*. Believed to have been invented in Los Almendros restaurant (Ticul), but now a standard across the peninsula.

Puchero: a rich stew made with two or more meats – typically pork and chicken – and pumpkin, carrots, rice, bananas, bitter limes and oranges, *habanero* chili and herbs.

Sopa de lima: not just a lime soup: shredded chicken, strips of fried *tortilla*, tomato, sweet peppers, oregano, garlic and lots of lime, which infuses into the meat. A gentle, very satisfying dish.

Tamales: steamed maize dough stuffed with meat, beans, and any one of a whole variety of vegetables, chilis and seasonings, then baked in corn-husk or banana leaves.

Mexican Dishes

Caldo tlalpeño: soup of chickpeas, vegetables and chicken.

Carne a la tampiqueña: char-grilled beef with assorted accompaniments: guacamole, refried beans, *quesadillas*, onions and salad.

Fajitas: strips of meat or seafood, pan-fried and served sizzling hot for you to create your own *tacos*; the *tortillas*, onions, beans, guacamole and other necessaries are all provided on the table.

Machaca: shredded beef or pork with peppers, tomatoes, onions, medium chilis and herbs.

Pescado a la veracruzana: any fish cooked in a tomato, caper and olive sauce.

Pollo con mole: fried chicken in thick chocolate *mole* sauce; usually spicy but not searing.

Pozole: from Jalisco, a butch stew of chickpeas, tomatoes, chilis and pork or offal. Very cheap, if you like that sort of thing.

Puntas de res a la mexicana: strips of beef, char-grilled and served with tomatoes and onions.

there are now very refined versions available. A 'legendary' drink of Highland Chiapas is **posh**, though you'll never see it advertised. This is the home-distilled cane hooch of the Highland Maya, traditionally drunk by Mayan men to open the doors of perception. It has never been produced legally, but is made in every village, and those in the know with a little asking can usually find the local distiller, usually an old lady (take a plastic bottle if you want to buy). It's actually a pretty coarse rum, but not dangerous.

Drinks are served either in cafés, bars (unusual outside big towns) and restaurants, all of which are quite calm, or in **cantinas**. The *conquistadores* related that in all the Mesomerican cultures men used periodically to drink themselves senseless to make contact with the other world; this tradition of binge-drinking survives today. Drinking also has a clear position in the dark-and-light nature of Mexican society, between the controlled courtesy of everyday life and the need for release. The home of the latter, for men, has usually been the *cantina*. Not everyone gets drunk, but heavy drinking is certainly a distinct cultural phenomenon, and when Mexican men get going the concept of 'one more for the road' doesn't exist. Most tourists don't go near *cantinas*, but, while many still fit the shabby, drunken model, in major towns there are also more elegant ones that are actually quite comfortable, and some that even have women clients.

Non-alcoholic drinks: Mexico is a major **coffee** producer, but the bulk of the crop goes for export, and coffee-culture is strictly a regional matter. In the Yucatán it is spectacularly absent, and in Mérida there are only a few cafés that offer decent fresh coffee. In many cheap and country places if you ask for coffee you will be given *'agua para café'*, a cup of hot water, followed by a jar of instant coffee for you to add. If you are lucky, the coffee will arrive before the water's got cold. An exception is Cancún, as there are so many people there from the coffee-devoted state of Veracruz. Of the southern states, only Tabasco and Chiapas have a real coffee tradition. An older Chiapanecan tradition is ***pozol***, a cold drink of unfermented maize liquor, sometimes with cocoa powder added. Those who are used to it are near-addicted to it, and find it enormously refreshing, but it's an acquired taste. **Juices** (*see* below) are available in all towns and cities, and then there are **colas**. If Latin America really wanted to deal a body-blow to *gringo* power, all they would have to do is boycott Coke and Pepsi for one week. They are everywhere, even where nothing else is available. With regrets to the other brand, the generic name for a cola is *una coca*.

Fantastic Fruit

It would be a great blow for human values if someone would replace the national anthem, *Mexicanos, al grito de guerra* ('Mexicans, at the war cry'), with a hymn to the nation's **fruit**. It is the Yucatán's greatest symbol of abundance, and it is wonderful. Tropical fruits abound, but others that might seem completely familiar are just as, if not more, impressive. You've had pineapples before, but not like these pineapples.

Fruit can be taken chopped up straight on a plate, bought peeled or unpeeled from street sellers, or as juices. There are specialized **juice shops**, labelled *juguerías* or just *jugos*. Juices in turn come in one of three ways: as straight juice (normal for orange juice); as a *licuado* – with the fruit put fresh through a blender and then mixed with a little water (a *licuado de agua*) or milk (a *licuado de leche*); or as an *agua*, with the juice diluted with water and ice (both nearly always of purified water). Certain local fruits, such as the *mamey* and *guanábana*, are unimpressive when eaten but make very enjoyable *aguas*. Others are only available as drinks, such as *agua de jamaica*. Made with an infusion of the dried flower of the *jamaica*, a type of hibiscus, it is diluted to make an exceptionally refreshing, healthy drink; *agua de tamarindo*, tamarind water, is similar. *Agua de chaya*, an infusion of the Yucatecan vegetable, is another that's virtually a health-food concentrate, best drunk mixed with a little lemon. Not a juice, but sold in juice shops, is ***horchata***, a speciality of Tabasco: this is not the same as the Spanish nut-drink of the same name, but instead is made with rice, cinnamon and milk. A speciality of Chiapas is ***tascalate***, a powder combining ground maize, cocoa, cinnamon, sugar and *achiote* that is beaten into water or (better) milk.

As well as in *jugos* shops, a selection of fruit *aguas* (but not *licuados*) will also be on offer in *paleterías* and *neverías*, **ice cream shops**. There are at least a couple in every town. At their best they sell beautifully fresh, home-made ice creams in a range of fruit flavours, in pots (*copas*) or on a stick (*paletas*). There are also ice cream chains in cities, which while not bad are not the same thing.

Travel

Getting There

By Air

Cancún is the main gateway airport for the whole of southern Mexico, with air and road links to everywhere else in the region. If, however, you are only travelling to Chiapas, it may be more useful to fly in via Mexico City.

If you intend to take internal flights within Mexico during your stay, it's worth considering the **MexiPass** scheme (see p.113) before you go, as this can only be arranged from abroad.

From the USA and Canada

Scheduled Flights

It is easy to get to the Yucatán from anywhere in North America. All the airlines listed (see box, right) fly from various parts of the USA to Cancún. There are no direct scheduled flights from Canada to Cancún, but **Mexicana** offers connections from Toronto or Montreal, with one change at Mexico City. There are also some direct flights to other airports in the region other than Cancún, for those who really want to avoid the place. **Continental** has flights from Houston to Mérida and Cozumel, and **Aeroméxico** has a daily Miami–Mérida service. If you travel via Mexico City, there is a very wide range of flights available from many different cities.

Charter Flights

Here the choice expands enormously; thanks to the numerous flights available, it is often possible to pick up a return to Cancún for around $200 or less. The best times to find budget charters are the Spring Break season (Feb–April) and into the summer. From Canada there is a popular Toronto–Mérida charter.

From the UK and Europe

Scheduled Flights

Since **British Airways** gave up its service from London Gatwick in March 2002 there are no direct scheduled flights to Cancún from Britain. The best ways to travel there by scheduled flight are with a change in the USA or via Spain with Iberia, which has frequent flights from Madrid. The quickest route is via Miami

Major Air Carriers

From the USA and Canada

Aeroméxico, t 1 800 237 6639, *www.aeromexico.com*.

American Airlines, t 1 800 433 7300, *www.im.aa.com*.

Continental, t 1 800 523 3273, *www.continental.com*.

Mexicana, t 1 800 531 7921, *www.mexicana.com.mx*.

TWA, t 1 800 892 4141, *www.twa.com*.

United, t 1 800 241 6522, *www.united.com*.

US Airways, t 1 800 428 4322, *www.usairways.com*.

From the UK and Europe

Aeroméxico, t 020 8492 0000.

American Airlines, t 0845 778 9789.

British Airways, t 0845 773 3377, *www.british-airways.com*.

Continental, t 0800 776 464.

Iberia, t 0845 601 2854, *www.iberia.com*.

Virgin Atlantic, t 01293 747 747, *www.virgin-atlantic.com*.

Flight-only Operators

Payless Travel, t 020 7436 6900.

Dialaflight, t 0870 333 2266.

Flightline, t 0870 040 1757.

(around nine hours): good fare deals are often available on **Virgin Atlantic** (in association with **Mexicana** for the Miami–Cancún leg) or **American Airlines**. Flying with **Continental** via Houston takes a bit longer. The usual price for an economy return to Cancún via the US or Spain is officially around £500, but there are frequent offers available and agencies can often get flights for around £400 or less.

Travelling via Mexico City gives a much wider choice: with **British Airways** direct, **Air France** via Paris, **KLM** via Amsterdam, **Iberia** via Madrid, or **Aeroméxico** from Madrid or Paris. However, if you are heading for the Yucatán this is a much longer way around.

Charter Flights

It is still quite easy to fly direct to Cancún from Britain because of the frequent charter flights that operate from several airports around the country, all year round. It is possible to find prices of around £250 return or less, especially in the low season (roughly Mar–Nov). Check **Teletext** on TV (*www.tele-text.co.uk*) or flight websites for current offers. It's also worth calling the low-price specialists listed under 'Flight-only Operators', (*see* box, facing page). Check if they have flight deals that include one or two nights at a hotel, very handy on arrival in Cancún.

Getting to and from Mexican Airports

Only **Transporte Terrestre** airport taxis and minibuses, recognizable by a special colour scheme with a plane on the doors, are allowed to pick up passengers from Mexican airports. Their fares, posted up by airport taxi ranks, are higher than those of standard cabs, but there is no alternative unless you or the travel agent have made arrangements to be collected. This scheme only applies on arrival; when you are leaving, any local cab can take you to the airport. There are no airport **bus** services.

By Road

To take a US- or Canadian-registered vehicle into Mexico beyond the *zona fronteriza* (roughly 20km from the border, except in the states of Baja California and Sonora, where special conditions apply) you must obtain a **Temporary Import Permit**, which you should keep with your Tourist Card (*see* 'Entry Formalities', p.111). AAA offices near border crossings have the forms required, and help members with paperwork. To get a permit you will need to have the originals and at least two photocopies of each of the following: your passport or birth certificate; a Mexican Tourist Card (which you should therefore obtain first); a current driving licence; and the car registration papers, which must be in the same name as the licence and passport. At a Customs (*Aduana*) post at any of the main border crossings, take these documents to the **Módulo de Control de Vehículos** desk. The permit costs just US$11.50, but to get one it is effectively essential to have a credit card. This is because your card details are taken as a guarantee against you selling the car in Mexico or over-staying the allotted time, in which case import duty and a fine will be charged against the

card, and the vehicle can be confiscated. The alternative to using a card is to take out a cash bond, which is refundable but can amount to almost the whole value of the car. The permit will name the drivers authorized to use the car, and will be valid for six months (a dated car-sticker comes with it), during which time you can leave and re-enter the country as many times as you like. Because of the card or cash bond guarantee, though, it is important that when the six months is up and/or you finally leave Mexico, you remember to revisit a *Control de Vehículos* desk at the border to have your permit officially cancelled.

With hard driving it's possible to get from the Brownsville/Matamoros border crossing around the Gulf Coast (the most direct route) to the Yucatán in four days (or even three), and fast toll roads make the going quicker in some stretches. Most people, however, make a trip of it, and allow at least a week.

It is not usually permitted to take any US-rented car into Mexico. For **Car Hire**, *see* 'Getting Around', p.114.

Insurance

You will also need Mexican **insurance**, since US and Canadian policies are not valid here. Again, the AAA assists members with tourist policies, and there are plenty of insurance company offices near every border crossing.

The following companies offer a range of short-term policies at reasonable rates:
DriveMEXICO, t 1 800 557 1977, *driveinmexico@ aol.com.*
Amisi Mexican Insurance Services, t 888 420 0086, *www.AmexInsurance.com.*

By Ferry

It's been promised for so long many thought it would never happen, but it does appear that in June 2002 a passenger and vehicle ferry service will finally get going between the US and Yucatán. It's operated by **Mayalines** (*www.mayalines.com*), with three modern ships running between Tampa and Progreso, with a future route promised between Miami and Puerto Morelos. Each trip takes around 24 hours each way. Fares begin at $250 per vehicle, plus $150 per person, one-way.

Tour Operators and Special-interest Holidays

For a list of selected websites with general and specialized information on Mexico, *see* the box of 'Useful Websites', **Practical A–Z**, p.136. A great many **dive** hotels and services operating in Mexico now advertise directly on the Internet. Simply run a search on *dive Mexico* on the websites listed or any decent search engine.

Abroad

Hundreds of agencies across the **USA** and **Canada** offer flights or all-in packages to Cancún and other parts of the region and it's impossible to mention more than a few of them here. An enormous range of flight deals is available on the web.

Many large-scale **UK** tour operators – Kuoni, Thomson's, Unijet and Cosmos among them – now include Cancún, Cozumel and Playa del Carmen in their brochures.

See box, below, for a selection of companies offering a more extensive range of tours and contacts in the area.

In Mexico

Within Mexico there are many local, small-scale tour agencies and organizations that are a great help in getting around the more remote parts of the country and, in particular, provide a rapidly expanding variety of **environmental** and **adventure tours** (*see* below). Most of the UK-based **trek** companies offer 'Mayan Route' small-group tours, combining the Yucatán with Chiapas and parts of Belize and Guatemala, with variations in the details.

Special-interest Tour Operators

In North America

eXito, t 1 800 655 4053, *www.wonderlink .com/exito*. Latin American specialists, offering a wide variety of flight-only fares, package trips, adventure tours and so on.

Mayatour, t 1 800 392 6292, *www.maya tour.com*. A leading specialist in tours through Mexico and Central America, with some of the most extensive and sophisticated knowledge of the area. They can organize wildlife, diving, adventure and pure leisure tours, and archaeological tours are a particular speciality.

José Sales Tours, t 1 877 639 2296, *www.mex tours.com*. Hotel bookings and packages throughout Mexico.

Budget and Student Deals

Airhitch, t (212) 864 2000, *www.airhitch.org*. Last-minute, bargain-basement ticket specialists.

STS Travel, t 1 800 648 4849, *www.ststravel .com*. Major student travel service with a great range of spring break deals for the student fun market.

USA Springbreak, t 1 877 460 6077, *www.usa springbreak.net*. Another low-cost student and spring break specialist.

The following **websites** are also worth checking for budget deals:
www.xfares.com
www.smarterliving.com

In Britain

Bales Worldwide, Bales House, Junction Road, Dorking, Surrey, RH4 3HL, **t** 0870 241 3208, *www.balesworldside.com*. Their 'Mayan Heritage' tour takes in Guatemala, while 'Treasures of Mexico' includes Mexico City.

Cathy Matos Mexican Tours/Mexicana, 75 St Margaret's Avenue, Whetstone, London N20 9LD, **t** 020 8492 0000, *www.cathy-matosmexico.com*. The leading Mexico-only specialists in the UK, with the widest range of tours, made-to-measure itineraries and contacts throughout the country. They are also UK representatives for many *haciendas* and special hotels, and are UK agents for **Mexicana**, and so provide Mexipass discount passes for domestic flights (*see* p.113).

Club Med, 115 Hammersmith Road, London W14, **t** 0700 258 2932, *www.clubmed.com*. Club Med has a large resort at Cancún but also runs the attractive 'Villas Arqueológicas' hotels at Chichén Itzá, Cobá and Uxmal.

Cox & Kings, Gordon House, 10 Greencoat Place, London SW1P 1PH, **t** 020 7873 5000, *www.coxandkings.co.uk*. Prestigious travel service providing bookings at a portfolio of *haciendas* and other distinctive luxury

Tours and Guides

In any town with more than a few tourists there are local agencies that run guided tours to archaeological sites, nature reserves, etc. **Bus tours** are an easy way of seeing the region's treasures, above all if you don't want to hire a car, but in the most visited parts of the Yucatán they have notable limitations. They usually give you two hours at a major Mayan site such as Chichén Itzá, which is too short, and always seem to shepherd everyone together at the hottest times of day. Also, while there are some enterprising tour companies that offer fresh trips, many of the tourist itineraries remain unchanged and unimaginative, and rarely go near recently opened but lesser-known sites. Bear in mind that many big sites are quite easy to get to under your own steam, giving you all the time

you want; especially Chichén, which is on a major bus route.

It's best to be selective with tours, and use them for places otherwise hard to get to. At the other extreme, if expense is a minor consideration, there are **air tours**. Aerocaribe runs occasional one-day tours from Cancún, Cozumel or Mérida to Chichén, Palenque or Tikal in Guatemala (about $200 per head). The air-taxi services Aerobanana, in Cozumel, and Aerosaab, from Playa del Carmen, run light-plane charter-tours to the likes of Isla Mujeres, Chichén, Holbox and San Pedro, in Belize.

Where tours really come into their own is in **Chiapas**. The distances, and the state of many roads, make independent travel into many fascinating but remote areas daunting and slow even if you have a car. One tour worth taking is the two-day trip from Palenque to

hotels, and tailor-made itineraries and an exceptional variety of tours, with the possibility of customized options and extensions.
Hayes & Jarvis, Hayes House, 152 King Street, London W6 0QU, t 0870 898 9890, www.hayes-jarvis.com. Efficient, helpful company offering tours and hotel packages.
Journey Latin America, 12–13 Heathfield Terrace, Chiswick, London W4 4JE, t 020 8747 3108/8315, www.journeylatinamerica.com; 2nd Floor, Burton Arcade, 51–63 Deansgate, Manchester M3 2BH, t 0161 832 1441. One of the best sources for flight-only deals, budget escorted trips through the major Mayan sites and into Guatemala, and bespoke trips.
South American Experience, 47 Causton Street, London SW1P 4AT, t 020 7976 5511, www.southamericanexperience.co.uk. Helpful specialists offering a 'Yucatán Highlights' tour, tailor-made trips, flight-only deals and 'Soft Landings', flight deals with the first two nights' hotel included.
Trips Worldwide, 9 Byron Place, Clifton, Bristol BS8 1JT, t 0117 987 2626, www.tripsworldwide.co.uk. An imaginative range including wildlife tours, fly-drive combinations (an innovation here) and tailor-made itineraries.

Adventure Tours and Treks

Dragoman, Camp Green, Debenham, Stowmarket, Suffolk, IP14 6LA, t 01728 861 133, www.dragoman.co.uk.

Exodus, 9 Weir Road, London SW12 0LT, t 020 8675 5550, www.exodustravels.co.uk.
Explore Worldwide, 1 Frederick Street, Aldershot, Hants, GU11 1LQ, t 01252 760 000, www.exploreworldwide.com.
Funky Tours, www.funkytours.com. A small-scale operation set up by young Canadians with a lot of regional knowledge, whose small-group trips in Mexico, Guatemala, Belize, Cuba and Costa Rica have been very warmly praised. Itineraries are very flexible, according to the wishes of each group.
Mexico Adventures Ltd, 10427 Janway, El Paso TX 79925, USA, t 1 800 206 8132, jrood@mexmail.com. Accommodation bookings, group trips and tailor-made itineraries.
Travelbag Adventures, 15 Turk Street, Alton, Hants, GU34 1AG, t 01420 541 007, www.travelbag-adventures.co.uk.

Scuba Diving

Hayes & Jarvis Diving Worldwide, Hayes House, 152 King Street, London W6 0QU, UK, t 0870 903 7737, www.hayes-jarvis.com. H&J have specialized diving staff and offer full dive packages to Cozumel and sometimes other places nearby.
Scuba Voyages, 595 Fairbanks Street, Corona CA 92879, USA, t 1 800 544 7631, www.scubavoyages.com. A highly-regarded company offering a big range of all-in scuba trips to Cozumel and throughout the Caribbean.

the Mayan forest sites of Yaxchilán and Bonampak, camping overnight in a Lacandón Indian village. Agencies in Palenque offer this tour for around $80–100 a head. In **Highland Chiapas**, you are strongly recommended to visit villages such as Chamula and Zinacantán with a guide from San Cristóbal, as they open doors for you that otherwise stay firmly shut.

Of the other kinds of trips available, some of the most valuable are **nature tours**, which explore the landscapes, wildlife and natural attractions of the region. The Biosphere Reserve of Si'an Kaan, south of Tulum, can only be visited by guided tour (*see* p.217). Most such trips are run for a minimum of four, six or eight people, so if there are fewer of you it's advisable to look around for other interested parties. This kind of trip blends in with using **local guides**. In many towns and villages there

are men (and even women) who make a bit of extra money by guiding visitors around local forests and ruins. A few have a surprising level of English, others none. They are a great help when exploring remote Mayan sites and areas with little infrastructure, and on the coast it's essential to hire local boat-owners (*lancheros*) in order to see birds or wildlife. To have somebody's services for several hours rarely costs more than about $20 ($25–$30 with a boat), but you can cut costs by going as a group.

At the largest **Mayan sites**, you will find officially licensed independent guides available for hire. They are impressively skilled linguists and often very informative; their tours last 1½ hours for a set fee of about $30, which means they're usually only of interest to groups. At more deserted sites you may be approached by local kids who will follow you around as

World of Diving & Adventure Vacations, 301 Main Street, El Segundo CA 90245, USA, t 1 800 900 7657, *www.worldofdiving.com*. A wide range of Cozumel diving packages, covering all experience levels.

In Mexico

Eco-tours

Pronatura Yucatán, C/ 17 no. 188-A, Colonia García Gineres, Mérida, Yucatán, t (999) 925 3787, *www.pronatura.org.mx*. Not actually a tour agency as such but the major local conservation organization, which is a very good source of information.

Crucero Tours, C/ 1 Poniente 10, Tapachula, Chiapas, t (962) 625 2257, *www.crucero tours.com.mx*. Tapachula agency that is developing interesting trips such as rafting in the Sierra Madre and wildlife trips into the Encrucijada reserve.

Ecocolors, C/ Camarón 32, SM27, Cancún, Quintana Roo, t (998) 884 3667, *www.eco travelmexico.com*. Bird-watching, kayaking, cycling, camping and other trips mainly in Quintana Roo and Yucatán state.

Ecoturismo Yucatán, C/ 3 no. 235, between 32-A & 34, Mérida, Yucatán, t (999) 920 2772, *www.ecoyuc.com*. The longest established local specialists, offering a very wide range of trips with able guides, car and mountain-bike hire and hotel bookings.

Explora Ecoturismo y Aventura, C/ 1 de Marzo 45, San Cristóbal de Las Casas, Chiapas, t (967) 678 4295, *explora@prodigynet.mx*. San Cristóbal agency that doesn't follow the standard local routes, but offers adventure trips to three main destinations: Lacanjá, near Bonampak and Yaxchilán, where it has its own camp site; kayaking and hiking in the Lacandón jungle, and rafting down La Venta gorge west of Tuxtla.

Maya Dreams, Av. Palenque 6, SM26, Cancún, Quintana Roo, t (998) 884 3502, *www .gerardotheguide.com*. Local guides offering tours to many parts of the region, including more remote Mayan sites on request.

Mayan Quest, Av. Acanceh 1-01, SM15, Cancún, Quintana Roo, t (998) 887 1578. Highly regarded local company offering nature and bird-watching trips in Sian Ka'an and other locations in Quintana Roo.

Orbitur, C/ 6 no. 480-A, between Av. 19 & Av. Colón, Colonia García Gineres, Mérida, Yucatán, t (999) 925 4566, *orbitur@prodigy .net.mx*. Tours to Celestún, Río Lagartos and other reserves, and also windsurfing trips.

Universo Maya, Hotel Maya Tabasco, Blvd Adolfo Ruíz Cortines 907, Villahermosa, Tabasco, t (993) 314 3696, *www.amtave .com/univmaya*. Organizes guided trips, horseback rides and river trips to the forests and waterfalls of Huimanguillo and to Tabasco's swamps.

your guide, even though they may show little knowledge of what they're looking at. If you wish you can make them go away by paying them off with a few pesos in advance.

Eco-tours

A growing number of agencies organize specialist trips to see the region's wildlife and visit the most remote areas. These are mainly day trips, such as visits to the flamingos at Celestún or Río Lagartos; areas for longer trips, usually including one or more nights camping, are south Quintana Roo, Calakmul and the Río Bec in Campeche, Humanguillo in Tabasco and especially the Lacandón forest in Chiapas. *See* box, facing page, for some of the best local specialists. Information can also be found on 'Eco Travels in Mexico' and other websites (*see* box, 'Useful Websites', p.136).

Entry Formalities

Passports and Visas

Citizens of the USA, Canada, Britain, Ireland and other EU countries, Australia and New Zealand do not need visas to visit Mexico. US and Canadian nationals can officially enter Mexico with only their birth certificate or a certified copy of it, but it's simpler to take a passport. On entering the country all visitors must fill in a **Mexican Tourist Card**, which will be completed and stamped by an immigration officer with the length of your permitted stay. You should keep the card in your passport, and give it up when you leave the country. If you arrive **by air** you will be given the form on the incoming flight, and the airline staff will collect them at check-in when you leave.

If you **drive** into Mexico from the US you are not required to have a card in the *zona fronteriza* (*see* p.107) for stays of up to 72 hours, but if you stay longer or travel further you should ask for one from border officials. There is no charge for a Tourist Card if you arrive by air (the nominal cost is included in the ticket), but if you enter overland from the US, Guatemala or Belize you may be charged 185 pesos or around US$20 for one. This can take time, as you must pay the fee into a Mexican government bank account and then return to the Immigration Office to collect the card.

Standard Tourist Cards are only valid for a maximum of six months, but immigration officers at Cancún and Mérida airports give 30 days to most visitors. Mexican bureaucracy, though, is very inconsistent: in Mexico City most new arrivals are given three (or six) months, while if you come in from Belize to Chetumal, or to Tapachula from Guatemala, you may only be given 15 days, because of suspicions about drugs in those countries. If you want to stay more than 30 days, make this clear to the immigration officer when you arrive, and if this doesn't work, apply for an extension in Cancún, at the office of the **Instituto Nacional de Migración (INM**; *corner of Av. Nader and Av. Uxmal, **t** 884 1749; open Mon–Fri 9–12*). The staff are helpful and efficient, and generally provide extensions to 90 or 180 days without much question. Apply early at 9am and you can probably collect a revised card before lunch. Offices in other cities can be much slower, and may demand obscure documents or charges for permits that in Cancún are free. There are **immigration offices** in many cities, listed in phone books under Secretaría de Gobernación–Instituto Nacional de Migración. Note also that it is particularly important to have your tourist card in order in Chiapas, because of heavier security checks there (*see* 'Crime, Security and Drugs', pp.119–20).

Customs

On arrival visitors are required to fill out a **customs form** (given out on incoming flights). At airports, as you go through customs with your bags, you will be asked to press a button at a thing like a small traffic light; if it comes up green, you walk straight through, if it's red, your bag will be searched. This is intended to guarantee that baggage checks are absolutely random. As elsewhere in the world, checks are more frequent than pre-September 2001.

Departure Tax

On leaving Mexico, airline passengers are required to pay tax of about 145 pesos (US$16). Most airlines now include this in the ticket price, but with some flights it's still necessary to pay in cash at check-in, so it's a good idea to have some cash with you (the fee can be paid in dollars).

Getting Around

By Air

Mexico has an extensive domestic airline network. All the state capitals have daily links to Mexico City, and generally to Cancún and between each other as well. In this region, Cozumel, Ciudad del Carmen and Tapachula airports also have regular services. There are small airports at Palenque, Comitán and San Cristóbal de Las Casas which take scheduled turboprop flights, but they are infrequent, and for Palenque, for example, it's often more convenient to use Villahermosa, a 2–3-hour drive away. There is a small new airport near Chichén Itzá, and airstrips at Playa del Carmen, Isla Mujeres, Isla Holbox and Xcalak, which are used mainly by light-plane air-taxi companies operating out of Playa or Cozumel.

Domestic flights can be very useful for avoiding too many long land journeys, especially between Yucatán and Chiapas, but list prices have risen a lot in recent years and for some routes are surprisingly expensive (around $450, Cancún–Tuxtla return). It's a good idea to make the most of the **MexiPass** system (*see* box, right). Within Mexico, airlines also have occasional offers, advertised in local travel agencies, that are worth looking out for.

By Bus

The bus system is one of the great wonders of Mexico, the glue that holds the Republic together. Wherever you are, no matter how remote the village, there will always be some kind of vehicle that will come chugging along to take you to the nearest town, from where there will be buses on to the nearest city – so that for the traveller there's scarcely anywhere that's completely impossible to reach.

Unless you hire a car buses will be your main means of getting around. There are different grades of buses, giving a choice of prices and comfort levels. In most cities, first- and second-class have separate stations (one exception being Cancún); in smaller places stopping-points are usually shared. When in a taxi or asking directions, specify *la estación de camiones de primera clase* (or *de segunda*).

First-class buses are air-conditioned, modern and comfortable, with reclining seats, ample leg-room and videos of variable quality; many have on-board toilets, and free coffee and soft drinks too. They run between main towns and cities, with only a few set stops on each route. They're inexpensive by international standards, but prices have risen notably in the last few years: Mérida–Cancún costs around $17.50.

In Yucatán, Quintana Roo, Campeche and Tabasco the main first-class company is **ADO** (so the station may just be known as *el ADO*), but there are plenty more. In a few cities there is no single first-class station but each company has its own base. Most companies also offer grades of extra-luxury services, such as the ADO-GL and top-range UNO buses. First-class services are pretty punctual, but very few companies issue printed timetable leaflets, so the only way to find out about which services go where is to phone or, usually easier, just go to the main station and check the timetable board. The routes of different companies are listed separately, which may be confusing but allows you to compare prices.

It is not usually necessary to book first-class buses ahead, except at Mexican holiday times (Christmas and Easter), but you can if you wish. Baggage on first-class buses is rigorously checked in and out. Top-grade buses can be the only place in the Yucatán where you need a sweater; full-strength air conditioning seems to be part of the luxury package.

Second-class buses provide local services and often follow similar routes to those of the first-class buses, but stop in just about every village and are generally older, do not have air conditioning and are around 25–30% cheaper. Second-class buses are essential for getting to any smaller places, but taking them long-distance can be a false economy, given the extra time and discomfort involved.

There are also services called *intermedios*, especially the **Riviera** and **Mayab** buses along the Cancún–Chetumal highway, which do not stop quite as often as second-class buses, and similarly offer an *intermedio* level of comfort, in many cases not much different from that of first class.

It's not usually possible to book ahead for second-class buses, and they're more likely to be full; you just have to queue for a ticket.

Booking Information for Internal Flights

The MexiPass

Operated jointly by Mexicana/Aerocaribe and Aeroméxico, the MexiPass gives foreign visitors discounts of around 50% on internal flights, such as $115 for Cancún-Tuxtla one-way. You can enter Mexico with any airline, but you must book your MexiPass tickets outside the country at the same time as you buy your main ticket, specifying the routes you wish to travel, and take at least two domestic flights per person on the same trip (three, if travelling from North America). However, you can change dates, and destinations within the same price brackets, for no extra charge.

For further information, contact:

In the USA and Canada: t 1 800 531 7921.

In the UK: Cathy Matos Mexican Tours, t 020 8492 0000.

Major Domestic Air Carriers

Aerocaribe, t (998) 884 2000 (Cancún); t (999) 928 6790 (Mérida); www.aerocaribe.com.mx. The regional subsidiary of Mexicana, with the most comprehensive route network in the Yucatán and Chiapas. Particularly useful is their daily 'bus flight' between Havana, Cancún and Oaxaca, with stops at Mérida, Villahermosa and Tuxtla Gutiérrez. Aerocaribe also operates turboprop services most days into Palenque from Cancún, Mérida and Tuxtla Gutiérrez, and includes **Aerocozumel**, which runs an eight-flights-a-day shuttle between Cancún and Cozumel. Aerocaribe's **international service** flies from Cancún to Belize, Havana and Guatemala City and Flores in Guatemala (inc. one-day Tikal tours); parent **Mexicana** operates from Cancún, Cozumel and Mérida to Mexico City.

Aeromar, t 5133 1107 (Mexico City); t (961) 615 0552 (Tuxtla Gutiérrez). Turboprop flights between Mexico City and San Cristóbal de Las Casas and Comitán in Chiapas. It also hopes to begin Mérida–San Cristóbal flights.

Aeroméxico, t (998) 884 3571 (Cancún); t (999) 920 1293 (Mérida); www.aeromexico.com .mx. Flights from Cancún and Mérida to Mexico City, Villahermosa and Tuxtla Gutiérrez, and from Cancún to Chetumal; it is also virtually the only airline serving Campeche, with flights to Mexico City.

Aviacsa, t (998) 887 4214 (Cancún); t (999) 946 2164 (Mérida); www.aviacsa.com.mx. Flights between Mexico City and Cancún, Mérida, Chetumal and Tuxtla, as well as several cities in the north of the country, and many services to Tapachula.

Again, there are no printed timetables; different services are signed up on a board above the ticket windows. Baggage is not checked in; you place it yourself in the side compartments or overhead racks inside the bus. Watch over your bags, especially in the south of Campeche and northern Chiapas.

Colectivos, also known as *combis*, fill in any gaps left by the other two. Villages that cannot sustain a second-class bus route have at least one or two *combis* that run up and down to the local town, perhaps once or twice a day, but often more frequently. Other *combis* run long distances along the same routes as second-class buses, but are even cheaper. In many places *combis* are licensed as taxis, in others it may just be somebody who has a van. *Combis* stop wherever anyone wants them to. They are becoming more organized in places, but to a great extent *colectivos* still form a word-of-mouth system. In towns, there are known places where *combis* from a particular village arrive and depart, usually near markets and often in a particular square. These *combi*-points are acknowledged, and may even have a battered sign, but tourist offices often know nothing about them. The only way to find one for a particular village is to wander around and ask: '*¿Por favor, dónde salen los colectivos para...?*' Similarly, at the other end you will have to ask when there is a *colectivo* for town B and where it leaves from (usually the main square).

This is not a quick mode of transport, and being prepared to be told that there isn't one for hours and taking the wait as an opportunity to absorb the atmosphere is part of the experience. When you squeeze into a *combi*, ask the driver how much it is to where you want to go, and, if you're at the back, pass the money to other passengers to hand forward. Change is passed back just as punctiliously.

Local Buses

Most cities have local bus services. In fact, in some places it can seem that the traffic is made up of nothing but buses of all sizes: roaring, full-size models, van-size microbuses, and *combis*. In most towns buses do not have route numbers. Instead, since the same buses always ply the same route, their destinations are painted on the windscreen. Using them involves a little knowledge of local geography, and it's best to pick a street or landmark that you're heading for, and look for that. Again, it helps if you can ask around, or ask the driver. Fares are the same for each route no matter how far you travel, rarely more than 3–5 pesos. Urban *combis* are even cheaper. Some towns have set bus stops with blue and white signs, but more usual practice is simply to flag buses or *combis* down at street corners.

By Car

It's possible to get to just about anywhere in Mexico by bus – eventually. However, if you don't have infinite amounts of time, a car is an enormous asset. It is especially so if you wish to visit remoter parts of the Caribbean coast or more out-of-the-way Mayan sites, including even some well-known ones such as those on the Puuc route: bus and *combi* routes answer the needs of local people, not tourists, so there may be very few that go near isolated sites.

Car Hire

To hire a car you must be over 21 and have a driving licence, your passport and a credit card. Some agencies give discounts if you pay in cash, but you will still need a credit card to use against a deposit. The basic Mexican hire car is the Volkswagen Beetle (Bug), still in production in Puebla; the next grade up, usually a small Chevy hatchback or a Nissan, may give the option of air-conditioning. In Cancún and on the coast many agencies offer small 4-wheel-drives, at around $80 a day.

Hiring a car is much easier in some places here than others. The main concentrations of rental agencies are in Cancún and on the 'Riviera Maya', in Mérida and in Villahermosa, with others scattered around other towns such as Ciudad del Carmen, San Cristóbal de Las Casas and Tapachula. Car hire rates in

Cancún are no longer all as expensive as they once were but, in general, if you intend to drive any distance, it is best to go to **Mérida** and hire a car there. In Mérida there are small local agencies, such as **México Rent a Car** (*see* p.266), which offer by far the best prices in the region (from about $30 a day) and give good discounts for weekly or longer-term rents.

Cancún has a great many hire-car agencies among which there are now small agencies that offer rates from around $40 a day, but overall you still find the best deals in Mérida; in Playa del Carmen and other coast towns rates still tend to be high-ish. Car hire is particularly difficult, and expensive, in Chetumal and Campeche. Mérida agencies will often arrange for a car to be dropped off in Cancún, if you are leaving from there; they cannot arrange drop-off in Chiapas or Tabasco, but if you need a car in that area and do not want to return to Mérida agencies in **Villahermosa**, while not as cheap, are still reasonable. Local agencies also tend to keep their cars in better condition than the big franchises in Mexico.

Driving in Mexico

Driving here presents no great difficulties, if a few peculiarities. Main roads are mostly in good condition; on secondary roads look out for potholes and sudden lurches in the road surface, which make it inadvisable to drive at night. Sooner or later you will have to negotiate a few dirt tracks, which may be slow but except after rain are usually passable in an ordinary car. The biggest peculiarity of driving here is the *tope*. This is a speed bump, but not as you know it. In Mexican villages old men chew the fat and kids run around in the street, and cars do not have automatic priority. The *tope* is designed to keep things that way. They may be gentle humps, or upturned bricks that, if attempted in anything higher than first gear, will bring you down the other side with a spine-jarring crash. In towns, they double as pedestrian crossings. On the outskirts of many villages they are announced well ahead (signs saying '*Topes a 200m*'), but in remoter places (especially in Campeche State) you can come upon them completely unawares. It is impossible to drive around Mexico for more than two days without being caught out by at least one *tope*.

Flat tyres are relatively frequent, due to debris on roads and stones on dirt tracks. When you hire a car, the agency should check the spare and ensure it is in good condition. If you have to stop for a flat on a main highway, you are required by law to place behind the car a red warning triangle, which should also come with the car. Once you've changed the wheel, in the nearest village there will almost certainly be a tyre repair shop, called a *llantera* or a *vulcanizadora*, which will fix the tyre and put it back on for you for about 20 pesos.

Local road habits include a strange convention that, when two vehicles approach on a narrow road, the one who flashes their lights first claims the right of way. Another is that Mexican drivers rarely indicate when about to turn, but often put on hazard warning lights as a vague sign that some manoeuvre is imminent. On the other hand, if you are behind a slow-moving vehicle such as a big truck on an open road, it may indicate left: this is a helpful gesture, to tell you it's clear to overtake.

Speed bumps aside, official speed limits are generally 80 to 110kph on main highways, 60kph in the outskirts of towns and 40kph or less in town centres. Fines can be levied on the spot. Also, as everyone must know, police here occasionally pull cars over, find things wrong with them, stand around, threaten undefined prosecutions and otherwise waste the driver's time. This is the application of the *mordida* ('bite'). In such cases, you can if you wish stand on your dignity, refuse to take the hint, and see whose nerve will crack first; otherwise, the standard procedure is to say something like '*Tengo mucha prisa, ¿no se puede arreglar esto?*' ('I'm in a hurry, can't we sort this out?'), and proffer 100–200 pesos. Bear in mind, though, that it's very easy to drive around the Yucatán for days on end without anything this picturesque ever happening to you. You will have to stop at army checkpoints (*see* 'Crime, Security and Drugs', pp.119–20), but they are not usually interested in foreigners.

There are two toll **motorways** in this region. The most important is the *180-Cuota* part of the way between Mérida and Cancún. This must be one of the least-used major roads in the world: the toll, at over $25, is seen as too much by most Mexicans, and it has too few exits. Unless you're in a real hurry, it's far more interesting, as well as cheaper, to take the parallel old road, the *180-Libre*. At each end the roads are signposted *Mérida-Cuota* and *Mérida-Libre*. There is a more useful *Cuota* road south of Campeche to Champotón.

Parking is restricted in city centres. Where this is so, the kerb is painted yellow (sometimes red), and police reaction if you park there can be surprisingly swift. Many hotels have car parks and there are also private car parks (marked **E** or **Estacionamiento Público**). When a street has unrestricted parking it will often be staked out by an *aparcacoches*, a man with a red rag who stops the traffic for you, waves you in and offers to watch over your car for a few pesos. This is one of many ways the very poor have of making a little money.

Petrol/Gasoline

All petrol/gasoline in Mexico is sold by the state oil company, **Pemex**. Prices are climbing and now higher than in the USA, but still below European levels (about 60 US cents a litre). All Pemex stations sell unleaded (*magna* and higher-grade *premium*) and diesel fuel. Petrol stations (*gasolineras*) are easy to find around cities, and there is usually one in each town in Yucatán state and the Cancún area. There are rarely any between towns along main highways, and they are very thinly distributed in many rural areas, especially in southern Quintana Roo and Campeche. It pays to know where they are, and above all to fill up whenever you get the chance. In villages without a *gasolinera* there will usually be someone who sells fuel unofficially from a tank, a ramshackle but practical arrangement; ask in shops if there's anyone selling *gasolina*.

To ask for a full tank, just say '*lleno, por favor*'. There is an 'etiquette' to follow at *gasolineras*. It is not unknown for unwary tourists to be short-changed or, especially, for attendants to start the pump with 50 pesos or so already on the gauge. This is not to say that all staff will do this, as many are perfectly friendly, but it's advisable to do what Mexicans themselves do: when you drive in, get out of the car, and look straight at the pump. The attendant will then demonstrate that the pump is properly set at zero before turning it on. It also makes it clear that you know what you're doing, and should discourage most other scams.

By Ferry

Frequent passenger-only ferries run to **Isla Mujeres** from Puerto Juárez, north of Cancún, and to **Cozumel** from Playa del Carmen. There are also more expensive boats to both islands from Cancún. Car ferry services are separate: the Isla Mujeres car ferry runs from Punta Sam, a little further north from Cancún, and the very inefficient Cozumel car ferry operates from Puerto Morelos. There are also daily passenger launches between **Isla Holbox** and Chiquilá on the north coast of Quintana Roo.

By Taxi

There are taxis in all cities, towns and even villages, and they're never hard to find. In smaller places, they blend indistinguishably into *colectivos* (see 'By Bus', p.113). If you have a car to yourself, it's a taxi; if you share, it's a *colectivo*. Similarly, in towns like Villahermosa where taxis are used by locals almost as much as buses, don't be surprised if after you've got into a cab the driver then stops to pick up somebody else going the same way. You will probably still be asked to pay the normal fare.

Taxis do not have meters. Instead, in each area there are officially set rates for journeys within a town, to the outskirts and so on. This could be expected to create problems, but in fact with one big exception usually works very well on trust: in towns with few tourists like Villahermosa or Chetumal drivers rarely overcharge you, even though they must realize you probably don't know what the official rates are. The exception is Cancún and the Riviera. Cancún taxi drivers have a bad reputation for trying out inflated *gringo* rates on any foreigner. It's useful to know what the current correct rates are (see p.150): these are posted at taxi stands at the bus station and in Puerto Juárez, and given in free magazines such as *Cancún Tips* and *Playa del Carmen* that are distributed in many hotels. The other rule is always to agree the price to your destination **before** you get in a cab, and be firm about rejecting anything outrageous.

In most places taxis are cheap: within most towns, the standard fare is around 15 pesos ($1.70) or less. In Mérida cabs are more expensive, with a minimum fare of 30 pesos ($3.30).

In Cancún official rates are cheap for trips within Ciudad Cancún, but more than double for anywhere in the Hotel Zone or to the airport. Cabs will travel long distances, such as the whole length of the 'Riviera Maya', so long as you agree a price first. For a group, this can work out cheaper than taking a bus. For taxis to and from airports, *see* 'Getting There', p.107.

By Train

After years in which Mexico's once-famous railway system slid towards total dereliction, it finally gave up the ghost in 1997, when the whole network was privatized. In the south, the new company gave up passenger services completely, and the lines now carry only freight. A plan has been mooted to provide an 'Orient-Express'-style luxury tourist service on the old line between Mérida and Palenque via Campeche, but it's taking a long time getting going (*see* www.expresomaya.com for an optimistic vision of the project).

Cuba for the Weekend

Mexico has never severed its links with Cuba, and the Yucatán has acquired a significant position as a jumping-off point for trips to the island. There is a daily **Aerocaribe** Oaxaca–Mérida–Cancún flight which goes on to (and returns from) Havana, and there are also **Cubana** services. Since most things in Cuba are very cheap, so too is a trip there: a four-day package from Mérida, hotel included, can cost around $250 US, and flight-only deals are also available.

Many local agencies offer bargain trips to Cuba, including the following:
Mérida: Yucatán Trails, C/ 62 no. 482, x 57 & 59, t (999) 928 2582 (*see* p.268).
Cancún: Viajes Divermex, in the Plaza América mall, Av. Cobá 5, t (998) 887 5005.

Visas

As well as a flight you will need a Cuban **visa**, which costs $20. You do not have to seek out a Cuban consulate to obtain one, as the same agency that sells you the ticket will get it for you, usually within 24 hours. You need only provide photocopies of your passport.

Practical A–Z

08

Children

The Highland Indians of Chiapas often ask why *gringos* never seem to have any children. Away from beach resorts, foreign children are seen relatively rarely; Mexican children, on the other hand, are everywhere.

Brave parents who venture into the Mexican interior with young children often find that they represent a point of contact with locals that's lost to the childless traveller. Children get smiled at and indulged and their parents are accorded added respect.

On a practical level, Cancún and the Riviera offer all the facilities associated with a family holiday: hotel pools, water parks, rides and, of course, beaches. **Eco-theme-parks** like Xcaret are quite expensive, but provide an enjoyable and very safe introduction to snorkelling in Caribbean lagoons. There are also **dolphin pools** (*see* p.94). Of the beach areas, Cozumel is probably the best for kids, with the most tranquil waters and most to see just offshore. Away from the Caribbean there are fewer child-oriented attractions, and keeping kids entertained is more a matter of involving them in local sights. The big Mayan ruins such as Chichén provide huge spaces for exploring, while Palenque is surrounded by real jungle. Villahermosa and Tuxtla Gutiérrez have great zoos, with otherwise hard-to-see local wildlife. It's best to travel with a **hired car**, as long bus journeys are perfect for getting kids bored, and it will also work out cheaper.

No Mexican **hotel** objects to a whole family sharing a room, at only marginally higher prices. **Restaurants** will often try to cater for special requests. If your children are inflexible, there are pizzerias (and burger chains) in most towns. As regards drinks, local milk is thin, and if you really need it stick to the best (most expensive) brands available in supermarkets. Try to interest kids in the local fruit juices; otherwise, Coke or Pepsi are always available.

Climate and When to Go

The whole of the Yucatán and Chiapas is below the Tropic of Cancer, and the region's climate follows the usual tropical pattern of a dry season building up in heat from roughly October to May, followed by a rainy season

Climate Calendar

Mid-December–February
Temperatures throughout the Yucatán, and in most of the rainforest areas, are ideal: hot but not oppressive. In the Highlands, it can get pretty cold at night. This is the peak tourist season, above all at Christmas and New Year.

March–mid-June
The heat picks up, though it's still a good time to travel around. The number of fellow-travellers drops rapidly from early February (except around the equinox in Chichén Itzá, and during Easter). Prices are also off-peak. The truly hot *seca* ('dry spell') doesn't usually start till mid-May. In Highland Chiapas the weather from February to early May is superb.

Mid-June–September
June and September are usually the rainiest months. In the Yucatán peninsula the rain is by no means continuous, temperatures are high, and in Cancún and on the coast the July/August period is actually busy. In the forest and highland areas the rains are much heavier, and travel may be difficult, and tours cancelled, due to the state of the roads.

Mid-September–December
The rains tail off in most areas. This is when the Yucatán gets fewest visitors, in part because it's also the peak hurricane season. But once the rains are done the weather is delicious, nowhere is crowded, and prices are at their lowest point in the whole year. Come from mid-November to early December, when the hurricane risk is negligible.

from late May to September, although in recent years the weather has become noticeably more volatile. If you want to see wildlife, it's actually better to come in the rainy season, but the downside is that along with creatures you do want to see there also emerge some you probably don't (bugs and snakes), and dirt roads in remote areas may be impassable.

There are also major differences in climate from one area to another. Roughly speaking, there are three climatic zones across this region. The whole of the **Yucatán peninsula** is hot, with dry-season daytime temperatures climbing from a mild mid-20s °C (about 75°F) in January up to 40°C (103°F) by late May, but dry, with humidity rarely much over 70°. **Tabasco, southern Campeche**, the lowlands of **northern Chiapas** around Palenque and the Pacific coastal strip of the **Soconusco** are real rainforest territory – or were, before huge swathes were cut down. Temperatures are a few degrees higher than in the peninsula, and the atmosphere is often very steamy. In both these zones nights are cooler, but the difference in temperature is not that great. In the third zone, **Highland Chiapas**, the mountain air is crisp and cool: around 12°C (55°F) by day Dec–Jan, and rarely much above the low 20s°C (70°F) at any time. Temperatures drop sharply at night. Rainfall is particularly heavy in June and September, but the weather is erratic.

Hurricanes

Should your visit be disturbed by a hurricane warning, the best thing to do is simply get to somewhere else. Mexico has now developed considerable anti-hurricane precautions, particularly in Cancún, where many buildings carry an orange sign identifying them as an official *Refugio Anticiclón* (Hurricane Shelter).

Crime, Security and Drugs

Is Mexico Dangerous?

There is a long-standing preconception that Mexico is a violent and dangerous place, in which you need to watch your back. The US State Department advisories to travellers customarily give a long list of warnings and things not to do. A few hours after arriving in the Yucatán, though, you wonder what they're talking about. This is a very peaceful and tranquil place, and many of the Americans and Canadians who retire here cite the absence of crime as a prime reason for coming.

Diplomatic warnings and TV reports have in common that they take their references overwhelmingly from the urban crisis zones of Mexico City and the northern border cities. This blanket approach obscures a distinctive, gentle decency noted by many as characteristic of the Yucatán region. The crime rate in most of the Yucatán peninsula is actually very low. There are few firearms in circulation, and violent crime of any kind is rare.

There are some places where the risks are higher. Parts of Cancún City – away from the more touristy areas – are developing a little of an edgy, urban atmosphere, and the level of petty crime, assaults, beach thefts and so on has sadly been increasing in Playa del Carmen and in parts of Tulum. There is a greater likelihood of street thefts in Tabasco and northern Chiapas. However, so long as you keep to some standard, sensible rules – stay where there are people around, watch your bags – even in these areas it's easy to travel around without anything happening to you.

If you are robbed, report the incident to the police to get an official statement for an insurance claim. In Mérida, Cancún, Playa del Carmen and some other towns there are special **Policía Turística** units with English-speaking officers. *Cancún Tips* (*see* p.150) is handy for its list of emergency numbers.

Political Violence and Military Checks

Since 1994 there has been an ongoing conflict in parts of Chiapas involving the Zapatista rebels, the Mexican army, right-wing paramilitaries and others. Most of the time this has had the nature of a 'low-intensity conflict', with murders, harassment and so on occurring sporadically, in secret and often with no clear evidence as to those responsible. From 2000, the new government's willingness to negotiate was reflected in a marked reduction in tensions in Chiapas. However, their proposed Law on the Rights of Indigenous Communities (April 2001) failed to meet the expectations of the Zapatistas and other Indian groups, causing renewed uncertainty (for more on the politics of Chiapas, *see* p.466).

The implications this situation has for travellers need to be viewed from two distinct angles. One is from the point of view of one's feelings about travelling in a region of social conflict, which is really a matter of personal opinions and attitudes. The other is strictly with regard to whether it creates dangers for travellers themselves. It's wise to avoid any shaky predictions, for the situation could still deteriorate back into open violence. The best advice when you travel in the area is to check on current circumstances through the press, other travellers or local agencies. Palenque is a good place to get first-hand information on conditions further south, and it's also worth looking up the Mexico Channel (*www.trace-sc.com*) for up-to-date news and travel advice.

In this author's opinion, the circumstances as they stand do not create special dangers for foreign travellers. The Zapatistas have never engaged in attacks on tourists or hostage-taking. They have been more concerned with retaining the moral high ground and their favourable standing in international opinion. A direct danger is more likely to come from the shadowy right-wing groups, but so far they haven't attacked any tourists either. The foreign visitor in Chiapas is actually in a position of greater safety than locals. San Cristóbal de Las Casas and the main villages visited by travellers are peaceful, and most foreigners are unlikely to go near the real conflict areas (or any paramilitaries) unless they go looking for them. There is very little ordinary crime in central Chiapas. Perhaps most importantly, the main sides in the conflict are all concerned that nothing should happen to you: the Zapatistas believe that having foreigners around helps mobilize international opinion in their favour, while the military are concerned that you should go on your way with the least unpleasantness.

Wherever you travel you will encounter **military checkpoints** on country highways. In Quintana Roo, Yucatán state and Campeche their main stated function is to help prevent drug trans-shipments through the peninsula. Don't be spooked: the soldiers cause little trouble to foreigners, and usually just ask you where you're going and wish you a good day. They may ask to look at your bags and check your passport and tourist card (especially in Chiapas), which should be in order.

Drugs

It is well known that Mexico is a major marijuana producer (mostly in the north) and a conduit for drugs on their way to North America. In the region covered by this book there are persistent stories of remote parts of the Quintana Roo coast being used as staging posts and fuel stops for boats and planes carrying drugs from Colombia to the US. In response to both US pressure and a growing domestic drug problem in Mexican cities there are severe penalties for possession or trans-porting of marijuana or narcotics. The primary purpose of army checkpoints on roads in the Yucatán is to look for drugs. Anyone arrested in possession is usually refused bail. The safest thing is, of course, not to touch them.

Disabled Travellers

Special facilities for disabled people, such as handrails and ramps, have been relatively scarce in Mexico but their provision has improved enormously in the last few years – especially in Cancún, where there are now wheelchair ramps in many streets. The lack of specific facilities may be compensated for in part by people's willingness to be helpful: bus drivers and ferry crews will often make great efforts to find space for a chair and baggage. There are also nice surprises: most state **museums**, such as the Anthropology Museum in Mérida, have access ramps, and more are being installed. Of the **archaeological sites**, Chichén Itzá and Uxmal have smooth-ish walkways in main areas that are chair-accessible, but most have earth and stone paths where the going is difficult. **Hotels** with decent access include many upscale places in Cancún and Cozumel. Smaller and colonial-style hotels tend to be less suitable, but some have good-sized ground-floor rooms.

In the UK

RADAR, 12 City Forum, 250 City Road, London EC1V 8AF, **t** 020 7250 3222, *www.radar.org.uk*.
UK Disabled Living Foundation, **t** 020 7289 6111/0845 130 9177, *www.dlf.org.uk*.

In the USA

Mobility International USA, PO Box 10767, Eugene OR 97440, USA, **t** (541) 343 1284, *www.miusa.org*.

Eating Out

Throughout the guide restaurants are arranged in three **price categories** (*see box, p.121*), based on price per head for an average three-course meal with drinks. However, there is no obligation to have multiple courses, so meals can easily work out cheaper. Bear in mind that the *expensive* range is an open-

Price Categories
Note: *Prices based on the cost of a three-course meal*

Category	US Dollars ($)	UK Pounds Sterling (£)	Mexican Pesos ($)
expensive	Over $20	Over £14.50	Over $180
moderate	$8–20	£6–14.50	$70–180
cheap	Under $8	Under £6	Under $70

ended one, so that while in Cancún there are places where you can easily spend over $30 a head, in Chiapas it may be hard to part with over $20 even in the best restaurant in town.

Tipping in Bars and Restaurants
It's normal to tip in all restaurants, and at bars if you've had more than one drink. The going rate is 10%, though on the Cancún coast waiters may expect more. Wherever you are, tip more if the service has been especially good. A growing number of restaurants add service charge (usually 10%) to the bill, in which case you're not expected to add more.

See **Food and Drink**, pp.95–104, for a glossary of related vocabulary and more detailed information on Mexican cuisine and tastes. For advice on drinking water, see 'Heath and Insurance', pp.124–5.

Electricity
Electricity in Mexico works on a 110v system, as in the USA and Canada, with the same flat-pin plugs. Newer equipment has three- rather than two-pin plugs; adaptors from three to two pins can be bought in any *tlapalería* or ironmongers (in Calle 58 x 61 in Mérida there are several). If you wish to use any British or European 220/240v equipment you should take a current transformer and plug adaptor with you, as these are impossible to get here.

Embassies and Consulates
Besides their embassies in Mexico City, many countries also operate consular sections in Cancún and other towns in the southern states (see below for contact details).

Entertainment
Every Mexican town has a few discos, and cities have air-conditioned cinemas that show Hollywood movies, as on TV, in English with Spanish subtitles; this is rarely stated on advertising, so the only way to find out is to ask. However, just as life on the street is often more interesting than anything you

Embassies and Consulates

In Mexico City and Southern Mexico
Belize: Consulates in Cancún and Chetumal (for details, see under individual towns).
Canada: Mexico City: Canadian Embassy, C/ Schiller 529 (Rincón del Bosque), Colonia Polanco, CP 11580, Mexico D.F., t (55) 5724 7900;
Cancún: Canadian Consulate, Plaza Caracol II, Third Floor, room 330, Blvd Kukulkán Km8.5, Hotel Zone, CP 77500 Cancún, t (998) 883 3360.
Cuba: Consulate in Mérida. (note: it is not necessary to go in person in order to travel from the Yucatán to Cuba, see *Travel*, p.116).
Guatemala: Consulates in Chetumal, Comitán and Tapachula (for details, see under individual towns).

UK: Mexico City: British Embassy Consular Section, C/ Río Usumacinta 30, Colonia Cuauhtémoc, CP 06500, Mexico D.F., t (55) 5242 8500.
Cancún: British Vice-Consulate, Royal Sands Hotel, Blvd Kukulkán Km13.5, Hotel Zone, CP 77500 Cancún, t (998) 881 0100.
US: Mexico City: US Embassy, Paseo de la Reforma 305, Colonia Cuauhtémoc, CP 06500, Mexico D.F., t (55) 5209 9100;
Cancún: US Vice-Consulate, Plaza Caracol II, Second Floor, room 320–23, Blvd Kukulkán Km8.5, Hotel Zone, CP 77500 Cancún, t (998) 883 2450;
Cozumel: Villa Mar Mall, office 8, Av. Juárez 33, CP77600 Cozumel, t (987) 872 4574;
Mérida: US Consulate-General, Paseo de Montejo 453, near corner of Av. Colón, CP 97000 Mérida, t (99) 925 5011.

have to pay for, in Mexico a lot of live entertainment is on offer informally and with no set timetable. Music can be found in all kinds of places; in bars and restaurants, or individually commissioned in the troubadour style of the Yucatán trios or *mariachis*. It's also a real community experience: as well as *fiestas* (*see* facing page), many towns organize free concerts, folklore displays or street dances in central squares on one day or more every week (usually Sunday).

There are also two very specific kinds of 'show' on view in the region. The Spanish-style **bullfight** has a long tradition in the Yucatán, and is a customary feature of village *fiestas* (*see* p.124). There are bullrings in Mérida and Cancún.

The other distinctive spectacle found in most cities is the **charrería**. A *charro* is a Mexican cowboy, dressed in the classic wide *sombrero*, embroidered bolero jacket and tight trousers with buttons and more embroidery down the leg. Like those other elements of typical Mexican-ness, *mariachis* and tequila, their real home is the state of Jalisco in central Mexico, and in the Yucatán they're something of an artificial imported article. Nevertheless, a *charrería* can be genuinely impressive. A kind of rodeo, it features horse-wrangling, steer-wrestling and displays of extraordinary horsemanship and rope tricks by the *charros* and *charras* (whose feats can be even more impressive, since to remain ladylike they must ride side-saddle in flouncy skirts). There are *lienzos charros* (special grounds for the shows) outside most large towns, holding *charrerías* on occasional weekends. Tourist offices have details of upcoming events.

Calendar of Events

January

1 Jan *Año Nuevo* (New Year's Day). Celebrated with parties and parades in the main cities.

6 Jan *Día de Reyes* (Feast of Three Kings, or Epiphany). Children all over the Hispanic world receive their Christmas presents; *Fiesta Mayor de Tizimín* (**Yucatán**). The town sees especially big festivities as Epiphany coincides with its Saint's day.

20 Jan *San Sebastián*. Celebrated in San Juan Chamula, in the **Chiapas** Highlands; also the main *fiesta* in Chiapa de Corzo, the most elaborate and colourful of the festivals of *ladino* (non-Maya) Chiapas.

23 Jan *San Ildefonso*. The patron saint of Tenejapa, **Chiapas**. Celebrations get going several days beforehand, making this the first major Highland Maya village festival.

February

2 Feb *La Candelaria* (Candlemas). A major religious festival, with night processions (with hundreds of candles) and *fiesta* entertainments. Celebrated all over the **Yucatán**, but above all in Campeche and Tekoh.

Late Jan/Feb *Carnival*. Most spectacular in Mérida, where it's the biggest *fiesta* of the year, but there are events in most **Yucatán** towns. A rather synthetic one is gradually gaining momentum in Cancún.

Late Jan/Feb *Carnival of San Juan Chamula* (**Chiapas**). The most remarkable of Highland Maya festivals (*see* p.494).

March

21 Mar *Equinox*. The only annual 'celebration' that could be called 'pre-Columbian', if its existence was not a modern revival: traditionally observed at Dzibilchaltún and Chichén Itzá (**Yucatán**), the latter of which is getting too big for its own good.

April

Mar–April *Semana Santa*. Holy Week is low-key in much of the **Yucatán** and **Quintana Roo**, as everyone makes a bee-line for the beach, but celebrations are a bit more elaborate on Cozumel. Further south, Easter is a much more important traditional celebration. There are spectacular processions and ceremonies all week in San Cristóbal and other towns, and a typical Chiapanecan mix of rituals in the outlying villages (**Chiapas**).

Late April–May *Feria de Tabasco*. The Tabasco State Fair takes over Villahermosa (**Tabasco**); it may not be traditional or religious, but it is great fun.

June

Early June (or late May) *Corpus Christi*. Another significant festival in that city *of fiestas*, San Cristóbal de Las Casas (**Chiapas**).

Festivals and *Fiestas*

We are a ritualistic people.

Octavio Paz, *The Labyrinth of Solitude*

Paz, the classic collective psychoanalyst of modern Mexico, is just one of many writers who have pointed to the immense importance of *fiestas* throughout the country. Every town or village has at least one major festival each year, nearly always on the day of its patron saint, and different districts, churches, trades or other groups often have their own patrons too.

The *fiesta* is one of the essential features of Mexico, the ultimate synthesis of the country's two primary traditions, Spanish Catholicism and pre-Columbian culture.

Local festivals are spectacular. In towns, the streets are garlanded in livid colours, there are even more food stands, balloon-sellers and crowds than on a normal Sunday and music is provided by traditional groups, *mariachis*, pop groups and salsa and dance bands. Fireworks go off all over the place. The village *fiestas* are similarly colourful but more low-key, although they can be wilder. As the *fiesta* is usually in honour of a saint, there is normally a religious procession on the main day of the feast.

A few *fiestas*, such as the **Virgin of Guadalupe**, are celebrated across the entire country. Most, however, are strictly local. Moreover, it is here in the heavily 'Indian' states that local festivals stray most from the conventional Catholic calendar and show the strongest pre-Columbian, pre-Christian influences.

24 June *Fiesta* of St John the Baptist. San Juan Chamula's actual Patron-Feast (**Chiapas**).

July
16 July *Fiesta de la Virgen del Carmen.* The little oil town of Ciudad del Carmen (**Campeche**) throws a big *fiesta* for its patron on her day.
25 July *Santiago (Saint James).* Yet more celebrations in Highland communities (**Chiapas**).

August
15 Aug *La Asunción* (Feast of the Assumption). One of the most important religious festivals in **Yucatán**; the Mayan town of Oxcutzcab has a lively *fiesta* in the week preceding the Assumption, while Izamal sees religious celebrations on the day itself.
10 Aug *San Lorenzo.* The Patron-Feast of Zinacantán (**Chiapas**), giving the best opportunity of the year to hear the Zinacantecos' strange, unearthly festival music.

September–October
27 Oct–13 Oct *Cristo de las Ampollas* (Christ of the Blisters). Throughout this period Mérida (**Yucatán**) has a religious festival, featuring devotional processions.

November
2 Nov *Día de los Muertos* (Day of the Dead). Perhaps the most famous of all Mexican *fiestas*, one of the select few events common to every part of the country. It's actually part of a three-day holiday, beginning on the Eve of All Saints' Day, *Halloween* (**31 Oct**) and continuing through *All Saints'* (**1 Nov**). At the culmination of this celebration of the dead, during which toys, sweets and multi-coloured decorations formed in the shape of skeletons and coffins can be seen on every street and in every kid's hand, families troop off to the cemetery with a picnic to have a party with their own departed, a marking of the continuity between the living and the dead that can be traced to pre-Columbian times. Foreigners are not likely to be invited along, but few can avoid being fascinated by the pink sugar skulls, death's-head garlands and other souvenirs that fill the shops, presenting death not so much as something to be feared than as an integral part of life.

December
8 Dec *Immaculate Conception.* Particularly important in Izamal (**Yucatán**), with pilgrimages and ceremonies in the Virgin's honour.
12 Dec *Virgin of Guadalupe.* Major celebrations are held throughout Mexico, but especially in San Cristóbal de Las Casas (**Chiapas**), and each of the Highland communities has its own way of paying their respects.
25 Dec *Navidad.* A wide range of celebrations take place everywhere throughout the whole Christmas period.

In the Yucatán (including Yucatán state, Quintana Roo and Campeche), **Carnival** is a major event, but curiously **Easter** goes by with relatively few ceremonies: for most people it's just the main break from work in the year, when just about everyone heads to a beach or somewhere cool. Local *fiestas* in honour of patron saints are most frequent between February and September. A feature of nearly all Yucatán town fiestas is **bullfights**. This, obviously, is a Spanish introduction, but the links between the regulated ritual presented in Madrid or Mexico City and the Yucatecan village affair can be pretty tenuous. For one thing, the bull (or, sometimes, cow) doesn't always die; it may be too valuable for that. Animal rights supporters are unlikely to find it much more acceptable, however, as instead the beast is just tormented for half an hour or so. It may be something of a consolation to know that, statistically, the 'bullfighters' are actually in greater danger of serious injury than the bull. Announcements of upcoming *fiestas* always appear in the *Diario de Yucatán*.

Among the Highland Maya of Chiapas, whose whole life is dominated by ritual, the notion of the festival reaches another level still. They are the most overt, vivid demonstration of the survival of the Mayan past, an extraordinary synthesis of Catholic ritual and an ancient Mayan essence that has given dream material to generations of anthropologists. The **Carnival of Chamula** is the most famous and most spectacular, but there are many more. Some of the main fiestas of southern Mexico are listed in the Calendar of Events (*see* pp.122–3), though inevitably the list is far from exhaustive. For more detailed information, *see* those chapters covering the places mentioned.

Health and Insurance

Mérida: *call t 066 for all emergency services.*
Elsewhere: *call the local Red Cross (Cruz Roja).*
See *relevant chapters for emergency numbers and addresses of local clinics.*

There are no obligatory **inoculations** required for travelling in Mexico. However, as a precaution it's advisable to be immunized against polio, tetanus, typhoid, hepatitis A and, if you really want to be sure, cholera.

The risk of these diseases is low, but they are present in the area. It's also a good precaution to take malaria tablets, especially if you're going to forest areas of Quintana Roo, Campeche, Tabasco and Chiapas. Be aware, though, that they can cause secondary effects. The type containing **chloroquine** tend to be the most effective with the least threat of side effects; check with your doctor on the varieties currently recommended. Bear in mind that Malaria tablets need to be taken for at least a week before you enter a risk area, and for some time after you leave.

Insurance and Emergencies

You should also have full travel insurance covering all medical eventualities including repatriation as a last resort. If you have a medical emergency or need to see a doctor, the best place to turn will be one of the well-equipped **private clinics** in the main cities and beach towns. Smaller towns and country areas have **public health centres** (*centros de salud*) which, while they may lack some sophisticated equipment, respond perfectly adequately in emergencies.

For more usual, minor eventualities you should also have a **first-aid kit**. This should contain your remedies for diarrhoea and stomach complaints. The risk of these hitting you is much exaggerated, but it's advisable to take along standard remedies (eg. Imodium and Dioralyte), along with rehydration mixtures to aid recuperation, although ideally it's better to survive an attack without them and build up your resistance. If you have children travelling with you, the need for medication will be greater, but do check the dosage carefully.

Drinking Water

Traditionally, Mexican guide books come with a lengthy list of don't do's related to water. Again, the risks are greatly exaggerated, as the standard of mains-supply water has improved considerably. Drink only purified water (*agua purificada*); this is not mineral water, just guaranteed clean. It is available from grocery stores and supermarkets, and all pharmacies. You're unlikely to catch anything from taking in a bit of tap water while you wash. Most bars and restaurants use purified water to make ice, and as long as you exercise reasonable care when choosing foods like shellfish or meat, and steer clear of dirt-cheap *loncherías*, you should avoid most dangers.

Pharmacies

Pharmacies are peculiarly abundant in cities and even small towns. In most places a few open 24 hours a day. They stock a wide range of goods including purified water, cosmetics, sanitary products, aspirins and a huge range of medicines, some of which are only available on prescription in other countries and should be treated with care. Local people often ask the advice of a pharmacist rather than go to a doctor. They also provide different forms of contraception, including condoms (*condones*).

Language and Communication

Around Cancún and the Caribbean strip it's really not hard to spend a week or even more without giving the slightest recognition to the Spanish language. The level of English falls dramatically, however, as soon as you head inland, and you will gain immeasurably on your trip if you can handle even basic Spanish. Local guides in forest areas rarely know more than limited English and, in any case, Mexico still operates far more of an oral culture than North America or Europe. Bus timetables are unreliable, street names are not signposted, opening times are nowhere to be seen: in all kinds of situations where you are used to reading or following signs, you have to ask.

Communicating Effectively

Communication here is not just a matter of the meaning of words, but of how you use them. Mexicans in general, but the Maya above all, are by tradition extremely polite and lay great importance on courtesy. Observing unhurriedly the old forms of courteous and ceremonious Spanish, and apparently strange practices such as preceding a question by a question ('*¿Le puedo hacer una pregunta?*', 'May I ask you a question?'), forms an essential bridge to being heard. The Yucatán Maya can appear impenetrable and stony-faced, but greet someone with a proper '*Buenos días*' and

you may be rewarded with the most dazzling of smiles. Despite its formality, this can often be a more amiable and effective means of communication than the self-conscious, brash upfrontness that has grown up in Mexico's tourist zones. In Cancún and Playa del Carmen, many workers veer from traditional formality to the opposite extreme of forced, overdone and slightly self-defensive good cheer, with the 'Dyou wanna beer *amigo*?', that often comes over as just pushy.

The Joys of Getting Lost

Taking on board the need for a courtly style of speech doesn't mean your communications will all then be crystal clear. This stems in part from courtesy itself: rather than disappoint you by admitting they cannot help, people will often send you off somewhere with apparent certainty, even if they haven't a clue what you're asking for. Another trait is imprecision: no matter how well you define your question, as in 'Is this the road to the bus station?', the standard response will be '*P'allá*', 'Over there' (from *por allá*) accompanied by an undefined hand gesture; whether this means *p'allá* to the left (*izquierda*) or *p'allá* to the right (*derecha*) can involve real mental gymnastics. Getting lost at least a few times is inevitable in Mexico, it goes with the territory. This also means you find yourself in all sorts of places you never thought to visit. It's best to enjoy it.

Learning Spanish and Local Languages

San Cristóbal de Las Casas and Mérida are the two main centres for Spanish courses. Schools offer courses on a tuition-only basis, for those who have arranged their own accommodation, or in conjunction with homestays with local families, providing immersion in the language and closer contact with local people. Most schools also run extra activities, such as classes in local handicrafts and trips to Mayan sites. Courses in San Cristóbal are cheap: often around $180 per week, with 15 hours of classes and accommodation and all main meals with a family; discounts are available for couples or group bookings. Mérida is more expensive. There are also opportunities to learn indigenous languages such as Tzotzil and Yucatec. For schools, *see* sections on the cities named.

Media

Newspapers

The only English-language newspaper widely on sale is the *Miami Herald*, which has a 'Caribbean Edition' produced in Cancún with local news and features. It's most easily found on the coast and in Mérida. Competition is provided by *The News*, an English-language daily owned by the Mexican paper *Novedades*. There are swathes of Mexican papers. Most states have one main paper; *Diario de Yucatán* in Yucatán. In main towns, the Mexico City press goes on sale mid-afternoon: the erudite *La Jornada* is the main liberal paper; *Excelsior* is the most traditional heavyweight daily.

Television and Radio

The most omnipresent means of communication in modern Mexico, TV can reach into the remotest village and, quite often, the cheapest hotel. Programming is dominated by Mexico's popular *telenovelas* (soap operas), lurid crime reporting, movies and sport, in particular football. The changing political situation of the last few years has generated more serious discussion-time programmes. In addition to Mexican networks, cable and satellite TV are developing rapidly. Many hotels receive US channels (CNN, ESPN), and Rupert Murdoch is getting a grip on the Latin American market, with Sky channels in Spanish and the Fox Sports Americas network.

Snatches of Mexican **radio** fill the air in every street: boisterous *banderos* and phone-ins head the popularity stakes.

Money, Banks and Tipping

The Mexican currency is the **peso**, which for some time has stood at around 9 to the US dollar (about 12.5 to the pound sterling). In view of the peso's occasional instability all prices in this book are quoted in US dollars. There are **coins** for 1, 2, 5, 10 and 20 pesos, and **notes** for 20, 50, 100, 200, 500 and 1,000 pesos. Each peso divides into 100 *centavos*, with little coins for 5, 10, 20 or 50. Confusingly, the most common symbol for the peso is the same as the dollar sign ($), although to differentiate this may be written after the amount (20$).

In Cancún, Cozumel and on the Caribbean coast prices are often given in US dollars as well as (or sometimes instead of) pesos, and dollars are widely accepted for all sorts of transactions, but note that if you pay in dollars you will normally end up paying slightly more.

If you are travelling to Mexico from Britain or anywhere in Europe take money with you in **US dollar** travellers' cheques or cash. Mexican **banks** still give very bad rates against non-dollar currencies, and even after exchanging your money twice you will still be better off. Away from the main tourist areas, bank staff will be unaccustomed to changing these currencies and take a very long time over it, or even refuse to try. Canadian dollars are less of a problem and are exchanged fairly readily.

Credit cards (MasterCard and Visa, less so American Express) are widely accepted in larger shops, diving schools and hotels of mid-range and above, and near-essential for hiring a car. They are less common in restaurants, and the street and market economy is cash-only. Most city bank branches and even many in small towns also have ATM cash machines, which may well be the best way of obtaining cash, as you get the best exchange rate and avoid hefty bank commissions. Most ATMs take all major cards. If you forget your PIN and want to withdraw cash over the counter, you must provide a photocopy of your passport.

It is not wise to rely solely on cards or ATMs, as you can get stuck when the only ATM for miles is out of action, as can happen. It's best to have at least some travellers' cheques too.

Opening Hours and Changing Money

At **airports** there are exchange offices open whenever there are incoming flights, although they tend to give very poor rates. Change only as much as you need to get into town, then go to a bank or exchange office. Medium-sized towns should have at least one bank, but city branches will be more efficient and hassle-free. Virtually all banks will exchange dollars in cash or travellers' cheques.

Bank hours are traditionally Monday to Friday 8.30–1, and all banks are closed on Sundays and public holidays. Many branches now stay open until 4 or 5, and on Saturdays from 9 till 1, but Mexican banks seem to be following an annoy-the-tourist scheme by refusing to exchange money at certain times. This is rarely signposted, so check ('*¿Se puede cambiar dinero/dólares?*') before joining the line; larger branches are usually best. Dollar rates change daily and, like commission, vary between banks, so it is worth comparing. In any tourist town there will also be small private exchange offices (*casas de cambio*), open every day.

Note: When changing money, make sure you're not left with only large-denomination notes (ie. 500 or 1,000 pesos), which are hard to break for any transaction smaller than a hotel bill. Try to keep some change in coins.

Estimating Costs

Travelling costs depend entirely on what you aim to do, but the following may be helpful in making an estimate. There are roughly three price zones in this part of Mexico. The 'Riviera' along the Caribbean coast, and above all Cancún itself, is one of the most expensive parts of the country, with prices close to US levels. In the rest of the Yucatán peninsula and most other parts of the region prices are generally about 70% of Cancún levels or less: they tend to decrease the further south you go. Highland and central Chiapas forms its own price zone, and remains very cheap. These differences are most marked in accommodation prices; they're not so clear in food.

In the largest, middle one of these zones, two people travelling together without any package bookings can stay in pleasant inexpensive-range hotels and eat in mid-range restaurants for about $40 a day each (for price ranges, *see* p.138 and p.121). On top of that are travel costs – $17.50 each for a first-class bus from, for example, Cancún to Mérida, or from $40 a day for a hired car – plus anything you want to buy. It's still possible to travel for a good deal less, staying in cheaper hotels and taking advantage of the huge range of cheap food. Aim to spend $60 a day, on the other hand, and you can be very comfortable.

Tipping

Tips are an essential supplement to low wages for many Mexicans. For **hotel porters** the usual tip is 3–10 pesos (depending on the hotel); it's also normal practice to leave something for the maid. It's a good idea to keep a stock of loose change (especially if you're driving), for all the other service providers for whom there are no fixed charges, such as windscreen washers, men who watch over your car, etc. Petrol station attendants do not expect a tip for putting fuel in your car, but it is normal to give them a few pesos if they've checked the oil, put air in the tyres and so on. The exception is **taxi drivers**, who do not normally expect tips, except if they've gone out of their way, or helped with bags.

For tipping in restaurants and bars, *see* 'Eating Out', p.121.

Opening Hours and National Holidays

Opening Hours

Shops generally follow the siesta pattern: they open early, are busiest in the morning and close from 1–2pm to 4–5pm, and then stay open until dark, around 9pm.

Set timings are not part of Mexican culture, so there are exceptions. In **cities**, several shops stay open all day, until late at night or round the clock. There are always one or two 24-hour pharmacies. In **small towns** and villages, shops are often just open from morning till night. **Markets** get busy very early, and mostly close by 2pm. City shops usually close on Sundays, but in smaller towns Sunday morning can be the busiest shopping time of the week.

Churches are always opened at sunrise and invariably close in the afternoons, from about 12.30–1.30pm until 4 or 5pm, when they will be opened again until after dark.

For bank hours, *see* 'Money', facing page.

For museum/site hours, *see* 'Visiting Archaeological Sites and Museums', p.136.

National Holidays

The country's official holidays (*see* box, overleaf) are important events in the life of the Mexican state, which observes them with parades and patriotic rhetoric, above all in the capital. On the ground, curiously, they attract nothing like the interest shown in traditional *fiestas*, and many people treat them just as a day off work. Exceptions are the Virgin of Guadalupe and Christmas, which are national and religious celebrations. In Holy Week,

National Holidays

1 Jan	*Año Nuevo* (New Year's Day)	
5 Feb	*Día de la Constitución* (Constitution Day)	
21 Mar	*Nacimiento de Juárez* (Birthday of Benito Juárez)	
1 May	*Día del Trabajo* (Labour Day)	
5 May	*Batalla de Puebla* (Battle of Puebla)	
16 Sept	*Día de la Independencia* (Independence Day)	
12 Oct	*Día de la Raza* (Discovery of America)	
20 Nov	*Día de la Revolución* (Anniversary of the Revolution)	
12 Dec	*Nuestra Señora de Guadalupe* (Our Lady of Guadalupe)	
25 Dec	*Navidad* (Christmas)	

Easter Thursday, Good Friday and Easter Saturday are also official holidays. The only institutions that consistently mark national holidays are banks and government offices, all of which close.

Packing

Clothing

Local attitudes to **clothes** are fairly laid-back, but so as to avoid looking weird in non-beach areas it's better not to expose too much flesh, especially when visiting churches. Topless and nude bathing are tolerated in a few places on the Riviera such as Playa del Carmen and Tulum, but elsewhere swimming costumes are not particularly skimpy. The Chiapas Highlands are usually the only area where warm clothing is needed, but it's useful to have long trousers and a long-sleeved shirt to minimize sunburn, scratches and bites when exploring forests and Mayan ruins.

You definitely need a **sunhat**, but many people pick one up on the spot, along with sunglasses and yet more T-shirts.

Accessories

Sunblock, high-factor **suncream**, aftersun and **lip balm** are all available in Mexico. **Insect repellent** is best brought with you. The best kinds contain the ingredient DEET. More natural equivalents are kinder on the skin and smell better, but unfortunately they are not as effective. It's also useful to take a basic **first-aid kit** (*see* 'Health and Insurance', p.124).

Among those less obvious things worth acquiring ahead are: **film** (cheaper outside Mexico); a **torch**/flashlight; a **snorkel mask** (expensive to buy/hire on site); and especially a **bath plug**. It's customary to advise travellers to take a money belt, but many give up on them within a few days after finding that the natives aren't hostile.

Laundry

In larger towns and tourist areas there are service laundries, where you leave your clothes to be washed for you; for a small extra fee they can also be crisply ironed. Laundries vary in efficiency, and it pays to be selective.

Photography

International brands of film are available throughout Mexico, but since prices are relatively high it's best to stock up at duty-free. There are restrictions on the use of video cameras at archaeological sites (*see* 'Visiting Archaeological Sites and Museums', p.137). Otherwise photography in most of the region poses no special problems, although Yucatán village Maya tend to be shy of the camera. The major difference is in central Chiapas, where Highland Indians often actively dislike it and refuse to have their picture taken. Contrary to what tourists are regularly told, this is not because they think cameras 'steal their souls'. The beliefs of the Maya are more complex than that. However, they do resent involuntary photography as an aggressive intrusion. There is an absolute ban on taking pictures in the churches of villages such as Chamula and Zinacantán, as any guide will remind you.

With individuals (but not in the churches, or at some ceremonies), this reluctance to be photographed may be overcome by politely asking permission beforehand, or offering a little money. If you're with a guide, they will tell you when you may and may not take pictures. Unfortunately, once they've been 'contracted' to be photographed, bright and giggly kids tend to go immensely solemn as if they were posing for a Victorian portrait.

The other people you shouldn't photograph are soldiers at army checkpoints.

Post Offices and Couriers

There are **post offices** (*oficinas de correos*) in all towns, and small offices that open a few hours a day in many villages. These sell stamps (*estampillas*), as does any shop with a sign saying *Expendio de Estampillas*. Post boxes are small metal boxes in two shades of blue marked *Servicio Postal Mexicano*; they're usually attached to walls, but often quite hard to find. Outside post offices there are often big red boxes optimistically labelled *Buzón Expreso*, but post office staff claim that mail in these is dumped in with everything else, so it goes no faster; at best, they'll have more frequent collections.

Receiving Post

All post offices have a **poste restante/general delivery service** (*lista de correos*). Any mail sent this way should be addressed to you with the post code, e.g. your name, Lista de Correos, CP 97000 Mérida, Yucatán, Mexico. When collecting mail, ask for it under every possible combination of your name (first name, last name, backwards, and so on); nowadays, it's much easier to keep in touch via e-mail (*see* 'Telephones, Faxes and the Internet', p.134).

Sending Post

The Mexican postal service is cheap but very, very erratic: letters to North America or Europe might arrive in two weeks, or two months (businesses operate purely by courier, fax or e-mail). For anything important it's best to use the **Mexpost** express courier service, run by the post office but efficient and reliable. Charges are higher than for regular post but still lower than those of commercial couriers. Packages within Mexico arrive the next day, to North America in about two days, to Europe in about three days to a week. In most cities there are Mexpost desks in the main post office, but in some places they have separate offices. It is not available at small post offices.

Shopping

The **market** is one of the very oldest of Mesoamerican institutions, and there are still many Mexican towns in which buying and selling seem to take up more time than any other visible activity. The Yucatán is also one of the world's great souvenir mines; Cancún itself can seem like one giant bazaar. Most people take away at least one T-shirt; more problems may arise with the the supposedly traditional craftwork, as many items are now mass-produced, and often poor quality.

With due respect to the souvenir outlets of the coast, the two great places for finding original craftwork are **Mérida**, for panama hats, hammocks, and embroidery, and **San Cristóbal de Las Casas**, for the weaving of Highland Chiapas. Some towns have their own specialities: Valladolid embroidery, Ticul ceramics, Becal hats. In the main towns there are museum shops and official craftwork stores (usually the *Casa de Artesanías*) where you can see an array of high-standard local pieces. Their prices are higher than average, but they do allow you to compare quality against the goods offered in markets and independent shops.

Books

For books in English, the Librería Dante in **Mérida** has a small selection, particularly on Mayan history and regional topics. The only real general English-language bookshop is the Alma Libre store in **Puerto Morelos**, a *gringo* home-from-home, while two Internet cafés in **Tulum** and **Isla Mújeres** have second-hand book-exchange shelves. The other place to try is San Cristóbal de Las Casas, which has more bookshops than anywhere else in the region.

Ceramics

Large quantities of earthenware pots are produced in Yucatán state, although many are not very skilfully made. The main centre is the little town of **Ticul**; its most characteristic pots are big water vessels, but local shops also offer smaller, finer pieces. There are also makers in Ticul who use pre-Conquest techniques.

In Chiapas, the remarkable town of **Amatenango del Valle** has a pottery-making tradition believed to date back 2,000 years. It's continued by women, using an open-fired technique to make pots of all sizes and small figures. The **Lacandón Indians** of the forest near Bonampak also have their own, basic ceramics tradition, producing simple but engaging earthenware figures and animals.

Clothing, Embroidery and Textiles

In textiles more than any other craft the two main areas with distinctive traditions are the Yucatán and the Chiapas Highlands. For more on this, *see* 'Mayan Textiles', p.88.

Across the Yucatán the *huípil*, a spotlessly white shift dress with bands of bright flower embroidery around the yoke and the bottom of the skirt, is still everyday wear for many women. Simple, light, loose-fitting and pretty, *huípiles* are ideal for a hot climate, and still worn by all ages from little girls to wizened old ladies. Market stalls and shops have a huge variety, from mass-produced models to dazzling *ternos* for special occasions. *Huípiles* seem to fit Mayan women like an extension of the skin, but the jury is still out on whether *gringas* can look good in them. In response to modern demand it's possible to find blouses with *huípil*-style yokes, as well as embroidered handkerchiefs and tablecloths. Besides Mérida, Valladolid is famous for embroidery.

For men, the Yucatán's most distinctive product is the *guayabera*, a light, elegant shirt-jacket, with four pockets, that is accepted as tropical formal wear. Mérida is again the main centre of production and sales.

Some shops in the region now use Mexican cottons and traditional fabrics in modern designs that make great, stylish hot weather wear. Flapping in the breeze at stalls all over Cancún and the coast there are also multi-striped *sarape* blankets and throws, which are made in giant quantities in northern Mexico.

Other parts of the region have their own traditions. Campeche has its own, slightly sober variation on the Yucatecan *huípil*. In Villahermosa a few shops sell the traditional off-the-shoulder blouses and embroidered skirts of Tabasco (for that Rita Hayworth look).

Weaving is one of the strongest traditions of the Highland Maya of Chiapas. Each village has its distinct style, but in San Cristóbal, where Indian women come to sell their wares, they are often jumbled up together. Articles vary greatly in quality, from those created with the full array of traditional skills to others produced for quick tourist sales. To get a feel for the best traditional work, it's a good idea to go first to a weavers' cooperative such as **Sna Jolobil** (*see* p.480). Prices will be higher than on the street, but the weaving is of very fine quality, and bear in mind that one of the objectives of these cooperatives is to ensure that Indian women receive a fair price for their work. Blankets (suitable either as throws or wall-hangings), belts, blouses (confusingly also called *huípiles*) and small decorative cloths are the most traditional products, but in response to demand you now find such things as tablecloths and napkins.

As well as in San Cristóbal, there are village markets in Chamula, Zinacantán and other communities. The non-Mayan region towards Chiapa de Corzo has its own tradition in textiles, weaving bright *sarape* blankets.

Foods

All markets have plenty of stalls offering good picnic ingredients, especially very fresh, cheap **fruit**. Most things on show are not an option as souvenirs, but fans of ferocious food may want to take away some local **chilis**. Livid red and green trays of them, in many shades and varieties, flare in every market; as a rule, the smaller they are, the stronger. In Mérida and other Yucatecan markets you can buy local seasonings such as *achiote* and *chirmole* as powders already made up. Markets also have aromatic selections of fresh **herbs**. Small quantities of peppers and **spices** can usually be brought into Britain as long as they're in a sealed bag; US Customs are much more restrictive. For drinks to buy, *see* pp.100–104.

Hats, Hammocks and Shoes

The **panama hat** (known as a *jipi*) and other articles made from *jipi* palm – bags, mats – are some of the Yucatán's best-known products. *Jipis* are available in all sorts of styles and sizes, and make the best sun hat for travelling. Any hat worth buying can be rolled up and packed, and should regain its shape naturally when unrolled. Panamas have traditionally been made in the town of Becal, but most of these are now shipped out directly to markets elsewhere, and you'll find a wider range of hats at low prices in Mérida.

The **hammock** is the second great product of the Yucatán to take home. Once again, the best place to buy is Mérida's market area. For more on hammock-buying, *see* p.269.

Equipped with sun hat and hammock, you may still be after hot-weather footwear. Hard-wearing, cheap leather *huarache* **sandals** can be found pair upon pair in any market, and especially in Cancún, Mérida and Chetumal.

Jewellery

Cozumel specializes in jewellery stores aimed at cruise passengers, offering fine silver and settings of Colombian emeralds, Mexican opals and other gems at low (a relative term here) prices. There are also outlets on Isla Mujeres and in Cancún and Playa del Carmen. Most of the stock is international in style, but some feature pieces made with the region's **obsidian**, the deep-black, diamond-hard stone considered so precious by the Maya, and **jade**.

Amber is one of the traditional treasures of Chiapas. Several shops in San Cristóbal offer fine amber jewellery, and boys will probably approach you on the street offering coarser pieces. Amber can also be bought in Palenque, Chiapa de Corzo and Tuxtla Gutiérrez.

Markets and Bargaining

The markets of Mérida and San Cristóbal may be the most spectacular, but there are others in every city. An 'ordinary' Mexican market is remarkable in itself. It may not have much original craftwork, but will look, instead, to satisfy every possible need or desire. You can find 20-litre cooking pots, watch parts, or an impossibly huge stock of shoes. Two of the most extraordinary markets are in the border towns of Chetumal and Tapachula.

In most local markets bargaining is still common, especially for bigger articles such as hammocks. Like most public interactions here it's pretty relaxed, and a figure is usually agreed after only a few offers and counter-offers. It is not the norm to bargain in shops, but many will offer discounts if you show an interest in buying more than one of any item.

Useful Stuff and Mexican Junk

The market in Mérida is the best place for just about any practical item you might need, though Chetumal and Tapachula give it close competition. Plus, if you're not entirely wedded to craftwork for souvenirs, you might consider the myriad options thrown up by the day-to-day Mexican markets: plastic shopping bags (or anything in plastic), table-cloths, whole stands of party decorations, giant fruit-squeezers and indeterminate cooking implements.

Sports and Activities

Diving and Snorkelling

The late Jacques Cousteau brought the coral reefs of northeast Yucatán to the attention of the world in the 1960s, describing them as one of the richest undersea environments in existence, on a par with Australia's Barrier Reef. **Cozumel** is the largest dive centre, but there are others in Cancún, Isla Mujeres, Puerto Morelos, Playa del Carmen, Akumal, Tulum and smaller places. South of the main 'Riviera', by Xcalak in Quintana Roo, is **Banco Chinchorro**, a giant reef that's increasingly drawing in divers in the know. There are reefs of every grade of difficulty, from shallow, gentle waters to those strictly for experienced divers. The sea is beautifully clear, and the range of coral and marine life spectacular. For more on this, *see* 'Sealife and the Reefs', p.94.

Diving Instruction

Most dive centres offer a full range of services, from 'resort courses' – an introduction to scuba for complete beginners – through certification courses to accompanied dives and equipment hire for already-certified divers. Most diving in this area is **drift diving** (i.e. in the main you let the current carry you, rather than swimming), so it is very important to follow a guide. You should only dive with an instructor holding an international PADI or NAUI certificate. This is fairly academic, as you are unlikely to see anyone present themselves as a dive-master here without PADI or equivalent qualifications (or one who doesn't speak English), but the number of clients entrusted to an instructor can vary: look for the lowest ratio possible, and with beginners' courses never accept more than four students per dive-master. New measures have recently been introduced to improve diving safety, especially on Cozumel (*see* p.178), and on the whole accidents are pretty rare here.

Very roughly, 'resort courses' here **cost** around $60–80 per person; four–five-day basic certification courses about $300–350; and a half-day two-tank dive for a certified diver from about $40, with more complicated prices for extra tuition, special and night dives. Discounts and packages are nearly always on offer for diving over several days or for groups. Schools are usually most expensive in Cancún; this is also where the seas are most crowded. For better diving, head south to Puerto Morelos or Playa del Carmen. Complete beginners will probably be best off in Cozumel, Isla Mujeres or Puerto Morelos, which offer the best combination of shallow, tranquil reefs that still have plenty to see. However, you can take introductory courses at almost any dive centre on the coast, even in Xcalak.

Diving Accidents

24-hour Emergency: **t** 872 1430/872 2387

Cozumel has a world-class divers' emergency centre with hyperbaric chamber and helicopter evacuation. Dive-masters will have their own contacts with it, or you can call the number above. The Total Assist medical centre in Cancún also has a hyperbaric chamber.

Cave Diving

The Yucatán is one of the world's key centres for cave diving, in its thousands of *cenotes* or cave systems and underwater rivers (*see* p.84). The main area is just inland from the southern end of the 'Riviera', behind Akumal and Tulum, with the **Dos Ojos** *cenote*, the longest underwater cave system yet discovered in the world. More systems are being explored all the time. To go on a cave tour divers must have at least basic open-water certification; cavern trips generally cost from about $120, but prices are lower if you make up a group (maximum four). For more on cave diving near Akumal and Tulum, *see* pp.206–7. If you're not already a diver but still want to sample the unique environment of a *cenote*, cave-diving centres and some other places offer snorkel tours of the upper levels of some caves (from about $30, all transport included). *Cenotes* are also being explored in Yucatán state, south of Mérida, and diving and snorkel trips are beginning to be offered there too, in a much more rustic setting than on the Riviera (*see* p.268).

Snorkelling

If you don't want to be bothered with tanks and other scuba technology (and the cost), snorkelling is by no means second-best. The same centres that offer scuba courses commonly offer snorkelling trips to inshore reefs (most cost around $15, with equipment included) and hire out snorkels; if you have your own you can just organize yourself. Cozumel, Isla Mujeres and Puerto Morelos are generally best for easy, offshore snorkelling, and off Cozumel you can sometimes see as much with a snorkel as on a full dive. For a more expensive but no-effort alternative, there are the 'snorkel parks' in the lagoons of Xcaret, Xel-Ha, Tres Ríos and Yal-Ku in Akumal, which are very commercialized but can still be fun, especially for kids. Arrive early to avoid the crowds.

Fishing

Before Mexico's Caribbean coastline was discovered by divers or sunbathers, the first tourists to appreciate the area were sport fishermen. Both **deep-sea** and **inshore** fishing are possible. The deeper waters offshore contain snapper, amberjack, bonito, kingfish, shark, barracuda and tarpon (found all year round) and sailfish, marlin, tuna and dorado (best Mar–June). The inshore waters further south attract plenty of pompano, and also contain the richest **bonefishing** grounds in the world.

Many dive centres (especially on Cozumel and Isla Mujeres) organize fishing trips, and there are fishing specialists with boats for hire and brokering agencies that arrange longer-term charters and all-in packages. **Licences** are needed for deep-sea fishing, which brokers also obtain. On the mainland, Puerto Morelos is a good fishing base, and many of the more expensive companies use Puerto Aventuras. A must for flyfishing fans are the specialized fishing lodges on the remote Punta Allen road south of Tulum, the bonefishers' mecca.

The Caribbean coast is not the only spot you can fish. On the Gulf Coast, fishing is more rustic; getting a boat is a matter of finding a local fisherman and striking a deal over a drink. Some of the best undeveloped fishing lagoons and friendliest fishermen are in Holbox, El Cuyo and Río Lagartos.

Golf

There are three opulent golf courses in Cancún, one in Playacar at Playa del Carmen and one at Puerto Aventuras, and, in Yucatán state, a golf club just north of Mérida. More of these sharply manicured upheavals in the landscape may appear in the next few years.

Horse Riding

South of Cancún near **Puerto Morelos**, there is a ranch, Rancho Loma Bonita, offering group rides on horseback, with guides, through forests and along the beach, swim optional; on **Cozumel**, Rancho Buenavista organizes similar tours. No experience is necessary.

In Yucatán, Hacienda San Antonio Chalanté near **Izamal** has horses available for its guests. In Chiapas, tour agencies in **San Cristóbal** run horseback treks up to Highland villages such as Chamula, while Rancho Esmeralda, near **Ocosingo**, offers easy rides through a much lesser-known part of the Chiapas countryside.

Sailing, Windsurfing, and Kayaks

Sailing boat hire is oddly underdeveloped, with very few permanent agencies. It is easiest to find boats for rent on Isla Mujeres and Cozumel.

Inshore **windsurfers** are better off: windsurf boards can be rented at many hotels, at any of the marinas and waterparks and at several places along the beach in Cancún, on the southwestern beaches of Cozumel and on the beach at Isla Mujeres. They may also be available for hire from dive schools at Tulum.

If you prefer the kind of boat that allows you to slide silently through marine environments there are outfits that rent **kayaks**. Hotels near Punta Allen arrange kayak tours in the Sian Ka'an reserve, and many hotels in Xcalak have kayaks for exploring the nearby mangroves. One of the best places for tranquil kayaking is the remote lake of Bacalar, where camp sites on the lake shore have boats available.

Skydiving and Other Esoterics

You can **skydive** on to the beach at Playa del Carmen with Skydive Playa. In Cancún it is possible to **parasail** from AquaWorld, Tiki Island by Playa Tortugas (which also offers **bungee-jumping**, from a crane) and other places along the beach.

Trekking and Climbing

In Chiapas, as well as the village tours run from San Cristóbal by conventional agencies, treks are sometimes organized to more remote areas by individual guides. Contact the main tourist office and Na Bolom museum for information. Individual expeditions are the only means of trekking into the Chiapas mountains; there are no regular tours.

Telephones, Faxes and the Internet

In cities and tourist areas, and nowadays in many villages as well, there are white **Lada** (for *larga distancia*, long distance) public phones, which operate with phone cards (a *tarjeta de teléfonos* or *tarjeta Lada*). They can be bought to the value of 30, 50 and 100 pesos from phone company offices and shops with the blue and yellow *Ladatel* sign (pharmacies often sell them). In villages where there are still no phone boxes there is virtually always a local phone office (*caseta*), identified by the blue-on-white logo of **Telmex**, the national phone company, and *Teléfono Público* or *Larga Distancia*. You write the number down, and they dial it for you. The village *caseta* is an institution in rural Mexico, taking messages for anyone in the community, and naturally knowing everyone's goings-on.

Local calls are cheap, but charges go up steeply for anywhere defined as long distance (which can be just 2km outside a city) and are very expensive for international calls. With a

National Dialling Codes

To call anywhere in Mexico outside your immediate area, dial **01** and then the area code, before the numbers shown in this guide.

International Dialling Codes

From Mexico:
Canada: **00 1**
Ireland: **00 353**
UK: **00 44**
USA: **00 1**

To Mexico:
(Intl access code)+52+(area code)+(number)

100-peso phone card you can make a very short call to North America, and talk for a few seconds to Europe. International calls are best made from local *casetas* or, in cities, from the private phone offices found in central areas, where, similarly, you give the number and the call is dialled for you. They're still not cheap: an average price is about $3 a minute to Europe, and $1 to the US or Canada. The best thing to do is have someone call you back at a hotel.

In some areas there are Portatel coin-operated cellular pay phones, and in tourist places there are often separate black phones used only for making international calls with a credit card. **Mobile phones** are widely used in Mexico. All work on a 1900 band, as in the USA, so a European mobile will not work here unless it has a Triband facility (even then you may find that coverage is very patchy).

Most private phone offices and even village *casetas* send and receive **faxes** as well. Charges are the same as for phone calls.

Dialling Codes within Mexico

Whether using a Lada phone or a hotel or private phone, to call any number in Mexico outside your immediate area you must first dial an access code (**01**) followed by an area code. The codes for each area are indicated throughout this guide, but the country's phone code system has undergone two major changes since 2000, which (to put it mildly) can cause confusion. Area codes and numbers are shown in this guide in line with the new system, which we are assured will not be subject to any further alterations in the foreseeable future. However, the recent changes have not yet fully filtered through into local guides and advertising, so you may see the same number written in different ways: eg. in Playa **(987)** 30176 (pre-2000 style) or **873 0176** (new style, but without the new area code, 984, introduced in 2001). However, to make a local call within the town, you dial the latter number, 873 0176. Calling from outside Playa, you now must dial **01 984 873 0176**.

Internet

Unsurprisingly, given the cost of phoning and the state of the postal system, Mexico has become highly Internet and e-mail-conscious. Internet cafés and basic internet-access shops are now plentiful in cities and can even be found in small towns. They usually charge around $1 an hour, going up to $2.50 or so in expensive places such as Playa del Carmen. Connections with the server can be volatile (particularly in central Chiapas), but as elsewhere e-mail has become by far the easiest and cheapest means of keeping in touch while travelling, and can be the most reliable means of making hotel reservations.

See box, p.136, for a list of useful websites.

Time

Most of Mexico is on the same time band as US Central time (six hours behind GMT). However, Mexico moves on to daylight saving time in early May, over a month after the USA and Britain, and goes back to winter time earlier in September (the actual dates are still a matter of national controversy), so that in April and September the Yucatán is usually at the same hour as US Rocky Mountain time, or seven hours behind British time.

Toilets

There are not usually any public lavatories in Mexican cities, but bars and restaurants have toilets. Ask for *los servicios* or *el lavabo*. There are also toilets at bus stations, and most first-class buses have on-board toilets. Museums of any size have decent toilets, and whenever the INAH plans to make an archaeological site more accessible they have toilets installed by the entrance. Otherwise, there's always the bushes, and in Cancún you're never too far from a shopping mall, endowed with spanking shiny toilet facilities.

Tourist Information and Maps

In 1990, Mexico, the authorities of five Mexican states and the governments of Belize, Guatemala, El Salvador and Honduras set up the *Mundo Maya* ('Mayan World') scheme for the joint promotion of the whole Mayan region. Scores of leaflets appeared vaunting the red Mundo Maya logo, but few joint projects took shape on the ground; most information is still produced separately and, within Mexico, on a state-by-state basis. Mexican tourist offices abroad have a wide range of information, but there are always local initiatives they are unaware of.

Inside Mexico there are official **tourist offices** in all state capitals and main towns. Their staff may be helpful and well informed, or they may just be leaflet-pushers who smile sweetly but show no specialist knowledge of their area. At times they can be positively misleading, so check transport details with relevant companies rather than tourist offices. They should at least be able to give you a free town map. One notable exception is the useful office in **San Cristóbal de Las Casas**. In general, though, local private travel agencies can be as useful as tourist offices, and several are recommended in this guide.

It's useful to pick up the English-language magazines distributed free in hotels, tourist offices and travel agents, such as *Cancún Tips* in Cancún and *Yucatán Today* in Mérida. These are advertising-led free sheets, but contain useful information and maps.

Mexico's awakening to the Internet age means that online information is some of the most reliable on offer. *See* 'Useful Websites', p.136, for a list of recommended sites.

See **Travel**, pp.108–110, for information about specialist tours and guides in the region.

Maps

One of the peculiarities of travelling in Mexico is the difficulty of finding reliable maps. Tourist offices sometimes have decent free maps of some areas, and useful orientation maps are provided in the free magazines (*see* above), but anyone exploring the countryside will probably want extra maps.

If you plan to drive around it's wise to stock up on maps in **Mérida**, as they are far harder to find elsewhere. In Cancún, the Fama bookshop sometimes has a small selection. Mexican maps are nearly always published by state, and show the next state over as blank. The best available are the *Mapa Turística* series published by the official Secretaría de Comunicaciones y Transportes (SCT), but even they have inaccuracies, and in this region cover only Yucatán, Campeche, Tabasco and

---

Mexican Government Tourist Offices

In the UK
Britain: Wakefield House, 41 Trinity Square, London EC3N 4DJ, **t** 020 7488 9392.

In the USA and Canada
Call toll-free (within USA and Canada) on **t** 1 800 44 MEXICO, **t** 1 800 446 3942.
Canada: 1 Place Ville-Marie, Suite 1931, Montreal, Quebec H3B 2C3, **t** (514) 871 1052; 2 Bloor Street West, Suite 1502, Toronto, Ontario M4W 3E2, **t** (416) 925 0704; 999 West Hastings Street, Suite 1110, Vancouver BC V6C 2W2, **t** (604) 669 2845.
USA: 300 N., Michigan Ave, 4th Floor, Chicago IL 60601, **t** (312) 606 9252; 4507 San Jacinto, Suite 308, Houston TX 77004, **t** (713) 772 2581; 2401 West 6th Street, 5th Floor, Los Angeles CA 90057, **t** (213) 351 2075; 1200 North West 78th Ave, Suite 203, 33126 Miami, Florida, **t** (305) 718 4095; 21 East 63rd Street, 2nd Floor, New York, NY 10021, **t** (212) 821 0367.

Chiapas. The best map for Quintana Roo is the one published by Ediciones Independencia with a yellow and red cover, although it too has errors. Also, Mexican states often have road-building schemes up their sleeves, and it may be a year or two after they open before new roads appear even on official maps.

Hustling and Begging

As in many countries where there are a lot of people with insecure incomes and large numbers of tourists, many people try to make money by wandering around selling things to foreigners, especially in Mérida. Yucatecos, though, tend to be among the world's worst ever hustlers. If, in answer to the standard question, '*¿Quiere hamaca?*' ('Do you want a hammock?'), you say politely '*No gracias*', or better '*Ya tengo una*' ('I've already got one'), most will just say '*Bueno*' and walk on. Alternatively, speak a bit of Spanish and the chances are they'll express surprise and start a conversation, all thoughts of making a sale apparently forgotten. Begging, again, is rarely

Useful Websites

http://mexico-travel.com: Main website for the Mexican Federal tourist authorities.

www.mexicanwave.com: Well-presented site with travel info, links and features on culture, food and all other aspects of Mexico.

www.mexicotravel.co.uk: Information site for Europe based at the Mexican tourist office in London.

www.yucatan.gob.mx: The Yucatán state government's official website.

www.trace-sc.com: Mexico Channel, the most comprehensive site for general and travel information on Mexico, with loads of links.

www.mexonline.com: Mexico Online, a similar site with useful travel information and links.

www.go2mexico.com: Mexico Travel Guide, with information on all parts of the country.

www.planeta.com/ecotravel/mexico: Eco Travels in Mexico, a great means of finding out about less mainstream, smaller-scale and adventurous travel possibilities and tour operations on offer.

http://amtave.com: Spanish-only site of the Asociación Mexicana de Turismo de Aventura y Ecoturismo, with links to a mixed bag of small hotels and tour companies.

www.cancun.com: Cancún Online, with information and links on hotels, dive centres, things to do and all kinds of other services in Cancún and along the Riviera.

www.cozumelonline.com: Cozumel's equivalent to Cancún Online, above.

aggressive. Street selling is more intensive in Chiapas, especially in Palenque and at Agua Azul, where kids selling craftwork or fruit are far less ready to accept no for an answer.

Visiting Archaeological Sites and Museums

Usual Opening Hours: *daily 8–5.*

Virtually all archaeological sites in Mexico are administered by the **INAH** (Instituto Nacional de Antropología e Historia). Most have a standard timetable, 8 till 5, although less prominent sites may open later and close earlier, and/or are closed one day a week. Entry charges vary; admission to the most famous sites in Yucatán state (Chichén Itzá, Uxmal) costs around $9, but for smaller sites is usually $2–$3. Admission is free on Sundays at all sites. The disadvantage of this is that Sunday is the only day when big numbers of people visit some sites, and the major ruins can be seriously crowded. INAH sites have standard signs to look out for along the roads: blue with white lettering and a silhouette of a pyramid.

Excavations are continuing at many sites, and the INAH and state governments have an ongoing programme of opening up sites, so it is now possible to visit more Mayan sites in Mexico than ever before. Among the areas recently opened up are some major sites of great archaeological importance, such as Santa Rosa Xtampak and the great city of Calakmul, both in Campeche. This increase in accessible sites is also related to the enormous growth in our understanding of the sheer complexity of Mayan society over the last 30 years. One aspect of the programme is also controversial, in that it often involves large-scale restoration work. The INAH, however, assures that only the original stones have been used in all restored structures, and only after painstaking research.

There are Mayan sites for all tastes in this region. The most visited are Chichén, Tulum and, some way behind, Uxmal and Palenque. Away from this well-beaten path, visitor numbers fall radically (especially mid-week), and there are awe-inspiring sites where you can wander undisturbed among the forests, birds and ancient stones, and get a real sense of exploration. Some are very hard or near-impossible to reach without a car, often at the end of bumpy dirt tracks. Wherever you go, there will be an INAH watchman waiting with his book for you to sign. As-yet unsated ruins enthusiasts can also look out sites that have not yet been brought under INAH administration, some of which can be reached with the help of local guides.

For an introduction to the Maya, it still makes sense to look first at the 'classics': **Chichén Itzá**, **Uxmal** and the **Puuc hill cities**, and **Palenque**. The two great Yucatán cave systems of **Loltún** and **Balankanché** are also easy to reach, and fascinating. Mention apart goes to **Yaxchilán** and **Bonampak**, two fabulous sites – the latter with the only surviving series of Mayan mural paintings – that are best visited in a two-day camping trip from Palenque. Less known but hugely impressive are **Cobá**, and the most important recent discovery in the Mayan world, **Calakmul**, properly excavated only since 1990, but which may have been the largest of all Mayan cities. Others worth highlighting include **Mayapán, Ek-Balam, Kohunlich, Becán, Edzná** and **Toniná**.

Getting around a large site like Chichén Itzá or Palenque with any appreciation (and all the walking involved) requires at least a morning, and can easily take a full day. At Chichén, Cobá, Tulum, Uxmal and Palenque there are multilingual guides who take you round for about $30. Bus tours with guides are the easiest way to see these ruins, but they have their limitations (*see* 'Tours and Guides', p.109). At smaller sites the watchman may accompany you (a tip is in order); sometimes this is a necessity, as the ruins are hard to find without a guide. Most sites have slabs set into the ground with information in Spanish, English and the local Mayan language. Larger sites have visitor centres with restaurants, shops and bookshops of variable quality; at others there may be little or no printed material, nor refreshments. It's useful to have the site leaflets (5–8 pesos) published in Spanish and English by the INAH itself, although, like most local guide books, they are often out of date. They are oddly hard to find, too, but there are stocks at Uxmal and the museum in Mérida. At any site, it's best to start early, to avoid the heat and any crowds. Take water, a sun hat, sunblock, and – especially in southern Quintana Roo, southern Campeche and Chiapas – plenty of insect repellent.

There are no restrictions on photography (except where sites are still being prepared for opening), but you are required to obtain a permit at each site to use a video camera (normally around 30 pesos or $3.75). Staff at major sites check on this punctiliously, but lone watchmen at smaller ones may not bother. And, at any site, don't even think of taking away any souvenir stones. Arrest is immediate and arranging bail and a lawyer very expensive.

The INAH also has the responsibility for **archaeological museums**. Opening hours are similar to those of sites, but several close on Mondays; they too are free on Sundays. The most important museums for Mayan artefacts are in Mérida, Dzibilchaltún, Campeche, Palenque and Tuxtla Gutiérrez. Villahermosa has two wonderful museums, dealing not only with the Maya but the Olmecs and the whole range of Mesoamerican cultures. Also extremely interesting are the collections in the innovative museum in Chetumal, the site museums at Comalcalco and Toniná and the regional museum in Tapachula; there are lesser museums in Cancún, Uxmal and Chichén Itzá, and several small, sometimes rather eccentric local museums.

Where to Stay

There is a choice of hotels at different price and comfort levels in all cities and most towns of any size, and at some major archaeological sites (Chichén Itzá, Uxmal, Cobá) there are luxury-grade hotels built for visitors to the ruins. In more remote country areas and small towns accommodation is much more scarce, and you may have to base yourself in the nearest larger town and make trips out. In colonial cities such as Mérida, Campeche or San Cristóbal de Las Casas there are many hotels in charming old buildings, with plant-lined patios; in more modern cities hotels tend to be more functional. Cancún and the Riviera coast have of course any number of big resort hotels, which are usually cheaper (and easier) to book from abroad as part of a package than by calling direct. Growing even faster are all-inclusive resort complexes, each with its own restaurants, pool, dive trips, beach and so on.

Any hotel in or above the *moderate* range (*see* 'Accommodation Price Categories', p.138) will provide ample comforts such as large beds, good bathrooms and air conditioning, although there can be surprises, generally due to poor maintainence. Places in the *inexpensive* range may similarly be charming, bright and enjoyable, or disappointing, depending mainly on the demeanour of the owners and how well it has been kept up. Below that there's the Mexican *cheap* hotel, with rooms that, if they're clean, decently sized and with good light, can be perfectly pleasant, or may be pretty cell-like. A consolation is that all but the very cheapest hotels have bathrooms (toilet, washbasin and shower) in every room.

Accommodation Price Categories

Prices based on the cost of a double room for one night.

Category	US Dollars ($)	Pounds Sterling (£)	Mexican Pesos ($)
luxury	Over $130	Over £95	Over $1,200
expensive	$80–130	£58–95	$730–1,200
moderate	$45–80	£33–58	$410–730
inexpensive	$20–45	£14.50–33	$183–410
cheap	Under $20	Under £14.5	$Under 183

Many (even *inexpensive* or *cheap*) hotels also offer rooms with air conditioning, which costs a little more. This can be a mixed blessing: it may be a relief at times, but the machines are often old and very noisy, and the cheaper, old-fashioned ceiling fan is more peaceful and can be just as efficient. Avoid rooms in *inexpensive–cheap* places that are sealed boxes with a/c only; the best option is one with a/c and a fan, so you can choose yourself.

It's advisable to book ahead during the high seasons (mid-Dec–Feb, at Easter and, to a lesser extent, July–Aug). In and around Cancún you should book at all times. At peak times in busier places (Isla Mujeres especially) don't expect any *inexpensive/cheap* hotel to hold a booking beyond mid-afternoon. The best rule is to get there as early as possible. Always ask to be shown a room before you take it, and if it's gloomy ask if there are any others with more light ('*¿Hay cuartos con más luz?*'). There are often larger, brighter rooms on the upper floors at the same price. Another feature of Mexican hotels stems from the way Mexicans travel. Families and groups often take one room between them, and many hotels have big, multi-bed rooms, and have no objection to large numbers sharing for only a marginally higher cost, so that travelling in a group, if you don't mind bunking in, can be very cheap.

Hotel Price Ranges

In hotel prices, more than any other field, there are three different economies in the region covered by this book. **Cancún and the 'Riviera'** make up the most expensive area in the whole of Mexico, above all in the high season (Dec–Mar). At that time it's difficult to get any room for much under $20, mid-range rates are comparable to the USA at about $40, while big hotels have public rates over $100 (these are much better booked in a package, not direct). At other times prices may drop considerably. In **most other areas** a lower set of prices applies, with some variations but broadly similar. A fair proportion of places are available for $15–$25, and hotels for $30 can be very comfortable. In **Highland Chiapas** prices drop again. A budget hotel in San Cristóbal de Las Casas means $12 a night, and magnificent colonial-style rooms can cost $60.

To avoid confusion the same price bands are used throughout, based on the middle one of the three ranges above. With this in mind, a hotel listed as *luxury* in Yucatán state will be more exceptional than one in Cancún, while a place on the coast listed as *inexpensive* may be no better than a really *cheap* one elsewhere.

Hacienda Hotels

Yucatán State and some other parts of the peninsula are peppered with *haciendas*, aristocratic estate-houses built between the 16th and the 19th centuries. In the last few years several have been beautifully restored into seductive upscale retreats, with exuberant gardens, rooms with high ceilings and wood beams, palm-shaded pools and restaurants on colonial-style verandahs, providing some of the Yucatán's most distinctive experiences. In a class of its own is **Hacienda Katanchel** near Mérida, the one true luxury hotel in the Yucatán, with a unique atmosphere. The Grupo Plan company *(www.grupoplan.com)* has restored several *haciendas*, which are now marketed by Starwood Hotels in their 'Luxury Collection' *(www.luxurycollection.com)*, and some others have opened around Mérida (*see* p.270) and in Campeche. Rooms at all these *haciendas* cost a minimum of $200 a night.

Following on from this upscale example, some less opulent *haciendas* have opened to guests, such as **Hacienda San Antonio Chalanté** near Izamal, **Hacienda San Miguel** near Valladolid and **Hacienda Blanca Flor** in Campeche (*see* p.258, p.230, p.379), enabling guests to experience their rural calm for a much lower price. Strange but true, there is also a *hacienda* hotel near Comitán in Chiapas, the **Parador-Museo Santa María** (*see* p.503).

Guest Houses

For a more personal atmosphere than in the average town hotel, Mérida features a clutch of old houses turned into relaxed guest houses by their resident owners. Some offer bed-and-breakfast, others have kitchens for guests' use. Among the most attractive are **Casa Mexilio** (*moderate*) and **Casa San Juan**, **Los Cielos** and **Luz en Yucatán** (*inexpensive*)

In many places on the Caribbean coast there are medium-sized bed-and-breakfast lodges. Several similar operations and independent hotels on the coast (and the Casa Mexilio) have a joint booking service in the USA, the **Turquoise Reef Group**, (**t** 1 800 538 6802, *www.mexicoholiday.com*).

Cabañas and Palapas

You would be missing out if you visited the Yucatán and did not spend at least a couple of nights under a palm roof by a beach. A *palapa* is that palm roof, and can be a big shelter for sleeping under, a shade over a bar or just a sunshade on the beach; with walls beneath the roof, it becomes a *cabaña*. The original, basic cheap beachside *cabaña* is just a stick and palm hut, the traditional Mayan *na* with sand floor, a simple mattress or hooks from which to sling a hammock, candlelight and a mosquito net, with communal toilets and showers nearby. The first great home of this kind of *cabaña* was the beach at **Tulum** (*see* pp.209–211), where due to demand huts like this now go for $20 a day (per hut, not per person) in high season. There are still some *cheap cabañas* around Playa del Carmen and in smaller bays along the 'Riviera', on Holbox and in south Quintana Roo near Mahahual. Budget *cabaña*-hotels also crop up in isolated spots on the Yucatán coast, such as **El Cuyo**.

From these beginnings the *cabaña*-concept has taken off, and there are now two main grades of cabin: the basic model described above, and the smart *cabaña* with solid walls, tiled floors and all kinds of comforts: excellent bathrooms and beds, roof fans and terraces on which to sit and watch the birds float by.

Tulum, again, has some beautiful *cabaña*-hotels in this style, at *moderate–expensive* prices. There are also luxury-standard *cabañas*, such as **Las Palapas** or the **Shangri-La** north of Playa del Carmen, or **Xixim** near Celestún in Yucatán. Inland, there is some *cabaña*-style accommodation at **Rancho Encantado** on Lake Bacalar (*see* p.346) and in some small hotels around Palenque (*see* pp.438–9). Nearly all the 'eco-tourism' projects recently mooted (*see* **Travel**, pp.110–11) also involve creating *palapa*-style, low-impact accommodation.

Staying in Villages

Amid all the talk about eco-tourism in this region there has naturally been discussion about low-level projects that directly involve and benefit local people. At present, though, the number of schemes in operation is still small, leaving aside small-town cheap hotels, which by their nature tend to be run by locals.

In Yucatán state, you can stay in Mayan villages at **Tinúm** and **Yaxuná** (*see* p.231, p.252). The two 'schemes' are very different from each other, but are both run by local people. In southern Quintana Roo **Tres Garantías**, near Belize, has its own jungle reserve with some *cabañas*, the **Campamento La Pirámide** (*see* p.355), and there are some attractive sites around Lake Bacalar (*see* pp.346–7). In Chiapas there are several communities with 'village tourism' schemes, especially **Misol-Ha**, **Agua Clara**, and (part of a Zapatista community) **Laguna Miramar**.

Apartments and Renting Longer-term

Thanks to all the condominium-building that has taken place on the Caribbean coast, there are many self-contained apartments with full facilities, and even whole houses, available for rent. These are concentrated chiefly in Cancún itself, Playa del Carmen, Puerto Aventuras and Akumal. Many condo rental agents advertise on the Internet (ie. *www.cancun.com*). Rents can be surprisingly reasonable, especially outside winter. A wide range of rentals is available on Isla Mujeres, and longer-term stays are something of a speciality in Puerto Morelos, where many places offer weekly or monthly rates. In small places, you can often find basic houses to rent cheaply just by asking around.

Away from the Caribbean coast, Progreso, Chicxulub and other towns on the north coast of Yucatán are largely made up of beach houses that are used by Meridanos for only a few weeks each year. The rest of the time they're rented out. There are always places available in Progreso, and the same agencies may have places in Mérida as well. In Chiapas, a range of cheap rents is available in San Cristóbal de Las Casas.

Camping, Trailer Parks and Youth Hostels

There are organized camp sites, most of them with trailer parks as well, on the 'Riviera' in Playa del Carmen, north of the town around Punta Bete and to the south at Paamul, although like turtles they are becoming something of an endangered species as hotel developers clamp their eyes on every decent stretch of beach. Some *cabaña*-owners at Tulum allow camping on their land at low rates, and many camp sites have spaces where you can just sling up a hammock beneath an open *palapa*. Inland, there are camp sites and trailer parks with facilities near Chichén Itzá and Uxmal, and there are a couple of very lovely, tranquil and remote camp- and hammock sites on Lake Bacalar. Elsewhere, there are fewer camp sites than places where you can camp: beaches in Mexico are public property, and along the Tulum–Punta Allen road, the 'Costa Maya' down to Xcalak or the Yucatán sand bar, lovers of lonely places can stop more or less anywhere, although you will have to take absolutely everything with you (including insect repellent).

In Chiapas, there are camp sites at Palenque and Misol-Ha and Agua Azul south of the town, and you can also camp in the grounds of some cheap hotels in San Cristóbal de Las Casas. It is not advisable to camp anywhere far from towns in Highland Chiapas; you will certainly need a guide and prior permission, due both to the political situation and to the very complicated local system of landholding.

The increasing relative cost of even *cheap* hotels has led to a revitalization of the youth hostel concept, and the AMAJ organization (*www.hostels.com.mx*) has opened several hostels in southern Mexico with dorm-style accommodation which, especially in Cancún, Mérida and Valladolid, are quite attractive and the cheapest places to stay in their areas. The older Mexican hostel organization still runs a few of its basic hostels; the only ones worth bothering with are in Cancún, Campeche and Chetumal. On Isla Mujeres and in Playa del Carmen, Palenque and San Cristóbal de Las Casas the cheapest options are the private hostels which also have dorm-style rooms.

Women Travellers and Sexual Attitudes

On the whole **women travellers** do not experience great difficulties in southern Mexico. Each individual experience will be different, but in general the pervasive *machismo* archetypically associated with Mexico is far less noticeable in the south: among Mexicans, Yucatecan men are associated with *suavidad*, 'softness'. Indian men are particularly likely to be shy and keep their distance; for *mestizo* (mixed-race) men, women travelling alone or in pairs may be an object of fascination and vaguely suggest availability, but this doesn't mean they'll try to do anything about it.

Sexual come-ons are most likely in Cancún and Playa del Carmen. Some sexual assaults have been reported in Cancún and tourist hot-spots on the coast. Wherever you are, it's best to follow the same sensible practice as in any country – avoid empty streets at night, and perhaps the isolated parts of archaeological sites. It is advisable to be more careful in northern Chiapas. Two women travelling together will rarely encounter harassment, and women can also enjoy advantages over male travellers in that they may have more immediate access to some areas of local life, such as the markets.

Attitudes to **homosexuality** are contradictory. As is evident on the street, a fair number of foreign gay men come here to meet young Mexicans, but alongside this is a strong strain of covert and overt, occasionally violent homophobia. There is a certain visible gay scene in Cancún, but elsewhere it's fairly subterranean.

Cancún, the Islands and the Riviera Maya

09

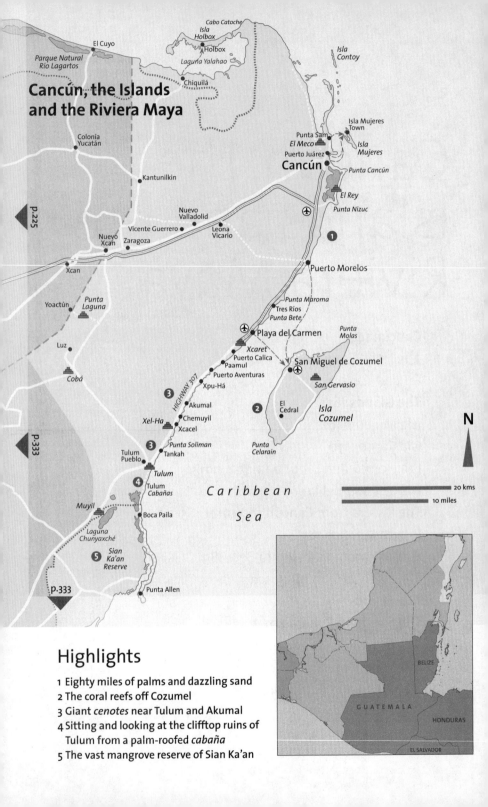

Cancún, the Islands and the Riviera Maya

Cabo Catoche
Isla Holbox
Holbox
Laguna Yalahao
El Cuyo
Parque Natural Río Lagartos
Chiquilá
Isla Contoy
Isla Mujeres Town
Punta Sam
El Meco
Puerto Juárez
Cancún
Isla Mujeres
Punta Cancún
El Rey
Punta Nizuc
Colonia Yucatán
Kantunilkin
Nuevo Valladolid
Vicente Guerrero
Leona Vicario
Nuevo Xcan
Zaragoza
Xcan
Puerto Morelos
Yoactún
Punta Laguna
Luz
Cobá
Punta Maroma
Tres Ríos
Punta Bete
Playa del Carmen
Punta Molas
Xcaret
Puerto Calica
Paamul
Puerto Aventuras
San Miguel de Cozumel
San Gervasio
Xpu-Há
HIGHWAY 307
Akumal
Chemuyil
Xel-Ha
Xcacel
El Cedral
Isla Cozumel
Tulum Pueblo
Punta Soliman
Tankah
Tulum
Punta Celarain
Tulum Cabañas
Muyil
Boca Paila
C a r i b b e a n
Laguna Chunyaxché
Sian Ka'an Reserve
S e a
Punta Allen

20 kms
10 miles

N

p.225
p.333
p.333

Highlights

1 Eighty miles of palms and dazzling sand
2 The coral reefs off Cozumel
3 Giant *cenotes* near Tulum and Akumal
4 Sitting and looking at the clifftop ruins of
  Tulum from a palm-roofed *cabaña*
5 The vast mangrove reserve of Sian Ka'an

BELIZE
GUATEMALA
HONDURAS
EL SALVADOR

Brilliant white beaches lining arc-like bays, lush tropical greenery and an impossibly turquoise sea make Mexico's Caribbean coastline one of the most beautiful in existence. One of its greatest features is the sand itself: made up of fine powdered fossils, it's wonderfully soft and doesn't retain heat, so that it's comfortable even when the temperature tops 35°C. Offshore in the always-warm sea lies one of the richest reef environments in the world, a paradise for divers and snorkellers. And in the northeast corner stands Cancún, modern gateway to the Yucatán, economic motor of southeast Mexico and one of the ten biggest resorts on the planet.

It wasn't always like this. Until the 1960s this area was virtually deserted, home only to a few turtle fishermen, *chicle* tappers and some of the least 'Europeanized' Mayan communities in the Yucatán. Then the foreign archaeologists and a few hippies wandered down, discovered this lost paradise and decided to hang around. Then, in 1969, the Mexican government noticed that the country had a Caribbean coastline, decided something should be done with it, and Cancún was born.

Since 1998, we are enjoined to call this 130-kilometre strip – from Cancún to Tulum, together with the islands of Isla Mujeres and Cozumel – the *Riviera Maya*, a name that has made its way irresistibly on to road signs and into brochures to replace its former, more prosaic identity as the *Corredor Turística*. The transformation of the Mexican Caribbean from undiscovered remote spot to mega-attraction is sometimes cited as a benchmark-case of over-development, of how not to do it. The statistics are overwhelming: the Riviera Maya has the highest population growth of anywhere in Mexico and receives 20 per cent of all visitors to the country, while Playa del Carmen is swelling so fast it has left any available statistics way behind. The region's developers, Mexican and foreign, often seem chronically unable to say enough's enough, and the only thing that has forced a pause in the pace of building plans has been the crisis in the international travel business after 11 September.

It's become a guidebook cliché to sneer at Cancún at this point, at how tacky it is, but a more destructive recent plague is that of the all-inclusive resort complexes, which often look to be out to gobble up the entire coast down to Tulum. This, though, hasn't happened yet, and there are still many beautiful places along this coast, and people concerned that they stay that way. Come here expecting somewhere out of the way of the modern world and you'll be disappointed. But take Cancún, for example, for what it is – a brash, flash resort – and it's fun. Places like Isla Mujeres and Puerto Morelos retain a laid-back, beachtown atmosphere, there are still wonderful reefs full of life nearby, and dazzling canopies of stars at night. The diving is still superb. Elsewhere you can find isolated, small-scale hotels looking on to miles of empty beach, and towards the southern end of the Riviera there are wonderfully clear *cenotes* to swim in, and major Mayan ruins at Cobá and Tulum – which has to count as one of the most beautiful places on earth. Beyond Tulum is the Sian Ka'an reserve, one area where development is still held back. And in 2001, the Mexican Federal Environment Ministry actually prevented an all-inclusive project from going ahead on a turtle-breeding beach at Xcacel, the first time such a decisive intervention has happened in Mexican history.

Go on, do it again.

Cancún

People are very nasty about the city of Cancún. Hotel proprietors along the rest of the 'Riviera' tell you with great self-esteem, 'of course, we're not Cancún'. The implication is that Cancún is big, brassy, 'oh, so tacky', Miami-South, a cross between a beach and a freeway. Well, Cancún is big and unsophisticated, and horrifies some people. But, to say something on behalf of the old place, consider these two points:

A few years ago Friends of the Earth put out the suggestion that people who were really concerned about the environment should take their holidays in established, commercial tourist towns rather than forever demand new remote and 'unspoilt' places into which to extend airports and air conditioning. By these standards Cancún is the most eco-place in the whole Riviera. It is a purpose-built, industrial estate of fun. Until the late '90s some 90 per cent of Cancún's visitors never left Cancún island, let alone venturing beyond the town: if you made the effort to go a few kilometres inland or down the coast, your fellow-tourists would often number no more than 10 to 30 in each place. Cancún is a specialized facility, a piece of old-fashioned seaside, to be made use of or not as you wish. It does not pretend to be anything else.

Secondly, people often complain that Cancún is 'not the real Mexico', which presumably exists in some ideal adobe-state of immobile third-worlddom. In fact Cancún is actually the most Mexican city in the whole of the Yucatán, in that, in contrast to the very distinct, traditional Yucatecan culture of Mérida or Valladolid, people from all over Mexico live here. From being purely a necessary dormitory for chambermaids and gardeners, Ciudad Cancún has become a real city, population 600,000 and counting, gathering its own momentum as well as tourism. It has the *barrios*, bustle and street life and some of the tensions of a modern Mexican city, as the country teeters between 'developing' and 'first world' status. OK, you say, this is not actually the Mexico we came to see. But you can't say it's not authentic. Mexicans take holidays too and, at some times of year, foreigners share beach-space with crowds of locals and big family groups.

Having accentuated the positive, this is not to deny that Cancún can be an acquired taste. The Hotel Zone along Cancún island is forever being compared to Miami, but it has a lot of similarities with Las Vegas, being so new and pleasure-centred, with so much architecture that's downright silly, such as banana-shaped restaurant signs in luminous pink. Charm is not the strip's most obvious characteristic, and the traffic density can be atrocious. Cancún is a bit like any modern city, in fact, although crime and similar signs of urban decay are still fairly small-scale.

Because Cancún is preeminently the main entry point to the Yucatán, most people find themselves spending at least a night here on arrival or departure. Even though it has over 25,000 hotel beds, it fills up. The busiest times are Christmas, winter and Easter. Part of the folklore nowadays is Spring Break, a great American institution, which traditionally sees US college students have a wild time before serious exam business starts. Think Club 18–30, and multiply the numbers by several thousand.

Things to do in Cancún? Go with the flow. The city's reason for being, its beach, is one of the world's finest, a spectacular strand of white sand and surf running for miles. For a quick immersion in the Cancún experience, book a couple of nights here, see that view, and sample that other great Cancún institution, a pool with a swim-up bar. Have three margaritas and then roll mellowly backwards into the water, with your ears half-in and half-out. With luck they'll be playing some bouncy Mexpop that you can hear vibrating through the pool as you float around and look straight up at the perfect azure sky. It can be a transcendental experience. If then you must have culture, Cancún has a small but informative anthropology museum, and two Mayan sites, at El Rey, on Cancún island, and El Meco, at Punta Sam.

History

In the afternoon we steered for the mainland, passing the island of Kancune, a barren strip of land, with sand hills and stone buildings visible upon it...

John Lloyd Stephens

History? There isn't any, surely. When Stephens and Catherwood came along this coast by boat in 1842, looking for Tulum, they were told there was not a single road through the entire great triangle between Valladolid, the Bahía de la Ascensión and Yalahao (modern Chiquilá), and that the only settlement anywhere on the coast was a small *rancho* that had been the home of a retired pirate. It was, Stephens wrote, 'a region entirely unknown; no white man ever enters it'. And this was before the Caste War, which led non-Mayan Yucatecans to keep even further away. Cancún and the coast as a whole had seen much greater human habitation many centuries earlier. Archaeological research has shown that there were fishing communities on Cancún island from the Preclassic period, from about 300 BC. It was not, however, until the Late Postclassic in about 1200 that the town now known as El Rey was built, around the same time as other coastal communities such as Xcaret (Polé), Xel-ha and Tulum. They were important points on a vigorous trade route that ran from the Gulf of Honduras around the coast to Campeche and the Gulf of Mexico, bartering dried fish, cotton, honey and sea shells (a valuable commodity for the Maya), either for obsidian from Guatemala and gold from Panama, or for cacao, grinding-stones and salt from western Yucatán. By the 15th century this trade had gained considerable sophistication, and small temples along the coast were often built as aids to navigation. It was fatally disrupted, however, when the Spaniards conquered the lordship of Chetumal in the 1540s. Deprived of their livelihood, the local Maya abandoned their town and moved inland looking for places to farm, leaving the coast all but empty.

After the Caste War, the northeast corner of the peninsula was left as something of a no-man's-land for decades. In the 1900s, when the trade in *chicle*, the raw ingredient of chewing gum, finally brought a new population into the area, Puerto Juárez was built as a ferry port to Isla Mujeres, although traffic was still never more than sluggish. Quintana Roo was so underpopulated it remained a federal territory rather than a state until 1974. A few sport fishermen and people seeking a very out-of-the-way retreat built houses in the area, but that was it until the great transformation began in 1969. There is a story put around that, once the Mexican government decided that it should have a resort on the Atlantic as a counterpart to Acapulco on the Pacific, Cancún was chosen by a computer, as having the optimum combination of natural advantages: climate, proximity to major markets and so on. Probably of more immediate influence – as well as the beach – was the fact that the only building on Cancún island at that time was the holiday hideaway of Luis Echeverría, a leading figure in the PRI who would be president of Mexico from 1970 to 1976. Echeverría was considered very left-wing in PRI terms, which means that he was very much in favour of Mexico's state enterprises and the party unions, and liked to make statements about the Third World and goad the *gringo* by hobnobbing with Fidel Castro; but this didn't stop him from recognizing the deal of the century when he saw it. He sold the island to the nation, and a public corporation, Fonatur, was set up to oversee the creation from scratch of the new resort. The first hotel, the Camino Real (*see* p.152), opened in 1971, and the builders have been hard at work pretty much ever since.

The Hotel Zone

Cancún's two halves can be taken one at a time, or entirely separately, but since the beach was the start of it all it's only fitting to begin with the Hotel Zone. And an awesome sight it is. Cancún island is one of the great display cases of end-of-the-millennium kitsch-pleasure architecture, a giant park in which architects have been let loose to create some of the largest buildings on the planet in a tutti-frutti of corporate-fantasy styles. As you travel along Blvd Kukulcán, the hotels give out a real mixture of signals: some retire behind imposing driveways and primped lawns, others are placed up front beside the street. The balconies of the Fiesta Americana Coral Beach drip with vegetation, while the two halves of the Sheraton Towers want to reach out and give you a hug. If leisure is a religion of the modern era, the builders of Cancún have followed up the sacred temples of the Maya with pyramids on a scale the ancients never dreamed of: a stepped pyramid with a three-pointed-star ground plan at the Caesar Park; three massive, squat pyramids at the 1,000-bed Gran Oasis. Other buildings take less note of their location. The French-owned Meridien mixes up Parisian Art Deco with a few Mayan motifs on top, while the Ritz Carlton is a picturesque combination of Italian Renaissance and US penitentiary architecture.

Apart from the hotels and the most prominent restaurants – one of the best-known reference points is Fat Tuesday, by Playa Tortugas beach – the other landmarks of the Hotel Zone are its giant malls or plazas (not to be confused with squares), spaced out along the boulevard. **La Isla** at Km12.5 is the most gleamingly recent addition, with upmarket international fashion names among its stores. A lot of Cancún development also works on a slash-and-burn principle like that of Mayan agriculture, in that once a hotel becomes a little worn it's left to slide, then built over with something bigger. Along the strip you can also find some modest shopping centres from the Cancún of the 1970s, now shabby and forlorn, half-empty and waiting to be knocked down and forgotten.

The busiest section of the Hotel Zone is along the north side, running roughly down to the Flamingo mall. At Km4 there is another glossy attraction at the **Embarcadero**

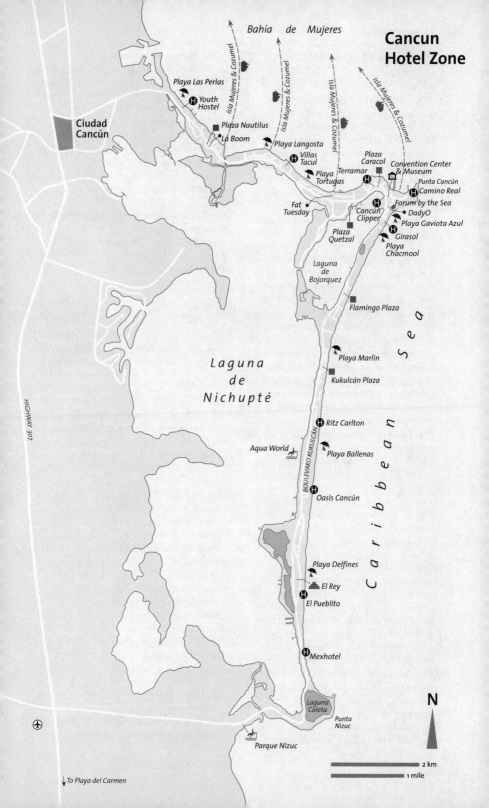

Getting There

By Air

Cancún **airport** is 15km south of Ciudad Cancún, on the mainland parallel with the southern end of Cancún island. The **arrival halls** for international and domestic flights are at either end of the terminal; for **departures**, all passengers can use the same entrances, in the middle. Arrival is not a triumph for Mexican PR. Baggage reclaim can be very slow. There is a **money exchange office** in the arrivals lounge which always gives the worst rate; change as little as possible.

Getting To and From the Airport

In the arrivals hall there is a ticket desk for the *Transporte Terrestre* **airport minibuses**, which are the only means of transport into town unless you have a transfer arranged by a tour company. Buy the ticket, and the buses are on the other side of customs; current rates, which are the same for all the different *colectivo* companies, are posted by the desk (about $8.50 per person); the buses run through the Hotel Zone and then on to Ciudad Cancún (taking nearly an hour), dropping each passenger at their hotel door (drivers expect tips). Passengers going only to Ciudad Cancún are sometimes told that a bus will take them straight there, but this is scarcely ever true, and *colectivos* are not obliged to leave until they have at least eight passengers, so that you may have an irritating wait. In theory it's possible to take an **airport taxi** ($30–$40), but these can be hard to find (*see* below).

When you're **leaving**, any city cab can take you to the airport (about $11 from Ciudad Cancún; $15 from the Hotel Zone) but, as usual, agree a price before you get in (*see* below, 'By Taxi'). Along Av. Tulum there are bus-stop signs marked *Aeropuerto*: ignore them; these buses are for airport workers and run only occasionally at inconvenient times.

The transport situation has improved for anyone heading directly to **Puerto Morelos** or **Playa del Carmen**. There is now a Riviera bus (about once an hour; fare around $7) to Playa, passing Puerto Morelos, usually on the half-hour 10.30am–7pm daily; from Playa del Carmen 8am–7.30pm. It leaves from outside Domestic Arrivals; from International Arrivals,

go out of the main exit, turn right and then walk along the length of the terminal building (the ticket desk is inside the Domestic Arrivals hall). There are also hourly *colectivos* ($15) to and from Playa between 6am and 6pm, which are similarly easier to find at Domestic Arrivals, and even individual Cancún airport cabs are also more readily available there than at International Arrivals. A cab to yourself from the airport to Puerto Morelos will cost around $40, to Playa del Carmen over $55.

Contact Numbers for Leading Airlines

Aerocaribe, t 884 2000.
American Airlines, t 883 4460.
Continental, t 886 0006.
Iberia, t 886 0158.
Mexicana, t 887 4444.

By Bus

Cancún conveniently has only one long-distance bus station for first- and second-class buses (the two booking halls are side by side), in the centre of Ciudad Cancún at the junction of Av. Tulum and Av. Uxmal. There are services to most parts of the Yucatán peninsula and to cities throughout Mexico, and only some are detailed here. As usual, they are run by different companies, but ADO (**t** 886 8604) has the most long-distance services.

Campeche (*7hrs*): one GL, three first-, two second-class daily, via Mérida. First-class fare about $27.

Chetumal (*6hrs*): three ADO GL luxury services and at least eight regular first-class daily; 23 *intermedio* or second-class services. Most first-class services and all others stop at **Playa del Carmen, Tulum** and **Felipe Carrillo Puerto**; one first-class and all *intermedio* and second-class buses stop at **Bacalar**. First-class fare to Chetumal about $18.

Chiquilá, for **Holbox** (*3½hrs*): two second-class buses daily (8am and 1.30pm). Fare about $6.

Mérida (*4¼hrs*): 20 luxury services (12 ADO GL, eight UNO) daily, and normal first-class almost hourly 1am–11.30pm with ADO or Super Espresso. Fares from $17. Second-class buses run hourly, 3am–7pm, and slightly less frequently at night. An unusual (but longer) route is with Autobuses del Centro de Yucatán, which has 15 buses daily going via Valladolid and **Izamal**. Fares around $14.

Mexico City (*28hrs*): three ADO GL and two UNO luxury services and four regular first-class daily. Fares from $86.

Palenque (*12¼hrs*): five or six first-class daily via **Chetumal** and **Escárcega**, with Altos (2.15pm, 6.30pm (Fri–Mon only 8.30pm); Cristóbal Colón (3.45pm); Maya de Oro (5.45pm) or ADO (7.30pm). The 2.15pm and 6.30pm Altos buses and C. Colón and Maya de Oro continue on to **Ocosingo**, **San Cristóbal de Las Casas** (*17hrs*) and **Tuxtla Gutiérrez** (*21hrs*); the 8.30pm Fri–Mon Altos bus goes from Palenque to **Comitán** and **Tapachula** (*24hrs*). Fares vary significantly, Altos being cheaper, but more cramped: the range is about $37–$46 Palenque, $46–$58 San Cristóbal.

Puerto Morelos and **Playa del Carmen** (*1¼hrs*): Riviera shuttle service every 10mins 5am–11pm daily, and 22 Mayab *intermedio* services daily; fares to Playa about $3.50; 11 Riviera services and 13 Mayab continue on to **Tulum** and **Chetumal**. Playa Express buses, slower but a little cheaper, run on the same route every 30mins 6am–8pm daily, and many also go on to Tulum. First-class buses via Chetumal also stop at Playa del Carmen.

Valladolid and **Chichén Itzá** (*1½hrs*): 12 first-class buses a day to Mérida stop in Valladolid, and some also stop in Pisté (for Chichén Itzá). All second-class Mérida buses (hourly, 3am–7pm) stop in both destinations, and can leave you by the ruins entrance instead of in Pisté. Second-class fares around $6.50 Valladolid, $8 Chichén.

Villahermosa (*14hrs*): three luxury and 10 ordinary first-class buses daily. Fare about $45.

Orientation

Cancún is made up of two parts. The **Hotel Zone** (*Zona Hotelera* or *Zona Hoteles*) is the prosaic name for Cancún island, the 23km spit of sand, looking like a giant '7', that encloses Laguna Nichupté and is held to the mainland by bridges at each end. It has only one road, **Boulevard Kukulcán**, measured by kilometre markers (used as locators in addresses) to make it easier to distinguish one part from another. There are hotels, restaurants and other attractions all along the strip, but the

biggest concentration is around the angle of the '7', close to Punta Cancún and the Centro de Convenciones.

Ciudad Cancún, often called 'Downtown', is the mainland town originally built to provide services for the hotels and somewhere for their employees to live. The north end of Blvd Kukulcán meets the town's north–south artery, **Av. Tulum**, which at one end runs up to the ferry landing at Puerto Juárez and at the other runs away to the airport and the coast road south. The centre of town is the stretch of Av. Tulum between two large roundabouts at Avenidas Cobá and Uxmal: the bus station, town hall, main banks and other essentials are on this block or within easy walking distance. Cheaper hotels, cheaper restaurants – in fact, cheaper anything – are all in Ciudad Cancún.

As a new city Ciudad Cancún has an addressing system that can be uniquely incomprehensible. It is made up of several wide avenues, most named after Mayan cities. The areas between them are called *Super Manzanas* or 'Super Blocks', each of which has a number. The smaller streets within the SM blocks are named or numbered too, but in some parts of town, especially in north Cancún (the location of several budget hotels), this has yet to be done. Instead, addresses are given as lot numbers, as in SM 64, Mza 3, Lote 8, which is meaningless to anyone fresh off a plane. If you have such an address the only way to find your way there is to trust in a cab driver, and/or call ahead and find out if there are landmarks close by. Note that many named side streets are not through streets but only enclosed rectangles around a small block, so that exits next to each other on an avenue often have the same name.

Getting Around

By Bus

Cancún has a user-friendly local bus system. Routes R-1 and R-2 run continually between the Hotel Zone and Ciudad Cancún from about 5am to 2–3am, running from Av. Tulum along Blvd Kukulcán and turning back at the very bottom of Cancún island by Parque Nizuc. They are pretty full in the mornings and early evenings, but they come every few minutes.

There's a standard fare no matter how far you travel, long pegged at 5 pesos. Some R-1 buses and route R-13 run from Av. Tulum (there is a stop opposite the bus station) to the Isla Mujeres ferry at Puerto Juárez.

By Car and Bike

Petrol/gas stations are plentiful in Cancún, and going south there are *gasolineras* at Puerto Morelos, Playa del Carmen, Puerto Aventuras, Xpu-Ha and Tulum. **Cycling** is not something associated with Cancún, but there is now a cycle track (*ciclopista*) along almost the length of Cancún island. There do not, though, seem to be any cycle hire shops, but many hotels have bikes.

Car Hire

There are any number of car hire agencies, with offices in hotels, all the Hotel Zone malls and along Av. Tulum. Rental has been expensive (from $50 a day), but good value deals can be found, although you will get better rates in Mérida (*see* p.266). All agencies offer a range of vehicles, including jeeps. The best place to find good value agencies is in Ciudad Cancún, especially on the corner of Av. Tulum and Av. Uxmal opposite the bus station. Agencies generally stay open in the evenings, for clients wishing to book a car for the next day.

Auto-Rent, Av. Tulum 77, **t** 887 0709. Next to the Novotel on the bus station corner, this is about the cheapest, with VWs from $35–$40 a day, regular offers and big discounts for more than a few days, but their cars may be pretty well-worn.

Econo-Rent, Edificio Atlantis, Av. Bonampak, corner Av. Cobá, **t** 887 6487, *www.econocar-rental.com*. Rates usually begin at about $35 a day, and can be highly negotiable in low season, or for longer-term rents. The office is by the entry into Ciudad Cancún, coming from the Hotel Zone.

Localiza, in Cancún **t** 849 4680 (*see* p.193). This Mexican chain offers frequent special deals.

By Taxi

Cancún has hundreds of taxis. As usual in Mexico, they do not have meters, and there is a complicated structure of official rates based on the idea that tourists can and should pay more than locals. Any journey within Ciudad Cancún is quite cheap (about $1.20), but trips are more expensive to or from the Hotel Zone (around $5). Similarly, a taxi to the airport from the Hotel Zone costs more than one from Ciudad Cancún, even though it may be a shorter journey. Current rates are posted at Puerto Juárez and outside the bus station, and are listed in local free magazines (*see* below); the basic rule is always to agree the price **before** getting in the cab.

Tourist Information

Cancún t (998–)

There are scores of tours, special club nights, trips and so on advertised in Cancún at any time. Useful things to pick up are the free magazines *Cancún Tips* and *Cancún Nights*, available in hotels and shops as well as tourist offices (you'll usually be offered one in the airport as you arrive). As well as masses of ads they have the current taxi rates, maps and discount coupons to soften the blow of Cancún prices. Also useful is the free *Hotel Guide*, which is not a guide at all but consists only of discount coupons for hotels along the Riviera. An avalanche of information is also available online: **Cancun Online** (*www.cancun.com*) is about the most comprehensive site.

Tourist Offices: Municipal Office, in the town hall on Av. Tulum (*open Mon–Fri 9–3 and 6–8; closed Sat and Sun*). Hidden away to the right of the main stairs, beyond the lobby. There are also information kiosks in La Isla and Forum malls, by the ferry in Puerto Juárez and by the highway in Puerto Morelos. They are staffed by students.

Quintana Roo State Tourist Office, C/ Pecari 23 in SM20, off Av. Tulum south of Av. Cobá. More professional but inconveniently sited. Along the length of Av. Tulum there are kiosks advertising 'Information'. These are usually only interested in selling you tours, tickets to bullfights and other attractions and time shares, but if you ask a straight question you might get an answer.

Banks: The main bank offices are also on the central stretch of Av. Tulum; the big Banamex, on the east side, is usually the quickest at changing money. All have ATM cash machines, and most are now open on

Saturday mornings. There are also banks in the Hotel Zone near the Convention Center, in Flamingo Plaza and Kukulcán Plaza malls, and there are *cambio* offices (*open Sun*) on Av. Tulum and in the malls. **American Express**, Plaza América, Av. Tulum 208, **t** 885 2001, south of Av. Cobá in Super Manzana 4.

Consulates and Immigration: **Canadian Consulate**, Plaza Caracol II, third floor, room 330, **t** 883 3360; **US Consulate**, (in the same building) Plaza Caracol II, third floor, room 320–323, **t** 883 0272; **British Vice-Consulate**, Royal Sands Hotel, **t** 881 0100.

The **Mexican Immigration Office** is at Av. Nader 1, **t** 884 1749 (*open Mon–Fri 9–1; closed Sat and Sun*), at the corner of Av. Uxmal. The best place in the region to get an extension to your stay (*see* p.111).

Health: If you need a doctor, the **American Hospital**, C/ Viento 15, SM 4, **t** 884 6133, is the best place to call, with a 24-hr emergency service. It is off Av. Tulum in the next block south of the central section, near the American Express office. **Total Assist**, C/ Claveles 5, **t** 884 8116, off Av. Tulum, is another 24-hr medical service with English-speaking staff. There are several **pharmacies** in the malls and the town centre; note that **Farmacia Unión**, on Av. Uxmal opposite the bus station, is open 24hrs.

Internet Access: Two well-priced places are **Cyber-Office**, Av. Uxmal 19, Local 6-1, handily sited by the Av. Uxmal entrance into the bus station, which charges by the time used, not a flat hourly rate (*open daily*), and **Internet Kids**, C/ Gladiolas 18, off Av. Yaxchilán.

Newspapers and Books: The *Miami Herald* and the English-language, Mexico City paper *The News* are available at most news-stands on Av. Tulum and in the malls. The best book and magazine store is **Fama**, Av. Tulum 105.

Phone Office: There are long-distance *casetas* on Av. Tulum and Av. Yaxchilán (quite pricey).

Police: The main police station is next to the Town Hall, Av. Tulum, **t** 884 1913. There is another in the Hotel Zone beside Kukulcán Plaza. Cancún has special 'tourist police' officers who speak English.

Post Office: Corner of Av. Sunyaxchén and Av. Xel-Ha (*open Mon–Fri 8–6, Sat, Sun and hols 9–12.30*). There is a **Mexpost** office (*closed Sun*) alongside the main building.

Shopping

Cancún has thousands of places to shop, but how much you might want to buy is another question. Mexican handicrafts here are mostly of production-line standard, and more expensive than anywhere else in the Yucatán. The Hotel Zone's giant malls can be of most interest just for looking around and buying silly souvenirs. Plaza Caracol has some good **toy shops**. **Jewellery**, made with Mexican silver, jade and imported gems, is a traditional buy, but prices in the malls are now little different from international levels. **La Fiesta**, Km9, and the **Coral Negro**, Km9.5, are slightly cheaper: two flea-market type malls selling jewellery and all sorts of Mexicana, with some fine pieces as well as an awful lot of junk. The real signature product of Cancún is the **T-shirt**, and the **Ki-Huic souvenir market** on Av. Tulum in 'Downtown' has enough to clothe a whole city. For more sophisticated designs, look for the **Miró** shops on Av. Tulum and in the main malls. Have a look in **Deportes Martí** in the Flamingo Plaza, Las Américas and La Fiesta malls for Mexican football shirts. There are shops offering tequilas and other Mexican alcoholic specialities in all the malls, but **Bodegas La Sevillana**, Av. Sunyaxchén 38, is one of the best, with an interestingly varied stock. Cuban cigars are another sought-after Cancún commodity, and **La Casa del Habano**, Flamingo Plaza, has as good a stock as any.

Sports and Activities

Diving and Snorkelling

There are a few diving schools in Cancún, and introductory scuba-diving trips are available at attractions such as Aqua World, but diving here is more expensive than at other places nearby and since the Cancún reefs are in a poor state, you may well be taken from here to those same areas on a fairly long boat trip. It is usually more enjoyable to go straight to Puerto Morelos, Playa, Isla Mujeres or Cozumel. Two established companies are: **Scuba Cancún**, Blvd Kukulcán, Km5, **t** 883 1011. **Ocean Sports**, Av. Cobá 51, **t** 884 6034.

Lagoon snorkel trips can be made from Aqua World and other venues (*see* below).

Golf

Hilton Cancún Golf Club, Hilton Hotel, Blvd Kukulcán Km17, t 881 8000. Eighteen holes, and the most opulent facilities.

Club de Golf Pok-ta-Pok, on Pok-ta-Pok island in the lagoon by Blvd Kukulcán Km7.5, t 883 1230. A very high-standard, 18-hole course.

Meliá Cancún Hotel, Km15, t 881 1100. Has a 13-hole course.

There's also a mini-golf course at the **Cancún Palace** hotel, Km14.5, t 885 0533.

Swimming and Swimming Safety

Lifeguards are posted along the long, east-facing beaches, which attract a strong swell. Look out for red flags, and caution is especially recommended when a *norte* (north) wind is blowing. The beaches facing north, along the top of the '7', have calmer waters (*see* p.158). Another good place to swim outside of hotel pools is in the tranquil lagoon on the other side of the island, where there are several landing stages. Locals often swim from the park alongside the lagoon near to the Plaza Nautilus mall (Km3) – also a nice place to walk – but most foreigners seem to ignore it.

Other Watersports, Rides and Fun Parks

An essential Cancún tradition is getting around on the water by different means: try **wave runners** (jet skis), **water-skiing**, **banana rides**, **parasailing**, **kayaks** and **windsurfing**. **Aqua World**, Blvd Kukulcán Km15.2, t 885 2288, *www.aquaworld.com.mx*. The largest venue, offering every one of the above activities and more. Boats are taken out into the lagoon more than the open sea; they also offer scuba instruction, sport-fishing trips, dinner cruises, 'jungle tours' including snorkelling at 'Paradise Island', and what they call a 'submarine ride', not in fact a sub, but a boat with a glass-sided hull where you look out from beneath the water level.

Smaller-scale operations can be found all along the Kukulcán strip, especially around Fat Tuesday on Playa Tortugas.

Parque Nizuc fun park, t 881 3000, *www.parquenizuc.com*, right at the very bottom of the island (Km25). Cancún's best watery attraction, this has a swim-with-dolphins pool (*see* p.94), and another big salt-water pool where you can snorkel among rays and (small and harmless) sharks. The real star is the huge **Wet 'n' Wild waterpark**, which has spectacular rides and slides.

There are regular **excursions** from Cancún to places out of town, especially Isla Contoy, Dolphin Discovery on Isla Mujeres and Xcaret. For these, *see* the relevant sections.

Where to Stay

Cancún t (998–)

Even with their 25,000 beds, Cancún's hotels are still often expensive. Those in the Hotel Zone are designed to be booked as part of a package, and off-the-street public rates are very high (many do not take non-agency bookings). If you want to stay by the beach it is always best to book a package from home rather than trying to reserve direct through the hotel. Independent travellers who need or want to spend some nights here nearly always stay in the simpler hotels in Ciudad Cancún, but even there prices are higher than in places inland. Given the limitations of town hotels it can be more enjoyable to cut your losses and splurge on a beach hotel to sample the Cancún experience, and even on an average budget this isn't out of the question. In the main winter and Easter seasons rates are at their highest, but at other times smaller hotels often have offers. The *Hotel Guide* of discount coupons (*see* p.150) is also useful.

With so many hotels in Cancún, the listing here can only be a selection. Those listed in the Hotel Zone are only those particularly worth looking out for and more amenable to individual travellers. It is always advisable to book ahead.

Hotel Zone

Luxury

El Camino Real, Punta Cancún, t 848 7000, *www.caminoreal.com/cancun*. It requires mention most as a monument, since it's the place that started Cancún off back in 1971, but it's been very well maintained, and has big, bright rooms and every kind of service.

Villas Tacul, Blvd Kukulcán Km5.5, t 849 7060/ 883 0000, *www.villastacul.com.mx*. Of a similar vintage as the Camino, made up of

23 attractive self-contained villa-apartments in a lush and pretty garden, with its own beach, pool and other extras. Prices drop substantially off season, and for a family it can be quite economical; the main hitch is that there's much more traffic noise than when the hotel was built.

Expensive–Moderate

Cancún Clipper Club, Blvd Kukulcán Km9, t 883 1366, *salesccc@cancun.com.mx*. Faces the lagoon (near the Convention Center) rather than the sea, so no beach frontage, but this otherwise has comfortable, well-equipped rooms and a pleasant pool. Prices may be *moderate* in low season.

Mexhotel, Blvd Kukulcán Km20.5, t 885 0361, f 885 0236. A pleasant independent hotel, with a good pool and sea views. Prices are upper-*expensive* in peak season, but may be *moderate* at other times.

El Pueblito, Blvd Kukulcán Km17.5, t 881 8800, *www.pueblitohotels.com*. One of the most attractive of the smaller beach hotels, with suite-style rooms mostly with great ocean views, a three-level pool (with swim-up bar) and pretty Mexican-traditional-style public rooms. It's run on an all-inclusive basis, but is still open to non-package-booked guests, and prices are quite reasonable.

Suites Girasol, Blvd Kukulcán Km10, t 883 2151, f 883 2246, One of the cheapest places on the beach, a suite complex in a 1970's tower with well-used but well-equipped apartments for a maximum of four, with ocean view and a pool. Prices *moderate* off-season.

Ciudad Cancún

Expensive

Best Western Plaza Caribe, Av. Tulum and Av. Uxmal, t 884 1377, *plazacbe@cancun .com.mx*. Right opposite the bus station, but despite being so central, behind the façade it has very pretty gardens with a good pool, and pleasant rooms. On the *expensive–moderate* border (lower off-peak), making it very good value.

Moderate

Hotel Antillano, Av. Tulum and C/ Claveles 1, t 884 1132, *antillano@mpsnet.com.mx*. Very

handily located on the main drag, and accordingly popular. The rooms could do with some modernization, but they're still comfortable and spacious. Be sure to book well in advance.

Hotel Batab, Av. Chichén Itzá 52, t 884 3822, *www.hotelbatab.com*. One of a bunch of hotels on the north side of the city centre, in a functional '70s building; it's unspectacular but reliably decent value, with big, well-lit rooms all with a/c, TV and phone, and a pleasant **restaurant**.

Hotel Caribe Internacional, Av. Yaxchilán 36–37, t 884 3999, *www.caribeinter nacional.com*. An 80-room, modern hotel in an enjoyable location away from Av. Tulum on the corner of Yaxchilán and Sunyaxchén. The rooms have no great character, but they're light and spacious and there's a nice pool and **restaurants**, making this one of the best-value mid-range hotels.

Novotel, Av. Tulum 75, t 884 2999, f 884 3162. Has a well-established niche thanks to its convenient location on the corner of Av. Uxmal by the bus station. Rooms are functional but quite pretty and surprisingly quiet, and there's a small pool. Fan-only rooms are a little cheaper.

Suites Cancún Center, C/ Alcatraces 22, t 884 2301, *www.suitescancun.com*. In the middle of SM22 by Las Palapas park, this has big, functional rooms with kitchenettes, most with a/c, and you have access to a 'beach club'. Built in the 1970s, it's showing its age, but has a good pool and is decent value, especially off-peak.

Inexpensive

Cancún's *inexpensive* hotels (there are few in the really *cheap* range) are mostly a few blocks from the central stretch: the most economical (and more basic) are in the blocks north of Av. Chichén Itzá towards the Crucero. All the hotels listed have showers en suite.

Hotel Alux, Av. Uxmal 21, t 884 6613, f 884 0662. A very short walk from the bus station and refurbished in the last few years, this has 30 rooms with a/c.

Hotel Chichén, C/ 2, SM 63, t 884 4440, f 887 3292. On a side street off Av. Chichén Itzá by the junction with Av. Uxmal, this motel-style hotel is a bargain. Rooms have more comforts than most (easy chairs, fridges in some rooms, a/c throughout).

Hotel Hacienda Cancún, Av. Sunyaxchén 39–40, t 884 3672, *hhda@cancun.com.mx*. One of the most popular upper-*inexpensive* hotels. Rooms are a little small but all have both fans and a/c, and it has a pool in a pretty garden.

Hotel María Isabel, C/ Palmeras 59, t 884 9015. A long-running favourite, a short walk up Av. Uxmal from the bus station. Its 12 small but snug rooms, all with a/c, are not as well kept as they once were (and some of the lower ones are very dark) but they need to be booked well ahead.

Hotel Piña Hermanos, C/ 8 no.35, SM 64, t 884 2150. A basic but quite likeable hotel with some of Cancún's cheapest acceptable rooms: very *inexpensive* with a/c, or *cheap* for very simple, fan-only rooms. If you know any Spanish, call for directions.

Hotel Progreso, C/ 31, SM 63, t 884 6700. One of the more welcoming budget options, a simple but well-kept hotel with bright, quite comfortable, mostly fan-only rooms, and friendly owners.

Cheap/Camping

Hotel-Hostel Las Palmas, C/ Palmeras 43, t 884 2513. A pleasantly cosy hotel and hostel up the street from the Hotel María Isabel (*see* above), run by a slow-moving but very amiable local family. Recently converted, it has big, bright double rooms (some with a/c) for lower-*inexpensive* range prices, and six-bed hostel rooms, with lockers and new showers, for $10 a night per bed. There's also an open kitchen and café area.

Mexico Hostel, C/ Palmeras 30, t 887 0191, *www.mexicohostels.com*. Opened in 2000, this AMAJ hostel has 50 beds in dorm-style rooms for $10 each (20 beneath a *palapa* shelter on the roof), plus six double rooms (around $20), with continental breakfast included for all. It's very clean and well cared for, with good showers, and there's an open kitchen, a lounge space with TV, Internet access and lockers, but deposits or extra charges must be paid for a range of basic facilities (sheets, towels, soap, etc.). To find it from the bus station, turn right up Av. Uxmal.

Villa Deportiva Juvenil, Blvd Kukulcán Km3.2, t 883 1337. Cancún's older, more 'official' hostel is the cheapest place to stay near the beach. However, it's a very drab, school-like building, with beds in an 8-bed room for $10, or camping in the grounds for less. This is the cheapest camp site around Cancún.

El Meco, next to the ruins of the same name. A big, modern RV and camp site.

Eating Out

Cancún has even more restaurants than hotels. Along the Hotel Zone boulevard you can find every cuisine (usually as filtered via the USA), and all the big noises of modern theme eating – Planet Hollywood, the Hard Rock, the Rainforest Café. Cancún's tourist restaurants have a reputation for paying more attention to flashy décor than to their sometimes production-line food, and their prices are generally over double the Yucatán average. In amongst them, though, there are places where the expense can be worth it for a special meal and, since locals eat out too, there is a far bigger price range in eating-places than in hotels. In Ciudad Cancún there are plenty of decent local restaurants, and even by the beach you can still eat cheaply at cafés and *taco*-stands.

Expensive

This category is necessarily open-ended: whereas in many Mexican cities it's hard to spend much over $25 per person even in the best restaurants, in anywhere remotely smart here this is an average price.

Blue Bayou, Hyatt Cancún Caribe Hotel, Blvd Kukulcán Km10.5, t 883 0044. Award-winning Cajun/Creole cooking, prepared by Mexican chefs and served in a pretty, soothing dining room.

La Fisheria, Plaza Caracol (Km8.5), t 883 1395. Big, bright and light, serving (surprise) a high-quality, US and international-style fish and seafood menu.

La Habichuela, C/ Margaritas 25, t 884 3158. In a tranquil location in Ciudad Cancún next to Parque de las Palapas, this long-running place offers superior traditional Yucatecan and Mexican dishes with original touches, charmingly served in a pretty garden.

La Joya, Fiesta Americana Coral Beach Hotel, Blvd Kukulcán Km9.5, **t** 881 3213. One of Cancún's most prestigious venues for refined Mexican food.

Perico's, Av. Yaxchilán 71, **t** 887 4884. A Mexican theme restaurant 'downtown' that's almost an institution, as year after year taxi-loads of tourists have been taken there to sample an 'authentic' fantasy-*cantina* atmosphere, live music, waitresses in bandit-girl outfits and all. Get there early if you don't want to stand in line.

Moderate

There is a clutch of fun Mexican restaurants on Av. Yaxchilán – the same street as Perico's (*see* above) – which are among the prime places for Cancún locals to go to for a night out or Sunday lunch. They have shaded terrace or garden tables, occasional live music and an ample choice from simple *tacos* to giant all-inclusive buffets (for two or more persons only). Two of the busiest are **Las Yardas** and **Cielito Lindo**, where if you get into the spirit you can join in singing all-time Mex-classics like *Guadalajara* and *La Bamba*.

Los Braseros, Av. Yaxchilán 34. One of the best of the Yaxchilán restaurants, with classic Mexican dishes in very generous portions, and a speciality of huge set platters for two (chargrilled meats, mixed fish and seafood) at bargain prices. Service is fast but charming, and non-pushy.

El Café, Av. Nader 5. Parallel to Av. Tulum behind the town hall, this attractive modern terrace café is a favourite meeting-point for middle-class Mexicans. The house speciality is excellent Veracruz coffee, but the classic Mexican dishes are very good too.

Carlos'n'Charlie's, Blvd Kukulcán Km5.5. Cancún is one of the great homes of the chain restaurant, and among the corporate identities some are worth singling out. Grupo Anderson, a Mex–US restaurant group that has now gone global, has four places in Cancún with similarly silly names: Señor Frog's (Blvd Kukulcán Km9.5), the Shrimp Bucket and so on. OK, they're very much a chain, but they do what they do well: present standard Mexican dishes with the heat slightly taken off for *gringo* tastes, well-prepared and in a fun atmosphere.

100% Natural, Av. Sunyaxchén 62, corner of Av. Yaxchilán. A Mexican-owned chain to be taken note of by all vegetarians, with three of its pleasant health-food restaurants in Cancún: this one in town and two in the Hotel Zone, in Plaza Terramar (near the Convention Center), and Kukulcán Plaza. As well as a big choice of salads and other light dishes made with fresh produce (vegetarian and non-) they have fabulous juices and juice cocktails.

El Parador, Av. Tulum 26. A popular hotel restaurant near the bus station, serving decent local favourites out on its lively outside terrace.

Rosa Mexicano, C/ Claveles 4. Just off Av. Tulum is this pretty, slightly old-fashioned central-Mexican restaurant with enjoyable food and very charming service so far uninfected by Cancún fake have-a-nice-dayism.

Sanborn's, Av. Tulum, corner of Av. Uxmal. Opposite the bus station is this branch of the famous Mexico City café (there are two more in Plaza Terramar and Plaza Flamingo). They're great for breakfast, and for insomniacs, it's the best place to get a coffee and a snack and find café-style animation. *All open daily 24hrs.*

La Villa Rica, Av. Yaxchilán, opposite Av. Sunyaxchén. Smoothest of the outdoor restaurants on Yaxchilán, with a smart, comfortable terrace. Refined, Veracruz-style fish and seafood is the house speciality.

Cheap

Cancún's biggest concentration of cheap eating-places is in the central court of the **market** at the end of Av. Sunyaxchén. Its 20 or so restaurants, with outside tables under shady canopies, are not quite as basic as market *cocinas* in older Mexican cities, but they're more comfortable and they're still cheap. Reflecting Cancún's Pan-Mexican population, the food of every part of the country is represented: the **Restaurant Veracruz** has Gulf fish and seafood, **El Rinconcito del DF** (Distrito Federal, or Mexico City) offers strong, classic Mexican food, and there's even **Cocina La Chaya**, with Yucatecan *chaya*-based dishes and vegetarian options. Go for Sunday lunch, when they're full of family groups, and you'll never again be able to say that Cancún is lacking in Mexican atmosphere. A full meal will rarely cost over $9.

Other good places to look for cheap eats in the centre are the popular snack- and *taco*-stands in **Parque de las Palapas**, and **Calle Tulipanes**, with its line of unfussy small bars and restaurants.

Belinda's/Los Antojitos, C/ Tulipanes 23. The best of the small cafés on Tulipanes, with charmingly attentive service. It has excellent $3–$4 all-in traditional breakfasts that make a fine welcome to Mexico after arriving on a late-night flight, and Yucatecan dishes at other times. It comes warmly recommended by readers. *Open all day.*

Gory Tacos, C/ Tulipanes 26. A classic, straightforward *taquería* with plenty of outside tables and many fans for its juicy, fiery Mexican classics and cold beers.

Entertainment and Nightlife

Live Entertainment

Naturally enough, there's loads of it. One fixture on the programme is **bullfights**, every Wed at 3.30pm, which include a preceding *charrería* (*see* p.122) and folk music display. Tickets can be booked from a stand on Av. Tulum, near the Ki-Huic market. There are also occasional full-scale *charrería* shows at the *Lienzo Charro* south of the city, information on which is available from the tourist office.

Another Cancún speciality are **theme dinner cruises** (Pirate's Night, the Columbus cruise, etc.), including live entertainment, dinner, disco, karaoke and other forms of fun for around $45 a head. Places like the **Hard Rock** and **Planet Hollywood** (which have large dance spaces as well as restaurants) fairly regularly present live rock shows by US and international acts.

If you want to see a show, try the following resident companies:

Ballet Folclórico de Cancún, Centro de Convenciones (reservations t 883 0199, ext. 193). Performs an anthology of Mexican music and folk dances every night at 8pm (cocktails and dinner included, beginning at 6.30pm).

Teatro de Cancún, El Embarcadero, Km4 (t 849 4848). A similar venue hosting two shows every night (Mon–Fri): *Voces y Danzas de México* with more Mexican folklore at 7pm, and the more Cuban-carnivally *Tradición del Caribe* at 9pm.

Clubs and Bars

The permanent hubs of Cancún nightlife are its Hotel Zone clubs, mostly clustered in the same block as the Convention Center. These tend to be vast, with several spaces, a/c that's a miracle of modern science and regular hot body contests, bikini nights and similar to draw in the crowds. If on the other hand you want something more Mexican (and cheaper), head for the Yaxchilán/Sunyaxchén junction in Ciudad Cancún, where in the block to the north there are enormously popular places like the **Buena Onda** and **Bum Bum** discos and the **Canta Canta** Mexican karaoke bar. There's also a smallish nightlife cluster around C/ Tulipanes, with **El Chat Cancún**, an Internet café by day and buzzing rendezvous by night, and **Roots**, which promises Food, Music and Art and has a tad of a BoHo feel. Both have live bands and offer food as well as booze.

La Boom, Blvd Kukulcán Km3.5. Closest to town, the most 'English-style' club in Cancún, with the best and most sophisticated choice of music. It also has one of the best ever open-air chill-out and restaurant areas, with a view across the lagoon.

Coco Bongo, Blvd Kukulcán Km9.5, in the Convention Center block. Giant, multi-level mega-venue that of late has displaced its older competitors in the most-popular club stakes with eye-boggling show nights and a combination of live acts and a funkily eclectic music policy.

Dady'O, Blvd Kukulcán Km9.5. Still the biggest club of them all and retaining the loyalty of Spring Breakers, despite the challenge of the Coco Bongo across the street.

Dady Rock, in the same building as Dady'O. With live bands.

Ma'ax'o, a little way up the road beside Plaza La Isla mall (Km12.5). Run by the same organization as Dady Rock, with international-Balearic style club music rather than the all-American boogie favoured by the others. A free shuttle bus runs between the venues.

activities centre, with a giant rotating tower which you can go up for a panoramic view (*open daily 9am–11pm; adm*). The bend in the '7' around Km8–9 is the hub of the strip and the site of the city's biggest clubs and bars, and so the spot where Cancún's nightlife is most dazzling. To give a public focus to the area there is another giant mass in the centre of the same block, the **Centro de Convenciones**, housing the theatre that hosts the nightly *Ballet Folclórico* show. Sometimes unnoticed in one side of the Convention Center is Cancún's **Museo de Antropología e Historia** (*open daily 8–5; adm, Sun adm free*), the archaeological museum. Though small, it has an informative display on different aspects of Mayan life, labelled in Spanish and English, with ceramics, jewellery, tools and other artefacts mostly gathered from Postclassic sites in northern Quintana Roo, including *stelae* from Cobá and a head in stucco that was found in the ruins on Cancún island, after which the site was named *El Rey*.

Beyond the Flamingo Plaza the traffic and the atmosphere become quieter as the road (and the cycle track) rolls down to **Punta Nizuc**. The area between the south end of the island and the Parque Nizuc water park (where the buses turn back) is so far fairly empty, but there are always plans to build something in this city.

Beaches

Its magnificent sand strip is obviously the be-all and end-all of Cancún, but the city has a problem: the beach is shrinking. Recent hurricanes and tropical storms are believed to have changed the pattern of tidal drift along the coast, accelerating a tendency to beach erosion. Very gradually, the beach is getting narrower and steeper, especially around Punta Cancún.

While the hotels each have their own beach frontage, the beaches themselves, as everywhere in Mexico, are public property, and there are several public access points dotted along Cancún island (*see* box, 'Public Beaches', p.158). Being long and open, most of the east-facing *playas* along the longest stretch of the island have a lot of surf and sometimes a strong swell and undertow, and are best suited to jumping around on rather than swimming (*see* 'Swimming and Swimming Safety', p.152).

El Rey

By Km17 on Cancún Island; open daily 8–5; adm.

The buildings that make up the ruins of El Rey are not individually impressive by the standards of the great Mayan cities. However, it's still an interesting site to visit because of the clear impression it gives of a Mayan settlement as a potential real community. Like other Postclassic settlements along this coast El Rey grew up from about 1200, as a subordinate community of the lordship of Ecab, the capital of which was to the north near Cabo Catoche. No one knows what it was originally called, and it owes its current name to a stucco head found in one of the temples, now in the Cancún museum (*see* above), which has been labelled a 'king'. However, the site has been of considerable importance to archaeologists in reconstructing the pattern of Postclassic trade: it has been demonstrated that El Rey had links with places as far away as Colombia and the Aztec territories of central Mexico.

Public Beaches

Cancún's public beaches are as follows, from the top of the '7'. Those facing north are the most popular:

Playa Las Perlas (Km2): A small, quiet beach (except for the traffic on the boulevard), mostly surrounded by condo developments.

Playa Langosta (Km5): Much bigger, a big stretch of sand that's good for swimming and about the busiest public beach, with restaurants and a landing stage for boats to Isla Mujeres and other trips.

Playa Tortugas (Km7, by Fat Tuesday): Similarly big and busy, with plenty of attractions and a departure point for the Cozumel Shuttle.

Playa Caracol (Km8): A narrow but pleasant beach on a sheltered mini-lagoon with a palm-roofed bar, and a water-taxi to Isla Mujeres.

Playa Gaviota Azul (Km9): Around the corner from Caracol, near the point, but now severely eroded.

Playa Chac-Mool (Km9.5): A narrow beach with a simple, cheap bar and a few rather shabby shops; it seems a bit like a little island that goes unnoticed by the tourist hotels alongside it.

Playa Marlin, much further down at Km13 (behind the Kukulcán Plaza): A big, open stretch of sand and surf. No bars or shops, so take everything with you.

Playa Ballenas (Km14): Less attractive than Marlin and squeezed between two big hotel projects.

Playa Delfines (Km17), near the El Rey ruins: About the best of the surf beaches, a tall, steep bank of sand with a great view. No facilities, so take everything with you.

Playa Mirador, about 500 metres to the left of Parque Nizuc, near a little park: A sheltered, south-facing beach that few people seem to know about, for anyone who wants a beach more or less to themselves. Another one where you must take everything with you, as there are no bars or shops.

The **entrance** is at the southern end of the site. Like other small communities in Quintana Roo, El Rey differs from the grander Mayan cities, with their multi-plaza layout, in having a recognizable main street running from north to south, called the *Calzada*. This path leads north from the entrance past several small platforms – some of which are the bases of temples and others of houses – into the main plaza. Forming the south side of the square is the largest building at El Rey, a low platform with 18 columns that once supported a wood and palm roof, known as Structure 4 or **El Palacio**. In the middle of the square is a temple platform, and on the right as you enter are three temple buildings (known as **Structures 3a, b** and **c**) which are the most intact on the site. The head of 'El Rey' was found in 3b, which also has carved glyphs and wall paintings that are still visible. To the left of these temples is the single **Pyramid of El Rey** (Structure 2), a fairly crude pile that was built over an older base dating from the Terminal Classic. Excavations into it have revealed a tomb, almost certainly of the town's ruler, buried with offerings of copper vessels and conch, jade and coral jewellery.

The L-shaped building next to the Pyramid, forming the north side of the plaza, is another colonnaded platform (**Structure 1**), with a raised stone bench around the back wall. This too would have had a palm roof and is believed to have been the town's fish market. On the north side of it is another smaller plaza, with another platform-type building (**Structure 7**), probably a residential complex for the ruling lineage, and beyond that more small temple and house platforms. Again, the small size of the squares is a clear indication of the limited size of El Rey, its population numbering a few thousand at most. The small scale, however, also makes it easier to imagine comings and goings across the plaza.

Ciudad Cancún

Even people who really like Boulevard Kukulcán rarely suggest it's much good for strolling. For that you must go into town, where the streets and street life are more or less normal, despite an ever-increasing traffic density. The hub of the town is the tree-lined central section of Av. Tulum, with the bus station at the top and the Town Hall (the **Ayuntamiento Benito Juárez**, the official name of the municipality of Cancún) in a square on the east side. Av. Tulum also catches the most tourist movement. Walk down any of the streets on the west side such as Claveles or Tulipanes and you will come to a pleasant, park-like square in the middle of the SM 22 block called **Parque de las Palapas**, with a clutch of simple cafés and a big stage for occasional free live entertainment (especially at Carnival time). From there you can carry on through to Av. Yaxchilán which, along with Av. Uxmal, is one of the best areas to seek out cheapish restaurants and cheaper, less tourist-dominated nightlife. On the far side of Av. Yaxchilán, Av. Sunyaxchén runs away to SM 28, which contains the post office and the **market**, sometimes called **Mercado 28**. By Mexican standards this is not an impressive market, but inside there is a collection of the cheapest restaurants in Cancún, packed with locals at weekends.

Av. Tulum runs all the way through the city. North of the bus station it runs up to meet Av. López Portillo, the main road out towards Mérida on the one side and Puerto Juárez on the other. If the Hotel Zone and the centre stretch of Tulum are the centres of tourist Cancún, this junction, known as **El Crucero**, is the new heart of the Mexican city (it's only fitting that, while every tiny Mexican village has its plaza, Cancún has as a major focus an anonymous road junction). Around it cluster the *taco*-stands, overstocked shoe stores, street-corner dentists, tyre shops, ice cream shops, crowds of kids and innumerable pharmacies so characteristic of modern, working-class urban Mexico.

Av. López Portillo leads after three kilometres to the Isla Mujeres passenger ferry at **Puerto Juárez**. The road continues another three kilometres to the car ferry dock at **Punta Sam**. Previously neglected, the narrow beaches along this shore are another area where hotels and condo developments are expanding as the main Cancún strip becomes oversubscribed. For details of boat sailings, *see* 'Isla Mujeres', p.163.

Ciudad Cancún

500 metres
500 yards

N

To Mérida

To Puerto Juárez &
Punta Sam

To Puerto Juárez &
Punta Sam

EL
CRUCERO

Piña Hermanos

SM64

AV. CHICHEN ITZA

AV. LOPEZ PORTILLO

SM63

AV. GARCIA DE LA TORRE

AV. BONAMPAK

Progreso Chichén

AV. CHICHEN ITZA

Batab

JABI

GRANADILLO
GRANADILLO

CEIBO
CEIBO

SM23

CEDRO

CEDRO

FLAMBOYAN

AV. TULUM

SM2

SM2-A

AV. UXMAL

ROBLE
ROBLE

PALMERA
PALMERA

LAUREL

LAUREL

FLAMBOYAN

CHACA

CHACA

México
Hostel

Maria
Isabel

Plaza Caribe

Bus Station

Immigration Office

SM24

NICCHEHABI

ROSAS

ROSAS

MARGARITAS

MARGARITAS

Cielito
Lindo

Novotel

AZUCENAS

AZUCENAS

YOQUEN
CONOCO
NICCHEHABI

SARANU
TAUCH

AV. SUNYAXCHEN

JAZMINES

Hacienda
Cancún

100% Natural

JAZMINES

Parque
de las
Palapas

TULIPANES

Belinda's

Ayuntamiento
and Tourist Office

SM28

Post
Office

GROSELLA
TAUCH

LLO

GLADIOLAS

Perico's

MARANON

AV. YAXCHILAN

SM22

GLADIOLAS

TULIPANES

Bank

AV. TULUM

Bank

El Café

Market

AV. XEL-HA

GROSELLA

ORQUIDEAS

ORQUIDEAS

CLAVELES

Antillano

CLAVELES

Rosa Mexicano

SM5

AV. J.C. NADER

SM25

CRISANTEMOS

CRISANTEMOS

AV. TANKAH

AV. YAXCHILAN

AV. COBA

AV. COBA

AV. XCARET

AV. COBA

AV. COBA

To
Hotel Zone

SM20

PECARI

AV. TULUM

Tourist Office

To Airport &
Playa del Carmen

El Meco

Open daily 8–3; adm, Sun adm free.

A little south of Punta Sam is the Mayan site of El Meco, only opened to visitors in 1998. It is older than El Rey, since parts of its buildings date back to AD 300, but it grew to a significant size at around the same time in the Postclassic after 1100, when El Meco seems to have become a significant religious centre and an important link in Yucatán coastal trade. Compared to El Rey (*see* p.157) the site is small, but the buildings are bigger and the **Pyramid** (*visitors may not climb up*) is taller and more solid. It stands at the centre of three very well-structured plazas, ringed by the remains of temples and palace complexes, the largest of which, **Palacio 12** in Plaza C, was a much more opulent structure than the similar colonnade-fronted palace at El Rey. The chief interest of the settlement lies in its layout, but on Palacio 12 and the Pyramid steps you can still see some distinctive decoration and animal carvings.

The Islands

Each of the three inhabited islands around the coast of Quintana Roo is distinct from the others. **Isla Mujeres** has managed to retain much of its easy-going, beach village atmosphere, as well as being a diving centre. Tiny and little-known **Holbox**, around the cape north of Cancún, remains a remote, far-away spot. **Cozumel**, largest of the three, has a more conventional resort feel, and is shared between package holidaymakers and diving devotees.

Isla Mujeres

The 'Island of Women' is all of eight kilometres long, a narrow, rocky strip running southeast from the small triangle at the top that contains the only town. A fork of land along the west side encloses a sheltered lagoon, the Laguna Macax. The best swimming and snorkelling beaches and diving reefs are all on the western, landward side; on the eastern, ocean side the island is much rockier and more windswept, and the sea much rougher. When Cancún was beginning to be developed for mass tourism, the sleepy fishing community of Isla Mujeres was the first place along the coast to be discovered by backpacking travellers. Since then the pace of development has picked up, but the little town with its sandy streets still has a lot of its laid-back, Caribbean, vaguely hippyish feel. Outside the town and its beaches, on the other hand, the island does not have many attractions.

History

As a small monument in the town plaza recalls, this was the site of the Spaniards' first landfall anywhere in Mexico in 1517, when Hernández de Córdoba's expedition came upon the island after a storm. The idols that Hernández' men saw on the island which they recognized as figures of women (and so the origin of its Spanish name) were images of Ixchel, Goddess of Fertility, and other female deities. It seems likely that Isla Mujeres was a secondary place of pilgrimage, associated with the shrine of Ixchel on Cozumel (*see* p.174).

After the Conquest the island was of little interest to the Spaniards, and like other settlements along this coast was also largely abandoned by its Maya inhabitants. For three centuries it was home only to a tiny community of turtle fishermen. However, its remote location and the shelter of its lagoon did make it attractive to pirates, in particular to the last of the great Caribbean pirates, the Louisiana-born brothers Jean and Pierre Lafitte. They made it their favourite refuge, but their career was also brought to an end here when Isla Mujeres was attacked by the Spanish navy in 1821. The brothers escaped, but both were fatally wounded, and one is said to be buried at Dzilam Bravo (*see* p.301). After this brief excitement Isla's population grew a little more at the end of the century, when *chicle* tappers favoured it over anywhere on the mainland. The island's varied past and population – more *mestizo* than Maya, and with a lot of contact with Cuba and other islands in the Caribbean – are reflected in the traditional houses still seen in some streets: wooden, brightly painted, clapboard houses with porches, to contrast with the plain palm huts of the Yucatán.

Isla Mujeres

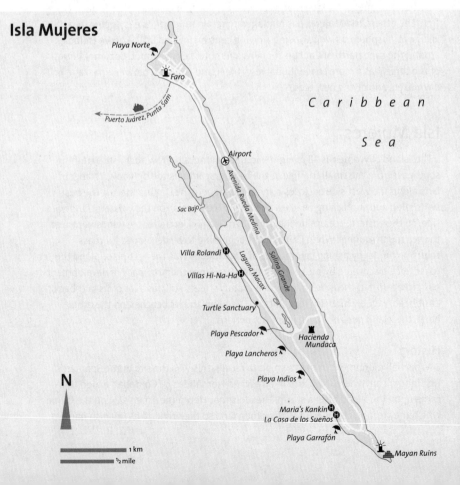

Getting Around

By Air

Isla's **airstrip**, along the neck of the island south of town, is used for light plane tours by Aerobanana, **t** 877 0331, and Aerosaab (from Playa del Carmen, **t** (984) 873 0804. A luxury air-taxi and transfer service between Isla and Cancún airport is also run by Aerobanana.

By Sea

The most usual way of getting to Isla Mujeres is by **passenger ferry** from Puerto Juárez. Several local bus routes (some R-1 buses, R-13) run from Av. Tulum in Cancún to the ferry dock; there are also *colectivos* (cab around $2). Fast-boat sailings from Puerto Juárez run approximately every half-hour 6.30am–11.30pm daily (6am–8.30pm, from Isla), but timings can vary (journey 20mins; around $4 per person). Older, slow boats with open-air decks cost half as much, take 45mins and make for a more charming ride (usually 5am–11.30pm from Puerto Juárez; 6am–11.30pm from Isla). There are five **car ferries** each way daily from Punta Sam (8am–8.15pm from Punta Sam; 6.30am–7.15pm from Isla Mujeres). A car and two people costs about $22. There are also fast **shuttle boats** four times daily each way from Playa Linda, Playa Langosta, Playa Tortugas and Playa Caracol in Cancún (more expensive than the ferries).

By Road

Isla Mujeres has the usual complement of **taxis**. A trip to the furthest point is around $4 each way, or $15 for a 'taxi tour' all around the Isla. There are also *tricicleros*, tricycle-cart drivers, who will carry your bags anywhere in town (5 pesos), and an infrequent local **bus** service that runs around town and down to Garrafón. For getting around on your own, given the size of the island, cars seem a bit excessive, and the fad form of transport is four-seater electric **golf carts**. **Scooters** and **mopeds** are faster, but it is very easy and more peaceful to take an ordinary **bicycle**. The same shops normally rent out carts ($40–50 a day; $15 an hour), scooters ($20–30 a day; $6–$8 an hour) and bikes ($6–$10 a day). When hiring you will need to pay in advance and leave a document or cash deposit, so take something else if you don't want to leave your passport. Get there early to have the best choice (some vehicles have been round the island many, many times), and check the machine over before you take it, especially the brakes and saddles on cycles. Take a hat and plenty of sun block too.

Ciro's, Av. Guerrero 11, near the corner of Av. Matamoros. A wide choice of quite new carts, scooters and bikes.

Motorent El Zorro, Av. Guerrero, between Matamoros and Abasolo. About the cheapest for bikes/scooters, but get there very early, as they have some real wrecks.

Tourist Information

Isla Mujeres **t** (998–)

Like other places on the Riviera, Isla Mujeres has its free ads-and-information magazine, the *Isla Mujeres Tourist Guide* which, with free maps, is available at the tourist office and in shops and restaurants. About the best of the Isla-based websites is *www.islamujeres.net*.

Tourist Offices: Isla Mujeres has a small official office at Av. Rueda Medina 130, near the ferry quay (*usually open Mon–Sat 9–5; closed Sun*). Usually more useful is **Mundaca Travel**, Av. Hidalgo 15-A, **t** 877 0025, *www.mundaca-travel.com*. Provides information and organizes tours, diving, snorkelling and fishing trips, boat charters, hotel bookings and airport transfers to Cancún; also has an accommodation/real-estate service.

Banks: There's a Bital branch on Av. Rueda Medina; changes money Mon–Fri 9–2.30, Sat 9–4.30. There are *cambio* offices on Av. Juárez and Av. Hidalgo (*open Sun*).

Health: There's a **pharmacy** on Av. Juárez between Morelos and Bravo, and an English-speaking **doctor**, Dr Antonio Salas Torres, Av. Hidalgo 18-D, **t** 877 0477/877 0021; the **medical centre**, on Av. Guerrero between Madero and Morelos, has a hyperbaric unit in case of diving accidents.

Internet Access: Cosmic Cosas, Av. Matamoros between Guerrero and Hidalgo. Combined backpackers' hangout, English- and other languages second-hand bookshop and Internet shop, with noticeboards offering *cabañas* for rent, unusual tours, lifts etc.

Laundry: Tim Pho laundry, Av. Juárez, corner of Abasolo. Very efficient and cheap.

Post Office: Towards the beach, corner of Guerrero and López Mateos.

Shopping

Isla town has plenty of souvenir shops and markets, with goods from all over Mexico and Guatemala, including a lot of junk. The **Casa Isleño II** on Av. Guerrero, off the Zócalo, has its own hand-painted T-shirts and locally made shell and coral jewellery, and every Sunday afternoon in the plaza there's a **Gran Feria** market where island artists and craftspeople sell their wares. There are several **jewellery stores** offering fine gems at only slightly bargainish prices (**Van Cleef & Arpels** is on the corner of Juárez and Morelos). For general shopping, besides the market there are supermarkets on the Zócalo (**El Bético**) and on Matamoros by the waterfront (**Capricornio**); good bread and pastries can be found at **La Reina** wholefood bakery (Madero with Juárez).

Sports and Activities

Diving and Snorkelling

Isla Mujeres, more than Cancún, is the best base for **diving** in the northern part of the Maya Reef. Prices are lower, and the local divemasters have a better reputation for personal service. Despite the intensification of traffic in the area, Isla still offers beautiful diving conditions. The **Manchones** reef is popular for beginners and basic dives, a very safe reef about 10m deep upon which there is an undersea cross. There are other deeper reefs nearby, some with wrecks including that of one of the *conquistador* Montejo's ships, sunk in 1527. For more experienced divers, there is the **Sleeping Sharks cave** in a 20m reef northeast of the island, where an underground river flows out into the sea bed. The confluence of fresh and sea water is peculiarly attractive to reef sharks, and large numbers of them 'sleep' for hours on end on the cave floor. Properly dealt with they never attack anybody.

Even more popular than scuba diving are **snorkelling** tours. Most boat outings from Isla Mujeres go to the reefs off Sac Bajo, the little island at the northwest tip of Laguna Macax, or to Manchones, where it's possible to see plenty of underwater life even without scuba equipment.

Fishing and Sailing

Sport **fishing** trips are widely available. If you have your own boat, there are ample landing facilities at three marinas, one in town and two on Laguna Macax. For information on facilities and immigration formalities, call the tourist office on t 877 0307 or check *www.isla-mujeres.net*.

Dive Shops and Agencies

The same dive shops and agencies frequently offer diving, snorkelling and fishing trips. An introductory scuba 'resort course' costs around $60, a two-tank dive for certified divers about $40; going diving to the Sleeping Sharks Cave about $50–$60. Snorkel tours cost $10–$20, and fishing trips from about $200 a day. All the shops offer good value price packages for certification courses and for dives over two days or more. From their building near the ferry landing the local *Cooperativa de Lancheros* (boatmen) also offer trips around the island for $10 a head ($13 with snacks), for snorkelling or fishing.

Captain Tony García, Av. Matamoros 17, t 877 0279, *capitantony@latinmail.com*. Very experienced local boatman who runs fishing trips ($25 an hour) and snorkel tours ($10 per person).

Coral Dive Center, Av. Matamoros 13-A, near Av. Rueda Medina, t 877 0763, *www.coralscubadivecenter.com*. Large, well-equipped agency with some of the best rates for dives, dive courses and snorkel trips. Offers specialist courses (rescue, underwater photography) and sailing boat rental.

La Isleña, Av. Morelos, between Rueda Medina and Juárez, t 877 0578. One of several more basic hire shops, offering bargain snorkel tours for around $10 ($13 including food) and fishing trips.

Mexico Divers, Av. Rueda Medina, near the ferry landing, t 877 0274. Small-scale scuba-only specialists and highly respected dive-masters who offer a complete range of courses and speciality dives (night dives, underwater photography, etc.).

Mundaca Divers, Av. Madero 10, near corner of Hidalgo, **t** 877 0607, *http://travel.to/mundacadivers*. Friendly and reliable, with a full range of diving, snorkelling and fishing trips at very amenable rates.

Tarzan Water Sports, on Playa Norte. Offers cheap scuba diving (without as good facilities as the more 'regular' dive masters), relatively expensive snorkel tours, water skiing and a range of wave runners, pedalos, kayaks and windsurfers.

Where to Stay

Isla Mujeres **t** (998–)

Isla hotels are predominantly small and low-key. Nearly all are in town. Rooms fill up frequently Dec–early April, and are relatively expensive, if less so than in Cancún; prices climb again, but to a lesser extent, in July and Aug. Between these times it's rarely hard to get a room and prices drop considerably.

Luxury

La Casa de los Sueños, Ctra Garrafon, about 8km south of town, **t** 877 0651, *www.los suenos.com*. A US-style 'bed & breakfast' lodge, with spectacular contemporary Mexican architecture. Very secluded, it has nine utterly comfortable, stylish rooms, and a spectacular pool and terrace overlooking the ocean. Honeymoons are a speciality.

Villa Rolandi, Fraccionamiento Lagunamar, **t** 877 0700, *www.villarolandi.com*. Under the same ownership as the Hotel Belmar in town, but much smarter, this is on the west side of Laguna Macax, and sits above its own beach facing Cancún in the distance. Each room is beautiful, with a sea view from the shower and a Jacuzzi on the balcony. It's aimed at couples (no kids under 13). There's also a private landing stage and yacht; sea transfers from Cancún are included; the dining room, with mainly-Italian cuisine, has a spectacular view.

Expensive

Cabañas María del Mar, Av. Carlos Lazo 1, **t** 877 0179, *www.cabanasdelmar.com*. Very comfortable rooms divided between a main 'tower' building and slightly more expensive

two-room *cabaña*-style bungalows around a garden. Rooms have hammocks and fridges and there's a small pool. The beach's most popular bar, **Buho's** (*see* below), is attached, and massages and health treatments are a speciality. *Moderate* or *inexpensive* off-peak.

Na Balam Beach Hotel, C/ Zazil-Ha no. 118, **t** 877 0279, *www.nabalam.com*. The most opulent place in Isla town, spread out among palm trees behind Cocoteros beach. The large rooms all have sitting areas and balconies or terraces, but some are a little dark and do not all have direct beach access. It also has a pretty pool, one of the island's best **restaurants** (*see* below), and yoga and meditation courses. Prices *luxury* Dec–April.

Villas Hi-Na-Ha, on the road up the west side of Laguna Macax, **t/f** 877 0615. Self-contained apartments, very comfortably equipped and with full kitchens. All have a sea view and are very private, and there's a small beach and boat landing. Breakfast is included, and flexible weekly and longer-term rates (especially off-peak) mean it can be a bargain.

Moderate

Casa Maya, C/ Zazil-Ha 129, **t/f** 877 0045, *www.kasamaya.com.mx*. Has one of the most attractive locations on Isla Mujeres, facing Playa Secreto lagoon. Rooms are individually decorated with traditional textiles, some in the main house and some in *cabañas*; they vary a good deal in size and facilities (some have a/c, some are on the beach, some are quite simple; no. 11 is best), so there are several prices as well. There's a comfortable, homey lounge and a fridge and open kitchen for guests' use. Prices lower out of season; weekly/monthly rates are also available.

Hotel Francis Arlene, Av. Guerrero 7, **t** 877 0310, **f** 877 0861 (borderline *inexpensive*). One of the most individual hotels in town, with pastel-coloured, suite-style rooms that have lots of extras. All have fridges and a/c, balconies and big beds (around $45), some have kitchenettes ($50), and the top floor room is a real mini-apartment with a sitting room and a big roof terrace ($55). There are also attractive, airy patios, and the whole place has a cosy feel.

Hotel Playa la Media Luna, Punta Norte, t/f 877 1124. Recently built, on the ocean side of Playa Secreto, so that much of it faces on to a choppy and rocky open sea rather than a usable beach, but just beside it is the tranquil Playa Secreto lagoon. There's a pool, breakfast is included and all rooms have a/c and fridges.

Hotel Posada del Mar, Av. Rueda Medina 15-A, t 877 0044, *hposada@cancun.rce.com.mx*. On the main street next to the lighthouse, painted in pink and green (on the outside) with well-equipped, almost overdecorated rooms; main pluses are the views from most of the sea-side rooms, and one of the prettiest hotel pools.

Maria's Kankin, Ctra Garrafón, t/f 877 0015/877 0395. An eccentric place run since the 1970s by Frenchwoman Maria Llopet. There are nine quirky, beach-cabin style rooms, each different: the whole place shows its age, but the rooms are all big and have ample sitting space, fridges and other extras. It also has a beach and boat jetty, a terrace **restaurant** and free bikes for guests.

Su Casa, on the Sac Bajo road, west side of Laguna Macax, t/f 877 0180, *vicki@lost oasis.net*. Cluster of small, pretty beach houses on its own tranquil stretch of beach. The cabins are a few years old but have all the necessary comforts, a kitchen and a double and a single bed (more if required). *Moderate* Dec–April, *inexpensive* otherwise.

Inexpensive–Cheap

Budget hotels virtually all vary in price during the year, from *inexpensive* ($20–$27 a double) Dec–April, to significantly cheaper ($18–$20) at other times. This doesn't mean they offer more than the standard Mexican basic hotel. All are in town. You can book ahead, but don't expect these hotels to hold on to rooms for long at peak times; in winter, get to the island as early as you can, certainly by 1pm, to be sure of getting a room.

Hotel Berny, Av. Abasolo, between Juárez and Hidalgo, t 877 0132. A cut above most, with rooms (all with fan and a/c) that are a bit better cared for than many, and a small pool. Prices around $30 all year.

Hotel Caracol, Av. Matamoros 5, between Hidalgo and Guerrero, t 877 0150. Has a good

few years on the clock, but quite light and well-aired rooms on the top floor, though it can be noisy due to its proximity to Tequila disco. Peak prices go up more than most.

Hotel Carmelina, Av. Guerrero 4, between Abasolo and Madero, t 877 0006. One of the most popular, arranged on three floors around a wide patio, so all the well-kept rooms have good light. Rooms with a/c are slightly pricier.

Hotel María José, Av. Madero 25, corner of Rueda Medina, t 877 0245. Well-worn but quite bright hotel near the ferry landing with some of the lowest prices, for fan-only and a/c rooms.

Hotel Vistalmar, Av. Rueda Medina, on the corner of Matamoros, t 877 0209, f 877 0096. Impossible to miss with its island colours of pink, yellow and green, this is one of the best in this range, and a bargain. The owners are friendly, it has a terrace **restaurant** and the simple rooms (a/c or fan-only), are well kept. Prices *inexpensive* all year, but they don't charge extra for the rooms with a great sea view.

Poc-Na youth hostel, Av. Matamoros, corner of Carlos Lazo, t 877 0090, f 877 0059. Always cheap, this backpackers' favourite is a non-affiliated hostel with rooms of 8 or 14 beds; one is women-only, others are mixed. For around $5 (plus a $10 returnable deposit) you get a bed, sheet and locker, or can rent a hammock and locker (same price), or camp in the grounds (by the beach) for a little less. Reservations are required for groups of more than five or six, but are not taken for individuals; it's first come, first served.

Apartment and House Rentals

Many people want to settle on Isla Mujeres for weeks at a time, and many self-catering flats and villas are available for longer-term rents. Mundaca Travel (*see above*) has a rental service, with flats and houses of all sizes (from around $250 a month).

Cielito Lindo, Av. Rueda Medina, between Abasolo and Madero, t 877 0585, *joy@ cancun.com.mx* (*moderate*). A building with two fully self-contained, well-equipped apartments on the waterfront that can be rented for any period from three days to several months.

Eating Out

After Cancún Isla Mujeres represents a return to something closer to normal Mexican restaurant style and – within the limits of the Riviera – prices, with the extra element of some *gringo*-influenced health-food outlets.

Expensive

Casa O's, Ctra Garrafón. Next to Maria's Kankin, with a pretty beach view, this is an attractive, less cranky place with a superior traditional Mexican menu.

Lo Lo Lorena, Av. Guerrero 7, corner of Matamoros (no phone; near-*moderate*). French-run, in a pretty old house, serving an eclectically global range of dishes – French, Mexican, American and Italian influences all feature – presented with charm.

Maria's Kankin, Ctra Garrafón, t 877 0015/877 0395. No longer the island's best, but still quirkily enjoyable, with an idiosyncratic blend of Mexican and French cuisine served on a lushly tropical terrace overlooking the hotel's own little bay. Reservations essential.

Zazil-Ha, Na Balam Beach Hotel, C/ Zazil-Ha no. 118, t 877 0279. The top restaurant in town, serving locally-caught fish and organic and vegetarian dishes, and with tables in a beach-garden or a rather over-neat, air-conditioned dining room.

Moderate

There are plenty of beachside eateries along Av. Rueda Medina, mostly serving seafood. They tend to be overpriced, but make a fine place from which to watch the movement of boats and people. By day, Playa Norte bars like Zazil-Ha and Buho's are the place to be.

Buho's, Cabañas María del Mar, Playa Norte. Nearly always the most popular beach bar, with seats on swings dangling from the *palapa* roof, and a range of Mexican snacks, salads and seafood.

El Café Cito, Av. Juárez, corner of Matamoros. A mellow healthfood café specializing in fruit and yoghurt breakfasts, with vegetarian/wholefood dishes later in the day.

French Bistro Français, Av. Matamoros, between Hidalgo and Juárez. Likeable place with a suitably beachcomberish air that features French oriented, global cuisine,

making good use of local seafood and lobster, and breakfasts made with flair. *Open mornings till noon and eves after 7pm.*

Manolo's, Av. Juárez, between Matamoros and Abasolo. One of the most enjoyable; an unassuming restaurant in a pretty garden patio, run by a charming family who offer excellent fresh fish and Yucatecan fare.

El Sol Dorado, Av. Madero, between Hidalgo and Guerrero. The most extensive and varied menu of the vegetarian/wholefood places.

El Sombrero de Gomar, Av. Hidalgo, corner of Av. Madero. Reliably enjoyable Mexican classics are the staples of this large and perennially popular restaurant, with a pretty and airy *palapa*-roofed balcony overlooking the town's central crossroads.

Cheap

Budget standbys are the open-air *cocinas económicas* by the market. The best **ice cream and juice stand** is on the Zócalo, corner of Hidalgo and Nicolás Bravo.

Al Natural, Av. Hidalgo, between Madero and Abasolo. Fresh juice and wholefood café.

La Casita, Av. Madero, corner of Guerrero. A bakery-café with good sandwiches, coffee and cakes.

Cocina Económica Susanita, Av. Juárez, between Madero and Abasolo. For a filling Mexican-Yucatecan lunch, this wooden hut has *comidas corridas* for about $4.

Entertainment and Nightlife

This is a small island, and the round is pretty simple: after dark, the most hopping meeting place is the stretch of Av. Hidalgo just off the plaza, where there's a choice of bars (tequila-tasting a speciality), straightforward food (*fajitas*, pizzas, etc.) and, on most nights, live bands playing basic boogie rock, Bob Marley covers and the like. **Margarita Mama's** and **Yaya's** (really the same place), by Playa Caribe, corner of Av. Rueda Medina and López Mateos, are similar but bigger, and often don't have as much atmosphere. Towards midnight it's time to move back to the beach to the **Palapas** beach bar/disco, which often has live bands who will never be famous but, what the hell.

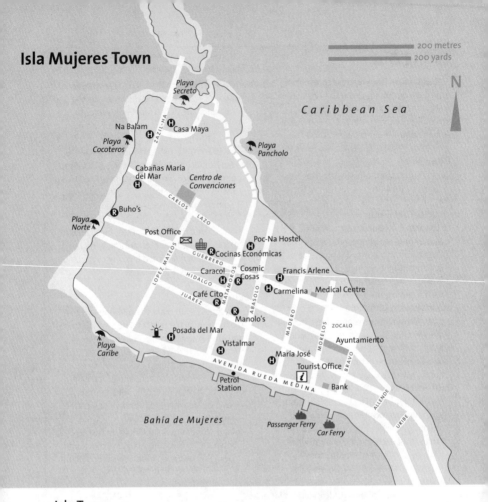

Isla Town

The ferries leave you on Av. Rueda Medina, the main road along the western side of the town. A walk up the streets opposite and just to the right, Morelos or Nicolás Bravo, will take you to the main square, with the town hall and the church, which runs right through to the east side of the island, so narrow is it at this point.

Inside the town, Avenidas Juárez and Hidalgo, north of the Zócalo, are the nearest things to 'main drags', with the main restaurants and souvenir markets. This is also where most of the beach-squatters gravitate to after dark. On Guerrero, next to the post office, there's a tiny **food market**, and nearby on Av. Carlos Lazo is a rather fancy **Centro de Convenciones**, although it doesn't seem to host many events. Among the more modern buildings there are still a few old Isla houses with wooden porches and balconies, and a few doors from smart jewellery stores there are places like the 'Fishermen's Cantina', brightly painted with a perky and drunk-looking tuna. A big part of the town's charm – carried over on to newer, concrete buildings – comes from its lurid paintwork in candybox greens, pinks, reds and yellows, which are almost an Isla trademark. It's hard to take things very seriously in any place that's bright pink.

Around the Island

Av. Rueda Medina continues south down the island, past the airstrip, at the end of which there's a left turn across to the eastern side (still only half a kilometre away). A kilometre or so further, at the island's main crossroads, lies the entrance to Isla's best known monument, **Hacienda Mundaca**. Fermín Mundaca, who built a mansion here, is often described as a pirate, but he was actually something far less romantic. One of the last of the Caribbean slavers, he ran Africans to Cuba until in 1860 the British Navy's anti-slavery patrols prompted him to call it a day. According to legend he chose Isla Mujeres for his retirement because he was infatuated with an 18-year-old local girl, *la trigueña* ('the fair one'), and so built the largest house ever seen on the island in the hope that it would impress her. She, though, was not interested one bit, and married a young islander, leaving Mundaca to go mad and die an embittered man. The story is really more interesting than anything standing on the site today, for only the entrance gate and the remains of a few buildings survive of the Hacienda. Its grounds have been made into an (often very bug-filled) **park** (*open daily 9–6; adm*), containing a little zoo with a jaguar, monkeys and other local wildlife.

A sharp right turn at the crossroads will take you up the west side of the lagoon, a gentle run past a few restaurants, beach clubs, hotels and smart houses with boat landings. A little north of the turn is the **Tortugranja turtle farm** (*open daily 9–5; adm*), an official turtle-breeding and repopulation centre. As well as the tanks and pools in which the sea turtles are bred and kept until they are big enough to be self-sufficient in the wild, there is a good display (in Spanish and English) on turtle and reef ecology and the inevitable souvenir shop, the profits of which go to support the centre. Further up the same road is an 'eco-attraction' that people tend to like or hate (*see* p.94), **Dolphin Discovery** (*swims daily 9–3; adm exp*), with a sea-enclosure in which dolphins are penned for visitors to swim with. Day trippers are brought here from Playa Langosta in Cancún (*reservations **t** (998)849 4748*).

Beaches in Town

Head left from the ferry landings and you will come to the beaches.

Playa Caribe: The long beach towards the lighthouse. Used by dive-masters and fishing guides to pull up their boats, but not the most popular for swimming and sunbathing.

Playa Norte and **Playa Cocoteros** (really just the one beach): The main town beaches, along the 'top' of the island, where many Isla-lovers spend a great deal of their time. Here, too, you'll find the beach bars like Buho's and Las Palapas. It's a fine little strip of white sand with shallow, permanently sheltered turquoise waters excellent for easy swimming, but can get crowded.

Playa Secreto: Around the corner at the eastern end of Playa Norte there's a little inlet that's shallower and more tranquil still. The sheltered waters make it ideal for paddling kids. It is crossed by a wooden footbridge to a small tributary island that's filled up by the Avalon Grand all-inclusive.

Playa Pancholo: A small beach further around the corner again which, since it faces east, suffers from rougher seas.

Back at the crossroads, the main island road continues to the right of Hacienda Mundaca. Almost immediately you come to **Playa Lancheros**, the longest beach on Isla, with beachside restaurants that are regularly visited by Cancún day trips. It's another sheltered beach that's good for gentle swimming, with enclosed shallow areas. The road winds on past other quiet beaches to **El Garrafón** nature park (*open daily 9–4; adm exp*), a user-friendly snorkelling centre similar to Xcaret or Xel-Ha (*see* p.200, p.204), with a big natural pool in the reef and equipment for hire. However, the facilities are shabby, it's often crowded, the place reeks of suntan oil and, most importantly, the reefs are now pretty dead, making it the most disappointing of the facilities of this kind around Cancún.

From Garrafón it's only a short distance to the point at the southern tip of the island, which since 2001 has been marked off as the **Parque Escúltorico Punta Sur** (*open daily 7–10; adm*). Beside the path to the point there's now a 'sculpture park' of multi-coloured modern works, often evoking Mayan themes, leading to the older monuments at the tip, a lighthouse and a small **Mayan temple** to Ixchel. Never very impressive, this crumbling cube was badly battered by Hurricane Gilbert in 1988, and a more substantial reason for going to the point is the sweeping view of the ocean and the island behind you. The east side of the island, along the road running back up from Punta Sur, is flat, bare and windblown, dotted with isolated clumps of private beach houses. Take some drinks with you, as any shops or bars along this route are only intermittently open.

Isla Contoy

The uninhabited island of Contoy, 30 kilometres north of Isla Mujeres, is Mexico's most important seabird reserve. It has particularly important populations of pelicans, cormorants and especially frigate birds, but there are also boobies, spoonbills and over 50 other species. Much of the island is made up of mangroves that contain many rare plants, and there are also important turtle breeding beaches. Around the island lie beautiful lagoons with intact coral reefs.

The areas open to ordinary visitors are the **visitor centre**, the main **lagoon** (with a fine white beach), an **observation tower** and a path that runs past one of the main frigate-bird nesting lagoons. Controlled fishing is also permitted.

Getting There

Most of the Contoy tours operate from Isla Mujeres (around $40 per person), though trips are also available from Cancún (**t** (998) 886 4847). A standard trip lasts a full day (journey 1½hrs each way), with (hopefully) some time to walk the path and snorkel in the lagoon (equipment provided); drinks and barbecue lunch are also included. However, these trips can be very disappointing: many are badly managed, and often all the boats arrive together, so you don't see many birds. You may be left on the public beach for much of the day, together with the other tours, to drink and splash around. Check carefully with the tour operator when booking. Other parts of the island can officially only be visited by study trips by prior arrangement with the **Instituto Nacional de Ecología** (Semarnap), Av. Insurgentes 445, CP 77500 Cancún, **t** (998) 835 0216, *qroo_deleg@semarnap.gob.mx*.

Isla Holbox and Laguna Yalahao

One of the greatest contrasts you can come across on the Mexican Caribbean is that between Cancún and Isla Holbox, a tiny sand-strip of an island across Laguna Yalahao on the north coast of Quintana Roo west of Cabo Catoche. Development has been catching up with Holbox, and it's gradually becoming better known, but so far it remains a delightfully friendly little place of about 1,000 people, whose main business, apart from passing the time of day, is still fishing. The pace of change is slow and, with its sandy streets and empty beaches, it is a lovely place to forget the world for a few days.

Getting There

Holbox's limited previous connections with the Riviera are primarily due to its remoteness. You get there via the little port of **Chiquilá**, after a long, bumpy drive (at least 2hrs from Cancún) 80km north of Highway 180 from a turn just east of the Quintana Roo state line. If you have a **car**, there are small parking lots near to the jetty that will look after it for about $2 a day (there is also a **petrol station**).

Passenger launches (about $3 per person) leave Chiquilá about every 2hrs, on the hour, daily 6am–7pm, with returns from Holbox 5am–6pm (journey about 25mins). If you miss the ferry there are often local boys with boats hanging around who will take you across for about $12–$15 per boat. A **car ferry** usually makes the crossing twice each way every Tues, Thurs and Sat, but this is always subject to change.

Second-class **buses** run to Chiquilá from Cancún and Mérida. Two buses daily leave Cancún (8am, 1.30pm) to connect with the ferries at noon and 5pm; going back, buses leave after the arrival of Holbox ferries at 7.30am and 1.30pm. From Mérida there is a bus nightly at 11.30pm, calling at Valladolid (2.30am) and arriving in Chiquilá at 5am for the 6am ferry; the return leaves at 5.30am after the first ferry of the day from Holbox. At other times, *combis* and taxis run between Chiquilá and Nuevo Xcan on Highway 180.

The opulent option is to go by **light plane** to the airstrip on the west side of the village. Aerosaab from Playa del Carmen, **t** (984) 873 0501, in Holbox, **t** 875 2157, offers one-day local tours (about $150) and air-taxi transfers to or from any airport or airstrip in the region.

Getting Around

Once on the island, there are very few cars, and it's easy to get anywhere on foot or cycle. However, Holbox's current craze is **golf carts**. Locals love them (there are golf-cart taxis), and several rental shops have opened, mostly on the main street. **Rentadora Alondra** (t 875 2052) and **Rentadora Moguel** (t 875 2028), both near the plaza, are two which offer a big selection. All charge similarly high prices ($9 an hour, $45 a day), though you may be able to strike deals for longer rents.

Bicycles are actually handier for getting to the places outside the village that you're most likely to want to visit. Sra Dinora at the **Tienda Dinora**, by Posada Los Arcos on the plaza, has bikes for rent (about $1.70 an hour, $6 a day).

Tourist Information

Holbox t (984–)

The island has its own free magazine, *Holbox*, packed with the usual ads and local information. It can be found in restaurants, hotels and so on on the island, and in tourist offices in Cancún and Playa.

Pharmacy: Just off the square on the main street next to Jugos La Isla.

Phone Office: There's a long-distance *caseta* one block further back off Av. Juárez to the right, going towards the ferry landing.

Post Office: Next to the town hall on the plaza.

There is **no bank** on Holbox, nor any regular money-changing facility closer than Cancún, Valladolid or Tizimín. Some hotels may be able to change money, but it's always best to come prepared.

Isla Holbox

On the way across, look out for dolphins jumping in the lagoon; the sight of them, glistening in the sunlight, is an exhilarating introduction to the island. Holbox is a long narrow strip, running east–west, with the village smack in the middle. From the ferry landing on the landward side the one main street (Av. Juárez) runs straight across for about a kilometre to end at the beach on the ocean side. Along the way you pass the noisy generator that provides the place with electricity, and the little **plaza**. Streets run off between palms on either side. At the ocean end there's a leaning lighthouse, a jetty, the Faro Viejo hotel and beach bar, boats pulled up on the beach and sand and dunes running away to the horizon. Since it faces the Gulf and not the

Sports and Activities

Dolphin Watching, Fishing and Tours

Virtually the entire male population of Holbox knows its way around the local fishing grounds and places to see dolphins, turtles, flamingos, sea birds and other attractions of the Yalahao lagoon, and if you ask around in any of the island's shops and hotels they will probably be able to recommend someone to act as a guide.

Dolphin Human Connection, Cancún, t (998) 880 9768, f 884 6991. Organized programme that aims to let visitors see dolphins in their natural environment, in the Yalahao lagoon. Run from Cancún, tours include transport to Holbox, accommodation and 4hrs spent touring the lagoon. It focusses on dolphin watching, but therapeutic activities that involve swimming with dolphins (*free*) are also available.

Hotel Faro Viejo. Runs well-organized tours.

Jugos y Licuados La Isla. Sets up boat tours of the lagoon including Isla de Pájaros, El Manantial and dolphin-watching, or fishing trips and longer itineraries as required. Guides are very reliable, and a 4–6-hr tour costs about $60 (max. 6 people per launch).

PUHAC, in a hut one street back from the beach on the east side of Av. Juárez, behind the Abarrotes Mariana store. A local conservation organization that can organize a range of fishing trips or eco-tours; the members seem a bit hard to find.

The owners of **El Parque** restaurant and **Rentadora Willy** cart-hire shop, both on the plaza, and of the **Villamar** restaurant by the beach are also very experienced boatmen and fishing guides.

Where to Stay

Holbox t (984–)

Room prices on Holbox drop a good deal outside the main seasons. If you really want to settle in, *cabañas* and houses are also often available for rent, at low rates. Finding them is a matter of asking around, and looking for ads.

Villas Delfines, about 1km east of the village, t 874 4014, or via Cancún t (998) 884 8606, *www.holbox.com* (*expensive*). Opened in 1997, with 10 positively opulent palm-roofed, beachside *cabañas*, and its own **restaurant**; there's a wide range of tours and activities (kayaking, fishing, dolphin watching, etc).

Villas Chimay, 1km west of town along the beach, t/f 875 2220, *chimay@holbox.com.mx* (*expensive–moderate*). Seven secluded, palm-roofed *cabañas* in splendid isolation. Swiss-owned, they're very comfortably and prettily fitted out, and are designed to be eco-friendly, with solar electricity and low-impact services. Some share (high-standard) bathrooms. There's also a **bar-restaurant**.

Hotel Faro Viejo, at the ocean end of the main street, t 875 2217, *www.faroviejoholbox .com.mx* (*moderate*). The most attractive rooms on Holbox are here: they're pretty, individually decorated and well-equipped. There are doubles and twins with balconies and sea view, or family-sized 'suites' with terraces, some with kitchenettes. Breakfast is included, and the French-Mexican management are very welcoming. It also has the island's best **restaurant** (*see* below).

Villa Los Mapaches, by the beach west of the village, t 875 2090, *holboxmapaches@ hotmail.com* (*moderate–inexpensive*). Pretty,

Caribbean Holbox does not have the crystal-turquoise waters of the Riviera, but it's a gentle, shallow beach that's great for a relaxing swim, with sandbars that allow you to 'walk on water' for what seem to be enormous distances out to sea. All along the beach there are huge numbers of pelicans, frigate birds and terns, and scurrying flocks of turnstones and other wading birds.

The long beach east of the village is where, as Holbox experiences its mild 'tourist takeoff', a palm-roofed line of smartish-looking hotels is extending itself along the shore. Continue past them along the track behind the beach toward Cabo Catoche, though (best done with a bike), and you can find long, long stretches of beach with nothing but brush, sand, sea birds and the breeze.

spacious and comfortable *cabañas* and apartments, all with kitchens and terraces. Very laid-back, and great for longer stays (good discounts). Bikes are free for guests.

Posada Los Arcos, on the left of the main square, looking seawards, t 875 2043 (*inexpensive–cheap*). The best decent budget option. Some of the big, light rooms, around a pleasant patio, have clanky a/c (*inexpensive*), but you can be as comfortable with fan-only (*cheap*); ask for *sra* Dinora, the owner, in the Tienda Dinora store next door.

Posada d'Ingrid, a block west of main street, t 875 2070 (*inexpensive–cheap*). A little box-like, but well cared for, and all rooms have a/c and fans.

Posada Mawimbi, by the beach east of town, t 875 2003 (*inexpensive*). Five comfortably beach-bum-style rooms in a big *palapa*-roofed house, plus two self-contained cabins. The Italian owners are very friendly and one is a dive master (experienced divers only). Fishing trips are a speciality.

Posada Yalahau, by the ferry dock, t 875 2005, *www.holboxyalahau.com* (*inexpensive*). On the lagoon side with a distinctive view, and five rooms that have been fully refurbished with new bathrooms (a/c or fan-only).

Eating Out

Hotel Faro Viejo (*moderate*). Holbox food is often simple but enjoyable, but for something a little more sophisticated, this is the best choice. It also has a delightful location, right by the beach and well shaded.

Jugos y Licuados La Isla/La Peña Colibrí, on a corner of the plaza (*moderate–cheap*). Very likeable little café, with excellent jumbo fruit salads. Owners Marco Antonio and Loly are charmingly friendly, it advertises tours of the lagoon (*see left*) and is a great place to find out what's going on. It's open for breakfast and lunch, but the owners also have a relaxed restaurant round the corner, **La Peña Colibrí**, offering multinational, bargain meals in the evenings. It also functions as a social centre of sorts, with occasional live music, video screenings and other surprises.

Pizzería Edelyn, on the plaza (*moderate–cheap*). Given Holbox's quirkiness it's only fitting that the island's biggest restaurant should be a pizzeria. A full range of local seafood dishes are available too.

Restaurante Villamar, opposite the Hotel Faro Viejo (*moderate–cheap*). Open-air, beneath a *palapa* right on the beach, with fine *ceviches*, conch and other local fish and seafood. *May not be open eves*.

Antojitos Dafne Guadalupe, right in the middle of the plaza (*cheap*). Basic, great value *lonchería* and *taco*-stand, surrounded by terrace tables. It's particularly popular in the evenings.

Entertainment and Nightlife

Naturally there isn't much, but there is a friendly 'night bar', **Disco Carioca's**, two blocks from the plaza, which is open intermittently. At the weekend, on no account miss the afternoon softball games, when everyone turns out to laugh at their neighbours. There are ten teams who have all played each other a thousand times, but games are very competitive.

Laguna Yalahao

Holbox is only one of several islands across the lagoon (mostly uninhabited). On the next island to the west there is **El Manantial**, a magical place where an underground river brings fresh water up into the middle of the sea-water mangrove, creating a delicious pool for swimming and a very special mix of flora and fauna. Further away to the east, **Cabo Catoche**, where the Gulf and Caribbean waters meet, is another unique spot. Birds are as abundant on the lagoon-side as by the Gulf, and south of Holbox across the lagoon is **Isla de Pájaros**, noted for a diversity of species that includes ibises and flamingos, and which now has two viewing platforms for people to use as they land there. The waters around Holbox are also excellent for sport fishing, and the island is full of fishermen who can provide personal tours of all the attractions of the lagoon, for reasonable prices (see p.172).

Holbox has one drawback, though: much of it is made up of mangroves, and its mosquitoes can be ferocious, especially around sundown. Take DEET.

Isla de Cozumel

Mexico's largest offshore island, Cozumel was an established holiday destination before there was a single hotel open in Cancún. However, the flows of tourist development are fickle. While Cancún's grandest palaces are monuments to 1980s–'90s opulence, many of Cozumel's big hotels have a certain '70s look to them, making it clear that the big money has moved elsewhere. Its position as an island means that it feels quiet and very safe, and it's more family- and cruise-passenger-oriented than Cancún; it has its clubs and chain restaurants, but they're less hectic, even a tad staid. Cozumel's long dependence on tourism also means that this is one place in Mexico where not only are prices posted in dollars but shop assistants actually don't seem to know the peso equivalents, and with the opening of a new liner terminal, still more of San Miguel (the only town) is being taken over by jewellery and souvenir stores. Away from its beaches and San Miguel, the island – despite many relics of Mayan occupation – is a thinly populated slab of Yucatán brush, and not instantly attractive.

The true riches of Cozumel lie not on the island but around it: it has the greatest concentration of inshore coral reefs in the whole Maya Reef system, and the colour and vibrance of the undersea life just offshore is utterly spectacular. The way to get the most out of Cozumel is to spend as long in the water as possible.

History

Although there had been small fishing settlements on the island for centuries, large-scale Mayan settlement of Cozumel did not begin until the Terminal Classic (in about AD 700), with the migration of Mayan groups around the peninsula from Tabasco. Cozumel reached its greatest importance in the Late Postclassic, from about 1100 until the Conquest. It was the seat of a major oracle and a shrine to the goddess Ixchel which, as Landa (see p.68) recorded, was with the great cenote at Chichén-Itzá one of the two most important places of pilgrimage in the Yucatán, 'held in as much veneration as Jerusalem and Rome are among ourselves'. Every inhabitant of the peninsula tried to visit it at least once in their lives, and lords and priests sought to go every year. Since Ixchel was the principal deity of fertility, a visit to the shrine was especially important for women before they had their first child.

This status as a pilgrimage centre, added to its role in coastal trade, made Cozumel a wealthy community. The layout of the island's capital, now known as **San Gervasio**, indicates that Cozumel had a small-scale version of the *multepal* system of collective government seen at Mayapán, with authority shared between a *halach uinic* or 'first lord' and three or four subsidiary lords or *batabob*.

Cozumel was 'discovered' for the Spaniards by Grijalva's expedition in 1518, but was conquered the following year by Cortés himself. Its people were pacific and offered no resistance, fleeing into the woods to avoid the strange new arrivals. Cortés saw how many ceremonies and processions were held on the island, and, as his chronicler Bernal Díaz relates, he called together the lords of Cozumel to tell them, 'making

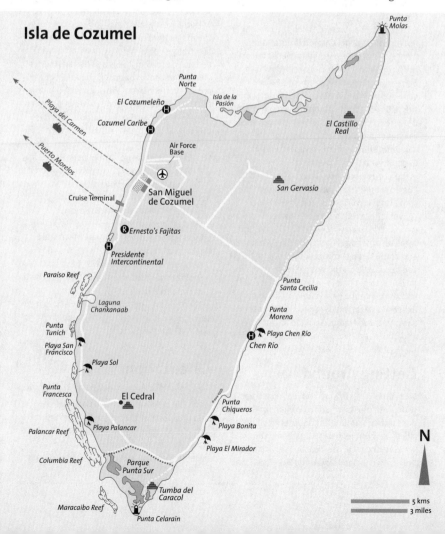

Isla de Cozumel

Getting There

By Air

Cozumel's airport, just north of San Miguel town, has regular direct flights from the USA, with **Continental** (t 872 0847) to and from Houston. There are also many charter flights. Within Mexico, **Aerocaribe/Aerocozumel** (t 872 3456) has a shuttle service to Cancún eight times daily each way, and **Mexicana** (t 872 2945) has flights from Cozumel to Cancún and Mexico City, and many other connections via Cancún.

There are official *Transporte Terrestre* taxis and *colectivos* (fare about $10) from the airport into town.

By Boat

The most popular route is on the **passenger ferry** from **Playa del Carmen** (information t 872 1508). Boats run roughly every hour on the hour (with some 2-hr gaps) from Playa 6am–11pm, and from Cozumel to Playa 5am–10pm. The fast boats take about 30mins; single fare is about $8, a return exactly double. It's wise to be at the dock 15mins in advance, as queues are often long. There is also a **'Cozumel Shuttle'** from Playa Tortugas in Cancún, for a hefty $32 return.

The Cozumel **car ferry** (t 872 0827) runs from **Puerto Morelos**, but unless you're staying for some time it will almost certainly be more convenient to rent a car on Cozumel. There are two sailings each way on Sun and Mon, and three on other days (generally at 4–5am, 10am and 2pm); timings can vary, so check first. Plus, you need to be on the dock at least 2½hrs in advance, to get on the list for the next sailing and complete the paperwork; it's also very expensive (a car and two people can cost over $80). Note too that on Fri and Sat, only cars and drivers, with no passengers, can cross.

Getting Around

Cozumel is 53km long and just under 14km wide, with one town and one main road that does a circuit around the southern half of the island. Anywhere in San Miguel is within walking distance. The local **bus** service runs only between San Miguel and the Hotel Zone

and Chankanaab lagoon south of the town, and is very infrequent. **Taxis** are the main form of local transport (from town to the north Hotel Zone, around $4; to Chankanaab around $8; a full tour of the island around $40). Agree the price before you get in the cab.

To see Cozumel with any freedom you need to **hire** a **bike**, **scooter**, **car** or **jeep**, and there are many rental agencies in town. Bikes cost $10–15 a day, scooters $25–$35, cars from $40 (or $30 off-peak), and 4WDs from $60. If you want to explore the dirt roads in the north of the island, you'll need a four-wheel-drive (check the insurance status for driving off normal roads). It's worth noting that, since traffic is light, rental companies seem to be under the impression they can send their stock out endlessly with minimal servicing, with the result that the island has some of the ropiest hire cars in Mexico. Check carefully for strange noises before you set off (if you do have a problem, the island has an *Angeles Verdes* breakdown patrol). If you take out a scooter you should be provided with a helmet (officially obligatory), and beware of potholes. If you're hiring a car or a jeep, note that it is officially illegal to have more than four people on board.

Localiza, C/ 2 Norte no. 99, between Av. Melgar and Av. 5, t 872 2111. Has some very battered cars, but is flexible about rates.

Rentadora Aguila, Av. Rafael Melgar 685, between Calles 3 and 5, t 872 0729, *aguila@cozunet.finred.com.mx*. Sizeable local agency with a big range of vehicles.

Rentadora Margón, C/ Adolfo R. Salas 58, between Av. Melgar and Av. 5, t 872 1318. Scooter specialist with a big stock: get there early to pick the best.

There are two **petrol/gas stations**, both in town on Av. Juárez, one on the corner of Av. 30 and the other at Av. 75.

Orientation

The Playa del Carmen ferry brings you right on to the main square, **Plaza Cozumel**, the meeting point of the seafront boulevard, **Av. Rafael E. Melgar** (or just Melgar) and the main street **Av. Juárez**, which runs off to the east to become the cross-island road. The big package hotels are lined up in two beach-side 'Hotel Zones' on continuations of Av. Melgar north and south of the town. San Miguel's layout is a straightforward grid, but it has one of those peculiarly Mexican street-naming systems: streets parallel to the seafront are Avenidas, numbered by fives (5, 10, 15, etc.), those running away from it are Calles. The same Avenida can be Av. 10 Norte or Av. 10 Sur according to whether it is north or south of Av. Juárez; Calles north of Juárez are even-numbered (C/ 6 Norte), those to the south are odd (C/ 5 Sur). There are also a few exceptions that have names.

Tourist Information

Cozumel t (987–)

The best sources of information are the local free magazines, especially the *Blue Guide* and *The Best of Cozumel*, distributed all around town. The best website for general tourist information about Cozumel is *www.cozumel online.com*.

Cozumel Tourist Office: In the government buildings on the east side of the plaza, facing the ferry landing (*officially open Mon–Fri 9–2 and 6–8; closed Sat and Sun*). Not much use unless you have a serious problem or a complaint.

Banks: There are several branches in the main plaza or on Av. 5, and all have ATM machines. There are also private *cambio* offices around the same area.

Consulates: There is a **US Vice-Consul** in Villa Mar Mall, Office 8, Av. Juárez 33, t 872 4574.

Health: There are several English-speaking medical services; the **Centro Médico de Cozumel**, C/ 1 Sur no.101, corner of Av. 50, t 872 3545, has a full emergency service (for special services for divers, *see* below). There is a also a **pharmacy** on the plaza, next to Bancomer bank.

Internet Access: Two decent value places are the **Calling Station**, Av. Melgar 27, by C/ 3 Sur, which also has a long-distance **phone office**, and **Cozunet**, Av. 5 Norte no.9, a little way off the plaza.

Post Office: Corner of Av. Melgar and C/ 7 Sur (*open Mon–Fri 9–6, Sat 9–noon; closed Sun*). Has a Mexpost desk.

Festivals

Easter is celebrated in San Miguel with processions and a passion play. Cozumel's biggest *fiesta* is **Santa Cruz** (3 May), held at El Cedral ever since the village was founded by Caste War refugees in 1848. Cedral is the island's centre of agriculture, and as well as music and dancing there's also a horse fair and country show.

Shopping

As anyone can see just by looking along Av. Melgar, shopping is a major attraction. Cruise-liner traffic is fostering a boom in new shops and malls selling souvenirs, glass, cameras, sunglasses and so on along the Malecón and around the Punta Langosta dock.

Craftwork comes from all over the country, and is often quite pricey. **Unicornio**, on Av. 5 Sur, just off the plaza, has a more varied and original range of handicrafts than most, with particularly good bags. **Almacenes Morales**, Av. Juárez 120, near Av. 15, is fun, big and colourful, with a huge stock of Mexican painted parrots, fish and baskets.

Jewellery has long been a speciality, and anyone into glitzy rocks can visit lush branches of **Van Cleef & Arpels** (Av. Melgar no.54), **Rachat & Romero** (Av. Melgar no.101) and others.

For **general shopping** there is a market at the junction of Av. Adolfo Rosado Salas and Av. 20 Sur, and the **Maxi** supermarket at Av. 10 Norte and C/ 2 Norte.

Sports and Activities

Diving and Snorkelling

There are over 20 diving reefs around Cozumel, many of which are not only full of life, but relatively close inshore and easily accessible. Complete beginners and novice divers are normally taken to the **Paraíso** or **Yucab** reefs just south of San Miguel towards Chankanaab, but they may also visit **Palancar** further south. Intermediate-level divers can handle reefs in between such as **San Francisco**, a 12m wall dive, **Santa Rosa**, Cedral and the rest of Palancar, with many caverns, tunnels and coral pillars. For advanced divers there are spectacular dives such as the 'Devil's Throat' cave at **Punta Sur**, and there are other reefs (towards the north point or on the east coast) that most dive-masters will warn anyone away from.

Many divers actually prefer **snorkelling** off Cozumel rather than bother with tanks, pressures and so on. Visibility is excellent, even off the beaches by the southern Hotel Zone, and you can see a lot just by putting your head in the water. Many dive shops offer snorkel tours, and there are also snorkel-only operators who run tours to the inshore reefs, equipment and refreshments included, for around $35.

Diving Courses and Operators

There are also over 60 diving operators. Most offer a full range of courses and dives, and many have special services such as Nitrox instruction and night dives. The same considerations apply on Cozumel as anywhere else: your dive-master should have a PADI certificate, and in beginners' 'resort' courses there should never be more than four people per dive-master. Prices are reasonable: resort courses from around $60, two-tank dives around $50. There are also specialized dive hotels (*see* below) and diving packages, which usually work out more economical still. For experienced divers looking to use their own equipment or needing any spares an essential port of call is **Pro Dive**, Av. Adolfo Rosado Salas 198, corner of Av. 5 Sur, a giant divers' store with every kind of diving equipment.

Deep Blue, C/ Adolfo Rosado Salas 200, corner of Av. 10 Norte, t 872 5653, *www.deepblue-cozumel.com*. Long-running, reliable and welcoming school and dive shop offering resort scuba courses, basic dives, full certification and Nitrox courses, cavern diving on the mainland, snorkelling trips, fishing, hotel and apartment bookings, packages with accommodation included and even post-dive massage.

Diving Adventures, C/ 5 Sur no. 22-D, just off Av. Melgar, t/f 872 3009, *www.diving adventures.net*. Friendly local company with reliable, personal service, good rates, and also snorkel tours.

Kuzamil Snorkelling Center, C/ 1 Sur no. 149, between Av. 5 and Av. 10, t/f 872 0539. good value snorkelling-only tours stopping at a minimum of two reefs, with the option of longer trips.

Roberta's Eco-Dive Cozumel, C/ 3 Sur, between Av. Melgar and Av. 5, t 872 4187, *www.rob ertasdivecozumel.com*. Excellent, friendly American-European dive shop with a strong concern for developing non-environmentally damaging methods.

Diving Safety

The local authorities' policy of favouring the cruise business above all else does no favours for divers. However, the Cozumel Reefs are officially a National Marine Park, and so far the increase in big-ship traffic has been relatively modest. Safety concerns have also been raised by the growth in small-boat traffic, and the death of singer Kirsty MacColl in a diving accident involving a yacht in 2000 led to new safety measures. Accidents of this kind are actually very rare here, but areas used for basic instruction are now generally roped off; dive masters should also make clear to their students that they should always look up and check what's above before surfacing, and their own boats should take great care to stay with their divers and so warn off other craft. In case of accidents, Cozumel has a state-of-the-art divers' emergency centre and recompression chamber, at t 872 1430 (24 hrs).

Fishing

The waters around Cozumel are known for marlin, sailfish, tuna, bonefish, snapper and especially billfish. Many dive shops also run fishing trips.

Aquarius Travel, C/ 3 Sur no. 2, between Av. Melgar and Av. 5, t 872 1092, *aquarius grandslam@correoweb.com*. Local fishing specialist with several boats available and very experienced captains, from $475 a day. They will arrange all necessary licences.

Marathon Fishing Charters, t 872 1986, *vogakin@prodigy.net.mx*. Flexible outfit with boats available for full- or half-days.

Horse Riding

Rancho Buenavista, off the main road near El Cedral, t 872 1537 (*closed Sun*). Runs very easy, guided pony treks (4hrs approx.), with no experience necessary.

Sailing

Cozumel Sailing, Av 10 Sur, corner of C/ 1 Sur, **t** 872 1449, *www.cozumelsailing.com*. Sailing yachts (with motors) for hire, from $100 for 2hrs, plus $25 for each additional hour and $15 per hour if a crew is required.

Windsurfing, Water-Skiing and Others

The best places to find water-skis, wave runners, boards and the like (plus parasailing) are **Playa San Francisco** and **Playa Sol**. There are often windsurfing boards for hire on other southwest beaches too.

Where to Stay

Cozumel **t** (987–)

Luxury–Expensive

Cozumel's big beach hotels are cheaper than those in Cancún, but they're still best booked as part of a package.

Casa Mexicana, Av. Melgar, between Calles 5 and 7, **t** 872 9080, *www.casamexicana-cozumel.com*. Sleek new building by the waterfront in town, with light, airy rooms, slightly Mexican-traditional décor and a fine terrace pool. The same company also runs the **Suites Bahia** and **Suites Colonial** (same phone/website, both *moderate*), with simpler but still very comfortable suite-style rooms with kitchenettes.

Presidente Intercontinental, 6.5km south of San Miguel, **t** 872 0322, *http://cozumel.inter-conti.com* (*luxury*). This 253-room complex dates from the '70s, but offers thoroughly refurbished rooms with every comfort and service, plus private beaches, a landing stage and marina, tennis, an in-house dive-shop, snorkelling, fishing and a beautiful pool.

Moderate

Amigo's B&B, C/ 7 Sur no. 571-A, between Av. 25 and Av. 30, **t** 872 3868, *www.akumal.net /amigos.htm*. Very pretty guest house run by Bob and Kathy Kopelman (who also have a house in Bacalar, *see* p.346), with three big, exceptionally well-equipped *cabaña*-style rooms (with a/c, kitchenettes, fridges, their own terraces) in a garden with a lovely pool. It's very good for families, with kid-friendly

features; breakfasts are served in a central *palapa*, which also serves as a games and lounge area. Prices *inexpensive* in low season. No credit cards.

Hotel Barracuda, Av. Melgar 628, **t** 872 0002, *www.cozumel.net/hotels/barracuda/*. By the water at the southern end of the Malecón, this long-established, specialist dive hotel is a favourite, with good facilities and very good value dive packages.

Hotel Flamingo, C/ 6 Norte, off Av. Melgar, **t** 872 1264, *www.hotelflamingo.com*. American-owned dive hotel that ranks as one of Cozumel's best whether you dive or not, with comfortable rooms, pleasant bar and rooftop terrace areas, breakfast included and a welcoming atmosphere. A variety of diving packages are available.

Inexpensive

Hotel Mary Carmen, Av. 5 Sur no. 4, **t** 872 0581. An old San Miguel standby with a certain quirky character. It has rooms around a small patio, with fans or a/c, and some eccentrically ornate furniture.

Hotel Maya Cozumel, C/ 5 Sur no. 4, **t** 872 0011. Well run-in, straightforward hotel, with good-sized rooms with a/c, fridges and TVs, and a pool.

Hotel Vista del Mar, Av. Melgar no. 45, next to C/ 5 Sur, **t** 872 0545, **f** 872 0445. Right on the Malecón, so the rooms with front balconies are superbly placed for enjoying the sunsets. Other rooms (all with a/c) are also big, bright and comfortable, and it has a pleasant pool and garden, a dive shop and other extras.

Hotel Pepita, Av. 15 Sur no. 120, corner of C/ 1 Sur, **t** 872 0098. Cozumel's best budget bargain; a big, pleasant place with a/c, fridges and fans in all its rooms, and also complimentary coffee. Run by a very friendly, helpful family, it's very well looked-after, and prices are exceptional. Popular, so call ahead.

Hotel Saolima, Av. Adolfo Rosado Salas 260, between Av. 10 and Av. 15, **t** 872 0886. The nearest thing to a real cheapo hotel, a motel-like building with 20 simple but well-kept, light rooms, some fan-only.

Tamarindo Bed & Breakfast, C/ 4 Norte no. 421, by Av. 20 Norte, **t/f** 872 3614, *www.cozu mel.net/bb/tamarind*. An exceptional choice, and also exceptional value, with the biggest rooms just nudging *moderate* in winter. Run by a charming Mexican-French couple, it's in a very pretty house with a garden in a quiet street, and the five rooms have lots of character. Generous breakfasts are included, there's an open kitchen, and the atmosphere is enjoyably cosy. The same owners run the **Palapas Amaranto**, C/ 5 Sur, between Av. 15 and Av. 20, with suites and self-contained apartments imaginatively designed by the owner himself with a striking mix of traditional Mexican fittings and many extras. Again, prices are exceptional.

Apartment Rentals

Longer-than-usual stays are popular, so that many hotels offer good longer-term rates. Any Cozumel website (especially *www.cozumel online.com* and *www.cozumel.net*) has a range of information on rentals.

Rentadora Isleña/Cozumel Vacation Homes, C/ 7 Sur, between Av. Melgar and Av. 5, **t** 872 0788, *www.cozumelhomes.com*. An agency with apartments and villas for rent at daily, weekly or longer-term rates.

Eating Out

Expensive

Morgan's, Av. Melgar, corner of Av. Juárez. In a corner of the main square, this big place decorated in Caribbean-colonial/pirate style has an expansive terrace and an international seafood menu.

Las Palmeras. Av. Melgar, corner of Av. Juárez. A big, popular restaurant on the main square. Its Mexican/Yucatecan cooking is enjoyable, but you pay for the view.

La Veranda, C/ 4 Norte, between Av. 5 and Av. 10, **t** 872 4132. A pretty bar-restaurant with tables in a lush garden, and a very internationally/US oriented menu of Caribbean seafood and other dishes.

Moderate

Casa Denis, C/ 1 Sur no. 132, off the plaza by Av. 5 Sur. A Cozumel institution, in a Caribbean wooden hut surviving from olden days on the island. It has outside tables and serves Yucatecan dishes mixed in with burgers and other internationals. *Open all day.*

Cocos Cozumel Café, Av. 5 Sur no. 180. A short walk from the plaza, this is one of the best places for a relaxing breakfast, with great juices. Choose either Mexican- or American-style, from breakfasts to other dishes.

Ernesto's Fajitas Factory, Av. Melgar by C/ 1 Sur. Ernesto's two branches – one here in town, and one under a big *palapa* 4km south – are consistently popular, both serving sizzling *fajitas* using very good-quality ingredients.

Island Gourmet de la Isla, C/ Adolfo Rosado Salas, corner of Av. 10. The pushmepullyou name seems to be a growing feature of international-run 'Riviera' restaurants: this laid-back bar-café offers a mixture of Mexican and Mediterranean-ish food, with a few vegetarian choices.

Restaurante Chen Río, on the Chen Río beach, on the east coast. A great location, and huge mixed platters of grilled seafood (easily enough for four, for $40), or more compact alternatives like great refreshing *ceviches*.

Cheap

As usual, the cheapest budget meals will be found at the *cocinas económicas* by the market, at C/ Salas and Av. 20 Sur.

El Amigo Chivo, C/ Adolfo Rosado Salas, by Av. 15 Sur. One of the remaining traditional local restaurants, with enjoyable local seafood.

Café del Museo, Av. Melgar, by C/ 4 Norte. On the rooftop terrace of the Cozumel museum, this makes a very attractive and good value place to eat or just spend time, with a great view, and good snacks and lunches, and you needn't go into the museum to use it.

Entertainment and Nightlife

Cozumel's nightlife is similar to that of Cancún, but there's less of it and less hysteria.

Hard Rock, Av. Melgar beside the plaza.

Carlos'n'Charlie's, in Punta Langosta mall.

Raga, Av. Salas between Av. 10 and 15 Sur. Palm-roofed restaurant-bar-club with a giant cocktail list and live rock bands.

Neptuno's, at the south end of the Malecón by C/ 11 Sur. A big, classic disco.

Platino's, closer into town, corner of Av. Juárez and Av. 25 Norte. The other main dance club.

himself understood as best he could', that their idols were evil, and that they had to abandon them. The Maya replied that he was wrong, and that if the Spaniards did attack them they would be punished by being destroyed at sea. Cortés ordered his men to smash all the idols they could and bury their remains, leaving in their place an image of the Virgin and a wooden cross. This may not have had such an immediate effect as Cortés expected, since pilgrimages to Cozumel were still being recorded by Landa 30 years later, but as Catholicism and Spanish rule imposed themselves more rigorously, they and Cozumel's other sources of wealth were gradually eliminated. By 1600 the island was virtually deserted.

Over the next 200 years Cozumel, like Isla Mujeres, was used as a base and bolthole by pirates, from Henry Morgan in the 1660s to the Lafittes (*see* p.162) in the 1820s. In 1842, when Stephens and Catherwood came here, the only settlement was a small *rancho* built by an escaped pirate called Molas, while the rest of the island was completely wild and overgrown. Cozumel was only resettled after 1848, when *mestizo* farmers from eastern Yucatán took refuge here from the Caste War, rightly assuming that the rebel Maya had lost the seafaring skills of their ancestors. Its population was under 1,000 in 1900, when it began to grow a bit more quickly thanks to the *chicle* trade. In the Second World War, a US base was established here, and US Navy divers discovered Cozumel's beaches and the treasures of its reefs. This information reached Jacques Cousteau, who came here in the 1960s and pronounced it one of the finest diving areas in the world. The tourist business largely took off from there, and on the back of it Cozumel now has a population in excess of 80,000.

San Miguel de Cozumel

The town of San Miguel is home to around 90 per cent of Cozumel's population. Its relative newness and tourist-town status give it a neatness atypical of Mexican towns, and Av. Melgar itself is being overpowered by jewellery stores, but for the most part it's a relaxed, pleasant and friendly place to stroll around, and what gloss there is fades away as you leave the main streets. There is a narrow beach along Av. Melgar (also known as the **Malecón**, the seafront), but the island's main beaches are outside the town to the south. The waterfront is best just for wandering along, and taking in spectacular sunsets. By Plaza Cozumel there's a navy monument and a giant Mexican flag, a rather desperate reaffirmation of national sovereignty in this tourist zone.

On Av. Melgar next to C/ 4 Norte there is an attractive local museum, the **Museo de la Isla de Cozumel** (*open daily 9–5; adm*), with a bookshop and a pleasant café (*see* facing page). Housed in a pretty building that used to be a hotel, it has interesting displays (in Spanish and English) on the island's ecology and its history: Mayan Cozumel (fine ceramics); the Conquest; pirates; the frontier island of the *chicle* trade.

In the opposite direction, south of the plaza along Melgar, the view is now dominated by the latest big innovation on Cozumel, **Punta Langosta**, the gleaming new cruise terminal that's intended to make the island a major player in the Caribbean cruise trade, with the obligatory mall at its landward end. To celebrate this new asset a new official town centre is being created just south of the mall, complete with a new plaza on Melgar between Calles 11 and 13 Sur and a new sports stadium, police

San Miguel de Cozumel

500 metres
500 yards

N

To North Hotel Zone
To Airport

CALLE 12 NORTE

CALLE 10 NORTE

Passenger Ferry to Playa del Carmen

Flamingo

Museo de la Isla de Cozumel

CALLE 8 NORTE

La Veranda

CALLE 6 NORTE

Tamarindo

CALLE 4 NORTE

Las Palmeras

PLAZA

CALLE 2 NORTE

5 AV. NORTE
10 AV. NORTE
15 AV. NORTE
20 AV. NORTE
25 AV. NORTE

AV. RAFAEL E. MELGAR

Church

Banks

Mary-Carmen

Casa Denis

AVENIDA BENITO JUAREZ

Cocos Cozumel

Island Gourmet

Pepita

CALLE 1 SUR

Petrol Station

Saolima

CALLE ADOLFO ROSADO SALAS

Market

To San Gervasio

CALLE 3 SUR

Maya Cozumel

Vista del Mar

CALLE 5 SUR

AV. PEDRO JOAQUIN COLDWELL (30 AV.)

CALLE GENERAL FRANCISCO MUJICA

AV. 35 SUR

AV. 40 SUR

AV. 45 SUR

CALLE FELIPE ANGELES

Cruise Terminal

Casa Mexicana

Post Office

5 AV. SUR
10 AV. SUR
15 AV. SUR
20 AV. SUR
25 AV. SUR

Punta Langosta

Palapas Amaranto

CALLE MORELOS

AV. 50 SUR

PLAZA

CALLE 7 SUR

Ayuntamiento

CALLE 11 SUR

CALLE 9 SUR

Barracuda

CALLE 15 SUR

CALLE 13 SUR

Amigo's B&B

AV. 50 SUR BIS

To South Hotel Zone

headquarters and town hall. Beyond that are the main diving piers, a naval base and the Puerto Morelos car ferry dock. The former town hall, which faces you across the old plaza as you get off the Playa del Carmen ferry, has been left as a shopping mall, which was sort of predictable.

Around the Island

As on Isla Mujeres, the sheltered beaches and reefs of Cozumel with their tranquil, clear waters are all on the western, landward side, particularly in the southwest corner. The eastern side is much more rugged, and the sea more ferocious. Outside San Miguel, Cozumel is often impressively empty. The one main road runs dead straight across the island from Av. Juárez, then makes a circuit around the southern coast. The northern half of Cozumel is only accessible by dirt track, and is mostly left to the birds. The name Cozumel comes from *Cuzmil*, Yucatec for 'island of swallows', and during the winter months places like San Gervasio welcome great flocks of them.

San Gervasio

Open Sept–May daily 7–4; June–Aug daily 7–5; adm, Sun adm free.

There are over 30 Mayan remains and ruins on Cozumel, most of them small, individual shrines, temples or navigational markers. The former capital, San Gervasio, is up a good road six kilometres north of the main road, from a turn about halfway across the island. Its surviving buildings are all from the last centuries of Mayan civilization, and architecturally crude compared to those of older Mayan cities. San Gervasio's layout, though, is unique, and like El Rey in Cancún it is most interesting for the impression it gives of a Mayan community as a whole.

At the entrance there's a small visitor centre, with handicraft shops and fairly insistent local guides. The site is quite spread out, its sections connected by *sacbé* paths, so a visit can take one and a half hours or more. This dispersal reflects both Cozumel's role as a place of pilgrimage and its *multepal* government. San Gervasio has a number of residential complexes, with frontal porticos (which once supported palm roofs) leading into interior rooms. Each of Cozumel's *batabs* would have maintained their own establishment of this kind, located outside the shared core of the city.

Near the entrance is the **Manitas** building ('Little Hands', so called because some of the red hands painted by the Maya as invocations to good health, now near-invisible, were found here), thought to have been the residence of the chief lord of Cozumel in about 1000; a little further on is the **Chichan Nah** complex, which was probably the seat of the *Halach Uinic* or first lord of the island from about 1200 until the Spaniards' arrival. Off to the west there is a *sacbé* that was the main entry road for pilgrims from the mainland. Across it there is an **arch**, with a small altar where arriving pilgrims left offerings to Ixchel. A little more towards the centre is the **Nohoch Nah**, a substantial temple with a Postclassic upper structure on a Late Classic base. Another place where offerings were made to the goddess, it was once richly decorated. Further on again are the **Casa de los Murciélagos** ('House of Bats'), most important of the older buildings at San Gervasio, a residential complex begun in about 700, and the **Pet Nah** or 'Round House', unusual for a Mayan building in being completely round. The **main plaza** is beyond that. With a little imagination it's easy to recreate this in your mind's eye as a Mayan colonnaded square, and some buildings still have traces of their blue and red colouring. A fair distance from the main site is the Postclassic **Casa Alta**, the largest pyramid, decorated in multi-coloured stucco, and it is possible that this was the principal shrine of Ixchel.

An added attraction of San Gervasio is the walk itself. The paths are lined with an enormous variety of succulents and other plants, and there's often an exhilarating scent of wild spearmint. In the air, as well as the swallows, you can see a great range of buntings, butterflies and spectacular red dragonflies.

The Coast Road

Returning to the main road, a left turn will take you to the east coast at **Punta Santa Cecilia**, as well known by the name of its lonely bar-restaurant, **Mezcalito's**. The east side of Cozumel is gaunt and windswept, with crashing surf, its gauntness further accentuated by the effects of hurricanes. There are beaches all along the coast, but swimming here can be dangerous, and it's advisable to be very careful, and swim, if at all, only in the more sheltered bays. From Mezcalito's a dirt track (4WD only: check your insurance when hiring if you want to go up this road) runs up for some 20 kilometres to the lighthouse at the northern tip of the island, **Punta Molas**, past miles of deserted beaches, and two Mayan temple ruins at **El Castillo** and **Agua Grande**.

Turning south from Punta Santa Cecilia, the road rolls on past more windblown beaches and isolated restaurants. **Punta Morena** is a big, open beach with a couple of beach bars; much more attractive is **Chen Río**, where a rocky headland gives extra shelter and creates an arching, little-used surf beach with a roped-off small lagoon for safe swimming. It also has one of the most enjoyable beach restaurants on this side of the island. **Punta Chiqueros** has a pretty, sheltered cove, and there are two cafés further down at Playa San Martín and Playa Bonita. A few kilometres further on, the newly-rebuilt main road turns abruptly towards the west side of the island. Beyond it, the whole southern tip of Cozumel has been made into **Parque Punta Sur**, an ecological reserve (*open daily 8–5; adm*), only accessible from the southeast corner of the coast road. From the main car park, the old dirt track continues to the hurricane-battered lighthouse on the southern point, **Punta Celarain**, which now contains a museum, and which you can climb up. Look out for the extraordinary **Tumba del Caracol**, a miniature Mayan temple with doors about half a metre high, dating from around 1200. Although it looks like a toy it is likely that it was built as a navigational aid or as a marker in rites involving the movements of the sun. Elsewhere in the park there are a turtle nesting beach, crocodile and flamingo lagoons, a snorkelling beach and areas full of birds, and 'exploration paths' have been laid out to enable visitors to get to see them.

The sea becomes calmer, and the beaches more usable, as soon as you round the point. The beaches of southwest Cozumel are well developed for tourism, with beach bar-restaurants that have facilities for scuba diving, snorkelling, kayaking and other water sports. Among the most attractive are **Playa Palancar** and **Punta Francesa**, down side-tracks from the main road, with a delicious, gently lapping sea overlooked by coconut palms. Just north of Palancar a turning inland will take you to the tiny community of **El Cedral**, which hosts the island's most important festival in May (*see* p.177). Back on the main road, the next stop is the **Playa Sol** beach club, Cozumel's biggest waterside fun centre.

About five kilometres north of Playa San Francisco is the **Chankanaab** nature park (*open daily 8–6; adm; adm plus snorkel hire $6*), one of the most popular places on Cozumel. It's centred on a coastal lagoon, originally home to an enormous variety of fish and coral, and there's also a lush botanical garden. Swimming is no longer permitted in the lagoon, damaged by overuse, but there are decent restaurants and an attractive beach with plenty of sea life just offshore, making it a user-friendly introduction to snorkelling that's very good for kids. Scuba diving facilities are also available. North of Chankanaab the road meets the southern Hotel Zone, and carries on past more beaches back into San Miguel.

Getting Around the Riviera

Highway 307 runs south from Av. Tulum in Cancún down the length of the Riviera, 1–3km inland. From Cancún to Xcaret (72km), 307 is a fast four-lane divided highway; from there to Tulum (59km) it is a wider-than-usual highway that's almost as fast, before it reverts back to a normal two-lane road from Tulum to Chetumal. There are no through roads inland off 307 anywhere between Cancún and the Cobá turn at Tulum: the roads shown on some maps as running inland from Puerto Morelos and Playa are so far still only dirt tracks in bad condition, though they may be paved at some point. There are **petrol stations** by Cancún airport and at Puerto Morelos, Playa del Carmen, Puerto Aventuras, Xpu-Ha and Tulum.

Buses are plentiful. Fast shuttle buses run between Cancún and Playa del Carmen, stopping at Puerto Morelos, every 10mins 5am–11pm daily (11 of these continue to Tulum); there are also over 20 Mayab *intermedio* buses daily (13 continue to Tulum and Chetumal), which stop at most places along the road. The clanky but cheaper **Playa Express** service also plies between Cancún and Playa del Carmen about every 30mins, 6am–8pm daily, stopping anywhere en route on request (about half of these continue to Tulum). Several first-class buses run daily between Cancún and Chetumal via Playa and Tulum. At most places other than Playa and Tulum buses stop only on the main road, so there is still a walk to the beach. A ticket all the way to Tulum will cost around $9.

Taxis from Cancún, Puerto Morelos, Playa del Carmen and Tulum will also take you anywhere along this coast, for a price (around $30–$35, from Playa to Tulum). Be prepared to do some haggling.

The Riviera from Cancún to Xcaret

The first section of the Riviera corridor south of Cancún is the least interesting, as the road runs some way inland west of the Cancún lagoon through what is now the service centre for the whole area, lined with warehouses that keep the hotels going. Beyond the airport and the southern end of the Hotel Zone road the Highway 307 freeway bends back toward the shore line, as mostly empty scrub and a few *ranchos* – where tourist developments may or may not be on the way – roll by alongside. The first attraction is at Km30, the **Crococun** 'regional zoo' (*open daily 8.30–5.30; adm*). This is primarily a crocodile and alligator farm, but despite the tacky name it's also a fairly well-organized and cared-for collection of local wildlife that includes spider monkeys, Yucatán white-tailed deer and a range of birds and snakes, in a natural forest setting. Bus trips go to the park daily from Cancún (*information t 850 3719*).

Puerto Morelos

Puerto Morelos, 36 kilometres south of Cancún, has another staggering Riviera-fact to state for itself. In the era pre-Cancún this little place of one square and just three main streets was for a very long time the most substantial town anywhere on the coast north of Chetumal, the primary centre for shipping *chicle*, then Quintana Roo's main export. This trade had gone into decline by the 1960s, and Cancún's arrival only hastened the fading of the town's importance. Today, it's still the vehicle-ferry port for Cozumel, and the plan to bring in ferries here from Miami (*see* p.107) may change things at some point, but don't let this fool you into expecting a bustling harbour.

Getting Around

Buses going between Playa del Carmen and Cancún drop passengers for Puerto Morelos at the turn-off on Highway 307, 2km from the town. If you don't want to walk, **taxis** run down to the town plaza (just over $1); sharing should cut the cost. There's a **petrol station** by the Highway crossing.

For the **Cozumel car ferry**, *see* p.176.

Tourist Information

Puerto Morelos t (998–)

Tourist Office: There is an occasionally-staffed official kiosk by the turn-off to Puerto Morelos on the highway, but the Marand agency (*see* below) is generally more useful.
Banks: There is a Bital branch on the plaza, with an ATM.
Health: There's a **pharmacy** next to the church.
Internet Access: There's an Internet shop on the land side of the plaza near Posada Amor.
Phone Office: Av. Rojo Gómez (north out of the plaza on the landward side).

Useful Local Organizations

Alma Libre Bookstore, on the plaza, t 871 0264. A beacon for English-readers throughout the region. Besides its books, it's a good place to meet people and find out about any new trips or activities. They also have a book-exchange service. *Open only Oct–May Mon–Sat; closed Mon and June–Sept.*
Goyo's Info Centre, Av. Rojo Gómez, t 871 0189 or t 810 6179, *www.goyosjungle.com*. American Goyo Morgan is a local institution, having accumulated a huge knowledge of the area over his 26 years spent living here. He provides all sorts of information, runs a range of tours (ie. the 'Jungle Adventure', $40), organizes sessions in a *Temazcal* (traditional Mayan sweat bath) among other activities and also produces a range of natural health products.
Marand Travel Agency, on the street parallel to the road in from the highway (landward side of the plaza), t 871 0332, *www.puerto-morelos.com.mx*. Provides travel services, money exchange, gift shop, car and bike hire, tours of the area and general information.

Sports and Activities

Diving, Snorkelling and Fishing

Diving facilities are more low-key here than in larger centres, but a full range of dives and courses is available, and the reef is wonderful for snorkelling. Puerto Morelos also offers very good fishing, as deep water and the Caribbean currents are unusually close to the shore.
Almost Heaven Adventures, on the plaza by El Pescador restaurant, t/f 871 0230, *almost heaven@puertomorelos.com.mx*. The dive master, Enrique Juárez, offers a wide range of trips and courses with expert instructors: reef snorkel tours; scuba dives, including a special introductory programme for kids; cavern dives; jungle tours and fishing trips, which have been highly recommended. Rates are variable for couples and groups, and he also speaks very good English.
Secret Reef Center, on the plaza, by Marand Travel, t/f 871 0244. The base of Fernando Cusi, a very experienced sport-fishing and snorkelling guide. Service is very personal.
Sub-Aqua Explorers, on the plaza, next to Alma Libre, t 871 0012, *nitosdivers@yahoo .com.mx*. Long-established dive shop with a full range of diving trips and instruction ($60, two-tank dive), they can provide reef-snorkelling tours ($30), trips to *cenotes*, and deep-sea fishing trips ($85 a day).

Where to Stay

Puerto Morelos t (998–)

Long stays are popular and several hotels offer self-catering and long-stay rates. Rooms may also be available for rent in houses; look for ads in Alma Libre and elsewhere in town.

Moderate

Acamaya Reef Motel/Campsite, northern end of the Puerto Morelos beach road, 2km from town, t 871 0132, *www.acamayareef.com*. Has a suitably beach-bohemian feel to it, pet spider monkey included. There are seven rooms, divided between a main building and *cabañas* (*moderate* with a/c) but there's cheaper camping space ($9) and an RV park with hook-ups (from $15). You're soothingly isolated, but meals are available.

Amar Inn, on the beach near the Ojo de Agua, **t** 871 0026. A wonderfully ramshackle house with a garden full of rusty anchors. It has four rooms with kitchenettes or three self-contained *cabañas* in the garden, with interesting touches like beds atop spiral staircases. Shiny comfort this isn't and it feels pricey for just a night or two, but much better weekly/monthly rates are available.

Cabañas Puerto Morelos, Av. Rojo Gómez **t** 871 0199, *www.cancuncabanas.com*. Four blocks north of the plaza, this big house in a garden contains individually furnished *cabañas* for two to three people, and a whole two-bed house for five. All are well-equipped, self-contained units; rates vary with the season. There's also a pool in the garden. It's very popular, so book well ahead.

Casita del Mar, north end of town, **t** 871 0301, *www.hotelcasitadelmar.com*. Popular beach hotel a 5–10-min walk from the plaza; it has spacious rooms with all mod cons and a lovely beachside pool and **bar-restaurant**, most recently hosting an Argentinian grill.

Hacienda Morelos, just off the plaza, **t** 871 0015. Attractive and friendly beachside hotel, with well-equipped, apartment-style rooms with kitchenettes, a/c and more. Its terrace houses Johnny Cairo's **restaurant** (*see below*). Note that not all rooms face the sea.

Hotel Ojo de Agua, a couple of streets north of the plaza, **t** 871 0027, *www.ojo-de-agua.com*. Beach hotel with bright, pretty rooms (a/c or fan-only), all well-equipped; they vary in size and so in price (several are *inexpensive*), but it's worth going for at least the $40 rooms to get more space and the beautiful view. Also has a **restaurant**, pool and dive shop.

Rancho Libertad, by the beach, south end of town, **t** 871 0181, *www.rancholibertad.com*. Mellow, *palapa*-roofed, *cabaña*-style (but extremely comfortable) rooms, in a great location. 'Hanging beds' – solid beds which swing on ropes with the breeze – are a trademark. Ample breakfasts and use of an open kitchen are included, and it has a **restaurant**. It has one of the best stretches of beach, and there are bikes and snorkels to rent, and a resident scuba instructor. Growth workshops and so on are a speciality, but if all you want to do is lie out on your terrace, it's a beautiful, peaceful and relaxing place.

Inexpensive

To camp or park an RV the best place in the area is the Acamaya Reef (*see above*).

Hotel Inglaterra, Av. Rojo Gómez, **t** 871 0418, *michael@hotelinglaterra.freeserve.co.uk*. Curious, small hotel with quite comfortable, well-equipped rooms; upper-floor rooms are almost mini-suites; most, though, are quite dark. There's also a pleasant breakfast bar/lounge with TV, and free coffee.

Posada Amor, just off the plaza, **t** 871 0033, **f** 871 0178. Long-running institution with pleasant fan-only rooms beneath *palapa* roofs. There's lots of variety (and prices): light, bright two- or one-bed rooms with showers, others with shared bathrooms, and four great, atmospheric rooms sharing a bathroom in a big, *palapa* hut (nearly *cheap*). The owners are friendly, and it has one of Puerto Morelos' most popular **restaurants**.

Eating Out

Johnny Cairo's Beach Bar & Grill, Hacienda Morelos hotel (*moderate*). Eclectic, very good food from a highly trained US chef, served in a very friendly atmosphere. Most Sundays it hosts an all-afternoon party drawing in most visitors in town, with a live band and a great value, eat-all-you-want barbecue.

Palapas Pizzas, on the plaza (*moderate*). Lively place with bumper-sized, classic pizzas.

Los Pelícanos, by the beach and plaza (*moderate*). An antidote to the crass pushiness of many resort restaurants. Impossible to miss, with a giant *palapa* roof and wide terrace, it offers first-rate local seafood and the charming service invites you to settle in.

El Pescador, on the plaza (*moderate*). Smarter than most, a seafood/steak house on a balcony beneath an impressive giant *palapa*, with a great view of whatever's going on.

Posada Amor (*moderate*). A favourite stand-by, especially for breakfast (good coffee), with an unusually varied menu later in the day.

Restaurant La Cordobeza on the plaza (*moderate–cheap*). Bright little restaurant with all the Yucatecan favourites and Mexican breakfast standards.

El Pirata, on the plaza (*cheap*). Puerto Morelos' best *tortería* and *taco*-stand, in a hut next to the taxi rank. Great juices and sandwiches.

Despite its good beach and its proximity to Cancún, Puerto Morelos, remarkably, is radically different in atmosphere from the city or Playa del Carmen. It's actually one of the most low-key places anywhere on the Riviera, inhabited by real fishermen and frequented by divers, snorkellers and sport fishermen. It has a sizeable international population of well-heeled bohemians, personal-growth therapists, artists and so on, who often say that Puerto Morelos is like Playa del Carmen *used* to be, and fervently hope their retreat is not set for a similar transformation. Many visitors come here not for a couple of weeks but for a couple of months, or a whole winter. As with anywhere on this coast, the town's attractions have not entirely escaped the stare of hotel developers, and a consortium is pushing to build a mega-resort (to be called El Cid) on the south end of the beach, but the surrounding mangrove lagoons and reefs offshore have officially been declared a protected area, and El Cid is being resisted tooth and nail by locals and incomers, so far with some success.

The Town

Belying the benign atmosphere it has today, Puerto Morelos has a hairy frontier past. It was founded in the 1890s, after the Díaz government responded to the US demand for chewing gum by granting exclusive rights to the *chicle* and any other resources they could find in a huge area between Cabo Catoche and Tulum to a Mexican-British venture, the Compañía Colonizadora de la Costa de Yucatán. Puerto Morelos was their principal base. The surrounding wilderness was still part-occupied by rebel Cruzob Maya, and in 1899 a group of armed Maya appeared at the camp and warned its occupants not to move any further into the forest. The company gave orders to tough it out, and eventually Maya rebelliousness faded away. Puerto Morelos contained around 1,000 workers – Mexicans, West Indians, Chinese, Spaniards driven out of Cuba – and had the wild, brutal life of a frontier camp.

All this has long been forgotten. The walk into town from Highway 307 can be gruelling when the sun is up, but the road leads you between peaceful marsh pools full of coots, herons and stately white ibises. It runs out in the town's **plaza**, facing the beach. Alongside it is Puerto Morelos' leaning tower, a **lighthouse** that was knocked out of true by Hurricane Beulah in 1966. It has been supplanted by a neat, white, upright tower next to it, but the old tower has been kept as a monument. The Cozumel ferry dock is at the end of the streets to the south (on the right). The reef stands only 600 metres offshore and is clearly visible from the beach. It is one of the richest coral environments along the whole mainland shore, rivalling Cozumel, and has been made into a protected *parque marítimo*.

Back on the beach itself, pelicans perch on mooring posts while the fishermen land their catch, reinforcing the impression of an easy-going tranquillity long lost by Playa del Carmen. A few new projects have appeared here, but for the most part these are all modest developments that haven't altered the feel of the place. Nightlife consists largely of sitting in cafés and watching the waves. From the north end of town a bumpy road winds past a few hotels, beach houses and a fair amount of empty coast, for around two kilometres until it reaches the Acamaya Reef *cabañas* and turns inland, providing an alternative route back to Highway 307.

Back on the highway, around one kilometre south of the Puerto Morelos turning there is the **Jardín Botánico Dr Alfredo Barrera** (*open daily 8–5; adm*), containing an exuberant variety of bromeliads, palms and other Yucatán plant-life (labelled in Spanish only); on the nature trail you can also see spider monkeys and birds. Insect repellent is essential. A more adventurous excursion is to take the (pretty slow) dirt road that turns inland off Highway 307 opposite the botanical garden for about half an hour to the village of **Colonia Vallarta**. Nearby are three beautiful *cenotes*, the **Tres Bocas** ('three mouths') which are great for snorkelling, and a forest 'nature trail' of paths. Sub-Aqua Explorers and Almost Heaven (*see* p.186) run snorkelling trips.

Punta Maroma and Punta Bete

Along the Highway south from Puerto Morelos tracks head into the woods towards the coast and secluded beaches. Until about 1997 this area was scarcely inhabited, but now more and more tracks are being staked out as the entrances to resort complexes, each announcing its presence with a giant gatehouse like a set for a particularly cheesy Arabian-nights fantasy movie. It's still possible to slip between them, though, to a turquoise sea bordering near-untouched forest bays, and to unfenced beachside tranquillity that's open to all.

Playa del Secreto, one of the first signposted entrances after Puerto Morelos, is a beach development lined mostly with individual houses on a lavish scale. At Km49 (counting from Cancún), there is **Rancho Loma Bonita** (*reservations in Cancún **t** (998) 887 5465/887 5423*), a ranch offering pony and horse treks through the forest, lunch and beach-stop included. About a kilometre further on the road passes a small, scarcely marked *palapa*-style hut by a wooden gateway. This is the very discreet entrance to the most luxurious hotel on the whole coast, the palace-by-the-sea that is the **Maroma**, at Punta Maroma. Another stretch of road beyond that brings you to the newest of the area's 'eco-parks', at **Tres Ríos** (*open daily 8–5; adm exp*) which, like those at Xcaret and Xel-Ha, offers easy, no-worries and family-friendly access to different aspects of the local environment. Covering a big stretch of jungle around a fine beach, mangrove inlets and *cenotes*, it's very well-organized and offers lots to do: scuba diving, snorkelling, kayaking, horse riding, cycling, forest walks and even paintballing. There's also a beach, and several restaurants. Day trips with transport included are available from Cancún (*t (998) 887 8077/t freephone 01 800 714 3643, www.tres-rios.com*).

Twenty-four kilometres from Puerto Morelos (Km62) is the impressive entrance to one of the most popular self-contained hotels on the coast, the **Posada del Capitán Lafitte**, on the tip of **Punta Bete**. The road actually signposted to Punta Bete is about a kilometre further south. From this turning three kilometres of track bring you out on to a series of bays with long, curving beaches lined with coconut palms. Developers have been moving in on Punta Bete, but this entry road is still a rut-ridden jungle track, helping to keep the point relatively little visited. Many of its beaches therefore remain beautifully peaceful, fronted only by a few small-scale operations among the

Where to Stay and Eat

Punta Maroma/Punta Bete t (984–)

Luxury

Kai Luum II, t/f 873 0212, *www.capitan lafitte.com*, or via the Turquoise Reef Group (*see* p.139) (*luxury–expensive*). An offshoot of Capitán Lafitte, reached via the same driveway, this is a place you'll either love or hate. It's called a 'camptel': the rooms are permanent, with good beds, fittings and maid service, but are in tents shaded by *palapas*, with shared showers. It's upscale camping, with most of the inconveniences taken away. The atmosphere is very chummy, and meals (breakfast and dinner are included) are taken together in a giant beach *palapa* (dinner 7pm only). A big range of activities is available. *Closed Sept–Oct*.

Maroma, t 872 8200, *www.maroma.net* (*luxury*). The peak of tasteful opulence on the Riviera, a secluded retreat chosen by the likes of Tony and Cherie Blair. It's set in 200 acres of exceptionally lush vegetation by the cape of Punta Maroma, with its own magnif- icent beach at the end of a near-endless driveway through thick palm groves. Most rooms have superb Caribbean views (some face the garden), terraces and all kinds of luxuries; every health treatment is offered, and there's a magnificent pool and sports facilities. The terrace **restaurant** (*expensive*) is gourmet-standard, and open to non-resi- dents; transport can be arranged for diners from Playa del Carmen.

Posada del Capitán Lafitte, t/f 873 0212, *www.capitanlafitte.com*, or via the Turquoise Reef Group (*see* p.139). Opened in the '70s, an unusually charming resort hotel with a superb and very long beach. Breakfast and dinner are included but it's less claustro- phobic than fully all-inclusives, with a friendly atmosphere. Rooms are in individual or two-room pavilions spread around the grounds, with **restaurants**, bars, pool, a library, games room and dive shop. Very

popular with families, it has many regulars and often gets booked up well in advance during winter.

Moderate–Inexpensive

If you arrive without a reservation, go to the road actually signposted to Punta Bete, about a kilometre south of the Capitán Lafitte along Highway 307 (look out for the Cristal water depository). Mayab and Playa Express buses stop there on request.

Coco's Cabañas, on the north fork of the Punta Bete road behind Los Pinos (*see* below), **t** 887 0785, *cchr@caribe.net.mx*. With five high- standard *cabañas* – good showers, pretty textiles and fittings, their own terraces – a small pool and a laid-back **restaurant**. Prices are *inexpensive* most of the year, *moderate* in winter. It's not quite on the beach, though, and a new hotel building nearby has taken away a fair bit of its secluded feel.

Bahia Xcalacoco, at the southernmost end of the Punta Bete road, *bahia-xcalacoco@ yahoo.com* (*inexpensive*). Ricardo Novelo and his American wife Rosa are holding on to their very pretty part of the beach despite the encroachments of resorts from Playa. They have six pleasant, good-sized rooms, all with new showers and a beach view, or you can camp or sling a hammock (around $3 a head).

Paradise Point, at the end of the south fork of the Punta Bete road, *www.knowAmerica .com/Paradise* (*inexpensive*). Very attractive, bargain *cabañas* right on the beach, built and owned by Americans Richard and Darlene Klenck. All are decorated with tradi- tional textiles, and have kitchenettes and beach terraces, and there's also a **restaurant- bar**. It's one of the best bits of beach here, especially good for fishing. *Usually closed May–Nov*.

Restaurante Los Piños, north fork of the Punta Bete track. The **restaurant** (*moderate*) has four basic rooms with showers (*inexpensive*), by the beach (and a new hotel 100m north). There's also a **camp site** (about $4 per head).

palms. About a kilometre from the beach there is a fork in the track, both sides of which (things are not yet that organized) have signs saying Punta Bete: the right fork leads down to Bahia Xcalacoco and Paradise Point; the left, skirting the perimeter wall of the new Ikal hotel, leads to Los Pinos and Coco's *Cabañas*.

Playa del Carmen

Once upon a time (around 1985), there was this sleepy little fishing village on the Yucatán coast with one sand street, under 1,000 people, reefs offshore, a fabulous beach lined with coconut palms, a passenger ferry to Cozumel and not much else.

Today, Playa del Carmen is the fastest-growing town in the whole of Mexico. No one knows how many people live here, but it could easily be over 100,000, with more arriving by the week, to work in hotels, restaurants or construction or just see what they can find. The single street of yore, now known as the **Quinta Avenida**, is a pedestrian walkway lined end-to-end with restaurants, bars, mini-malls and jewellery,

Playa del Carmen

Getting Around

By Air

For details of transport to Playa when arriving at Cancún airport, *see* p.148, and for buses from Playa to the airport, *see* below. A local cab from Playa to Cancún airport will cost $30–$40.

Playa has an airstrip, at the south end of Av. 20, mainly used by **Aerosaab**, t 873 0804/873 0501, *www.aerosaab.com*, which operates principally as an air-taxi service, providing light-plane transport on a to-order basis to places in the region such as Chichén, Mérida and, especially, Holbox (*see* p.171). They also offer aerial sightseeing tours (around $150 per person). Scheduled air services between Playa and Chichén Itzá, Cozumel and other destinations are currently suspended.

By Bus

Note that Playa del Carmen now has **two** bus stations (local publications are slow to show this). **ADO** and affiliated companies' first-class long-distance services now use a station (often called *Estación Alterna*) on Av. 20 between Calles 12 and 14. Most buses along the Riviera (the Riviera shuttle to Cancún, most Mayab services, Playa Express) and second-class services still use the recently rebuilt **'old' station** on the main plaza, at Av. Juárez and Av. 5. You can buy tickets for all services at either station, and some buses still call at both, but always check which station a bus will leave from.

As well as those listed here, there are several more long-distance services to central Mexico.

Cancún (*1¼hrs*): Riviera shuttle from the old station every 10mins 5.15am–midnight, and over 20 Mayab *intermedio* services daily; fare about $3.50. All buses stop off at **Puerto Morelos**. The cheaper Playa Express buses run every 30mins 6am–8pm daily, and they and Mayab buses stop anywhere en route on request. Many first-class buses stopping at the new terminal will also take on passengers for Cancún.

Cancún airport (*1¼hrs*): Eight Riviera buses daily from the old station 8am–7.30pm; fare about $7. *Colectivos* also run hourly 6am–6pm, also from the old station, although you can arrange to have them pick up from many hotels in Playa (t 873 2505). Fare around $15.

Chetumal (*5hrs*) via **Tulum** (*1½hrs*): one ADO GL luxury service and at least nine regular first-class buses daily from Estación Alterna; 11 Riviera (1am–11.55pm), 13 Mayab *intermedios* (1.15am–10pm) and frequent Playa Express services from the old station. Riviera calls at main stops (**Tulum, Felipe Carrillo Puerto**); Mayab and Playa Express call anywhere en route, such as **Akumal** and **Bacalar**. First-class fare about $15, Mayab $12.

Mérida (*5hrs*): two ADO GL and 11 Super Espresso or ADO ordinary first-class services every day from the new terminal, 5.15am–midnight; fare around $21. Also two TRP second-class daily from the old station via **Tulum, Felipe Carrillo Puerto, Peto** and **Ticul** ($19).

Palenque (*11hrs*): three or four first-class buses daily from the new terminal, via **Tulum, Chetumal** and **Escárcega**: Altos (3.30pm, Fri–Mon only 9.45pm); Cristóbal Colón (5pm); Maya de Oro (7pm). Altos and C. Colón also stop at **Ocosingo**, and the 3.30pm Altos bus, C. Colón and Maya de Oro all continue on to **San Cristóbal de Las Casas** (*16hrs*) and **Tuxtla Gutiérrez** (*20hrs*); the 9.45pm weekend Altos bus normally goes on from Palenque to **Comitán** and **Tapachula** (*23hrs*). Fares vary, as Altos is cheaper but more cramped: about $35–$45 Palenque, $44–$55 San Cristóbal.

Valladolid (*3hrs*) via **Tulum** and **Cobá** (*2hrs*): one Super Espresso first-class daily from the new station (5.30am), also one Riviera from the old station (7.30am). Fare about $10 Valladolid, $5 Cobá.

Xpuhil: one or more first-class daily, from the new station (usually 7.15pm). Fare about $19.

By Car or Bike

Playa now has three **petrol/gas stations**, one on Av. Juárez one block in from Highway 307 and two along the Highway on the north and south sides of town.

Car Hire

Prices are quite high, and there are fewer deals available than in Cancún or Mérida. A growing number of shops offer scooters and bikes for hire. Machines are newer than on Isla

Mujeres or Cozumel, but it's still wise to get there early for the best choice, and check the machines over (*see* p.163, p.176).

Easy Way, C/ 4, between Avenidas 5 and 10, **t** (998) 704 5757. Helpful local agency with well-maintained cars at better-than-usual rates, from $36 a day.

Happy Rentacar, Plaza Tucán, Av. 10, between Calles 12 and 14, **t** 873 1739, *happycar@ caribe.net.mx*. Local agency with good weekly rates: VWs from $30 a day, and Nissans with a/c from $55.

Localiza, Av. Juárez, between Av. 5 and 10, **t** 873 0580. Generally has the best rates in the 'car-hire row' along Av. Juárez, from $35 a day. May be willing to negotiate rates, especially for longer-term rentals, and there are good drop-off facilities at Cancún airport.

Universal Motors, Av. 10, between Calles 12 and 14, **t** 879 3358. Bikes for hire at around $2 an hour or $10 for 24hrs; scooters for around $38 a day, or $200 for a full week. They also offer group scooter tours of local *cenotes*.

By Taxi

The main taxi rank is opposite the old bus station on Av. Juárez. Playa's taxi drivers will take passengers anywhere along the Riviera, but have a terrible reputation for making up rates as they go along (unusually, the official rates are scarcely ever posted up). Within town taxis should cost about $1.50, Playa to Cancún airport or down to Tulum about $30–$40 (280–360 pesos), but be prepared to negotiate and, as always, agree the price first.

Getting to Cozumel

The Cozumel ferry dock also runs off the plaza, in the opposite corner to the bus station. There are boats roughly every hour, daily, *see* 'Cozumel', p.176.

Orientation

The grid geography of Playa del Carmen is simple, even though street identification (away from the centre there are few number signs at street corners) may not be. **Av. Juárez**, the main street in from Highway 307, runs straight in to the main **plaza**, next to the beach. North from the landward side of the plaza runs the **Quinta Avenida** (Av. 5), the main drag. Streets parallel to the Quinta are called Avenues and confusingly numbered by fives: Av. 10, 15, 20, etc. Cross-streets are even-numbered north of Av. Juárez – C/ 2, 4, 6 – and odd-numbered to the south. **Avenida 30** is the main cross-street between the Quinta and the highway.

Tourist Information

Playa del Carmen t (984–)

Playa's main free magazine is simply called *Playa del Carmen*, and is available at the tourist office as well as in many shops and restaurants around town.

Tourist Office: Playa's official tourist office is in the old town hall on Av. Juárez, corner of Av. 15 (*open Mon–Sat 9–9, Sun 9–5*). Along Av. 5 there are several independent 'tourist offices', but their main aim is to sell tour tickets and/or timeshares.

Banks: Most banks are on or near Av. Juárez, between Av. 5 and Av. 30. Only Banamex (between Av. 20 and 25) normally changes money in the afternoons or on Sat mornings, but all have ATM machines. There are also plenty of *cambio* offices (*open daily*).

Health: An **emergency medical service** is run by Dr Víctor Macías (who speaks English) at Av. 35 between Calles 2 and 4, **t** 873 0493. There are also plenty of **pharmacies**, and Farmacia Betty's, Av. 15 between Calles 4 and 6, is open 24hrs.

Internet Access: There are plenty of Internet shops, although they tend to be pricey: two with good rates are the unnamed shop on Av. 30, corner of C/ 2, and **Internet Point**, C/ 12, between Av. 5 and 10.

Laundry: There is a good, unnamed laundry on C/ 4, between Av. 10 and Av. 15.

Phone Office: The one at the corner of Juárez and Av. 25 usually offers the best prices.

Police: The main police station is in the old town hall, on Av. Juárez and Av. 15. Playa's growth has attracted petty crime: watch out for pickpockets and bag thefts, especially around the old bus station, and do not leave bags on the back of chairs or on the ground out of sight. Robberies have also occurred from lockers in some of the backpacker hostels. Take care when you leave anything on the beach when swimming, especially along the north section of the beach beyond the Porto Real hotel.

Post Office: Av. Juárez between Av. 15 and 20 (*open Mon–Fri 8–5, Sat 9–1*). Has Mexpost.

Shopping

Playa has plenty of places offering **Mexican handicrafts**, but many are not of a standard to justify the prices. **Telart**, Av. Juárez 105, by the plaza, has some good original textiles, and **La Calaca**, with two shops on Av. 5 between Calles 6 and 8 and at C/ 4, has colourful masks, ceramics and other craftwork. Recently the Quinta has acquired a swathe of stores offering Mexican silver and amber jewellery, but there's little to choose between them.

For general **food shopping**, there's a San Francisco de Asis **supermarket** on Av. 30 at C/ 14. Also, Playa still has its share of cranky little shops around the back streets. One of the most handy is the **Licorería El Campeón**, at Av. 10 and C/ 4, which seems to be open at any hour of the day or night, which is also a general supermarket.

Sports and Activities

Diving, Snorkelling and Fishing

Playa is one of the best **diving** centres on the mainland, with several operators who run trips to the local reefs, most of whom also offer cavern dives, night dives, etc. Costs are a bit higher than on the islands, although as usual there are good value packages for several days' diving. Introductory resort courses cost from about $65, two-tank dives from about $60 and night dives from around $50. With a **snorkel**, you can just walk up to Chunzubul and launch into the water, but for a better view operators such as Phocea, Tank-Ha and several others offer snorkel trips to the nearby reefs or Xpu-Ha (around $20–25 a day, refreshments included). Snorkels can be hired from Tank-Ha and some other operators.

Fishing trips can be arranged with Aqua Venturas and several specialist operators, for deep-sea fishing off Cozumel or bonefishing in the Sian Ka'an area.

Aqua Venturas, Av. 5, by C/ 2, **t** 873 0969. Respected local dive operator offering a wide range of dives, snorkelling and also fishing trips.

Club Naútico Tarraya, C/ 2, by the beach, **t** 873 2040, *www.tarraya.com.mx*. Arranges fishing charters with experienced captains. Sailfish are a speciality.

Phocea Caribe, Hotel Colibrí, Av. 1 between Calles 10 and 12, **t/f** 873 1024/873 1210, *www.phoceacaribedive.com*. Small, highly recommended dive operation run by dive master Henri Pérez and offering a complete range of dives. Clients receive personal attention from friendly dive-masters, and Henri is a very expert, able teacher.

Tank-Ha Dive Center, Av. 5, between Calles 8 and 10, **t** 873 0302, *www.tankha.com*. One of the longest-running operations, very well-equipped and offering a complete range of dives and instruction. It has international staff, so that courses can be taught in over seven languages.

Yucatek Divers, Av. 15, between Calles 2 and 4, **t** 803 1363, *www.yucatek-divers.com*. Highly regarded dive operator with international staff offering reef dives, courses and snorkel trips as well as a special programme for disabled divers. They have a branch at **Casa Tucán** hotel (*see* below), where accommodation packages can be arranged.

Golf

Playacar golf course, t 873 0624. Has 18 holes and every other facility. Green fees begin at around $65. *Open daily 6.30–6.*

Skydiving

Sky Dive Playa, just by the entrance to Playacar from the plaza, **t** 873 0192, *www.skydive .com.mx*. Plummet on to Playa from a great height; novices make a freefall 'tandem dive' on the back of a certified instructor.

Where to Stay

Playa del Carmen t (984–)

Prices – particularly for *moderate–luxury* hotels – tend to go down a good deal outside the mid-Dec–April and (sometimes) July–Aug seasons. The big resort hotels in Playacar

(Continental Plaza, Reef Club and others) are generally run on an all-inclusive basis, and best booked as part of an agency package. Details of several more individual, independent hotels around Playa can be found on the Turquoise Reef Group website (*www.mexicoholiday.com*).

Luxury–Expensive

Baal Nah Kah, C/ 12, between Av. 1 and 5, **t** 873 0040, *www.cancunsouth.com/baalnahkah*, or through the Turquoise Reef Group (*see* p.139). Has one of the most friendly atmospheres in Playa, in a big house full of traditional Mexican textiles, run on a B&B basis. The five rooms are all charming but vary a lot in size and price (the smallest may be *inexpensive* off-peak). Minimum stay of three nights at busy times, but discounts for five nights plus. Other hotels have grown up around it, but it's still a pretty, relaxing place.

Blue Parrot Inn, Av. 5, by C/ 12, **t** 873 0083, *www.blueparrot.com*. Once a hub of old beach-bum-Playa, with its celebrated bar (*see* below), this began life as a set of basic *cabañas*, but is now a solid structure that offers a choice between 'studio rooms', the same with kitchenettes, and self-contained suites with kitchens and every other convenience. They still have *palapa* roofs, ocean views and a great beach location, but it can be noisy (because of the bar), so don't come if you're a determined party-pooper.

Chichan Baal Kah, C/ 16, between Av. 1 and 5, **t** 873 0110, or bookable through Turquoise Reef (*see* p.139). Very attractive, modern building with self-contained apartments with kitchens around a small pool. Furnished with traditional Mexican fittings, they're extremely pretty and comfortable, and breakfast, maid service, bicycle-use and many other extras are included. They're also very good value, especially off-peak.

Deseo, Av. 5, by C/ 12, **t** 879 3620, *www.hotel deseo.com*. In 2001 the internationally-lauded Mexico City design hotel Abita created this 'branch' in Playa, and so gave the town a real style hotel, much as you can find in Tokyo, London or New York. The trendy style is familiar – all minimalism, contrasting hard and soft surfaces, Japanese-ish dark woods – and some of its features are the kind that dazzles in magazines ahead of being practical (a pool deck so shadeless that it's virtually unusable), but if you seek post-millennium elegance there's really no other choice, and your fellow-guests will include some of Mexico's wealthiest, most fashion-conscious and best-maintained young bodies. Choose from standard rooms, balcony rooms or suites. Downstairs is Playa's trendiest bar, **Fly** (*see* below).

El Faro, C/ 10, **t** 873 0970, *www.hotelelfaro.com*. Small, striking and deliberately stylish, the 'Lighthouse' is made unmistakable by its white spiral-staired tower, which has never been a real lighthouse. The very tasteful rooms have every convenience and are set around a very lovely pool, looking out on to the beach; those with sea views (especially the lighthouse suite) are often spectacular (*all luxury*), but the smaller garden rooms (*expensive*) are less exciting. Very good deals in low season.

Mosquito Blue, Av. 5 and C/ 12, **t** 873 1245, *www.mosquitoblue.com*. Just as cool as the Faro in its way, with a pool, terrace bar and garden patio that together make up a *tour-de-force* of beachfront chic. The very stylish and well-equipped rooms are divided between 'standard' rooms and suites. It's aimed at couples (no children). Prices often drop off-peak.

Las Palapas, C/ 34, **t** 873 0584, *www.cancun .com/hotels/laspalapas*. By the beach to the north of town there are two 'hotel-villages' that combine the palm-roofed *palapa* idea with every luxury. Having arrived ahead of their neighbours, these boast the prime beach front locations, and have a style that the competition just can't match. Rooms are arranged in one- or two-storey palm-roofed villas, or in impressive *cabaña*-suites. The beach bar and pool are very pretty, all the required watersports are available, and the whole place has an enjoyably calming, welcoming atmosphere.

Shangri-La Caribe, **t** 873 0611, *www.shangri-la.com.mx*, or through Turquoise Reef (*see* p.139). Just north of Las Palapas (and a bit more expensive), this also opened when there was still open country between Chunzubul and Playa town, and offers the most stylish cabins on one of the best beaches. It consists of 70 upscale *cabañas*, divided into 'Playa' and 'Caribe' sections (Playa rooms are best). They vary a lot in size and view, and so in price: the beachfront cabins are really lovely, and the penthouses completely seductive (30P is the real tops). Breakfast and dinner are included, and there's a suitably attractive pool, an on-site dive shop and so on.

Moderate

Hotel Acuario, Av. 25, between Calles 2 and 4, t 873 2133, *www.elacuariohotel.com*. Though small and some way from the beach, this has a welcoming, homey atmosphere. The rooms, around a garden with a small pool, are very pretty, and three have kitchenettes. Off-season prices *inexpensive*, with lower weekly or monthly rates.

Hotel Corto Maltés, C/ 10, by the beach, t 873 0206, *www.cortomaltes.com*. Announcing itself as 'the last of old Playa', this enclosure on the sand has *cabañas* with a beach-comberish air, so that the comfortable, Mexican-traditional fittings and showers inside come as a surprise. Each has a terrace with hammock and the place has a mellow feel. Has its own boat and kayaks and runs snorkelling trips for guests.

Posada Las Iguanas, Av. Constituyentes, by Av. 1, t 873 2170, *www.posadalasiguanas.com*. Another survivor of 'old Playa', with many devoted customers, easily identifiable by its jokey iguana mural up one wall, Las Iguanas has kept its mellow feel. The two-storey hotel stands in an unkempt garden full of trees, and rooms (recently done up) are simple but cosy, with hammock-space outside each one (the top floor rooms are especially nice).

Villa del Sol, Av. 15, between Calles 12 and 14, t 873 1144, *www.villadelsol.de*. Friendly little rustic hotel, with pretty, comfortable rooms and a self-contained cottage for 4–5 people that's a spectacular bargain, set in a leafy garden to create a suitably laid-back feel.

Inexpensive–Cheap–Camping

Cabañas La Ruina, C/ 2, between Av. 5 and the beach, t 873 0405. A survivor from Playa's wild days, astonishingly holding on to its prime site not so much next to as actually on the beach amid all the surrounding development. A cross between a *cabaña* hotel, camp site and collective sleeping space, it offers several options: rustic *cabañas* with showers (*inexpensive*); *cabañas* without bath (*cheap*), or camping/hammock space and a locker under big, gregarious, mixed-sex *palapas* ($5–$6 per person). Not great for privacy, but you couldn't be closer to the beach, and there's **Café Sofía** alongside for breakfast. What's more, it has its own little Mayan ruin in the grounds.

Casa de las Flores, Av. 20, between Calles 4 and 6, t 873 2898, *www.hotelcasadelasflores.com*. In a quieter part of Playa with a friendly owner, spacious, airy rooms with Mexican-rustic décor and good facilities, at good value prices.

Casa Tucán, C/ 4, between Av. 10 and 15, t 873 0283, *www.casatucan.de*. One of the best-value options in central Playa; Rooms (*inexpensive*) are bright, pretty and spacious and there are three apartments (*moderate*) with kitchenettes. Deceptively small-looking, inside it contains a lovely garden and pool, and runs Spanish-language courses in a room on the roof. Also has good facilities for divers, and is used by the **Yucatek Divers** dive school (*see above*).

Hostel El Palomar, Av. 5, between Av. Juárez and C/ 2, t 873 0316, *hostelelpalomar@ myrealbox.com*. Private hostel aimed at backpackers; it has beds in dorms, with lockers (*cheap*) or simple rooms with shared showers (*inexpensive*, negotiable off-peak). It's airy and brightly painted, but the area is noisy, and the staff seem smart-alecky.

Hotel Hul-Ku, Av. 20, between Calles 4 and 6, t 873 0021, *kantunchi@hotmail.com*. Relaxing, excellent value hotel run with slightly old-fashioned and un-Playa-ish slow-moving charm by the same family who have set up the Cenote Kantun-chi park (*see* p.203). Bigger than it looks, with well-kept rooms and features that you often don't get at this level (fridges and kitchenettes in many rooms, TVs, balconies overlooking the garden) and a small pool and **restaurant**. Good discounts for longer stays.

Hotel Maya Bric, Av. 5, between Calles 8 and 10, t 873 2041, *mayabric@playa.com.mx*. Popular, long-running hotel, recognizable by its ersatz 'Mayan Arch' entrance (and the Diesel fashion store). It has light, white rooms and a small but welcome pool in its garden, and all rooms have two beds, bathrooms and fans, while some have full a/c.

Mom's Hotel, Av. 30, by C/ 4, t 873 0315, *www.momshotel.com*. A first-choice hotel, the kind of place people come back to, and a friendly home-from-home. As well as comfortable, characterful rooms (a/c or fan-only), it has a tiny pool and a terrace bar (which sometimes has food). The bar's a great place to meet people, and you may be able to arrange sailing or snorkelling trips and excursions to *cenotes* and other less conventional locations.

Posada Melissa, Av. Juárez, on the plaza, t 873 0485. One of Playa's eccentric survivors, a little hotel with simple but well looked-after double rooms, with fans and showers, half-hidden among all the shops and right on the town plaza, but still with very low prices. Ask for a top-floor room, with a sea view.

Posada Mariposa, Av. 5, between Calles 24 and 26, t 873 3886, *www.posadamariposa.com*. A new, Italian-owned *abobe*-style inn in north Playa with fairly attractive rooms and six suites, in a three-storey building around a leafy patio with a little **café**: most rooms, some with a/c, are *inexpensive*, but the best are the suites, with kitchenettes, balconies and (until they build something in front) a sea view (borderline *moderate*).

Posada Sian Ka'an, Av. 5, by C/ 2, t 873 0202, *jaguar@playa.com.mx*. A big, white, beach-comber-style house with pleasant rooms in the main block and more in *palapa*-roofed cabins spread around a garden, all with bathrooms, and terraces or balconies on which to sling a hammock and listen to the waves breaking a few yards away. Rooms (fan-only or a/c) vary in size and price, and there are also two self-catering rooms available, with kitchenettes (*moderate*).

Urban Hostel, Av 10, between Calles 4 and 6, t 879 9342, *urbanhostel@yahoo.com*. Of the backpacking-as-refugee-experience school of budget accommodation, in a shed-like building with a huge *palapa* roof. Bunk beds are very close together, in separate sections for men and women divided by a curtain. Showers, toilets, lockers and so on are quite well-maintained, but prices are steep for these conditions: $10 in high season, basic breakfast included. Included here as a warning, not a recommendation.

Apartment and House Rentals

With all the building there are always places available to rent. Many more services also advertise on the Internet.

Oasis del Caribe, Av. Juárez, by Av. 40, t 873 0060. Apartment complex offering short-term lets.

Siete Aluxes Too, Av. 30, between Calles 20 and 25, t 873 0637, *aluxes@playa.com.mx*. Agency handling rental villas and apartments of all sizes around the town.

Eating Out

Playa's restaurants multiply as fast as its hotels, and offer a more international range of food than anywhere else on the coast. The Quinta contains a line of cafés and restaurants, most with tables in front from where you can watch everyone else go by, and as you go further from the plaza more of them are contained within deep-green gardens. The town's hustling atmosphere, though, means that service along the main drag is sometimes irritatingly pushy.

Expensive

Ambasciata d'Italia, Av. 5, by C/ 12 (no phone). Playa's popularity among Italians means it has several genuinely Italian restaurants. This pretty place has Bologna-based cooking, and better service than most.

La Casa del Agua, Av. 5, by C/ 2. Rather incongruously placed a few steps away from a giant fast-food outlet, this 'café-restaurant-art gallery' occupies a large, airy and distinctly elegant balcony up above (and so slightly removed from) the bustle of the Quinta. It offers refined versions of Mexican cuisine and some international dishes.

Tierra, Av. 5, by C/ 12, t 873 1245. On the same corner as the Deseo hotel and its very hip bar, **Fly**, this stylish restaurant offers a fashionably eclectic 'Mediterranean-Mexican' genre of cooking, presented in a coolly comfortable setting.

Moderate

Café Sofía, C/ 2, by the beach. Long-running, and one of the liveliest cafés in Playa. Good for bargain breakfasts, lobster and juices, and open late.

Coffee Press C/ 2, by Av. 5. American-style coffee house with some of the best coffee in town – espressos, lattes and so on – plus snacks. Very popular.

Karen's Grill and Pizzas, Av. 5, between Calles 2 and 4. Usually-friendly pavement café with Mexican-Italian-American food.

Media Luna, Av. 5, between Calles 12 and 14. Once hippyish, now smart and trendy-looking terrace café with decent, eclectic menus – light salads and pastas, and larger dishes combining Mediterranean and Pacific flavours with local ingredients – including vegetarian and health-food options. Service, once friendly, has become much more anonymous of late.

100% Natural, Av. 5, between Calles 10 and 12. Playa branch of the local health-food chain (*see* p.155), with great juices, sandwiches and light meals, on a lovely garden terrace.

El Sabor, Av. 5 between Calles 2 and 4. Relatively small pavement terrace standing out among the over-priced mediocrity of much Playa catering for food, value and unaggressive service. Highlights are its seafood dishes and better-than-usual vegetarian choice, and you can eat very cheaply if you don't want too much.

La Vagabunda, Av. 5, between Calles 24 and 26. Pleasant, modern breakfast, lunch and juice bar a block back from the beach. *Closed eves.*

Cheap

For a really budget meal, head away from the tourist route; **Calle 4** between Avenidas 5 and 15, in particular, contains several good value small restaurants.

Cafetería Danae, Av. Juárez, between Av. 20 and 25. Café-hut with excellent breakfasts and great juices.

Restaurant-Coctelería Las Brisas, C/ 4, between Av. 5 and 10. A great find; a big terrace-restaurant, plain and simple in style but with excellent fresh local seafood – especially the *ceviches* and cocktails – at non-Playa prices. Much appreciated by locals and any foreigners who discover it.

Tacos y Quesos el Sarape, Av. Juárez, between Av. 20 and 25. Classic, hot terrace-*taquería* with the fiery classic Mexican snacks.

Entertainment and Nightlife

The **Pez Vela** and some other places at the junction of Av. 5 and C/ 2 have live rock bands each evening, often chugging away at the inescapable Bob Marley covers, and many restaurants have *mariachis* or other music. Traditionally, though, there has been the **Blue Parrot**, the Blue Parrot, and the Blue Parrot, once lauded as 'among the world's best beach bars'. With Playa now so big the scene is more diffuse, but the Blue Parrot (bottom of C/ 12) still holds its own: it's an obvious place to start an evening, there's always a crowd, and there's a great view of the moon over the beach. Later the crowds move on to Playa's club scene, also mainly concentrated towards the beach.

Apasionado, Av 5, by C/ 12 bis. A few steps from Fly is this 'jazz bar-restaurant', above the street beneath a huge *palapa*, with live jazz and Latin music.

Calypso, C/ 6, between Av. 10 and 15. A walk away from the beach, this is the favourite club in Playa for salsa and Latin fans, with frequent live bands.

Capitán Tutix, C/ 4, on the beach. Ever-popular place to call in post-Parrot, a club in a giant beach *palapa*. Far less trendy than Fly, but wilder. The music covers a wide, dance-to-Latin-to-mainstream pop range, and there are also live bands, fire-eating, party nights and other specials.

Fly, Deseo hotel, Av. 5, by C/ 12. If **Deseo** (*see* above) has brought a new hipness to Playa hotels, its big terrace bar has also become by far the trendiest mingling spot in town, with international club music blasting across the street. Food is available, but extravagant cocktails look to be much more popular. Budget travellers note: this is also probably the most expensive bar in town.

Starzz, Av. 5, on the plaza. The non-chic alternative: a big, rumbustious rooftop disco overlooking the old square, popular with locals, which hosts a big range of events (live acts, salsa nights...).

artesanía and dive shops. This is a story of the 1990s, for the transformation really took off with the Playacar development in 1991. Since then, Playa has been through several identities: backpacker beach hangout ('95); internationally hip and trendy mingling spot ('97); nowadays, since an all-new building boom took off in '99, it's going full-throttle to become the Benidorm of the Caribbean. Local brochures still peddle the line that Playa is somehow more sophisticated and has a more relaxed, small-town feel than Cancún, but its concentrated size can actually make its main drags just feel more hassled and intense.

Playa del Carmen still has its assets. It can be strolled around in a way that the Cancún hotel strip can never be, and this gives it an intimate bar and beach life that makes it easy to run into people. The pace of its transformations has been such that traces of earlier eras have been left behind, from mellow backpackers' *cabañas* still gripping on to their prime beach spots to elegant small style hotels. Its range of hotels and easy-to-locate dive shops, markets and other services still makes it a convenient base for travelling round the region. And as a party town Playa is a lot hipper than Cancún, and far livelier than Cozumel; the beaches and the deep-turquoise sea are still fabulous, especially if you walk half an hour or so to the north. So long as you don't get sick of hearing 'boy, it wasn't like this when I was here 2/5/8/10 years ago...'

The Town

Contained within the plaza there's a testimony to Playa's former size that can't help but amaze: its original church, a tiny white chapel that often overflows on Sunday mornings. Leading away from the square is the main people-watching drag of Quinta Avenida, with Italian restaurants and American-style coffee shops as well as *taco*-stands, and high-fashion beachwear stores amid the Mexican souvenir junk. All along it streets run down to the beach.

From the main town beach by the plaza, the view is cut off by the bizarre bulk of the Hotel Porto Real, at the seaward end of Av. Constituyentes. The area behind the beach north of here is where hotel construction is currently proceeding at the most feverish pace (so that you can find the familiar 1980s Spanish phenomenon, of one pretty hotel being finished while on the next lot drills and diggers chug away most of the day). There is another hitch in that unless you just walk along the sand from the town, the only places where you can easily get down to the beach are 'beach clubs' such as Playa Tukan, Mamita's and others at the bottom of Calle 28, with bars, restaurants, loungers and so on. Continue on along the beach past the much more striking Shangri-La and Las Palapas hotels and you'll reach the main topless beaches and Playa's favourite spot for snorkelling, **Chunzubul**, where the reef comes close inshore. More white beaches stretch away to the north; the further you walk, the fewer people you'll have to share them with (but it's still a good idea to be wary of leaving things unattended on the beach, see pp.193–4). Parts of this beach also offer very little shade for anyone who's not a serious sun-worshipper.

Back in town, along C/ Juárez and Av. 30 you can find the *taco* stands, *abarrote* stores and fruit shops of any Mexican town. In the streets nearby the new city of

Playa is also finally being 'consolidated', as Mexican official terminology puts it, after years of getting by: a rather imposing neo-Mayan town hall has appeared, there's a family-size new church, and since 2000 Playa has acquired all of two new bus termi-nals. Eight blocks from C/ Juárez, Av. 30 meets Av. Constituyentes, which in 1995 was pretty much the northern limit of Playa, but which now has over 50 blocks stretching away beyond it on the map. In these blocks a still-ragged, tough-edged new city is being created, as people build their own houses, badger the local authorities into laying on services, open up corner stores, *loncherías* and car-repair shops and carve out little corners of domestic comfort such as patios ringed with flowers.

Head south from the town plaza and you see a completely different side to Playa del Carmen. From the square a walkway leads directly into the eerily perfect avenues of **Playacar**, an enormous development of quiet, winding streets lined with clipped hedges and neat flowerbeds, an alien world like some Caribbean Bournemouth. Along the streets there are luxury houses and condominiums, and on the three kilometres of narrow beach there are five giant resort hotels, while at its centre is a champi-onship-standard golf course.

Playacar also contains an **Aviario** or aviary (*open Mon–Fri 9–5; adm*), with the region's bird species (and a lot of mosquitoes) in a well-created natural setting. To find it, follow the main road into Playacar (Av. 10), and head left at the first roundabout/ traffic circle. Scattered around the development there are also, rather bizarrely, the Mayan ruins of **Xaman-Ha**, a series of small Postclassic temples of a similar style to those at El Rey or Tulum. They were some of the first Mayan buildings to be seen by the Spaniards, as Grijalva used them as a navigational marker in his exploration of the Yucatán coast in 1518. Today they have been landscaped into Playacar, so that access is free.

Xcaret

About six kilometres south of Playa del Carmen is one of the Riviera's most visited attractions, the 'eco-archaeological' theme park of Xcaret. It is centred on one of the natural coastal lagoons, around which a large area has been landscaped into areas representing different elements of the local environment. Within the park there are also a few remains of the Postclassic Mayan port of **Polé**, once the main departure point for pilgrims to Cozumel. Some environmentalists detest Xcaret as a profanation of a natural beauty spot, but from the visitor's point of view the main sections of Xcaret are undeniably impressive, providing a unique, easy – and, on first experience, overwhelming – opportunity to see the sheer richness of a tropical environment. It's very well organized and well geared to families; prices are high, but it seeks to provide a complete day out, and offers lots to do.

Beyond the entrance is a small **museum** of Mayan archaeology but many people head straight for the partly underground '**snorkelling river**' that winds through the park to come out by the beach. It's one of the more controversial parts of the project, as a natural underground river was blasted and remodelled to create the required effect, but it does provide a very safe environment for kids and snorkelling novices. Equally controversial (and popular) is the **dolphin enclosure** in the lagoon, where visitors may swim with the animals. Only small numbers are allowed in at a time, and each day's slots are often booked by 10am; however, some visitors have complained that the dolphins are still 'over-used' and in poor health.

Other parts of Xcaret include a fine **aviary**, a dense **botanical garden**, **jaguar** and **puma** 'islands' and an **aquarium** and **turtle-breeding farm**. There's loads of information available in both Spanish and English, if you take the time to read it. Perhaps most impressive of all is the *mariposario* (butterfly garden), claimed to be the largest in the world. Among the park's kitschier features is a fake 'Mayan village'. Every evening except Sunday the day ends with a showbiz spectacular that begins with some 'ancient Mayan' rites, moves on to a *charrería* cowboy show and ends in a (pretty long) tutti-frutti of Mexican music, dances and traditions.

The Southern Riviera

South of Playa del Carmen the road rolls on through the green scrub, lined by a palisade of giant billboards held up on poles in the sky, past more entrances to the beach. About 17 kilometres from Playa another coastward sign indicates the track to **Paamul**, a small bay with one of the best beaches on the coast. Its main occupant is a big *cabañas*, camping and RV site – the largest on the Riviera – but even the big RVs are fairly discreet, tucked away under *palapas*, and they don't dominate the view of palms and curving sand. It's a breeding spot for turtles in July and August.

For a complete contrast, from there it's another couple of kilometres to the largest heavy-duty tourist development in the area after Cancún, **Puerto Aventuras**. Created from nothing, it's a collection of hotels, shops and condos in Mediterranean holiday-village style, centred around a purpose-built yachting marina with beaches on either side. It's based on the unspoken principle that you can sell anything you build, but there's something about this 'Venice on the Caribbean' (as the brochure says) that suggests that the calculations of Riviera developers might not quite add up; it's never quite full. Besides a lavish tennis centre and the obligatory golf course, a wide range of activities is available – ultralight-flying, and, a major speciality, fishing charters – and in the marina there are some tame dolphins, and even some manatees.

Tourist Information

Akumal t (984–)

Tourist Information: Akumal has a free magazine, *Info-Akumal*, and a local website, *www.info-akumal.com*.

Internet Access: In the TSA travel agency, next to the Centro Ecológico.

Post Office: In the middle of Akumal village.

Sports and Activities

Diving, Snorkelling and Fishing

There are dive shops by nearly all the (open) beaches on this stretch of coast, and this is also the prime area for cave diving in *cenotes* (*see* p.206).

Aquatech-Villas de Rosa hotel, Akumal (*see* p.206). The foremost cave diving specialist in the area, also offering open water diving.

Captain Rick's Sportfishing, lobby of Omni Hotel, Puerto Aventuras, t 873 5195. Four different sport-fishing and sightseeing trips available, on a day- or half-day basis. User-friendly, but very pricey.

Dive Center Akumal, to the right of Akumal beach, t 875 9025, *www.akumaldive center.com*. Well-regarded dive operation. Instruction, open-water and cave diving, snorkelling and fishing trips.

Dive shop (unnamed), on the X-7 track at Xpu-Ha. Diving, snorkelling or fishing trips at low prices.

ScubaMex Dive Shop, on the beach, in Paamul village, t 873 0667, *www.scubamex.com*. Long-established dive operation; it's also possible to arrange accommodation in a house nearby for clients.

Tankah Dive Inn, Tankah. The hotel has in-house dive masters.

Turtle Tours

Centro Ecológico Akumal, t 875 9091, *cea94@ caribe.net.mx*. Runs turtle tours of Akumal beach on most nights for up to ten people, for around $8 per person (bring your own torch and camera). Other tours such as night snorkelling, jungle walks or bike rides and bird-watching can also be arranged. Another locally-based conservation organization is SAVE, based at the **Aquatech-Villas de Rosa** hotel (*www.cenotes.com/save*).

Where to Stay and Eat

Paamul t (984–)

Cabañas Paamul, t 875 1051, *paamulmx@ yahoo.com* (*moderate–cheap*). The best-equipped RV park on the Cancún–Tulum coast, with a pretty beach **bar-restaurant**, a laundry and the ScubaMex dive shop alongside (*see* above). RV spots cost about $18 a day, or $395 a month; longer term rates are available. Camping space is also available. There are also some comfortable *cabañas* (Dec–Easter *moderate*; otherwise *inexpensive*), all with good facilities, fans and their own terraces. And the RVs don't even spoil the view.

Puerto Aventuras t (984–)

Apartment rentals t 873 5110/873 5100, *www.puertoaventuras.com*. Studio and larger apartments are often available from around $550 a week, see website for details.

Xpu-Ha t (984–)

Bonanza Xpu-Ha, X-7 (no phone, *inexpensive*). Five simple rooms with showers – rather than *cabañas* – and RV or camping space for under $3 per person. It's still right on a

Xpu-Ha and Akumal

Anyone who travels independently nowadays can begin to feel distinctly unwelcome along stretches of the Riviera, as you pass one new bloated piece of theme-park architecture after another announcing another all-inclusive named El Dorado or Copacabana, each with a barrier across it to limit the inmates' visiting rights.

A case in point is **Xpu-Ha**, about 10 kilometres from Puerto Aventuras. With a line of fabulous beaches in small bays and some of the area's best reefs for diving and snorkelling, this is one of this coast's most beautiful places. However, of the seven beautiful beach, despite the encroachments of all-inclusives, the owners are friendly, there's a dive shop, and snorkelling and fishing trips can be arranged.

Hotel Villas del Caribe/Café del Mar, X-4, t 873 2194, *www.cafedelmarxpuha.com* (*inexpensive*). Mexican-owned beach hotel hanging in there slightly quixotically despite having the wall of the Copacabana all-inclusive looming behind it. As well as pleasant rooms in beach cabins or a main block, all with sea view, it has a beach bar and **restaurant**.

Akumal t (984–)

There are more apartment complexes than hotels, but many rooms with self-catering facilities are available at reasonable rates, and while prices are especially high around Christmas–New Year they drop off-season, above all April–Nov. Many short-term rents are available: **Akumal Real Estate**, t 875 9064, *www.info-akumal.com/real-estate*, is one central source of information.

Aquatech-Villas de Rosa, Aventuras Akumal, t 875 9020, *www.cenotes.com* (*expensive–moderate*, according to room size and season). While they are diving specialists (*see* p.206), Tony and Nancy de Rosa also run a very pleasant hotel that's popular with families and non-divers, with a great rooftop bar, pool and a beach almost to itself. It gives a choice of self-contained beach villas, apartments or rooms, with fine views.

Hacienda de la Tortuga, Media Luna bay, t 875 9068, *htortuga@prodigy.net.mx* (*expensive* Dec–Jan; *moderate–inexpensive* otherwise). A 'condo-hotel' in a wonderful location on the beach, with well-used but airy self-contained apartments combined with a pool and other hotel features and a pleasant Mexican **restaurant**.

Qué Onda, near the end of the North Akumal road towards Yal-Ku lagoon, t 875 9101, *www.queondaakumal.com* (*moderate*). Very relaxed, this is primarily a garden-patio **restaurant**, with a mostly-Italian, eclectic menu. It also has six very pretty, ultra-light rooms under palm roofs. Not actually on the beach, but only a short walk away.

Vista del Mar, near Media Luna beach, t 875 9060, *www.mexico-vacation.com* (*luxury–inexpensive*). Similar to La Tortuga, with pretty apartments and 'hotel suites', most with kitchens and all with great sea views. Rates vary enormously, and off-peak it's great value, especially for families.

Punta Solimán t (984–)

Oscar y Lalo (no phone, *moderate*). Very enjoyable, mellow **bar-restaurant** right on the beach, with great fresh seafood, and a camp site and RV park (*cheap*). Kayaks and snorkels are available for hire, and there are more *cenotes* nearby.

Tankah t (984–)

Casa *Cenote* (*moderate*). Surprisingly large and comfortable beachfront restaurant at the end of the road right by the Tankah Cenote itself.

Tankah Dive Inn, on the beach, t 874 2188, *www.tankahdiveinn.com* (*expensive–moderate*). Especially friendly, laid-back hotel, which has five big rooms with plenty of character and comfort, run by Texans Jimmy and Shaleh Clark. Diving and kayaking are specialities – there is nearly always a resident dive-master – but it's equally enjoyable if you want to laze around for a while, with a great bar and an above-average **restaurant**. Very good rates for weekly stays, families, dive packages, etc.

entrances to the beach off Highway 307, each strangely signed with an 'X', only two now remain open to public access (X-7 and to a lesser extent X-4), with independent hotels and camping spaces by the beach.

On the landward side of Highway 307 at Xpu-Ha there are three swimmable *cenotes*. The largest of these, **Cenote Kantun-Chi** (*open daily 7–6; adm*), down a track a kilometre off the road, is run as a low-key private 'nature park'. The centrepiece is the broad and lovely *cenote* itself, with snorkel gear for hire (but no food facilities), but you can rent horses or bikes, and there's a mini-zoo of local wildlife. Two pools just to the south, the **Cenote Cristalino** and **Cenote Azul** (*adm cheap*) have no extra facilities, but are still delicious for swimming, especially the Cristalino. The only drawback is the inescapable traffic noise from the Highway on the other side of the trees.

Akumal, 40 kilometres from Playa del Carmen and 105 kilometres from Cancún, is another condo-land like Puerto Aventuras, with beach-front apartments spread along several beautiful bays on a very gentle sea. However, in contrast to the Puerto there was a small community here before building began, and the new buildings are much more spread out, so that it feels less isolated and claustrophobic. Also, since more people live here throughout the year, it has more of a consistent life to it. Based on self-catering more than hotels, it's a peaceful, relaxing place to settle into for a while (note, though, that you need a car to get around).

The northernmost entrance – looking deceptively like a private driveway to the Casitas Akumal resort – leads to the main Akumal 'village', with a very pretty beach. Akumal means 'place of the turtles', and turtles still breed on several of the beaches in the summer months: a **Centro Ecológico Akumal** seeks to ensure their survival and encourage eco-respectful tourism. From the village's sand 'plaza', follow the road to the left for about one kilometre, around the arc of Media Luna bay, to reach the **Laguna Yal-Ku** (*open daily 8–5.30; adm*), one of the most beautiful of the coastal coral lagoons, with sufficient marine life to make it wonderful for snorkelling.

South of Akumal village there are more condos and a clutch of all-inclusives, among them the **Hacienda Santa Isabel**, sure winner of the Riviera all-time kitsch award, built to suggest a traditional *hacienda* but three times the size and in a riot of sugary colours. The Aventuras Akumal turn-off leads to another superb beach with condos and some smallish hotels, facing one of the richest of the inshore reefs on this coast. On the landward side of the Highway about two kilometres further south is **Aktun-Chen** (*open daily 8.30–5; adm exp*), a private nature park at the end of a dirt track (3.5km) through impressively unmolested jungle, created around one of the Yucatán's biggest caves and *cenote* systems (*not suitable for swimming*). The guided tours (in English) are highly informative, and as well as a spectacular range of birds there's a collection of local animal life, especially monkeys and wild boar.

A little beyond Akumal are **Chemuyil** and **Xcacel**, two places that are illustrative of the way in which the Riviera could develop. At the first there is for once a turning west, inland, signposted to Ciudad Chemuyil, where a new housing development is to be built for the Riviera's fetchers, carriers and cleaners, relieving some of the pressure on Playa del Carmen. **Xcacel** meanwhile is the most important turtle-breeding beach in the whole region, considered a site of worldwide scientific importance, and the place where, in 2001, Mexican authorities actually blocked the plans of Spanish hotel conglomerate Meliá to build one more mega-resort on the beach.

Xel-Ha

Information t (984) 875 4070; www.xelha.com.mx; open daily 8.30–6; adm exp.

After Akumal, signs promising 'Snorkel Heaven' announce that you're nearing another of the most popular places on the Riviera at **Xel-Ha**, an 'eco-park' run by the same organization as Xcaret. It was created around the largest of the coastal lagoons, a long inlet of turquoise-crystal water, coral and brilliantly coloured tropical fish. It gets crowded, and the accusation is frequently made that overexploitation is killing the lagoon off, but if you swim away from the main landing stages a little (which not many people do) it's still full of fish. It's a superb natural swimming pool and, like Xcaret, very user-friendly and child-safe. Snorkel hire is additional to the entrance fee. As well as the lagoon itself, the park contains some swimmable *cenotes*, a beach, a forest trail, some Mayan remains and a choice of restaurants. Get there early.

It was from here that the Adelantado Montejo first tried to conquer the Yucatán in 1527, founding a settlement called Salamanca de Xel-Ha, of which nothing remains. Across Highway 307 from the park entrance, though, are the ruins of the Mayan city of **Xel-Ha** (*open daily 8–5; adm, Sun adm free*). This was once the largest of the Mayan towns on the Quintana Roo coast, and has the longest record of continual settlement, from the Preclassic until the Conquest. It extended all the way out to the lagoon and the 'wharf group' of buildings, now within the park, from where traders and pilgrims set off along the coast or to Cozumel. Several areas have never been excavated.

It's a pleasant site among woods, and interesting even though most of its buildings are in a very poor state. The largest set of buildings, **Group B**, formed the main plaza. The largest parts of it were built in the Early Classic, after about AD 300, but additions were made right up to the end of the city's history. Another path further to the left leads to the most fascinating building at Xel-Ha, the **Casa de los Pájaros** (Structure 8b or 'House of Birds'). It's only a small ruin, but on one side there are two well-preserved mural panels in sienna and white of birds in flight, including some very clearly drawn parrots. Dating from the Early Classic, they are among the oldest Mayan murals in existence. On the other side of the building is a much fainter mural, with a checkerboard pattern around a figure of a man in an elaborate headdress. It shows strong central-Mexican influences, indicating that as early as 300–400 even a place as apparently remote as Xel-Ha had contacts extending over thousands of kilometres.

From the plaza itself, a path parallel to a Mayan *sacbé* leads west through the woods for nearly a kilometre to the much later **Jaguar Group**, mostly from the Late Postclassic after 1200. The most important temple, called the **Casa del Jaguar**, has some faint murals in blue, black and red, especially of the Diving God seen at Tulum.

Punta Solimán and Tankah

Around three kilometres after Xel-Ha there is another turning off the Highway, signposted to **Bahias de Punta Solimán**, where at the end of a dusty track there is a narrow but peacefully palm-lined beach, with a simple camp site and a likeable beach restaurant. A little further on, the last accessible beach before Tulum, at **Tankah** (difficult to turn into heading south), is indicated only by signs for the Casa Cenote restaurant and the Tankah Inn, and a small, scarcely excavated Mayan temple by the roadside. It's another long, curving beach, which has been acquiring a clutch of condos, houses and smallish hotels in the last few years. The best place to swim is by the Casa Cenote beach bar, where there's an impressively large, swimmable *cenote*.

Cenote-Swimming and Cave Diving

The area just inland from the lower Riviera has the largest concentration of explored *cenote* pools, cave systems and underground rivers in the Yucatán, with 57 known systems extending through 480 kilometres of water-filled caves. Naturally, this also makes it the region's – if not the world's – most important area for cave diving. *Cenotes* are among the Yucatán's most magical features (*see* p.84). Some of these are only accessible to divers, but others are easy to swim in or to explore with a snorkel. The further you go in, the more you'll see, but swimming in the deliciously fresh, crystal-clear water of the surface pools, with the sunlight filtered through towers of lush vegetation, is always a wonderful experience. *Cenotes* are mostly on *ejido* (*see* p.79) land, and an admission fee of $1–$2 is usually charged for swimming.

Cave Diving and Snorkelling Specialists

You can enjoy the entrance pools at *cenotes* like Tankah or Aktun-Ha entirely under your own steam, but to make the most of the experience and see any of the less accessible caverns it's good to go with a snorkel and a guide. Many operators offer snorkel tours – equipment provided, no experience necessary – and easy, low-cost tours can be booked at the **Weary Traveler** in Tulum (*see* p.209). Most dive operators also offer cave-diving trips, but those listed here are the best-prepared cave specialists which also offer snorkel tours. In order to try any cave dives, divers must already have open-water certification.

Aquatech-Villas de Rosa, Aventuras Akumal, **t** 875 9020, *www.cenotes.com*. These are the longest-running and most comprehensively equipped cave-diving specialists in the area. US owners Tony and Nancy de Rosa have been pioneers in opening up the local caverns, and are familiar with every one of them. They offer a complete range of open-sea, reef and cave diving courses and dive trips (from $55), snorkel tours (around $30), equipment rental and deep-sea fishing trips (from $100). They also have a very attractive hotel (*see* p.203), publish a newsletter called *Cenotes* and are prime movers in the SAVE conservation organization.

Aktun Dive Center, El Mesón, Tulum, **t** 871 2311, *www.aktundive.com*. By the Cobá turning in Tulum, offering a complete range of cave dives and instruction, open-water and reef diving, 'fun dives', cavern snorkel tours ($30)

and sightseeing boat tours of the local reefs. They also have an eight-room hotel and restaurant, **El Mesón** (rooms *inexpensive*) especially for clients.

Cenote Dive Center, on main street, opposite the bank, Tulum, **t** 871 2232, *www.cenote dive.com*. Owner Per Dovland and his colleagues are very highly qualified and well-equipped, and offer a complete range of cave dives (from $60) and cave diving instruction – for British/European as well as US certification – as well as accessible cave snorkel tours (from $30). They also offer reef and open-water diving at very reasonable rates ($35).

Hidden Worlds/Dos Ojos Dive Center, well signposted off Highway 307 south of Xel-Ha, **t** 877 8535, *www.hiddenworlds.com.mx*. Based at the Dos Ojos *cenote*, this is the operation run most like a conventional tourist attraction, but for the same reason offers some of the most accessible, good value tours. Non-divers can take the 'Tak-Be-Ha Snorkel Tour and Jungle Adventure' ($40 per person), a high-quality, 3½-hr tour with a 'junglemobile' ride through the forest and a forest walk between the caverns – with helpful guides and lots of birds and wildlife – as well as swimming and snorkelling through a stunning series of caverns. Divers can take introductory tours over a similar route, which descend into the 'stalactite forests' of the vast Bat and Dos Ojos caves and the channels that connect them (from $50). Reef diving and a full range of courses are also offered. All tours are run three times each day (at 9am, 11am and 1pm) and bookings are advisable but not essential.

There is a clutch of small, easily swimmable *cenotes* further north at **Xpu-Ha** (*see* p.202), but the most spectacular of all the Yucatán caverns is about two kilometres south of Xel-Ha: the *cenote* of **Dos Ojos**; at over 600 kilometres, it has for years been considered the longest underwater cave system in the world, until the recent discovery that the **Nohoch Nah Chich** (Great Bird House) cave nearby may be even bigger. Large sections of Dos Ojos and the adjacent **Murciélagos** ('bat') *cenote* are close to the surface and can be visited independently (*adm*), but if this is your first time here you'll get more out of it if you take one of the tours provided by the Hidden Worlds facility (*see* facing page). Just behind the beach at **Tankah** (by the Casa Cenote restaurant) there is a broad, open *cenote* that's great for easy swimming, with no problems of access. Three kilometres south of Tulum is the **Cenote Cristal** (which, though, can be dirtier and more bug-ridden than the best *cenotes*). There's a lovely *cenote* by the Sian Ka'an entrance lodge on the Tulum beach road (*see* p.218), but some of the best known accessible *cenotes* are on the Tulum–Cobá road. About three and a half kilometres north of Tulum is the **Gran Cenote** (*adm*), one of the best for casual swimmers and snorkellers, with an idyllically beautiful entrance, a wide open cavern with a collapsed roof surrounded by rock columns and exquisite flowers and plants. The large main pool runs into a wide, arching cavern where you can swim a long distance without need of scuba diving equipment, even as far as a second *cenote* entrance at the other end of the cave. Two more signposted *cenotes*, the **Cenote Sagrado** and the **Vaca-Ha**, are really only of interest to divers, but **Cenote Aktun-Ha** (*adm*), some four kilometres from the Gran Cenote, is another wonderfully tranquil, broad pool, with plenty of small fish, that leads into an extensive cave system. Divers often refer to it as the 'Carwash'. More *cenotes* are continually being opened up.

Tulum

We were amid the wildest scenery we had yet found in Yucatán; and, besides the deep and exciting interest of the ruins themselves, we had around us what we wanted at all the other places, the magnificence of nature.
John Lloyd Stephens on Tulum

The established Riviera-corridor comes to a spectacular end at Tulum. This is both the furthest point reached by most tour buses from Cancún, and the beginning of a less well-trodden Yucatán. Architecturally the city of Tulum is by no means the most distinguished of Mayan ruins, but its location is magnificent, on a clifftop above a dazzling sea, the only Mayan site with a beach. Below it, miles of shoreline stretch away to the south, lined with palms, dunes and beach *cabañas*, a magical place from which to count the birds and watch the sunrise.

At the beginning of the 20th century Tulum was under the control of followers of the Talking Cross (*see* p.71), and when Professor Sylvanus Morley came to investigate the ruins in 1914, he did so by boat from the island of Cozumel with an armed guard, and concluded that work could only begin when there was 'no danger of attack'. To

Getting Around

By Bus

The bus station is towards the south end of the Avenida in Tulum Pueblo, but some buses will let you off at the ruins themselves or the crossroads on request (ask the driver for *las ruinas* or El Crucero).

Cancún (*2½hrs*) via **Playa del Carmen** and **Puerto Morelos**: three ADO GL luxury services, nine regular first-class, at least nine Riviera (10am–11pm), more frequent Mayab (hourly, from 7.30am) *intermedio* buses and Playa Express second-class approximately every hour, daily. Mayab and second-class will stop at all points en route. Fares around $3 Playa, $6 Cancún.

Chetumal (*4hrs*) via **Felipe Carrillo Puerto**: three ADO GL luxury services, nine regular first-class and around 20 *intermedio* and second-class buses daily. *Intermedios* and second-class also stop at **Bacalar**. Fare to Chetumal around $13.

Cobá and **Valladolid**: one or two Super Espresso first-class daily, continuing on to **Mérida** ($15), plus usually three Mayab buses terminating in Valladolid, and one Riviera service (8.30am) which also goes on to **Chichén-Itzá**. Fares to Cobá around $2.50, to Chichén $8.

Mérida via **Felipe Carrillo Puerto**, **Peto** and **Ticul**: seven second-class buses daily. Fare around $14.

Mexico City (*25hrs*): one ADO first-class daily (1.10pm). Fare $89.

Palenque (*10hrs*): three or four first-class buses daily, via **Chetumal** and **Escárcega**: Altos (4.15pm, and Mon–Fri only 10.45pm); Cristóbal Colón (6pm); Maya de Oro (8pm). Altos and C. Colón also stop at **Ocosingo**, and the 4.30pm Altos bus, C. Colón and Maya de Oro all continue to **San Cristóbal de Las Casas** (*15hrs*) and **Tuxtla Gutiérrez** (*19hrs*). The 10.45pm Altos bus normally continues from Palenque to **Comitán** and **Tapachula** (*22hrs*). Fares vary, as Altos is cheaper, but less comfortable: the range is about $30–$40 Palenque, $40–$50 San Cristóbal.

Villahermosa: two ADO first-class daily, fare around $39.

Xpuhil: one ADO first-class daily stops there (1.10pm). Fare about $18.

By Car, Bike and Taxi

Tulum has plenty of **taxis**, which will take you between the Pueblo and anywhere on the beach for about $2–$3. There is no *combi* service between the Pueblo and the beach, so that if you're staying by the beach without your own transport you're pretty dependent on the cabs. People often hitchhike between the village and the beach road, but this is not a way of getting anywhere fast.

Car Hire

Car hire has been slow to develop, but more agencies have been opening up. Alternatively, a **motor scooter** or a **bike** are just as handy.

Ana y José Car Rental, Tulum Pueblo, two blocks north of the bus station, t 871 2477, *www.tulumresorts.com.mx*. Run by the same people as Ana y José's hotel (*see* below). Well-maintained cars at decent rates for the area (VWs from $40 a day, Nissans from $60); prices negotiable for longer rentals.

La Estación, by the bus station. Well-used bikes from around $6 a day, or much less for a few days. Get there early to have the best choice, and check bikes over when you hire.

Maya Motos/Los Cocos Locos Scooter Rental, to the north of the Pueblo by the post office, t 877 7529. Motor scooters from around $30 a day; bicycles from $4 a day, but prices are 'always negotiable'.

Nohoch Tunich, Beach road, Km3.5. Outside the Nohoch Tunich hotel (*see* below) there are bikes for rent, for around $6.50 a day, with discounts for longer rents.

Playa Mambo Car Rental, opposite the bus terminal, t 871 2030. About the cheapest car hire shop, with a small stock of well-used VWs from $35 a day, or less at slack times.

Orientation

There are two parts to Tulum. Driving from the north you first meet the smartly landscaped entrance to the ruins, on the left. Just beyond it by the **petrol station** there is a crossroads, called El Crucero. The road to the right leads to Cobá, while a turn left will take you to the beach, the *cabañas* – spread over a long distance – and the road to Punta Allen. The village, Tulum Pueblo, now straggles all the way along 2km of Highway 307. Being the one main street, it is called Av. Tulum within the village; cross-streets across it now have rather fancy names (planets, Greek letters), but as they're little used it's more practical to orient yourself by landmarks along the Avenida.

Tourist Information

Tulum t (984–)

As Tulum has developed into a major back-packer destination, bag thefts, break-ins into *cabañas* and so on have also become more common. Be especially careful in the cheapest beach *cabañas* and, to a lesser extent, in the Pueblo; in more expensive beach places theft-incidence is much less. The **police station** is in the same block as the bank and the town hall in the Pueblo, but it may be just as useful to turn to the Weary Traveler for advice.

Tulum Pueblo

Tulum's free magazine, distributed in the usual hotels, restaurants, etc., is *Info.Tulum* (*www.info.tulum.com*), and an essential resource is the free **map** produced by the Weary Traveler. Several hotels and *cabañas* have a joint website at *www.hotelstulum.com*. Near the north end of Av. Tulum is **Sian Ka'an Tours**, running tours of the reserve (*see* p.217).
Banks: The town has a full-service bank (Bital), with ATM, by the town hall a block north of the bus station. There are three more ATM cashpoints on Av. Tulum; one is by the bus station. There are **money exchange offices** at the Acuario hotel by the Crucero (Tulum Pueblo) and by the Nohoch Tunich *cabañas* (on the beach) which tend to give poor rates.
Health: There is a **pharmacy** in the shop at the Hotel Maya, opposite the bus station.
Laundry: Lavandería Tulum, across the Highway from the post office.
Post Office: Towards the north end of the Avenida, on the inland, west, side.

Useful Addresses

Savana: Three blocks north of the bus station, t 871 2081, f 871 2092, *www.tulummx.com*. **Internet shop**, long-distance **phone/fax office**, travel agent and courier office.
The Weary Traveler, at the southern end of town in the block south of the bus station,

t 871 2461, *hostel@tulum.com*. An essential service for travellers, open 24hrs daily and combining Internet access, café, second-hand bookshop, video patio and general social and information centre. Guiding light John Kavanagh and his team are very friendly and helpful with any traveller's problem, providing a very useful free local map of Tulum, and you can book low-cost *cenote* tours. Plus, they have bargain hostel-style beds (*see* below). There's a 'branch' Internet café on the beach just south of the T-junction by Cabañas Copal, **Blue**.

Sports and Activities

Diving and Snorkelling

Tulum is a prime cave diving centre, but there is also fine diving and snorkelling around the reefs just offshore and to the north and south. The two best-equipped local dive operators are **Aktun Dive Center** and **Cenote Dive Center** (*see* p.206).
Dive Tulum, in Cabañas Santa Fe, on Tulum beach, t 871 2096, *www.divetulum.com.mx*. A low-cost but friendly dive operation, with bargain introduction courses for $55, and easy snorkel tours for $12 (snorkels available for hire). Diving around nearby reefs is their *forte*, but they can also provide cave dives.

Where to Stay

Tulum t (984–)

Tulum's first *cabañas* were stick and palm huts, and spending time by the beach with just the palms and the waves was a BoHo-backpackers' preserve. Over time, though, they have developed, so that Tulum can offer a whole range of grades of comfort on the beach. There's also a whole range of prices, although these have gone up for even simple huts: the most basic *cabaña* is $10–$12 a night, with many places at around $18, while at the other end there are $80–$100 beach houses (prices drop considerably April–mid-Dec). So far, though, all the new places have remained relatively low-key and stayed with the basic *cabaña* idea. One Tulum tradition that has been kept up – deliberately in some cases – is the lack of permanent electricity. Most places turn off their generators at 10–11pm, although some now have 24-hr solar power. Others only have candles. Mosquitoes can be irritating, so take repellent. A good source for mid- to upper-range places is *www.hotelstulum.com*.

As the beach has filled up, more places to stay have opened in Tulum Pueblo. Obviously, you can't get straight into the sea, but prices are lower, and there's a bigger choice of places to eat. Also, if you arrive late, you can always take a room in the village the first night and try again at the beach the next morning.

Getting to the *Cabañas*

From the Crucero the beach road runs seawards for nearly 2km before it meets a T-junction. The left arm runs north for 3km up to a back (footpath only) entrance to Tulum ruins, while to the right the road runs down for another 8km to the entrance to Sian Ka'an (paved for about the first 2km, a fairly smooth dirt track after that). Note that **kilometre markers**, often used as address locators, are numbered for the full 11km from the ruins, not from the T-junction. The *cabañas* are strung along the beach in either direction, and taxis are the only public transport, so that getting between *cabañas* without your own transport can take time, although many drivers give lifts. The first sites that opened, closest to the ruins up the road left of the T, have the best spots, with the best (if busiest) beaches and a superb view of the Castillo, but have mostly remained the most basic and the cheapest. The downside is that these cabins are also the places where thefts and other hassles have been most frequently reported.

The Beach *Cabañas*

Hotels and *cabañas* in each price category are listed from north to south (with kilometres numbered from Tulum ruins). Nearly all Tulum hotels (but especially those on the beach) change their price slot according to season: *cabañas* that charge *upper-moderate* or *expensive* rates in the winter high season ($60–$90) may drop into *inexpensive* in spring or autumn ($45 or less), and basic cabins that are *cheap* most of the year may jump into *inexpensive* (over $20) Dec–Jan. Prices vary according to size and location of the rooms.

Expensive–Moderate

Piedra Escondida, Km3.5, **t** 871 2221, *piedra escondida@tulum.com*. One of the most enjoyable beach hotels; slightly upscale *cabañas* on the beach, consisting of eight very comfortable, pretty rooms with bath in *palapa*-roofed buildings, each room with its own terrace balcony and a superb outlook on a sheltered beach. Italian-owned, it has a charming Italian-Mexicn **restaurant**.

La Perla, Km3.5, **t** 871 2387, **f** 871 2092. Not as pretty as the Piedra Escondida, this has comfortable *cabañas* with good bathrooms, and an enjoyable **restaurant**.

Zamas, Km4, **f** 871 2067, *www.zamas.com*. A smart *cabaña*-development at the south end of the Punta Piedra group, offering beachfront cabins, similar cabins in a tropical garden and smaller *cabañas* with shared bath. There's also another Italian-oriented **restaurant**, headlining on seafood.

Maya Tulum (formerly Osho Tulum), Km5, **t** 877 8638, *www.mayantulum.com* (*luxury– moderate*). Just after the paved surface ends comes one of the longest-established of the Yucatán's New Age hotels. It has very comfortable *cabaña* rooms with characteristic meditative 'hanging beds' and all kinds of treatments, sessions and workshops. The **restaurant** has the best vegetarian menu in a very wide radius, and excellent seafood.

Cabañas Ana y José, Km7, **t** 887 5470/880 6022, *www.tulumresorts.com* (*luxury–expensive*). Feels distinctly secluded, with 15 of the plushest rooms along the whole beach (not all have a sea view). It also has bikes for hire, a lovely pool and a pretty, sand-floored seafood **restaurant** with charming, traditional service. The beach is fabulous.

Cabañas Tulum, Km7, **f** 871 2092, *savana@ tulum-mexico.com* (*moderate*). Another longer-established option, though it's much less smart, and the big beach-house-style rooms, while regularly done up, are a bit time-worn. Even so, it has a certain charm and plenty of relaxed Mexican atmosphere.

Dos Ceibas, Km9.5, **t** 877 6024, *www.dosceibas .com* (*moderate*). A *posada ecológica* with seven pretty rooms in bungalows. There's solar electricity, as well as a range of therapies and activities (meditation, massage), a lovely **restaurant** and snorkelling trips.

Moderate–Inexpensive

El Paraíso, Km1, t 871 2006, *elparaiso_tulum@ hotmail.com*. One of the longest-running and most 'solid' beach hotels on the north stretch of beach, with a main building and pleasant rooms in beach-house-type blocks and four self-contained bungalows. Recently attractively renovated, it also has a very pleasant **restaurant** (*see* below). The reef here is one of Tulum's best for snorkelling.

Cabañas Diamante-K, Km2.5, t 871 2283, *www.diamantek.com*. One of the most attractive larger *cabaña*-clusters, with pretty wooden cabins of different sizes with hanging beds and other features; there's also a communal, dorm-like hut (*cheap*). There's also a **restaurant**, a shop, massage facilities and a vegetarian juice bar, and the beach, while more rocky than those to the north, is nicely sheltered; the place is clean and well-kept, and feels more tranquil than the backpacker cabins further up the road.

Cabañas Copal, Km3.5, t 871 2482, *copal@ tulum.cc*. A good budget choice affiliated to the AMAJ hostel association, with some 40 cabins spread around a forest garden and along the beach, either with double beds and shared showers, or double or big family-sized cabins with their own showers, with or without a sea view. There are also cabins with bunk beds (*cheap*). No electricity but there is a **café-restaurant**, and the cabins and the site are very well looked after, with an unhassled atmosphere. Just alongside there's also the **Blue** Internet café.

Nohoch Tunich, Km3.5, t/f 871 2470. Simplest of the Punta Piedra cluster, with plain but cosy separate *cabañas* or rooms in two-storey buildings with balconies, with showers and with or without fans. The owners also rent bikes, and have a **mini-supermarket** and **money-exchange** desk, a boon to anyone staying nearby.

Rancho Hemingway, Km5.5 (no phone). A *cabaña*-cluster with one of the best atmospheres along the beach, run with friendly, slightly piratical verve by long-term New York resident Juan Chio. There are double- and twin-bed cabins with shared showers, and six with bathrooms and kitchenettes. There's a convivial beach bar for breakfast, and dinner can be fixed with advance notice.

Cheap

Don Armando, Km0.47, t 871 2417. Best-known of the simpler *cabañas* on the north fork, a guidebook institution and a hangout for 'generations' of backpackers. There's a choice of sand- or concrete-floored *cabañas*, less basic than at the adjacent Santa Fe or the Mar Caribe, but you don't get a lot more for your money. Service is chronically offhand. But it's a reference point, and fine if you want to mingle more than stay tranquil. The entry sign is marked only **Maysal SA** and **Acuatic Tulum**, the on-site watersports shop.

Mar Caribe, Km0.7 (no phone). Simplest of those along the north road, and so about the best choice if you're looking for the original-model, sand-floored beach hut, with simple beds or hammocks and no electricity at all. Their own bit of beach is great, and the atmosphere is more peaceful than at the sites closer to the ruins, although there can still be a certain amount of hassle.

La Flor, Km5.5 (no phone). Next to Rancho Hemingway, a very simple site run by local people, with mostly hammock-only *cabañas* and camping, and communal showers. If you stay there, stock up on water, candles and food before making the trek.

Tierra del Sol, Km10 (no phone). Almost at the end of the road, one of several half-hidden entrances leads to ideally beachcomber-ish *cabañas*. There's 24-hr solar electricity, and the ultra-laid-back owners cook up breakfast and lunch. Down here you're especially isolated without transport, but as compensation you get superbly wild, open beaches, and very few people to share them with.

Tulum Pueblo

Inexpensive

Hotel Acuario, at the crossroads north of the village, by the old entrance to the ruins, t 871 2195, *www.acuariotulum.com*. Cranky establishment, oft-extended, which has had ornate details added that give it a vaguely showbiz-oriental-palace look. Its large rooms are well equipped, with good bathrooms and TVs, but box-like. It also has a **bar-restaurant**, a **supermarket**, **Internet café** and **money exchange**, a handy resource for visitors to the ruins, just a short walk away.

L'Hotelito de la Isla Natural, on the Avenida, three blocks north of the bus station, t 871 2061, *hotelito@tulumabc.com*. Italian-run, with cabin-style rooms (some with a/c) in a garden, and a pretty **restaurant**. Peak prices go up, but are better-value than the beach.

Cheap

Diana's Cabañas, signposted up C/ Centaurio, almost opposite the post office (no phone). One of several small *cabaña* groups in the village, offering simple but quite well-kept palm cabins with shared showers.

Rancho Tranquilo, at the very south end of Tulum Pueblo, t 871 2092. Welcoming place run by an American couple, with pretty *cabañas* in a fruit-filled garden. Bathrooms are shared, guests have use of the kitchen and almost free run of the family house, and fishing and snorkelling trips and tours can be organized. A tremendous bargain.

The Weary Traveler, t 871 2461, *hostel@ tulum.com*. The most economical decent accommodation by a long way, with dorm rooms sleeping five in bunks or hammocks and an unbeatable $5 deal that includes a simple breakfast and dinner and kitchen use, in a welcoming, sociable atmosphere.

Eating Out

On the Beach

Given their isolation, most places along the beach road also have restaurants.

Expensive–Moderate

Maya Tulum, Km5. By far the best vegetarian food in the area.

Cabañas Ana y José, Km7. The prettiest Mexican restaurant.

Las Ranitas, Km9. The most sophisticated food on the final part of the road.

Moderate

El Paraíso, Km1. The best Mexican-Yucatecan food on this stretch, and a great setting for watching the sea and catching the breezes.

Diamante-K, Km2.5. Good vegetarian/health-food option.

Gringo Dave's, Km2.5 (*moderate–cheap*). Impossible to miss with its mock-Mayan

temple entrance north of the T-junction, by the Diamante-K, is this excellent value bar-restaurant with tables around little terraces above the beach. It specializes in platters of fish, seafood and spare ribs, flame-grilled, and contrary to what you might think, the food is much more Mexican than Gringo.

Piedra Escondida, Km3.5. Pleasant Italian food.

La Perla, Km3.5. Next door to Piedra Escondida, this is more Mexican and maybe pips it for prettiest setting, on a bluff over the beach.

Cheap

Don Armando's, Km0.47. Permanently busiest and noisiest, an ever-popular beachbums' rendezvous before the lights go off at 10pm.

Mar Caribe, Km0.7. Simpler, with traditional *ceviches* and similar, and good for lunch.

Tulum Pueblo

Plenty of eateries are spread along the main road, from *loncherías* to wholefood cafés.

Moderate

Don Cafeto, midway down Av. Tulum between the post office and the baseball field. Almost a landmark, with a big terrace, unpushy service and some of the best Mexican standards – especially seafood – around.

La Nave, halfway along Av. Tulum, near Savana. Contending for first prize in the Tulum pizzeria championships, with great, fresh, woody-flavoured dough. You can eat cheaply too, on the (very adequate) smaller portions.

Paris de Noche, Av. Tulum, in the block north of the town hall and bank. Another novelty, bringing an enjoyable combination of French and Mexican cooking styles. It has a big bar-terrace and service is charming.

Son y Café, C/ Orion Sur, south of Av. Tulum. Pretty, unusually tranquil restaurant with classic Mexican-rustic décor and some of Tulum's best classic Mexican dishes.

Cheap

Charlie's, opposite bus station. Pretty, deeply relaxed and good value little patio-café.

Helen's, C/ Orion Sur, off Av. Tulum. Great value breakfast bar with a few outside tables, run by a Mexican-German couple (so there are home-made German breads and sausages, as well as above-average coffee).

this day, behind the travellers' den façade, there are still people in Tulum who perform Cruzob rituals. Until about 1999, there was a pretty easy three-way split between the main centres along the Riviera: Cancún was the big-scale tour destination, Playa del Carmen was for people who preferred something a little smaller, and Tulum was the backpackers' capital. It has largely kept its beach-hangout character, but now it also attracts the more well-heeled traveller, looking for a mellow tropical hideaway and non-Cancunized beaches; it too has had its boom, not in hotels but in *cabañas*. Today there are *cabaña*-clusters virtually all the way along the 11 kilometres from the ruins to the Sian Ka'an reserve. The atmosphere is no longer as sleepily relaxed as it once was (and some prices can be distinctly unfriendly). Nevertheless, if you pick your spot the old beach-breeze calm is still easy enough to track down.

The Tulum Ruins

...the next day toward sunset we saw a burg, or town, so large that Seville would not have appeared larger or better. We saw there a very high tower...
From the report of Juan de Grijalva's voyage to the Yucatán, 1518.

The name Tulum, from the Yucatec for 'wall', is fairly recent, and it is likely that the city's original name was something like *Zama* or 'place of the dawn', an obvious reference to the cliff's dramatic outlook toward the east. The site was probably occupied from the Early Classic, as a carved *stela* found at Tulum, now in the British Museum, has a Long Count date from the year 564. It was in the Late Postclassic, though, that it developed into an important city, and its main buildings are the clearest example of the relatively crude, square 'East Coast' style of Mayan architecture also seen at El Rey, San Gervasio and other late-period Quintana Roo sites. In the 13th century Tulum had links with Mayapán, and was still a thriving trading community when the Spaniards arrived. It remained occupied for several decades after the Conquest, longer than other places on the coast. Its ruins were partially uncovered by Stephens and Catherwood, but permanent excavations were begun by Morley in 1916. In the interim, in about 1890–1910, Tulum was occupied (or reoccupied) by a breakaway sect from the Talking Cross Maya, led very unusually by a woman 'high priestess', who held rituals in the temples of the Castillo and clashed many times with the *chicle*-tappers.

As you walk up the impressive approach it becomes very apparent that Tulum, like Mayapán, is one of the walled Mayan cities. Opinions differ as to whether this wall was a defensive rampart or simply used to mark off an aristocratic core from the surrounding city. The only entrance is through a narrow passage in the wall. Another

Site Information

Open daily 8–5; adm, Sun adm free.
Tulum is one of the most visited of all Mayan sites. By the main entrance there is a visitor centre and full-scale souvenir shopping mall, and a tractor-driven 'train' is provided for those who don't want to walk the 800m or so to the ruins. Because of pressure of numbers some buildings are now roped off, and can only be viewed from a distance. To avoid the crowds, get there early, and forget the Sunday free days. After examining the ruins you can go for a swim, from the beautiful palm-lined cove beneath the Castillo, where the city's trading canoes once landed.

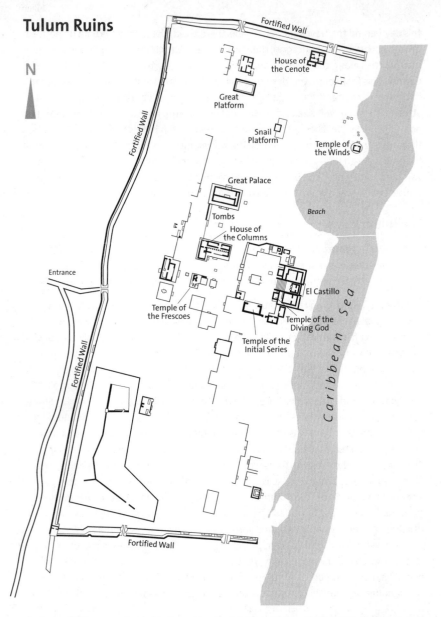

Tulum Ruins

N

Fortified Wall

House of
the Cenote

Great
Platform

Snail
Platform

Temple of
the Winds

Great Palace

Tombs

House of
the Columns

Beach

Fortified Wall

Entrance

El Castillo

Temple of
the Frescoes

Temple of the
Diving God

Temple of the
Initial Series

Caribbean Sea

Fortified Wall

Fortified Wall

feature of Tulum, easily visible from the rise by the entrance, is that it has a very
distinct layout, with a north–south main street running through two central plazas.

Unlike other Postclassic cities such as Mayapán or San Gervasio, with their collective
multepal authority system, Tulum seems to have had a single ruler clearly superior to
his subordinate lords, as one of its residential complexes is much bigger than all the
others. The first major group of buildings beyond the entrance includes the **Great
Palace** or **House of the Halach Uinic**, the first lord. It has within it a small sanctuary

with a battered carving of a recurrent image at Tulum, the 'Diving God', an upside-down figure who looks to be jumping headfirst out of the sky and into the sea. The most widely accepted theory is that this was a Postclassic variation on the older Mayan maize god, the Hero Twins' father Hun-Hunahpu (*see* p.49). Facing away from the palace across a small plaza to the south stands the **House of the Columns**, a colonnaded building where the Halach Uinic probably did business with his lesser lords. Across the street, back towards the main entrance, there are the remains of a much smaller residential building, called the **Reservoir House** (Structure 20) because it has a *chultún* artificial water cistern. Opposite this on the sea-side of the street is one of the most fascinating buildings at Tulum, the curious two-level **Temple of the Frescoes**. As well as more carved Diving Gods on the upper frieze, it has within the lower portico on the west side some remarkably complete mural paintings, showing the goddess Ixchel in the underworld amid animals, gods and everyday objects. Unfortunately you are no longer allowed close enough to see them fully, but if the light's right you can still see a lot of the fine outline and colours of green and red.

Further along the 'street' there are many more platforms, the bases of shrines, residential buildings or trading platforms. Isolated by the north wall is the **House of the Cenote**, because it stands above a natural *cenote*, although its water is not drinkable. Nearby is a small temple impressively placed on a rock overlooking the beach, the **Temple of the Winds**, believed to have been a shrine to Kukulcán.

The largest group of buildings is centred on the great temple-pyramid of the **Castillo**, a majestic presence on the tallest crag above the beach. According to the Spaniards a flaming beacon was lit on the top of the temple, visible for miles along the coast. It faces inland, and Stephens, who took up residence in the main temple, initially bemoaned the fact that its builders had not provided for a sea view, only to be grateful when night fell and he realized how strong the ocean winds could get here. It's no longer permitted to climb up the Castillo, but you can still see the carved Diving God on the upper temple frieze, and images of Chac on the corners. South of the Castillo is one of the oldest parts of the complex, the **Temple of the Initial Series** (Templo de la Estela), where the British Museum *stela* was found. North of Castillo is the later **Temple of the Diving God**, with the clearest carving of the god at Tulum. Its walls are not at all straight, due purely to the crude techniques of Postclassic builders; it's always been that way.

Tulum Pueblo

Tulum village used to have two separate parts, but these have now more or less joined up. Virtually everything – the bus depot, the small chapels of Protestant sects (very popular among the Maya), a host of backpackerish services – is along the main road, with rough streets of concrete houses and a few *na* palm huts running off it. Despite a tentacular growth Tulum has long remained a pretty ragged, chaotic place – which is part of its charm – but the pace of 'urban improvement' has picked up notably in the new millennium, with more solid kerbs, street name signs and, above all, a bank and an all-new town hall, in Tulum's growing 'civic centre', a block north of the bus station.

Muyil

Open daily 8–5; adm, Sun adm free.

About 25 kilometres south of Tulum along Highway 307 and just inside the limits of the Sian Ka'an reserve there is another, little-known archaeological site, Muyil. Despite its proximity to Tulum this Mayan city had a very different history, as it came to prominence in the Early Classic era from about AD 300–600. Little has been definitely established about Muyil, but it appears to have been closely associated with Cobá. When Cobá was overwhelmed by Chichén Itzá, Muyil slipped into decline with it, but revived in the Postclassic after 1200 to reach its greatest size. Consequently the ruins reveal a broad architectural mix, from Classic-era buildings similar to those of Cobá to others in the plain and square East-Coast style of the Quintana Roo coastal settlements. A path beside the ruins leads to Lake Chunyaxché (*see* p.219).

Only a part of the Muyil site is open to be visited, so it is not possible to get a real impression of the city's size and importance. On most days any visitors will have it to themselves, except for the insects. The first group of buildings is to the right of the main gate, the **Entrance Plaza** group, with the remains of three pyramids and several other structures around a small square. Most of the buildings are thought to be among the oldest at Muyil, begun in the Early Classic. The grandest structure here is the steep, 17m-high pyramid known as the **Castillo** (*cannot be climbed*), which shows a strong Petén influence. It's also very distinctive, with a peculiarly complex temple at the top with a unique – and unexplained – circular inner core. A little north of the Castillo is a more conventional pyramid, **Temple 8**, with a squat Postclassic temple – similar to but larger than the Castillo at Tulum – on top of a base of several layers dating back to the Preclassic era. In the sanctuary of the temple it's still possible to see some of the original painted stucco in yellow, red, black and Mayan blue.

Sian Ka'an and Punta Allen

The Riviera-strip of potential tourist development is effectively brought to an end by the **Sian Ka'an Biosphere Reserve**, the most comprehensively protected natural environment in Mexico. It extends over 530,000 hectares around the Bahía de la Ascensión, a huge area of all-but-uninhabited lagoon, reef, mangroves, lake, tropical forest and savanna. Somewhere within Sian Ka'an (Yucatec for 'where Heaven is born') there are examples of nearly every kind of the region's wildlife: jaguars, jaguarundis, howler monkeys and tapirs; crocodiles, turtles and manatees; and millions of birds. There's an extraordinary biological diversity, and the fixed plant life is as fascinating as the elusive fauna. As you enter the reserve the road is surrounded by more and more of the giant fan palms called *chit* in Yucatec, one of the species peculiar to the Yucatán. Also common on the coast road is the *chechen*, an apparently innocuous tree with a poisonous sap that can affect humans and animals even if they only stand near it. Close by, though, there will be a complementary *chakah* bush, which produces a natural antidote.

One particular feature of Sian Ka'an is that conservation has generally been given precedence over exploitation for tourism. There are very few roads, none of them paved: the one from Tulum to Punta Allen, a very little-used road from Felipe Carrillo Puerto to Vigía Chico on the coast, and one from Mahahual to the south (*see* p.342). It's always best to visit the reserve with a **tour** (*see* below), as it's very hard to find your way around by yourself.

Getting There

The Punta Allen track is a great, bumpy roller coaster of a dirt road, with some of Mexico's champion potholes. Taking its time, a standard car can get down the road when it's dry, but at many times of year it's 4WD only; ask about current conditions before you try it. In any vehicle, the 48km from Cabañas Tulum will take 2–3 hrs. **Fuel** is only available in Punta Allen from unofficial village sellers, so it's best to fill up in Tulum when you have the chance.

Even Punta Allen, though, has a *colectivo*, a big 4WD van that normally leaves Tulum once a day, usually at around 11am from outside **Savana**. Times may vary, so do check ahead.

Tours

Punta Allen **t** (984–)
Cooperativa Los Gaytanes, Punta Allen, **t** 877 8405. As you come into the village by the beach road you'll see the hut of this local guides' cooperative. Among their (flexible) tours they offer flyfishing (from $150 for 6hrs), tours of the reefs and lagoons offshore to see birds, dolphins, turtles and other wildlife ($100 for a 3-hr trip) and snorkelling trips. You'll also see signs around the village for other tour operations.

Sian Ka'an
Only a few organizations are fully authorized to take tours into the reserve. Some companies in Playa del Carmen offer tours with very limited environmental safeguards, but there are also agencies that run trips with more ecological awareness, allowing you to experience Sian Ka'an without snarling motors. Most tours are relatively expensive ($60–$75 per person, for a full trip) but all organizers of fully-equipped tours insist that it's impossible to offer them for less.

Amigos de Sian Ka'an, C/ Crepúsculo 18, SM 44, Fraccionamiento Alborada, Cancún, **t/f** (998) 848 2136/848 1618, *www.amigosdesiankaan.org*. After an interruption due to bureaucratic problems the most important conservation organization working in Sian Ka'an expects to resume its tours during 2002 (around $75 per person). Tours are run any day, according to demand (min. 5 people, so in low season you may have to wait). Tours leave Tulum from Cabañas Ana y José (who provide information and sell tickets) at 9am; tours last around 6hrs or more, with a bilingual qualified botanist or earth scientist as guide, and include a forest walk and boat trip, with a swim. There's also a night 'crocodile adventure' tour, run intermittently according to the number of people interested and the availability of guides.

Cooperativa de Chunyaxché, *camaltours@hotmail.com*. Boatmen's cooperative in Chunyaxché offering more basic tours. For around $200 a boat (or $30 per head for 6–7 people) you can spend a full day amid the lakes and mangroves, with a swim. Guides are less widely informed than those on the more organized tours (some speak some English). Contact them at the hut opposite the Muyil ruins entrance (at least a day or two in advance) or try e-mailing.

Sian Ka'an Tours, Av. Tulum, between Calles Géminis and Satélite, Tulum, **t/f** 871 2363, *siankaan_tours@hotmail.com*. Private agency run by Sergio Hernández, a biologist and former Amigos guide, providing excellent tours in association with the Centro Ecológico Sian Ka'an. There are two main trips: one is from Tulum, with a forest walk and boat trip through Lake Chunyaxché ($68); another includes a drive down to Punta Allen, and a boat tour taking in mangroves, Ascension Bay, bird-watching and reef snorkelling ($80). Lunch and all equipment are provided.

There is also one small but beautiful part of the reserve that can be visited without need for any guide, right by the official entrance to Sian Ka'an. The reserve warden may ask you to sign a book, but there's no admission charge, and just behind his lodge there's a short nature walk to a deliciously clear and fresh *cenote* called **Ben-Ha**, which is great for swimming. Most 'proper' tours of Sian Ka'an continue on from there down to the fishing lodge at Boca Paila, with stops to look at the forest. You then take

Where to Stay and Eat

A scattering of places lie along this road, small-scale *cabaña*-hotels permitted within the reserve. Most specialize in fishing packages, and are quite expensive. You can stop and **camp** almost anywhere that isn't fenced off, but remember to take everything you need, and take it out again when you leave.

In Punta Allen, as well as the places listed here there are often a few signs up offering rooms to rent in the village. If you ask at Posada Sirena or Serenidad Shardon they will always try to search out a room for anyone who makes it down to Punta Allen, even if they themselves are full.

Boca Paila Fishing Lodge, t 874 0989, *www.bocapaila-lodge.com* (*expensive*). Longest-established specialized fishing lodge, 11km south of the Sian Ka'an entrance. It has nine superior *cabañas*, its own boats and a gift shop and **restaurant**. In low season rooms may be available to non-fishermen. Reservations essential.

Bonefish Bum, Punta Allen, *www.bone-fishbum.com* (*expensive*). Home of an Alaskan couple who in winter run bone-fishing and eco-tours with accommodation in three well-equipped rooms in their house in the village. Reservations essential.

Cuzan Guest House, Punta Allen, reservations via Apartado Postal 24, Felipe Carrillo Puerto, CP 77200 Quintana Roo, t (983) 834 0358, *www.flyfishmx.com* (*expensive–moderate*). Punta Allen's main hotel, with *cabañas* with bath and a likeable **restaurant** (*moderate*) with sand floor and catch-of-the-day fish. Though it's mainly a bonefishing lodge, it also arranges bird-watching and snorkelling, kayaking and other eco-trips in Sian Ka'an.

Marr del Greco, f (984) 871 2092, *www.marrdelgreco.com* (*moderate*). Beach-side lodge only a kilometre north of Punta Allen, with very high-standard *cabañas*. Bonefishing is the speciality, but they also provide other fishing trips, diving, snorkelling and packages.

Posada Colibrí, Punta Allen, t (984) 877 8078 (*inexpensive*). Simple, cheap rooms with showers. Don't expect restrained décor; they've been 'graffitied' by nearly everyone who's stayed there. The owners are very welcoming, and they also serve up local dishes on long wooden tables facing the beach (*moderate*).

Posada Sirena, Punta Allen, f (984) 879 7795, *www.casasirena.com* (*inexpensive*). Sirena runs her bohemian beach guest house with very friendly verve: she has two cabins in the village, both self contained with kitchens, hammocks and all sorts of distinctive fittings. They're a great bargain (sleeping up to 6 or 8 for $30–$40). She can also arrange all the local excursions at low prices.

Rancho Sol Caribe, around 35km south of the Sian Ka'an entrance, t (998) 874 1858, *www.cancun.com* (*expensive*). Little *cabaña* hotel, which with its beach bar appears bizarrely neat and tidy in the middle of emptiness. It's owned by Michael and Diane Severeign, who have two very well-equipped, family-size beach cabins, and 24-hr solar electricity. They cook up great fresh fish, and arrange fishing, snorkelling and diving trips and packages, with expert guides. A complete beach retreat (*moderate* July–early Dec).

Serenidad Shardon, Punta Allen, t (984) 879 7715, *serenidadshardon@aol.com* (*moderate–inexpensive*). Big house in the middle of the village run by Shon and Nikki, who offer a range of accommodation: very attractive *cabaña* rooms, a simple room in their own house, or a whole, huge separate beach house with space for 12 people in comfort and very high quality kitchen facilities, bathrooms etc. ($250 a day, less for longer-term stays). The owners are very friendly, and try to ensure that anyone who reaches Punta Allen gets a room for the night.

a boat through the mangrove lagoon and up a channel that separates it from the freshwater **Lake Chunyaxché**. This is one of the Yucatán lakes fed only by underground rivers, which can be seen bubbling up from the lake bed in little 'eruptions'; just as remarkable is the point where sea and lake water meet, with a complex, teeming combination of fish and plants. There is also usually time to stop for another swim, and to visit one of the 27 scarcely explored Mayan sites in the reserve, a tiny Postclassic temple on an island. Whether you will see any of the rarer Sian Ka'an animals is a matter of luck, but you will always see plenty of birds – orioles, ibises, blue and tricoloured herons, storks, frigate birds and many more.

The Punta Allen Road

If even the most distant Tulum *cabañas* feel too busy, much greater remoteness can be found by carrying on down the dirt road along the sand spit to the pirate village of Punta Allen, a wild, empty track that meanders through jungle to swing back again to meet the sea. It's completely deserted for miles, with nothing but windswept palms, wheeling pelicans and empty dunes on the one side, and the deliciously still channels and islets of the coastal lagoons on the other. Along the way lie stretches of beach that are spectacularly beautiful.

One of the most accessible spots is just three kilometres south of the reserve entrance, an open area behind the beach that's one of the (relatively) popular places to stop and camp. Fishermen, though, are the area's true devotees. The flats in the lagoons and Ascension Bay are considered the best bonefishing grounds in the world, while offshore there's good deep-sea fishing for snook, tarpon, barracuda and others. Permits are required, which can be arranged by the fishing lodges. Eleven kilometres from the entrance is the longest-established and most prestigious, at **Boca Paila**, from where many Sian Ka'an tours set off into Lake Chunyaxché. The next organized stopping-place is some 20 kilometres further at **Rancho Sol Caribe**, a very welcome spot to stop for a drink. Beyond there the road is just a little more inhabited for the last ten kilometres into Punta Allen, with the **Pesca Maya** and **Marr del Greco** fishing lodges.

Punta Allen, 44 kilometres from the Sian Ka'an entrance, is a tiny collection of houses amid dunes and giant palms facing a huge open sea in variations of colour from turquoise to deep ultramarine blue. It has a beach with a few landing stages where giggling kids play in the waves, a plaza, a school, a basketball court, four or five shops and a few very laid-back restaurants. One theory goes that it owes its non-Hispanic name to the *Allen*, the ship of Edward Teach, Blackbeard the Pirate, who in the 18th century used Ascension Bay as a bolt hole, and (some say) founded the village. Today its 450 or so inhabitants make a living from lobster fishing. In among them there's a sprinkling of mostly American beachcombers. You can tell locals' houses from *gringo* homes: the former are Caribbean-style painted wooden huts or more modern Mexican concrete-block houses: the latter are put together from upturned boats and driftwood, with wind chimes and all sorts of other junk out in front. A walk south out of the village will take you to the lighthouse at the tip of Punta Allen. Staying here, protected from the outside world by that road, is for those who want to sink into some really deep tranquility.

Cobá

Despite its proximity to the coastal tourist areas Cobá, 45 kilometres north of Tulum, is much less well known than any of the other great Mayan cities, yet it is one of the most intriguing. Its location and layout are different from any other, for it stands beside five lakes, the largest set of lakes in the Yucatán. Instead of the concentrated plaza-structure of cities like Chichén Itzá or Uxmal, Cobá, one of the oldest Mayan cities, was made up of many separate groups of buildings spread over a huge area of some 70 square kilometres. Within this lie the remains of over 15,000 structures spread between 20 identifiable groups, only a small part of which have been excavated. They were linked by the most complex network of *sacbés* or stone roads anywhere in the Mayan world.

Far enough from the coast to have lost the sea breezes and yet with the lakes alongside to raise the humidity, Cobá is also a powerfully hot and sticky site. Being lost among jungle paths, it's also a great place to see birds and sometimes other wildlife.

History

As a source of water Cobá's lakes attracted Mayan settlers from earliest times, but a city beside them first came to prominence toward the end of the Preclassic, in about

Getting Around

Cobá is 45km from Tulum, 45km from Nuevo Xcan on the Highway 180 Cancún road, and 58km from Valladolid via Chemax. There are no petrol stations between Valladolid and Tulum. At least one first-class and several *intermedio* or second-class **buses** daily run between Valladolid and Tulum, and all stop at Cobá. Tours are also available from agencies on the coast.

Cobá is one of the most widely dispersed of the large Mayan sites, with walks of over a kilometre between building groups, and you can now rent **bicycles** (around $2.50) or **tricycle carts**, with 'driver' ($8) to get around. They can be found just inside the site, by the first ball court.

Site Information

Open daily 8–5; adm, Sun adm free.

Only a few of the most important building groups make up the main site that is normally visited, but even so Cobá's dispersal means that a visit involves a healthy hike (or bike ride) over forest paths. **Guides** (at the entrance) will take you round the main areas

in about two hours (around $30), but it's best to allow at least a whole morning.

Where to Stay and Eat

Cobá village is tiny, but it has two good value places to stay that allow you to see the site at its best, first thing in the morning. For real tranquility you can also **camp** or stay in hammocks nearby in the spider monkey reserve at **Punta Laguna** (*see* p.224).

Club Med-Villas Arqueológicas, t/f 874 2087, *www.come2clubmed.com* (*moderate*). Like its fellow Club Med-owned Villas Arqueológicas at Chichén and Uxmal, this offers upscale accommodation at lower-range prices, and is great for a splurge. Right by the lake, it has pretty, colonial-style rooms, **restaurant** and bar, and a delicious pool in a tropical garden.

Posada El Bocadito, by the bus stop, no phone (*cheap*). Also a good deal, with decent rooms with showers and fans, and a **restaurant**.

There are also several *cheap–moderate* **places to eat** around the ruins car park, and in the village there's **Restaurant-Bar La Pirámide** (*moderate*), with enjoyable Yucatecan snacks served on a relaxing terrace with the same lake view as the Club Med.

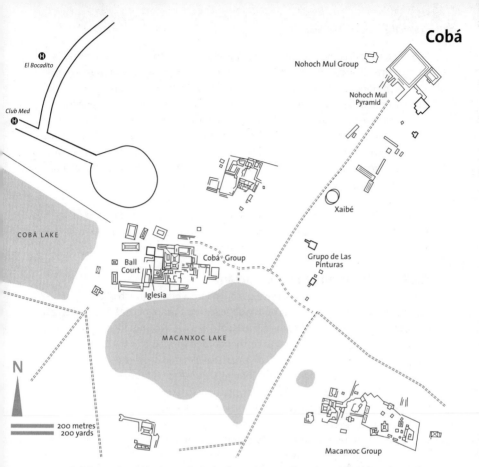

El Bocadito

Club Med

Nohoch Mul Group

Nohoch Mul Pyramid

Xaibé

COBÁ LAKE

Ball Court

Cobá Group

Grupo de Las Pinturas

Iglesia

MACANXOC LAKE

N

200 metres
200 yards

Macanxoc Group

AD 250. Cobá remained the largest city in the entire northern Yucatán throughout the Classic era, reaching its peak from about 650 onwards when it dominated the northeast of the peninsula. Compared to Dzibilchaltún, Uxmal and other northern cities, Cobá clearly had closer ties – cultural and economic – with the Classic Mayan centres of the Petén to the south, reflected both in its architectural style and in the presence of a great many carved *stelae*. It is widely believed, but hard to demonstrate, that as representatives of the Classic Maya tradition the lords of Cobá considered themselves superior to other, less literate peoples in the north, especially those of Chichén Itzá.

The decipherment of Cobá's *stelae* is limited by their poor condition, and so it does not yet have as personalized a 'history' as the southern cities. Archaeological evidence indicates that by the 8th century it had as many as 50,000 people, living in innumerable clusters of house-enclosures between the *sacbeob* and building complexes, and with a very sophisticated system of water management. Some of its *sacbé* causeways extended far beyond the vague limits of the city to link Cobá with subsidiary cities such as Muyil and Polé (now Xcaret) and other settlements on the coast, and Yaxuná to the west. Examination of these causeways from Cobá has played an important part in demonstrating that Mayan *sacbéob* had a military and trading role as well as being built for use in rituals or pilgrimages.

Cobá's downfall came with the rise of Chichén Itzá, and the long war between the two cities is one of the titanic confrontations of Mayan history. In the early 9th century the longest of all Mayan *sacbeob*, over 100 kilometres in length, was laid all the way from Cobá to its western stronghold at Yaxuná, an extraordinary operation that must have involved the mobilization of thousands of people. This reinforcement was only temporarily successful, however, and the destruction of Yaxuná by Chichén in about 860 was rapidly followed by the defeat of Cobá itself. Its decline as a major city was terminal and preceded the main Collapse in the region, although Cobá was to revive a little some centuries later in the Postclassic, when some more buildings were added.

Cobá was lost in the forest for centuries in a very thinly inhabited part of the Yucatán, until it was rediscovered in 1891 by Teobert Maler. Excavations were carried out by Eric Thompson in the 1920s and then the INAH in the 1970s.

The Cobá Group and the Nohoch Mul

As you approach Cobá the road swings round into a broad stretch of open grass, with the site parking area at one end and the glazed surface of the largest lake, Lake Cobá, below you. The ruins, behind a barrier of trees, are not immediately obvious. Walk up a short rise from the entrance, though, and you come to the **Cobá Group**, a large complex of temples centred on a massive pyramid of sweeping steps above a plaza. It's known as the **Iglesia** (the Church), because for centuries the local Maya continued to hold ceremonies here. Sadly, it's now so deteriorated, in parts almost a formless cone, that ordinary visitors are no longer allowed to climb it. It has as many as nine different levels of construction, but the largest part was built in the Classic era, in a very Petén-influenced style with rounded corners, and at its foot on the west side there are two other small pyramids, together forming a typical Petén-style three-sided plaza. Around the Iglesia there are also several Mayan-arched passageways, and in the plaza there are several *stelae* in poor condition, placed under *palapas* for their protection. On the north side of the Iglesia there is a Classic-era **Ball Court**, with some recently installed and rather obviously modern reconstructed scoring rings.

The main path continues past the Ball Court around the northern side of Lake Macanxoc, hidden behind the trees, although some of the paths leading off to the right will take you through to the lake shore. After about 500 metres a fork around the Pinturas group (*see* below) gives you a choice of places to visit first, the Nohoch Mul pyramid or the Macanxoc Group; to do the most strenuous part before it gets hotter, follow the left fork for a walk of around one kilometre to the Nohoch Mul. The density of Cobá's forest is such that even excavated areas can seem almost reclaimed by the brush, and makes it doubly hard to imagine thousands of people living here. Temples appear through the woods as if they've only just been discovered, and as a natural landscape, with soaring *ceiba* trees filtering luminous patches of dappled sunlight, it's fascinating.

Partway along this path there is another ball court, and a very unusual pyramid known as the **Xaibé** or 'Crossroads' because it stood at the junction of several *sacbeob*.

Built almost like a massive, conical drum, it has only recently been excavated, and is believed to have been of special importance in the life of the city. Easier to see coming is the huge **Nohoch Mul** ('Big Mound') itself, by far the tallest pyramid in the northern Yucatán, 42m high, in seven levels of diminishing width. Again, it is in a Petén-like, rounded style, and begs comparison with the giant pyramids of Tikal. This one you can climb up, and those who do so are rewarded with a really fabulous view over the lakes, the Iglesia and the sea of forest. Having made the gruelling scramble up there, most people stay to take it in for at least a while, and at the very top there's a late addition, a small Postclassic temple with a Diving God carving. Near the foot of the Nohoch Mul is a small temple platform, **Structure 10**, with some fairly well-preserved *stelae*. One of these, **Stela 20**, has a particularly fine carving of an unidentified *ahau* shown standing over two captives, and the latest Long Count date yet found at Cobá, corresponding to 30 November 780.

The Grupo de Pinturas and Macanxoc

If you retrace this path you can cut across to the Macanxoc track through the **Grupo de Pinturas**, which stands between the two sides of the fork. The last large group of buildings erected at Cobá, from the Late Postclassic around 1200, it was built in the East-Coast style of Tulum, partly by 'recycling' the stones of older temples, such as Classic-era *stelae*. Some of its buildings, especially the largest (**Structure 1**), still have sections of the murals that gave the group its name, but you're not allowed close enough to see them much.

Another 500 metres or so will take you to the **Macanxoc** cluster itself. There are several small buildings and temples, but the centrepiece is an area with over 20 *stelae* scattered among the trees, each on its own small platform and sheltered by a *palapa*. Some of them appear to be lost in the woods, and take some clambering to get to. The concentration of so many *stelae* in such a small space suggests that this was a place of great ceremonial importance, almost a collective 'archive' of Cobá. Some of them are very worn and hard to distinguish, but in others the carving is quite clear. One as yet unexplained feature of them is that they depict an unusually large number of women, as if Cobá had several women rulers. The most spectacular of all is **Stela 1**, which has an account of the Mayan creation myth with a time-cycle that corresponds to 41 thousand, million, million, million, million years, the longest Long Count date ever written and one of the largest finite numbers ever conceived by a human being.

If you still want to see more of Cobá, there are many more semi-excavated building clusters that can be found by wandering on down the forest paths. The official guides at the gate, on request and if you strike a deal, will also take you to lesser-known parts of the site. Continuing on past Macanxoc for about one and a half kilometres will eventually take you to the **Zacakal** group, and there's another good track that leads off south from the path between Macanxoc and Las Pinturas. If you can take the heat you could easily explore for a whole day without exhausting the possibilities, amid the unearthly giant *ceibas* and the birds. Just don't get totally lost.

Tours

Villagers will be willing to guide you around the reserve and ruins for between $3 and $5, according to the length of tour you request; the best times to see monkeys are 6–8am and 2–4pm.

Where to Stay and Eat

There is also an area by the lake where you can **camp** or sleep in a hammock beneath a big communal *palapa*, for around $10–$15, all meals included. It's a pocket of complete, rural tranquillity.

Punta Laguna

About 20 kilometres north of Cobá on the road toward Nuevo Xcan is the village of Punta Laguna. There is another small Mayan site just outside it, one of the tributaries of Classic-era Cobá, with buildings in a similar style. The village is of more interest to most visitors today, though, for its **Reserva del Mono Araña** or spider monkey reserve (*villagers will guide you to the ruins and the best places to see wildlife*). In the middle of dense forest and with a beautiful small lake, Punta Laguna is one of the best places to see wildlife in northern Yucatán, and in the surrounding area there are alligators, deer, peccaries, howler as well as spider monkeys and all kinds of birds.

Yucatán State

Yucatán State

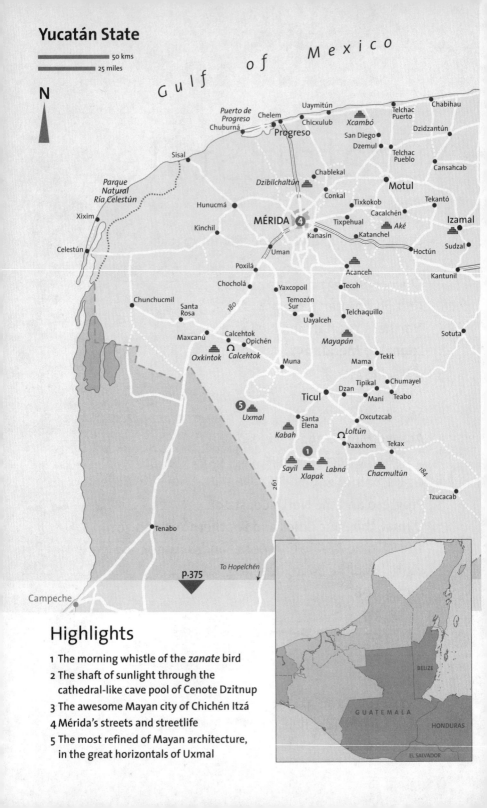

N

50 kms
25 miles

Gulf of Mexico

Puerto de Progreso
Chuburná
Chelem
Chicxulub
Uaymitún
Telchac Puerto
Chabihau
Xcambó
San Diego
Dzidzantún
Dzemul
Telchac Pueblo
Cansahcab
Progreso
Sisal
Chablekal
Motul
Tekantó
Dzibilchaltún
Conkal
Tixkokob
Cacalchén
Izamal
Hunucmá
MÉRIDA
Tixpehual
Aké
Sudzal
Xixim
Kinchil
Kanasín
Katanchel
Hoctún
Uman
Parque Natural Ría Celestún
Celestún
Poxilá
Acanceh
Kantunil
Chocholá
Yaxcopoil
Tecoh
Chunchucmil
Temozón Sur
Telchaquillo
Santa Rosa
Uayalceh
Sotuta
Maxcanú
Calcehtok
Opichén
Mayapán
Oxkintok
Calcehtok
Muna
Mama
Tekit
Tipikal
Chumayel
Dzan
Maní
Teabo
Ticul
5
Uxmal
Santa Elena
Oxcutzcab
Kabah
Loltún
Tekax
Yaaxhom
1
Sayil
Labná
Chacmultún
Xlapak
Tzucacab
Tenabo

P.375
To Hopelchén

Campeche

Highlights

1 The morning whistle of the *zanate* bird
2 The shaft of sunlight through the cathedral-like cave pool of Cenote Dzitnup
3 The awesome Mayan city of Chichén Itzá
4 Mérida's streets and streetlife
5 The most refined of Mayan architecture, in the great horizontals of Uxmal

BELIZE
GUATEMALA
HONDURAS
EL SALVADOR

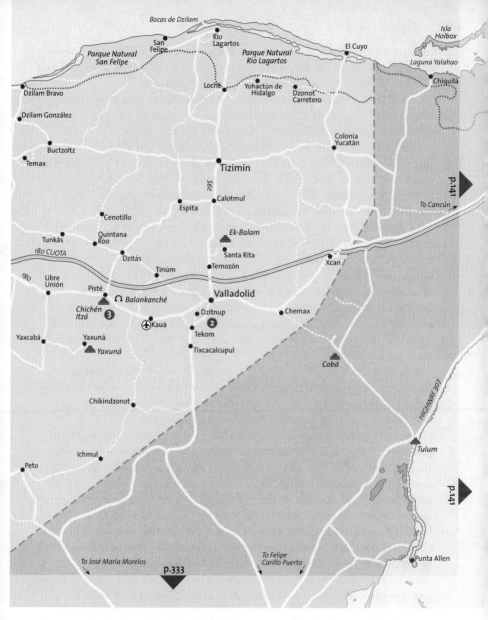

Anyone who can leave Yucatán with indifference, has never been an artist and will never be a scholar.

Desiré Charnay

Glimpsed flashing by from a bus window, the Yucatán can appear like one continuous expanse of flat green scrub, each stretch the same as the last: all those kilometres with not a single river, not a single hill. The Yucatán does have rivers, huge ones, but they flow under the ground not over it, passing through giant caverns as at

Loltún or Balankanché, and into cathedral-like subterranean pools such as Dzitnup near Valladolid. It has hills too, but they're the man-made, massive temple-platforms of the Maya, now often overgrown contours in the countryside.

Yucatán State is the heir of the old Spanish *Audiencia* which once governed the whole of the peninsula, until the Mexican government separated off Campeche and Quintana Roo, a 'truncation' that still rankles with some Yucatecans. The Yucatán did not even have proper communications by land with the rest of Mexico until the 1940s; contacts were carried out by ship or, lately, air. Self-contained, it developed its own history, its own food, its own music, becoming one of the most distinctive parts of Mexico. Compared to the newly minted world of Cancún and the coast, it has a very solid sense of its own historic culture.

The presence of the Maya is fundamental to the Yucatán, as alive in the present day as it was in the past. The state contains many of the greatest creations of Mayan culture – Chichén Itzá, Uxmal, the Puuc cities – but also many more sites that are little known and only recently excavated, such as Oxkintok or Ek-Balam. There are other attractions from other eras as well. The state is exceptionally rich in Spanish colonial architecture, from the great monasteries of Maní or Izamal to once-aristo-cratic *haciendas* (some of which are now very special hotels). At the centre of it all is Mérida, hub of everything in the Yucatán and one of the most distinguished of Mexican colonial cities.

All these features are very concrete and specific, but people who love the place recall something much less tangible. Yucatán towns have a unique set of visual asso-ciations, a very particular combination of street life, tricycle taxis, unhurried pace, bright flowers and fruit, women in embroidered white *huípiles* and solid colonial architecture. Behind it all there is a pervasive sense of amiable, courteous gentleness. In Mexico as a whole, Yucatecans are known as sentimental romantics. The Yucatán Maya for their part are very special, very self-possessed, aware of their own culture, impassively reserved one moment and enormously friendly the next, with a quiet, straightforward, almost palpable decency. Put these elements together and the result is an atmosphere that can leave the new arrival distinctly disoriented. Perhaps the greatest attraction of Mérida is that, even as a city, it manages to main-tain this charm and tranquillity. The Yucatán really has no right to be so benign, for it has often had a terrible history. This is the great Yucatecan paradox.

This chapter is ordered as if you are continuing west from Cancún, though it can be just as practical to travel straight to Mérida and tour outwards from there.

Valladolid

If you enter the Yucatán through Cancún and head west, the town of Valladolid comes as a sudden blast of local life after the multi-national, Pan-Mexican world of the coast. It's the first real Yucatecan town you come to, a first encounter with the region's distinctive way of being. Tourists come through here, and Valladolid has lately taken to displaying its charms rather more self-consciously, but the town's main business is still to fulfil, for the villages around it, the role that Mérida carries out for the whole state: that of place to buy and sell, meet up, catch a bus, hear what's going on, sort out any official business and pick up anything they can't find at home.

Experiencing this way of life is an attraction in itself, but the town also has the finest of the easily swimmable *cenotes* nearby. Valladolid also makes a good (and economical) base for visiting Chichén Itzá, or Ek-Balam and Río Lagartos to the north.

History

As often in the Yucatán, Valladolid's current likeable calm belies a bitter history. It stands on the site of *Zací*, capital of the Mayan lordship of the Cupules, although next to nothing remains of the pre-Hispanic settlement. A new 'city' of Valladolid was first

Getting Around

By Bus

Valladolid's main **bus station** is at the junction of Calles 37 and 54, but as this is several blocks from the centre most buses also stop at the old terminal at Calles 39 and 46 (except 3am–6am). Along Highway 180, there are 13 first-class and 17 second-class (hourly or half-hourly) buses daily to **Mérida** (first-class about $8). Several first- and all second-class buses stop at **Chichén Itzá/Pisté**. In the opposite direction there are nine first-class and almost hourly second-class buses to **Cancún** (about $5), of which six first-class and three second go on to Playa del Carmen.

There are also four buses a day to **Izamal** via **Dzitas** (all second-class). Going south, there are three first- and three second-class buses each day to **Cobá** and Tulum ($4.50), and two second-class services daily to **Chetumal** ($10.50) via **Felipe Carrillo Puerto**. Valladolid is also a good jumping-off point to northern Yucatán: there are buses hourly to **Tizimín**, a few of which continue to **Río Lagartos**, and one daily at 2.30am to **Chiquilá** (for **Holbox**, *see* p.171), all second-class. Valladolid is also the hub of abundant *colectivo* traffic to all the surrounding villages and further afield. Most leave from C/ 44, just west of the plaza. Some run all the way to Cancún.

By Bicycle

Bikes can be hired for 5 pesos (55c US) an hour or $3 a day for trips around town or out to Dzitnup Cenote, from **Antonio 'Negro' Aguilar** (*see* below). Valladolid is easy to cycle around, with dedicated cycle tracks along the main roads into town, and out to Dzitnup.

Orientation

Valladolid has a straightforward grid street system centred on the main plaza (even numbers run north–south, odd numbers east–west). Highway 180 west from Cancún becomes C/ 39, which runs along the north side of the plaza between Calles 40 and 42; eastbound traffic runs along C/ 41, and the south side of the plaza. Because streets are long, cross-streets are often indicated with addresses, i.e., C/ 46, x 39 & 41 (between 39 and 41). The most central *gasolinera* is on C/ 41 west of the plaza between Calles 46 and 48.

Tourist Information

Valladolid t (985–)

Tourist Office: In the **Ayuntamiento**, beneath the arcades on the east of the plaza (Parque Principal), on the corner of Calles 40 and 41 (*open daily 8–8*). Helpful.
Banks: Two on the plaza, both with ATMs.
Internet Access: Two central places on the square are **Modatel**, by the Hotel María de la Luz, and **The Mexican**, among the restaurants in the Bazar.
Phone Office: There is a (relatively) well-priced phone office just off the plaza on C/ 42.
Police Station: In the town hall; the **post office** is alongside.

Tours

Viajes Valladolid, C/ 42 no. 206, near Hotel San Clemente, t 856 1857, *viva@chichen.com.mx*. Useful local agency, running tours of the town and Chichén Itzá, Ek-Balam, Río Lagartos and some other locations.

founded in 1542 by Montejo el Sobrino in a place called Chauacá, closer to the coast, but its colonists found it unhealthy, and in 1545 it was decided they should take over the old Mayan town. For its first 300 years Valladolid was a colonial frontier town, a white island amid a sea of Mayan villages. Scarcely a year after it was established, in 1546, Valladolid was besieged in the first great Mayan revolt of the colonial era.

Its distance from Mérida meant that Valladolid developed into a regional centre of its own, with distinguished colonial architecture. It was a place where little changed after the first decades of the Conquest, and its finest families were known for their extreme conservatism. In the same way that the élites of Mérida or Campeche rejected interference from central Mexico, the *ladinos* of Valladolid resented control

Antonio 'Negro' Aguilar at C/ 44 no. 195, x 39 & 41, t 856 2125, one block from the plaza. El Negro (Antonio's baseball nickname) is what you call a character: a one-time police chief of Valladolid, and prior to that a pro baseball player. Today he rents out bikes, rooms (*see* below), and also provides any information he can to passing visitors in booming, self-constructed English.

Where to Stay

Valladolid t (985–)
Valladolid remains by far the best place to find good value, low-priced accommodation in central Yucatán, especially if you don't mind not having a/c.

Moderate
Ecotel Quinta Real, C/ 40 no. 160-A, x 27 & 29, t 856 3472, *www.ecotelquintareal.com.mx*. A recent addition in a quiet area six blocks north of the Parque Principal. It occupies a new but colonial-style building combining traditional décor with modern comforts. The 'eco' tag means mainly that it's rustic-looking, but it does have an exuberant patio garden, with a wonderful orchard that supplies all fruit and herbs used in the hotel. There's also a lovely pool and tennis court, and pretty restaurant.

Hacienda San Miguel, about 8km west of the town on the Dzitas–Izamal road, t 858 1539, *sanmiguel@chichen.com.mx*. A distinct alternative is provided by this 19th-century *hacienda*, though similarities between it and 'luxury *haciendas*' elsewhere are mainly architectural. Until recently it was purely

agricultural, and it still has the feel of a working ranch, with plenty of cattle about. Its owners have built eight large *cabañas* in the grounds, sleeping up to four, with roof fans and shady porches. There are also plainer rooms attached to the main house which have a/c, costing a bit more. There's a pool, a bar and verandahs for lounging, and you can rent horses or bikes for exploring the paths around the estate. The owners have a charming country courtliness.

El Mesón del Marqués, C/ 39 no. 203, x 40 & 42, t 856 3042, *h_marques@chichen.com.mx*. Not as spick and span as the Quinta Real, but has a distinctive charm (and lower prices). It's in an old colonial house on the plaza, with restaurant and lounge areas around a flower-decked patio, and a pool in a garden. Rooms all have a/c, fans and cable TV, and are all quite bright; some have balconies overlooking the garden.

Inexpensive
Hotel María de la Luz, C/ 42 no. 193-C, x 37 & 39, t/f 856 2071. Occupies a colonial-style house on the Parque Principal with an airy patio, attractive restaurant and a nice pool, but the rooms are a bit worn and often dark. However, all have baths, a/c and TV, and the low prices make it good value for the price. No credit cards.

Hotel San Clemente, C/ 42 no. 206, x 41 & 43, t 856 3161. On a corner just off the plaza, this is one of the best-known hotels, but its large rooms could be better cared for. There's more light but no a/c on the upper floors; it also offers a pool, a restaurant, and TV in every room, but it's not such a good deal as its competitors.

from Mérida. At the same time, the old wealth on which they based their social pretensions was really very meagre. When Stephens arrived here in 1841 he found a town semi-paralyzed in time, which bore 'the marks of ancient grandeur, but is now going to decay', with streets overgrown and roofless, and collapsing houses even in the main square.

It was only fitting that this symbol of old Spanish rule should see the outbreak of the great upheaval of the Caste War. It was in nearby Tizimín that, in 1838, Captain Santiago Imán began his anti-Mexican revolt and, against all previous practice, hit upon the secret weapon of recruiting the Maya for his revolutionary army. In January 1847 Valladolid was attacked and taken in yet another white-led, anti-centralist rising,

Hotel Zací, C/ 44 no. 191, x 37 & 39, t 856 2167, f 856 2594. A block west of the plaza, one of the most enjoyable *inexpensive* options, with a small pool, a/c in some rooms, parking and friendly management. All rooms are quite well lit (choose upper floors for more light and a view of the cathedral, lower floors for a/c) and comfortable.

Cheap

'Negro' Aguilar (*see* facing page). Basic rooms, with fans and showers, in a former school, costing from $6–7 per room, with discounts for longer stays. They're very simple, but big, and you can make them cosy; amazingly, they also have access to a pool, a basketball court and a patio where tenants can lounge on hammocks and cook up barbecues. You couldn't have a friendlier and more decent host: he and his son-in-law are ultra-helpful, and will drive people to the bus station and set up their own 'tours'.

Albergue La Candelaria, C/ 35, no. 201-F, x 42 & 44, t 856 2267, *candelaria_hostel@hot mail.com*. A new hostel affiliated to the AMAJ federation. Well run and a lot brighter than many bargain-basement hotels, it has beds in dorm rooms for around $7 (discounts for IYHF card holders), one double room or you can hang a hammock in the garden for $3. There's an attractive patio and lounge area, with TV, free water and coffee, and Internet access ($2 an hour). It's next to a church on Parque de La Candelaria square, two blocks north of the Parque Principal.

Hotel Lily, C/ 44 no. 192, x 37 & 39, t 856 2163. Founded in 1928, with plain, much-used but very cheap rooms with fans and showers, and a few cell-like rooms with shared bath.

Staying in a Mayan Village: Tinúm

Anyone wanting to get close to the reality of modern Mayan life might wish to stay in the village of **Tinúm**, 22km from Valladolid on the Izamal road. Since the 1970s, when a US college anthropology department sent study groups here, people from many countries have stayed here, from ones and twos to groups of 40 or more, and for one or two days or months at a time. The scheme is run by one of the elder citizens of the community, Don Jacinto Pool (known as Don Chivo).

Guests share the space within a palm-roofed *na* with a local family, their kids and dogs, and join in meals. There are *cenotes* nearby, and excursions to Chichén Itzá or further afield can be organized with village *combis*. Visitors are also welcome to take part in the chores of daily life. It's not obligatory, and the Maya are too courteous to ask you to do anything unless you offer first.

Villagers speak only Yucatec and Spanish, but Don Chivo has an English phrase book for emergencies. Be aware that sleeping in a hammock can be trying on the back if you're not used to it. Staying in Tinúm costs around $12 per person per day, meals included.

If you are interested in staying there, you should write, in Spanish, to **Don Jacinto Pool Tutz**, C/ 24 no. 102-A, Tinúm, Yucatán CP97750, Mexico, allowing at least six weeks for a reply. Alternatively (as mail is very unreliable), you can just turn up, and efforts will be made to accommodate you. Ask for Don Chivo, and by and by you'll be directed to him.

Tinúm can be reached by *colectivo* from Valladolid, and is also on the second-class Cancún–Mérida bus route of Autobuses del Centro de Yucatán.

but this time Indian troops got out of control, unleashing their anger in a brief orgy of looting and destruction. The following July a local Mayan leader, Manuel Antonio Ay, was executed in Valladolid's main square, but this only spurred other village *batabob* into action. Once the revolt began Valladolid was cut off from Mérida and besieged, until in March 1848 the order was given to evacuate the 10,000 people left in the town up the road north to Espita. Once on the open road they were easy prey to Mayan guerrillas, and the withdrawal from Valladolid was the greatest catastrophe suffered by *ladino* Yucatán in the entire war.

After the Mayas' apparently inexplicable failure to achieve final victory Valladolid, deserted, stripped and looted, was reoccupied in 1849. The Yucatán state legislature

Eating Out

Valladolid has its own prized specialities within Yucatecan cuisine, above all *pollo oriental de Valladolid* (roast chicken with a sauce of chilis, garlic and bitter orange juice) and *lomitos de Valladolid* (diced pork cooked with tomatoes, garlic and chilis, often eaten *taco*-style).

Moderate

La Chispa, C/ 41 no. 201, x 42 & 44. Style comes to Valladolid: a youth-oriented restaurant, with a smartly redesigned patio, metallic seating, primary-coloured décor, low lighting, loud Hispanopop much of the time and a menu of decent but pricey *tacos* and Mexican standards.

Hotel María de la Luz, C/ 42 no. 193-C, x 37 & 39. Not as traditionally pretty as the Mesón del Marqués, but the patio is still a very pleasant place to eat, serving enjoyable traditional Yucatecan and local dishes, including good seafood.

El Mesón del Marqués, C/ 39 no. 203, x 40 & 42. This long-established patio-restaurant is the classic place to eat in town; it is home to a very highly regarded version of *pollo oriental*.

El Mexicano, Ecotel Quinta Real, C/ 40 no. 160-A, x 27 & 29. Less atmospheric than the places right on the plaza, but pretty, and offering an interesting and varied menu of Mexican, Yucatecan and international (Italian-oriented) food.

Yepes II, C/ 41 no. 148. Off the plaza opposite the Museo de San Roque, with high-quality *tacos*, steaks and other Mexican, rather than Yucatecan, dishes served out in a garden.

Cheap

Best for a cheap meal are the 20 or so open-air *cocinas económicas* around a kind of self-service food court in the Bazar handicrafts market on the plaza, next to the Mesón del Marqués. They offer everything from Yucatecan traditionals to familiar *burritos* and *enchiladas*, and even burgers. They share the Bazar with a lot of music shops, so even breakfast can get surprisingly noisy.

La de Michoacán, C/ 41, x 42 & 44. A combination ice cream stand, bakery and restaurant that's a backpackers' favourite, with bargain set meals. It's almost next door to Restaurant El Parque.

Los Portales, C/ 41, corner of 40. Atmospheric place from which to survey the plaza, with a terrace in the shady colonnades across the street from the tourist office, fine for breakfast or substantial Yucatecan dishes. Inside, the dining room is equally pretty.

Restaurant El Parque, C/ 41, corner of 42. A long-running institution on the plaza, providing decent Yucatecan specialities at friendly prices, including a nicely punchy *pollo oriental*.

Entertainment and Nightlife

Some of the best local entertainment is free, at weekends. On Sunday evenings the plaza fills up with families, couples and bunches of kids, and at 7.30pm every week the Banda del Ayuntamiento gives a free concert, playing Latin American favourites – *rumbas*, stately Mexican *danzón*, Yucatecan *boleros*, cha-cha-cha – and sometimes even big-band jazz.

awarded it the title of *Ciudad Heroíca*, which the town crest retains to this day, despite the fact that much of the current population is as likely to be descended from besiegers as besieged. In more modern times events in Valladolid have been far less spectacular, and today it seems one of the best organized of Yucatán towns.

The Plaza and Cenote Zací

Everything in Valladolid homes in on the plaza, or **Parque Principal**, a classic Yucatán colonial square with its *confidenciales* love-seats, laurel trees, several *taco*-stands and a Franciscan cathedral, tall and plain on the south side. Valladolid used to wear its historic state fairly casually, but in 1999 the last (probably) PRI governor of the Yucatán, Víctor Cervera Pacheco, decided the old town wasn't quite pretty enough and gave the square and several streets around it a Campeche-style refurbishment, with façades painted in pastel colours instead of the traditional whitewash, gothicky lettering on shop signs and so on. Since then the town looks slightly as if it's always having to look its best and straighten its collar, but for the most part Valladolid is happy enough being itself rather than dressing up for tourists. It still fulfils with dedication its role of local market and repository of every kind of necessity for country people, with the busiest shopping time being Sunday morning. The main **market** is a few blocks east of the plaza (Calles 32 and 37). Since the repainting the Parque Principal has been heavily colonized by souvenir stores, but C/ 39 either side of the square is much more local, alive with crowds, bikes, buses and shops. One block west at the corner of C/ 44 is the semi-official **Mercado de Artesanías** (craft market).

In the middle of the plaza the railings are lined with *huípiles* and other embroidery that Mayan women from surrounding villages hope to sell to the occupants of the tourist buses that turn up every morning from Cancún. Valladolid is a noted centre of *huípil* embroidery; there's even a rather cute statue of a lady in a *huípil* emerging from the fountain in the middle of the plaza. On the north side of the plaza there's another small handicrafts centre, known simply as the **Bazar**, but the goods on show are generally less interesting than the cheap restaurants in the patio.

Valladolid has some of the finest colonial church architecture in the Yucatán, with a lighter, more elegant style than many churches elsewhere. The Cathedral of **San Servacio**, begun in the 17th century and finished in the 18th, is tall and white, with delicate twin towers above a façade as grand in some ways as that of Mérida. Alongside it, the sides of the square are sheltered by deep, whitewashed colonnaded porticoes. On the east side is the colonial-style **Ayuntamiento** (*adm free*), which has a pretty patio inside; above one can see the plain 19th-century council chamber, while on the stairs there is a monument to the original Spanish settlers of the city in 1545. Behind the Ayuntamiento on the same block, a short walk along C/ 41, is the church of San Roque, which now houses the **Museo de San Roque** (*open daily 9–9; adm free, discretionary contributions requested*), an engaging local museum that makes the most of its setting inside the airy old church. Highlights among its displays are fine ceramics and other artefacts from the Mayan ruins of Ek-Balam, the amount of which has increased rapidly with the accelerating pace of excavations there; from later eras there are fascinating documents on the *conquistador* founders of Valladolid and rare anecdotes about 17th-century pirate raids, as well as thorough exhibits on colonial rural society and Mayan folk traditions. However, it's only labelled in Spanish.

In the middle of town, occupying the block between Calles 37, 39, 34 and 36, is an extraordinary natural attraction, the **Cenote Zací** (*open daily 8–6; adm; swimming not permitted*). This was the original water source of Mayan Zací and the early settlement of Valladolid. It's now a park, and steps lead down into the cavern mouth, at the top of which is a bar/restaurant and an underused crafts market. It's a huge, dramatic sink-hole, with fascinating patterns of light, even if the water is now grubby with algae.

San Bernardino Sisal

Officially open Mon and Wed–Sun 8–noon and 5–7; closed Tues;
outside service times a small adm fee may be charged;
alternatively, you may find the church has simply been left open.

Two blocks west of the plaza on C/ 41, C/ 41-A (another street that has been painted-up, and given the rather fake name *Calzada de los Frailes*), cuts off southwest to the *barrio* of Sisal and the finest of Valladolid's colonial monuments, the monastery and church of San Bernardino de Siena. Begun in 1552, San Bernardino is the oldest permanent church – as opposed to a *capilla de indios* – in the Yucatán. Like those at Maní and Izamal, the work was supervised by the Franciscans' ever-energetic architect Friar Juan de Mérida. The location of the massive, fortress-like convent outside the town was due in part to the presence of a good *cenote*, but also to the fact that it had to fulfil two functions: catering to the Spanish population of Valladolid and acting as a missionary convent for the Mayan villages in the surrounding countryside. This was reflected in a unique feature of Sisal, in that the open altar of the *capilla de indios*, rather than being placed alongside the monastery chapel as at Maní, was built on to the side of the church, facing south, so that the two groups could worship without coming into contact (the remains of the Indian chapel can be seen if you walk round to the right, from the main entrance of the church).

The monastery was closed, and San Bernardino converted into a simple parish church, as long ago as 1755. Recently it has been extensively restored and, in line with other changes in Valladolid, the blockhouse-like main façade has been unhistorically part-painted in white and yellow. It's an unusual, slab-fronted building, with the frontal gallery in its massive limestone walls giving it a distinctly medieval appearance. Inside, the highlight is the church's giant altarpiece in polychrome wood, a dramatic combination of high Baroque with a Mexican sense of colour. On the left-hand side a door leads to a two-storey cloister of massive stone colonnades, housing a beautiful garden full of giant palms. There is also a four-square 'well' dating from 1613, which was built over the mouth of the natural *cenote*.

Due east of San Bernardino, at Calles 40 and 49, there is another fine 17th-century church, **San Juan**, with an unusual twin-spired façade and a beautiful, bougainvillaea-filled garden. Anyone wishing to do a fuller tour of Valladolid's colonial churches should also take a look at the **Candelaria**, at Calles 44 and 35, **Santa Ana** – another missionary chapel – at 34 and 41, and **Santa Lucía**, at 42 and 27.

Cenote Dzitnup and Cenote Samula

One of the most spectacular of Yucatán *cenotes* – and the best of the well-known, swimmable ones – lies only seven kilometres west of Valladolid. It's most widely known as **Cenote Dzitnup**, although Yucatec *dzitnup* is a form of the word that gave rise to the Spanish *cenote*, so this means nothing more than 'Cenote-Cenote'; in Maya it's ungraciously called the Cenote Xkekem or 'Pig Cenote'.

At the entrance, you can begin to wonder where the *cenote* has gone, but the way in is down a narrow ramp and still narrower passageway that only has room for one crouching person at a time (although steps and path are well kept and easy to nego-tiate). Then, below, the passageway suddenly opens up into a dramatic vision of the underworld, a cave of basilica-like proportions with a huge, arching roof filled with turquoise water; the thought occurs that, despite the Franciscans' best efforts, the *cenotes* and caverns are the true cathedrals of the Yucatán. A hole in the roof casts a shaft of light dead into the centre of the pool, creating a wonderful contrast of light and shade. A small stepped area leads down to a muddy 'beach', or you can swim directly from the rocks. The water is clear, clean and at a perfect temperature; few can resist swimming into the shaft of light, while all around strange forms of rock hang into and rise out of the pool.

When the main *cenote* is crowded, there is another sinkhole on the other side of the road into Dzitnup, **Cenote Samula**. Though not quite as dramatic, it's still spectacular, with the roots of a huge *ceiba* tree stretching straight down from the surface some 40ft to the precious water below, a vivid image of the mystical powers that the Maya attributed to these trees. There's also a little landing stage, for easy swimming.

Ek-Balam

Little known and formerly very overgrown, the ruined Mayan city of Ek-Balam is one of the sites where very recent excavations (since 1998) have produced extraordinary results, in the shape of some of the finest of all Mayan sculpture. It's also one of the most unusual, with an architectural and sculptural style that seem entirely of its own.

Ek-Balam has one of the longest records of occupation in the northern Yucatán, from the Preclassic, about 100 BC, right up until the Conquest. The name means 'black jaguar', and a Spanish land grant of 1579 relates that the settlement was founded by a 'great lord' also called Ek-Balam, a story that must have come from the local Maya. It appears to have grown into a significant city above all in the Terminal Classic, around 700–1000. Many of its most impressive structures were built very late, after 800, in or around the time of a powerful ruler called Ukit-Kan-Lek-Tok, whose tomb has been the most dramatic discovery of all. The size and grandeur of Ek-Balam's buildings indicate that it was a powerful, wealthy city, and there is much speculation as to how much this wealth was related to the control of salt beds near Río Lagartos. Like other cities in the region it suffered a collapse around the year 1000, but it seems to have remained inhabited to an unusual degree throughout most of the Postclassic and pre-Conquest eras. In the modern era it was first explored by Desiré Charnay in 1886, but thorough excavations only began in 1987 and 1994.

The excavated site covers only the ceremonial core of Ek-Balam. The whole city covered a much wider area, and in 1987 *sacbé* roads were discovered stretching out two kilometres in every direction. The most distinctive feature of central Ek-Balam is immediately apparent as you approach: its compactness, contained within a perimeter wall. It is not clear whether this was purely to mark off the 'official' area or whether it was also for defence. Superficially it can seem similar to the walled Mayan city of Becán (*see* p.365), but Ek-Balam's internal layout is different again. Within the wall are massive, rectangular temple-platforms around connecting, quadrangle-like plazas, giving a much more inward-looking feel than is usual in Mayan squares.

From the caretaker's hut you enter the ruins along an impressively ramp-like *sacbé*, facing north. Unmissable as you go through the gap in the wall are two of the most enigmatic structures at Ek-Balam. The first is a unique, **four-sided arch** that looks as if it served as a kind of ceremonial, ritual entrance over the *sacbé*. To the right of it is the **Palacio Oval** ('Oval Palace', also known as La Redonda), a semi-spiral-shaped round tower that from this angle looks more Middle Eastern than Mayan. Instead of the square symmetries of Mayan temple platforms it seems to be made up of a series of round drums of different sizes and even at different angles, an almost abstract combination of interlocking shapes and spaces. Why it was built this way is a mystery. Relics of wealthy burials, including one of a child, have been found here, and it may have been used in astronomical ceremonies. From the Redonda or the arch you get a good view of the layout of the three squares of Ek-Balam, with the first and smallest below you. Beyond it on the left, sideways-on, is the first of the three huge platforms that form the sides of the main plaza, **Structure 2**, which has scarcely been excavated. Forming a boundary between the squares is a **Ball Court**. A date found here indicates

Site Information

Open daily 8–5; adm, Sun adm free.

Ek-Balam is reached via a right turn off the Highway 295 Tizimín road, about 16km north of Valladolid. From there, you follow a winding country road for another 10km, and turn left in the village of **Santa Rita**. There are no regular bus services to Ek-Balam, but **tours** are run from Valladolid (*see* pp.229–30), and drivers of *colectivos* from Valladolid to Santa Rita may be open to offers to go on to the ruins.

that it was completed in 841, and other discoveries have included some very hard stone balls (now in the Mérida museum) apparently used in the game.

Dominating the view, though, and filling the whole north side of the main plaza is the looming mountain known as **Structure 1** or the **Acropolis**, the part of Ek-Balam most dramatically transformed by recent excavations. Until 1998–9 this was only an indistinct mound like Structure 2 and 3 on either side of it; today, it has been revealed to be a multi-level combined palace and temple complex, similar to the equally imposing Palacio at Sayil or the Five Storeys at Edzná. Climbing up the middle there is a typically awe-inspiring, very steep stairway, either side of which are temples, long Puuc-style friezes with (still undeciphered) stucco inscriptions and doorways leading into unusually deep, spacious chambers. The truly unique discovery here, though, is the temple three-quarters of the way up on the left, now sheltered for its protection beneath an equally huge *palapa* roof, and called **El Trono** ('The Throne'). It is believed to have contained the tomb of Ukit-Kan-Lek-Tok, who was clearly a major figure in Ek-Balam's history. Astonishingly complete, this is the largest, best-restored and most theatrical of Mayan monster-mouth temple entrances, but one that stands all on its own since, while in the more common Chenes style monster-elements run all around the entrance, here a giant-toothed jaw actually forms the floor of the doorway. Around it there are superbly modelled figures – yet to be identified – that rate among the finest Mayan carving. The seated figure above the doorway, who has lost his head, is believed to be Ukit-Kan-Lek-Tok himself. More large rooms are being excavated further up on the Acropolis, but are not yet open to visitors.

From the upper levels of the Acropolis you also get the usual fabulous view, and can pick out more *sacbés* and unexcavated platforms on the plain around the city. You also get a good view of the Puuc-like buildings, the remains of residential complexes, that stand on top of Structure 2, and the similarly still-unexcavated Structure 3 on the east side of the main plaza. The last square, the southeast plaza, forms a smaller, separate area just beyond Structure 3. Back at ground level, **Structure 17**, which forms one side of this plaza by the Ball Court, is known as **Las Gemelas**, 'The Twins', because of its pair of near-identical small temples. **Structure 10**, opposite them on the east flank of the square is a wide platform with an almost complete raised plaza on top of it. The base dates from the Late Classic, but the structures on top were built by much later occupants of Ek-Balam, after 1200. On a platform in the middle of the plaza is an impressively clear, carved *stela* – another rare discovery in northern Yucatán – that is still under interpretation but is believed to show King Ukit-Kan-Lek-Tok.

Chichén Itzá

Chichén Itzá is the most extensively excavated and the most famous of all the great Mayan cities. This is a little ironic, for its most imposing buildings are not at all typical of Classic Mayan architecture, and show strong influences from non-Mayan central Mexico (just how much is one of the great debates). It is also the most developed site, and the current number of visitors sometimes appals those who knew the place

Getting There

Chichén Itzá t (985–)

Chichén Itzá is 119km from Mérida, 42km from Valladolid, and just south of the Highway 180 Mérida–Cancún road. Pisté, which has a petrol station, is 1½km (an easy walk before the sun gets high) west of the ruins.

Buses are abundant along this road. Second-class buses pass hourly in either direction, stopping in Pisté and at the ruins entrance; some first-class buses also stop in Pisté.

There is now a fully-fledged Chichén Itzá airport near Kauá, 10km towards Valladolid. However, this flight of fancy currently has no scheduled flights and is only used for pricey day trips from Cozumel and Playa del Carmen.

Site Information

Open daily 8–5; adm exp, Sun adm free.

Many people visit Chichén on coach trips from Cancún, with a standard 1½hrs at the ruins, and it can be taken in as a stop-off along the road. However, it's far better to stay overnight. Get to the ruins early to avoid the crowds and heat, and forget the free Sundays unless you're really short of cash. To see the site at all well requires a full morning and can easily fill a whole day, with plenty of rest and water stops (buy water in Pisté; facilities at the site are relatively expensive). Most tour groups arrive at about 11am, and are less noticeable after 2pm. Increasing visitor numbers means that some sections are closed off for conservation reasons; hopefully this won't be extended to too many more areas in the future.

The site admission ticket now obligatorily includes the evening Sound and Light Show, which is why Chichén (and Uxmal) is a good deal more expensive than other Mayan sites (around $9). At the main (western) entrance there is a visitor centre with a restaurant, shops, and a small museum; by the big hotels is another entrance with limited facilities. Handicraft-sellers are now confined to a mall in the visitor centre, leaving the ruins neatly empty of Maya except for guides. The centre stays open for the Sound and Light show until 9–10pm (*see* below). Official guides run a 1½-hr tour for up to 20 people (about $30).

Where to Stay

Chichén Itzá t (985–)

In recent years, two of the upscale hotels on the eastern approach road to Chichén (the first turn, coming from Cancún) have upped their prices sharply. Two others, the Dolores Alba and the Ikkil Cenote, are 3km further east of Chichén Itzá, while all other hotels are in Pisté, 1½km from the ruins (about a 20-min walk). Despite its dependency on the site and ever-growing 'souvenir-ization' Pisté still has a good deal of the laid-back charm of a normal Yucatán village, especially in the evenings.

Hotel prices in Chichén and Pisté tend to be relatively high. An alternative is to base yourself in Valladolid (45mins by bus). It is rarely hard to find a room at Chichén except around the equinoxes, when places are booked up across the whole area, including Valladolid.

Luxury–Expensive

Hacienda Chichén, t 851 0045, *www.yucatan adventure.com.mx.* More characterful and prettier than the Mayaland, with a faded colonial elegance: it occupies part of the old *hacienda* of Chichén, which was rebuilt for the Carnegie archaeologists in the 1920s. The attractive rooms are in *cabañas*, most of them also built at that time.

Hotel Mayaland, t 851 0071, *www.mayaland .com* (*luxury* Nov–April). The biggest of the luxury hotels, the closest to the ruins, the traditional VIP first choice, and also the most expensive. It's a great barn of a resort hotel with a slightly neo-colonial look, and rooms with a wonderful view of the ruins on one side, or over a patio and pool on the other.

Parque Ikkil, t 851 0000. New, plush *cabañas* (whole bungalows) set in the park around the Ikkil *cenote*, 3km east of the ruins (*see* p.251). A first five cabins opened in 2001, and it's due to have 120. They're very spacious, all with porches and the obligatory palm roofs, plus state-of-the-art comforts, but the place seems more organized around the coach-trippers' restaurant than room guests.

Moderate

Club Med-Villas Arqueológicas, t/f 851 0034/851 0018, *www.come2clubmed.com.* The third of the big hotels by the eastern ruins entrance, but like its near-identical sister hotels at Cobá and Uxmal, Club Med hasn't jacked up its prices as much as its neighbours. The rooms, **restaurants**, lovely pool and beautiful gardens, though, are the same standard (or better), making this a wonderful bargain. All three Club Meds have the same neo-colonial *hacienda* charm, with rooms in *cabañas* or a main building.

Hotel Chichén Itzá, Pisté, t 851 0022, *mayaland@valladolid.com.mx*. A modern hotel in Pisté, not as attractive as those nearer the ruins and a bit short on character, but its rooms have recently been renovated, and it has a big pool and **restaurant**.

Inexpensive

Hotel Dolores Alba, on Highway 180 some 3km east of Chichén (5km from Pisté) towards Balankanché, reservations via Mérida t (999) 928 5650, *www.doloresalba.com*. The best value hotel near Chichén, with very pretty rooms. They're bright, comfortable and in better condition than most of those in Pisté, but cheaper (with or without a/c). There are two great pools, a bar and a **restaurant**. It's a bit isolated, but free transport is provided to the ruins every morning, so you'll only have to get a taxi back (about $3). Second-class buses on the Highway also stop outside. The owners run a sister hotel in Mérida.

Pirámide Inn, by the side of the road in Pisté, t 851 0115, *www.piramideinn.com*. Impossible to miss, this pastel-green travellers' institution is big and motel-like, with its own photo gallery of Mayan excavations, a garden and daffy details like a fake Mayan pyramid by its pretty, relaxing pool. There's also a pleasant **restaurant**, and the rooms (all with a/c) are bright and recently redecorated.

Stardust Inn, Pisté, t 851 0122. Next door to the Pirámide, but now more run-down. It's also motel-like, and has a pool and a/c in all rooms; there's a trailer park and camp site attached. Official prices are quite high, but there are big discounts if you pay cash.

Cheap

Posada Novelo, Pisté, t 851 0122. Little, bargain-basement *posada* attached to the Stardust next door. Rooms are very simple and dark, but guests can use the Stardust's pool.

Posada El Paso, C/ 15 no. 48-F, Pisté (no phone). Best of the real budget options in Pisté, with rooms with fans and showers. They're basic but reasonably well kept, and those on the upper floor, around a courtyard with palms and bougainvillaea, have decent light.

Eating Out

The big hotels all have restaurants (all *expensive–moderate*) that are open to non-residents, with traditional local food. The one in the Hacienda Chichén is most attractive, while the one in the Hotel Chichén Itzá, big and barn-like, is good value. Piste's main street is lined with restaurants, all fairly similar. For really cheap food there's **Lonchería Las Cazuelas** and **Lonchería Fabiola**, two decent snack restaurants on the village's cleaned-up, main plaza. Both cater to a steady stream of foreigners, so their food can't have troubled many of them.

Las Mestizas, near the Stardust and Pirámide, Piste (*moderate*). Most attractive of the small Pisté restaurants, with tables under a *palapa*, good local dishes such as a generous *sopa de lima* and charming waitresses in regulation *huipiles* who go about their business with a Yucatecan hush.

El Carrousel, on Piste's main street (*moderate–cheap*). A reliable standby for enjoyable local fare.

La Palapa, beside the entrance road coming from Pisté (*moderate*). The best place to eat near the ruins: a pretty, traditional restaurant with decent local fare at only slightly inflated prices.

Entertainment

Chichén Itzá's **Sound and Light** spectacular is presented nightly, at 7pm (Nov–Mar) and at 8pm (April–Oct). Commentary is in Spanish, but headphones and a cassette commentary are offered in other languages (an extra $2–$3). Despite its high kitsch-quotient, the show is visually quite effective, and for most of the year this is your only opportunity to see the Descent of Kukulcán (electrically induced) down the Castillo. And since you're obliged to pay for it with the ruins, you might as well go...

years ago. This does not mean, however, that it is no longer worth visiting; other, older Mayan sites may be more subtle architecturally, but the combination of giant scale, monumentality and the mysterious, precise astronomical calculation in the buildings of Chichén make it truly awe-inspiring.

History

Nothing has sparked off more argument among archaeologists and other investigators of the Maya than Chichén Itzá. Until around 1980 it was widely stated with a fair degree of confidence that there had been three successive 'occupations' of Chichén: one that was purely Maya, in the Terminal Classic; one by an illiterate non-Mayan people called the Toltecs, who migrated to the Yucatán from central Mexico in about 1000 and built the largest part of the city (often referred to as 'Toltec-Maya'); finally, another by the still less cultured Itzá in about 1200. The links between them were never clear, and it was sometimes suggested they were entirely separate, and even that the city had been abandoned in the interim. It is clear that Chichén at its peak was far less publicly 'literate' than the Classic cities of the south, and in particular did not erect *stelae* or many other glyph-inscribed monuments (one reason why unravelling its history has been particularly difficult). Architecturally the most spectacular buildings at Chichén have a style of their own that is unquestionably related to those of central Mexico, and distinct from older Mayan styles. However, recent archaeological research has shown that the great 'Toltec' structures at Chichén, such as the pyramid known as the High Priest's Grave, were built in the mid-9th century, during the same years as clearly 'Mayan' buildings nearby like the Casa Colorada. At the same time, Mayan carvings and glyphs have been found on Toltec buildings. Few now believe it possible to draw a line in time or space between the different occupiers of Chichén. Instead, it appears that Chichén Itzá – in contrast to its great rival, purely Mayan Cobá – was always a hybrid, 'cosmopolitan' community, inhabited simultaneously by a mix of peoples from different parts of Mesoamerica.

Discussion is ongoing, and even the 'Toltec-Maya' theory still has its defenders, but in the most widely-shared current view Chichén Itzá emerged as a significant city in around 700, as a result of the convergence of several different groups in the northern Yucatán, driven there by a series of crises in other parts of Mesoamerica. In about 650 the giant, central-Mexican capital of Teotihuacán was sacked and overthrown, and it is likely that some 'refugees' from this collapse migrated towards the Yucatán. With them, according to another theory, came the Putún Maya of Tabasco, who had long formed a link between the Mayan world and central Mexico. In the Yucatecan chronicles that survived after the Spanish Conquest the founders of Chichén Itzá (meaning 'the well of the Itzá') were always identified as a group of 'foreigners', the Itzá. Some say that the Putún and the Itzá were one and the same, but in their book *The Code of Kings* Peter Mathews and the late Linda Schele argue that the new arrivals came north from the other region associated with this name, around Lake Petén-Itzá in Guatemala, and may have been refugees from Tikal and its ally-cities who had lost out in the late-7th-century Petén wars with Calakmul.

At the same time, the founders of Chichén also included people who were clearly fully situated within more traditional Yucatán Mayan culture. As well as the square-cut 'Toltec' pyramids there are many entirely Mayan-style buildings in the city, and carved inscriptions with Long Count dates, confined to a relatively short time from 832 to 909. Over time, Chichén Itzá moved further away from Classic Mayan culture, leaving behind the Long Count calendar as well as other earlier traditions. However, it retained others, and instead of the city being 'illiterate' throughout the Postclassic period, Mayan glyph writing continued to be used in bark manuscripts. Rather than an entirely foreign body, Chichén appears as an adaptation within Mayan civilization.

Chichén Itzá, though, differed from the Classic Mayan cities in other ways besides its heterogeneity. Nowhere in the city are there any images glorifying a single *ahau* ruler and his lineage, the near-obsessive theme of carvings at Palenque or Yaxchilán. Instead, a prime feature of Chichén is the representation of large groups of people of the same size and so, presumably, the same status: lines of seated lords on the Temple of the Chac-Mool, hundreds of carved figures in the Temple of the Warriors. The few deciphered inscriptions refer to several lineages, with no clear sense of precedence. This fits in entirely with the image of Chichén as a 'new' city created by diverse, wandering groups, none of their leaders willing to grant any of the others clear supe-riority. Instead of being ruled by a hereditary *ahau* Chichén had a complex system of government called a *multepal*, in which authority was shared between leading figures of several lineages. This emphasis on the collective is also seen in the giant scale of Chichén's public spaces, as ceremonies must have involved huge numbers of people. Another consequence of Chichén's collective orientation was in its style of sacrifice. Early idealizers of the Maya believed it was the Toltecs who introduced human sacrifice into pacific Mayan cities, but this has been shown to be thoroughly mistaken. What there does appear to have been is a difference in scale: whereas in cities under one *ahau* the sacrifice of a few noble captives was often sufficient, ceremonies at Chichén seem to have demanded the killing of large numbers.

Chichén Itzá's period of glory was relatively short – from about 800 to 950 – but the *multepal* system gave the city great collective strength, and during that time it became pre-eminent across the whole of northern Yucatán. Much has been learnt about the history of Chichén from excavations at Yaxuná, about 20 kilometres to the south. This was the main western vassal of Cobá, and was massively reinforced in around 800 to resist the expansion of the new city (*see* p.222). The conquest of Yaxuná in about 860 was the prelude to a decisive victory for Chichén over Cobá, leaving it with few rivals. Like other Mayan cities it was a sprawling place, extending over 30 square kilometres. It traded widely, and precious materials – turquoise, gold – have been found here from as far afield as modern New Mexico and Colombia. On the coast at Isla Cerritos, near Río Lagartos, the rulers of Chichén built the most sophisti-cated harbour in the Mayan world, from where they controlled the salt trade.

Nevertheless the effects of the collapse still reached Chichén, around 950, and no major buildings were erected in the city after 1000. According to the Yucatecan chronicles some kind of Chichén state survived until the 1190s, when a ruler called

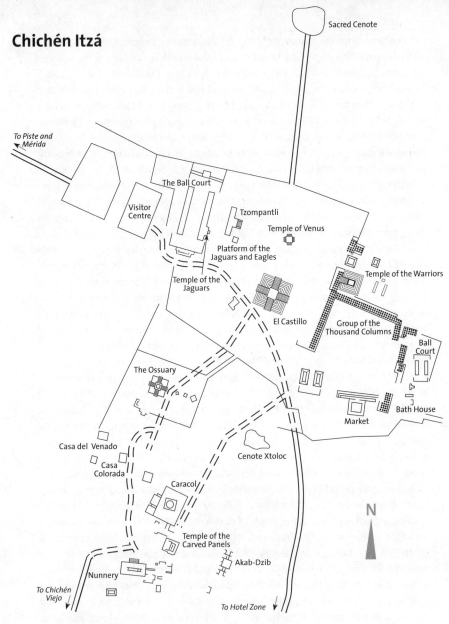

Chichén Itzá

Sacred Cenote

To Piste and
Mérida

Visitor Centre

The Ball Court

Tzompantli

Temple of Venus

Platform of the Jaguars and Eagles

Temple of the Jaguars

Temple of the Warriors

El Castillo

Group of the Thousand Columns

Ball Court

The Ossuary

Bath House

Market

Casa del Venado

Cenote Xtoloc

Casa Colorada

Caracol

N

Temple of the Carved Panels

Akab-Dzib

Nunnery

To Chichén Viejo

To Hotel Zone

Chak-Xib-Chak was expelled from the city by a lord of Mayapán. Nor was it ever completely abandoned, for Bishop Landa wrote that at the time of the Conquest the great *cenote* of Chichén, with Cozumel, was still one of the two great pilgrimage centres of the Yucatán. In 1532 Montejo el Mozo briefly occupied the ruins, and tried to make them into a Spanish fortress. Due to its size and location Chichén was never entirely forgotten, and did not need to be 'discovered'. Stephens and Catherwood made the first serious examination of the site in 1842. In the early 1900s the US

Consul in Mérida, Edward Thompson, bought the estate around the ruins for about $100 and began excavations by trying to dredge the Sacred Cenote, an operation for which he has since been greatly criticized. Chichén Itzá was the first Mayan city to be systematically excavated, by Morley and the Carnegie Institution, beginning in 1923.

The Castillo and the Ball Court

As you enter the site from the visitor centre you come over a slight rise, the remains of a wall that ran around the centre of Chichén. Given its small size it does not appear to have had any defensive purpose, but rather formed the boundary of the ceremonial core of the city. Straight ahead of you is the great plaza, and just to the right the giant bulk of the great pyramid, **El Castillo**, also known as the Pyramid of Kukulcán. This is now established as a standard image of a Mayan pyramid – and a symbol of the Yucatán – although its severe geometry is, in fact, very central-Mexican. Its square, symmetrical plan, with steps on all four sides rather than the one giant stairway of most Mayan pyramids, is reminiscent of buildings at the original Toltec capital of Tula, or at Teotihuacán.

The pyramid is actually a giant representation in stone of the *haab* calendar. It is made up of nine flat, square levels, on top of each other. Each side is divided by a massive staircase, making the number of terraces visible on each side 18, the number of months in the *haab* year. Worked into the slab sides of the terraces there are lines of flat panels – all originally painted, like the rest of the pyramid – which add up to 52, the number of years in the Calendar Round. The number of steps in each staircase is 91, which with the one step to the temple at the top totals 365, the number of days in the year. Most extraordinary of all is the famous phenomenon known as the 'Descent of Kukulcán' (*see* 'The Descent of Kukulcán', overleaf).

Whichever day you arrive, the first thing to do is join the throng making its way up between the two serpent-tails on the majestic north stairway. Climbing up the pyramid is essential to an appreciation of the theatricality of the architecture, towering out of the Yucatán plain. From the top you have a complete overview of the city, and can appreciate the pervasive cosmological layout it shares with all Mayan cities, with a sacred mountain (the Castillo) facing a sacred space (the plaza) leading to power points and entrances to the underworld (the Sacred Cenote, the Ball Court).

On the top platform of the Castillo there is a squat, square temple, with an inner sanctum reached from the portico facing the north side. The two columns of the main entrance are more plumed serpents, with heads at the bottom and hook-shaped rattle-tails at the top. Like much of 'Toltec' Chichén, this temple is an ingenious combination of different architectural traditions. Central-Mexican peoples such as the Toltecs made great use of multiple square columns, but the only roofs they used had been timber frames supporting flat stones or palms; the Maya, meanwhile, had developed their characteristic V-shaped arch, but only used it directly on top of walls, producing distinctive narrow rooms. In the Chichén Itzá synthesis, Mayan pointed vaults were placed on top of a structure of square columns and wooden beams, a combination that made possible much larger spaces, even though it was not ultimately stable (which is why so few roofs from Chichén's columned buildings have survived). The antechamber behind the north entrance of the Castillo temple is one of the best remaining examples, still with its original beams.

The Castillo of Kukulcán was probably given its final form in the late 9th century, and appears massively solid. It is, though, really a casing, for inside it, in the common Mayan pattern, a smaller pyramid has been discovered. This has usually been dated to a century earlier, although one theory maintains that the new pyramid was built precisely 52 years after the first one, in order to mark the ending of a Calendar Round. Although it is sometimes closed due to pressure of numbers, the temple of the first pyramid can usually be visited (*entrance at the back of the upper temple, open only 11am–1pm, 4–5pm*), by climbing down an extremely steamy staircase where the sweat of videoing visitors becomes part of the dank atmosphere. In the first chamber is a large Chac-mool, the characteristic Chichén reclining figure with its head looking fixedly sideways towards anyone approaching, and its hands apparently forming a flat space on its belly where offerings – the hearts and heads of sacrificial victims, and jewels and rich feathers – were placed. The posture of the Chac-mool, like that of the dying Pakal as depicted on his tomb-lid in Palenque, represents a figure descending into the underworld. Beyond this statue is an altar called the **Throne of the Red Jaguar**, a red-painted stone jaguar inlaid with jade roundels, sacred mirrors and bone teeth.

The Descent of Kukulcán

The main, north, staircase of the Castillo is lined on either side with carvings of plumed serpents – an obsessive image in Chichén – leading down to giant serpent-heads at the bottom. On the spring and autumn equinoxes (21 Mar and 21 Sept) the afternoon sun coming round the corner of the pyramid exactly picks out the snake, which 'comes alive' – descending to finish at the head in March (when the effect is clearest), climbing up from it in September. The feathered serpents of Chichén are commonly associated with the mythical god-king Kukulcán, the Yucatecan form of the Teotihuacán god Quetzalcoatl, who was introduced from central Mexico some time around 900–1000 and had become a major cult in the Yucatán by the time of the Spanish Conquest. However, they are just as likely to represent the vision serpents that in Mayan mythology had always formed the most direct conduit to the Otherworld. The descent of the sun represented in the most graphic way possible the community's contact with the heavens.

On the equinoxes the phenomenon begins around 4pm, and lasts about an hour. It's an astonishing demonstration of Mayan astronomical, mathematical and building skills, and the lengths to which they were prepared to go in combining them. It's also very famous, and around 80,000 people go to Chichén for the spring equinox each year; admission is free for the day, and in the last few years the authorities have put on a programme of music, folkloric shows and so on to accompany the event. For anyone who complains that Chichén is becoming a Mayan theme park, this is probably a day to avoid. The effect can also be seen for a shorter time and with smaller crowds during the weeks preceding the equinoxes, and is also reproduced artificially every night of the year in the 'Sound and Light' show (*see* p.239).

Back at the bottom of the Castillo, across the plaza to the left, is the equally monumental great **Ball Court**. Formally 'dedicated' in rituals held in 864, this is the largest ball court anywhere in Mesoamerica, and radically different from the smaller, sloping-sided courts of Classic Mayan sites or even the seven other ball courts around Chichén. It has great, vertical slab walls 160 metres long, on top of low, slope-sided base platforms and with two huge stone rings halfway along each side that formed the 'goals' of the game. From the carved reliefs on the lower platforms it appears that in this central-Mexican-influenced form of the game there were seven players on each side. The giant size of the court is an indication of the extra importance given to the Ball Court at Chichén, as a portal to *Xibalba*. Built on to the southeast corner of the court are two temples on top of each other, one facing the plaza and the one above it looking into the court, the Lower and Upper **Temples of the Jaguars**. They are some of the most densely carved buildings in the city, covered in elaborate images that place the founders of Chichén within the Mayan creation myth, so that the city gains its energies from the first makers of men: the First Father and First Mother. The door columns of the **lower temple** have intricate panels showing a series of still unidentified individuals together with gods such as Sak Ixik, the mother of the Hero Twins, while inside there is an astonishing carved mural of the foundation of the city in semi-mythological form. The interior of the **upper Temple** (*often closed to visitors*) once contained an extraordinary series of painted murals on the history and triumphs of Chichén, which included some of the most vivid Mayan depictions of warfare. However, these murals, recorded in drawings in the 1900s, gradually became all-but-invisible during the 20th century.

Inside the Ball Court, the carvings along the base are also of exceptional quality, many with monstrous images. Around each corner are sinuous feathered serpents, winding intricately through several metres, within which are extravagantly dressed figures of warriors, discs with mythical images and scenes of the ball game. It's a prime illustration of the Mayan love of repetition, of the use of recurring motifs to create an unremitting visual rhythm. In each of the six panels one of the ball players is being beheaded, and of the seven snake-like spurts of blood from his neck one is being transformed into a flowering vine, a vivid image of the Mayan idea of death (and so sacrifice) as an essential stage in the cycle of rebirth and new life. This beheading could also be, more directly, an illustration of the possible fate of losers in the game. One other feature of the ball court is its remarkable acoustics: echoes resound like a gunshot, while it's possible to hear a normal voice quite clearly from one end of the court to the other. This is just as enigmatic as the Descent of Kukulcán, for it must have been achieved deliberately, and presumably for a specific purpose.

The Tzompantli, Temple of Venus and the Sacred Cenote

Around the plaza there are several smaller structures. Alongside the Ball Court is the **Tzompantli**, a Nahua word meaning 'Wall of Skulls', one of the most gruesome shrines of Chichén's sacrificial cult. It's a low, T-shaped platform, 60m long, covered on all sides by rows of carved skulls, four deep, lightened by scenes of eagles devouring human hearts. Similar platforms are found in central Mexico. The heads of sacrificial victims were displayed here, together with those of losers in the ball game. Next to it is the **Platform of the Jaguars and Eagles**, a small altar-platform with steps on each side and carved, as the name suggests, with images of these animals tearing open the chests of human victims to eat their hearts. This platform was probably associated with the military 'orders' of the Jaguars and Eagles, a tradition brought from central Mexico, who played a major role in Chichén in capturing prisoners for sacrifice. Almost in the middle of the plaza is a similar but slightly bigger platform, the **Temple of Venus**. All these platforms probably served as 'stages' for ritual dances.

From the north side of the plaza a white *sacbé* leads through a gap in the perimeter wall for 300 metres to the great **Sacred Cenote** of Chichén. This is one of the essential stops on tours of the city, for this awesome well, 60m in diameter and 24m deep from the top to the level of the water, is one of the most spectacular natural phenomena in the Yucatán. The siting of the city, called 'the well of the Itzá', was almost certainly due to the presence of two large *cenotes*: one, the Xtoloc Cenote to the south, provided its main water supply, while the great *cenote* seems to have been used only for sacred ceremonies, as an opening into the underworld and the home of the rain god Chac.

On the south side of the great pit there is a small Toltec-style platform jutting over the water, and one of the eternal legends of the Sacred Cenote is that of the young virgins thrown off here as sacrificial victims. When Edward Thompson acquired Chichén in the 1900s one of the first things he did was to try to find the bottom of the *cenote* (it was reputed not to have one) and to dredge it. The bottom was discovered (at about 13m, with a thick layer of mud beneath), and his and subsequent explorations have produced some 4,000 objects that had been thrown into the *cenote* as ritual offerings, mostly during the dry seasons to hasten the return of Chac. Among them were several human skeletons, both male and female, but these were outnumbered by a mass of other artefacts: jade and amber jewellery, ceramic pots and figurines, bells, animal bones, mirrors, and sculptures in alabaster and turquoise. Landa wrote that human sacrifices were thrown into the *cenote* only occasionally (with the belief that they did not die, but would be resurrected after three days), and a high proportion of small children suggests that some may have fallen in by accident. Among the relics there were spectacular pieces in gold and copper, which must have been imported from Mexico, Costa Rica or Panama. Unfortunately, few can be seen at Chichén; most of the objects found by Thompson and other early investigators were taken off to the Peabody Museum in Harvard or to private collections, long before the Mexican authorities got organized to stop it. Other finds are in the National Museum in Mexico City or in Mérida.

The Temple of the Warriors and the Thousand Columns

Heading back into the plaza from the Sacred Cenote, on the left stands the greatest creation of Chichén's 'Toltec-Maya' style, the **Temple of the Warriors** and the huge building complex alongside. Sadly, the main temple is the most important building at Chichén that you are no longer allowed to climb up to. This is because the top of the steps is the site of one of the symbols of Chichén Itzá (reproduced in a million souvenirs): here stands the figure of Chac-mool, where everyone used to have their picture taken, placing their head on the spot where sacrificial victims were once laid. Unfortunately, no more. Many features of the temple at the top can, however, still be seen: it's a large, squat building which had only one opening at the main entrance, and a Chichén-style vaulted roof that collapsed centuries ago.

The Temple of the Warriors takes its name from the dense rows of columns in front of it, each one carved on all four sides with images of over 200 warriors and other figures, which you're free to wander around at will. They are the foremost example of Chichén's preference for group, collective monuments, arranged in ceremonial groups as if in an eternally frozen procession. They do not, though, simply depict the generic images of warriors, for each carving on the columns is different, seeming to be a real, individual portrait. Most are warriors, some showing their wounds, but some are captives with bound wrists (to the right of the temple steps, looking towards them), while near the corner of the colonnade into the Court of the Thousand Columns there is a line of priests, carrying offerings. Together they form a unique picture gallery that has proved a vital source in reconstructing the history of Chichén Itzá.

At the south corner the warriors' pillars meet with still more long rows of columns, forming one side of the giant quadrangle called the **Group of the Thousand Columns**. As you wander into this forest of pillars – which like the Warriors once supported stone roof-vaults, in a huge colonnaded hall – you are not immediately aware of just how rambling it is. In place of the narrow, dark rooms of Classic Maya cities, the arch and column roof allowed the builders of Chichén Itzá to create spaces of a completely different size. These colonnade-halls (125m long on the north side of the Columns Group, 50m long by the Temple of the Warriors) served many other purposes as well as that of giant ceremonial spaces: public business, the settlement of disputes and buying and selling all went on between their arcades.

When first constructed, like most buildings at Chichén they would have been painted in bright colours, predominantly red and blue, a very few faint traces of which can still be seen. There are also examples of fine carving. On the east side (furthest from the Temple of the Warriors) is the **Temple of the Sculptured Columns**, made up of individually carved square pillars like those of the Warriors', only in far worse condition. Forming the south side of the courtyard is the colonnade-fronted building known as the **Market** (El Mercado), although no one has been able to demonstrate that this is really what it was. Next to it, in the far southeast corner of the courtyard, are the remains of a Mayan **bathhouse**, built in a semi-Puuc style. These sweat-baths were regularly used in purification rituals before religious ceremonies. From the north side of the Columns quadrangle, a Mayan-arched passageway leads to another small group of buildings outside the main colonnaded hall, one of them a small ball court.

The High Priest's Grave, the Casa Colorada and the Caracol

By the southwest corner of the Thousand Columns, near yet another ball court, you meet up again with the main path through the middle of Chichén Itzá, between the two entrances. By the rear of the Castillo a path runs off it to the south. On the right about 300 metres down this track is another pyramid, the **High Priest's Grave**, also known as the **Ossuary**. It is a smaller version of the Castillo, almost a prototype of the larger model. This building has been of major importance in forcing a reconsideration of the 'three stage' idea of Chichén's history, since despite being 'Toltec-Maya' in style it has a Long Count inscription dated 20 June 842, clearly within what had been seen as the 'Mayan' period at Chichén. From the top there is a near-vertical shaft down to a natural cave at the base of the pyramid (*not open to visitors*), in which human remains were found with funeral offerings of jade, crystal and copper. It was clearly a tomb-chamber for high-ranking lords and priests of Chichén, hence its name.

The area south of the High Priest's Grave is what used to be thought of as 'Mayan Chichén', separate from the Toltec city, although this division is no longer seen as valid (*see* above), and the buildings here now appear as one more element in the eclectic architectural mix of Chichén. Most, however, are in a recognizably more Mayan style than the Castillo and the buildings on the plaza.

The first substantial building you come to after the High Priest's Grave, right of the path, is the **Casa del Venado** ('Deer House'), so called because until the 1920s it was possible to see in one room a painted mural of a deer, now sadly lost. Just past it is the **Casa Colorada** ('Red House'), where it's still possible to see traces of the original red wall paint. Inside there is an antechamber and three small rooms, and also, though they're now very hard to see, some of the most extensive glyph inscriptions found at Chichén. They record that on 15 September 869 several lords of Chichén, among them two important figures named Kakupakal and Hun-Pik-Tok, took part in bloodletting rituals, presumably around the time the 'house' was built. Next to it there is another ball court, which may also have been connected with the building.

Across the path from here rises up the **Caracol** (the Snail) or **Observatory**, one of the most fascinating buildings of all at Chichén. It is a round drum-tower, on top of a large, low, two-level platform with side-temple attached. The whole structure was altered and added to over many centuries, and against all appearances large parts of the platforms were actually built after and around the main tower, not vice versa. It's now fairly well established that its first sections were built by 800. The lower stages of the tower are in a typically Mayan style, with Puuc-style *atadura* mouldings between different levels topped by Chac masks. One other feature of the whole structure is that, in contrast with the symmetrical precision so common in Mayan buildings, none of its parts – the approach staircases, the angles of the platforms – is aligned with each other, nor are they quite square.

Inside, the Caracol tower is one of those Mayan buildings that seems incorrigibly obscure. Though often referred to as a spiral, it is really a series of concentric circles. The first 'room' is a very narrow outer corridor, with the remains of a vaulted roof; this connects through four entrances to a similar inner ring, from which another four entrances, not in line with the previous set, lead to the inner core. From here, a spiral staircase (the 'Snail') leads up to the upper level (*closed to visitors*). Much of the small top-tower has collapsed, but in its sides there remain three window-slots. Sylvanus Morley showed that one points due south, a second towards the setting of the moon at the spring equinox (21 Mar), and a third, slightly wider slot points due west toward the setting of the sun on the spring and autumn equinoxes or, according to which side of it you stand to look from, the setting of the sun on the summer solstice

(21 June). These astronomical observations were made with the naked eye alone, for the only equipment Mayan astronomers had to use was the cross-stick, to check the movements of stars against each other at specific times.

By the south side of the Caracol platform there are the remains of another steam bath. The path up the east side of the Caracol runs back to the Group of the Thousand Columns, passing the **Xtoloc Cenote**, the source of water for practical purposes in Chichén, together with some *chultun* artificial cisterns dotted around the site.

The Nunnery and the Akab-Dzib

From the Caracol platform there is a great view of the grandest buildings in this part of Chichén, **Las Monjas** or the Nunnery Complex (as with the 'Nunnery' in Uxmal, this Spanish name has no relation to the buildings' real function). This is a group of connected buildings, all with spectacular Terminal Classic carvings, around a platform 60m long. Between it and the Caracol stands the very different **Temple of the Carved Panels**. Its name is due to the carved reliefs in its northern chambers, now very faint, showing birds, gods, serpents and three figures in a hut among jaguars and warriors.

The 'Nunnery' is believed to have been the main palace and administrative area in the early years of Chichén. Much of it is in a relatively restrained style similar to that of the Puuc region – plain lower walls separated by *atadura*-type mouldings from upper friezes of geometric patterns and Chac-masks – but several parts of it have far more extravagant, Chenes-like carving, with a mass of intricate decoration that seems ready to overwhelm the buildings to which it is applied.

Inside there is what seems an enormous number of very small rooms, with benches around the sides. The most impressive parts of the Nunnery are the two smaller sections on the east side (on the left, coming from the Caracol). The addition to the main building, known simply as the **Annexe**, has adjacent façades in very different styles. The face that you see first as you walk towards it is a continuation of the same, Puuc-like style of the main block; walk around to the east end, though, and you are confronted by the most remarkable Chenes-style carving in Chichén Itzá. The wall is covered top to bottom in Chacs and other carvings that seem almost mobile, and the doorway, as in all Chenes building, is the mouth of a beast-god, with a row of hook-like stones to represent the teeth. Above the door sits a god-king, with a fabulous feather headdress. Around the lintel are glyphs, dating the façade to the year 880.

Forming a corner with the Annex, but entirely separate, is the strange structure the Spaniards called **La Iglesia** (The Church), because it had only one chamber inside. It is one of the oldest parts of La Monjas, probably from the early 8th century. The lower walls are completely plain, and seem about to be crushed by the towering frieze and roof comb above. Massive Chac-masks form the corners, and appear in the middle of the longer walls. Between them there are images of the four *Bacabs* that sustained the sky at the cardinal points, represented by a snail, an armadillo, a turtle and a crab.

A little east of the Nunnery Platform there is another large building, the **Akab-Dzib**, an 18-room complex that probably served as a lordly residence. It owes its name – meaning 'Obscure Writing' – to its southern chamber, which has a lintel clearly carved with an image of an enthroned priest and several glyphs, with a date from 870.

The Nunnery, from Désiré Charnay's book, Les Anciennes Villes du Nouveau Monde *(1885)*

Chichén Viejo

From the west side of the Nunnery Platform a path leads into the woods toward 'Old Chichén'. Should you wander down here you'll soon forget that Chichén is a major tourist attraction, for only a few conscientious guides bring their charges down, and most of the time you'll be alone with the trees and the birds. It's at least a 15-minute walk, or 500m, to the main group of buildings: paths crisscross each other along the way, with few signs, and it's almost impossible not to get lost at least once (on the way down, make a mental note of the right crossings for the route back).

The name 'Old Chichén' is a misnomer, for it has been shown that buildings here are no older than those in the central area. They stood at one end of the north–south *sacbé* that ran through the middle of the city; however, they were outside the area of the Hacienda of Chichén when studies began, and have never been fully excavated. If you can keep to the main path the principal buildings almost mysteriously appear in front of you from the forest. Though little known, they are of great importance to Mayanists, for they have the largest concentration of dated inscriptions at Chichén. The **Temple of the Four Lintels** has carved lintels marking the building's dedication on 13 July 881; nearby, the **Temple of the Initial Series** has carvings from 878. By the latter is the **House of the Phalli**, a Classic-era building with phallic sculptures from a later period. There are also structures with massive, Toltec-style roof-columns of carved warriors inside and, part-concealed in the brush, more semi-excavated buildings.

Around Chichén Itzá

Ikkil Cenote

Information, t (985) 851 0000; open daily 9–4; adm, discounts for under-16s.

Some three kilometres east of Chichén, opposite the Hotel Dolores Alba, is a giant *cenote* – scarcely noticed until a few years ago – that is now the centrepiece of an 'ecological park'. The *cenote* itself is spectacular: a giant, circular pit with creepers hanging down, crystalline water 13 metres below ground level and shafts of brilliant sunlight illuminating it from holes in the *cenote* roof. However, the park development around it is aimed squarely at coach-tours from Cancún, and in peak seasons it aims to get 1,000 or more visitors a day. At the top there's a giant restaurant, with an all-you-can-eat buffet (*moderate*). The *cenote* itself is not open to being expanded, and access to it is by a path that only allows a few people to pass at a time, so if you actually want to swim rather than just catch a glimpse it's best to avoid midday and weekends. Ikkil also has a *cabaña* hotel (*see* p.238), and around the *cenote* there are 25 hectares of forest that you are free to explore (though most coach visitors only have time to see the *cenote* and have lunch).

The Balankanché Caves

This is one of the great Yucatán cave systems, but one that was entirely forgotten until it was discovered by accident by a local guide in 1959. Subsequent searches revealed that offerings had been left here throughout the Classic and Postclassic eras,

Site Information

Open for guided tours; adm.
Balankanché is 5km east of Chichén towards Valladolid on Highway 180 (marked Grutas de Balankanché). If you don't have your own transport, second-class **buses** stop at the caves entrance (about once an hour); the caves are also included in many day-tours to Chichén. The caves can be visited only with an obligatory **tour** (about 1hr) and Sound and Light show at 11am, 1pm and 3pm (English); at 9am, 12 noon, 2pm and 4pm (Spanish), and at 10am (French); adm $4.50.

suggesting that, like Loltún, it was seen as an important point through which to make contact with and invoke the lords of the underworld. There is a botanical garden of local flora, a small museum and a café by the entrance.

The Balankanché caves are a little less extensive than the giant catacombs at Loltún (*see* p.324). Apart from turning on the 'Sound and Light' recorded commentary the guides tend to leave you to your own devices within the cave, so that a visit here is generally less informative than tours of Loltún. These limitations, though, cannot detract overly from the fascination of the cavern, a labyrinthine series of chambers leading dramatically into each other. One of the most remarkable is the 'sanctuary', where the stalactites and stalagmites meet to form a giant central tree. It was surrounded by over 100 Postclassic ceramic incense burners – many of which have been left exactly as they were found – of which the larger, hour glass-shaped pieces all have the face of Tlaloc, the central-Mexican equivalent of the rain god Chac. The most magical part of Balankanché is the very end of the cave, a chamber with a pool of extraordinarily still, crystalline water, in which the cave bottom seen through the water appears almost a perfect mirror image of the cavern roof.

One thing should be mentioned: if you have a metabolism that's responsive to heat and/or humidity, don't go in if you're not prepared to come out like a wet sponge.

Yaxuná

In the opposite direction from Balankanché and to the south lies Yaxuná, site of the bastion-city of Cobá, and the most important battle in the war between Chichén and Cobá. Major excavations were undertaken there during the '90s, and several large pyramids uncovered that show clear similarities with those of Cobá. The site has never been opened to visitors on a regular basis, but it is now possible to visit the ruins if you stay in Yaxuná village with its community tourism scheme (*see* below).

Getting There

Yaxuná is reached by turning south off Highway 180 in Libre Unión, 23km west of Piste, and continuing to the colonial town of Yaxcabá, where another road cuts eastwards to Yaxuná, some 20km south of Chichén Itzá.

Where to Stay and Eat

Staying in a Mayan Village: Yaxuná

The remote little Mayan village of Yaxuná, deep in the countryside south of Highway 180, has a village ecotourism scheme making use of six simple cabins that were built for the archaeologists working at the ruins (with showers, some with hammocks, some with beds). For $30 a day (less for longer stays) you get accommodation, all meals, and the help of local guides to visit attractions in the area: the Yaxuná ruins, other, uncharted Mayan remains, abandoned *haciendas*, beautiful *cenotes*, woods full of wildlife and the village beehives. Immersion in modern Mayan village life is guaranteed, and your hosts have a very amiable charm. It's advisable to book ahead, although they will try and fit any arrivals in: they can be contacted direct, **t** (mobile) 01 98 58 58 14 82, or maybe more easily via the Fundación Cultural Yucatán, an NGO that supports this and other village schemes (and also assists the Hacienda Tabí near the Puuc Route, *see* p.307), in Mérida on **t** (999) 923 9453. If you don't have transport, there are occasional buses at weekends to Yaxuná from the Autobuses de Oriente depot on C/ 50 in Mérida, or you can get any second-class bus on Highway 180 to Libre Unión, from where *combis* run to the village.

Northern Yucatán and Río Lagartos

North of Valladolid is the cattle country of Yucatán, a sultry landscape of wide, flat, open fields of scrub grass with lines of single palm trees marking the horizon like beacons, and where the movement on the roads is likely to be cowboys on horseback. For a visitor, its main attractions are the flamingo colonies of Río Lagartos, and the remote villages of the coast.

Tizimín

The dead-straight road north from Valladolid, Highway 295, is surprisingly one of the best in the Yucatán, rolling on from the Ek-Balam turn-off through broad, hot fields. Some 20 kilometres further on is **Calotmul**, as slow-moving as so many villages round about, with a wide, slightly ragged plaza, and another big, plain Franciscan church. From there it's a short distance to the capital of the cattle country, Tizimín.

The name Tizimín supposedly comes from a Yucatec word for a type of devil, *tsimin*, apparently used to describe the Spaniards when the Maya first saw them on horseback. As the main centre of the cattle region Tizimín has an occasional bustle and sense of movement that can be quite surprising in rural Yucatán. The broad central

Getting Around

Tizimín's **bus station** is near the market area on C/ 47, between Calles 46 and 48, two blocks from the plaza. There are five *intermedio* and hourly second-class daily between Tizimín and Mérida, many via Izamal, five *intermedios* and seven second-class to/from Cancún (one goes on to Playa del Carmen and Tulum), and services hourly to/from Valladolid. There are also many local services: ten daily to Río Lagartos, five to San Felipe and five to El Cuyo. *Combis* also run to all the coastal villages from around the bus station area.

The northbound road from Valladolid runs along C/ 50, southbound on C/ 52; they run into the main plaza between Calles 51 and 53. The main **petrol/gas station** is three blocks east of the plaza on C/ 49, between 44 and 46.

Orientation and Tourist Information

Tizimín t (986–)

Tizimín is a sprawling town, with the usual colonial grid (even numbers north–south, odd numbers east–west), although some streets have sub-sections (ie. 'C/ 49-A'). There are several **banks** around the central plazas.

Festivals

Tizimín's spectacular main *fiesta*, the **Feria de los Tres Reyes** (Three Kings), runs for a month from 15 Dec. This includes a stock fair as well as the more usual celebrations.

Where to Stay and Eat

Tizimín t (986–)

Hotel San Carlos, C/ 54 no. 407, x 51 & 53, t 863 2094 (*inexpensive–cheap*). Tizimín is not geared up to tourists, but the most pleasant place to stay is one block west of the plaza. It has 25 modern, light rooms around a pretty patio, and a/c rooms are just *inexpensive*.

Hotel San Jorge, C/ 53 no. 412, t 863 2037 (*cheap*). Similar to the San Carlos, but more ramshackle, on the plaza by the bank. All the rooms have bathrooms and TVs, some have a/c and cost a little more, and they're clean but otherwise run down.

Tres Reyes, C/ 52, corner of C/ 53, t 863 2106 (*moderate*). A great restaurant to find in a small town, on the Parque Principal and run with amiable energy by *sr* Willy Canto. Prices are a little above the norm for rural Yucatán, but the food is above average too, with great Mexican-style steaks.

plaza is particularly attractive, with plenty of room for strolling and people-watching; unusually it's divided into two, between the main Parque Principal and a smaller offshoot, the Parque Juárez. Dividing the plazas are two huge colonial edifices, both Franciscan monasteries, the **Convento de los Tres Reyes** and **Convento de San Francisco**. They seem very medieval, and give the centre of the town a noticeably Mediterranean look, so that at times you could think you were in Spain or Italy. Weekday mornings see the market packed with country people buying and selling.

Río Lagartos and San Felipe

From about 40 kilometres north of Tizimín the savanna grasslands and tall palms are interspersed with more and more patches of reeds and marsh, and then mangrove lagoons and ghostly 'petrified forests' of dead mangroves, before the road runs out in **Río Lagartos**. This fishing village and its spectacular colonies of flamingos and migratory birds are mentioned in every book and brochure on the Yucatán, but because of their remoteness not so many people actually make it up here, and while facilities are expanding it still scarcely rates on the scale as a tourist town.

Río Lagartos really is the end of the road, for Highway 295 comes to a stop when it runs into the waterfront, along which the town is stretched out on either side facing lines of tethered fishing launches. In front of you there's only the opal-coloured lagoon, with a long strip of sand and mangrove brush on the far side, and more pelicans and terns than there are people to be seen. Getting to see the flamingos here is not nearly as 'packaged' an experience as at Celestún, but has become more organized since the area was made a national park (the **Parque Natural Río Lagartos**). Setting up tours with local boatmen used to be complicated by the fact that there

Getting There

The largest number of buses to **Río Lagartos** runs from Tizimín (*1hr*), but there are also direct services from Mérida (Autobuses del Noreste de Yucatán, C/ 50, *see* p.265) and Valladolid. Many agencies in Mérida and some in Cancún offer day-tours to see the flamingos (*see* 'Tours and Guides', pp.109–111).

Río Lagartos now has a full-scale *gasolinera* on the way in to the village.

Tourist Information

Flamingo Watching

The flamingo lagoons, which cover an area over 20km long, are divided into four rough 'zones'. Getting to them involves travelling a fair distance over open water, so hats and sun block are very advisable (as are water and insect repellent). A trip of about 2hrs to the first zone costs about $33 per boat; 4hrs covering all four about $40–$55. Boats hold a maximum of six: individuals may find it best to go at a weekend, when you're more likely to run into other people trying to make up a boat. The best times to see birds are mornings or late afternoon, and the best season is August; busiest times for the boatmen are Easter and weekends in December, January, July and August, when several tour groups may turn up at the same time.

Flamingo Tours, on the waterfront, just left of the end of the main road in Río Lagartos, t (986) 862 0158. The main local boatmen's cooperative, which operates in association with the reserve authorities and has good boats and experienced, very helpful guides, some of whom speak English. They come highly recommended.

Alternatively, ask at any of the **restaurants**, but the guides may not be as knowledgeable and prices are not likely to vary much.

was no accommodation closer than Tizimín, but nowadays the best thing to do is get there a day ahead, stay the night in Río Lagartos or San Felipe and arrange a trip for early the next morning. Bird-watching attractions aside, both are among the most deliciously relaxing, peaceful places to spend some time anywhere in the Yucatán.

On the waterfront in Río Lagartos is the little kiosk of **Flamingo Tours** (*see* opposite). The flamingo colonies are to the east, along the 'river' (actually a lagoon between the mainland and the sandbar). The name Río Lagartos ('Lizard River') was given to it by the Spaniards because of the crocodiles they saw here, and though now very rare there are still a few about. On the way you travel at times across broad stretches of water, at others through narrow mangrove creeks. After nearly an hour you approach the mudflats that in the summer breeding season host a pink expanse of 20,000 flamingos, and flocks of several hundred throughout the year. In the past boats have been accused of disturbing breeding flamingos, but since the establishment of the national park some areas are closed to tours (*see* 'Celestún', p.294, for general information on seeing flamingos). Less celebrated is the enormous variety of other birds: herons, ibises, ducks, egrets, and pelicans. As a rule, the further from Río Lagartos, the more birds you'll see.

Río Lagartos itself doesn't have a beach, but there is one across the lagoon on the sand-spit of **Punta Holohit**. The same launch-owners will take you there and come back to pick you up, for about $10. There are better beaches at **San Felipe**, 12 kilometres west, which also has a waterfront information hut where you can hire *lanchas* for trips to see flamingos or around the lagoon, on similar terms to those in Río Lagartos. This tiny, beautifully tranquil village, with wonderful sunsets, has been something of a secret of Yucatecans. It has a slightly ragged beach alongside it and a better

Where to Stay and Eat

The Río Lagartos lagoon used to be so out of the way it didn't have any hotel at all for some years, but things are finally changing (a little) with the opening of three pleasant small hotels between Río Lagartos and San Felipe and the promised construction of a bigger, smarter development. Finding places to eat has never been a problem.

Río Lagartos t (986–)

Hotel Villa de Pescadores, C/ 14 no. 195, t 862 0020 (*inexpensive*). On the waterfront near the lighthouse, recently-built with spacious, fan-only rooms (no need for a/c, thanks to sea breezes). Prices go up a bit at weekends, but all the rooms have balconies and great views over the waterfront and the lagoon.

Posada Leyli, C/ 14 no. 104-A, t 862 0005 (*inexpensive–cheap*). Basic hotel one street back from the waterfront, with plain fan-only

rooms that are a slightly dark, but clean and well kept.

Isla Contoy (*moderate–cheap*). Great local restaurant, under a big *palapa* on a jetty over the sea, with a great view and cocktails of local seafood, limes and fresh coriander. To find it, go on along the waterfront around the bend past the Flamingos Tours kiosk.

San Felipe t (986–)

Hotel San Felipe, C/ 9, x 14 & 16, t 862 2027, *sanfelip@prodigy.net.mx* (*inexpensive*). An attractive addition; new and quite smart-looking with big, comfortable rooms, all with a sitting area, and a pretty, waterside **restaurant**. Room prices are very reasonable and vary according to the view, which can be fabulous, especially at sunset.

Restaurant Vaselina (*cheap*). This big place by the village quay (also signed as Restaurante La Playa) is utterly relaxing, and serves up exceptional local seafood at very low prices.

deserted one across on the sandbar, also accessible with local boats. Once again the bird life is abundant, and it's one of the best places to swim on the Gulf coast.

In the last few years, possibly due to the effects of hurricane damage and salt mining, many flamingos have been moving west from their old breeding grounds in Río Lagartos lagoon to a still-more remote area from San Felipe west to Dzilam Bravo, the **Bocas de Dzilam**. This is now also protected, as the **Parque Natural San Felipe**. Getting to it is difficult, but boat trips can be arranged from San Felipe or Río Lagartos (around $100, for a whole day) or from Dzilam Bravo on the other side (*see* p.301).

El Cuyo

Around 60 kilometres east of Río Lagartos along the coast is the lost-looking and idiosyncratic village of El Cuyo, sitting on a dead-straight beach with a jetty in the middle. You approach it after a long run through the savanna and cattle ranches of northern Yucatán, and then on a narrow causeway across the Río Lagartos lagoon and miles of sand and salt flats, which give it a feel of complete isolation. Most of the men of El Cuyo live by fishing. They go out before dawn and are often back by noon; from then, many of them spend the rest of the day in La Conchita's bar. They're naturally surprised to see foreigners turn up, but are very friendly.

El Cuyo has some of the feel of Holbox, not far away in Quintana Roo (*see* p.171). It also has its surprises – given the time it takes to get there – namely a line of holiday homes along the beach, kept by Mérida families and usually only used from June to

Getting Around

Five **buses** daily each way serve Tizimín and El Cuyo. More frequent *colectivos* run to El Cuyo from Tizimín and Colonia Yucatán.

Some maps show a coast road to El Cuyo from Río Lagartos via Las Coloradas, but even locals say this is barely passable even by 4WD. The main route **by car** from Valladolid is to take the road east towards Colonia Yucatán from Tizimín, and turn north in Colonia (85km in total). From Río Lagartos, a turning east (signposted to San Francisco) in Loché, 25km south on the 295, leads on to a potholed but decent road that runs 70km through lonely villages to join the El Cuyo–Colonia road.

There is no petrol station in the village.

Where to Stay and Eat

El Cuyo t (986–)

Phone calls to El Cuyo are usually made through the local *caseta* (t 853 0048), from which some places have their own extensions, for which you have to ask.

Cabañas Mar y Sol/Restaurante La Conchita, t 853 0048, ext 122 (*inexpensive–cheap*). The village's longest-running 'facility', on the last street to the left before the road reaches the beach. It has the best **restaurant**, serving generous platters of fresh fish and seafood. It's open through the day but closes at around 7.30pm. Behind the restaurant are eight quite cosy *cabañas* with beds, electric light, and their own bathrooms. Prices vary by size, and they're right on the beach.

Hotel Aida Luz, t 853 0048, ext. 172 (*inexpensive*). One block from the beach on the main road into the village, this small hotel opened in 1998, and has quite bright, airy rooms with fans and a/c.

Posada La Almeja, t 853 0048 (*cheap*). Almost next door to La Conchita, by the beach, are these five *cabañas*. They're more basic and a bit dark, but the Polanco family who own it are real fishing people and though quite shy at first, are soon very friendly.

Dos Hermanas (*cheap*). The alternative place to eat, a basic *lonchería* on the main street. The attraction, though, is that it stays open a bit later in the evenings.

August. A few more foreigners now find their way here as well, but it's still far enough from madding crowds to make a fine beach refuge for anyone looking to lose themselves a while in empty horizons. Beaches stretch away for miles on either side, lined with clumps of palms. There are no secluded bays as on the Caribbean coast, but if you want a beach to yourself and are ready to walk to get to it, this could be the place.

Izamal to Mérida

In central Yucatán, from about 50 kilometres west of Chichén Itzá, the villages become thicker on the ground as you enter the core of the state. East of Mérida there are two major attractions: **Izamal**, one of the most fascinating of colonial towns and an ancient Mayan city, and – far less well-known – the unique Mayan site of **Aké**. Both are usually visited as stop-offs on the way to Mérida, or as day trips from the city.

Between Izamal and the state capital lies one of the most populated areas of the Yucatán, a stream of villages and little towns with plazas, palm-roofed huts, Cristal water ads, children, dogs and flashes of bougainvillaea. The most interesting route to take from Izamal is to turn north up to Tekantó and then follow the back-country road through Tixkokob, a friendly little place with a market.

Izamal

Izamal is the most complete and most attractive of the Yucatán's Spanish colonial towns. If Mérida is the 'White City', Izamal is the *Ciudad Amarilla* or *Ciudad Dorada*, the yellow or golden city. Its elegant houses and arcades are painted a uniform, yellow-ochre wash that gives it a unique feel and charm, while characteristic tricycle carts or horse-drawn *victorias* clip-clop along wide, quiet streets, all helping to maintain its old-world tranquillity. Still dominating the town is the grandest of all the Franciscan buildings in the peninsula, the monastery of **San Antonio de Padua**. Izamal also has another label, though, as the 'City of the Three Cultures' – Mayan, Spanish and the Yucatecan-Mexican synthesis. Here more than anywhere else in the Yucatán the superimposition of Catholicism and Spanish culture on top of Mayan tradition is visible in stone, for the pyramids of ancient Izamal are still very intact, incorporated into the streets of the town.

History

There is here in Izamal one building among the others, of such height and beauty that it is frightening... I climbed to the top of this chapel and, since Yucatán is a flat land, one can see from there as much land as the eye could reach, and can see the sea...
Father Diego de Landa, *Relación de las Cosas de Yucatán*.

Because modern Izamal stands on top of the Mayan city, archaeological excavations have been limited. Nevertheless, it is clear that this was one of the oldest of Mayan settlements, occupied continually from about 300 BC till the Spanish Conquest. It

Getting Around

By Car

Izamal is north of Highway 180, 72km from Mérida and about 270km from Cancún. To get there from the east, turn right off 180 in the village of Kantunil (where the 180 *Cuota* motorway ends); from the west, take the well-signposted road from Mérida via Tixkokob, or take 180 as far as Hoctum (48km) and turn left. The main Mérida road through the middle of the town becomes C/ 31; Av. Itzamná is a kind of bypass that runs around the south of the central area. The *gasolinera* is at the corner of Calles 31 and 34.

By Bus

The **bus station** in Izamal is on C/ 32, one block from the monastery. There are buses from Mérida with Autobuses de Oriente, every 45 minutes daily, 5am–9pm, with returns 5am–7.15pm, and rather less frequently with Autobuses del Centro and from the main second-class station on C/ 69. Around 17 buses daily run to Izamal from Cancún via Valladolid.

By *Victoria*

Pretty much everywhere in Izamal is within walking distance, but among the traditions of the town are the *victorias*, the same kind of horse-drawn carriages which in Mérida are called *calesas*. A ride around the town from the main plazas will cost $10–$15.

Tourist Information

Izamal **t** (988–)

There is no **tourist office**, but information is available from the museum (*see* p.260).
Bank: On Plazuela 2 de Abril, the square with the Landa statue south of the monastery.
Post Office: On one side of Parque Itzamná.

Where to Stay

Izamal **t** (988–)

Due to Izamal being thoroughly established as a day-trip destination, it has been peculiarly poorly set up with hotels. However, as everywhere, some new possibilities are opening up.

Hacienda San Antonio Chalanté, about 8km south of Izamal via a turn east in the village of Sudzal, on the Kantunil road (well signposted), **t/f** 954 0287, *www.macanche.com* (*moderate–inexpensive*). A great way to experience the charm of the Yucatán's old *haciendas* without paying luxury prices. Owned by American Diane Dutton Finney and her Mayan husband José Francisco, the atmospheric 17th-century manor has been beautifully restored and has lovely, very individual but very comfortable rooms, at exceptional prices. There's a pool, breakfast is included and generous meals can also be provided. Horse riding is a speciality, but it also makes a very enjoyable, peaceful base for exploring the Yucatán countryside.

Macanché, C/ 22 no. 305, x 33 & 35, **t/f** 954 02 87, *www.macanche.com* (*inexpensive*). Izamal's best accommodation, run by the same owners as the Hacienda San Antonio (*see* above). Rooms are in small bungalows in a very pretty garden; all are individually decorated and very comfortable, and one is a self-contained cottage with kitchen (*moderate*). They are also building a pool. Breakfast is included and enjoyable meals are available at other times; low prices and a friendly welcome make this a real bargain.

Green River, Av. Itzamná 342, **t/f** 954 0337 (*inexpensive*).An eccentrically likeable motel-style hotel, with large rooms in bungalows in a garden, all with a/c and TV and recently painted in a very breezy mix of Mexican-bright and Hallmark-pastel shades. There's also a small pool. The disadvantage is that it's a 20-minute walk from the town centre.

Eating Out

There are also cheap, open-air *loncherías* just off the main square by the market.
Kinich Kakmó, C/ 27 no. 299, **t** 954 0153 (*moderate*). One of the best in the whole of the Yucatán for classic traditional dishes, presented at their best in all their variety. It's also very pretty, with tables around a shaded garden. It's to the left of the entrance to the Kinich Kak Mo pyramid. *Open lunch only.*
Restaurante El Toro, Plazuela 2 de Abril (*cheap*). Pleasant little place with enjoyable local classics, below the monastery. *Open all day.*

developed powerfully as a city-state from around AD 600. In the Classic era Izamal was allied with Aké, and a long *sacbé* was built between them, although this alliance was subsequently broken for reasons unknown. By the time of the Spaniards' arrival it was politically less significant, as the seat of *Akinchel*, one of the weaker Mayan lordships. However, it remained an important pilgrimage centre. The great pyramid of Izamal, the Kinich Kak Mo, is the largest pyramid-platform in northern Yucatán, and was a major shrine of Itzamná, the paramount god among the Yucatán Maya.

The arrival of Catholicism and the Franciscan order in Izamal is inseparably associated with Bishop Diego de Landa (*see* p.68). According to his *Relación*, the friars first came here in 1549 at the invitation of local Mayan chieftains, who urged them to build a monastery amid the old shrines. With its 12 large pyramids, like so many mountains, Izamal made a deep impression on the missionary brothers. A Franciscan chronicler relates that the precise site of the new monastery, one of the largest platforms and known as the *Paphol'chac* or 'Home of Chac', was chosen by Landa himself, in order that 'a place that had been one of abomination and idolatry, could come to be one of sanctity'. Intended as a symbol of the triumph of Christianity, the monastery was far the most ambitious of the Franciscan projects in the Yucatán, and the majestic *atrio* (courtyard) in front of it is the largest such church square anywhere in Mexico. Between the desire of the Mayan lords that a centre of the new religion should be on the same site as the shrines of Itzamná, however, and Landa's belief that he was 'sanctifying' a pagan place, the potential for confusion and ambiguity of motive and imagery was obviously spectacular.

Not long after the completion of the monastery in 1561 an image of the Virgin, almost certainly painted in Guatemala, was brought to Izamal by Landa. As the first 'official' Catholic focus of pilgrimage in the Yucatán, **Nuestra Señora de Izamal** ('Our Lady of Izamal') played an important part in the Christianization of the peninsula, and was credited with several miracles. In 1829 the original image was destroyed in a fire, and was substituted by another that had supposedly been brought from Guatemala at the same time and then preserved in a private home in Mérida. Its authenticity has often been questioned, but it is this image that is in the monastery today. On the *fiesta* of the Virgin, the Immaculate Conception (8 Dec), *Izamaleños* traditionally visit her at the monastery and then take a walk up the Kinich Kak Mo, a neat example of having it both ways (also known as 'syncretic religion').

In modern times the Virgin of Izamal has been somewhat displaced by the Mexican cult of Guadalupe, but she remains the Yucatán's official patron. In 1993, Pope John Paul II came to Izamal for an 'encounter with the indigenous peoples of the Americas'.

The Monastery of San Antonio de Padua

Whether you come into Izamal by bus or by car along C/ 31 – which more or less follows the line of the old *sacbé* from Aké – you automatically come up against the great focus of the town, Bishop Landa's monastery, currently in beautiful condition after extensive restoration work. Its great atrium stands squarely across the old platform of Chac, flanked on three sides by squares with shady arcades, in the same yellow and white colours, that mirror the colonnades of the quadrangle and give the town centre a particular sense of harmony and spaciousness. On the south side is the smallest square, with Izamal's lively little market; to the west is the town hall (with bus station behind it), and to the north is the largest square, the **Parque Itzamná**.

Massive ramps of steps lead up to the grass-covered *atrio*. On some Sundays and *fiesta* days open-air Masses are held on the quadrangle (measuring 520m by 420m), but on other days it's a huge, atmospherically empty space where the only noise will be from giggling kids who appear and offer to show you around. The church on the eastern side is the finest work of the Franciscans' architect Friar Juan de Mérida. Only a section of the atrium arches, the part directly in front of the church, was built by him, the rest being added later and completed by 1618. They effectively block off the original *capilla de indios*, to the right of the main façade as you face it. On the walls of the quadrangle arcades, near the church doors, there are the remains of 18th-century frescoes, as well as carved inscriptions commemorating miracles performed by the Virgin of Izamal. More interesting are the frescoes in the passage from the atrium to the cloister, some of which date from 1554, showing monks purging another monk with sticks, or friars adoring the Virgin. Elsewhere, the decoration shows a combination of Spanish techniques with very pre-Hispanic colours and flower imagery.

The lines of arches give Izamal a lightness that is not found in many early colonial churches in the Yucatán, but inside it's still a plain, simple Franciscan building. The massive, two-level **cloister**, on the north side of the church, has a very pretty garden courtyard on one side. Also off the cloister is a room with a small exhibit on the visit of the Pope in 1993, and nearby there's a portrait of Bishop Landa, although it's not believed to be contemporary. Our Lady of Izamal currently resides in a small sanctuary to the right of the main church. At the very back of the church is another separate chamber, the **Camarín**, built as a sanctuary for the Virgin in 1650–56 and reached by a romantic-looking set of stairs from which there's a great view over the town.

Returning to the atrium, in the little plaza below the south side there's a statue of Landa himself in all his dourness. Back on the north side, the corner overlooking the Parque Itzamná has one of the best views of the Kabul pyramid (*see* below). In the wall below, facing the Parque, there is a small local museum (mostly in Spanish only), the **Museo Comunitario Itzamal-Kauil** (*open daily 8–1 and 6–9; adm free*).

The Kinich Kak Mo and the Pyramids of Izamal

From Parque Itzamná, take C/ 28 (in front of you to the right, from the monastery) for a couple of blocks to meet C/ 27. A little to the right are some steps and an alleyway forming the entrance to the great pyramid, the **Kinich Kak Mo** (*open daily 8–5; adm, Sun adm free*). Getting to the top involves a stiff but gradual climb over several levels, since it consists of one pyramid base with another whole pyramid on top. The oldest parts date from the Early Classic and the latest from the Postclassic, a difference of nearly 1,000 years. In Mayan times the entire space between it and the *Paphol'chac*, where the monastery now stands, was just one great square, which must have been one of the largest of all Mayan plazas. According to one legend the Kinich Kak Mo is the burial place of the head of Itzamná, while his right hand was buried on the Kabul pyramid and his heart on Itzamatul. Another explains the name Kinich Kak

Mo, which means 'Fire Macaw – Face of the Sun': supposedly, Itzamná came down in the form of a fiery macaw to collect offerings left on the pyramid.

Nowadays, most of the pyramid's masonry is in a fairly poor state. Once you get up there, though, you still have the same view that so impressed Landa.

Returning to Parque Itzamná, a turn left on C/ 31, through the arch, will take you to the entrance to another pyramid, the **Itzamatul**, on C/ 26 (*open daily 8–5; adm, Sun adm free*). It's a smaller version of the Kinich Kak Mo, similarly built in stages in 400–600, 700–850 and 950–1150. The final platform at the top is quite overgrown, a strangely wild and beautiful place within the town, with a very good view back to the larger pyramid. The third pyramid, the **Kabul** on the western side of Parque Itzamná, is enclosed within a block and cannot be visited, so that it's best seen from the atrium. When Stephens and Catherwood visited Izamal in 1842 it had on one side a huge stucco mask, shown in one of Catherwood's most impressive drawings. Some 40 years later in 1886 Desiré Charnay looked for it using Stephens' account but found that it had already been destroyed, possibly in the Caste War.

These three are the only intact survivors of the 12 pyramids of Izamal counted by Landa. However, the remains of others are all around the town (the market is on one).

Aké

Aké is one of the strangest and most enigmatic of Mayan ruins, for its location and its unique architectural style. One of its most remarkable features is that the ruins and the current village are all within a 19th-century *henequen* estate, as if the community was no more than an adjunct to the *hacienda*. The great main estate factory, a giant neo-French construction, is to the left of the entrance. Still more extraordinary is that machinery can often be heard inside, for this is still a working *hacienda*. Don't miss wandering in: the foremen and few remaining workers have no objection, and a few village kids will appear to show you round for a few pesos. The huge c. 1900 machinery, all iron, cogwheels, grease and leather belts, still clatters away in the crumbling sheds, and the process by which the tough *henequen* leaves are stripped and turned into fibre can be seen in every detail.

The ruins begin just beyond the *hacienda* sheds. The largest structure at Aké, the **Edificio de las Pilastras** ('Temple of the Columns'), is ahead and to the left. It is only

Site Information

Open daily 8–5; adm, Sun adm free.

The most interesting route from Izamal is to turn north up to Tekantó and then follow the back-country road through Tixkokob (the route used by many Izamal buses). On the eastern side of Tixkokob, a turn off the main road to the south (hard to see if you're coming in from Izamal) leads to Ekmul and Aké. Aké is surprisingly remote. The road from Tixkokob is rough and bumpy, and convinces many visitors they must be going the wrong way (note also that the road to Aké from Highway 180 shown on some maps and signposted on the Highway itself is only a dirt track, and rougher than the Tixkokob road). If you don't have a car there are occasional *colectivos* from Tixkokob. Eventually, after passing through the village of Ekmul, you reach Aké, which at first looks like a gated private estate, although the gate is left permanently open.

one of several massively monumental buildings at Aké that are unlike anything else in the Yucatán. Most Mayan temple platforms were built steeply upward, with many narrow steps; the great ramp of the Temple of the Columns is instead a gradual climb of huge, flat stone slabs, leading up to strangely crude free-standing drum columns, which probably held up a palm roof. It seems built to a different scale. While it is unlike Mayan styles, it is similar to some central-Mexican temples, which has led some to speculate about Toltec-Mexican influence. However, it has also been shown that this is a very old site, inhabited from around AD 100, and it has not been made clear if, when and how Toltec influence was exerted here, or even whether the Aké platforms do not pre-date the 'Mexican' presence at Chichén Itzá.

The Temple of the Columns formed the north side of the **Great Plaza** of Aké, the centre of a city that covered four square kilometres. Only a few other buildings have been excavated. What is known about Aké is that it was an important link between Ti'ho (Mérida) and Izamal. It was initially allied with Izamal, and in about 600–700 a *sacbé* was built covering all the 32 kilometres between them (still visible on the east side, the left looking from the Columns). Later this alliance must have broken down, for at some point in the Terminal Classic or Early Postclassic a rough wall was built around the central area of Aké, crossing and so closing off the *sacbé*.

To the right (west) of the Temple of the Columns there are two more partially excavated buildings: **Structure 2**, an overgrown pyramid with the remains of Puuc-style masonry, and beyond that **Structure 3**, opposite the *hacienda*, another platform of massive stone slabs. Some of the most exceptional buildings at Aké are outside the main site. Reached from a separate entrance off the village square is a pyramid, **Structure 14**, which astonishingly has the local church built on top, neat and white-washed in its pagan setting and with a brightly coloured altar. Many other remains are scattered around the village, combining with the remains of the *hacienda*.

Mérida

Mérida, capital of Yucatán state and, in former times, of the entire peninsula, is a city of immense charm imbued with a pervasive romanticism. Beneath the arching palms and laurel trees of its squares are numerous *confidenciales*, the S-shaped love-seats in which couples sit whispering and giggling in the cool of the night, and the city's favourite music is the lilting *bolero* of the Yucatán trios, wistful and unashamedly nostalgic songs yearning time and again after lost loves and dark eyes. *La Ciudad Blanca*, the 'White City', as it is known, is the Yucatán's colonial city *par excellence*, with grand stone portals opening on to patios of lush plants and deep shadows that recall the Moorish towns of Andalucía. This is only part of Mérida's languid theatricality.

The colonial heritage is everywhere in Mérida – in the giant cathedral, in countless smaller churches, in carvings above gateways and faded inscriptions recalling long-forgotten governors – but the modern culture of the city always seeps through between the stones. It still fulfils very visibly the original role of a city, as market and commercial hub of its region, and every day people from villages and small towns

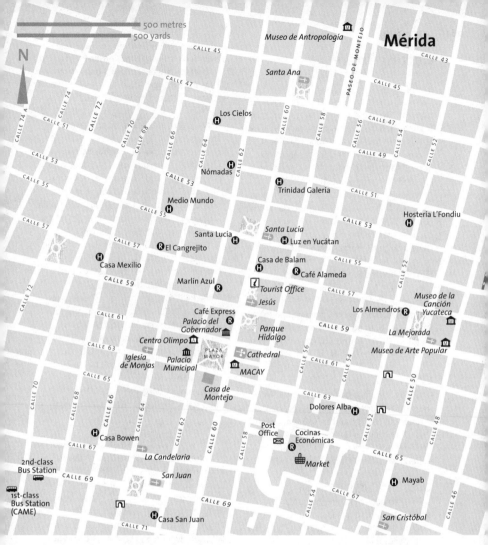

flood into Mérida to buy and sell (the cause of its sometimes overwhelming bus traffic). Come into Mérida from the quiet of the surrounding villages and its urban tone comes as quite a shock. Walk around a little more, though, after the crowds have gone home, and a gentle, much more small-town feel asserts itself.

An essential way to appreciate the atmosphere of *la Ciudad Blanca* is to wander around it at night, when it is at its most mysterious. Churches loom white at you out of the darkness, the details on 18th-century houses are sharply etched, couples chat in their *confidenciales* with whole squares to themselves, while small groups of drivers murmur away beneath taxi stands. This exploration involves very little risk, for along with the romanticism for which Yucatecos are known throughout Mexico is the gentleness apparent in every area of life here, making for one of the least threatening cities you are ever likely to be in. Mérida is a city that invites you to drop your guard, and experience a type of urban life that's near lost elsewhere.

Getting There

By Air

Manuel Crescencio Rejón airport is 4km from the town centre on the southwest road to Umán and Campeche, Highway 180, called at this point Av. Aviación. There is a tourist information desk at the airport. Mérida has direct international flights with Continental (t 946 1888) to/from **Houston** and with Aeroméxico (t 920 1260) to/from **Miami**, and there is a daily Aerocaribe flight to **Havana** via Cancún. Within Mexico there are direct flight connections to many cities (*see* pp.112–13). **General airport information**: t 946 1530.

Getting To and From the Airport

As usual at Mexican airports only official *Transporte Terrestre* **taxis** are allowed to take incoming passengers into town. A taxi to yourself is about $9, a place in a *colectivo* about $4. On departure, any city cab can take you to the airport (about $5).

By Bus

Mérida is the hub of an extraordinarily intricate bus network with services to cities throughout Mexico, and to just about every town and village in the Yucatán. There is a bewildering variety of services running to major destinations, from various termini.

CAME First-Class Bus Station

On C/ 70 between Calles 69 and 71. The primary terminus for first-class buses, used by ADO and several other companies. This is the main depot for long trips. Most of the 'luxury' services (ie. UNO and ADO-GL, and the frequent Super-Espresso buses to Cancún) also pick up and drop off at a depot behind the **Fiesta Americana** hotel (*see* p.271).

For information contact **CAME**, t 924 8391, or the **Fiesta Americana**, t 925 0910. Main services from the CAME are as follows, although all timetables can change at short notice:

Campeche (2½hrs): two ADO GL daily, normal first-class hourly, 6am–11.30pm. Fare $9.

Cancún (4¼hrs): 12 luxury services (six ADO GL, six UNO; some only run from the Fiesta Americana) daily, and normal first-class hourly every day 5.30am–midnight with ADO and Super Espresso. Fares from $17.50.

Chetumal (*9hrs*) via **Felipe Carrillo Puerto**: four Super Espresso buses daily 7.30am–11pm. Fare around $19.

Mexico City (*24hrs*): one ADO GL and six normal ADO services daily. Fares $78–$88.

Oaxaca (*22hrs*): one bus daily, at 7.10pm. Fare about $62.

Palenque (*10hrs*): via **Campeche** and **Escárcega**, three ADO buses daily, plus two daily with Altos (7.15pm) and Maya de Oro (9.30pm) that stop at Palenque and continue on to **San Cristóbal de Las Casas** (*16hrs*) and **Tuxtla Gutiérrez** (*20hrs*). ADO and Maya de Oro are more comfortable than Altos, and cost a little more. Fares around $26–$30 Palenque, $34–$44 San Cristóbal, $37–$50 Tuxtla.

Playa del Carmen (*5hrs*): two ADO GL buses and ten normal first-class daily, via Valladolid, 5.45am–midnight. Three buses continue to **Tulum**. Fare to Playa from $20.

Valladolid (*3hrs*) via **Chichén Itzá** (2½hrs): 14 Super Espresso buses daily, of which four (6.30am, 8.45am, 9.30am, 1pm) stop at Chichén. Fares around $7 to Chichén, $9 to Valladolid.

Villahermosa (*10hrs*): one ADO GL, one UNO and ten normal ADO buses daily. Fare $31.

Terminal Maya Kiin

Calle 65, between Calles 68 and 70. Used by Autotransportes Tuxtla's Elite/Nuevos Horizontes first-class buses, with six daily to **Cancún**, four to **Playa del Carmen** and five to **Campeche**, two of which (at 10.15am and 9pm) continue to **Ciudad del Carmen** and **Villahermosa**. There are also two Elite buses daily to **Palenque**, **San Cristóbal de Las Casas** and **Tuxtla Gutiérrez**. All services pick up and stop outside the Fiesta Americana. These buses are slightly cheaper than ADO services.

Second-class Terminal de Autobuses

Around the corner from the CAME on C/ 69 between Calles 68 and 70. The base for a great many routes run by many different companies, of which some of the most useful are as follows; many longer-distance routes are now *intermedio* services rather than 'traditional' second-class, with a comfort level not so far behind first-class. All second-class buses on the main road to Cancún and Playa del Carmen stop at **Chichén Itzá** and **Valladolid**.

Campeche: Autotransportes del Sur, buses every half-hour 4am–10.30pm, on Highway 180. Some are *semi-directos* and don't stop everywhere en route. Five daily buses serve the 'Slow Route' via **Hopelchén** and **Uxmal**.

Cancún: Buses hourly, 4am–midnight; nine buses daily also continue on to **Playa del Carmen**. Autobuses del Centro de Yucatán has six buses daily to Cancún that do not take the main Highway 180 but go via Tixkokob, Izamal, Tinum and Valladolid. Average fare around $14.

Chetumal: via **Muna**, **Ticul**, **Felipe Carrillo Puerto** and **Bacalar**, seven buses daily, 7am–midnight.

Chiquilá/Isla Holbox: via **Valladolid**, one bus nightly at 11.30pm. Fare around $12.

Puuc Route: An ATS/Mayab bus leaves daily at 8am and returns at 2.30pm, stopping at **Uxmal** and all the main sites on the route, with time allowed for each visit. Tickets cost around $11. For **Uxmal** and **Kabah** there are also six buses daily along Highway 261 to **Hopelchén**, from where five continue to **Campeche** on the 'Slow Route', while one carries on to **Dzibalchén**. A second-class return to Uxmal only will cost around $7.

Autoprogreso Depot

At C/ 62 no. 524, between Calles 65 and 67. Buses to **Progreso** go every 10mins 5am–10pm, and the same company has several services daily to **Dzibilchaltún** (*see* p.295). *Colectivos* to Progreso can be found one street over, on C/ 60, also between 65 and 67. Autobuses del Centro de Yucatán also has a frequent service to **Izamal** via **Tixkokob** from the same depot.

Autobuses de Occidente Depot

On C/ 71 no. 585, between 64 and 66. Buses to **Celestún**, roughly hourly 5am–8.30pm, with returns 6am–7pm. These are stopping buses (two hours for the full trip); there is also a special direct service at 8am and 10am, with returns at 5pm and 7pm (*1½ hrs*). The same company has 13 buses daily each way to **Sisal**.

Autobuses de Oriente Depot

Calle 50, between Calles 65 and 67. Second-class routes to **Izamal** (almost hourly), **Tizimín**, **Valladolid** and other places in eastern Yucatán. Some routes continue to **Cancún** and **Playa**.

Autobuses del Noreste de Yucatán Depot

On the other side of the street from Oriente, at C/ 50 no. 527. Serves the northeast and the Yucatán coast, including **Motul**, **Tizimín**, and the coast from Telchac to **Río Lagartos**, **Dzilam Bravo** and **Colonia Yucatán**. Some buses also continue to **Cancún**.

Combis and *Colectivos*

Mérida's authorities plan to rationalize the sometimes chaotic overkill of public transport in parts of the city by providing garages for the *colectivos* and *combis* that run to villages all around Yucatán state. But, for the time being, most *combi* collecting-points are in the street, often in squares and mostly not too far from the market. The **Parque San Juan** is used by *combis* to many locations south and west of Mérida, especially places near the Puuc Hills such as Ticul, but also by some that run to the north, notably to Dzibilchaltún and Chablekal. **C/ 69 between 56 and 54** and **C/ 67 between 50 and 48** are the main *combi*-points for Tixkokob, Izamal, Sotuta and other points to the east, and for Umán to the south.

By Car

If you are **driving into Mérida** from Cancún and Valladolid on Highway 180 you will first meet the *Anillo Periférico*, the city ring road. Here, you cross straight over to get on to C/ 65 for *Mérida-Centro*, or turn left for Campeche and the south, or right for Progreso and the Yucatán coast.

On C/ 65 you reach an inner ring-road, the *Circuito Colonias*. Continue across it and you enter Mérida's central grid (*see* 'Orientation', below). To get to the centre turn right at C/ 52, then go up two blocks before turning left on to C/ 61 for the Plaza Mayor and C/ 60.

Coming in from Campeche, Uxmal and the south on Highway 180-west, you will join Av. Aviación, a long, busy road that runs past the airport until it becomes the Av. Itzaes. Follow this till you see a sign to the right for *Mérida-Centro* on to C/ 59 (a surprisingly abrupt turn).

Driving out of Mérida can be more complex. To get on to the Cancún road east from the city centre, the best way is to get on to C/ 63 to the *Circuito Colonias*, turn right, and then look for signs to the left for Cancún. For Campeche and Uxmal, take C/ 65 west from the centre as far as Av. Itzaes, turn left, and follow signs for Umán and Campeche. For Progreso and the north coast, get on to C/ 60 or Paseo Montejo and take them out of town.

Orientation

A classic Spanish colonial grid, central Mérida has a comprehensible system of long, straight streets anchored on the **Plaza Mayor** or Zócalo, and the main street, **Calle 60**, that runs across it. Even-numbered streets run north–south, odd numbers east–west. This grid is interrupted to the north by the Paseo Montejo, and other larger streets with names rather than numbers. Away from the centre the grid breaks down, streets divide (31-A, 31-B, etc.) and *colonias* and *fraccionamientos* exist with their own numbering systems.

Since the streets of the grid are so long, in addresses it's usual to indicate the block as well as the house number, as in C/ 57 no. 436, x 56 & 58 (between Calles 56 and 58).

The compactness of central Mérida means the easiest way to get about is to walk, but if you need to get anywhere fast, a staggering range of transport is on hand to take you.

Getting Around

By Bus

It can seem that every street in the city has its own bus, *micro* or *combi* route. Stops and destinations are written on the windscreen, so to find a bus for any part of town requires a little knowledge of local geography. However, given the walkability of Mérida the only area most visitors use a bus to get to is the north side of the centre, the Paseo Montejo and the Anthropology Museum, and it's fairly easy to find a bus marked 'Paseo Montejo'. For the return journey, look for any bus with 'Centro' on it. Many routes to north Mérida begin and end on the blocks of C/ 59 between Calles 58 and 54, which have their own microclimate of 110°F and 50% CO2. Buses for Montejo run up C/ 60, C/ 56 or C/ 52, while buses for shopping areas in north Mérida, labelled 'Prol. Montejo' and 'Gran Plaza', run up C/ 52 or C/ 60. Many buses to the west of the city run along C/ 61, or from C/ 65 south of the Plaza Mayor.

Away from route termini buses stop at street junctions: in a few places there are blue and white bus stop (*parada*) signs, but otherwise just stand at a corner and flag a bus down. There is one set fare for each route, normally 3–4 pesos in full-size buses and 2 pesos or less in *combis*.

By Car

Parking in central Mérida is heavily restricted, and if you have a car it's advisable to find a hotel with off-street parking. Where parking is not allowed the kerb is painted yellow, and restrictions are strongly enforced. **Angeles Verdes** roadside assistance: t 983 1184.

Car Hire

Rental rates in Mérida are, overall, lower than around Cancún, and this is always the best place to hire a car if you aim to drive around the Yucatán. Most car hire agencies are on or near C/ 60.

Balam Rent a Car, C/ 60 no. 486 Local M, x 55 & 57, t 924 2483, *balamrentacar@latinmail .com*. Not so cheap for small cars, but good rates for higher-grade vehicles, all with a/c.

Kimbila Car Rental, C/ 58 no. 485, x 55 & 57, t 923 9316. Quite a large agency with a wide range of vehicles from around $45 a day.

Mexico Rent a Car, C/ 57-A (Callejón del Congreso) Depto 12, x 58 & 60, and C/ 62 no. 483 A, x 57 & 59, t 923 3637, *mexico rentacar@hotmail.com*. A local company that can be completely recommended: rates are consistently the best in the region, beginning at under $30 a day for a VW Beetle with unlimited mileage (other models, some with a/c, are also available). Costs are even lower for longer-period hire, and drop-off can be arranged in Cancún. On top of that you get very personal, friendly service: getting your vehicle from the Alonzo family is not so much like hiring a car as borrowing one. The main office is in the Callejón del Congreso pedestrian alleyway alongside the Teatro Peón Contreras, just north of the Iglesia de Jesús.

Mundo Maya, C/ 62 no. 486-A, x 57 & 59, t 924 6521, *mundomayarent@hotmail.com*. Another friendly local agency with decent rates, from $35–$40 a day; discounts for longer rents.

By Taxi

Ranks are in the Plaza Mayor, by Parque Hidalgo, at the bus stations and several points around the centre. Each taxi stand has a phone: to call a cab from Parque Hidalgo, phone **t** 928 5326. Taxis are more expensive than in most cities (min. fare around $3.30).

By *Calesa* (Horse-drawn Carriage)

A favourite way of seeing Mérida is from a *calesa*, one of the traditional horse-drawn carriages that ply for trade from the Plaza Mayor, near the junction of Calles 60 and 61. The most popular trip, from the square up C/ 60 and Paseo Montejo and back again, costs around $10 (per *calesa*), and other routes are open to negotiation. Some drivers speak some English and can be fountains of anecdotes on the city's history and its buildings, and the ride is especially enjoyable at night. Neither is it a purely touristy affair; on Sundays the *calesas* are full of local families and couples, who, as with the *confidenciales*, are as devoted to Mérida's romantic touches as any visitor.

Tourist Information

Mérida **t** (999–)

Tourist Offices: There are official offices in the Teatro Peón Contreras, on the corner of Calles 60 and 57 (**t** 924 9290), at the corner of Calles 59 and 62, and on the Paseo de Montejo, corner of C/ 39 (*all open daily 8–8*), and an information kiosk in the Palacio Municipal (City Hall) on the Plaza Mayor. They provide rudimentary street maps and leaflets on various attractions, but the most useful thing is the free magazine *Yucatán Today*. Mérida's travel agencies provide useful supplements to official services; for specialized eco-tourism agencies, *see* p.111.

Banks: Mainly concentrated around Plaza Mayor and on C/ 65, between C/ 60 and C/ 62. Virtually all have ATMs. Of the exchange offices (*casas de cambio; also open Sun*), **Cambiaria del Sureste** in the Pasaje Picheta, on the north of the Plaza Mayor next to the Palacio del Gobernador, offers competitive rates. **American Express** is at Paseo Montejo no. 492 (**t** 923 4974), corner of C/ 43 and opposite the Museo de Antropología.

Consulates: The **US Consulate** is at Paseo Montejo no. 453, **t** 925 5011, near corner of Av. Colón. There is a **Cuban Consulate**, C 1-D no. 320, X 42 & 4-D, **t** 944 4216, but note that local travel agencies selling flights to Cuba can provide visas directly.

Health: Mérida has a 24-hr number to call for emergencies (**t** 066), but it is usually best to call individual services (police **t** 925 2555, fire **t** 924 9242, Red Cross ambulances **t** 924 9813). Mérida has **tourist police**, identified by their cream shirts and brown trousers, or ask for *Policía Turística* (ext. 260) on the central number. If you need a **doctor**, the **Clínica de Mérida**, Av. Itzaes 242, x 27 & 29, **t** 925 4100, in the Colonia García Gineres west of Paseo Montejo, is a well-established private clinic with English-speaking staff. One highly regarded **dentist** is Dr Javier Cámara Patrón, C/ 17 no. 170, x 8 & 10, **t** 925 3399. **Pharmacies** are abundant, and Farmacia YZA (Plaza Mayor) is open 24 hrs.

Internet Access: Mérida has plenty of choice: **Internet House**, C/ 62 no. 487, x 57 & 59, **t** 928 1531, *www.internethouse.com.mx* is well-organized with generous opening hours and good a/c. Prices (around $2 an hour) are halved 7am–9am; **Cibercafé Santa Lucía**, C/ 62 no. 467, x 55, is cheaper, and very popular.

Laundry: A good, cheap one is **Lavandería La Fe**, C/ 64 no. 470, x 55 & 57.

Mérida English Library: C/ 53 no. 524, x 66 & 68, **t** 924 8401. Excellent place for books, to check the recent press and/or make contact with the local English-speaking community (also has Internet access). Run by volunteers, it has a wide range of books including a good stock on the Yucatán and Mayan culture. It hosts international community parties every other month. **Catholic Mass** is said in English in the church of Santa Lucía, every Sat at 6pm.

Phone Offices: Many phone/fax offices are on or near C/ 60; the cheapest is usually in the Edificio Conesa on C/ 62, x 59 & 61; **Telworld** at C/ 60 no. 486, x 55 & 57 (plus several other branches) also generally offers decent rates.

Post Office: In the market area, junction of Calles 65 and 56 (*open Mon–Fri 7–7, Sat 9–1; closed Sun*). **Mexpost** has an entrance in the same building. Not all services are available all the time, so it's best to go in the morning.

City Tours

For a quick introduction to all of Mérida's sights take the **Paseo Turístico**, a 2-hr bus tour in an open-sided bus that runs from Parque Santa Lucía, at C/ 60 x 55, Mon–Sat at 10am, 1pm, 4pm and 7pm, Sun at 10am and 1pm ($8); you can book on **t** 927 6119, but it's not usually necessary. A 4-hr tour includes Dzibilchaltún (*see* p.295) and the 17th-century *hacienda* of San Antonio Cucul, departing Santa Lucía at 9am (except Mon), for an expensive $29.

Yucatán Trails, C/ 62 no. 482, x 57 & 59, **t** 928 2582, *yucatantrails@hotmail.com*. Especially handy to know, an agency run by Canadian long-term resident Denis Lafoy. As well as providing the usual city and local tours, he can organize snorkelling or diving trips to *cenotes* (*see* p.84), has a lot of information on the area in general and provides luggage lockers and a free English book-exchange service. Together with the Mérida English Library (*see* above) he also organizes international community parties each month that are a good opportunity to meet a wide range of people (not only resident Anglos).

Festivals

Carnaval (*Jan or Feb*): Mérida's biggest annual celebration, climaxing in several days of parades up to Shrove Tuesday.

Easter Week: Low-key, with few celebrations other than that everyone goes to the beach.

Cristo de las Ampollas (*Oct*): The most important religious festival culminates on 13 Oct, when the blackened image of Christ is carried in procession through the streets.

Learning Spanish

Mérida is popular for Spanish lessons, though courses here are more expensive than in San Cristóbal de Las Casas or Guatemala.

Centro de Idiomas del Sureste (CIS), C/ 14 no. 106, x 25, **t** 926 9494, *www.cisyucatan .com.mx*. Well-established school with three centres in the city that offers a full range of courses, with or without homestay accommodation with local families. Tuition fees begin from around $330 for two weeks; with homestays, an additional $120 a week.

Shopping

Mérida is the best place in the whole of the Yucatán to pick up traditional local products: embroidery, panama hats, ceramics, *guayabera* shirts and, most of all, hammocks. As the great market of the peninsula, Mérida is in fact the best place to shop for just about anything, ancient or modern. For more conventional shopping, the place to head is **Prolongación de Montejo** (beyond the Paseo itself), where you'll find several malls.

Books and Maps

Mérida has by far the best bookshops in the peninsula, and it's the place to look for background reading in English on the Maya and the region in general.

Librería Dante, Centro Cultural Olimpo, C/ 61 no. 502. The Dante branch in the Plaza Mayor has the largest stock of English-language editions; there are others in the city centre on Parque Hidalgo and on C/ 59, and four more in other parts of the city.

Librería-Papelería Burrel, C/ 59 no. 502, x 60 & 62. Best for maps: if you intend to travel around the region, you are strongly advised to stock up here while you can.

Crafts and Markets

Should you take up the invitation of any of the men proffering cards advertising *artesanía* at the corner of C/ 60 and the Plaza Mayor and follow them to their shop, you will almost certainly find some quality items mixed in with a lot of dross, and goods from all over Mexico as well as strictly local embroidery and hammocks. A much better place to look for all craftwork is in and around the market area, although even here quality is very variable.

Bazar de Artesanías, above the main market building, reached by a ramp from C/ 67 at the junction with C/ 56. The most organized outlet for local handicrafts, aimed directly at tourists. It's interesting to look around to get an idea of the range of goods on offer. You'll find fine work and engaging curios such as the *maquech*, live scarab beetles decorated as costume jewellery (a Maya tradition) alongside near-production-line items. Prices are a bit higher than elsewhere in town, but stallholders are often prepared to haggle.

Artesanías Maya, C/ 60 no. 502-C, x 63 & 63-A. A big all-sorts-of-everything handicrafts store, south of the plaza, with a huge stock running from panama hats and *huípiles* to every sort of ornament. The staff are very keen, but also knowledgeable and friendly.

Casa de las Artesanías, C/ 63 no. 503, x 64 & 66. A place to see and buy local handicrafts in more tranquil surroundings is this official Yucatán state handicrafts store, next to the Iglesia de las Monjas. Not as high quality as it could be, but it does have some very attractive, often usable pieces, in textiles and other media as well as the Yucatecan classics like ceramics, basketware, and artificial flowers. Prices higher than average.

Hammock-buying

The Yucatecan hammock is one of the most cherished local institutions, and the state of contented contemplation it induces has been celebrated by local poets in verse. There may be a mystique attached to it, but buying one is a logical process rather than impossibly complicated. Most hammocks today are made of nylon, light but often uncomfortably sweaty, cotton, the most popular material, or mixes of the two; you can also find hammocks of traditional sisal, which is very strong but very scratchy. They come in three basic sizes, single (*sencillo*), *matrimonial* and *familiar*. Within each size, the fundamental determinant of quality is the number of pairs of end strings used to produce a given width. Fifty is the minimum number of end-loops for a single hammock, and anything under that will lack strength and wear out quickly. The more strands that are used of finer material over the same area, the softer and more comfortable it will be. This naturally affects the weight, and a single hammock should weigh at least 1kg to be worth buying. You should also check the end loops, which should be large, tightly bound and well-finished. Another thing to look out for is the length, since many hammocks are made for Yucatecan height. To check, hold one end of the hammock up with one arm until the far end of the body of the hammock (i.e. without the end strings) is by your feet. The body of the hammock should be at least as long as you are, and as wide as you can afford.

It's a good idea to ask for a demonstration on how to repack your hammock, and try to memorize it. Local lore states that the two ends of a hammock should never touch, not so much a matter of avoiding bad luck as of preventing some infuriating tangles.

Hammock Specialists

There are some good hammock stalls in the Bazar, but the best places to buy this essential item are the specialist hammock shops, which are also in the market area, especially near the junction of Calles 65 and 56. The quality of hammocks varies greatly, and it pays to buy with care. Sadly, the vendors who approach you with with bags of hammocks in the streets rarely have much that's worth buying.

La Poblana, C 65 no. 492, x 58 & 60. Huge choice of quality hammocks in all sizes, and won't try to sell you a dud. Once you're past his bluff exterior, owner *sr* Razu gives very helpful and knowledgeable service (partly in English). Satisfied customers are spread around the world: the adult-size cotton hammocks go from about $15.

Tejidos y Cordeles Nacionales, C/ 56 no. 516-B. Another shop with a vast stock, on the plaza opposite the post office. Stacks of mixed cotton and nylon hammocks for around $12.

Hats

Panama hats can be bought in any of the C/ 60 craft stores and in the Bazar, but you will generally find a better choice at lower prices if you seek out some of the panama-specialist stalls in the main market and in the neighbouring streets.

El Sombrero Popular, C/ 65 Depto 18, x 58 & 60. Half-shop, half-stall outside the market, with a very friendly owner and fine panamas for absolutely every size of head.

Textiles and Clothing

Mérida's market and the shops around it naturally contain many other things as well as hammocks and ornaments: *huarache* sandals, embroidered *huípiles*, rows of *guayaberas* for men. The best places for *guayaberas*, though, are the factory outlets run by manufacturers themselves. The same consideration applies to traditional embroidery and *huípil* dresses as with hammocks and hats: there are very good examples in the Bazar, but a wider range and better prices in the stalls in the main market.

Guayaberas Jack, C/ 59 no. 507, x 60 & 62. The factory outlet of a highly regarded, long-established *guayabera* manufacturer. Prices are very reasonable.

Maya Chuy, C/ 60, x 47 & 49. A local women's embroidery cooperative that seeks to maintain high standards and has a beautiful display of fine, original work for sale.

Mexicanísimo, C/ 60 no. 496, x 59 & 61. Not traditional, for once, but an attractive shop on the corner of Parque Hidalgo with very distinctive ranges of light-weight clothes for men and women, made with Mexican cottons and using traditional techniques in stylish, entirely modern designs that make them very wearable hot-weather clothing.

Peletería Castañeda, C/ 56 no. 519, x 65. Neither traditional, nor strictly textiles: a specialist plastic-products dealer with huge quantities of the multi-coloured plastic materials – bags, sheeting, shower curtains – that are a distinct Mexican phenomenon.

Sports and Activities

Club de Golf La Ceiba, 14½km north of Mérida beside the road to Progreso. The club has an 18-hole golf course, as well as tennis, basketball and volleyball courts, a gym, a pool and games for kids. Hotels frequently have concessions whereby guests are able to use the club's facilities for only a small fee.

Exploring *Cenotes*

They're far less well-known than the divable and swimmable *cenotes* near the Riviera coast around Tulum (*see* pp.206–7), but Yucatán state actually has far more *cenote* sinkholes and underwater caverns than Quintana Roo, above all in the area south of Mérida towards Muna and Mayapán. The state government, mindful of their fascination, has begun to develop ecotourism schemes to help villagers open their *cenotes* to visitors. An **International Cave Diving Conference** (with dives included) is held in Mérida each November, and some information on visitable sinkholes (especially a booklet called *Cenotes*) should be available from the Yucatán state **Ecology Department**

(t 923 1033, *secol@prodigy.net.mx*). With all such schemes there's a gap between projects and facilities on the ground (most village *cenotes* are still not signposted), but anyone who enjoys exploring, can handle Spanish and doesn't mind taking their time can spend many happy hours searching out *cenotes* around the Yucatán's back roads.

Maybe more practically, guided trips to *cenotes* have begun to be run from Mérida. Very complete one-day *cenote* snorkelling (from $38 per person, with discounts for children) and scuba diving ($100) trips, and cave visits ($40), meals and all equipment included, can be booked through **Yucatán Trails** (*see* above) and some other agencies.

Where to Stay

Mérida t (999–)

Mérida's hotels are among its great attractions: many are in buildings – some genuinely colonial, some more recent – with deliciously peaceful interior patios, a fair number of which, even in the cheaper ranges, also contain swimming pools. Mérida hotel pools tend to be small (in cheap hotels, tiny), but are still wonderfully refreshing after a day's tramp. In the last few years the range has also been significantly broadened with luxury *haciendas* at the top, and some very attractive, individually-run guest houses lower down.

Hacienda Hotels

Not in the city itself but in the countryside near Mérida are three of the most striking of the old *hacienda* estates, now converted into very special luxury hotels. All are within their own grounds, and offer an indulgent combination of aristocratic colonial architecture, lush tropical gardens and luxurious, stylish modern comforts; as you might expect, prices are top-scale too ($200–$400 a night). *Haciendas* are naturally quite isolated, but all offer transport and a range of excursions (into Mérida, to Mayan sites, etc.). The Plan Group, which runs San José Cholul, also runs three more *haciendas* south of Mérida, **Temozón** (*see* p.306), **Santa Rosa** (*see* p.303) and **Uayamón** in Campeche (*see* p.384) and the **Hacienda Ochil** restaurant (*see* p.307).

Hacienda Katanchel, entrance on the north side of Highway 180; at the end of a 3-km driveway, t 923 4020, *www.hacienda-katanchel.com*. First of the 'new' *haciendas* and still the most impressive, this is the one true luxury hotel in the state, with an individuality the others lack. Some 24km east of Mérida, it's an oasis in the Yucatán brush, a colonial-era *hacienda* that with its 300-ha estate has been transformed by architect Aníbal González and his wife Monica Hernández with verve, imagination, taste and investment. The 17th-century main house has been superbly restored, and outer buildings converted into 40 pavilion-style rooms; around them, a virtual microclimate of magnificently lush gardens are home to over 100 species of birds and many rare plants. With the owners' involvement comes an impressive attention to detail, in the use of handmade linen, natural colognes and antique furnishings. There is also a magnificent pool and one of the finest **restaurants** (*open to non-residents*, *expensive*) in the region. Coming upon this opulent Shangri-La in the midst of the dusty woods can be disconcerting, but is undeniably seductive.

Hacienda San José Cholul, 30km east of Mérida on the Tixkokob–Tekantó road, reservations via Mérida, t 944 3637, *www.grupoplan.com/www.luxurycollection.com*. One of four *haciendas* converted by the Plan Group, in a very peaceful part of the Yucatán countryside. The 17th-century house has been imaginatively restored, the gardens are delightful, there's a pretty terrace **restaurant** and a spectacularly designed pool. The 15 rooms are in buildings spread around the gardens, in four sizes from large to very large; all have terraces and giant bathrooms, and the master suite has a pool to itself.

Hacienda Xcanatún, just east of the Progreso road 12km north of Mérida, t 941 0213, *www.xcanatun.com*. Closest to Mérida, Xcanatún is also (just a little) less expensive. The 18th-century house was converted in 1999; surrounded by the luxuriant gardens there's a deliciously pretty **restaurant**, the Casa de Piedra (*expensive*), which ranks as one of Mérida's best, with refined, classic Yucatecan cuisine. Shielded from restaurant clients are 18 plush and spacious suites, in three different sizes but each with its own terrace with Jacuzzi (honeymoons are a speciality). There also two pools, a very stylish terrace bar, and a spa with all sorts of health and beauty treatments, but those who expect total seclusion should note that the *hacienda* is actually surrounded by the village-suburb of Xcanatún.

Luxury

Mérida's top-of-the-range hotels are oddly, yet conveniently near to each other on Av. Colón, by Paseo Montejo. All, of course, offer very comfortable rooms with state-of-the-art a/c, TV with cable and satellite, minibars, etc., as well as excellent service, bars, restaurants, tennis courts, pools and business facilities.

Fiesta Americana, Paseo de Montejo 451, t 942 1141/reservations t 326 6900, *www.fiestaamericana.com*. Most impressive to look at, a giant mansion built on to a much older building. The luxurious feel is sustained inside with a spectacular atrium topped by a splendid stained-glass roof; its large, traditionally styled rooms are also very attractive.

Hyatt Regency Mérida, Av. Colón x C/ 60, t 942 0202, *www.hyatt.com*. At the other end of the block, the Hyatt is still luxurious, but more functionally modern. However, it offers a more ritzily opulent rooftop pool, with several different sub-pools and that great asset a swim-up bar, and has **Spasso**, the more happening nightclub, in the basement.

Hotel Villa Mercedes, Av. Colón 500, x C/ 60, t 942 9000, *www.hotelvillamercedes.com.mx*. Opened in 2001, the Villa Mercedes is slightly smaller than its neighbours and seeks to evoke a rather more discreet, old-world style of luxury. Suites are especially opulent, and all rooms are also very well equipped with up to the minute electronics.

Expensive

Casa del Balam, C/ 60 no. 488, x 57, t 924 2150, *www.yucatanadventure.com.mx*. Charming, long-established and very central hotel, with a colonial 19th-century patio which has been skilfully blended into a modern addition. Rooms are attractive, and the suites in the old building (with original woodwork) are truly lush. The owners, the Mayaland Group, also own hotels at Chichén Itzá and Uxmal.

Hotel Misión Mérida, C/ 60 no. 491, x 57, t 923 9500, *www.hotelesmision.com.mx*. Opposite the Casa del Balam, this opened in the 1920s as the Hotel Mérida. The first two floors are part of a colonial building, while the rest is more modern; it now has over 150 rooms. Its opulent public areas are the chief draw, from a giant atrium-like main patio-restaurant to the garden beside the (relatively small) pool.

La Misión de Fray Diego, C/ 61 no. 524, x 64 & 66, t 924 1111, *www.lamisiondefraydiego.com*. Another example of the current trend to make the most of Mérida's colonial heritage, this recently opened venue occupies a partly 17th-century house opulently converted to contain rooms combining 'old Mérida' fittings with mod cons, as well as a pool and garden patios. Four 'special' rooms provide the full colonial mansion experience, and there are two very lavish suites; standard rooms are comfortable but less distinctive.

Moderate

Casa Mexilio, C/ 68 no. 495, x 59 & 57, t 928 2505, *casamexilio@prodigy.net.mx*. In a quiet area, this beautiful old house is more of a personally-run guest-house than a hotel. It has only eight rooms, each attractively and individually decorated by Jorge Manzanero and his American partner, with antiques, traditional furniture and artwork. Rooms lead into each other in labyrinthine fashion, and there's a delightful, grotto-like pool and two bars, one in a snug room and another on the roof. Several rooms have their own balconies, but there's a common breakfast room and a distinctly homey atmosphere. It's part of the Turquoise Reef Group (*see* p.139), and most bookings are made from the USA, but you can book direct. April–mid-Dec prices are extremely reasonable.

Hotel Caribe, C/ 59 no. 500, x 60, t 924 9022, *www.hotelcaribe.com.mx*. Popular and pretty traditional hotel on Parque Hidalgo, forming a corner with the Gran Hotel. It's in a fine, old 19th-century building, with rooms on three levels around a stone-columned patio, and has a lovely little rooftop pool with views of the cathedral. While all attractive the rooms vary in standard and price, the best ones being those around the pool.

Hotel MedioMundo, C/ 55 no. 533, x 64 & 66, t/f 924 5472, *www.hotelmediomundo.com*. Recently-opened creation in an old Mérida house of Uruguayan-Lebanese owners Nelson and Nicole, who arrived here after living in many parts of the world. Spacious rooms are decorated in warm, tropical colours, and there's a small patio pool with café-bar alongside where delicious fresh breakfasts (included) are served. A warmly individual welcome also marks it out from many of Mérida's older, more routine hotels.

Maison Lafitte, C/ 60 no. 472, x 53 & 55, t/f 923 9159, *www.maisonlafitte.com.mx*. One of the growing selection of small-scale, 'old-mansion' hotels, opened in 2001 in a historic patio house near the Santa Lucía church, and under the same ownership as the Posada del Capitán Lafitte near Playa del Carmen. Rooms combine a certain amount of old-Mérida style with state-of-the-art mod cons (a/c, TVs, bathrooms), but the atmosphere is more functional than in smaller guesthouses nearby.

Inexpensive

Casa San Juan, C/ 62 no. 545, x 69 & 71, t 923 6823, *www.casasanjuan.com*. One of the most charming of the guest houses, and also a great bargain. This 19th-century house near Parque de San Juan, the home of an old landowning family until the 1980s, has been beautifully restored by Pablo Da Costa. It has seven rooms, all different and some with a/c, but all with giant high ceilings and traditional fittings. There are also delightful patios, a garden providing home-grown lemons and an open kitchen. Breakfast and other extras are included, and the house is deliciously peaceful.

Los Cielos Guest House, C/ 49 no. 513-A, x 62 & 64, t/f (*messages only*) 923 1061, *www.los cielos.8m.com*. Home of Canadian Mérida resident Lorna-Gail Dallin, a few blocks from the centre in a peaceful part of town. She has one single room and one with two beds, both very comfortable and with their own bathrooms, and the house has a tranquil garden. It's a place to settle into and feel at ease; longer-term rates can be arranged. She can also be contacted through the English Library.

Hotel Aragón, C/ 57 no. 474, x 52 & 54, t 924 0242, *www.hotelaragon.com*. Pleasant patio hotel a three-block walk from C/ 60. Rooms are large, bright and comfortable, if a little pastel-shaded, and all have a/c. Basic breakfast, served in the patio, is included and tea, coffee and water are provided free. Prices are a bit lower than average, but there's no pool.

Hotel Dolores Alba, C/ 63 no. 464, x 52 & 54, t 928 5650, *www.doloresalba.com*. A four-block walk east of the Plaza Mayor, but consistently among the most popular of Mérida hotels. A large and leafy patio and a pool are some of the attractions; another is the atmosphere, which makes it an easy place to meet other travellers. The best rooms are those in the new annexe around the pool at the back, which are plain in style but have very good a/c, TV and other facilities; rooms in the main building have a bit more character and are cheaper, but are a bit time-battered. Good breakfasts are provided, for around $4. The same owners' hotel (with the same name) near Chichén Itzá can also be booked from here (*see* p.239). Both are often full, so call ahead or be there before lunch to get a room.

Hotel Mucuy, C/ 57 no. 481, x 56 & 58, t 928 5193, f 923 7801. Near the bottom end of this price slot, this is a long-term favourite with budget travellers. Spanish owner *sr* Alfredo Comín is a little severe on first encounter, but softens, and his wife is very friendly. The 24 rooms, with showers and fans (no a/c), are straightforward but bright and well kept. No pool, but a leafy patio.

Hotel San Juan, C/ 55 no. 497-A, x 60 & 58, t 924 1742, f 924 1688. One of the best value lower–mid-range hotels, with light, bright and comfortable rooms with good facilities (TV, phone, all with fans and a/c), and a neat little pool. It's in the block just behind the church of Santa Lucía.

Hotel Santa Ana, C/ 45 no. 503, x 60 & 62, t 923 3331, *www.hotelsantaana.com.mx*. Recently-converted, in an old house in a quiet area north of the centre. Rooms are a little small, but contain a full range of newly-fitted comforts, and there's a smart lobby and a small patio pool. There's no restaurant, so for breakfast the nearest options are the little cafés around Parque Santa Ana.

Hotel Santa Lucía, C/ 55 no. 508, x 60 & 62, t 928 2672, f 928 2662. On Parque de Santa Lucía and under the same ownership as the San Juan across C/ 60, this is a similar-style, pleasant, good value hotel with light, airy rooms and a pool. It's slightly older, not quite as comfortable, and a smidgeon cheaper.

Hotel Trinidad Galería, C/ 60 no. 456, x 51, t 923 2463, f 924 2319. Mérida's most eccentric/funky (or just cranky) hotel. In the lobby you're greeted by a riot of vegetation, dolls, inflatable superheroes and expressionist paintings; inside, there's more eclectic artwork in a maze of interlocking patios. The rooms are more basic (most fan-only, some with a/c). They vary a lot, and if you don't like one you're shown ask to see one with more light. A great plus is the palm-shrouded pool, with a wonderful hidden-glade quality, even if it is a tad murky. Left open at night, it's a magical place from which to take in starscapes. The same management also owns the cheaper **Hotel Trinidad**, C/ 62 no. 464, x 55 & 57, t 923 2033, *ohm@sureste.com*, an old house two blocks away with a García Márquez-ish charm, and a patio that's less plant-lined than overgrown.

Luz en Yucatán, C/ 55 no. 499, x 58 & 60, t 924 0035, *www.luzenyucatan.com*. Part of the old 17th-century convent building behind the church of Santa Lucía was transformed into an art gallery a few years ago, but is now the home of American Madeline Parmet. The beautifully shady old house is huge, and within it there are several fully-equipped apartments, with kitchens. There's also a small pool, but nevertheless she lets them go at exceptional prices. A real home from home, it's ideal for settling in and enjoying a completely hassle-free stay, especially if you're planning on staying for a while; a range of activities and wellbeing treatments – massage and health therapies, Spanish courses, exercise programmes – are also available.

Cheap

Mérida's cheapest hotels rarely have such things as swimming pools, but most offer showers in most rooms. Several are in one area near the main bus stations, south of the Plaza Mayor and west of the main market.

Casa Becil, C/ 67 no. 550-C, x 66 & 68, **t** 924 6764. Popular budget hotel in a modern, slightly motel-style building near the bus-station. Rooms are quite plain but all have showers and roof fans (no a/c), the management are very friendly, and it has a brighter feel than some bargain-basement hotels. Breakfast is often included in the (low) price.

Casa Bowen, C/ 66 no. 521-B, x 65 & 67, **t** 928 6109. Another cheapie favourite: it has one of the most attractive patios of the budget hotels, and while there's no pool there's a little café alongside. As well as fan-only rooms there are ten with a/c (*inexpensive*).

Hostería L'Fondiu, C/ 52 no. 469, x 51 & 53, **t/f** 924 9149. A few blocks' walk from Mérida's main drags, this little guest-house-café is a real find. In the garden at the back of the café (*see* below) the charming owners have four bright, delightfully airy rooms, with brand-new facilities, all available at an exceptional price. You can sit out and enjoy Mérida tranquility in the garden, and the upper rooms even have a fine view.

Hotel del Mayab, C/ 50 no. 536-A, x 65 & 67, **t** 928 5174, **f** 928 6047. Motel-style hotel just east of the market, seven blocks from Plaza Mayor. Rooms are a bit shabby, but big and airy, and all have their own showers (some have clanky a/c too, still *cheap*) and the management are friendly; the biggest plus, though, is that it's about the cheapest hotel in Mérida with a pool. It also has parking.

Hotel Meridano, C/ 54 no. 478, x 55 & 57, **t** 923 2614. Three blocks from the Plaza Mayor, with a well-looked after patio and plain rooms; from some that are dark to others that are quite roomy: all have showers, some a/c, and four people can have inter-connecting rooms at special rates. Prices are near *inexpensive*, but breakfast, served in the patio, is included.

Nómadas, C/ 62 no. 433, x 51, **t** 924 5223, *www.hostels.com.mx*. With 'backpackers' written on the façade this hostel, part of the AMAJ federation, couldn't be more clearly targeted. Beds in 8-bunk dorms cost around $7, or a little less with a IYHF card; one room is women-only, the others are mixed. You can hire camping or hammock space for a bit less, and there are also a few double rooms with and without showers ($16–$21).

It's not spacious, but bright, well kept and very clean, and newer and airier than many cheap hotels; there's also a kitchen, Internet access, TV, a garden and lounging space.

Eating Out

The classics of Yucatecan cuisine – *cochinita pibil*, *sopa de lima*, *poc-chuc* – are everywhere, but the city also offers many other cuisines: central-Mexican, Italian, Middle-Eastern (due to the sizeable Lebanese community), Chinese, multi-national chains. Prices are generally low; however, in Mérida still more than in most Mexican cities, price differences don't necessarily reflect differences in quality. Fresher, better meals are often found by seeking out special places rather than paying more; try avoiding the most touristy areas of the centre and venture into places favoured by locals on Paseo Montejo. Most are not expensive.

A peculiarity of some of the most traditional, upscale Mérida restaurants (but not most *haciendas*) is that they only open for lunch, not dinner.

Hacienda Restaurants

In the same way that several of Yucatán's colonial *haciendas* have been converted into upscale hotels, others, with rather less of a transformation, have been turned into restaurants where you can sample Yucatecan cuisine on an arcaded terrace, and see a little of the gardens and *hacienda* ambience. Most offer tours of some kind if you don't want to organize your own transport. All are *expensive* and reservations are advisable. The best and most beautiful *hacienda* restaurants, though, are those in the hotels of **Katanchel** and **Xcanatún**, also nearby (*see* above, p.271).

Hacienda Kancabchén, Ctra Baca-Tixcuncheil Km2, **t** 984 1851, *www.kancabchen.com.mx*. Striking old *henequen hacienda* a few kilometres north of Tixkokob, about 25km east of Mérida. As well as a garden restaurant it has other (optional) attractions such as a wildlife collection, handicraft shops and displays of rural skills like cattle-wrangling.

Hacienda San Antonio Cucul, C/ 28 no. 340-A, **t** 944 7571. The only *hacienda* within Mérida's *periférico*, in the northeast corner of the city (any cab driver knows the way). Founded in

1626, it has kept its lovely gardens; the restaurant is fairly touristy, but still pretty.

Hacienda Teya, Ctra Mérida-Cancún (Highway 180) Km12.5, t 988 0800, *www.hacienda teya.com*. One of the first *haciendas* to open its gates to visitors, just 12½km east of the city. It's pretty well oriented to the larger-scale trade, so the atmosphere is not very intimate, but its classic Yucatecan dishes are highly regarded by locals.

Expensive

Alberto's Continental, C/ 64 no. 482, x 57, t 928 5367. Quirky place in a classic old Mérida house from 1727, which owner Alberto Salum has filled with a huge collection of religious images, mirrors and other Baroque bric-a-brac. The family are Mérida-Lebanese, and the menu includes such things as tabbouleh and kebabs, and distinctive salads, alongside Yucatecan standards, accompanied by wonderful home-baked Lebanese bread.

Los Almendros & Gran Almendros, C/ 50 no. 493, x 57, t 928 5459, and C/ 57, x 50, t 923 8135. Mérida's most celebrated restaurant, facing the church on Parque de la Mejorada. It's actually a branch of a small 'chain' that began life in Ticul (*see* p.327). Traditionally the foremost showcase for Yucatecan cuisine, the Almendros are credited with actually inventing *poc-chuc* (pork marinated in garlic and bitter orange juice), now a standard on menus all over the peninsula. Their approach, with a dance show every Friday and waitresses in lavishly embroidered *ternos*, has become pretty tourist-kitschy, and standards are irregular, but on a good day it's still a pleasant place to sample local dishes. Service is charming. The larger Gran Almendros is around the corner on C/ 57.

Muelle 8, C/ 21 no. 141, x Prolongación de Montejo, Colonia Buenavista, t 944 5343. Generally regarded as the very best in town, a seafood specialist with superbly fresh fish and seafood, beautifully presented with an innovative combination of local tradition and modern styles. *Open lunch only.*

Portico del Peregrino, C/ 57 no. 501, x 60 & 62, t 928 6163. A likeable option for a more comfortable-than-usual dinner, offering a choice between an air-conditioned, traditionally furnished dining room and an intimate patio; the menu features refined versions of Yucatecan and Mexican standards and Italian and international dishes.

Moderate

Amaro's, C/ 59 no. 507, x 60 & 62. A good first choice for vegetarians, and extremely pretty. It's set in the house where Andrés Quintana Roo, Yucatán's most important participant in Mexican independence, was born in 1787, and the patio is dominated by a magnificent giant orchid tree that explodes into flower in winter. Aside from a few Yucatecan meat dishes, it mostly serves vegetarian specialities such as *crêpes de chaya*, made with the spinach-like *chaya*, as well as sandwiches, pizzas and conventional Mexican dishes.

Bella Epoca, Hotel del Parque, C/ 60 no. 495, x 57 & 59. On the first floor – with an almost trendy-looking 'video bar' on the ground floor – the Bella Epoca for once offers no pavement tables but instead a view of Parque Hidalgo from its chandeliered dining room. The Yucatecan–Mexican–Lebanese food is not quite as luxurious, but pleasant.

Las Brasas, Paseo de Montejo no. 462, x C/ 37. One of several restaurants worth checking out along the Paseo, with a rooftop terrace overlooking the roundabout. It has enjoyable, snacky Mexican dishes, but the big attraction is the buzzy, relaxed atmosphere.

Café-Restaurant Express, C/ 60 no. 502, x 59. Facing Parque Hidalgo from across C/ 60, the Express was the height of sophistication when it opened in 1936. It still has an air of café-society today, with twirling roof fans, long shadows, wrought-iron chandeliers and dark wood-panelled walls decorated with faintly odd paintings of Mayan scenes and local wildlife, and provides a wonderful vantage point on all the movement around the square. In its early days it was an important meeting point for everyone who was anyone in Mérida, and especially the local bohemians who wrote the songs of the *Trova Yucateca*, and it's still patronized just as much by locals as tourists. A good place for breakfast, and for sitting over a drink for as long as you need, and they also provide good salads and satisfying Mexican dishes.

Café El Rincón, Hotel Caribe, C/ 59 no. 500, x C/ 60. Several of Mérida's most frequented restaurants (especially by foreigners) are in a clutch around Parque Hidalgo. Though pleasant, you go there to crowd-watch more than for their food. This is about the best, with enjoyable Yucatecan and Mexican standards, decent service and great juices by the jug. If you don't fancy the bustle of the square you can sit inside in a lovely patio.

Pane e Vino, C/ 62 no. 496, x 59 & 61. You may not have come looking for Italian food, but for a change this popular, modern restaurant off the Plaza Mayor offers high-quality pasta (with several vegetarian options) and other Mediterranean favourites.

Los Vaqueros, Paseo de Montejo, x C/ 35. Popular *taquería* with a big terrace on the Paseo and carefully prepared *tacos* that make the standard model seem a little poor. *Open eves only.*

La Vía Olimpo, Centro Cultural Olimpo, Plaza Mayor. The café in the new-minted Olimpo centre next to the Palacio Municipal may be a bit over-bright and modern, but it has charming service, pavement tables, effective a/c inside and an all-purpose menu, from Mexican classics to crêpes, burgers and salads. *Open 24hrs; also 24-hr Internet café.*

Cheap

Several of the most popular places for cheap eats-and-pavement-terrace-sitting are in the colonnades of the Plaza Mayor. The cheapest places, though – as usual in Mexico – are the *cocinas económicas* attached to the market. They are all in a row, at the top of the ramp facing C/ 67 that leads to the crafts market. A few years ago they were done up with tiled tables, but most still have their painted signs with names like Carmita La Mestizita or La Huachita, offering *tacos*, *enchiladas* and other specialities such as *mole con arroz*, *mondongo* or *cochinita pibil*. You give your order at one of the stands, then find a space at the nearest table, lined with salads, fierce *salsa verde* and other bright things you may or may not wish to add to your food. There's no alcohol, but stands offer fresh juice *licuados*. A filling meal can be had for $2–$3, snacks for less. Opening early in the morning every day (*except Sun*), they close, like the market, by mid-afternoon.

Café Alameda, C/ 58 no. 474, x 55 & 57. Very friendly old Mérida-Lebanese café with a lofty interior and Arab specialities (superb fresh bread) as well as local standards. Quality is reliably high, and it's a delightfully tranquil place to collect your thoughts.

El Cangrejito, C/ 57 no. 523, x 64 & 66. Proof of the rule that in Mérida price and quality can often be strangely disconnected. The traditional seafood dishes prepared by Don Felipe Santos Ché and his crew at this cranky little café have a high reputation, but despite its fame it's still cheap and unpretentious, and you can put together a fine meal with *tacos* of fresh octopus, *camarones* or lobster for under $5. Some of the staff can also be pretty brusque, and they have a tendency to close unpredictably for a day or so. *Open daily for lunch only until 5pm.*

Hostería L'Fondiu, C/ 52 no. 469, x 51 & 53. A few blocks' walk from C/ 60, this soothing little café is worth the trip for a relaxing breakfast or lunch. Owner Enrique de la Garza and his wife take more trouble than most: they're especially welcoming and attentive, and their dishes – from Mexican and Yucatecan standards to fine fish grills – are made with superior ingredients above the local norm, still at very low prices. They also have four similarly exceptional guest rooms (*see above*). *Closed Sun and eves.*

Marlín Azul, C/ 62 no. 488, x 57 & 59. Another great bargain: a simple, street-side bar, but its Yucatecan seafood dishes – especially the *ceviche mixto*, with prawns, octopus and conch – are among the best you'll find.

Pizzeria Vito Corleone, C/ 59 no. 508, x 60 & 62. A few steps from Parque Hidalgo, this basic little place looks like a standard Mexican snack-house, except for the bicycles hanging above the entrance, its flame-fired pizza oven and the name. This eccentric hybrid will provide you with fine standard pizzas with a well-baked thin crust, or you can try their *pizza mexicana* incorporating *jalapeño* peppers and refried beans.

Restaurante Café-Club, C/ 55 no. 496-A, x 58 & 60. Likeable, laid-back and eclectic café by Santa Lucía church with an Iranian owner and a mixed, at least 50%-vegetarian bill of fare that includes Mexican standards, classic breakfasts, pizzas, salads and great sandwiches. It's also very airy and comfortable; the vegetarian set lunch is an ultra-bargain.

Drinks, Cafés and Juices

Always a favourite for a drink is the Express (*see* above), which allows you to get a real sense of the life of the city. For non-alcoholic, daytime refreshment, Mérida also has an exceptional range of juice specialists.

Dulcería-Sorbetería Colón, C/ 61. Branch of Mérida's leading ice-cream makers, with terrace tables on the north side of the plaza.

Jugos California, C/ 63-A (the pedestrian alley parallel to C/ 63), corner of C/ 58. The local best-juicer award has to go to this company. It has another branch on the Plaza Mayor (corner of C/ 63 and C/ 62), and several more around the centre. Make your way through the kids and resting shoppers to find every possible local fruit ready to be juiced.

La Michoacana, C/ 61, x 56. A wonderful, classic city ice cream, juice and *agua* shop in the middle of the shopping area north of the market. Staff are very friendly, and if you spend a day going through the full range you'll be in vitamin overdrive.

El Trapiche, C/ 62 no. 491, x 57 & 55. Brightly coloured old café and juice shop with wonderfully refreshing *licuados* of watermelon, *mamey* and other fruits. It also has all kinds of other things, from international breakfasts (with lots of fruit) to an eclectic range of vegetarian dishes.

Entertainment and Nightlife

Entertainment

The best entertainment in the city is free, and open to all on the streets. Free events take place nightly: current programmes are available from tourist offices. The **Teatro Peón Contreras**, C/ 60, also puts on folkloric shows fairly frequently, for which you have to pay.

Mérida en Domingo (Mérida on Sunday). Every Sunday the whole of the Plaza Mayor and C/ 60 as far as Santa Lucía are closed to traffic to make way for a great weekly, all-day *fiesta* organized by the city council. There are *jarana* displays in the Plaza Mayor, and other performances, and opportunities to dance yourself, in the Plaza, Parque Hidalgo and Santa Lucía.

Ponte Chula Mérida (roughly translatable as 'Put on a show, Mérida'). Usually held on one Saturday each month, when C/ 60 is closed off at night to make space for stages, dancing and extra restaurant tables, with live music from 8pm into the early hours.

Serenatas Yucatecas. Held every Thursday without a break for over 35 years, on the stage in the Parque de Santa Lucía, these feature an ever-changing, ever-charming programme of all the classic elements of Yucatecan music: *jaranas*, folk dancing, trios, and even poetry recitals. If you've never seen one, this is an essential date. And it's free.

Folk Dancing: Most Fridays at 8pm, Mérida's student folk-dance society presents demonstrations of traditional dances from all over Mexico, in the University patio on C/ 60.

Bars and Clubs

Less folkloric nightlife is not so apparent but also not far away.

L'Atelier, Prolongación de Montejo no. 454, x 13 & 15. Good option for a late-night chat over a drink or a light meal. Near the junction with Circuito Colonias and C/ 11, this bar-café is in a fine old house with a garden, where mellow Latin jazz bands perform, and pleasantly stylish without being fussy.

Ay Caray!, C/ 60, x 55 & 57. Making up much of the block along C/ 60 is a Mérida institution, a building with four loud night-spots full of 'local colour' that draw a noisy Meridano crowd more than foreigners. The Ay Caray!, a big *cantina*/dance bar (with food), generally has the best (boisterous) atmosphere; next door, **El Nuevo Tucho** is a glitzy cabaret-restaurant with poor food but (sometimes good) live salsa and Latin dance music, **Azul Picante** on the upper floor is a smaller salsa bar and the **Xtabay** is a grungy, dive-like disco-bar that still draws in the crowds.

Pancho's, C/ 59 no. 509, x 60 & 62. Mexican-theme bar-restaurant, with pictures of Pancho Villa and Zapata everywhere and waiters in *sombreros* and crossed bandoliers; the most consistently popular hangout in the heart of town. It has two big bars, open to the stars and the Christmas lights that supplement them, and one of the world's tiniest dance floors. The staff are on the ball, and there's always a good atmosphere.

History

Mayan Ti'ho

When the Spaniards arrived in 1540 the city known as *Ichcansiho* or *Ti'ho* was already partially abandoned, with a population much smaller than fitted its imposing ruined pyramids and buildings. These ruins have long since been obliterated and their remains incorporated into the later city. Recent investigations, though, suggest that there had been a settlement here since the Preclassic, in about 300 BC.

As a city Ti'ho reached its apogee between about AD 500 and 900, when it had about 10,000 inhabitants. Politically, though, it was probably subordinate to Dzibilchaltún, just to the north. Like other cities in the northern Yucatán it was not completely abandoned at the time of the great Collapse like the Mayan cities in the south, but by the time of the Conquest it was only a tributary settlement of *Chakán*, one of the 19 Mayan chieftancies into which the Yucatán was divided. It did, however, retain a giant square, surrounded by some of the region's largest pyramid-platforms.

The City of the *Conquistadores*

In 1540 Francisco de Montejo el Sobrino, youngest of the three identically-named conquerors of the Yucatán, arrived in Ti'ho with under 50 men after a bloody, water-less march from Campeche. It was probably chosen because its population was too small to offer resistance, while its massive ruins provided an ideal place to set up a fortified camp. He was shortly joined by his cousin Montejo el Mozo with reinforce-ments. Still with only 200 men, they were besieged within Ti'ho for long months by an army brought together in a rare moment of cooperation by the Yucatán lordships, until in June 1541 the Mayan chiefs launched a frontal assault.

In the bloodiest battle of the conquest in Yucatán the Spaniards held back attack after attack, until one climactic day when Mayan morale collapsed. They never again came together for joint resistance, and at the beginning of 1542 Tutul Xiú of Maní was the first of a string of Mayan chieftains to come to Ti'ho to accept Spanish rule.

On 6 January 1542 the city of Mérida was formally founded as capital of the new colony. The name was chosen by Montejo el Mozo because its ruins reminded him of the ruins of Roman Mérida in Extremadura, near his home in Salamanca. He immedi-ately began drawing up the city's grid, centred on its Plaza Mayor or Plaza de Armas. The plot on its east side was set aside for a future cathedral. The first Spanish stone building in Mérida, however, was the residence built for El Mozo and his descendants, the Casa de Montejo, completed in 1549.

As the colony was pacified, the conquerors settled down into reproducing the aristocratic way of life they had seen at home in Spain. Yucatán was a down-at-heel colony, which unlike central Mexico or Peru gave its new lords no El Dorado of precious metals. Mérida's leading citizens, though, did not let this blunt their ambitions. Like so much in the *conquistador* saga, this bordered on dreamland. Early colonial Mérida was a very peculiar settlement. Across it there were still plenty of Mayan pyramids, especially the glowering mass of the *Xbaklumchaan*, a huge platform that filled the west side of the Plaza, where the Palacio Municipal is today.

Around them most of the 'city' consisted of stick huts with palm roofs, between which there stuck out a growing collection of solid, stone buildings more or less in line with European styles of the late Middle Ages and Renaissance – the Casa de Montejo, the Hospital of San Juan de Dios, the Franciscans' Monastery of the Assumption – virtually all built by Mayan hands under the system of one day's compulsory unpaid labour each week.

Greatest among them was the towering mass of the cathedral. Juan Izquierdo, Bishop of Yucatán at the time of its consecration in 1599, reported to his king in Spain that in 30 years of service in the Americas he had 'never seen anything like it, or close to it'. An austere Franciscan, Izquierdo complained of the extravagance of building a cathedral 'so large and sumptuous that it would satisfy any populous city in Spain' in a settlement he referred to as an *aldea*, a village. Mérida's pioneer aristocrats, on the other hand, were immensely proud of having the first cathedral completed in Mexico, and enthusiastically subscribed to it and other new church buildings in the city.

Colonial Mérida

As the conquest era faded into the past, the streets of Mérida became less dramatic in their contrasts, filling up with more solid houses of stone and masonry, and yet more churches. They were built by pilfering the stones of the old Mayan ruins and platforms, which consequently dwindled away to nothing.

In the original city the first streets built in the grid, around the plaza, were reserved for the population of wholly European, Spanish origin. Communities of other races were confined to separate *barrios* on the fringes of the official city – Santiago and Santa Catarina to the west for local Maya, Santa Lucía in the north for African slaves and mixed-race mulattos. For each of them the Franciscans built separate churches.

Mérida's inland position protected it from the constant harassment by pirates and other European powers suffered by Campeche, and the city settled into the slow-moving life of a somnolent colonial centre. Governors and officials became much more active in the last decades of Spanish rule, in response to the reforming impulses coming from King Charles III. Most energetic of all Spanish governors was Lucás de Gálvez, who in only three years from 1789 gave Mérida an unprecedented set of urban improvements. He was a great road builder, and rebuilt Mérida's defences with a city wall which had eight lofty gateways, three of which still stand. He also completed the unfinished colonnades on the Plaza Mayor. For his pains he was assassinated – for reasons never made clear – in his *calesa* in the Plaza Mayor in 1792, but he became the only Spanish governor to have a monument erected to him by locals, the Cruz de Gálvez by C/ 28 on the road towards Valladolid.

Independence and Caste War

At the end of the 18th century Mérida in its modest way also acquired a greater cultural life. Erudite gentlemen wrote and studied local traditions, and like others in more prominent Spanish American colonies founded discussion clubs. They had little effect on the city's life until Napoleon's invasion of Spain threw the empire into turmoil, and local liberals launched a campaign for the recognition of the new

Spanish constitution of 1812. After the restoration of King Ferdinand VII in 1814, leading liberals were imprisoned, but this only radicalized opinion. In February 1821 the governor marshal Echéverri carried out the last important measure of Spanish rule in the Yucatán, dissolving most houses of the religious orders. In September of the same year, the governor himself made his departure.

As the capital of a semi-independent Yucatán Mérida was the focus of all the factional intrigues of the new state, but its social life changed little. It was this city, small, remote and with a life still revolving around religious festivals, that John Lloyd Stephens visited in 1840. Falling in love apparently on a daily basis with 'charming young ladies', he wrote after an afternoon watching the *paseo* on the Alameda – a colonial-era promenade swallowed up by the modern market area – that, 'as the sun sank behind the ruins of the *castillo*, we thought that there were few places in the world where it went down upon a prettier or happier scene'.

This city was accustomed to treating the Mayan villages around it at arm's length, and the upheaval of the Caste War came as an utter shock. In May 1848, as town after town fell to the Maya bands, refugees flooded into the capital, camping out in the Plaza Mayor and anywhere they could find. Gálvez' city gates were shut up against attackers for the first (and last) time, although to the north the road to Sisal was full of an endless line of escapees from the city, desperate to find a boat. At the end of the month the bishop left, and military leaders declared further defence unsustainable.

Then, when the Maya inexplicably turned back from the very brink of victory and returned home (*see* p.72), the jubilation was naturally immense. Bells rang, fireworks were set off and, as the hostile Maya were pushed back into the remote east Mérida received a sudden shot of brio. In the years following the siege the Plaza Mayor was relaid, the Palacio Municipal was rebuilt and an 'Academy of Science and Literature' was founded.

The Boom Town of the Porfiriato

In 1865 Mérida welcomed Empress María Carlota, the Belgian wife of Maximilian, with 11 days of lavish celebrations, balls, concerts and *fiestas*. After the upheavals of the previous 40 years many of the city's good families liked the idea of having a monarchy under a real European royal house again, and María Carlota remembered Mérida as the most genuinely loyal place in Mexico. What's more, this loyalty was put to the test in 1867 as the Empire crumbled, when a force advanced from Republican Tabasco. The imperial commander, Colonel Traconis, somewhat quixotically decided to carry out his duty at all costs, and fought on even after Maximilian himself had been taken prisoner. The Republican army subjected Mérida to a 55-day siege.

After this imperial interlude there would be no more battles in Mérida. Under the Díaz regime after 1876, the great transformation in Mérida was not political but economic. Railways and the new port at Progreso greatly facilitated exports of the sisal rope from Yucatán's *henequen* plantations, the 'green gold' for which the world had an insatiable demand. Money and people poured into sleepy Mérida, which doubled in size between 1870 and 1910 from a population of around 30,000 to over 60,000. The influx included 'exotic' communities from China and the Lebanon. A great proportion of the wealth of Yucatán's 'Gilded Age' also went straight to the *henequen* barons themselves. Yucatecan magnates became familiar figures in European resorts, while at home they picked up imported luxuries at stores with names like *Au Petit Paris* and *La Ciudad de Londres*.

The *henequen* oligarchs also set about improving their home town to suit their new tastes. Mérida was the first Mexican provincial city to have fully paved streets and a comprehensive sewerage system, tramways were laid, and the crumbling remains of the colonial Citadel and Monastery of the Assumption and their Mayan-platform base were all swept away to make space for a new business area on C/ 65, with shockingly modern, multi-storey buildings. Mérida's leading citizens also resolved to break out of the old colonial grid and give their city a modern, elegant avenue on a par with those of the great cities of Europe. Paris was the benchmark in sophistication for the élite of the Porfiriato, and their new boulevard, the Paseo de Montejo, was intended to resemble the Champs-Elysées. Begun in 1904, it became the new centre of elegant society. The *henequen* boom saw the greatest transformation of Mérida since its foundation, the stamp of which can still be seen all over the city.

Revolution and the Modern Era

The power of Mérida's *henequen* barons was such that they were able to ensure that local life went on pretty much as normal through the first five years of the Mexican Revolution. Consequently, when General Salvador Alvarado was sent to bring the Revolution to the Yucatán in 1915, he sought to change things very visibly. In September 1915 he closed all churches in response to the anti-revolutionary activities of Catholic priests. On 15 September a revolutionary mob invaded Mérida cathedral, burning its images and leaving the interior as bare as it is today.

Alvarado also introduced immediate improvements in the conditions of workers on *henequen* estates. In the 1920s, Yucatán's short-lived Socialist government under Felipe Carrillo Puerto brought in educational reforms and urban improvements. He also introduced an ultra-liberal divorce law that for a time made Mérida the divorce capital of the western hemisphere, annoying right-thinking American legislators so much that special measures were taken to declare 'Yucatán divorces' invalid in the USA. The last major violence of the Revolutionary era came in January 1924, when right-wing soldiers in Mérida executed Carrillo Puerto. A popular hero, he is commemorated in town and street names and monuments throughout the peninsula.

Since then Mérida life has been far less eventful. The main change over the next decades was the decline in the *henequen* trade, which was only counterbalanced when the creation of Cancún brought tourism and a whole new source of wealth.

The Plaza Mayor

A near-automatic starting point is the grand main square, most commonly known as the Plaza Mayor but also referred to as the Plaza Grande, Zócalo, Plaza de la Independencia and, historically, Plaza de Armas. This was the centre of Mayan Ti'ho, surrounded by pyramids, and so the point that Montejo el Mozo took as the hub of the city's grid when he founded Christian Mérida in 1542. On each side of the square,

Moonlight Serenades

Sit under the colonnades of the Plaza Mayor as it gets dark and you may notice groups of men gathering on the pavements in the centre of the square and by the Palacio Municipal, carrying guitars, always in threes and dressed in white *guayaberas* and black trousers. These are members of the Yucatecan trios, available for hire, as they have been for over a century, to play *serenatas* (serenades). As you watch, cars drive up, kerb-crawling for musicians; a deal is agreed, and the three men get in the car and drive off to their booking for the night. Sometimes, the couple may only want one song, and the trio performs there and then at the car window.

Each trio has its own regular spot around the plaza, and turns up each night without any idea whether they might be facing five performances or none. This unpredictability is met with typical Yucatecan disregard. Angel López, one of a trio whose pitch is opposite the Casa de Montejo, took one engagement from a passing car for a party in Chetumal, involving an eight-hour drive, playing at breakfast time and getting back to Mérida the following night.

The music they play – some international intrusions aside – is the languid, dreamy, nostalgic, Cuban-influenced *boleros* and similar rhythms of the Yucatán. There is a huge repertoire of Yucatecan songs, nearly all with utterly romantic lyrics in which a whole soul is given in a kiss and the light of the stars is reflected in flashing eyes. Tourists hear this music in hotels or at the Thursday *serenatas* in Parque Santa Lucía, but few seem to contact trios off the street in the traditional way. The clientèle that keeps them going is overwhelmingly local and of all ages. It's traditional to have a trio for weddings, christenings, and family parties, but couples also go down to the plaza on their own to pick a trio on anniversaries or birthdays. Should you wish to hire one yourselves, the normal rate is about 200 pesos and up for a full *serenata*.

in accordance with Spanish colonial practice, he and the first mayor Gaspar Pacheco founded major buildings: a cathedral on the east side, the *Casas Reales* (centre of government for the whole of the Yucatán) to the north, and the *Casas Consistoriales* (municipal government) to the west, while on the south side the *conquistador* built himself the most distinguished private residence in the city, the Casa de Montejo.

Dominating the vista is the giant, perpendicular mass of the **Cathedral of San Ildefonso**, begun in 1562 and completed in 1598. It is the oldest cathedral on the American mainland, and only Santo Domingo (in the Dominican Republic) is older in the whole continent. Its most important architect was Juan Manuel de Agüero, from Cantabria in northern Spain, who worked on it between 1585 and 1590, but the cathedral was the work of many minds and hundreds of Mayan labourers. Its completion was often delayed, especially by the practice of successive governors of appointing their own protégés (and children) to the post of *Veedor* or supervisor of the works.

Like many smaller churches of the Yucatán it is a severe work of plain stone, in an austere Spanish Renaissance style with limestone walls lightened by elaborately carved Plateresque details. Although its builders were in touch with architectural ideas in Europe they were not without their eccentricities, such as the fact that the two towers on either side, despite appearances, are not actually identical. Between them are three portals, with an imposing main entrance flanked by figures representing St Peter and St Paul, and two smaller doors on either side. Above the entrance the façade used to be dominated by a giant Spanish Habsburg crest but, in 1822, during Mexico's ephemeral 'First Empire', this was replaced by an equally sizeable crest of a Mexican eagle, still with crown, that remains there today.

The cathedral is still plainer inside than outside, with whitewashed walls, having lost most of its images in Mérida's many revolutions, especially in 1915. At the end of the nave on the left is one of the most revered shrines the cathedral does retain, *El Cristo de las Ampollas* (Christ of the Blisters), a statue of Christ on the cross in blackened wood, in an ornate Baroque altarpiece. The legend goes that it was made in Ichmul, deep in central Yucatán, from a tree struck by lightning that had burnt for a whole night without being destroyed. Then, after the statue survived a second fire that destroyed the church of Ichmul – albeit with a little blistering in the wood – it was attributed miraculous powers, and brought to Mérida cathedral in 1645. A third conflagration, that of 1915, saw the figure remade again. Outside and at the back of the cathedral, on C/ 61, there is a small, separate chapel, the **Capilla de los Apóstoles**, with a set of bizarre life-sized painted figures of Christ and the said apostles at the Last Supper.

Forming a right angle with the cathedral on the plaza is the **Palacio del Gobernador** (*open daily 8–8*), seat of the state government of Yucatán, built in 1892 to replace an earlier colonial governors' palace. It is open to anyone to wander around its main patio and public rooms. Apart from the airy, neo-colonial patio, its main attraction is the series of intensely dramatic murals and paintings carried out by the Yucatecan artist Fernando Castro Pacheco in the 1970s, giving a fiercely felt synthesis of Mayan and *mestizo* history. Particularly impressive is the mural on the main staircase, representing the Mayan creation myth whereby man arose out of maize (*hombre de maíz*).

The western side of the plaza, running down from C/ 62, is dominated by the **Palacio Municipal**, the town hall (*open daily 8–8*). Only its main doorway, slightly lost beneath its later portico, remains from the original 16th-century *Casas Consistoriales*. The façade is now dominated by an elegant ten-arched colonnade, with matching loggia above, begun in 1735 and one of the finest creations of late-colonial Spanish architecture in the Yucatán. The Palace has been rebuilt several times, and its patios are plain, but on the second floor next to the loggia there is the *Sala de Historia* or old council chamber, a dark, wood-panelled room full of relics of local citizens and great events in the saga of Mexican independence.

Complementing the Palace, alongside it toward C/ 61, is the **Centro Cultural Olimpo**, built in 1999 but more or less in the style of a 19th-century theatre and indoor circus that stood on this spot until it was knocked down in the 1960s. It now contains attractive exhibition spaces, a café and a good bookshop, and from the upper floor you get a great head-on view of the Cathedral across the plaza. Look a little way up the next block on C/ 62, though, and your eye is caught by the **Teatro Mérida**, an Art Deco juke box of an old cinema that was restored in 2000 as a public theatre.

The south side of the square is mainly taken up by 19th-century buildings, but the eye is drawn to the much older portico of the **Casa de Montejo**, built in 1549 as the residence of the Adelantado and his descendants, and retained by the Montejo family until the time of independence. It was still a private house in the 1970s. Very little of the present building is original, since it has been almost entirely rebuilt over the years, and now houses a Banamex bank. Still intact, however – despite the crumbling that is inevitable in limestone – is the extraordinary portico, one of the finest examples in Mexico of the Spanish Plateresque style. The lower section, around the main gateway, has a Renaissance elegance: above it, though, is a giant frieze, around a balconied window, which gives the whole façade its unique character. At the centre is the Montejo coat-of-arms; on either side are giant bearded warriors, in suits of armour, each of whose feet bears down on a screaming head. Beside them, there are two much smaller bearded figures with strange, scaled skin. The two warriors have long been believed to represent the Montejos, father and son, and the screaming heads the Yucatán Indians, making the façade a portrayal of the Conquest in the most brutally graphic manner possible, although it's conceivable they have a more mythological significance. In either case, the façade is still a remarkable combination of the Renaissance and Gothic imagination, transplanted to the Americas and almost certainly carried out in small or great part by Mayan craftsmen.

The plaza also has other attractions. Big as the cathedral is, it was once even larger, for until the 20th century it and its annexes occupied the entire block between the plaza and Calles 61, 63 and 58. The southern half of the block contained the Bishop's Palace, which was rebuilt during the Revolution to become the **Ateneo Peninsular**, a cultural centre for the new era. As part of a drive to polish up the Plaza Mayor, the pedestrian alleyway called **Pasaje de la Revolución**, between the Cathedral and the Ateneo, has recently been restored, and is used as an exhibition space for large-scale sculpture by the Museo de Arte Contemporáneo de Yucatán. Better known as **MACAY**, this now occupies most of the old Ateneo (*entrance on Pasaje de la Revolución, t 928 3236, open Wed–Mon 10–6; closed Tues; adm, Sun adm free*). As well as hosting shows of contemporary art, the museum has permanent exhibits. There are more works by Fernando Castro Pacheco, not as dramatic as his murals in the Palacio del Gobernador but similarly reflecting on the relation between the Indian past and the Mexican present; in complete contrast is the work of another Yucatecan artist, Fernando García Ponce, abstract and international in style. There is also *El Bordado Yucateco*, a display of Yucatán embroidery and, as usual in older buildings in Mérida, there's a patio, which hosts a café with tables shaded by giant *huaya*, *caymito* and laurel trees.

In the streets around the Plaza Mayor there are plenty of other reminiscences of the colonial city, often in small details. Walk around to the back of the MACAY on C/ 58 and you can admire the neoclassical portico of the **Seminary of San Ildefonso**, built in the 1750s. Usually ignored by the crowds below, it is topped by two engaging statues of the Virgin and Child and the Bishop-Saint Ildefonso. On C/ 61, opposite the Capilla de los Apóstoles of the cathedral, stands one of the very earliest colonial buildings in Mérida, the **Capilla del Hospital de San Juan de Dios**. Begun just after the cathedral but finished much earlier, in 1579, the chapel was built in a remarkably archaic, almost plain Romanesque style that make up one of the most authentically medieval

European buildings anywhere in the Americas. As the name suggests it was originally part of a hospital, but it now contains the **Museo de la Ciudad**, the city museum (*open Tues–Fri 10–2 and 4–8, Sat and Sun 10–2; closed Mon; adm free*). The collection, though small, is a mine of information, and has recently been reorganized (fully labelled in English). It gives an illuminating introduction to the city's past, with artefacts from Mayan Ti'ho and a big range of carvings, paintings, prints and photographs, including the spectacular original 16th-century painted-wood altarpiece from the Cathedral, and an early portrait of Bishop Landa himself.

Calle 60

After a circuit of the Plaza Mayor, a natural first step in getting to know Mérida is a stroll up Calle 60, off the square to the north between the Governor's Palace and the cathedral. The city's main thoroughfare ever since its foundation, it is still the site of cultural institutions, hotels, restaurants and the best places for people-watching. There's also a big concentration of shops selling *artesanía*, hats, hammocks and other knick-knacks, especially in the block next to the plaza, and as you cross to enter C/ 60 you will almost inevitably be approached by someone proffering a card and praising the bargains to be had at their particular bazaar. They're rarely persistent if you reply that you've bought enough junk already. From the same corner, the horse-drawn *calesas* depart on their tours around town.

At the end of the first block on the right by C/ 59 is the **Parque Hidalgo**, Mérida's second most important square and one of the best places to take in the local scene. Full of exuberant fan palms that give it a delicious lushness, it has on a plinth at its centre a statue of General Manuel Cepeda Pereza, a major player in Yucatán and Mexico's 19th-century wars. Around him there are benches and *confidenciales*, newspaper sellers, tourists, young couples, old men spinning out conversations, more tourists, taxi drivers waiting for fares, students, and men collecting their thoughts. One of the best and most characterful vantage points of all is from the Express (*see* p.275), Mérida's nearest equivalent to a grand café.

Across C/ 59 from the square stands the second most distinguished of Mérida's colonial buildings, the **Iglesia de Jesús**. Built as the local seat of the Jesuits, relative latecomers to Yucatán, and consecrated in 1618, it is also known as the *Iglesia de la Tercera Orden*, after the Third Order of Franciscans to whom the church passed after the expulsion of the Jesuits from all Spanish dominions in 1767. As befits its Jesuit origins it is more ornate than its Franciscan neighbours, of more delicate proportions. Like other colonial churches the Jesús was built out of the stones of Mayan temples. In such cases the Spaniards made every effort to ensure that no trace of their former use remained visible, destroying carved surfaces or placing them inside the wall. Here, however, in the massive wall of the church facing Parque Hidalgo (opposite the taxi stand), one can see, quite easily, two stones bearing recognizable Mayan carvings. Regarded as the prettiest of the city's churches, the Jesús usually has the most beautiful flower displays, too, and is a favourite place for weddings. The most popular time for them is after seven on Saturday evenings, taking advantage of the evening cool, when the church's spectacular decorations – from altar flowers to garlands in the aisles – are brilliantly illuminated against the night.

Alongside the Jesús is another small square, forming a pair with Parque Hidalgo, the **Parque de la Madre**. A pedestrian alleyway, the Callejón del Congreso or C/ 57-A, separates this square and the Jesús from the giant bulk of the **Teatro Peón Contreras**, which takes up the rest of the block facing C/ 60. By the time of the *henequen* boom, Yucatán's magnates decided that the city's humble theatre, built on this site in 1831, was no longer adequate, and in the 1890s the vastly expanded building you see today was commissioned from two of their favourite architects, the Italians Pio Piacentini and Enrico Deserti. Deserti's grand style won him many clients in Mérida at that time, and he was also responsible for the Palacio Cantón, now the Museo de Antropología. No expense was spared in building the theatre, inaugurated in 1908.

It was restored in the 1990s, although it still seems underused in terms of number of performances. At most times visitors are free to wander around to examine its luxurious fittings, especially the grand loggia overlooking C/ 60. On the ground floor the theatre also contains a tourist office, a bookshop and an attractive if slightly expensive café. Outside, forming a trio with the theatre and the Jesús, at the far end of C/ 57-A, is the 1970s-modern **Yucatán State Congress** building.

Back across C/ 60, the Peón Contreras faces another cultural institution, the main building of the **Universidad de Yucatán**, begun in the 1920s. Its traditional-style patio hosts folkdance displays every Friday. The next block up, between 57 and 55, is dominated by two big hotels, the Casa de Balam and the Misión, but also contains more grungy night-spots such as the ¡Ay Caray! (*see* p.277). Continue on up C/ 60 and you will see, on the left at the junction with C/ 55, one of Mérida's prettiest squares, the **Parque de Santa Lucía**. Parts of it date from 1575, and, lined on two sides with a low, single-storey colonnade, it has a deliciously romantic ambience that sums up the essence of colonial Mérida. In the opposite corner from the street junction is a small stage, surrounded by busts of the great figures in *la Trova Yucateca*, Yucatecan song. Every Thursday this is the venue for the *Serenatas Yucatecas*, free performances of traditional songs and dances, for which Santa Lucía is ideally suited.

Facing the square is the 17th-century church of **Santa Lucía**, slightly hidden by trees. In colonial Mérida, the surrounding *barrio* was reserved for black slaves and mulattos, and the church was first built to serve them. One of the simpler colonial churches, it's also one of the prettiest, and rivals the Jesús as a Saturday-night wedding venue.

Beyond Santa Lucía C/ 60 becomes more functional, but further along at C/ 47 lies another engaging square, the **Parque de Santa Ana**, with a small food market and a line of cheap *loncherías* and cafés. On the north side of the square is the **Iglesia de Santa Ana**, a pink-painted church with 1730 on its façade and two squat spires that can look like a pair of crude rockets or salt cellars by moon- and street-light. On the façade a stone commemorates the burial here in 1734 of Don Antonio de Figueroa, Governor and Captain-General of Yucatán, who died in August the previous year on his way back from Bacalar; there he had undertaken the 'extermination of the English', the Belize pirates who plagued Yucatán's colonial masters. From Santa Ana, it's only a two-block walk to the Paseo de Montejo and the Anthropology Museum.

The *Jarana*

The music that accompanies the *jarana*, best-known of Yucatecan folk dances, can almost represent the distinctiveness of the region in itself. Played by a band with plenty of trombone, cornets and drums, it has some of the bouncy regularity of Mexican traditional music, but with an obvious touch of the more sensuous rhythms of the Spanish Caribbean. Its recurrent rhythms, meanwhile, give it a flavour that is different again from either.

The dance developed among the *mestizo* population of the *haciendas* of Yucatán, as part of the annual *vaquerías* or country *fiestas*. Like so many Mexican traditional dances it is a flirtation dance, but one with an extra delicacy. The man courts rather than teases the woman, and at times the flirtation element is lost within the movement of the dance. Men and women enter in separate ranks, break up into couples and then re-form, in a great variety of set patterns. Also popular are the different 'prowess' dances: one involves threading and unthreading ribbons around a kind of maypole; another includes dancing with bottles on a tray on the head.

Several groups regularly dance *jaranas*, in the Plaza Mayor, Santa Lucía and at other venues. All the dancers must wear the same uniform: high-collared *guayabera*, plain trousers and panama hat, all in white, for the boys; magnificently embroidered *ternos* for the girls, with plenty of traditional jewellery and their hair up in a bun, held by a silk band adorned with roses, carnations and daisies, bunched on one side of the head.

East of the Plaza Mayor

The Plaza Mayor, C/ 60 and its squares are really the only parts of Mérida that could be considered 'tourist haunts'. The traffic becomes thinner and the atmosphere more placid as soon as you move away from the central area. To the east of C/ 60, C/ 59 leads straight on for five long blocks until it reaches the **Parque de la Mejorada**, another shady square, laid out in 1745. This is the location of Mérida's branch of Los Almendros restaurant (*see* p.275), but the square's most impressive feature is one of the most imposing of the colonial churches, **La Mejorada**. A stone inside the portico commemorates its consecration in 1640, in the reign of King Philip IV, when it was built as part of a monastery of the same name. This was the only one of the many Franciscan houses in Mérida that was allowed to remain after the dissolution of religious houses in the Spanish Empire in 1821, but it too was closed by the Juárez *Reforma* in 1857. Later used as a hospital, most of its buildings have remained intact, if repeatedly altered, and now house Mérida's School of Architecture.

Behind the church there are also two very individual museums. In a part of the former monastic buildings is Mérida's main folk museum, the **Museo de Arte Popular** (*open Tues–Sat 9–6, Sun 9–2; closed Mon; adm*), entered from C/ 59. It now has a rather direction-less feel and its collection is a bit neglected (labelling is Spanish-only), but even so it still contains a fascinating (if confusing) range of textiles, musical instruments, day-of-the-dead offerings and other artefacts not just from the Yucatán but also from indigenous peoples from all over Mexico and even the USA. On the other side of the block, meanwhile, is one of the city's most charming museums, the

Museo de la Canción Yucateca, C/ 57, x 48 & 50 (*open Tues–Fri 9–5; Sat and Sun 9–3; closed Mon; adm free*), the 'museum of Yucatecan song' and a vivid indication of the Yucatecan's devotion to their own style of music. Since 2001, it has been spaciously housed here in a former school. The many composers and performers who have contributed to the tradition are all lovingly recorded, and the music itself can be heard playing in the rooms of the museum. It also hosts live performances at least once a month.

South of the Mejorada on C/ 50 there are two more very solid relics of old Mérida, a pair of the eight huge gateways that formed the entrances to the city's 18th-century defensive wall. Most imposing is the **Arco de Dragones** across C/ 61, so called because next to it there was a barracks for Mérida's garrison of Spanish dragoons. The **Arco del Puente**, on C/ 63, has on either side two small doorways, built to allow people to pass through on foot when the main gate was closed. They are scarcely four feet tall, not to fit the average height of the local Mayan population, but to make it more difficult for unwanted interlopers to force an entry. Along Calles 61 and 63, the arches can be seen towering above the streets from several blocks away, and can easily give the impression that you still are within a walled city.

West of the Plaza Mayor

On C/ 63 one block west of the Plaza Mayor, at the junction with C/ 64, stands the **Iglesia de las Monjas** (Church of the Nuns), so called because it was built as the chapel of a closed Convent of the Order of the Conception. Most of the building still exists behind the church. The ex-soldiers and officials who made up Yucatán's 16th-century aristocracy sought to give their rudimentary town all the institutions of a Spanish city of the Golden Age, and this convent was founded in the 1590s on the initiative of one old *conquistador*, Francisco de San Martín. Like aristocratic families back home, he and other important citizens had pious daughters who wished to enter nunneries, and until then had been obliged to send them all the way to Mexico City. The church's most unusual feature is the watchtower or *mirador* above the apse, visible from C/ 63, with a pillared loggia built to allow the nuns to take some air without leaving their enclosed world. Inside, although it's now only a parish church, Las Monjas still has in place the impressive metal grilles, the oldest in Mexico, that separated the nuns from visiting lay worshippers.

The other surviving convent buildings of Las Monjas were converted in the 1970s into a cultural centre, the **Casa de Cultura del Mayab**, which among other institutions houses the **Casa de las Artesanías**, the state handicrafts store (*see* p.269).

Northwest of Las Monjas at Calles 59 and 72, the solid walls of the cityscape give way to another shady square, the **Parque de Santiago**, with a local market, and a 17th-century church, Santiago. To the outsider Mérida's *parques* are more like tree-lined squares than real parks, but another six blocks west is the **Parque del Centenario** (*open daily 6–6*), at the junction of C/ 59 and Av. Itzaes. Built to mark the centenary of Mexican independence, in 1910, it's a formal garden typical of the era. A big attraction for locals is Mérida's **zoo** (*open daily 8–5; adm free*), featuring mainly local wildlife, together with exotics such as lions, tigers, llamas and antelopes.

South: the Market District

The streets south and immediately east of the Plaza Mayor form the commercial heart of Mérida, on which, every weekday, what seems like half the entire population of Yucatán converge to buy, sell, do any other business and look for anything else they might need (as a result, this is also the area with the most bus congestion). They will almost certainly find what they're after, for it's difficult to think of anything you *can't* buy here. On C/ 56, between C/ 59 and C/ 61, you can find car parts, cheap trainers and lots of watches, and buy and sell gold; continue on down between C/ 61 and C/ 63, and there are ranks of fridges, cookers and other electricals, sewing machines, yet more shoes, and toys. Since people here still expect to repair rather than replace things when they go wrong, there are plenty of repairers and shops selling spares for every kind of item, from radio parts to sewer pipes and bags of cement.

Busiest of all the business streets in Mérida is C/ 65 between C/ 60 and C/ 64, although for a change, just east next to C/ 56, the street is largely given over to multi-coloured shops selling jokes, *piñatas* and anything else you might fancy for a *fiesta*. Shabby though it may look today, C/ 62 south from the Plaza Mayor towards C/ 65 was, in the 19th century, one of the most prestigious residential streets of Mérida, with several grand patio-style mansions. The most distinguished is that of the (now shabby) Hotel Sevilla, with stone lions beside a grand, beautifully tiled staircase.

The greatest hub of activity (and congestion) is the junction of Calles 65 and 56. Not quite a square, more an open space developed slightly by accident, it's given a focus by the **post office**, built in 1908 as the federal government building. It is on this stretch of C/ 65 and the side-streets 65-A and 63-A that you'll find the best hammock shops (*see* p.269). Behind the post office is the market proper, officially known as the **Mercado Luis de Gálvez**. Theoretically between Calles 65, 67, 56 and 58, it actually sprawls over several more blocks. Opposite the post office on C/ 56 is a battered but elegant colonnade, in terracotta and white, which is the oldest part of the market: the 18th-century **Portal de Granos** ('Grain Gate'). Beneath its columns there are Mayan women sitting amid selections of vivid peeled fruit or fresh chilis, and stalls selling T-shirts, hats, bags or cutlery; this is only a taster, though, for the truly extraordinary variety inside.

Some of the market's crisscrossing lanes are quite broad, while others are narrow alleys that barely allow two people to pass at a time, with stalls held up by ropes that catch the taller wanderer unawares. In some of the main lanes there are dazzling displays of fresh flowers, or superbly bright fruit – mangoes, oranges, pineapples – and multiple varieties of fierce red chilis. Elsewhere there are lanes full of nothing but leather sandals, every possible size of metal pot, or hundreds of varieties and colours of plastic bags. As outside there is a huge variety of sometimes eccentric repairers, and some great panama hat stalls.

Above the main market, reached by a ramp from the junction of C/ 56 with C/ 67, is the main handicrafts market, the **Bazar de Artesanías** (*see* p.268). On the same level are the *cocinas económicas*. On its south side, towards C/ 69, the market becomes more open air and provisional, and runs in a vaguely chaotic way into the ranks of *combis* that come in from villages to the south and east.

The market may dominate this area, but it still has its monuments. At the corner of Calles 50 and 67 is the church of **San Cristóbal**, another limestone blockhouse. By contrast, eight blocks west along C/ 67 by C/ 64 – easy to miss, and unfortunately also often locked – there is one of the most discreet of Mérida's colonial church buildings, **La Candelaria**, a tiny, beautifully peaceful early Franciscan chapel with a Baroque altarpiece. This is near the other focus of south-central Mérida, the main **bus stations** near the junctions of Calle 69 and 70. A block south of the Candelaria at C/ 69 and 64 is another colonial square, the **Parque de San Juan**. Today its most noticeable feature may be the mass of *combis* that leave from there, but look around and you can see 18th-century houses and another church, naturally enough **San Juan**, in an unusual neo-Moorish style. This has been an entry point into Mérida for centuries, as demonstrated by the presence of another of the 1790 city gates, the **Arco de San Juan** on C/ 64, which was originally the Camino Real or 'Royal Road' to Campeche.

If you continue through this gate, cross over to C/ 66 and carry on down to C/ 77, you will come to one of the most atmospheric relics of colonial Mérida, the little **Ermita de Santa Isabel**. A plain rustic chapel, it was built, as an inscription states on the façade, in 1748, and a similarly simple cloister was added in 1762. It was established as a stopping point outside Mérida on the Camino Real, where those arriving could give thanks for a safe deliverance, and those leaving could pray for an equally trouble-free arrival at their destination. There's a pretty square in front of the church, and the gardens behind the cloister have been made into a secluded park.

The Paseo de Montejo and North Mérida

North Mérida has a very different atmosphere. In place of the narrow pavements and stucco-walled houses of the old city, there are long, tree-lined, very quiet streets with broad pavements. In some, there are striking residences with wide driveways. At the heart of the district is a broad, elegant avenue, the **Paseo de Montejo**, beginning at C/ 47 two blocks east of C/ 60. This was where Mérida's leading citizens decided to create their own Champs-Elysées. It's nowhere near as long as its Parisian model, but with its wide green lawns and promenades a vague similarity can be seen.

Paris provided the Yucatán magnates not only with a model of urban elegance but a suitably opulent style of architecture for the mansions they built around the new avenue, a tropical adaptation of the Beaux-Arts style of the French Second Empire. European architects were brought to Mérida to provide the final touch of refinement. The most extravagant of all these buildings, the great wedding cake of the Palacio Cantón at the corner of the Paseo and C/ 43, now houses the **Museo de Antropología e Historia** (*open Tues–Sat 8–8, Sun 8–2; closed Mon; adm, Sun adm free*), one of the most important collections of pre-Hispanic artefacts in Mexico after the national museum in Mexico City.

The house was built between 1909 and 1911 for General Francisco Cantón, former servant of the Emperor Maximilian and leading figure of the Díaz era. The design, by Enrico Deserti, is typically Frenchified, with a Mansard roof, and Italian marble and other fine materials were specially imported to give it its finer touches. By the time it was finished, though, in 1911, the Díaz regime had fallen, and Cantón himself died six years later. The museum collection includes artefacts from Mayan sites in Campeche and Quintana Roo as well as from all over Yucatán state. From the caves at Loltún, the oldest settlement in the Yucatán, there are Preclassic carvings; from Tulum there are fragments of Mixtec-influenced murals; and from Chichén Itzá there are sacrificial items from the great *cenote*, including three cases of fine jade. The very extensive collection of ceramics covers all the eras of Mayan culture in the region. Individual highlights include delicately coloured pottery from Mayapán, figurines that show very clearly and in colour Mayan styles in textiles and clothing, and several of the wonderful, tiny burial figurines from the island of Jaina in Campeche. The museum is a particularly good place to get an overview of every aspect of Mayan society, to fill out impressions gleaned from visiting actual sites. Displays deal with agriculture, hunting, trade, warfare, architecture and cooking, bones from tombs illustrate the diseases to which the Maya were prone, and another exhibit demonstrates very vividly the apparently bizarre practices associated with beauty that can make the Maya appear very alien: scarification, the filing of teeth into sharp points and, strangest of all, the deliberate deformation of the heads of babies to produce a flattened, elongated forehead. There is also a great deal to read. The museum was renovated a few years ago, with the (welcome) addition of air conditioning and more labelling in English, but the translated texts still cover less than the Spanish originals.

Outside, the shady pavements of the Paseo de Montejo make a fine place for strolling, but if you want to cogitate on what you've seen at a pavement restaurant you need to head a couple of blocks in either direction. Along the Paseo and in the streets around it there are many more examples of Yucatecan-Beaux Arts architecture. Many have been obliterated or greatly altered over the years, but there are still some fascinating houses. The **Cámara house**, at Paseo de Montejo 495 in the block south of the museum, is not so much in Beaux-Arts style as a faithful reproduction of an 18th-century Parisian *hôtel* of the *ancien régime*, even though it was built in 1906.

Beyond C/ 35 the Paseo opens up into one of its grandest junctions, a Parisian-style meeting point of several wide streets presided over by a statue of Justo Sierra, a 19th-century intellectual and one-time ambassador to Washington of an independent Yucatán. This part of town is especially atmospheric to walk around at night, with its houses all shuttered up as you go past. Its peculiar, tropical neoclassicism then becomes most apparent and most ghostly, while the bats twittering above you remind you that you're not actually in 16th-*arrondissement* Paris.

Alternatively, if you continue north on Paseo Montejo from the Sierra monument, you cannot miss the giant mass of the **Altar de la Patria**, Mérida's contribution to large-scale patriotic sculpture. Designed by sculptor Rómulo Roza – originally, in fact, from Colombia – and built between 1945 and 1956, it typifies the nationalistic 'Neo-Aztec' style favoured by the authorities of the Mexican Revolution at their most confident. Beyond this traffic circle the Paseo becomes **Prolongación de Montejo**, along which can be found many more offices, malls, middle-class residential areas, restaurants and international-style clubs.

Around Mérida

Mérida may have the feel of a big city by Yucatán standards, but go beyond the *Periférico* and everything becomes very rural. Within a short range of the city there are examples of all the state's prime attractions: the Mayan ruins of **Dzibilchaltún**, the flamingo breeding grounds at **Celestún** and the **beaches** of the Gulf coast.

The Yucatán coast west and north of Mérida is made up of a long, thin strip of sand, originally covered in coconuts and other palms, virtually unbroken for over 150 kilometres and separated from the mainland by a mangrove lagoon. This sandbar and the shallow sea beyond it has been a problem for all the region's modern rulers, since they make it exceptionally difficult to establish ports on the Yucatán coast, but the lagoon provides breeding grounds for an enormous range of water birds, above all flamingos. The flamingo lagoons west of Mérida around Celestún are now a national park.

The fishing towns along the sand bar, apart from Mérida's port of Progreso, are small, dusty and feel noticeably apart from the world, with no harbours but lines of fishing launches pulled up on the beach. In the last few years the Yucatán authorities have been making an effort to lure some of the beach-seeking masses across from Cancún. In all honesty, the sandy shallow seas of the Gulf coast will never have quite the same attraction as the clear turquoise waters and coral reefs of the Caribbean, and the Yucatán coast is prone to high winds, especially the *Norte*, which can blow in at any time from November to April. These problems aside, the Gulf beaches still fill up with Mérida families at weekends, Easter and in the hottest weeks of summer. Either side of the towns, there are miles of empty sand, while in the lagoons behind them you can get an immediate sense of wild, remote nature.

Sisal and Celestún

Calle 59 from central Mérida becomes Av. Jacinto Canek, the road for Celestún. After an imposing beginning this dwindles into a quiet country road, running on through villages and small towns, each with a Franciscan church and a plaza. Biggest of them is **Hunucmá** (29km from Mérida), where the road divides. One fork runs 25 kilometres northwest to **Sisal**, once the main port of the Yucatán. In 1800 one of the last Spanish governors resolved to provide Mérida with its own port here; previously there was no harbour at any point along the sand bar, and all traffic in and out of the colony had to go via Campeche. It was never a great success as a harbour, as ships had to wait offshore, bobbing against the *Nortes*, to unload on to launches, but it entered the English language, since the first shipments of *henequen* rope were exported through here in bales marked with the word *sisal*, which thus became the international term for the rope itself. However, the inadequacies of Sisal were such that once a new port was opened at Progreso in 1872 its brief prominence came to an abrupt end. Today it is a particularly windblown, dusty little place that seems well forgotten by history.

Back on the main road west from Hunucmá, the landscape is more lush. Villages along the route exhibit all the abrupt contrasts of Yucatán village housing, from stick-and-palm *na* huts to neat concrete houses, and there is bougainvillaea everywhere.

Getting There

The road to Hunucmá, Highway 281, is well signposted from Mérida. **Buses** to Celestún and Sisal leave from the Autobuses de Occidente depot at C/ 71 no. 585, x 64 & 66. There are 13 buses daily each way to Sisal. For Celestún there are buses roughly every hour from Mérida, 5am–8.30pm, with returns from Celestún 6am–7pm. Most are stopping buses (*2hrs*), but there is a direct service at 8am and 10am, with returns at 5pm and 7pm (*1½hrs*).

Drivers from Mérida should take Calles 65 or 57 west to Av. Itzaes and briefly turn right, to the north, before taking a left turn on to the Celestún road.

Tourist Information

Flamingo Watching

The *lanchas* that take you out to the lagoon leave from the **Embarcadero** (*open daily 6am–5pm*), and the trip lasts about 1½hrs. Boats take a maximum of six, and there's a set charge of about $40 per boat plus about $2 per person, although *lancheros* may still come up to you and offer to negotiate a deal (often, at peak times, to try to argue the price up rather than down). If you're travelling alone it's best to go on a Sunday, when it may be a bit crowded but you're more likely to be able to link up with someone to share costs. They have canopies to provide some shade, but exposure to sun and wind is inevitable, so take sun block and a hat.

There are regular all-in **tours** to Celestún from Mérida, including bus, a launch to the flamingo grounds and a meal, leaving Parque Santa Lucía daily at 9am and returning around 4.30pm (around $30 per person). They can be booked through any Mérida travel agency.

Where to Stay

Celestún **t** (988–)

Eco-Paraíso Xixim, **t** 916 2100, *www.mexon-line.com/eco-paraiso.htm* (*luxury*). Rooms in this area could be expected to be basic, but 9km north of Celestún is one of the region's 'eco-retreat' hotels. Getting there is a trek in itself, over a dirt track that's a test for a non-4WD car. It has 15 palm-roofed cabins by a huge Gulf beach, each with a terrace facing out to sea, and all utterly comfortable; there's also a restaurant with an international, semi-vegetarian menu and a big pool, and many trips are offered, including the Celestún flamingos and archaeological tours, as well as lesser-known aspects of the area. Low-impact technologies are used as much as possible, but electricity is available 24 hours. Turtles breed on the beach and dolphins can be seen offshore, and it feels utterly remote.

Hotel María del Carmen, towards the south of the beach at the junction of Calles 12 and 15, **t** 916 2051 (*inexpensive*). More conventional little hotel in the village with clean, white and bright rooms, all with nice bathrooms and balconies with fine sea views, and a beach **café** for breakfasts.

Hotel San Julio, just north of the main square at Calles 12 and 9, (*no phone*, *cheap*). Has clean, simple rooms with fans and showers, arranged around a sand patio that opens directly on to the beach. Lying in his hammock in the patio you'll often find the owner, who's slow-moving but very friendly.

You can **camp** for free at **El Palmar**, about halfway between Celestún and Sisal, but it's very isolated, so take all water, food and other supplies in with you.

Eating Out

Las Palapas, by junction of Calles 12 and 11 (*moderate*). Best by some way of Celestún's eating-places, with a bar and a beach terrace beneath *palapa*-palm roofs. It's moderately touristy, but the local fish and seafood – *ceviches*, *camarones*, octopus and mixed platters – are excellent.

Restaurante Avila, near junction of Calles 12 and 11 (*moderate*). Almost next door to the Palapas, similar and still enjoyable, but cheaper and less sophisticated.

Restaurante Celestún (*cheap*). A big beach-front restaurant – again, near the other two – with bargain *ceviches* and other seafood.

About 40 kilometres from Hunucmá there is a turning south on to a dirt road that makes an interesting short cut (a relative term, given the safe-but-slow road) to the Campeche road at Maxcanú and the Puuc Route (*see* p.301), passing through **Chunchucmil**, lost in birch woods around one of the grandest of decaying *haciendas*.

As you approach the coast the trees become thicker, so that when you emerge on to the long bridge across the lagoon to **Celestún** it catches you almost by surprise. A sharp left turn after the bridge leads to the official **Embarcadero** for boat trips to the flamingo grounds. Since the building of this facility in 1998 visiting the Celestún flamingos has become a lot more organized, more 'processed', and more expensive; if you want to see flamingos in a more relaxed way, it's worth making the trip to Río Lagartos (*see* p.254). Once you have joined your *lancha* it will hare off, driven by a noisy outboard, at a ferocious pace into the lagoon. The lagoon is very shallow in places, so hair-raising twists and turns and changes of pace are part of the trip (accidents and groundings, though, are virtually unknown). Along the way you glimpse fishermen's huts amid the mangroves, egrets, ibises, herons and many other birds. The flamingos first become visible as a pink streak on the horizon, gradually taking on form and a richer colour. They are at their densest from May to August, but hundreds can be seen all year round. The best time to see them is in the morning.

Flamingos are shy, nervous creatures, and the *lancheros* of Celestún have come in for a lot of criticism for their working practices. Since this is now a national park they are under instructions not to disturb the birds unnecessarily, especially when breeding. Some responsibility, however, lies with the tourist, for the local boatmen provide a service, and you get what you ask for. If you make it clear you do not want to disturb the birds or go too fast (try, '*No queremos molestar a los pájaros, OK?*' and '*Queremos ir tranquilamente*'), the *lanchero* will comply, and if you ask '*¿Se puede parar el motor?*' ('Can you stop the motor?') you may be able to sit in relative silence for a while to take in the flamingos' strange, immobile elegance (this involves more time, and deserves a tip). If, on the other hand, you ask for the boat to get closer and whether you can get photos of the birds up in the air, then the boatman will do that too. On weekends, you may find that whatever deal you make with your *lanchero*, someone else will always have their boat roar straight in to get a flock of flamingos in flight on to their video.

Most people come to Celestún just to see flamingos and leave again, but it is also a likeable beach village. Its long, white beach is the best in the Mérida area and has a string of little restaurants that make a popular weekend target for locals, although if you stay here overnight or mid-week you'll have the place pretty much to yourself. As well as the flamingos there are other birds out to sea, especially pelicans and frigate birds, and the white sands are great for beachcombing. Also, since Celestún faces west, the few who do stay here are often rewarded with superb sunsets, followed by astonishing starscapes after dark.

There is a dirt road, passable in a 4WD or with difficulty in an ordinary car, that runs north from Celestún behind the beach to Sisal, through miles of deserted dunes, scrub and coconut groves that house an enormous variety of birds. It's possible to stay in this wilderness (for a price) at **Xixim**, or camp for free at **El Palmar** (*see* p.293), where there is a lighthouse, a bird reserve and very little else.

Dzibilchaltún

The Mayan city of Dzibilchaltún, 20 kilometres north of Mérida, doesn't have the giant pyramid complexes of the best-known sites, but still has its special features: a Franciscan chapel blending in with the older ruins, a beautiful *cenote* that you can swim in, and one of the cosmological tricks that fascinate in Mayan architecture, the Temple of the Seven Dolls, through which the sun appears at dawn on the spring and autumn equinoxes.

History

Dzibilchaltún – translatable as 'the place where there is writing on the stones', a modern Mayan name that, as so often, has no relation to what it was called in its heyday – has one of the longest histories of unbroken occupation of any Mayan site, extending over 2,000 years from around 500 BC to shortly before the Conquest. Its growth well preceded that of Uxmal and the Puuc centres further to the south, and Dzibilchaltún was the most powerful city-state in the northwest Yucatán throughout most of the Classic era. It was also a wealthy port and centre of Mayan coastal trade, controlling salt beds in the lagoons to the north, and had a population of as many as 20,000 around the year 800. Like others in the region Dzibilchaltún declined precipitately in about 900–1000, but the site continued to be occupied on a smaller scale.

Dzibilchaltún was very widely dispersed, and the complete site covers around 30 square kilometres, although the central nucleus is much more concentrated. There has been much more to see since extensive excavations were carried out in 1993–4, and the museum and visitor centre added.

Getting There

Surprisingly isolated, Dzibilchaltún is an easy short trip away from Mérida, but it seems to be pretty much expected that you will get there with your own transport or with a tour. It is easy to find **by car**, signposted on the right-hand side of the Progreso road just outside the Mérida *Periférico*, about 15km north of the city centre. From there it is about 5km to the turn-off to the ruins, on the right after Dzibilchaltún village.

Getting there **by bus** is less advertised but easier than it used to be. Autoprogreso runs buses about every two hours daily, 5am–8.10pm, from its Mérida depot at C/ 62 no. 524, x 64 & 66, with returns at similar times, and *colectivos* to Dzibilchaltún village and Chablekal leave from or near Parque San Juan (look for *combis* marked Chablekal, or ask around). Both will leave you at the turn-off for the site, from where it's under 1km to the actual entrance. Leaving the ruins, walk back to the turn-off and flag down a bus or *combi* (last return about 7pm). Note that while *combis* run quite frequently Mon–Sat there are very few on Sun.

Virtually all Mérida travel agencies offer **tours** to Dzibilchaltún, and there is a sightseeing bus tour that leaves Parque Santa Lucía every day except Monday at 9am and costs around $29. The trip lasts four hours and includes a visit to the restored *hacienda* at San Antonio Cucul.

Site Information

Open daily, **site** *8–5,* **museum** *8–4; adm, Sun adm free.*

The same ticket admits you to both site and museum. Since its refurbishment the site is arranged so that you pass first through the **museum** before meeting the path to the ruins, although you can easily do the tour in reverse. There's also a **café** and **shop**.

The Museo del Pueblo Maya

In a spacious semi-open-air building, this is one of the best of the site museums, with artefacts from sites all over Yucatán State as well as Dzibilchaltún itself, and from the colonial era as well as pre-Conquest Mayan culture, giving an imaginative view of the region's past that places this and other sites in context. The display begins with some of the largest objects, carved columns from Dzibilchaltún and Uxmal, some important relics from Chichén Itzá, and an impressively powerful figure of a warrior from Oxkintok, but there are also less common items that show how Mayan artisans could handle the small-scale as well as the massive. Small ceramic vases are finely decorated with flowers, a reminder of the colour that has now been lost from virtually all Mayan sites.

Artefacts from Dzibilchaltún itself have a room to themselves. Most important is a fine *stela* of Chac, Stela 19, dated to 716. Perhaps most intriguing are the 'Seven Dolls', seven crudely modelled little figures that look very much like gingerbread men. The Temple of the Seven Dolls, where they were found, owes its name to them, and it is believed they were placed there as offerings. Later rooms feature the colonial and later eras – from *conquistador* armour to a first edition of a Yucatec-Spanish vocabulary book, and carriages, prints and weapons from the 19th-century Caste War.

The Ruins and the *Cenote*

Leaving the museum, you emerge into the Yucatán brush. There are two paths, one that takes you fairly directly to the ruins and the other a *sendero ecológico* that meanders through the woods and gives you the opportunity to see and hear a wide range of birds. On the direct path, you emerge after 400 metres on to the main *sacbé*, the long path that linked the two key centres of Dzibilchaltún, stretching away on either side and looking exactly like what it is, a road abandoned in the middle of the woods.

The *sacbé* runs almost exactly east–west. Away to the left, the east, at the end of an impressive approach is the smaller of the two centres, around the **Temple of the Seven Dolls**. A small altar and the remains of four other buildings block the path, and behind them rises the temple itself atop a low square platform. Because of its long history of occupation, at Dzibilchaltún still more than at other Mayan sites buildings

Dzibilchaltún

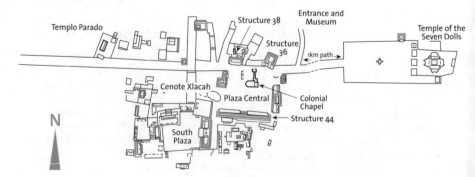

were superimposed on top of each other in different eras, and the base-platform here dates from the Early Classic, prior to 600. The temple on top is in a markedly different, more squared-off style, reminiscent of the 'Toltec-Maya' buildings of Chichén Itzá, and has been dated to around 700. This temple was in turn submerged beneath a larger temple platform in the last years of the city, and it was in this temple that the 'Seven Dolls' themselves – dated even later, to about 1200 – were found. This last structure, though, has been dismantled to reveal the 8th century temple. At dawn on the spring and autumn equinoxes (20 and 21 Mar and 20 and 21 Sept), the rising sun strikes directly through its east and west doors and along the line of the *sacbé*. This effect was known but could not be fully appreciated until the 1994 restoration. The site is now opened at 5.30am on these days for visitors to see the sunrise, best appreciated at 6–6.15am. Still more mysterious is the phenomenon at full moon in March and April, when the light of the moon similarly strikes through the doors (*check with a tourist office for each year's dates*).

From the temple platform the other main section of Dzibilchaltún can just be seen, about one kilometre away at the western end of the *sacbé*. This path of stones, sand and gravel was laid in about the year 600; in addition, excavations have revealed 11 other *sacbés* running through Dzibilchaltún. On one side of the path there are the badly deteriorated remains of a simple stone platform, which you pass before you reach the much larger western group of buildings around the broad **Plaza Central**.

Again, the buildings are of many different eras, mixed up and on top of each other. On the right as you enter the plaza is one of the largest buildings, a Classic pyramid (**Structure 36**), near which Stela 19 was found. Nearby there are some cruder buildings from about 1200, while beyond the pyramid is one of the oldest buildings on the site, the residential complex known as **Structure 38**, from about 600. The south side of the plaza is entirely dominated by one of the longest of Mayan buildings, a 130-metre bank of steps topped by the remains of columns that once formed three large chambers. Officially **Structure 44**, this is often referred to as the **Palacio**, and was almost certainly a residential complex for the rulers of the city.

Most curious of all the buildings in the plaza, in the middle of the grassy space and impossible to miss on the left as you enter from the *sacbé*, is the remains of a Catholic **chapel**, built for Franciscan missionaries between 1590 and 1600. This was a *Capilla Abierta* ('open chapel'); in contrast to the *capillas de indios* attached to missionary monasteries it was free standing, but similarly consisted only of a round stone apse to cover the altar, attached to a rough nave of wood and palm leaves. The apse was decorated with rare murals of saints, but in the last 50 years these have decayed into invisibility. Alongside, it's still possible to see the remains of the meagre friars' house, as well as some walls from a 17th-century ranch.

Just west of the Plaza Central is the main attraction of Dzibilchaltún for most locals, the **Cenote Xlacah**, the giant sinkhole that was the city's water supply. It was explored in the 1950s by divers from Tulane University, who found it to be 44 metres deep. This *cenote* can truly be called bottomless, for at that level it bends round into a large chamber, which in turn extends away beneath the Yucatán rock. They also found thousands of offerings thrown into the waters, mostly ceramic shards but also some more precious pieces, although they have found no trace of human sacrifices. On one side it is obvious from its intense blue just how deep the water is, but on the other it is shallower and more inviting for gentle basking. On Sundays the rocks around it are taken over by family outings and kids doing bomb-dives, but on other days it has a wonderful air of tranquillity.

Like other sites, Dzibilchaltún tails off into the woods. Almost hidden in the brush west of the *cenote* is Structure 57, known as the **Templo Parado** or 'Stopped Temple' because only half of its arched roof is still intact. It is assumed, but not known, that it was a temple, and it was built in the Late Classic in about 800–850.

Progreso and the North Coast

Progreso

Progreso, the modern port of Mérida, was created by the reforming followers of Juárez who governed Mexico in the years after the overthrow of Maximilian. The inadequacies of Sisal as a port had been obvious for years, and as *henequen* exports multiplied it was decided to give the Yucatán a completely new gateway to the world. The *Juaristas* were strong believers in progress, and so the new town got its name. They got over the great problem of this coast, the shallowness of the water, by building the harbour out to sea, at the end of an extraordinarily long pier, the **Muelle de Altura**, which now stretches into the distance for over six kilometres. The view from the far end might be an attraction in itself, but unfortunately you're not usually allowed to visit unless you have business there. As a trading harbour Progreso has never entirely recovered from the decline in the *henequen* trade, but its port-town bustle is expected to pick up significantly with the arrival of cruise ships and a ferry service from Tampa, Florida (*see* p.107).

What Progreso means most to people in Mérida today, though, is the seaside. Since the harbour is effectively over the horizon it doesn't interfere with the beach at all. At the height of the heat in July and August and on many Sundays the rest of the year, half the city decamps up the road to Progreso to flop on its sands and eat in its seafood restaurants. Large parts of Progreso and the villages alongside it are taken up by beach-houses owned by Meridanos, which are only really used during those two months of the year. The rest of the time most are shuttered up, and on weekdays in January or February, especially, Progreso is peculiarly quiet and empty.

Any image of Progreso as a 'resort' is limited by its pleasantly Yucatecan raggedness, an utter failure to be sleek or glossy. Calle 30 (80), running back from the Malecón to the Zócalo or main plaza, and C/ 32 (82) running up to the Muelle, are the main streets with banks and any businesses on them. The beach has little shade but fine, white sand (and wheelchair-access ramps) and the water stays shallow for a huge distance, so that it's a great beach for splashing around or easy swimming, especially for kids. Going to the beach on a Sunday in Progreso is a different experience from beach-squatting on the multi-national Riviera. Instead, it's as near as most foreigners are likely to get to being invited to a Mexican family party. All along the Malecón there

Getting There and Around

Getting to Progreso **by car** is easy: from Mérida, follow C/ 60 to Prolongación de Montejo, and keep going (33km). There is a **fuel station** by the entrance to the town.

Buses to Progreso go from the Autoprogreso depot at C/ 62 no. 524, x 65 & 67, in Mérida, every 10mins, 5am–10pm daily, and *colectivos* can be found on C/ 60, x 65 & 67. The terminus in Progreso is at the corner of C/ 32 (82) and C/ 29 (79). Returns run till about 11pm.

Taxis, *micros* and *combis* run from Progreso to outlying villages like Chicxulub or Chelem. You can also hire **mopeds: Sólo para su Moto**, C/ 29 (79) and 28 (78) is a hire shop with machines for rent for about $20 a day.

Orientation

Progreso has a straightforward grid running back from the beachfront road, the Malecón. Odd numbers run parallel to the Malecón, even numbers cross it. The added seasoning of Progreso is that it has two street-numbering systems, one older than the other, and no one has quite decided which should be definitive (lately, the lower-numbered one seems to be imposing itself for streets parallel to the Malecón, the higher numbers for streets running into town). Thus, the main road in from Mérida is both C 78 and C/ 28, the Malecón itself is C/ 19 or 69. Both can be seen on street signs and in addresses.

Where to Stay

Progreso t (969–)

Staying overnight in Progreso is a relaxing alternative to hurrying back to Mérida after the beach. Prices are generally low, and since they're geared to Mexican tourists one characteristic of Progreso hotels is that they all have big multi-bed rooms available for groups.

Inexpensive

Hotel Progreso, C/ 29 (79) no. 142, corner of C/ 28 (78), t 935 0039. Away from the beach, with some of the most pleasant rooms (fan or a/c) in town, with recently renovated bathrooms, but no sea view.

Hotel Real del Mar, on the Malecón, corner of C/ 20 (70), t 935 0798. On the seafront with a certain faded grandeur. Rooms (fan-only) are well kept and bright; half have a sea view.

Tropical Suites, Malecón, corner of C/ 20 (70), t 935 1263. On the same corner as the Real del Mar, but perhaps winning in the character stakes, this wonderfully named place has a certain Graham Greene-ish tropical-decadence, but inside the rooms are simple and pleasant, and some have a sea view.

House Rentals

Many houses and apartments in Progreso and villages alongside can be rented very cheaply. As places to spend a while, Chelem and Chicxulub are prettier than Progreso, but more isolated. Rentals around Progreso are advertised internationally, available to hire for the whole of the winter.

Agencies worth checking include:

Snowbird Accommodations, t (969) 935 1522, *snowbird@multired.net.com.*

Propriedades Las Pirámides, t (999) 986 1938, *www.miguelsmexico.com.*

Eating Out

There are the usual bargain *loncherías* near the market, at Calles 28 (78) and 25 (75) (all *cheap*). On the road through Yucalpetén and Chelem there are three big restaurants, **El Varadero, Las Palmas** and **La Terracita** (all *moderate*), all of which have tables on shady terraces. They're particularly good for *ceviches* and grilled fish.

Café-Restaurante Cordobés, Plaza Principal, corner of C/ 30 (80) & C/ 31 (81) (*cheap*). Not on the beach, but this attractive old-style café has good Yucatecan dishes.

Los Pelícanos, Malecón, corner of C/ 20 (70) (*moderate*). Fresh-fish restaurants are a Progreso tradition, and this is consistently one of the best, in front of the Real del Mar hotel. A friendly, outdoor terrace that gets packed with Meridanos at weekends, it serves great brochettes of *camarones*, conch or meat, and huge platters of grilled fish.

Flamingos, on the Malecón, corner of C/ 22 (*moderate*). An especially attractive terrace, with a fine view, friendly service and very enjoyable *ceviches* and grilled fish platters.

are vendors pushing *triciclo*-carts selling ice creams, fruit, *aguas*, fresh coconuts and little cakes. In the restaurants tables are taken over by huge family groups.

On the west side of Progreso there is a gap in the sand bar that forms the entrance to a broad, open section of lagoon, the **Laguna Yucalpetén**. The road out to the other, western side of this lagoon is reached by heading back out of Progreso on the Mérida road, then taking a right turn to rejoin the coast. The villages here, **Yucalpetén** and **Chelem**, have more attractive beaches than Progreso itself. Windsurfing boards can often be hired in Chelem. After another 20 kilometres the road reaches a village among the dunes, **Chuburna**, after which it dwindles into a track (*not passable in an ordinary car*) to Sisal.

East Along the Coast to Dzilam Bravo

East of Progreso the coast road continues for over 80 kilometres, lined by beach houses which very gradually fade away to leave slightly wind-battered fishing villages, between occasionally exuberant clusters of coconut palms. On the landward side there are more silent, bird-filled wetlands. Around 30 kilometres from Progreso a road leads a short way inland to a small Mayan site, Xcambó.

First along is **Chicxulub**, a relaxed little beach suburb of Progreso. The wetland lagoon behind it is another which has acquired large flamingo colonies. At **Uaymitún**, about five kilometres further east, there is a great watchtower or *mirador* (*adm free; binoculars available free but tips appreciated*), built to allow people to see the birds without disturbing them. The air is wonderfully fresh and clear, and as your eyes become accustomed to the light you can pick out whole flocks of flamingos and many other water birds spreading across the lagoons.

Getting Around

Autobuses del Noreste de Yucatán run **buses** along the coast road from C/ 50 no. 527 in Mérida, and there are frequent *colectivos* from Progreso. The only **petrol station** beyond Progreso is on the fish dock in Telchac Puerto.

There are no regularly organized trips to the flamingo-breeding lagoons in the **Bocas de Dzilam** (although some shops offer kayaks for hire), but Dzilam or Santa Clara fishermen will take you to the Bocas for about $40–50 per boat, and to places closer by for less. Finding a decent boat is a matter of asking around. This is a full day trip, so go prepared.

Where to Stay and Eat

There are still few places to stay along this coast, so that it retains an out-of-the-way feel. For eating, there are basic, cheap fresh-fish restaurants in every village.

Margarita's Villa, around 3km east of Progreso on the beach in Chicxulub Puerto, t (999) 944 1434, *www.margaritas.com.mx* (*expensive–inexpensive*). Attractive hotel – once a family beach house – with 12 rooms of different sizes, from comfortable doubles with balconies (*inexpensive*) to lovely self-contained apartments and beach houses (*expensive*). Rates are negotiable for longer stays and there's also a nice pool and a beach terrace **restaurant**. The owner, Margarita (who speaks very good English), is especially welcoming, and she has many return guests.

Posada Liz, C/ 23 no. 200, Telchac Puerto, t (991) 917 41 25, *posadaliz_telchac@hotmail.com* (*inexpensive–cheap*). Pleasant little budget hotel a short walk from the beach in Telchac, with simple but well cared-for rooms either with a/c (*inexpensive*) or just fans (*cheap*) – although with the winds around here a/c is not always a priority.

After San Benito, the next village along, the road becomes more empty. About 15 kilometres further east a road turns off inland, signposted to Dzemul, which leads in about one and a half kilometres to the Mayan ruins of **Xcambó** (*open daily 8–5; adm, Sun adm free*). This seems to be the preferred INAH spelling for this site, although you may see 'Cerros de Xtampu' on signs. Excavated in the 1990s, its central area consists of a large pyramid-platform facing a broad plaza, surrounded by smaller pyramids and buildings. They mostly date from the Late Classic, and it's likely that Xcambó was a salt-trading settlement, perhaps a subsidiary community of Dzibilchaltún. Its most fascinating feature, though, is the rustic Catholic chapel built alongside the main platform. It was used for years long before excavations began, and is the focus of a *fiesta* for the local villages on 19 and 20 May, an event of some solemnity.

Back on the coast road, just before **Telchac Puerto**, there is one of the stranger sights on this beach, the not-entirely-successful 'tourist complex' of **Nuevo Yucatán**. Part of local promoters' efforts to achieve tourist take-off along this coast, it has already seen one of its all-inclusive resort-hotels close down. **Telchac** itself is a more attractive, low-key little place, with a fishing harbour, good beaches and more restaurants.

Between **Chabihau** and **Santa Clara** the road twists away from the beach to run along the landward side of a lagoon. On the far side of it is a long, wooded island, **El Bajo**, where the beaches are naturally utterly secluded. Fishermen from Santa Clara or Dzilam Bravo will take you across and bring you back (*take everything you need for the day*). **Dzilam Bravo**, now quite a busy fishing town, is where the coast road ends. It has a certain claim to fame as the supposed last resting place of one of the Louisiana pirate brothers Lafitte. In 1821, after they were attacked by the Spanish navy on Isla Mujeres (*see* p.162), the two Lafittes, both severely wounded, escaped in an open boat and made their way along the coast. According to local folklore they stopped at Dzilam Bravo, where one of them died. It has always been said that it was the most dashing Lafitte, Jean, but it seems likely it was his less active brother Pierre.

Dzilam Bravo is also the closest point to one of the wildest, most remote areas of the Yucatán, the expanse of mangrove and lagoon known as the **Bocas de Dzilam**. This is a flamingo breeding area, scarcely visited but within the **Parque Natural San Felipe** (*see* p.256). Local fishermen will be able to take you into the area if you ask around (*see* facing page).

Uxmal, the Puuc Cities and Southern Yucatán

Directly south of Mérida are the Puuc hills, also known as the *Sierrita* or 'little sierra' of Yucatán, modest rolls in the ground that are the more noticeable (*Puuc* itself means hill) because of the contrast they make with the absolute flatness of northern Yucatán. This is one of the richest of all regions in Mayan sites: from some of the oldest (the caves at Loltún), to the grandest (Uxmal). It was also an important area throughout the Conquest and colonial eras. More than this, though, its towns and villages full of bicycles, dogs and *huípil*-clad women are also some of the most engaging places to get a feel of life in Mayan Yucatán today.

From Mérida a fast, surprisingly busy highway leads 17 kilometres southwest to **Umán**, where the roads divide, and revert into regular country highways. Highway 180 follows the route of the old Spanish Camino Real southwest to Campeche, while Highway 261, well signposted for Uxmal, turns off to the left, due south (also called the *Via Larga*, the 'long route', to Campeche). The established 'Puuc Route' (**La Ruta Puuc**) proper consists of Uxmal and the sites spread along the 60 kilometres between there and the town of Oxcutzcab (Kabah, Sayil, Xlapak, Labná and the caves at Loltún), and can be reached quickly on the 261 road. Archaeological work during the 1990s, though, potentially extended the 'route' with the opening up of two more sites, at Oxkintok, reached via the Campeche road, and Chacmultún to the east. The shape of the Puuc area has also been 'distorted' by early excavations having been concentrated in Yucatán state, and across the line in Campeche there are more ruins – Itzimté and Xcalumkín (*see* p.379) – which in terms of Mayan styles fall within the Puuc.

The Camino Real to Campeche and Oxkintok

From Umán Highway 180 runs through an area known as the *Zona de Cenotes* for its high number of sinkholes. A little before Maxcanú you enter the **Sierrita**, a welcome change in the landscape. Once on this road one feature of the Yucatán becomes very noticeable: the smaller a settlement is, the more solidly Maya it is likely to be.

Oxkintok

Open daily 8–5; adm, Sun adm free.

Oxkintok has been regularly open for some years now, but still does not get many visitors, and on most days you can have the place to yourself apart from the caretaker and some huge iguanas. These ruins are not a recent discovery – Stephens came here in 1841 – but it is only since 1990 that extensive excavations have been undertaken.

The main structures are at the top of a gentle rise, built on crests to give a more commanding view of the surrounding hills. Across on the north side of the road are more pyramids, unexcavated but clearly recognizable. As in many sites, the name Oxkintok ('three flint sun-stones') is an archaeologists' invention, and no one knows what it was really called, but it is believed that in its prime this may have been one of the largest cities in the region, with 20,000 inhabitants.

It is of exceptional interest to Mayanists because of the very long time it was occupied, and because Oxkintok exhibits a unique mixture of styles that reveals a great deal about the pattern of communications and trade in the Mayan world. Buildings have been discovered here from the Preclassic as far back as 300 BC, and from the very end of the Postclassic, on the verge of the Conquest. It has the oldest inscribed date this far north in the Long Count calendar (from 475), and one of the latest (859). It is believed that Oxkintok was a major city throughout the Classic era, from 300 to around 950, and so for much longer than the more famous Puuc sites to the east. Architecturally it was once considered an offshoot of the Puuc, but thanks to recent excavations it has been attributed an eclectic 'Oxkintok' or 'Pre-Puuc' style of its own.

Getting Around

By Bus
There are second-class buses every half-hour on the Mérida–Campeche road, which stop at **Maxcanú**. There you can get a *colectivo* to **Calcehtok** village, from where you can have a stiff hike or take a taxi to Oxkintok ruins. Returning, *colectivos* run from Calcehtok to Muna and the main Puuc road.

By Car
Shortly before Maxcanú (55km from Mérida) a left turn, signposted to Muna and Calcehtok, leads to the ruins at Oxkintok. In Calcehtok, take the turn right signposted to *Grutas de Calcehtok–Oxkintok* for Calcehtok caves and the ruins. After a sharp climb uphill and two kilometres, there is a turn right to Oxkintok.

After Umán there are **petrol stations** on the 261 and 184 roads in Muna, Ticul, Oxcutzcab and Tekax. If you are driving up and down the Puuc Route it's advisable to have a full tank.

Where to Stay and Eat

Hacienda Santa Rosa, off the road that turns towards Chunchucmil, south of Maxcanú, (reservations via Mérida) **t** (999) 944 3637, *www.grupoplan.com/www.luxurycollection .com* (*luxury*). The countryside around the Camino Real is not an area where many people care to linger – and there are no conventional hotels – but just off the Campeche road there is now this luxury retreat, one of the Plan Group's restored *hacienda* hotels (*see* pp.138–9). Built as a *henequen* estate in 1909, it opened as a hotel in 1998. Very secluded, it has 10 rooms, all featuring very high, wood-beamed ceilings, hammocks, traditional furniture, opulent bathrooms (a *hacienda* essential) and, in over half of them, their very own gardens; there is also a separate little cottage or *casita*. Moreover, there are two bars, including one in the old chapel, and a very pretty pool and **restaurant** (open to non-residents; *expensive*).

The excavated structures at Oxkintok mainly consist of three building complexes, arranged around plazas and sub-plazas in usual Mayan style. Largest of these is the **May Group**, centred on the slab-sided main **Pyramid**. The most complete buildings are in the **Canul Group** to the left, with several residential complexes of which the most impressive is the Puuc-like **Palacio Ch'ich** (Structure 7), with well-preserved bedchambers with raised sleeping platforms and niches for lamps. It fronts on to a small plaza, in which three column-like statues of warriors still stand; leading into this square from the main plaza there is a long building (Structure 6, or the **Palacio de la Serie Inicial**) in which the date inscription of AD 475 was found (on a lintel now in the Mérida museum). A *stela* of a warrior (**Stela 21**) with the last Long Count date at Oxkintok (859), now in the Dzibilchaltún museum, was also found near here.

The most famous building at Oxkintok, however, is the **Satunsat** or **Labyrinth** (also written *Tzat Tun Tzat*), a small squat pyramid built into the hill on the west side of the main plaza. It is entered from the other side, facing on to a large plaza leading to the little excavated **Dzib Group**. Once inside the very small doorway explorers must turn left or right, into pitch-dark, narrow passages that circle around each other and up and down steep inclines, and even narrower stairways; if you're lucky, you can find your way up to a second level and out again through semi-ruined entrances near the top of the building. Stephens came here in 1841, and, after hearing that local Indians believed it to be a bottomless pit and that no one in living memory had dared to enter it, set out to investigate by going in with a ball of string to keep track of his movements. He spent a day scrambling about the tunnels, only to conclude it was just a series of blind alleys. Current opinion is that the Labyrinth was a power point, part of one of the theatrical gestures central to Mayan kingship. It has openings on the west, north and south, but none to the east, the origin of the sun: the tunnels were perhaps an entrance to the Otherworld, into which only the *ahau* of Oxkintok could enter.

If you wish to enter now, it's eerie but not dangerous; take a powerful torch and expect lots of bats and a few bees. You may also wish to be aware, though, that local folklore holds that the Satunsat is a haunt of *aluxes*, Mayan goblins (*see* p.311), left there by the old gods and kings to guard the site.

The Caves of Calcehtok

Returning from Oxkintok, at the junction with the road back to Calcehtok village, a right turn will take you up steep hills to the **Grutas de Calcehtok**, one of the least-known of the Yucatán cave systems, and perhaps the more awe-inspiring for that very reason. The cavern is a vast basilica; whole trees are contained within it, along with flocks of birds whose shrieks echo off the cave walls. A rickety metal ladder helps you into the first part of the cave, from where a dirt path leads down as far as most casual visitors want to go, although the caves extend for another two kilometres (*should you fancy exploring further, ask the caretaker at Oxkintok*). Sudden changes in temperature and humidity are felt immediately on the skin, and the plants have an unearthly look, from the banana plants around the upper levels to giant ferns and moss lower down. Insect repellent is essential. Back at the entrance in the fresh air, as this is one of the highest points in the area, there is a great view south over the Yucatán plain.

After leaving Oxkintok and the caves, a right turn in Calcehtok village will take you in about 22 kilometres to Muna, to join the main Uxmal and Ticul roads.

Uxmal and the Puuc Route

The 261 road south from Umán runs more or less straight across flat brush. A place worth stopping at is **Yaxcopoil**, 33km from Mérida, where there is a rambling 19th-century *henequen hacienda* that has been turned into a museum (*open Mon–Sat 8–6, Sun 9–1; adm*). As you arrive it's impossible to see where village and *hacienda* divide, as the big square is entirely made up of former estate buildings, including the shop, formerly the *tienda de raya* or company store. Of all the *haciendas* open to view in the Yucatán, this best conveys how life functioned on these estates when 'green gold' dominated the life of the region. The caretaker, who shows you round, is a former *henequen* worker (he doesn't speak English). The tour begins with the big house, built in the 1860s, with its crumbling rooms with imported French tiles, 1920s swimming pool and fine gardens. There's a tiny chapel, and a room of Mayan ceramics discovered nearby. Also fascinating are the working buildings: Yaxcopoil produced *henequen* until 1984, and the giant machinery, built in Germany in 1911, is still in place.

A few kilometres further south on either side of the main road are two very different *haciendas*, the hotel at **Temozón Sur** and the restaurant at **Ochil**. Although no one would be aware of it from the highway, the surrounding area has one of the densest

The Puuc Cities

The Mayan cities of the Puuc Hills and their 'capital' Uxmal long represented an archaeological enigma. At one time this was one of the most densely populated of all the Mayan regions, and produced the most refined style of architecture. And yet the area seems unfit for human habitation. In the hills, the water problems of the Yucatán are multiplied 100 times: the water table is far below the surface and there are none of the *cenotes* that supported the Maya in other parts of the peninsula. The Puuc settlements had to create their own water supply by building *chultunes*, underground ceramic-lined cisterns, and *aguadas*, natural dips in the ground that were reinforced to form reservoirs. To found cities in these conditions seems perverse.

This is one of the regions where knowledge has been most extended by modern archaeological techniques such as soil surveys and radar mapping. It appears that because of lack of water the Puuc remained very thinly inhabited until AD 600 or even later. The Maya were highly aware of differences in soil quality. While the hills are very dry, their soils are exceptionally rich in minerals and, if watered, provide very productive land. It seems that the Puuc Hills were first 'colonized' at the end of the 7th century thanks to a combination of factors – overpopulation in lowland areas, the migration of Mayan groups from the Gulf Coast or maybe those 'exiled' by the wars in the Petén (*see* p.57) – but the Puuc cities only really 'took off' around 750 as the system of *chultunes* was refined to its highest level. An unprecedented number of settlements existed within a small area, surrounded by intensively cultivated fields that were maintained through an intricate system of land and water management. It has been calculated that towards the end of the Terminal Classic in around 900, the populations in the Puuc – 10,000 in Kabah, 9,000 in Sayil – had reached the very limit the land could support. In this fragile environment, it seems likely they fell victim to an acute version of the general 'Mayan Collapse', intensified by severe drought. Their highly organized agricultural and social systems imploded, and in the century after 950 the cities disintegrated. The Puuc has scarcely been inhabited ever since.

As such, the Puuc cities flourished for only 200 years, with the result that they are unusually homogeneous in style. Characteristic of Puuc style are an emphatic sense of design and geometry, particularly in contrasting plain and decorated surfaces; recurring motifs such as drum columns and *atadura* roof friezes (representing the roof of a thatched hut); as well as constant interplay between apparently abstract shapes and natural and everyday objects. An obsessive image in all the Puuc sites is a god-mask with a long, curling nose. This is commonly identified with the rain god Chac, but may also represent other supernatural figures such as Itzam-Ye, the animal manifestation of Itzamná that sits atop the World Tree at the centre of creation.

The short era of glory enjoyed by Uxmal and the Puuc cities formed part of an extraordinary late flowering in the northern half of the Mayan world, the same period that saw the rise of Chichén Itzá and the peak years of the cities in the Chenes and Río Bec. These areas were all in close contact with the Puuc, and 'exchanged' features of their architectural styles. One peculiarity of the Puuc cities is that they seem to have been the Mayan communities least devoted to the ball game: there is only one ball court at Uxmal, and none at some smaller sites.

Getting Around

By Bus

Buses here follow the needs of local people, not tourists, and as the Puuc is little populated there are very few regular bus and *colectivo* services. There are six second-class buses daily from **Mérida** (Terminal de Autobuses; five to Campeche, one to Dzibalchén) along the 'long route', passing Uxmal (*2hrs*), Santa Elena and Kabah, from 6am. About the cheapest way to do the full traditional route is on the Mayab **Puuc Route bus** that leaves Mérida (also from C/ 69) at 8am daily, passes Uxmal at about 9.30am and goes to Labná before turning back and stopping for 30mins at each of the four route sites, and 1½hrs at Uxmal (a bit tight). It brings you back to Mérida by 2.30–3.30pm and costs around $11 (not including site adm). In peak seasons and at weekends, book two or three days ahead. In **Santa Elena**, it's possible to find *colectivos* and taxis which run to **Ticul** and its abundant bus traffic (*see* p.327).

By Car

This is one region where a car is a big advantage. Roads are easy to follow and in good condition; Mérida to Uxmal direct takes about 1½hrs. *See* p.303 for **petrol stations** in the area.

Where to Stay

Uxmal and the Puuc Route t (997–)

It's possible to visit Uxmal and some smaller sites and return to Mérida the same day, but to see anything at all well you have to stay in the area for at least one night, preferably two. There is no village at Uxmal and no settlement anywhere along the Puuc road, so prices are relatively high. A cheaper alternative is to carry on to Ticul (*see* p.327).

Luxury

Hacienda Temozón Sur, halfway from Mérida, 45km north of Uxmal; a few km east of the 261 road, reservations via Mérida, **t** (999) 944 3637, *www.grupoplan.com/www.luxurycollection.com*. The first of the Plan Group's *hacienda* hotels, not really in the Puuc itself, but the most luxurious accommodation in the area (*see* p.270). The 17th-century main house, gardens, and **terrace restaurant** (*expensive*) are especially ravishing. Choose between 'Superior' (aka standard) rooms and four sizes of suite: all have giant bathrooms, lofty ceilings, old-plantation décor and opulent comforts (although some non-suite rooms are a bit dark). A broad range of excursions is available, and there's a superb pool and 36ha of grounds. For a brief taste of the *hacienda* experience, the Group have a separate **restaurant**, Hacienda Ochil, nearby at Ochil (*see* below).

The Lodge at Uxmal, in the woods beside the entrance road to the ruins, **t** 976 2102, *www.mayaland.com*. Owned by Mayaland like the Hacienda Uxmal, the Lodge is even closer to the ruins and intended to provide a more intimate experience, with 40 rooms divided between five palm-roofed villas, although they may not be opulent enough to justify the high prices. There are two pools and a pretty **restaurant**, and guests can use all the facilities at the Hacienda a short walk away.

Expensive

Hacienda Uxmal, t 976 2012, *www.mayaland.com*. Owned by the Mayaland Group like the largest of the Chichén hotels, but with more character, this is modern-ish (1950s) but colonial-style; it has airy rooms with traditional furniture and every comfort, bars on shady verandahs, a beautiful pool and gardens, tennis courts and fine **restaurants**. Peak prices of the best rooms are *luxury*.

Misión Uxmal, t 976 2022, *www.hotelesmision.com.mx*. A little blander than the Hacienda (and a bit cheaper), but still very comfortable. All the balconied rooms in the arc-shaped building, plus the **restaurant** terrace and the superb pool, are oriented to get a magnificent view of the Uxmal ruins.

Moderate

Club Med-Villas Arqueológicas, within the Uxmal site area, on the same driveway as The Lodge, **t/f** 976 2018, *www.come2club med.com*. The 'other' long-established upper-grade hotel at Uxmal has so far admirably refrained from pushing up prices. In return for this you get just as much comfort as you would at its neighbours, and there's also an especially pretty pool.

Inexpensive–Cheap

B&B (Flycatcher Inn), C/ 20 no. 223, Santa Elena (no sign; go up the track opposite Chac-Mool restaurant on the main road in the middle of Santa Elena, *dominguez_cuouh@yahoo.com*. American Kristine Ellingson and her Mayan husband Santiago Domínguez have four double guest rooms in their modern house, but they also hope to open a self-catering bungalow in the garden. The rooms are spacious and comfortable, with attractive décor and modern facilities. Evening meals can be provided by prior arrangement and they plan to have bikes for rent. It's an ideal way to experience Yucatecan country life, as the owners' extensive local knowledge can make a trip really special, with out-of-the-way *fiestas* or invitations to a local wedding.

Camping Sacbé, 16km along the road towards Kabah, just south of Santa Elena (no phone; it's possible to write to Familia Portillo, Apartado 5, CP97860, Ticul, Yucatán). The only genuinely cheap accommodation near Uxmal is a real find. Run by a very friendly Mexican-French couple, it's mainly a camp site, with good showers and solar electricity, where you can put up a tent or sling a hammock under a *palapa* shelter (about $2.50), but they also have a dorm-style room with beds (about $5.50) and four very pleasant double rooms in cabins, all with showers (around $15). They also offer bargain breakfasts and dinners. The camp site is on the west side of the road (the right coming from Uxmal); if you're on a bus, get off not in Santa Elena but beyond it, by the baseball field (*Campo de Beisbol*).

Hacienda Tabí, reservations via Fundación Cultural Yucatán, Mérida, **t** (999) 923 9453, *gabiort@hotmail.com*. A big, once-crumbling mansion run by a local community development organization as a nature reserve, study centre and simple hotel, with rooms (*inexpensive*) and camping space (*cheap*). Meals can be provided for a little extra, there's a pool, and the atmosphere is very friendly. As well as enjoying the house and woods around it, or visiting the Puuc sites, guests can visit other, scarcely excavated ruins, caves and forest areas with local guides. The same foundation supports the community tourism scheme in Yaxuná (*see* p.252).

Restaurante Rancho Uxmal, on the road 2km north of Uxmal, **t** 972 0277. Big, motel-like place with light but shabby rooms (fan-only) that cost more than you'd pay in Mérida, but they're still the cheapest this close to the ruins, and it has a small pool. There's also a **restaurant** and trailer park and camp site.

Eating Out

At Uxmal, the **visitor centre**'s bar-restaurant has straightforward, mid-price food. Better options are the restaurants in the big hotels, which are less pricey than their rooms. A little further from the ruins, the **Rancho Uxmal** (*moderate–cheap*) offers an extensive, standard Yucatecan menu, but the food can be poor. Instead, try the small, *moderate–cheap* restaurants beside the road just north of the Rancho, especially the **Hal-Tun**, which has a very pleasant terrace and charming service, and the **Papp-Hol-Chac**. There is also a decent restaurant by the road south at Santa Elena, the **Chac-Mool**.

Hacienda Ochil, about 30km north of Uxmal, down a well-indicated turning off the 261, **t** 950 1275, *ochil@grupoplan.com* (*expensive*). The Plan Group, owners of the luxury *hacienda*-hotels, have recently opened this smaller 17th-century *hacienda* as a restaurant and park alone. The menu features finely prepared, traditional Yucatecan dishes with modern touches, served on a delightful garden terrace. Prices are extremely reasonable for the quality of the food. In the park around it you can visit the gardens, a small museum, craft workshops and a *cenote*.

Entertainment

Uxmal stays open nightly for its **Sound and Light Spectacular**, at 7pm (Nov–Mar) and 8pm (April–Oct), for which, as at Chichén, you must pay with your entry ticket whether you fancy seeing it or not. However, this is the most effective of the shows of this kind, and while the commentary has the usual kitsch element it shows up the buildings to dramatic effect. Commentary is in Spanish, and speakers of other languages are offered headphones and a cassette commentary (an extra $2–$3).

concentrations of *cenote* sinkholes anywhere in the Yucatán. Few of them are sign-posted, but an official effort is underway to make village *cenotes* easier to visit, and snorkelling trips are now run to some from Mérida (*see* p.268). One *cenote* a little easier to find is **Sabak-Ha**, on the road between Abala and Sacalum, but it's always best to ask in the nearest village before going to any of the pools.

The 261 road stays pretty flat as you roll down towards **Muna**, where most local traffic takes Highway 184 towards Ticul, while most foreign travellers stay on 261 to Uxmal. Muna is the first of a string of engaging small towns across southern Yucatán, with a market, restaurants, a big plaza and a 17th-century church. From there the road winds up a steep ridge as you enter the Puuc Hills for the 16 kilometres to Uxmal.

Uxmal

Palenque may be richer in inscriptions and known history, and Chichén Itzá may triumph in awesome monumentality, but architecturally and aesthetically it is hard to challenge Uxmal as the most majestic of all the great Mayan cities. Its buildings have a special subtlety and sense of proportion: their powerful geometry could not be more emphatic, and they encapsulate the central strengths of Mayan architecture just as the Parthenon in Athens or the Pantheon in Rome do for Greek or Roman styles. The sense of design demonstrated by their unknown builders also makes them appear strangely modern.

History

The name Uxmal means 'three times built' and, unusually, is probably the original name of the city, since it was told to the Spaniards at the time of the Conquest. Its origins are cloaked in legend (*see* story box, p.311), and exactly how many times it was 'built' is not entirely clear. It is known, however, that this was one of the first large settlements in the Puuc, founded around 700–750. It is quite possible that a smaller community existed before then, and the oldest part of the Pyramid of the Magician has been carbon-dated to 560, but this date is very questionable. Uxmal is in one of the lowest parts of the Puuc hills, and its 'hilliness' was artificially accentuated, as most of the major buildings stand on man-made platforms. A difference is drawn in its architecture between 'Early Puuc', from 700–800, and refined 'Late Puuc' buildings such as the Nunnery Quadrangle, from around 900. This was not the only Mayan city where some of the finest buildings were created on the verge of its collapse.

Site Information

Open daily 8–5; adm exp, Sun adm free.

The site is more compact than Chichén, but 2hrs is still a minimum time to see it reasonably. Uxmal (like Chichén) is now more expensive to visit than most Mayan sites, at around $9, because the evening Sound and Light show is inescapably included in the ticket. In the **visitor centre** by the entrance there is a recently much-improved **museum**, a **café**, a **souvenir market** and a better-than-usual **bookshop** (at other sites similar facilities are very limited). The visitor centre stays open for the Sound and Light show until 9–10pm (*see* p.307). At the entrance there are official guides available, who charge in the region of $30 for a 1½–2-hr tour.

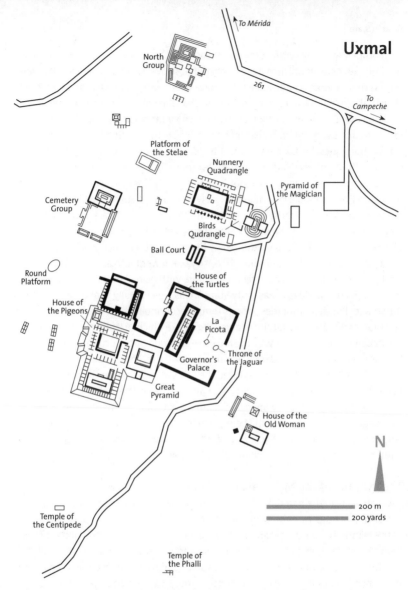

Uxmal

To Mérida

261

To Campeche

North Group

Platform of the Stelae

Nunnery Quadrangle

Pyramid of the Magician

Cemetery Group

Birds Qudrangle

Ball Court

Round Platform

House of the Turtles

House of the Pigeons

La Picota

Throne of the Jaguar

Governor's Palace

Great Pyramid

House of the Old Woman

N

200 m
200 yards

Temple of the Centipede

Temple of the Phalli

Uxmal has several glyph inscriptions and *stelae*. The city maintained literate Mayan culture, and has the second-latest date yet found anywhere in the Long Count calendar, in the Nunnery Quadrangle and from the year 907 (only Toniná in Chiapas has one later, from 909). These inscriptions, though, have not provided anything like as complete a history as has been built up at Palenque or Yaxchilán. In the Yucatecan chronicles written down after the Spanish Conquest the rulers of Uxmal, like the Itzá of Chichén Itzá, were described as a group of 'foreigners', called the Tutul Xiu, and the Xiu clan of Maní proudly told the Spaniards that they were the descendants of the lords of Uxmal. This story has often been questioned, but it now seems very likely that the dominant group among the founders of Uxmal were migrants and exiles from other Mayan regions further south, and could have included the Xiu. Unlike the similarly 'new' city of Chichén Itzá, Uxmal did not have a collective *multepal* leadership, as monuments to individual rulers have been found. The one prominent lord of Uxmal who has clearly emerged is Chan-Chak-Kaknal-Ahaw, better known as Lord Chak, who is shown as *ahau* of Uxmal on an altar (altar 10) now in the Mérida museum, and in an elaborate feather headdress on Stela 14, in the visitor centre. He was without question Uxmal's greatest builder, as the most emblematic buildings in the city – the Nunnery Quadrangle, the Governor's Palace and the Ball Court – were all built during his reign, between about 890 and 910. By this time Uxmal was evidently the 'capital' of the whole Puuc region, closely allied with Kabah, to which Uxmal is linked by a long *sacbé*. Its rise coincided with that of Chichén Itzá, and as the two most vigorous cities in northern Yucatán they seem to have been allies for a time in Chichén's wars against Cobá, although by the 10th century Chichén appears to have turned against Uxmal. Then, around 920–50 Uxmal went into a very rapid decline, leaving Chichén.to survive for a few years more with no real rivals in the peninsula.

Although Uxmal collapsed as a city-state it was never totally abandoned – unlike the smaller Puuc communities – for its temples continued to be used for special ceremonies. As an ancestral city of awe, Uxmal, like Chichén Itzá, figures strongly in Yucatecan folklore, which is why the Xiu were so proud of their connections with it. Because of its prominence Uxmal was never a 'lost' site. The Franciscan historian Father Diego López de Cogolludo visited the ruins in 1658 and, on the basis of Spanish equivalents, gave the main buildings the names – the Nunnery, the Governor's Palace – that have stuck to this day. Spanish documents from the 1680s also complained that pagan ceremonies were still being held in secret at Uxmal. The ruins were then largely forgotten until the 1830s, when first Count Waldeck and then Stephens and Catherwood arrived. Major modern excavations began in the 1930s.

The Pyramid of the Magician and Nunnery Quadrangle

As you walk up the path from the visitor centre, in the middle of it there is the entrance to a huge **chultún**. Rising up above the trees ahead of you is the giant mass of the **Pyramid of the Magician** (Casa del Adivino), also known as the House of the Dwarf (Casa del Enano). The most dramatic of the pyramids at Uxmal, 39m tall, it is rare for a Mayan building in that it is not square but oval, with massive rounded ends to the north and south. The east side, facing you, is dominated by a great ramp of steep steps reaching almost to the top. Uxmal may mean 'built three times', but the Pyramid of the Magician in fact contains five stages of building. Partway up the east side an opening has been made in the steps to give access to the dark, confined rear chamber of Temple II, previously buried under later building work.

Sadly, due to pressure of visitor numbers you're no longer allowed to climb up the steps to the top of the Pyramid of the Magician, which used to be an essential part of any visit to Uxmal. There's no option but to make the best of things and admire the giant tower by walking around it at ground level. The temples of the pyramid all face west, and from the side it is clear that the east face is very much its back, 'projecting' the whole structure towards the ceremonial centre of the city. At the very top is the last part to be added, Temple V, from around 900, with a façade of Puuc-style stone latticework panels. The platform in front of it is actually the roof of the older Temples II and IV – the same temples that ran through to the opening on the east side. Temple IV (from about 850) has a monster-mouth entrance like those of the Chenes style of Campeche, with the whole façade and doorway covered in carved decoration to form one giant image of Chac. This monster-temple is in local legend the House of the Dwarf himself. More curl-snout heads line the steps down. At the bottom on the west face there is a gap between the pyramid and the steps, buttressed with a Mayan arch, beneath which are the remains of Temple I, the very oldest part of the pyramid.

At the foot of the west face of the Pyramid there is the **Court of the Birds** (Cuadrángulo de los Pájaros), also known as the Antequadrangle, restored only in the last few years. In Late Puuc style, it is believed to date, like the main Nunnery complex,

The *Aluxes* and the Dwarf of Uxmal

An *alux* (pronounced al-oosh) is a Mayan leprechaun, a little spirit with the body of a baby and the face of an old man, born out of an egg. Always mischievous, they can be benign or malevolent. To this day, many Mayan farmers leave offerings in their fields as they plant their corn, to win the cooperation of the *aluxob*. According to one story, some *aluxes* are spirits of the old gods, driven from their temple-homes by the Spaniards, and have been taking revenge on *dzulob* (non-Maya, in Yucatec) ever since.

The most famous *alux* of all is the Enano de Uxmal, the Dwarf of Uxmal. His story, which crops up in different versions throughout the Yucatán, was told by local Maya to Stephens. Uxmal was then only a humble place, with nothing like the grandeur it later attained. It was ruled over by an old king, who lived in fear of a prophecy that he would be dethroned by a new lord, who was to announce his arrival by beating on a drum. Meanwhile, an old woman who lived alone in the woods, and cast spells, decided she wanted a child before she died. She spoke to some crows who gave her an egg. From the egg, there duly emerged a baby with an old man's face who already spoke and was 'as bright as a squirrel'; obviously he was an *alux*, the Dwarf. One day, the Dwarf found a drum in his mother's *na*, and began to play it. Hearing it, the old king was thrown into a panic, and sent all his men out to find the source of the noise.

The Dwarf was brought before the king, sitting beneath a sacred *ceiba* tree, and told him that he would be the new king of Uxmal. The king demanded that he prove it in tests of wit and strength, to which the Dwarf replied that he would, on the condition that the king matched every test himself.

The king was first confounded in a string of riddles, and left looking stupid. Then, the Dwarf said he would build a path to Uxmal from his house, suitable for a king and his mother; the *sacbé* from Nohpat and Sayil duly appeared. When the king challenged the Dwarf to build a house higher than any other in Uxmal, in one night he created the Pyramid of the Magician, worthy for a king. Finally, a crucial test saw both of them hit over the head with giant hammers. The Dwarf's mother placed a special *tortilla* over her son's head, and he survived; the king, of course, did not. The Dwarf ruled over Uxmal for centuries, transforming it into a great and wealthy city.

from around 900. Across it in front of you there is a perfectly formed Mayan arch, and on the façade to the left there are beautifully modelled carvings of birds amid feather-like patterns, a fine example of the naturalism of Puuc decoration.

Leave the Antequadrangle through the far-left corner from the Pyramid to walk around to the entrance of the **Nunnery Quadrangle** (Cuadrángulo de las Monjas). This is the most complete complex of buildings at Uxmal: each of its parts is impressive, but it is the complete ensemble that is extraordinary. Against the verticality of the pyramid, its geometry is decidedly horizontal, with long single-storey buildings, topped by friezes, that seem to parallel the flatness of the Yucatán countryside. It has 88 rooms, and its name was coined by Cogolludo because it reminded him of a convent, but there is no evidence that anything like nuns existed in Mayan society.

The four parts of the Quadrangle are all separate (and do not form an exact square), but this doesn't mean the complex is not a very integrated whole. Dates have been found indicating that the various sections were built simultaneously – over several years – and completed in fairly rapid succession: the South Building was dedicated in April 906, the East side in October the same year and one of the two temples in front of the great North Building in April 907. The main entrance is the arch in the **South Building**. Entering through it you immediately appreciate that the East and West Buildings on either side are at a higher level, with their platforms parallel with the South Building Frieze, and that the North Building facing you is higher again, giving the complex the authoritative quality that is a keynote in Mayan building. The vistas from the West Building across to the Pyramid of the Magician and from the North Platform to the Governor's Palace also seem to have been planned into its layout.

The carving on every one of the buildings is stunning, its effect heightened by the characteristic Puuc contrast between carved upper friezes and completely plain lower walls. The stone-mosaic friezes feature an intricate range of imagery with which Lord Chak's sculptors, as in so many Mayan cities, evoked the great Mayan creation myths and connected Uxmal's own rulers with them, in a complex that seems to have served as both an administrative and ritual centre for the city.

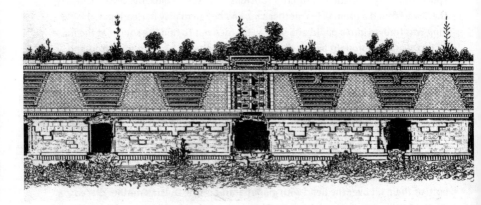

The East Building of the Nunnery at Uxmal, drawn by Frederick Catherwood

Especially striking is the very original Puuc combination of dynamic, apparently highly geometrical design and symbolism drawn from everyday Mayan life. The South Building is the only 'double-sided' part of the Quadrangle, and the simplest of the four sections. In its inner and outer friezes there are repeated lattice-pattern panels, reminiscent of the wooden latticework seen in Mayan houses, while above each doorway there is a realistic depiction of a *na* wood-and-palm hut, scarcely different from those seen in any Yucatán village today. Along the molding at the top of the frieze there are small flowers, symbols of magic, while above each *na* hut a spirit-monster-head sprouts bunches of flowering maize. This identifies the building as a magical one and links it with the place where the Maize God was reborn, and the house where the First Mother and First Father made the first men out of maize (*see* p.47). In the entry arch there are also two red handprints, left by the first builders as invocations to Itzamná, the paramount god known as 'Divine Hand'. The **East Building**, meanwhile, is the most spectacular as pure design – almost a piece of Art Deco – although even here the frieze is based on a homely latticework pattern. Again there are references to magic: the six grid-like, inverted triangles are made up of double-headed vision serpents, the conduit between men and the Otherworld, and in the middle of the frieze and in each corner there are stacks of Itzam-Ye masks.

The **West Building** opposite is the one that had to be most extensively restored, and has the most elaborate of all the friezes. Intertwined with great intricacy along its whole length are two giant feathered vision serpents (with rattler tails), which are believed to represent the War Serpent, bringing the power to make war from the Gods to the Lords of Uxmal. Only one snake still has its head, at the north end, but out of its mouth a human head is emerging, probably an ancestor of the Uxmal dynasty come via the serpent to advise the living. The background is a very complex lattice-pattern, with flower-symbols in each diamond-shape. This 'flower-lattice' pattern (also seen on the North Building), as well as invoking magic, is thought to indicate a *popol na* ('meeting house'), where important gatherings were held and decisions taken. Between and inside the loops of the snakes there are *nas*, stacks of God-masks, and squared-off, spiral-like panels that represent the Mayan glyph for *muyal* ('cloud'), another symbol of contact with the heavens. Above the three central doors there are niches with carved awnings representing the canopies of feathers held above Mayan lords, and in the middle niche there is a curious little king-like figure with the body of a turtle, one of the five *Pahauhtuns* or 'sustainer gods' who held up the sky at the moment of Creation, also related to the Cosmic Turtle from whose back the Maize Gods emerged in the same process. The **North Building** has similar imagery to the West, including repeated masks of Tlaloc, the central-Mexican war god, and flower-lattice panels indicating that this was also a 'meeting house', although given their position as the focus of the whole Nunnery Complex it is pretty clear that the North Building and the platform in front of it were much the more important section. Unlike the East and West sides it is also decorated at the back, with latticework panels and sculptures of naked, bound figures: war captives taken by Uxmal. On either side at the foot of the steps up to the North Building there are small temples, called the **Temples of Venus** because early investigators mistakenly interpreted their carvings as symbols of the planet Venus. In the very middle of the steps there is a very badly eroded *stela* which seems to have recounted events in the life of Lord Chak.

This remarkable combination of buildings and sculpture was intended to create a grand space for Lord Chak to hold court and for the celebration of rituals and the summoning up of supernatural forces, since these things were never separated in Mayan tradition. In the centre of the quadrangle there was also an altar and a monumental column, representing the *wakah-kan* (world-tree) at the centre of Creation. Early travellers also recorded the existence of a phallic monument in the quadrangle, but this was removed to avoid embarrassment to the first ever VIP visitor brought to Uxmal, Maximilian's Empress Carlota in 1865, and has never been seen since.

The Governor's Palace and House of the Turtles

> *There is no rudeness or barbarity in the design or proportions; on the contrary, the whole wears an air of architectural symmetry and grandeur... If it stood at this day on its grand artificial terrace in Hyde Park or the Garden of the Tuileries, it would form a new order. I do not say equalling, but not unworthy to stand side by side with the remains of Egyptian, Grecian and Roman art...*
>
> John Lloyd Stephens reporting on the Governor's Palace at Uxmal

From the arch in the south side of the Nunnery Quadrangle a path leads south, past some more, recently restored, colonnaded buildings, straight through the middle of the **Ball Court**. In style it is more or less midway between the Chichén Itzá-style ball court and the smaller ones of the older Mayan cities: although smaller than the one at Chichén, it had similar stone rings for scoring on either side. One of these rings, now kept in the Mérida museum, has an inscription mentioning Lord Chac and the dedication of the court, with a date from 901 (the rings now in place at Uxmal are replicas). The path continues towards the giant rock-and-earth platform on which the Governor's Palace and House of the Turtles stand. The building of this platform, extending over 180m by 154m and 17m high, involved transporting as much as a billion kilos of material.

As you walk up to the platform, immediately in front of you extends the great sweep of the **Governor's Palace** (Casa del Gobernador); for many, this is the pinnacle of Mayan architecture. It stands atop a second platform of its own, another 7m high. The palace is 100m long and made up of three parts, connected by exceptionally tall, false Mayan arches which once allowed access from one side to the other but were blocked off only a short time after the palace was built. As in the Nunnery buildings, there is a clear vision in the design that is emphatically horizontal. It may appear dead straight, but the two ends are in fact slightly lower than the middle. Mayan builders, like the Greeks, were aware of the optical principle that a truly straight and level building of this length actually looks as if it sags in the middle, and calculated their effects to compensate.

For once the Spanish name is fairly valid, for while there is no record of a specific 'Governor' at Uxmal it is near certain this was the main palace and residence of Lord Chak. It has 20 rooms, mostly small and arranged in two long rows, so those at the back are entered from those in front. In the middle there is an unusually long chamber with three entrances, which though by no means huge is actually the largest single space built by the Maya using their traditional arch technique. This was also the chamber in which Stephens, Catherwood and their ornithologist companion Dr Cabot camped out during their second visit to Uxmal in 1841, after first lighting fires inside for all of a day to clear out bats, bugs and the damp. Frederick Catherwood spent long periods alone here working on his drawings, while the others went off to explore. At that time a large section of the façade had collapsed, as can be seen in the drawings. This has since been restored, and with it most of the palace's frieze.

Like those of the Nunnery the frieze is an extraordinarily complex mixture of lattice patterns, *muyal* cloud images, masks of Chac, Itzam-Ye, Tlaloc and other gods, and human figures. In the centre a kingly figure, believed to be Lord Chak of Uxmal himself, sits surrounded by vision serpents as proof of his divine status. Over 20,000 individual pieces were used to create the frieze, an operation that involved a staggering degree of organization. There were originally 260 god-masks on the frieze, equalling the number of days in a *tzolkin* year, and it appears likely that the whole frieze symbolized the course of the year and the alternation of rain and sun.

Sharing the main platform with the Governor's Palace is the small, rectangular **House of the Turtles** (Casa de las Tortugas), which with its delicate proportions has often been compared to classical Greek architecture. It is the archetype of the pure Puuc style: above the usual plain, lower storey there is a frieze of Puuc drum columns, topped by an *atadura* frieze decorated with a string of very simple carved turtles. The turtle is another recurrent symbol at Uxmal. Its relation to the Cosmic Turtle aside, this is believed to be because turtles, like the people of the Puuc Hills, always relied desperately on the coming of the rains.

Around the platform there are a few more structures, most in fairly poor condition. Most apparent, in front of the palace steps, is a very worn monolith lying almost on its side, called **La Picota** ('the Whipping-Post'). It has on it some inscriptions that have long been completely indecipherable and is one of several clearly phallic monuments to have been found at Uxmal. It still leans at almost exactly the same angle as is shown in Catherwood's engravings. On the far side of the Picota from the palace there is an impressive altar, known as the **Throne of the Jaguar**.

From the east side of the platform, looking away from the palace, you can see amid the woods on the other side of a track a large pyramid called the **House of the Old Woman** (Casa de la Vieja), supposedly home to the Dwarf's mother. It's believed to be one of the oldest structures at Uxmal, from 680–750. It's in poor condition, but recent clearing work has made it easier to get to, with a scramble through the brush.

The Great Pyramid and House of the Pigeons

Forming a corner with the southwest angle of the palace platform is the **Great Pyramid** of Uxmal, a vast ascending pile of steps in a more conventional Mayan style than the Pyramid of the Magician. It is older than the palace buildings, probably from about 750–850, as is shown by the fact that part of the palace platform is built over the pyramid base; of the same age is a small temple with Chenes-style square pillars near the northwest corner of the platform, also partly covered by later building. At the top there is a temple with some fine carvings – especially of parrots and other birds, giving it the name **House of the Macaws** (Casa de los Guacamayas) – and in the centre an imposingly large, throne-like Chac-head. It is partially buried, almost certainly because in the 10th century they began to build a new temple on top of the existing one. For reasons unknown, this later temple was never completed.

From the Great Pyramid there is a view west over the **House of the Pigeons** (Casa de las Palomas), so called because its most distinctive feature, a long roof-comb of nine triangular crests perforated by square holes, looked like dovecotes to early travellers. Like the Great Pyramid it dates from around 800. It was the largest complex in the city, divided into three sections: to the north was a three-sided quadrangle, open on the north side into the central area of Uxmal. This led to the main, four-sided quadrangle of the House of the Pigeons, dominated by the roof-comb. To the south there is another area with a small pyramid topped by a temple. Like similar Mayan complexes elsewhere the Pigeons group was probably a combination of religious building (the pyramid) and lordly residence (the main quadrangle).

Other Buildings at Uxmal

Like most Mayan cities Uxmal had a considerable spread, and there are many other structures in the woods. From the House of the Old Woman a track leads for about 500 metres to a simple building known as the **Temple of the Phalli**. One part of the Puuc obsession with fertility in all its forms seems to have been a certain phallic cult. It is reflected here in penis-shaped tubes sticking out of the roof, which acted as drains to take off water, presumably into recipients to preserve the precious liquid. On the opposite, right side of the main track a path leads off to the **Temple of the Centipede** (Templo del Chimez), which is of more architectural interest as one of few 'multi-storey' buildings at Uxmal. Its name comes from its step-pattern frieze, which looks a little like a centipede.

Another 400 metres south along the main track, nearly a kilometre from the central buildings, stands an imposing, isolated Mayan **Arch**. It has long been put forward that this arch stood at the beginning of a *sacbé* running to the very similar arch at Kabah (*see* facing page). It may also have marked the southern boundary of Uxmal.

Returning to the central area, on the west side of the main open space opposite the Nunnery and the Ball Court there is another complex, called the **Cemetery Group** (El Cementerio) because of its many death's-head carvings. Another quadrangle, it has in its courtyard four altars, dated to about 880, covered in carved skulls-and-crossbones. To the south of the Cemetery a path leads from the Ball Court to the strange **Round Building** (Estructura Redonda), which is just that, a round drum platform. This was one of the last structures built at Uxmal, from the 10th century, and may have been partly inspired by Chichén Itzá's famous Caracol observatory.

Just a little further north than the Cemetery Group is the **Platform of the Stelae**, a low artificial mound with 15 monument-stones, lying on their sides. Most are in very poor condition. Lastly, a short walk from here is the **North Group**, another sizeable complex centred on a pyramid. So far, excavations here have been very limited.

The Puuc Road

From Uxmal it's 15 kilometres along the road to **Santa Elena**, the only village on the Puuc Route, which also has some of the area's most attractive places to stay (*see* pp.306–7). It has a plain village church from the 1770s, which has recently been (surprisingly) extensively restored. Attached is a village museum, and you can also climb up to the church roof for a wonderful view.

The ruins of Kabah are another eight kilometres south. While Uxmal had never been entirely lost from view, the existence of this and the other Puuc sites was utterly unknown to the outside world – including the rest of Yucatán – before Stephens and Catherwood came here in 1841, and their discovery, which was achieved by following the directions of village priests and local Maya, came as a revelation. As well as the four main Puuc sites there are plenty more ruins in the area (such as **Nohpat**, also visited by Stephens), scarcely excavated at all and accessible only by 4WD or on foot. If excavations are in progress they may be sealed off by the INAH, but if you are interested ask the caretaker at Sayil, who knows all the local sites and sometimes acts as a guide to out-of-the-way ruins.

Kabah

8km south of Santa Elena; open daily 8–5; adm, Sun adm free.

The ruins of Kabah straddle the Campeche road, although the main buildings are on the east side. Their feel of remoteness has diminished with the building of such facilities as concrete toilets, but even this site, between the times when buses arrive, can still feel far away from the world. From about 750 to 950 Kabah was the most important community in the Puuc after Uxmal, its political significance demonstrated by its being linked to the regional 'capital' by a finely constructed *sacbé*.

As you enter the main, eastern area of Kabah past the caretaker's hut, straight ahead at the top of a rise stands the long, low **Palacio**. It has a façade of multiple

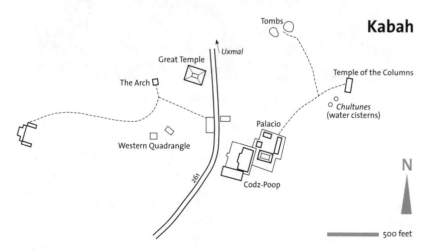

Kabah

Detail of the Codz-Poop, drawn by Frederick Catherwood, 1842

entrances supported by elegant columns, forming porticos to the usual small, dark inner chambers. If you look back from in front of the palace, you can have a first view of the Great Temple pyramid across the road, looming among trees and still almost entirely covered in brush. To the left of the Palacio, a path leads through woods to the **Temple of Columns** (called the 'Tercera Casa' by Stephens), a classic of the Puuc style. Before you reach it, just to the right of the path there are two well-preserved *chultunes* among the trees. To the north of the Temple of Columns there are some more unexcavated structures, believed to be **tombs**.

Each of the Puuc sites has its 'star attraction', and this leaves till last, on this side of the road, that of Kabah, the extraordinary **Codz-Poop** or 'Palace of Masks', to the right of the Palacio as you come up from the road. The normal Puuc style is for the lower walls to be entirely plain and topped by a frieze, with a noticeable sense of restraint, but here every inch is covered in decoration. The west façade, facing the road, is an absolute riot of Chacs, so that the whole building appears like one giant altar to the rain god. The current name of the palace means 'rolled blanket' and is only a post-Conquest Mayan reference to the 250 curling god-snouts that protrude from it. In front of this façade there is an impressive courtyard, containing rows of column bases, a *chultún* and an altar densely carved with glyphs (still scarcely deciphered). The Codz-Poop was almost certainly a residential and palace complex, and has an unusually large number of rooms, 27 in all. The east façade, away from the road, has undergone extensive restoration that has revealed superb carving. Halfway up, impressive king-like figures extend along the wall; on the sides of the entrance into the main chamber there are carved panels showing warriors in battle. The giant figures are unlike anything in any of the other Puuc cities, and a similar bust-like head of a man with a headdress, known as the 'King of Kabah' and now in the Mérida museum, was also found in the courtyard in front of the Codz-Poop.

From the Codz-Poop a bank of steps leads back to the entrance. Across the road, a broad path leads through a gate into the woods, past, on the right, the pile of rubble that is the **Great Temple**. Amid the brush to the left of the path there are the remains of another whole building complex, known as the **Western Quadrangle**, still almost entirely covered up. Further away again in the woods to the west – and very hard to find, off the main paths – there are the ruins of two more large buildings, where Stephens found intricately carved wooden lintels that would be priceless if they still existed today. He had them shipped to New York 'in order to preserve them', but they were then destroyed in a fire. Today, the most attractive monument on this side of the road is the **Arch**, standing alone across the track around a bend in the path.

After Kabah the Puuc Hills justify their name a little more, as the road runs gently up and down. Five kilometres further south, a sign (and, usually, an army checkpoint) indicates the left turn east on to the Ruta Puuc road. If you stay on Highway 261 here you continue down to **Bolonchén** and **Hopelchén** in Campeche, passing, in the first few kilometres, a much less-known continuation of the Puuc region (*see* p.394).

Sayil

Entrance 4km from the turning, on the south side of the Puuc road.
Open daily 8–5; adm, Sun free.

Sayil is quite an extensive site with buildings dispersed along thickly wooded paths. It was clearly one of the richest Puuc settlements but, like those around it, is almost entirely the product of one relatively short period. A lintel from its Palacio has been carbon-dated to about 730, while a *stela* inscription has a date from 810. The ceramics found here are all of the same era, from about 750 to 950. At around this time the population of Sayil and its satellite communities may have reached around 17,000.

From the site entrance the main path swings round in a wide arc through the woods. To the left, concealed by trees so that it comes up almost by surprise, is the greatest glory of Sayil, the magnificent **Palacio**, facing south. All of 85m long, it is a sweeping, three-level palace complex with similarities to the Five Storeys at Edzná (*see* p.393); as there, the 'floors' are not real storeys built on top of each other but tiers in a pyramid-like structure. Thought to have been built in several stages through the 8th and 9th centuries, it had over 90 rooms and could have housed over 350 people, served by eight water *chultunes* for their exclusive use, some of which can be seen by the northwest corner. The palace's drum facings and friezes, and the columns used in the entrances, give it a simplicity and elegance that has long been compared to

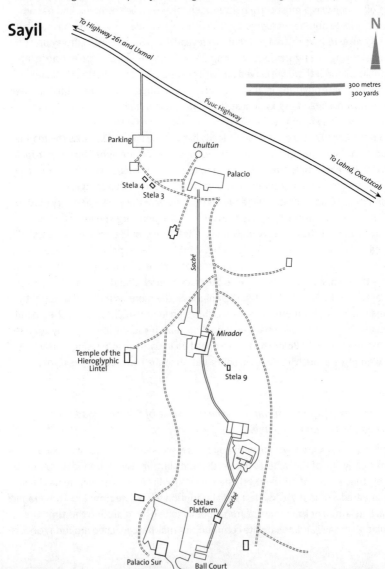

classical Greek architecture. Among the drum columns, as well as the usual Puuc god-masks, there are some carvings of a Diving God like those at Tulum (*see* pp.214–15). Apparently inexplicable so far from the sea, this has given rise to endless speculation.

The Palacio steps lead directly down on to an impressive *sacbé* that formed the main axis of the city, connecting its main areas along a north–south line. After 400 metres you see to the left of the path the **Mirador** ('Watchtower'). Thought to be older than most of the Palacio (dating from about 750), it occupies a small pyramid-platform, with a plain, five-room building supporting a massive roof-comb. What you see now is, mostly, only the rubble core, pierced by holes to reduce its weight; purely decorative, it must once have been covered with intricate stone and stucco carvings, in livid colours. Remains found nearby indicate that next to the Mirador there was also the main market area of Sayil.

Around the Mirador there are the remains of more *chultunes*, and amid the trees on the right (west) side of the path is the partly excavated **Temple of the Hieroglyphic Lintel**, with some quite well preserved inscriptions around the doorways. Back across on the other, left side of the path is the phallic **Stela 9**, a carving of a naked warrior with an erection that was probably part of a Puuc fertility cult. From here, back on the main path, it's a pleasant walk of 400 metres to the **Palacio Sur**, last of the main excavated complexes at Sayil. It had 18 rooms, several unusually spacious. Behind the Palacio Sur, to the west (right of the path), is a **Ball Court**. On the way to it you pass the **Stela Platform**, where the stone dated 810 was found. For a Puuc city Sayil has an unusually high number of *stelae*, more typical of 'classic' Mayan cities like Cobá.

Xlapak

Open daily 8–5; adm, Sun free. Five kilometres on from Sayil.

Xlapak is the smallest of the main Puuc sites. For this reason it's often missed out by tours, though it has plenty of attractions. So far it has pretty much missed out on site modernization. Its thick woods and undisturbed quietness make it the best site of all in which to see birds and even small mammals, worth visiting as much for a nature walk as for its ruins. First thing in the morning, especially, the range of bird song is quite wonderful.

The name *Xlapak* just means 'old walls' in Yucatec, and has no relation to its original name. The only large structure here, the **Palacio**, is a single, small palace building with three entrances on each of its two main façades. It's entirely Puuc in style, but here the local builders' sense of proportion appears to have gone astray. The base is very modest, while the frieze, of drum columns, geometric patterns and towering triple-Chac panels, looks much too big, seeming to bear down far too heavily upon it. Some of the carving, however, is very fine, and you can clearly see the method behind the Mayan technique of applying ornament as facings on to rubblework.

Seeing the Palacio on its own can make one think that the Maya had such a thing as an isolated country manor house, but in fact it was almost certainly the centre of a smallish, subsidiary settlement of about 1,500 people. The only other part-excavated structure is a stony, artificial platform in the woods about 300 metres south.

Labná

Open daily 8–5; adm, Sun free; three km from Xlapak.

For many Labná is a favourite among all the Mayan sites. Nestling in a small valley, it exemplifies the style of the Puuc hill settlements; it is also one of the places where the layout is most effective in conveying the sense of a community and the life that went on here rather than a set of scattered, separate buildings. It is a very peaceful site, if not quite so good for birds as Xlapak.

Like the other Puuc cities Labná was a prosperous community in about 750–950, but most of its buildings are in the Late Puuc style from the 9th to 10th centuries, when it probably had a population of about 4,500. They were supplied with water by 60 *chultunes*, which are dotted all around the site. As you reach the main area of Labná from the entrance you come up alongside the first of its major buildings, the grand **Palacio**, facing south. It has many similarities with the palace at Sayil, with two main levels built up pyramid-style and a bank of steps in the centre connecting with a *sacbé*. It had 67 rooms – fewer than at Sayil – but they were distributed over seven patios, and other levels as well as the main two. Above each level there is a frieze with the customary Chac masks, and on the southeast corner a sculpture of a human face emerging from a serpent's jaws, similar to those at Uxmal. On the northern side of the Palacio one of the Chac masks has an inscription on its nose with the date 862. Excavations suggest that the central patio was the palace's principal court and receiving space, while in the east patio (to the right, looking at the façade), *metates*, stones for grinding corn, have been found, indicating that cooking went on here and that this was probably the preserve of the servants. The west patio to the left was the living quarters of the lordly family of Labná.

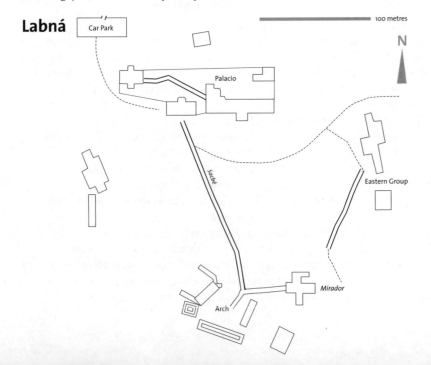

Labná

The Arch at Labná, drawn by Frederick Catherwood, 1841

From the Palacio a well-restored *sacbé* runs to the south group of buildings. To the right, at an angle to the *sacbé*, is the greatest of all Mayan arches, the **Arch of Labná**, subject of several of Catherwood's finest drawings. Structurally and aesthetically its builders showed a very high degree of sophistication, creating a wonderful solidity, and, instead of the abrupt lines of some Mayan arches, a finely crafted elliptical curve.

Although the arch now stands alone, it was not an isolated arch like those of Uxmal and Kabah but an interior passage within a complex of buildings that combined the functions of administrative building and aristocratic residence. On the east side, the remains have been traced of a sizeable quadrangular plaza. The arch connected this quadrangle with a smaller patio to the west, the main residential part of the palace.

A short distance from the arch, to the left of the *sacbé* going south and atop a very rubbly pyramid, is the **Mirador** of Labná. Similar to the Mirador at Sayil, and likewise thought to be from the Early Puuc period and therefore older than most buildings around it, it's a simple, three-room temple supporting a giant towering roof comb. When Stephens and Catherwood saw it in 1841 – 'the most curious and extraordinary structure we had seen in the country' – it still retained large sections of its high-relief carvings, and even some of their original colour. They were able to make out a line of death's-heads along the top and a giant, seated central figure with two smaller figures alongside him, while above their heads were two dynamic figures with balls, perhaps a reference to the ball game. However, between then and the time serious excavation began in the 1950s all this decoration disintegrated. Beneath the Mirador another building is visible, suggesting that the pyramid was built up in stages.

As usual, there are more buildings and structures around the woods that have only been excavated to a very limited extent. The most important are the **Eastern Group**, down a path to the right of the Mirador, looking towards the roof-comb.

The Loltún Caves

In some ways, the caves at Loltún are the most fascinating of all the sites on the Route. They are both the most awe-inspiring of the great Yucatán cave systems, and also the oldest and most mysterious of the peninsula's Mayan sites, used and occupied by local people from remote prehistory up until the 19th century.

The Loltún caves were 'discovered' for the outside world by the American consul Edward Thompson in the 1890s, and fully investigated in the 1950s. The local Maya seem to have been aware of them for ever. Remains found here have been dated to about 5000 BC, and are the earliest evidence of human occupation in the Yucatán; Preclassic carvings from about AD 100 are among the region's oldest identifiably Mayan relics. There are also many more carvings in the caves from the Classic period, contemporary with the Puuc cities on the surface, and others from the Postclassic. The caverns were important as the venue for rituals involving contacting or placating the subterranean gods – in many caves there are painted red hands, an invocation to the Gods for good health. They also played a part in virtually every other area of life. The rich clay of the cavern floor was greatly valued in making ceramics, and many of the stalactites have had their ends cut off, for use as weapons, or ground down for use in potions. During the Caste War of the 1840s the caverns were still of use to local Maya, as a refuge in which they hid from white armies.

And the caves themselves are staggering. The strata and different minerals make rich patterns in the rock, and all through the caves there are inexplicable draughts and cold air currents, while only a few steps away you can walk into a steam bath that can stop your breath. Sylvanus Morley thought that this was not a natural phenomenon but another product of Mayan ingenuity, refining the air-flows for their own purposes. The name *Lol-tun* means 'stone flower', and may refer to the caves' magical productivity, although in another theory it evokes only the echo made by hitting a stone on the stalactites. Throughout the caverns there is evidence of occupation at different times: of fires having been lit, god-heads and inscriptions, or rubble trenches from the Caste War.

Site Information

Guided tours at 9.30am, 11am, 12.30pm, 2pm, 3pm and 4pm; adm.

The caves, 12km east of Labná, have long been open to visitors, but are quite easy to miss. From Labná, take a short cut to the left signposted to Yaaxhom for about 4km, or stay on the main road till Emiliano Zapata and turn left; either way you will come upon the Loltún **visitor centre** fairly abruptly, round a left-hand bend. In the other direction, from Oxcutzcab, the entrance is more visible. Leaving Loltún, it is 8km to the left and downhill to Oxcutzcab.

You can visit the caves only with **guided tours** (around $5, plus $1 to park a car), but times can be imprecise; they officially include a Sound and Light show, which here does not feature any sound but only quite subtle lighting. The local guides are knowledgeable (and paid only through tips); several speak some English, and if possible it's worth checking when a tour in English will be leaving. Each tour lasts about 1–1½hrs and covers nearly 2km of caves; a further 2km of pathways are closed to visitors, and beyond that the caverns extend for more semi-explored kilometres into the ground.

There is a **restaurant** at Loltún. Located by the exit from the tour, its open-air tables are very welcome, since one other thing to note is that inside the caves the extraordinary variations in temperature and humidity can be genuinely overpowering.

Site Information

Open daily 8–5; adm, Sun adm free.
Chacmultún is quite hard to find: from Loltún, instead of heading for Oxcutzcab take the right turn south towards Xul. After about 6km there is a left turn signed to Tekax, which rolls for several kilometres through deep-Mayan villages until you reach Kancab, where there's a right turn for Chacmultún. It's easier to find coming the other way, from Tekax (10km). From the turn the road winds further uphill through Chacmultún, until, just when you think you're really lost, you hit the site.

Chacmultún

The ruins of Chacmultún are one of the least-known Puuc sites, and still little visited. Its buildings are in the now-familiar Puuc style, and it can best be recommended to Mayan completists and those who like their ruins to provide a sense of discovery and remoteness. Its greatest distinction is that it is the only visitable Puuc site to retain some painted murals, although these are now in very poor condition.

It is often the case with Mayan sites that their relative fame and state of preservation does not reflect what has been discovered about their original importance, and this is so with Chacmultún. As the most important city of the eastern Puuc, it covers a wide area, and was larger than, for example, Labná. It was also occupied for longer than many Puuc communities, with some settlement from the Early Classic, about AD 300, and limited occupation into the Postclassic.

One of its most distinctive features is that, whereas at other Puuc sites the 'hills' often seem only incidental elements, Chacmultún is built on some of the tallest hills in the whole region, with commanding views over the surrounding landscape. The largest group of buildings is up the hill behind the caretaker's hut. The **Edificio de las Pinturas** is the first of them (*ask the caretaker for 'los murales'*). Only three of its eleven rooms survive, of which one has the remains of the murals. They are very faint, but can just be seen to show men in headdresses and rich jewellery, in a procession. Above this building is the **Palacio of Chacmultún**, with some fine Puuc *na*-carving, and nearby, past the opening to a *chultún*, is the small **Structure 10** which also has some remains of painted decoration inside. To find the other groups of buildings, walk on up the road about 500 metres past the main site to the **Cabalpak** group, and then continue round the bend to the **Xethpol** group, the tallest building on the tallest hill in Chacmultún. Both are palace complexes, only partly excavated out of the woods.

Ticul and the Southern Yucatán Towns

The village of Ticul, to which we were thus accidentally driven, was worthy of the visit, once in his life, of a citizen of New York.
John Lloyd Stephens

When you emerge from the Puuc–Loltún road into Oxcutzcab, you leave the world of ruins behind to re-enter the land of the living. On a weekend, especially, there will be a slow but steady stream of traffic along the 184 road, mostly bicycles, and often whole families bunched up in the front of tricycle-carts propelled at a beautifully calm rhythm by the father or eldest son. The towns along the foot of the Puuc hills represent something of a Yucatecan heartland. A rich mineral content makes the land lush when water is applied to it, and this is one of the best fruit-growing areas of the state, with mango, papaya, lemons and sugar cane appearing between the more usual maize patches and brushwood. It is also a major centre for handicrafts. This does not mean that the pace hots up. Probably nowhere else in the Yucatán will you see so many tricycle carts: they seem ideally suited to the locals, for if they tried to ride regular, two-wheeled bikes quite so slowly they would almost certainly fall over.

The main southern towns are all Spanish foundations, established around Franciscan monasteries and churches. **Oxcutzcab** itself is known for the largest fruit and produce markets in the state, which take over its plaza on most days with succulent piles of oranges, pineapples, *mamey* and watermelons. Presiding over the scene is the whitewashed façade of the church of San Francisco, completed in 1645, one of three similar basilica-style churches in the area (the others are at Tekax and Teabo).

Seventeen kilometres to the northwest along Highway 184 is **Ticul**, the principal town in the district. Ticul has a bank, a post office, at least one fine restaurant and a few hotels that make it a good base for looking around the Puuc area. When John Stephens first saw the town's plaza, he wrote, 'it struck me as the perfect picture of stillness and repose'. He and Catherwood were given essential aid in finding Puuc ruins by the local priest, Padre Carrillo, and convalesced here from some of their bouts of fever. So taken was Stephens by Ticul that he declared that 'altogether, for appearance, society and conveniences of living, it is perhaps the best village in Yucatán', and in one memorable episode broke off from scrabbling among the ancient stones to ride through the day to catch the local *fiesta*, of which he wrote 'it was something entirely new, and remains engraven on my mind as the best of village balls'.

That was in 1841, and things change. One has to guard against romanticizing too much, but looking at Ticul it's easy to think some of the same air of benign contentment is around today. Nothing much happens in the town square, but it has an atmosphere that's enjoyable in itself, the very opposite of hassle and hussle. Ticul reveals the curious mixtures of Yucatán towns – palm *nas* stand alongside candy-coloured houses with a Nissan in the driveway, and while half the local women wear traditional *huípiles*, others are in lycra and ankle-threatening heels. It has its (slightly) busy side, and produces huge quantities of shoes, embroidery and ceramics.

From Ticul it's 22 kilometres to Muna and the 261 road back to Mérida. In the opposite direction, southeast from Oxcutzcab, Highway 184 runs on through more Mayan towns and villages. Largest of them is **Tekax** (18km from Oxcutzcab), which has one of the grandest of Franciscan basilicas, completed in 1692. Near the town there is a clutch of beautiful *cenotes* (*ask at the town hall for directions*). The next significant town is another 42 kilometres on, at **Peto**, from where those seeking strange, lost atmospheres can follow a narrow tarmac road another 37 kilometres east to **Ichmul**. The original home of the 'Christ of the Blisters' in Mérida Cathedral, the village has been partly abandoned ever since the Caste War.

From Peto and Tzucacab the road continues through little-populated backwoods to Felipe Carrillo Puerto (*see* p.336). Drivers should have fuel for the 130 kilometres from Peto, as there may be none in José María Morelos, the only other town along the road.

Getting Around

As this area is well populated there are lots of **buses** and abundant *colectivos*. At least 10 *intermedio* and second-class buses daily pass along this road from Mérida to Chetumal via Muna, Ticul, Oxcutzcab and Peto. All leave from the C/ 69 Terminal. From Oxcutzcab market, it's possible to find a *colectivo* to just about anywhere in the region, including a *colectivo* or taxi to **Loltún** and **Labná**.

There are **fuel stations** along the 184 road in Muna, Ticul, Oxcutzcab, Tekax and Peto.

Tourist Information

Ticul and Oxcutzcab t (997–)

Banks: In Ticul and Oxcutzcab, both alongside the main plazas.

Internet Access: There is a handy place in Ticul a short way south of the plaza on C/ 27, between C/ 28 and C/ 30.

Shopping

Ticul has many shops with locally produced **shoes** for sale, but most are only versions of international styles (though they are cheap). There are also any number of outlets for local **earthenware pots** and **ceramics**. A good deal of the stuff on offer is tacky, but one place that has quality higher than the norm is **Arte Maya**, C/ 23 no. 301, on the road in from Muna on the western edge of town.

Where to Stay

Ticul t (997–)

Hotel Plaza, C/ 23 no. 202, Ticul, t 972 0484, *www.hotelplazayucatan.com* (*inexpensive*). The best in Ticul by a long way. It's fittingly right on the plaza, and has large, functional, airy and comfortable rooms with good facilities such as bathrooms, fans, optional a/c and TVs, making them excellent value.

Hotel Real de Ticul, C/ 23 no. 291-A, Ticul, t 972 1368 (*cheap*). Motel-style hotel a long way from the centre on the 184 road (C/ 23 within Ticul) towards Muna at the western end of town. Its rooms have several years on the

clock and are quite dark, but several of them now have very state-of-the-art a/c.

Hotel Sierra Sosa, C/ 26 no. 199-A, Ticul, t 972 0008 (*cheap*). More basic but still decent, also just off the plaza. Some of its rooms have a/c (a little extra, just into *inexpensive*); they're all a bit dark but quite well kept, with reasonable showers.

Eating Out

Around the plaza in **Ticul** you'll find the customary line of *loncherías* and *taco*-stands, offering very cheap meals and soft drinks, and in **Oxcutzcab**, **Tekax** and **Peto** there are plenty of *loncherías* and simple restaurants around the markets.

Balnearios Cabo Cañaveral, west of Oxcutzcab, and **Balneario San Fernando**, on the Tekax side of Oxcutzcab (both *moderate*). Big, open-air *balneario* restaurants with *palapa*-shaded bars and tables around swimming pools which fill up with local families at weekends, but are open in the week.

Los Almendros, C/ 23 no. 207, Ticul, t 972 0021 (*moderate*). The fine restaurant in Ticul, a block from the plaza and the Hotel Plaza, and parent of the flashier branches in Mérida and Cancún. Opened in 1962, it is credited with being the first place ever to present Yucatecan country cooking '*para los dzules*', for non-Maya, and even with having invented dishes such as *poc-chuc* that are now accepted as utterly 'traditional'. As well as menu fixtures such as this and *pollo pibil*, this is also a fine place to try unquestionably traditional Yucatecan dishes such as *pavo en relleno negro* (turkey in a savoury black *chilmole* sauce with hard-boiled eggs). Cooking can be inconsistent, but there are more hits than misses, service is charming, prices are modest and a meal here is a near-indispensable part of a visit to the Puuc.

Los Delfines, C/ 27 no. 216, x 29 & 30, Ticul (*moderate*). A block south and a little west of the plaza, with a garden in which you can sample a good range of local favourites, and also several fish and seafood choices.

Pizzeria Góndola, C/ 23, corner of C/ 26, Ticul (*cheap*). Nearly opposite Los Almendros; very friendly, with decent standard pizzas and excellent breakfasts and Yucatecan snacks.

The Maní Road to Mayapán and Acanceh

The 'fast' route back to Mérida from the Puuc is via Muna, but there is also a back-country road that wanders north from Ticul and Oxcutzcab through more quiet, hot Mayan towns, *henequen* fields and long stretches of empty green scrub. This road has been labelled the **Ruta de los Conventos** ('Convent Route') by the local authorities, as a showcase for Yucatán's colonial church architecture. This is a little arbitrary, since there are Spanish churches in every part of the state. It is, though, truly steeped in history, for it contains some of the oldest and most impressive Franciscan foundations in the peninsula, and the remains of the last great Mayan city, Mayapán.

Maní

Only 10 kilometres north of Oxcutzcab (16km from Ticul) is Maní, oldest of all the Spanish missionary monasteries in the Yucatán and scene of one of the most dramatic episodes of the Conquest, Father Landa's *auto-da-fé* and bonfire of Mayan treasures in 1562 (*see* p.68). Maní was the seat of the Xiu, whose leader Tutul Xiu was the first of the Mayan lords to accept the authority of the Spanish crown in 1542. It was because of the loyalty of the Xiu that the Franciscans sent their first missionary expedition to this area in 1547, two years after the order had arrived in Yucatán. The friars originally established themselves in Oxcutzcab, but after rumours of a plot to murder them accepted the suggestion of Tutul Xiu to move closer to his centre of power in Maní.

The Monastery of Saint Michael the Archangel was dedicated in 1549. A major effort was made to build it as quickly as possible: the Franciscans' architect Friar Juan de Mérida oversaw the work, and a large part of it was built in six months in 1550. The friars established a school to teach Christian doctrine in Yucatec using Latin script, and even a choir school, where Mayan boys were taught to sing polyphonic Masses. The Franciscans, as Landa declared, sought to recruit into the school 'the young sons of the lords and principal people', in the expectation that when they returned to Mayan society they would carry back a full knowledge of the new religion.

It was some of these very children who in May 1562 informed the friars that their Mayan elders were celebrating old rituals in secret, and showed them a cave full of

Getting Around

This road has recently been upgraded, but **drivers** should have fuel for the 100km between Oxcutzcab and Kanasín on the outskirts of Mérida. Nor are there any official **petrol stations** along the 122km between Oxcutzcab and Chichén Itzá via Sotuta. Note also if you're visiting churches that they all close for lunch, from about 1pm to 4pm.

Bus traffic mainly consists of *colectivos*. They run fairly steadily in the morning, but are scarcer by midday. The main hub and best place to find an ongoing *combi* is Tekit.

Eating Out

All the towns along this route have one or two cheap *loncherías* or cafés with roadside tables that make good places for sitting and admiring church façades and watching the vultures go by, but **Maní** seems to be the only one with full-scale restaurants. Bear in mind that there is no overnight accommodation along this road.

Restaurant Los Frailes, C/ 27, x 28 & 30, Maní (*moderate*). Pretty restaurant not far from the monastery with a full range of Yucatecan standards. *Closed eves*.

idols and offerings. Investigations revealed a large-scale relapse into 'idolatry'. It appears likely that many Mayan lords simply had the wrong end of the stick. Used as they were to having many gods, who were flexible enough to admit others, it seems they had not quite understood how exclusive the new Christian god was intended to be. When the news was relayed to Landa, however, he was appalled. He resolved to root out the devil's work with no half measures, organizing a solemn *auto-da-fé* in the great square in front of the monastery of Maní. None of the 'idolators' was actually executed or burnt at the stake, but some died during the course of their tortures.

In later decades the monastery was supplanted as a missionary centre, and Maní was left as one more rural town. The great mass of the monastery still stands almost completely intact, though, over the grass expanse of the town square, which is now very quiet, with a town hall clock permanently at 8.15. The square is so big because it was once the ceremonial plaza of the Xiu capital. On the left of the monastery façade, looking straight at it, is the great open arch of the *capilla de indios*. The façade and bell towers of the church were not added until the 18th century.

Behind the Indian chapel and alongside the church is the two-storey cloister. It's a monument of Franciscan austerity, crude and powerful, with walls so thick they're almost cavern-like. Exuberant giant ferns soften the lines a little, and in one corner the remains are visible of a mural of the Visitation of the Virgin, probably from the 1580s. Contrary to some leaflets there is no museum here, only a very austere retreat house; the garden, still with its original well and waterwheel, is full of flowers, and in spring the crumbling upper arches are full of swooping swallows.

About six kilometres further along the road is **Tipikal**, from where it's six kilometres again to **Teabo**, with one of the most elegant Franciscan churches, from 1650–95. Ask the sacristan if you can see the wood-beamed sacristy, which has extraordinary mural paintings of saints. They were long covered in whitewash, and only discovered by accident in the 1980s. At Teabo the road splits. There is a long, slow road that runs northeast from here to the main 180 road and Chichén Itzá, via **Sotuta**, once seat of the Cocom, enemies of the Xiu of Maní and dogged opponents of the Spaniards. The main road from Teabo next runs through **Chumayel** (5km), place of origin of the *Book of Chilam Balam of Chumayel*, one of the Mayan chronicles written down in Yucatec in Latin script in the 16th century. From there it's nine kilometres to **Mama**, which has a church with a particularly grand belltower and a roofed-over 16th-century well (no longer in operation). Next is the slightly busier **Tekit**, from where it's another 20 kilometres through fairly empty country to the ruins of Mayapán.

Mayapán

Open daily 8–5; adm, Sun adm free; 20km from Tekit.

At Mayapán the Mayan past leaves the realm of archaeology and crosses over into recorded, conventional history. The city collapsed as capital of northwest Yucatán in the 1440s, only 80 years before the arrival of the Spaniards, and one of Father Landa's chief informants on Mayan ways, baptized as Juan Cocom, was the grandson of the last ruler of Mayapán.

There is evidence that the site had been occupied since the Early Classic, but scarcely anything remains from any time before the 12th century. Mayapán rose to prominence around 1200, the most vigorous product of the modest Postclassic revival in the northern Yucatán, and it seems that its growth triggered the final collapse of Chichén Itzá. At its peak the city had a population of around 12,000. In Yucatecan chronicles it was sometimes described as the seat of the 'League of Mayapán', and one legend maintains that the other members of this 'League' were Chichén Itzá and Uxmal, but this has now been discounted since it is clear these cities had both declined before most of Mayapán was built. Instead, it was the joint capital of a loose confederacy of small lordships – Maní, Chakan (around Dzibilchaltún-Ti'ho), Kin-Pech (Campeche) – into which the Yucatán had divided. The 'rulers' of Mayapán, the Cocom lineage, were not strictly kings but only the first among several lords in a *multepal* collective leadership, able to take decisions only with some consensus behind them.

This system involved a substantial bureaucracy. According to Landa, each of the local princes maintained their own establishment in Mayapán, headed by a *mayordomo* (*caluac*), responsible for overseeing communications with the home domain. This type of government was also inclined to instability. The authority of the Cocom was fairly effective for many years, but in the late 14th century the Xiu of Maní emerged as a centre of disaffection, accusing the Cocom of acting tyrannically. A 'coup' was staged in which the leading Cocom princes were murdered, except for one who escaped and returned to lead resistance. Civil wars went on for years, until in 1441 the Cocom withdrew to their own base at Sotuta, and Mayapán was abandoned. This Xiu–Cocom feud was still flaring up when the Spaniards arrived, and was enormously useful to them in the Conquest.

Mayapán is another place where major new excavation and restoration work has been carried out just in the last few years: important finds include several rare and richly coloured painted frescoes, and many fine ceramic pieces, most of which are now in Mérida's museum. Large parts of the site, though, remain scarcely excavated.

Mayapán's status as a confederal capital gave it a particular structure. The area that has been excavated is inside a rough perimeter wall, which swings round in a kidney shape. It seems clear that an etiquette designed to avoid flash points was a feature of relations between the lords of the League, so that the walled centre of Mayapán was a kind of collective 'no man's land' shared by all but belonging to no one in particular. According to Landa, each lord had the right to keep a residence within the wall, but kept most of their followers in separate areas outside, where there are enough semi-buried structures in the woods to intrigue any amateur archaeologist (the full area of Mayapán covers four square kilometres).

Looking at Mayapán it soon becomes clear that by the time the city was built many of the most sophisticated Mayan skills in carving and stoneworking had been lost. In their finish the buildings are much cruder than those at older sites. On the right, going in, is **Structure Q-62**, a residential area of stone walls making up only three rooms; behind it are three substantial pyramid-like temple platforms, the so-called **Cemetery Group** – the main focus of ongoing excavations – while to the left of the main path there is a substantial pyramid-platform with, at its top, fine frescoes of two

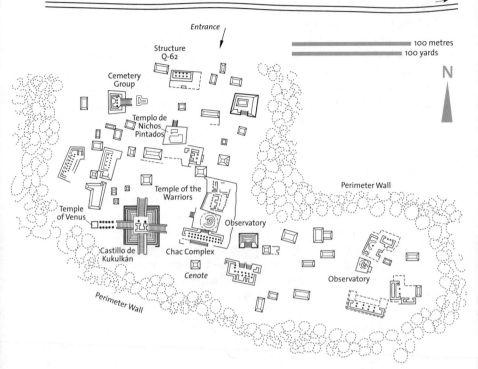

Mayapan

To Mérida →

To Maní →

Entrance

Structure Q-62

100 metres
100 yards

N

Cemetery Group

Templo de Nichos Pintados

Perimeter Wall

Temple of the Warriors

Temple of Venus

Castillo de Kukulkán

Observatory

Chac Complex

Cenote

Observatory

Perimeter Wall

monstrous god-like figures (although the protective fence around them makes it hard to get a good look). A little beyond Q-62 is a curious 'mini-pyramid' known as the **Templo de Nichos Pintados** ('Painted Niches', because it has faint traces of frescoes), which almost forms an entrance to the main Plaza of Mayapán, centred on the city's largest structure, the great pyramid or **Castillo de Kukulcán**, a cruder, smaller copy of the Castillo at Chichén Itzá. Recent restoration has made it much easier to appreciate that, however much Mayapán's builders may have been lacking in carving ability, in the structure of its Plaza the city had a curiously distinctive elegance, one more Mayan surprise. Forming the sides of the square around the pyramid are several almost Grecian colonnades, and lines of columns lead up to the steps on the Castillo's east and west sides, especially from the **Temple of Venus** platform to the west. The main fresco fragments are around the lower levels of the pyramid, protected by *palapa* roofs. Those in the northeast corner, facing into the Plaza, show warriors, some of them decapitated; fragments of skulls have also been found here, suggesting this was a place of sacrifice. Larger and more impressive are the scenes on the south side, outside the square, showing richly adorned figures carrying standards, surrounded by animals, stranger creatures and the inevitable death figure, in a style extraordinarily similar to modern Day-of-the-Dead souvenirs and the images of the great 19th-century Mexican folk artist Posada.

Just south of the Castillo is the walled town's main *cenote*, which had a temple platform built around its mouth. On the east side of the Plaza are the palace/temple buildings known as the **Chaac complex**, which this time seem to imitate the Puuc style, with a Chac mask in the centre. Beside them is the intriguing circular **Caracol** or **Observatory**, again very like the great Caracol tower at Chichén, although oddly it has none of the slots in its walls that would have been used for astronomical observations. Whether these round buildings were observatories is still not certain, but there were four such towers at Mayapán. The area outside the Plaza to the east can be recommended to anyone who wants to see Mayan ruins in their 'natural' state, with many more platforms and pyramids scattered around the woods.

Tecoh to Acanceh

Only three kilometres north of Mayapán is the next village, **Telchaquillo**, which has the entrance to a *cenote* in its main plaza. It is still in use by local people, and a flight of steps leads down into the cave. Eleven kilometres further on is **Tecoh**, another delightfully somnolescent town. Its twin-belfried church, from 1751, stands on another Mayan platform. It has a rival in the *Palacio Municipal*, a piece of peach-coloured Victoriana from 1904–6 which local jokers say was copied from Chicago City Hall.

The last stop on this road (8km from Tecoh) is the most extraordinary, **Acanceh**. Like Izamal, this is one of the places where the pre- and post-Conquest worlds exist side by side. As you enter the dusty village square from Tecoh, on the right is the 18th-century colonial church, while forming a corner with it is a Mayan pyramid, still substantially intact despite having been plundered to build the church and most of the other more permanent structures in town. Despite its proximity to Mayapán it is actually much older, and one of the most intriguing buildings in the Yucatán for the insight it gives on the links within the Mayan world.

The **Acanceh pyramid** (*open daily 8–5; adm, Sun adm free*) dates from the Early Classic, between about AD 300 and 600, and so is one of the oldest large structures in the north. There is evidence too that the site had been occupied for several centuries before then, from about 300 BC. Moreover, stylistically the pyramid has great similarities to buildings in the Petén far to the south in Guatemala and Campeche, indicating that Maya from the cities in the south may have travelled into the northern Yucatán even at this time. Most of the Acanceh site has been covered over by the later village, but two blocks south of the plaza there are two more survivors, the Palacio de los Estucos and the plainly named **El Edificio** ('The Building'). All three structures contain stucco friezes that, again, are unusual for the Yucatán and more typical of areas further south such as the Río Bec. Those on The Building show a rich decoration of animals, birds, and astronomical signs, retaining traces of their bright colours.

From Acanceh, a narrow country road runs 12 kilometres straight north to Ticopo to meet Highway 180, the Mérida–Cancún road going east, while to the west an all-new, widened road takes you quickly back along 19 kilometres to Kanasín and Mérida.

Southern Quintana Roo and the Río Bec

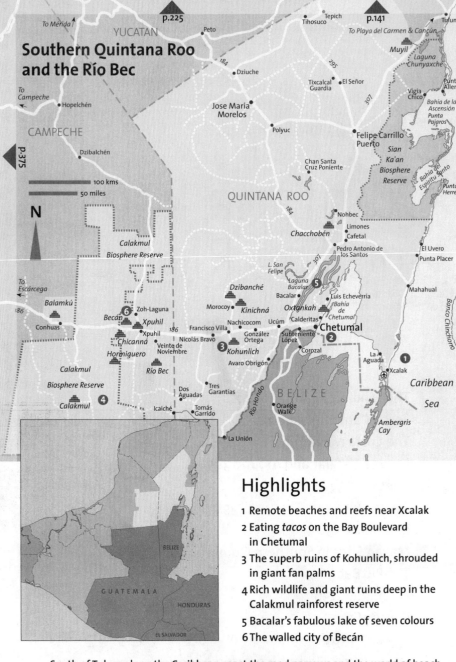

p.225
p.141
p.375

Southern Quintana Roo and the Río Bec

To Mérida
YUCATAN
To Playa del Carmen & Cancún
Tihosuco
Tepich
Peto
Tulum
Muyil
Laguna Chunyaxche
Dziuche
184
295
Tixcalcal Guardia
El Señor
307
Vigia Chico
Punta Allen
To Campeche
Hopelchén
Jose Maria Morelos
Bahía de la Ascensión
Punta Pajaros
CAMPECHE
Polyuc
Felipe Carrillo Puerto
Sian Ka'an Biosphere Reserve
Bahía del Espíritu Santo
Punta Herrero
Dzibalchén
Chan Santa Cruz Poniente
100 kms
50 miles
QUINTANA ROO
N
184
Nohbec
Limones
Cafetal
El Uvero
Punta Placer
Calakmul Biosphere Reserve
Chacchobén
Pedro Antonio de los Santos
307
To Escárcega
L. San Felipe
Laguna Bacalar
5
Mahahual
Balamkú
186
Dzibanché
Bacalar
Luis Echeverría
Banco Chinchorro
Conhuas
Becán
6
Zoh-Laguna
Xpuhil
Morocoy
Kinichná
Oxtankah
Bahía de Chetumal
Xpuhil
Francisco Villa
Nachicocom
Ucúm
Calderitas
Chetumal
Chicanná
186
Nicolás Bravo
González Ortega
Subteniente López
2
Hormiguero
Veinte de Noviembre
3
Kohunlich
Corozal
La Aguada
1
Calakmul
Río Bec
Avaro Obrigón
Xcalak
Biosphere Reserve
Dos Aguadas
Tres Garantías
BELIZE
Caribbean Sea
Calakmul
4
Icaiché
Tomás Garrido
Orange Walk
Río Hondo
La Unión
Ambergris Cay

BELIZE
GUATEMALA
HONDURAS
EL SALVADOR

Highlights

1 Remote beaches and reefs near Xcalak
2 Eating *tacos* on the Bay Boulevard in Chetumal
3 The superb ruins of Kohunlich, shrouded in giant fan palms
4 Rich wildlife and giant ruins deep in the Calakmul rainforest reserve
5 Bacalar's fabulous lake of seven colours
6 The walled city of Becán

South of Tulum along the Caribbean coast the road narrows and the world of beach bars, dive shops and holiday hotels comes, for the moment, to a pretty abrupt end. Highway 307 is pushed away from the coast by the great expanse of forest and lagoon that is the Sian Ka'an reserve; the population thins out drastically. Inland, the roads span huge distances through uninterrupted, lush forest between tiny villages, the domain of birds and butterflies. On the coast, despite the inevitable momentum toward development, there are still long miles of empty beaches and palm groves, between a few far-away *cabañas* and lost villages that once gave refuge to pirates.

The southern part of Quintana Roo – officially part of Yucatán until 1901, and a full state only since 1974 – was until recently one of the least-visited regions in the whole of Mexico. The Spaniards built only one major outpost here, a fort on the magnificent lake of Bacalar. In the 1850s, following the Caste War, this was the wilderness into which the undefeated Maya who followed the 'Talking Cross' retreated, establishing an independent community centred on Chan Santa Cruz (now Felipe Carrillo Puerto), which placed the whole area outside Mexican sovereignty for 50 years. They were only definitively incorporated into Mexico in 1930. Even today the state capital Chetumal still has something of a frontier-town look.

And yet, belying its isolation in modern times, in the Classic era of Mesoamerica this region was one of the major centres of Mayan culture. Not far from Chetumal there are the remains of major Mayan cities, such as Kohunlich. Further west they connect with the string of distinctive sites in the Río Bec area and Calakmul, one of the 'superpowers' of the Classic Maya world. Much later, at the time of the Conquest, the Mayan lordship of Chetumal was where Gonzalo Guerrero, the shipwrecked Spanish sailor seen as the father of the first *mestizo*, rose to lead Mayan warriors into battle against his former comrades.

Until the late 1990s the Mayan sites of this area were largely known only to archae-ologists, and its palm-and-white-sand beaches only to dedicated fishermen, divers and refugees from modern life who wandered down, found a few huts by a beach and settled in. People came to find what was getting into short supply further north: towns unaffected by tourism, scarcely known beach villages and great expanses of intact rainforest; Calakmul is the largest rainforest reserve in the Americas outside the Amazon. Change has come, in that since 1990 much more has been discovered about the region's Mayan sites than in the whole of the previous century, completely transforming estimates of the area's ancient importance. As well as Calakmul, sites such as Kohunlich, looming up out of thick jungle, can be a revelation, conveying a great sense of human habitation. Secondly, plans are afoot to open up the coast, now dubbed the 'Costa Maya'. As usual on the Mexican Caribbean, all kinds of schemes are tossed around of all different sizes and what the future may bring is an open question. For the moment, though, big projects are far more often heard about than seen. It remains a place for travellers who are prepared to explore and lose them-selves unhurriedly, amid a still intact atmosphere of sleepy, beachcomber isolation.

The Land of the Talking Cross

Three roads lead into southern Quintana Roo from the north: Highway 307 from Tulum, the 295 south from Valladolid and the little-used Highway 184 from Ticul via Peto. All three meet at Felipe Carrillo Puerto. Signs by the roadside warn drivers '*Cuida su vida, no se distraiga*' ('Look after your own life, don't get distracted'), and they're not kidding: the empty forest becomes a great green blur, and the combination of tree after tree, dead-straight road and sweaty heat is hypnotic. If you travel these roads between March and June, you're likely to be prodded out of your torpor by thousands of tiny white butterflies, splattering against windscreens like bullets.

If the country around Carrillo Puerto was where the rebel Maya carved out a place for themselves at the end of the Caste War, the region south of Valladolid is where the great conflagration actually began. Thirty-nine kilometres from Valladolid is **Tepich**, where the Caste War 'officially' started on 30 July 1847, while 15 kilometres beyond is the extraordinary village of **Tihosuco**. Towering up on one side of its baking hot plaza is the shell of a fire-blackened Franciscan church. Beside it, a street of Spanish colonial houses show the remains of grille windows and stucco mouldings, also blackened and roofless. It looks like 20th-century bomb damage, but this destruction, untouched and unrepaired today, was carried out during the Caste War, between 1849 and 1865.

Tihosuco was a substantial town under Spanish rule and in the first years of inde-pendence, with wealthy *ladino* planters. It was also the home of Jacinto Pat, *batab* of the local Maya and greatest of the leaders of the Caste War. Once the revolt began the town was taken quickly by the Maya, with little fighting; then, as the Maya retreated, it was reoccupied by the Yucatán army at the end of 1848. Tihosuco became the main base of the *ladino* armies in their efforts to advance against the followers of the Cross, and just as important a target for Mayan raids out of the forest. It was fought over time and again until, after a ferocious siege by the Cruzob in 1865, it was decided in Mérida that Tihosuco was not worth keeping, and the town was left deserted. It was only resettled after 1930. The 'new' village is completely Maya, and something of a memorial to Jacinto Pat: a statue of him, machete in hand, stands in the plaza.

This remote village is also the site of the **Museo de la Guerra de las Castas** (*officially open Tues–Sun 10–6; adm*), the only official museum dedicated to the conflict, just off the plaza. Although it was set up under state auspices, it's also a community project; if (as happens) it's not open when you arrive, ask any passer-by and great efforts will probably be made to find the key.

Felipe Carrillo Puerto

Eighty kilometres from Tihosuco, 95 from Tulum, is Felipe Carrillo Puerto. Official centre of the 'Zona Maya' of Quintana Roo, it is for the most part a nondescript town, with recent concrete buildings taking up most of the centre, fading into *na* huts like any Mayan village. For many travellers it's just a fuel stop between Chetumal and Tulum. It is, though, unique, for as Chan Santa Cruz this town was 'capital' of the last independent Maya semi-state in Mexico, called the **Cruzob** or Followers of the Cross.

History

José María Barrera, renegade *mestizo* leader of one of the Mayan bands wandering in the forest after the main Caste War, first announced that he had found a Cross by a *cenote* that spoke and offered leadership to the Maya in late 1850. He was then at

Xoccén, not far from Valladolid. Pursued by *ladino* troops, he retreated south to a still more remote place in the forest, and by May 1851 the 'Sanctuary of the Cross' was established next to the small *cenote* where it is today, in Chan Santa Cruz ('Little Holy Cross'). The Cross spoke only through its Mayan 'secretaries', the most important of whom was Juan de la Cruz Puc. The cross is of course a Christian symbol, but to the Maya it could equally represent the *wakah-kan*, the world tree, and Cruzob crosses, painted bright colours and surrounded by flowers, are very Mayan.

The Cross was first kept in a hut called the *Gloria*. Its messages told the Maya that their cause was righteous, and that if they followed the instructions of the Cross and kept themselves ready for war they would one day be victorious. Yucatecan troops who marched down to Chan Santa Cruz delighted in uncovering the chamber at the back of the *Gloria* from which the 'secretaries' supposedly performed their ventriloquist act. This, though, did nothing to stop the growth in the cult's popularity among the Maya, for hundreds of rebel bands converged on Chan Santa Cruz, and in 1852 the Cruzob launched a new offensive that sent a wave of fear rippling through Yucatán.

Getting Around

Highway 307 runs straight through Felipe Carrillo Puerto. Even numbered streets go north–south, odd east–west. It has the only real **fuel stations** between Valladolid or Tulum and Chetumal, one on the 307 north of town, another in the centre a block south of the junction with the Valladolid and Peto roads.

The **bus station** is on the plaza, by the town hall. Around 12 first-class buses each way between Cancún and Chetumal (via Tulum and Playa del Carmen) stop here daily, and many more second-class. Four *intermedio* and 10 second-class stop on the route to/from Mérida via Peto and Ticul, and there are two second-class daily to Valladolid via Tihosuco, which in the opposite way go on to Chetumal.

Tourist Information

Felipe Carrillo Puerto t (983–)
Banks: There's a Bital with ATM in the middle of town next to the 'old' petrol station.
Internet Access: In the cinema, on the plaza.
Post Office: North of the plaza on C/ 69.

Where to Stay

Felipe Carrillo Puerto t (983–)
Hotel Esquivel, C/ 65 no. 746, x 66 & 68, t 834 0344 (*inexpensive–cheap*). The most attractive in town, on the south of the plaza (main entrance around the back). Airy rooms have been recently renovated with a bright paint job (a/c *inexpensive*, fan-only *cheap*) and it has a very pretty garden patio.
Hotel-Restaurante El Faisán y el Venado, Av. Juárez 781, t 834 0702 (*inexpensive*). The biggest hotel, opposite the petrol station, with big, functional rooms.
Hotel San Ignacio, Av. Juárez 761, t 834 0122 (*inexpensive*). Decent choice on the highway a block south of the *gasolinera*, with bright, clean rooms and extras such as a/c and TV.

Eating Out

Next to that hub of town life, the old petrol station, there is a line of *loncherías* and *taco*-stands, for very cheap meals and fresh juices.
Hotel-Restaurante El Faisán y el Venado, Av. Juárez 781, x 69 (*moderate*). Big restaurant providing good breakfasts, snacks and a wide choice of Yucatecan and Mexican dishes; unhurriedly, like most places in Carrillo Puerto.
Parrilla Galerías, C/ 65-Plaza Principal (*moderate*). In the shady arcades on the plaza and next to the Hotel Esquivel, the most charming place to eat in the town, with good grilled meats.
Restaurante Mirador Maya, Av. Juárez, x 69 (*moderate*). Pleasant, semi-open-air eatery beneath the obligatory big palm *palapa*, on the same junction as the Faisán y el Venado.

The Adventures of Plumridge and Twigge

The Cruzob 'state' enjoyed a special, up-and-down relationship with Belize, then British Honduras. The British colony was an essential source of weapons, bought from traders and planters along the frontier and paid for with loot plundered from Yucatecan towns. The colonial governors in Belize City did not take part in this trade but did very little to stop it, thus convincing white Yucatecans of how truly perfidious Albion could be. The Cruzob, though, often made difficult neighbours. In 1861, after the Maya had been stealing cattle in British Honduras, the colony's Superintendent sent two army lieutenants, with the marvellous names Plumridge and Twigge, into the lion's den with a letter warning the Cruzob they were pushing the British Empire too far. They were also instructed not to put up with any nonsense about talking crosses, but to find the Indians' chief and talk to him. Once across the Río Hondo, and not knowing any Yucatec, they hired an interpreter, a *ladino* gun-runner called José María Trejo. The intrepid pair then presented themselves to the nearest Mayan chief, but were abused and obstructed at every turn, and took a week to get from Bacalar to Chan Santa Cruz. Taken before the current *Tatich*, the fearsome Venancio Puc, they presented their letter. Puc said he couldn't decide anything as they would have to talk to God. Plumridge and Twigge were stripped of their swords, and locked up.

At midnight they were led out through a huge crowd to the Balam Na, packed with Maya chanting in prayer. They were forced to their knees, until 'a rather weak voice', as Plumridge described it, was heard from nowhere, the Cross. It told them the letter was insulting, and that if the English wanted a fight with the Cross they could have it, and the first victims would be Plumridge and Twigge. The pair attempted to negotiate. Trejo, in fear of his life and clearly thinking his employers were missing something, decided to ignore what they were saying and told the Cross the letter meant nothing and they had really come to arrange trade. In that case, replied the Cross, the Cruzob wanted 1,000 barrels of gunpowder. Certainly, said Trejo.

The lieutenants were not at all grateful for his initiative. Moreover, they were not able to leave immediately, for Tatich Puc announced that he wanted to celebrate the 'deal' with a *fiesta*. When he saw that his guests weren't joining in the party spirit, he told Trejo that if they insulted his hospitality they were dead men. They were obliged to drink and eat until they vomited, and the three-day binge ended with Plumridge and Twigge hugging the Tatich and joining in drunken singing and dancing, sending their hosts into hysterics. When the two ragged lieutenants got back to Belize City, the Superintendent was not impressed, and their humiliation was recorded in detail by a board of enquiry. The Cruzob never got their barrels of gunpowder, but neither did they ever reply to demands for an apology for having mistreated British officers.

In Chan Santa Cruz the Cruzob established their own system of religious and political authority, mixing Catholicism, the village hierarchies of colonial Yucatán and older Mayan traditions. This gave them a cohesion that enabled them to survive the death of Barrera, in 1852, and many typically Mayan squabbles between different leaders. The most important figure was the 'Patron of the Cross', also known as the *Tatich* or *Nohoch Tata* ('Great Father'), originally Barrera, followed by the *Tata Polin* or

'Interpreter of the Cross', through whom the Cross spoke. Holders of these posts seem to have been chosen by concensus among the community's leaders, a little as in the old Mayan *multepal*. Another element was military organization, for an essential feature of Cruzob society was that they were permanently on a war footing, and all men had to take their turn in 'standing guard' over the Cross. Chief in the military hierarchy were the *Tata Chikiuc*, or General, and the *Tata Nohoch Zul* or 'Great Father Spy', who gathered information for raids deep into pacified Yucatán. These raids won the Cruzob booty and prisoners to be used as slaves; they grew most of their own food, and could trade with British Honduras for anything else they needed. In 1857 they took Bacalar, the only remaining *ladino* outpost south of Tihosuco. The Cruzob built a town around the Sanctuary of the Cross, and also in 1857 added a solid, church-like temple, the *Balam Na*. The Cross was moved to it as the focus of Cruzob rituals, another mix of ancestral Mayan tradition and a little Catholicism.

After the abandonment of Tihosuco by the Mexican army in 1866 the Cruzob were left virtually undisturbed in their control of a huge area almost from Valladolid to the Belize border. Over time, though, epidemics, crop crises, internal feuds and the non-appearance of the long-promised final victory led to a crisis in morale and numbers. In 1887 Tatich Aniceto Dzul tried to secure the community's future by asking to be admitted to the British Empire, but didn't get a reply. The death-knell for the Cruzob came with the Spencer-Mariscal treaty between Britain and Mexico of 1895. The British Honduras frontier was closed to them by 1898, and in 1901 General Ignacio Bravo took Chan Santa Cruz. The Maya fled into the forest – fortunately for them, as Bravo had intended to 'extinguish' them completely. In 1915 the Revolutionary General Salvador Alvarado ordered that the Maya should again be left to themselves, but not many returned to Chan Santa Cruz, which they considered 'defiled'. In the 1920s problems arose between the remaining Cruzob and incoming *chicle* tappers, which led some leaders of the Cross to feel they would be better protected by reaching a settlement with the Mexican state. This finally came about in 1930. The town was renamed after the Yucatecan socialist leader Carrillo Puerto, as a new beginning.

This was not the end of the Cruzob, though, for many did not accept the 1930 agreement. North of Felipe Carrillo Puerto there are villages – especially **Señor** and **Tixcacal Guardia** – that are still inhabited by followers of the Cross, who 'mount guard' over their shrines, reject all Mexican authorities and wait for their land to be returned to them. They are not hostile to foreigners, but have proved impermeable to occasional attempts to get them to act cute and perform their odd customs for tourists.

The Balam Na and the Sanctuary

Modern Felipe Carrillo Puerto is a ramshackle little place. Its busiest centre nowadays is a road junction, the meeting of Highway 307 (called Av. Juárez, or C/ 70, in town) and the Valladolid and Peto roads (C/ 71). Along 307 there is the vital *gasolinera* and a scattering of hotels, restaurants, *taco*-stands and rough-and-ready little shops. Half the people who go along the road just seem to be passing through.

If you walk one block west from the highway along C/ 67 you enter the main plaza, as laid out by the Cruzob in the 1850s. Today it's one of the most unusual of Yucatán town squares, surrounded by a complete range of buildings – from modern blocks to arcades and wooden verandahs. Look east and the view is dominated by the **Balam Na** ('Jaguar House'), the last pre-Hispanic pagan temple built in the Americas. As soon as you see it, it's clear that by the time they built it the Maya had lost all contact with their own architectural traditions after long domination by those of the Catholic church. It bears no relation to any pre-Columbian Mayan building, but instead is a massive, upright, round-roofed single-nave temple, as solid as an early Franciscan monastery, but without towers or belfry. Abandoned for years, the Balam Na was taken over as an official Catholic church in 1948, but only by an American/Irish order, because the local Maya would not accept Mexican priests.

Next to the Balam Na, a cloister-like building is now the **Centro de Cultura**. Little else of the buildings erected by the Cruzob survives. The modern town hall, facing the Balam Na, occupies the site of the *Chikinik*, residence of the *Tatich*, once an impressive building with arcades.

Go north from the plaza up C/ 66, however, turn left at the post office and walk four blocks along C/ 69 and you will reach the **Sanctuario de la Cruz Parlante**, the sacred *cenote* where the Cross was kept in Chan Santa Cruz. It's in a small, shady park, with a few huts that contain a small museum on the town's unique history. The Sanctuary is very like a missionary *capilla abierta*, an open altar, with just one massive wall with a round niche to contain the Cross, now just painted on. People still place flowers there, and the stones in front of the altar are blackened by the burning of recent offerings. Ceremonies are held here on 3 May, the day of the Holy Cross.

The Costa Maya

From Felipe Carrillo Puerto Highway 307 runs on south through trees and more trees, and villages with big *topes* where a few women and kids are always waiting patiently for someone to buy their *tortillas* and peeled fruit. Some 70 kilometres from Felipe Carrillo Puerto you reach a larger village, **Limones**. About 15 kilometres to the west (but actually easier to find via the village of Lázaro Cárdenas on the Mérida road, which turns off 307 18 kilometres further south) there is a recently excavated Mayan site at **Chacchobén** (*open daily 8–5; adm, Sun adm free*). Its central core consists of five large building-platforms arranged around an acropolis-platform, mostly dating from the Late Classic between AD 500 and 700; it is believed to have been a subordinate community of one of the great Petén cities, such as Calakmul.

About six kilometres south of Limones a sign points east to Mahahual, 56 kilometres away on the coast. Until about 1996 the coastline either side of it was known only to adventurous souls who were willing to bounce for hours over dirt tracks or, better still, came upon it by boat. Those in the know prized it as one of the undiscovered paradises of the Caribbean. Offshore is the fabulous reef of **Banco Chinchorro**. On land, there are bonefish lagoons, mangrove creeks full of ibis and blue heron that are completely unused to human presence, and miles of empty white beach still rimmed by lush, dense palms.

Getting Around

There are persistent plans for a ferry to Xcalak from Chetumal, but none has gone into permanent operation.

By Air

Xcalak has an **airstrip**, and one is being built at Mahahual, but so far there are no scheduled services. Private air-taxi trips are available from Aerosaab in Playa del Carmen (*see* p.192).

By Bus

There are two second-class **buses** daily from Chetumal to Mahahual and Xcalak, at 6am and 3.15pm, and several more *colectivos*; return buses usually leave Xcalak at 5am and 2pm.

By Car

Since 1998 a paved road has made it possible to get all the way from Chetumal to Xcalak in about 3hrs, and the stretch between Bacalar and Mahahual has also been significantly upgraded. There is, however, still no petrol/gas station closer than Carrillo Puerto or Chetumal, so you're dependent on village fuel sellers in Mahahual and Xcalak. The road meets the sea at Mahahual: outside it there is a fork northwards to Uvero, while another road turns south, running inland, to Xcalak.

Tourist Information

The Costa Maya **t** (983–)

As well as its beaches, another claim to fame of this coast, when it was just remote, has been as a drugs transhipment area, and there are military checkpoints outside Mahahual and on the Xcalak road. Keep your passports with you.

The Internet is usually the best way to make bookings here, given the problems with local phones. A range of information on hotels and other facilities can be found on *www.xcalak-info.com* and *www.bill-in-tulsa.com/xcalak*.
Internet Access: Check your e-mail at **Xcalak Properties**, in a hut by Hotel Caracol, Xcalak.

Sports and Activities

Scuba Diving, Snorkelling and Fishing

Aventuras XTC, by the beach road, north side of Xcalak village, t 831 0461, *www.xcalak.com.mx*. The only fully-equipped independent dive centre on this coast, run by two young Americans, Eric Adamson and Scott Brown, with an expert knowledge of the area. They offer good value scuba trips to Chinchorro or easier waters closer to shore, and also snorkelling trips, river and bird-watching tours, and fishing trips.

Chinchorro Charlie's, Ctra Mahahual–Xcalak Km8, on the beach road south of Mahahual. Two experienced local fishermen offer snorkelling and fishing trips to the inshore reefs or further out, all equipment included. Trips can also be arranged from Xcalak to San Pedro on **Ambergris Cay** in Belize, a short boat ride away.

Where to Stay and Eat

The Costa Maya **t** (983–)

Services along this coast have come slowly. People who have set up hotels here have had to make a considerable investment – their own electricity, water, etc. – and *cabañas* are pricier than you might expect. Electricity is often available only part of the day.

Undiscovered paradises, of course, are no longer undiscovered once they appear in guide books, any more than they are once investors notice that white-sand Caribbean beaches extend south of Sian Ka'an as well as to the north of it. The label 'Costa Maya' was thought up for this coast in around '96, and since then more effort has been put into improving communications than at any time in history. Talk, though, is always big in the tourism world, and those projects that have taken shape so far (that phrase again) are an odd collection: a few sleek, new facilities have popped up, but a little further on there are *cabañas*-clusters and small hotels motivated by a desire to get as

North of Mahahual

Sol y Mar, t (in Chetumal) 832 0535 (*moderate–inexpensive*). About 3km north of Mahahual, this Mexican-owned *cabaña*-style hotel and **restaurant** has a magnificent beach all to itself. You can have the whole place to yourself too, outside winter or Mexican holidays, but even so the caretaker will open up a beach *cabaña* for you (take food, as the restaurant may be closed). More seclusion is hard to imagine. Rooms in the main building are *inexpensive*, *cabañas* cost a little more; there's also camping and RV space. Diving, snorkelling and fishing trips (especially fly fishing) can be arranged, or *lanchas* to take you to still emptier beaches for the day.

The track off the road at **Río Indio** forks to lead to two simple places by the beach:

Cabañas Río Indio (*cheap*). There are very basic palm-roofed cabins, with no electricity and shared showers, and also camping space.

Restaurante Río Indio (*cheap*). Straightforward beachside restaurant, also with a camp site.

Mahahual

Fiesta Americana-Explorean Costa Maya, Punta Herradura, Ctra Mahahual–Xcalak Km14.5, **t** via Mexico City 5201 8333, *www.fiestamexico.com* (*luxury*). This *cabaña*-hotel is run by Fiesta Americana in line with their 'soft adventure' concept, combining all sorts of luxurious comforts (superb pools, fine **restaurants**) with all sorts of activities (jungle treks, diving, *cenote* tours, kayaking). In a very isolated setting between Mahahual and Xcalak, it's an all-inclusive; packages are available combining both this hotel and its sister Explorean near Kohunlich (*see* p.357).

Maya-Ha, Ctra Mahahual–Xcalak Km10, **t** (USA) 877 443 1600, or **t** 512 443 2977, *www.mayaharesort.com* (*luxury*). Very comfortable,

self-contained but modestly sized resort complex, run on an all-inclusive basis; the architecture is slightly camp neo-Mayan, but it has a fine pool, a good **restaurant** and its own beach, and the staff create a friendly atmosphere. Diving off Chinchorro is a speciality, with expert dive-masters on hand and good value dive packages; non-divers are also welcome. Many other activities are available, such as snorkelling, kayaking or swimming on Lake Bacalar, *cenote* visits, trips to Kohunlich and other Mayan ruins.

Susie's Place, Ctra Mahahual–Xcalak Km6.5, *www.SusiesPlaceMexico.com* (*moderate*). Centre of Mahahual's hanging-out-at-the-beach scene, a **beachbar-restaurant** run in friendly style by American Susie, who offers camping space (*cheap*) and is fitting out six rooms in the same building (*inexpensive*). Diving and fishing trips are specialities.

El Castillo, Ctra Mahahual–Xcalak Km11, **t** 831 5292, **f** 831 4396 (*moderate–inexpensive*). Solid little hotel in the middle of nowhere, with four very attractive rooms in the main building, with dazzling views, and three cheaper but comfortable *cabañas* outside. There's a **restaurant** with delicious fresh fish (*moderate*), and the beach is one of the best on this coast. Fishing can be arranged.

Hotel Mahahual Caribe, Mahahual, **t** 832 8111 (*inexpensive*). Main hotel in the village itself, brightly painted and with quite comfortable rooms, most facing the sea. Power runs 7pm–midnight; ask about hiring a boat for cheap fishing or snorkelling trips.

Cabañas del Doctor, Ctra Mahahual–Xcalak Km1.5 (*cheap*). Basic but good value cabins on the beach: some have electricity, and five two-bed cabins have showers, while one-beds share showers and are cheaper. You can also camp or sling a hammock ($3) and rent

far away from big-scale tourism as possible. Some of the loveliest places are still only accessible by bumpy dirt track. In between them, long stretches of this 130 kilometres of coast still feel distinctly remote, its peace and beauty impenetrable.

Mahahual and Around

The road across from the main highway traverses another very empty stretch of scrub, until you finally reach the coast at Mahahual (Majahual), now the main centre of the 'Costa Maya' and the most contradictory place of all. Mostly it is still a small, snorkels or bikes. A breakfast **café** is open in peak season, when prices may go up slightly.

Casa del Mar, Ctra Mahahual–Xcalak Km11.5 (*cheap*). A mellow little café on the beach track next to the *Cabañas del Doctor* run by a young German family, who've come here to escape the city. Popular for breakfast, with healthy vegetarian platters. *Closed eves.*

Xcalak

Costa de Cocos, 3km from Xcalak, **t** 831 0110, *www.costadecocos.com*, or via Turquoise Reef Group, *see* p.139 (*expensive*). Rustically decorated *cabañas* with every comfort, a pretty **bar-restaurant** (*moderate; open to non-residents*) and a fine beach. Room prices include breakfast and dinner. There are dive packages to inshore reefs, but not to Chinchorro; other options are snorkelling and, especially May–July, bone- and fly-fishing.

Casa Carolina, **t** 831 0444, *www.casacarolina .net*, 4km north of Xcalak (*moderate*). Easy going and likeable place, with just four very pretty rooms, all with kitchens, balconies and the sea right outside. The owners, Bob and Caroline, are very friendly, and Bob is a very experienced diver. Diving/fishing packages can be arranged and there are discounts for longer stays.

Marina Mike's, easily found by the beach, **t** 831 0063, *www.xcalak.com* (*moderate*). The best place to stay in Xcalak village itself, this has three suites with kitchenettes, one separate room, and one *palapa* alongside the main building. All are pretty, cool, spacious and comfortable, there's 24-hr electricity, and a lot of attention to detail. A fine bargain.

Playa Sonrisa, 10km from Xcalak, **t** (USA) 529 838 1872, *www.geocities.com/playasonrisa* (*moderate*). One of the longer-established places north of Xcalak – formerly the Villa

Caracol, but it has changed owners – with several comfortable, spacious rooms in a main block or beach-side villas, and a beach-side **bar-restaurant** in a great location. Bikes and kayaks are available for guests, and fishing and diving trips can be arranged.

Sin Duda, 10.9km from Xcalak, **t/f** 831 0006, (USA) **t** 1 888 881 4774, *www.sindudavillas .com* (*moderate*). The most characterful choice on this coast, a labour of love created by Robert Schneider and Margo Reheis. He designed the place himself, and the striking, apartment-like rooms, all different, are full of interesting touches. They're also hugely hospitable, and there's a beautifully sheltered beach. It's a seductive place just to flop, but diving, snorkelling, fishing, ruins visits and bird- and animal-seeking trips with local guides can all be arranged. Very enjoyable, and very reasonably priced.

Tierra Maya, 3.5km from Xcalak, **t** 831 0404, (USA) **t** 1 800 480 4505, *www.tierramaya.net* (*moderate*). Attractive, relaxing and modern with six ample rooms, some with fridges, all with traditional textile furnishings and a sea view. It has its own 24-hr electricity, so a/c is an option. It has a **restaurant**, a great beach terrace, and free use of bikes and kayaks. A full range of dive trips, snorkelling and fishing can be arranged.

Hotel Caracol (no phone, *cheap*). Blockhouse-like, but facing the beach, the community-owned Caracol is the only real budget place in town. Rooms are very plain, and can get very hot, but are only around $10.

Conchitas (*moderate*). The 'star' restaurant in Xcalak village, in a classic fishing-village-style wooden hut. On a good day there's wonderful snapper and conch, and there's always cold beer. There are also a few more basic *loncherías* around the village.

out-of-the-way Mexican fishing village, with a line of palms along the beach, kids playing in the waves, sand covering the road and a few shops and cheap *loncherías*. To the south, along the old beachside sand-and-dirt track to Xcalak, there are clumps of *cabañas*, camp sites and simple restaurants, attracting prospective beachcombers for whom the Tulum *cabañas* have become too crowded. The beach is not as beautiful as Tulum's, and there's more seaweed, but it's good for snorkelling and easy swimming. North of the village, however, a brand-new road leads to a brand-new quay for cruise liners, the **Puerto Costa Maya** (*open only to cruise passengers*), its glossy terminal filled with restaurants and the obligatory souvenir shops so the cruise passengers can be lined up to part with their cash. A mall in the jungle, it's like something out of a J.G. Ballard noveland is the biggest solid product of the Costa Maya development plans.

Alongside this strange new neighbour the rest of Mahahual carries on pretty much regardless for the time being, and at night there's little sound except the lapping of the waves. The road to the north skirts around the cruise terminal to cut back towards the coast and head up to the Sian Ka'an reserve. There are no regular buses on this road. It runs a little inland, amid empty brush and forest, with a few tracks off to the right to isolated camping sites and *cabañas*. At **Río Indio**, nine kilometres up, there's camping space, cabins and a basic restaurant. Beyond there there's nothing, but the road is being improved as far as **Punta Placer** and **El Uvero**, 28 kilometres from Mahahual. The paved road gives out at El Uvero, but a dirt track continues on through wild forest, lagoon and beach to the southern entrance to Sian Ka'an at Tampalam and a tiny settlement at Punta Herrero, over 70 kilometres from Mahahual.

South of Mahahual the old Xcalak sand road continues behind the shore, swerving occasionally to avoid fallen palm trees. Along it there are a few more beach hotels and bars, widely spaced out so they make no impact on each other's mellow isolation. The huge Fiesta Americana Costa Maya all-inclusive interrupts the course of the road; beside it, another dirt road cuts off to meet the new, paved road inland, while just beyond the hotel a track leads off left to go back to the beach road, so that you can carry on along a now neglected, rutted and very empty stretch of track to Xcalak (30km). Unless you're in a 4WD you will get there far quicker with the new road.

Xcalak and Banco Chinchorro

It was the reefs of **Banco Chinchorro**, 20–40 kilometres offshore, that first drew foreigners to Xcalak. Chinchorro consists of a great ring of coral, around 50 kilometres from north to south, with a few small, uninhabited sand and scrub islands. The difficulties of getting there have made them most attractive to experienced divers, but there are shallow-water reefs accessible to novices or snorkellers as well. The great attraction of Chinchorro is the sheer range of dives it offers: tunnels, wall dives, dazzling coral. It also has an extraordinary range of wrecks, from Spanish galleons and pirate ships to modern hulks, numbering over 100.

The paved road into Xcalak comes into the back of the village, while from the beach the old road turns up through the sand and palms back toward Mahahual (it's much less of a trek to reach this end of the dirt road via Xcalak, rather than driving all the way down it from the Fiesta Americana resort). Along the lower 15 kilometres or so of the old road are some of the coast's most enjoyable isolated small beach hotels; for those looking for an empty Caribbean beach in Mexico, this is the best place to go.

Xcalak itself, 55 kilometres from Mahahual, consists of a collection of small wooden houses, a plaza, palm trees, sand streets, a beach, a dazzling sea and one of the best sheltered anchorages in a long distance, where many a Caribbean yachtsman has taken refuge from storms. Its population is around 300, more *mestizo* than Maya, and with a number of resident *gringos*. A while ago Xcalak was expected to be the real big thing along this coast, but with the cruise terminal the focus has shifted to the more accessible Mahahual. As well as the Chinchorro reef, around Xcalak there is great snorkelling and inshore diving, deep-sea fishing for tarpon or snook and inshore bonefishing, and the nearby mangrove islands are alive with birds.

Laguna Bacalar and Around

Along the Highway south of the Mahahual turn the flat forest scrub gives way a little to rolling hills and broader, more open spaces. After a while you begin to glimpse flashes of water through the trees to the left, the Laguna Bacalar. This is the second-largest lake in Mexico, 80 kilometres long, but it's entirely fed by underground rivers. Its postcard name is *Laguna de Siete Colores*, the Lake of Seven Colours; whether that's the right number is up to you, but on any day it can easily run from Prussian blue and deep grey to sandy blue, opal and bright turquoise.

About 15 kilometres south of the Mahahual road is the straggling roadside village of **Pedro Antonio de los Santos** and beyond, the village of **Buenavista**, where roads lead off to lakeside *balnearios* with simple restaurants and landing stages.

Bacalar

From Buenavista, it's 35 kilometres to Bacalar itself, one of the most atmospherically tranquil small towns in the Yucatán, and with the only real castle in the peninsula.

'Salamanca de Bacalar' was founded in 1544 by a group of 28 Spaniards led by Gaspar Pacheco, the first mayor of Mérida, who had marched south from Valladolid to subdue the Mayan lordship of Chetumal. As a colonial town, however, Bacalar failed to develop. Its colonists soon realized they were in one of the least profitable parts of the Yucatán, and the town was gradually abandoned. Spanish interest in the area revived after British pirates established themselves in modern Belize in the 1670s. In 1725 an unusually energetic governor of Yucatán, Antonio de Figueroa, ordered the reoccupation of Bacalar as a bastion of Spanish power in the region. He died of disease in the same campaign, but not before he had ordered the building of Bacalar castle, and brought 700 migrants from the Canary Islands to establish a real colony. In spite of appearances there are channels that make it possible to sail from Lake Bacalar to Chetumal Bay, along an intricate, little-known route known as *El Recorrido de los Piratas* ('The Pirate Run'). As Spanish ships were able to get from the lake out to sea, so the pirates could get in to attack, and the castle saw plenty of action.

After independence Bacalar, still the only *ladino* town in the whole of southern Quintana Roo, led a quiet life until the Caste War, when it was fought over several times. After the Cruzob established themselves in Chan Santa Cruz Bacalar survived for a while, but in 1857 the Cross ordered a mass attack and the town fell to the Maya, with a massacre of *ladino* soldiers and civilians. Bacalar was not reoccupied until 1901.

Modern Bacalar doesn't feel at all like a military strongpost, but seems to gain an extra placidity from the lake. The town is long and thin, strung out along a ridge between the highway and the water with one long main street, **Avenida 7**, with the necessary plaza and town hall in the middle. Along the lake shore below there is a positively genteel boulevard, the Costera Bacalar, from which several rather distinguished houses look out across the water, and at the north end of the lake drive there are *balnearios*, lakeside areas where Mexican families go to swim and have lunch. Several things make swimming here a blissful experience: the cavern-fed water is crystal-clear, soft to the skin and wonderfully refreshing, the shallowness of the lake keeps it at a balmy temperature, the absence of current makes the waters very gentle. The view is exquisite. Some of the *balnearios* rent out kayaks, or run boat trips.

The castle, the **Fuerte de San Felipe de Bacalar**, is on the ridge above the lake-shore drive. It's an impressively squat and solid piece of 18th-century military engineering, with four massive bastions called, in Spanish fashion, after saints: San José, San Antonio, Santa Ana and San Joaquín. Around the walls there are several old cannon, once used against the pirates. Inside the castle is a local **museum** (*open Tues–Sun 10–6; closed Mon; adm*), with informative exhibits (in Spanish) and charming staff.

Getting Around and

Bacalar t (983–)

Highway 307 skirts around Bacalar town in a loop to the west; there are turn-offs to the centre and the lake at the north and south ends. There is no regular *gasolinera* in Bacalar. Ask around to find out whether any shopkeepers in town, if any, are selling fuel.

Second-class and *intermedio* buses on the Chetumal–Cancún route stop at Bacalar. There are frequent *combis* from Chetumal. Buses leave the main road and stop inside the town.

Internet Access: Bacalar does have an Internet shop, **Nave de Papel**, but it's hard to find; ask for the *centro Internet*.

Where to Stay

Bacalar t (983–)

Along the Costera in Bacalar there are often signs offering rooms to rent.

Rancho Encantado, 3km north of the town, t 831 0037, (USA/Canada) t 1 800 505 MAYA, www.encantado.com (*luxury*). Top of the line on Lake Bacalar, run by Ray Star, with upscale *cabañas* in a fabulous location in a lakeside tropical garden. A family villa is available, and there's an equally striking **restaurant**. Retreat groups, yoga courses, massages etc. are a speciality, as is a big range of trips including some to little known Mayan sites. Peak prices, though, are high

($150, standard cabin), even if they include breakfast and dinner; off season rates are *moderate*, but don't include meals.

Amigo's B&B, t in Cozumel (987) 872 3868, www.bacalar.net (*inexpensive*). Opened in 2001, this guest house on the Costera in Bacalar (about ½km south of the castle) has three attractive rooms with double beds, a/c and fans, very comfortable fittings and balconies with lake views. Prices are near *moderate*, but breakfast and the use of a nice lounge and TV room are included. Boats and kayaks can be rented, and tours organized to archaeological sites. The owners also have a guest house of the same name on Cozumel (*see* p.179).

Hotel Laguna, Av. Bugambilias 316, t 834 2206, f 834 2205 (*inexpensive*). One of the great hotels of the Yucatán, the Laguna sums up the combination of remoteness and tranquillity that is the prime appeal of Bacalar. It's also slighty nuts, in a very Mexican sort of way. On the lakeshore road just by the south turn off Highway 307 (it has a great hand-painted sign of a girl water-skiiing), it's hard to miss. In white and pastel Art Deco, it is arranged up a bluff between flower beds, as if it should be somewhere on the south coast of England; then, by the pool there's a chapel with an image of Christ, and lots of coloured glass. The rooms are a bit worn but comfortable, the **restaurant** has good local classics, and you get superb sunrises.

Puerta del Cielo, between Rancho Encantado and Bacalar town, t/f 837 0413 (*inexpensive*).

Cenote Azul and Xul-Ha

Just south of the Hotel Laguna at the southern end of the town a sign indicates the entrance and car park to the **Cenote Azul**. This is one of the very largest of the Yucatán *cenotes*, a giant green pit with water 90m deep. On weekdays there's hardly anyone around, but at weekends it's crowded with people from Chetumal out for the day, and teenage boys jumping into the water from the cliff-like edges. Another 12 kilometres or so further on, past El Paraíso, is **Xul-Ha**, not long before Highway 307 meets the 186 from Escárcega, where there's one last turn-off to the lake, down a bumpy road that ends on a bluff above the water, with a small *balneario*.

A few kilometres south of Bacalar town you pass the most regrettable innovation in this area, the site that is supposedly going to hold the 'Club Las Velas Bacalar'. Due to be an all-inclusive resort complex complete with golf course, it is laughingly billed as an 'Ecological Resort', but building proceeds at a pace that would embarrass a snail.

Pleasant, well-run hotel, offering big, comfortable rooms and two family-size suites arranged up the lakeside ridge, with fans or a/c and all with a lake view. It has its own landing stage and beach, with boats for rent, and an airily attractive **restaurant**. **Laguna Azul**, Pedro Antonio de los Santos, f 834 2035, *ecotrekpam25@hotmail.com* (*inexpensive–cheap*). Just south of Pedro Antonio village there's a ramshackle sign marked Laguna Azul on the east side of 307, above a dirt track. After a very bumpy 3–4km (signs saying 2½ are over-optimistic) you reach the camping and cabins site of Swiss traveller Fritz Vatter. There's camping and hammock-space (very *cheap*), RV hook-ups and also three pleasant cabins (*inexpensive*). Solar electricity panels provide hot-water showers. It's a very tranquil spot, with nothing around you but the forest and the serenity of the lake, and you can rent kayaks for about $10 a day. Insect repellent needed.

El Paraíso/Botadero El Pastor, about 10km south of Bacalar town, t 044 9831 3494, *botadero@yahoo.com/botadero@ecosur.com.mx* (*cheap*). Between the Km11 and Km10 markers on Highway 307 (which number from the south), look for signs on the lakeside of the road saying El Paraíso and/or Botadero San Pastor (easy to miss, but *combi* drivers should know it). This track leads in 1–2km to a magical spot on the lake, where the Martínez family have turned an old *chicle*-tappers camp into a small-scale ecotourism project and camp site. Activities in train include a project to cultivate 22 varieties of orchids; campers can help, but don't have to. You can sleep in one of their tents or hammocks, under *palapas*, or bring your own; free use of kitchen and kayaks is included. It's possible to arrange (with a little patience) guided kayak tours, such as an all-day lake tour, or a 3–4 day camping trip through the *Recorrido de los Piratas*, the pirate route to Chetumal Bay. Guided forest walks are also possible. Even if you do nothing but sit and swim, it's an utterly beautiful place, and the response of many visitors has been ecstatic. Bug repellent needed again.

Eating Out

The lakeside *balnearios* are great for lunch, offering mostly grilled seafood and fish, some of it from the lake: the best is the biggest, the **Balneario Ejidal** itself (*moderate–cheap*), with wonderful *ceviches* and a fine place from which to watch everybody swimming. **Rancho Encantado** (*expensive*) has more sophisticated (but not necessarily better) Mexican and international dishes, with vegetarian choices, and the restaurants at **Puerta del Cielo** and **Hotel Laguna** have lake views and good Yucatecan dishes (*moderate*).

At the Cenote Azul there is the **Restaurante Cenote Azul** (*moderate*), a big, traditional restaurant beneath a *palapa*, right at the top of the *cenote*.

Chetumal

Chetumal, state capital of Quintana Roo, sits beneath fan palms and giant laurel trees on the banks of the Río Hondo, northernmost river on this side of the Yucatán peninsula and the frontier with Belize. It is still the capital even though Cancún is now a great deal bigger and busier. Long isolated from the rest of the country, it is a very Caribbean town, with clapboard houses with painted wooden porches and tin roofs, wide streets, open skies and a very Caribbean pace.

The frontier-town location is an essential aspect of Chetumal. This is where most of Belize comes to shop, and on most days there will be some Belizeans along the main street, from black families talking *patois*-English to very white Mennonites talking old German. To aid border areas in the 1940s the Mexican government gave them a variety of duty-free concessions, and this became the best place in the whole of southern Mexico to find foreign goods at bargain prices: Japanese electronics, American sunglasses, Dutch cheeses. This trading attracted people from many parts of the world, which with the Belizean influence means that this is one of the most ethnically mixed towns in Mexico. It also attracted a cast of eccentrics fit for a lost town by a hot river, from the adventurer-archaeologist Thomas Gann in the 1930s to an aristocratic English lady who befriended everybody in town. Modern Chetumal has a very good museum of Mayan culture, but its greatest attraction is its amiable atmosphere, its ultra-laid-back air. It makes a great base for visiting the whole region.

History

Chetumal is one of the nicest towns founded on a drunken afternoon. In 1898 the Mexican navy, aided by the newly cooperative authorities of British Honduras, towed an armoured barge, named the *Chetumal*, into the Río Hondo. Commanded by Commandant Othon P. Blanco, its mission was to re-establish Mexican sovereignty on the border. After making a few forays on to land and not finding much resistance, his men built a small stockade. Corozal in northern Belize was then full of Yucatecan Caste War refugees, who had lived there for years. Part of Blanco's brief was to begin the repopulation of the north bank with Mexican citizens, and for the patriotic holiday of 5 May he invited the most prominent members of the Corozal Yucatecan community and several British officers to lunch aboard the *Chetumal*. After the meal, speeches and several toasts, the party were so inspired by Blanco's rhetoric that it was decided that there and then they should head for land, the British included, and found a new town at the stockade. Originally called **Payo Obispo** (Bishop's Point), the settlement was a broad mix from the very beginning, for its first residents included Mexicans, Belizeans and several German and English wanderers trying their luck.

Blanco sought to deal with the Santa Cruz Maya peacefully, in contrast to his geno-cidal successor General Bravo. Following Bravo's conquest of the Cruzob in 1901 the centre of administration moved to Chan Santa Cruz, but after 1915 it returned to Payo Obispo. In 1936 at the height of Mexico's nationalist 'cultural revolution' its name was changed to Chetumal, like the barge. Both recall the Mayan lordship of *Chetumal* or *Chectemal*, which, aided by Gonzalo Guerrero (*see* pp.64–5), fiercely resisted the

Spaniards in the 1530s and 1540s. However, Mayan Chetumal was probably located at Oxtankah (*see* p.356), or near Corozal in Belize, rather than on the site of today's town.

The most important event in the recent history of Chetumal has been Hurricane Janet, *La Juanita*, which in 1955 devastated the town and destroyed many of its old buildings, to be replaced by standard Mexican concrete. More recently still the town has been hit by a hurricane of another sort in the shape of the NAFTA agreement, under which its duty-free status has been cut back. This has hit Chetumal hard, and tourism is being pushed as one possible solution.

Héroes and the Malecón

The most impressive thing about Avenida de los Héroes, Chetumal's prime thoroughfare, is its extraordinary range of shops with gaudily painted signs, the number of them selling exactly the same thing, and their still more extraordinary amount of

Getting Around

By Air

Chetumal has a small airport, on the west side of town off Av. Obregón. Aerocaribe, **t** 833 0113, has regular flights to Cancún and Mérida, and Aviacsa, **t** 832 7676/832 7787, has flights to Mexico City.

Although only special **airport cabs** may take you from the airport into Chetumal, they're as cheap as ordinary taxis in many towns.

By Bus

Chetumal's main bus station (first- and second-class) is unusually far from the centre, on Av. Insurgentes near the junction with Av. Héroes. From there, you need to take a taxi into town (but they're very cheap). There are **luggage lockers** at the station.

Campeche (7hrs): one first- and two second-class daily via **Escárcega**. First-class fare $20.

Cancún (6hrs): three ADO GL luxury services and at least nine regular first-class daily; 19 *intermedio* or second-class services. Most first-class services and all others stop at **Felipe Carrillo Puerto**, **Tulum** and **Playa del Carmen** (5hrs); one first-class, all *intermedios* and second-class buses stop at **Bacalar** (45mins) First-class fare to Cancún $18.

Guatemala: five first-class daily to **Tikal** (6hrs) and **Flores** (8hrs) via Belize (three continue to **Guatemala City** (22hrs). Fare to Tikal $45.

Mahahual and **Xcalak**: two second-class buses daily, at 6am, 3.15pm. Fare to Xcalak $6.

Mérida (9hrs): four first-class, ten *intermedios* or second-class daily, via Peto and Ticul. First-class fare about $19.

Mexico City (22hrs): three first-class daily. Fare about $70.

Palenque (6¼hrs): five or six first-class daily via **Escárcega**, with Altos (8.15pm, 12 midnight (Sat–Tues only), 2.30am); Cristóbal Colón (9.15pm); Maya de Oro (11pm) or ADO

(1.30am). The 8pm and midnight Altos buses and C. Colón and Maya de Oro continue to **Ocosingo**, **San Cristóbal de Las Casas** (11hrs) and **Tuxtla Gutiérrez** (15hrs); the 2.30am Sat–Tues Altos bus goes from Palenque to **Comitán** and **Tapachula** (18hrs). Fares vary significantly, Altos being cheaper, but more cramped: the range is about $20–$28 Palenque, $29–$42 San Cristóbal.

Tomás Garrido and **Tres Garantías**: three second-class buses daily, and one to **Unión** and the Río Hondo. *Combis* to all these destinations run more frequently (*see* below).

Valladolid: two second-class daily via **Felipe Carrillo Puerto** and **Tihosuco**.

Villahermosa (9hrs): six first-class and one *intermedio* daily via **Escárcega**. Fare $27.

Xpuhil (2hrs): six first-class (**Escárcega** route) and six second-class daily. One second-class continues to **Zoh-Laguna**. First-class fare $7. For all **buses to Belize**, *see* p.356, 'Into Belize'.

Chetumal is unusual in having a *colectivo* **station** (corner of Avenidas Primo de Verdad and Miguel Hidalgo) in the centre, two blocks east of Av. Héroes by the Museo de la Cultura Maya. *Combis* run to virtually every village in the region, especially Bacalar, Luís Echeverría and Chetumal Bay, the Tomás Garrido–Tres Garantías road, and the Río Hondo to Unión. The *combis* that don't fit into the station leave from the streets outside, and some buses to villages nearer the city run from behind the market, at Av. Juárez/Av. Mahatma Gandhi.

By Car and Taxi

Chetumal streets are wide enough to make driving easy, and parking is less restricted than in most Mexican cities. There are *gasolineras* on the main road from the west, on Av. Obregón and Av. Insurgentes. **Taxis** are the main form of local transport. Any ride within Chetumal currently costs all of 7 pesos. Cab drivers also seem to be very honest here.

---

stock. Chetumal caters for all human needs, and does so in bulk. The centre of activity is the **market**, at Héroes and Av. E. Aguilar, a marvellous bazaar of dense alleyways.

As you walk down Héroes towards the bay there's a distinguished building on the right, by Av. Héroes de Chapultepec, the Belisario Domínguez school from 1936–8, a fine example of Revolution-era nationalist-modern architecture with a frieze bravely identifying it as an *Escuela Socialista*. In 1999 this was converted into Chetumal's

Car Hire

There are only three car hire companies, all relatively expensive and with only a few cars between them. It's better to hire in Mérida, Cancún or Playa.

Aventura Maya, Hotel Los Cocos, **t** 832 0544. In the hotel lobby: Fords from $70 a day.

Bacalar Tours, Av. Alvaro Obregón 167-A, **t** 832 3875, *licak@prodigy.net.mx*. Opposite the Hotel Caribe Princess, at the last count this had just two cars, from around $70 a day.

Continental, Holiday Inn, **t** 832 2411, ext 191, *www.holidayinnmaya.com.mx*. In the lobby, this has a wider range, from $50–$60 a day.

Orientation

In its rebuilt, post-Hurricane Janet form, Chetumal is a sprawling town of broad avenues, but the area of most interest is easy to handle. Highway 307 meets Highway 186 from Escárcega and Campeche south of Lake Bacalar 19km from the city, and enters Chetumal from the west. It becomes a broad boulevard, **Av. Insurgentes**, which runs around the north side of town. On this road, just as you enter the city, there is a roundabout-style junction with an exit right, marked *Centro*. This becomes **Av. Alvaro Obregón**, which runs to the centre of town. The main street is **Av. de los Héroes**, which runs back from the river, and crosses Obregón. Héroes also meets the **Malecón** or Boulevard Bahía, the attractive drive which skirts the river bank eastwards.

Tourist Information

Chetumal **t** (983–)

There is an official **tourist information** kiosk on Av. Héroes at the junction with Av. Efraín Aguilar (*officially open daily 9–2 and 6–9*), next to the Holiday Inn and opposite the

market, but it's spectacularly useless. Of more interest are local travel agencies (*see* below).

Banks:There are several near the junction of Av. Héroes and Av. Obregón, with ATMs, and many *cambios* along Av. Héroes specializing in changing Belizean dollars. There is also an exchange desk at the bus station. If you come in from Belize it's a good idea to change any leftover currency in Chetumal.

Consulates: There is a **Guatemalan Consulate** at Av. Héroes de Chapultepec (not the same as Av. Héroes) 356, **t** 832 3045, six blocks west of Av. Héroes by Av. Andrés Quintana Roo. The **Belizean Consulate** is at Av. Alvaro Obregón 226-A, **t** 832 0100, west of Héroes near the corner of Av. Juárez.

Internet Access: Try **Coffeeweb.com**, Av. Juárez 64, near corner of Obregón, and **Cybertec**, on Av. 5 de Mayo between Obregón and Othon P. Blanco, which is very cheap.

Phone Office: There is a long-distance phone office with good rates on Av. Ignacio Zaragoza, corner of Av. Héroes.

Post Office: One block from Av. Héroes, corner of Av. Plutarco Elías Calles and Av. 5 de Mayo (*open Mon–Fri 8–7, Sat 9–1*). **Mexpost** is on Av. Héroes beyond the museum, between Av. Primo de Verdad and Av. Carranza.

Tours

If you don't want to hire a car, agency tours are the easiest way to get to far Mayan sites and other attractions in the area. Bacalar Tours (*see* above, 'By Car') also offers local tours.

Ecoturística Xcalak, C/ 22 de Enero 167, **t** 832 1661, **f** 832 8479 *chuma_so@hotmail.com*. Enterprising agency run by young locals (English-speaking) offering well-priced adventure trips to Bacalar, Kohunlich, Xcalak, Chetumal bay and the Río Hondo; also offers tailor-made itineraries and kayaking.

Viajes Calderitas, Av. Primo de Verdad 121-A, **t** 832 2540, **f** 832 2006. Fairly conventional

official **Centro Cultural de las Bellas Artes** arts centre, which as well as exhibition spaces includes a good **bookshop** and the **Museo de la Ciudad** (*open Tues–Sun 9–7; closed Mon; adm*), an entertaining display on the region's Mayan past and the city's brief modern history.

Post-Janet rebuilding means that most of the rest of Héroes is made up of concrete, but in the streets alongside, especially Av. 5 de Mayo, parallel to Héroes to the left, tours to Kohunlich and the other local Mayan sites; prices are high for individuals, but more economical for groups (up to 10).

Shopping

Shopping in Chetumal is a way of life for the people of Belize, and this could be a place to stock up on cheap goods from the inevitable shoes, to leather goods, cooking pots, bright things in plastic and other Mexicana. If you're planning a picnic, the **food market** is towards the centre and back of the market building on Av. Héroes. Elsewhere, there is a supermarket attached to **El Fenicio** restaurant (*see* below), and the bookshop in the **Centro de Bellas Artes** is good for books on the Maya.

Where to Stay

Chetumal t (983–)

A luxury alternative has appeared in this area with the opening of the **Explorean** 'adventure hotel' near Kohunlich, but rooms are usually on an all-inclusive basis (*see* p.357).

Expensive–Moderate

Holiday Inn, Av. Héroes 171-A, t 832 1100, *www.holidayinnmaya.com.mx* and Holiday Inn reservations. Opposite the museum, this has the same reliable standards as other Holiday Inns, which makes it stand out the more in Chetumal. Prices are high midweek, but as it caters mainly to business guests there are good, *moderate* rates at weekends. Plus the staff are friendly and helpful, the **restaurant** is impressive, and the creature comforts make for a great splurge if you've done some time in sweaty, scratchy places.
Hotel Los Cocos, Av. Héroes 134, t 832 0542, f 832 0920. Two blocks down the hill from the Holiday, this is more characterful but a bit more battered. Its ornate 1960s lobby has been redecorated and is now dazzlingly bright, and its pavement-terrace **restaurant**, El Cocal, is permanently popular; inside, rooms are distributed around a magnificent pool in a palm-filled garden. Rooms and fittings are a little old, but well priced.

Inexpensive

Hotel Caribe Princess, Av. Obregón 168, t/f 832 0900. Very popular with foreigners and centrally located on Obregón by the corner with Av. 5 de Mayo. Its pastel-coloured rooms have seen a fair few years but they're mostly big, airy, light and decently comfortable, and all have phones, TV and good a/c.
Hotel El Dorado, Av. 5 de Mayo 42, t 832 0315, f 832 1441. More eccentric option around the block from the Princess, a 'hotel-piano bar' with a theatrical staircase between pink columns. Rooms with a/c are *inexpensive*, those without are *cheap*: outer rooms are pleasant and bright, but inner rooms costing the same can be gloomy and cell-like.
Hotel Marlon, Av. Juárez 87, t 832 9411, f 832 6555. Large-ish, pink-and-pastel modern hotel that's very central. Facilities (bathrooms, big rooms, TVs) aren't as shiny-new as they seem at first sight, but among its pleasant comforts are a small pool, a bar and a **restaurant**, and it has a nice, quirky appeal.

Cheap

Hotel Big Ben, Av. Héroes 48, t 832 0965. Irresistibly-named basic hotel with very cheap but quite light fan-only rooms, some of which have balconies overlooking Héroes.
Hotel María Dolores, Av. Alvaro Obregón 206, t 832 0508. Backpacker's standby and the best budget choice in the centre, with plain, fan-only rooms that have plenty of mileage on the clock but are well looked-after. It also has a likeable little **restaurant** for breakfast.

there are still many of the old clapboard, porched houses that make parts of Chetumal look very un-Mexican.

Héroes ends in a wide plaza, shaded by massive laurel trees, at the **Malecón** or Bay Boulevard, on the waterfront. In front of you there's a tall clocktower, and beyond that a view across the broad, green Río Hondo to Belize, an unbroken line of trees away in the distance. The largest presence on the plaza is the **Palacio de Gobierno**, the

Posada Pantoja, C/ Lucio Blanco 95, t 832 1781. Unchallenged as the most comfortable budget hotel in Chetumal, the Pantoja has very clean, neat rooms with fans or a/c (just *inexpensive*), good bathrooms, phones and (in many) TVs, and the owners are very obliging. It's some way from the centre, in a residential area (corner of Av. General H. Lara), but this also means it's very peaceful, and it's only a 20-min walk from town.

Villa Juvenil Chetumal, C/ Escuela Naval, corner of Calzada Veracruz, t 832 3465. Chetumal's official youth hostel is a lot more attractive than other Mexican hostels; the rooms have only four beds in each, and as it's rarely full you'll often get one to yourself. Showers are shared, and cheap meals are also available. IYHF cards are not essential, but with them it's even cheaper.

Eating Out

Moderate

Las Arracheras de Don José, Blvd de la Bahía, corner of Av. Othon P. Blanco. One of several restaurants along the bay boulevard where you can sit outside to enjoy the breeze: there are fabulous *fajitas* and Mexican classics with all kinds of trimmings, so you can eat a lot or a little, and pay more or very little, as you wish. Very popular, and very enjoyable.

El Cocal, Hotel Los Cocos, Av. Héroes 134. The big terrace hotel restaurant is a vantage point that's a centre of local life, and the fact that it now has positively over-the-top Las Vegas-junior décor doesn't seem to have harmed its popularity at all. Enjoyable, well-prepared Mexican and Yucatecan dishes are another attraction.

El Fenicio Super & Restaurante, Av. Héroes, corner of Av. I. Zaragoza. Travellers' standby (formerly Las Arcadas), serving Mexican and Yucatecan standards (including sizeable breakfasts) around the clock, and with a 24-hr **supermarket**. Its food, though, is more satisfying than interesting.

Sergio's Pizzas, Av. Obregón 182, t 832 2355. Food is a bargain in Chetumal, and Sergio's (also, inexplicably, known as María's) is its foremost restaurant: a neat, cosy and rather eccentrically smart little haven with stained-glass windows, dark woodwork, charming service and a/c, still at upper-*moderate* prices. You can have pizzas, steaks, or a refined range of Mexican and Yucatecan dishes, especially seafood with tropical seasonings. Excellent for breakfast, too.

Cheap

Cafetería Karla, Av. Carmen Ochoa de Merino 106. Chetumal has good coffee outlets, and standing out from the bunch is this unusual café near the bay boulevard. It's in an old wooden house, with a porch, and exceptionally pretty and peaceful; as well as a range of coffees including liqueur-combinations there are beers, sandwiches, snacks and home-made pastries. *Closed mornings but open late nightly till about 2am.*

Cafetería Los Milagros, Av. I. Zaragoza, just east of Av. Héroes. Another coffee-specialist with a big shady terrace where several of the gents go to play cards and dominoes. They also do bargain breakfasts, with great juices.

La Michoacana, Av. Héroes, near corner of Av. Lázaro Cárdenas. Best for ice-creams and juices in Chetumal.

Restaurant Campeche, Av. Obregón, west of Av. Héroes. A likeable piece of old Chetumal in a picturesque clapboard cabin. The set menus of Yucatecan fare are great value, but don't expect energetic service.

Restaurante Pantoja, Av. Mahatma Gandhi, corner of Av. 16 de Septiembre. Good bargain meals (above all *comida corrida* set lunches).

Quintana Roo state government, an attractive 1950s building with Caribbean-style arcades. At dusk, a welcome breeze comes in off the river, and a large part of the town comes down to meet up and enjoy it in the evening *paseo*. This is also the time to experience not a sight, but one of the sounds of Chetumal, as hundreds of *zanates* and *cauhil* birds roost in the laurels, producing a tropical cacophony that's truly astonishing. A block to the east (left), by Av. 5 de Mayo, a large sign announces the

Maqueta Payo Obispo (*normally open daily 9–6; adm free*). In a curious old clapboard pavilion, this is an engaging scale model of Payo Obispo in the 1920s, made entirely by one elderly local citizen with the very Chetumal name of Luis Reinhardt McLiberty.

The Museo de la Cultura Maya

Open Tues–Sun 9–7; closed Mon; adm. **Guided tours** *in Spanish and English.*

Chetumal's museum of Mayan culture is an impressive, slab-like modern building in the next block from the market at Av. Héroes and Av. Mahatma Gandhi. Opened in 1994, it differs from other museums in the region in that it has very few original Mayan artefacts. Instead, it seeks to present and explain every aspect of Mayan civilization through imaginative modern displays. The layout itself represents the three-level Mayan conception of the universe – the heavens, the physical world and Xibalba – and cosmology, agriculture, glyph writing and other fields are all covered. It's a very enjoyable and enlightening overview of the Mayan world, well labelled in Spanish and English. Besides very efficient air conditioning, the museum also has a **bookshop**, and hosts art and photography **exhibitions** on Mayan and local themes.

Excursions from Chetumal

As a small city Chetumal can still seem dominated by the lush nature around it, the reverse of what happens in most cities. Nearby there are still swathes of primary rainforest and untouched wetlands, some parts of which are at least partly accessible.

The Manatee Reserve

Chetumal bay contains one of the world's largest surviving populations of the manatee, a mangrove-dwelling aquatic mammal, like a slow-moving seal, which is

Getting There

The Manatee Reserve

Getting to see the manatee is currently a complicated procedure, as there are no regular manatee-watching trips. First place to enquire whether any are upcoming is the port administration (API) office on the Terminal Marítima quay (bottom of Av. Juárez), but you may get a better response if you go direct to the API main office at Av. Miguel Hidalgo 16 (corner of Av. Carmen Ochoa de Merino), **t** 832 6196, and ask for Lic. Jaime de Aguilar. Official API trips are run very intermittently, and often by appointment; a boat costs around $40 an hour and can take up to 10 people, and a reasonable trip takes 2hrs. Alternatively, you can enquire at **Ecoturística Xcalak** (*see* p.351), or at the **Club** Naútico, to the right of the Terminal Marítima, where fishing and manatee-seeking trips can sometimes be arranged (cost makes this only really practicable for groups). You can also get to the village of **Luís Echeverría**, up the bay north of Calderitas (accessible by *combi* from Chetumal), where some of the fishermen will take visitors to the manatee grounds. Prices are a matter of negotiation.

The Río Hondo

'Tourist infrastructure' here is virtually nonexistent, for there are no hotels, nor even many *loncherías*, but if you make your way to **La Unión** you can ask for Max Salas, an experienced jungle guide (second-class buses and *combis* run there from Chetumal). An easier alternative is offered by **Ecoturística Xcalak** one of only three related species in the world, collectively known as sea cows. The all-but-uninhabited northern end of the bay has been made into a manatee reserve.

Manatees are notoriously timid and dislike any disturbance; the best chance of seeing them is during a flat calm; if there's any swell, they'll be totally invisible. The best season is from October to January, and it's best to set out in the early morning.

The Río Hondo

About 10 kilometres west of the main crossing point into Belize (*see* overleaf) at **Subteniente López**, the Río Hondo, still the frontier but increasingly narrow, swings due southwest. A paved road runs with it from Ucum on Highway 186 for 90 kilometres down to **La Unión**, the last village on the Mexican side. Towards the top of this road villages extend along the river, but as you continue you enter scarcely touched rainforest. Toucans, parrots and monkeys are common, and even the elusive jaguar sighting is possible. The river by this point, after many meanders, is quite fast-flowing, with a few spectacular rapids. Near La Unión is the **Cenote Encantado** ('Enchanted Cenote'), a magnificent pool in the jungle at the foot of a giant rock cliff.

Tres Garantías

Tres Garantías is an *ejido* village 45 kilometres south of Highway 186 on the road to Tomás Garrido, from a turning 70 kilometres west of Chetumal. It's a sprawling, friendly settler village, with its own ecotourism project. In the 1980s the villagers took the brave decision, advised by local ecologists and international organizations, not to cut down the forest on the *ejido*'s land but to try to manage it to ensure its conservation. As part of this they built *cabañas* (the **Campamento La Pirámide**), with the idea that the 'hotel'-camp should contribute to making the forest a profitable resource for local people. Tapirs, monkeys, ocelots and jaguars are found nearby; as usual you may or may not see them, but there's always a wonderful range of birds.

(*see* p.351), the main company running trips up the Río Hondo. Their 2-day tour usually includes transport to La Unión, kayaking on the Río Hondo (forest river rather than rapids), a trek to the Cenote Encantado and a night camping in the jungle. Trips are for 4–8 people, so it's worth making up a group; cost is around $90 per person (for 4 it will be more expensive). The same agency offers trekking and camping in the still more remote forest of **Dos Aguadas**, near Tres Garantías, including a recently discovered, still unexcavated Mayan site at El Socorrito. Neither tour is possible during the rainy season (late June–Oct).

Tres Garantías

Campamento La Pirámide. The 'camp' consists of several simple but comfortable *cabañas*,

with showers. Guests are offered a wide range of tours and walks led by local guides and the English-speaking biologists who work with the *ejido*; all meals are cooked by Doña Olga, from the village. Suitable shoes and clothes (long sleeves, trousers and a hat) are absolutely necessary, and plenty of bug repellent. Bookings are taken for groups (min. 8, max.15), and the normal cost is $80 a day, everything included, though it may be possible to agree other rates at some times. It is essential to book at **Tres Garantías**, at least ten days ahead. Contact: **Sociedad de Productores Forestales Ejidales** (forestry office of the *ejidos* of Quintana Roo), in a battered wooden building at Av. Carmen Ochoa de Merino 143, Chetumal, **t** (983) 832 5232, *spfeqroo@prodigy.net.mx*.

Getting to Belize

Mexican **hire cars** are not usually allowed over the border into Belize. There are plenty of **buses** from Chetumal. From the main bus station, Novelo's has three first-class services daily to **Belize City** (*5hrs*) via **Corozal** (*1hr*) and **Orange Walk** (*2½hrs*), and four second-class on the same route. First-class to Corozal is about $3, to Belize City $6. Venus Bus runs its cheaper but clanky old buses from next to the Lázaro Cárdenas market at the corner of Calzada Veracruz and Av. Confederación Nacional Campesina, between the main station and the city centre. Some buses to Corozal also leave from or stop at the main market, on Av. Juárez.

Immigration and Visas

Citizens of Britain, other EU countries, the USA, Canada, Australia and New Zealand do not need a visa to enter Belize, but all passports are checked and you normally have to get off the bus and walk across the bridge. If you do have any problems, it is better to sort them out at the consulate in Chetumal rather than try to do so at Subteniente López. There are money-changing facilities on the other side of the border.

If you **enter Mexico** from Belize, you will probably be given a 15-day tourist card, and may be asked to pay for it (*see* p.111); if you want to stay longer, it's better to go to Cancún during that time and get an extension there.

Into Belize

The international bridge across the Río Hondo into Belize is in **Subteniente López**, eight kilometres west of Chetumal, well indicated off the main highway out of the city. This is one of the world's more humble and rustic border crossings, with a big, old iron drawbridge, although the customs and immigration buildings on the Mexican side have been rebuilt and now look much more impressive than those in Belize.

Mayan Sites in Southern Quintana Roo

In the most widely known accounts of Mayan civilization, southern Quintana Roo scarcely figured. Its most important Mayan site, Kohunlich, was only discovered in 1967, and by accident at that. During the 1990s excavations multiplied year by year, and more has been discovered in the last decade than in all the previous history of archaeology in the region.

Oxtankah

Open daily 8–5; adm, Sun adm free.

The road north of Chetumal, through Calderitas along the bay shore (not the wider road that veers inland), continues to become a winding country lane through a landscape of explosive vegetation, with fan palms, fields of horses and zebu cattle, and the milky-green waters of the bay off to the right. It then becomes an (easily passable) dirt track, which leads in 5km to the ruins of Oxtankah. The site was discovered in 1913, but only extensively excavated in the 1990s. It is of special interest because it was occupied for a very long time. Its largest structures are from the Early and Late Classic, but were built, Mayan-fashion, over much older buildings; abandoned after 800, it was resettled in the 14th–15th centuries, attracting the attention of the Spaniards, who tried to found a settlement of their own here at the time of the Conquest.

Oxtankah is laid out to combine a ruins visit with a nature walk, and you approach the site along a delightful winding path through the woods. The largest excavated structure is the first you come to, the **Plaza de las Abejas** (Plaza of the Bees), an impressive, Petén-influenced Mayan plaza with a pyramid, Structure IV, facing the sunrise, and smaller stepped platforms on two other sides. Beside the plaza there is also the unique **Structure I**, with steps only in one corner. To the south, a well-cleared path leads through the woods to the **Plaza de las Columnas**, another large Classic-era plaza; down a branch off the same path is the site's small *cenote*, still almost lost in the jungle. On the way back, to the north of Las Abejas, you come to a very different structure, the ruins of an abandoned **Franciscan chapel**. This chapel was not recorded in church archives and has given rise to a great deal of mystery, but it is now believed that it was built by the expedition of Alonso Dávila, one of the Montejos' lieutenants, who tried to establish a settlement somewhere near Chetumal in 1531. The settlement was abandoned after two years of struggling against the surrounding Maya, and did not get reoccupied even when the Spaniards finally conquered this area 15 years later.

Getting Around

By Bus

It is impossible to get to these sites directly by bus: buses toward Oxtankah only go as far as Calderitas; buses west only stop on the highway; while there are *combis* to Morocoy on the Dzibanché road, this is still several km from the ruins. Without a car the best way to visit the sites is with tours offered by hotels or agencies.

By Car

Getting around the sites is easy by car: Oxtankah is 6km up a continuation of the road through Calderitas; Dzibanché and Kinichná are both about 15km north of Highway 186 up a well-signposted, paved road which turns off about 50km west of Chetumal; the turn south for Kohunlich, 9km from the Highway and also well indicated, is another 10km west.

The last **petrol/gas station** going west is in Ucum, 26km from Chetumal.

Site Information

Not far beyond the village of Nachi Cocom on Highway 186, about 50km west of Chetumal, a turn north is signposted to Dzibanché and Kinichná. The road runs north through fields of maize and sugar cane to Morocoy (15km). Another 5km from the village the road divides: the main track continues 2km to Dzibanché, while Kinichná is up a fork to the right. You have to stop at the junction as the warden's hut for the two sites, with cold drinks on sale, is here.

Where to Stay

The Explorean, t (mobile) 015 201 8350, reservations via Mexico City t (55) 5201 8333, *www.theexplorean.com* (*luxury*). This area is an easy day-trip from Chetumal, but staying over is now a possibility with this luxury resort, built beside the Kohunlich access road by the Fiesta Americana hotel group. The opulent *cabañas*, main building and **restaurant** have been designed to make the most of a superb location, with a jungle-fantasy look; its slogan is 'soft adventure', and activities include kayaking, sailing, ruins tours, forest walks, health treatments and more. Rooms are let on an all-inclusive basis; the chain also owns the Costa Maya near Mahahual (*see* p.342), and it's possible to combine a stay in both. Some parts of it look as if they were designed more to dazzle in magazines than with an eye to actual guests' needs, but, if you want five-star comforts in the jungle, this could be it.

Dzibanché and Kinichná

Both open 8–5; adm, Sun adm free. Same ticket admits you to both sites.

Dzibanché and Kinichná are two more sites, far grander than Oxtankah, that were only opened up in the late '90s. Dzibanché was first explored in 1927 by Thomas Gann, who gave it this name, Yucatec for 'written on the walls', owing to its remarkable wooden lintels, some of the oldest and best-preserved Mayan woodcarvings. The smaller Kinichná is about two kilometres away, but it is now thought that with other unexcavated complexes nearby they both formed part of one widely dispersed city, rather like Cobá. The imposing size of their pyramids indicate that this was a powerful city state throughout the Classic era, from about 300 until the 8th century. Southern Quintana Roo, like the Río Bec further west, was an important channel in the flow of contact and trade between the Classic Mayan heartland in the south and the northern Yucatán. Dzibanché's massive architecture, like that of Kohunlich, suggests that from the Early Classic (AD 250–600) these cities had strong links with the great southern cities of the Petén, and an inscription from 495 suggests that Dzibanché, in particular, was an ally or vassal of Calakmul. Like other cities in the region Dzibanché (the name now commonly used for the whole city) entered into a decline later than the cities further south, around 850.

Just beyond the hut on the Dzibanché road a whole separate, slightly Río Bec-style temple-platform has recently been excavated, an indication of the complexity and richness of the whole site. As you arrive at **Dzibanché** itself you initially see nothing but vegetation, but the ruins take shape as you walk up through the trees. This is one of the most beautiful of Mayan sites, shrouded by giant *ceibas*, tropical birches and Spanish moss, and one of the best places to see tropical birds.

The core area of Dzibanché is made up of three giant connecting **plazas**, each at a different level. This is one of the truly monumental Mayan cities, a theatrical complex of massive, glowering pyramids built with an extraordinary sense of scale, their size now magnified by the towering trees. As you walk up the hill, the first large building you come to, on the left in the first plaza, is the towering pyramid-platform known as **Structure VI** or the **Building of the Lintels**, for it still contains its original wooden lintels found by Gann, including one dated 618. Their degree of preservation is quite extraordinary. The base of the platform dates from the Early Classic, while the upper levels were added between 600 and 800. In this case, though, the Mayas' skill in adding layer upon layer seems to have wavered, as at the back it can be seen that extra buttresses had to be added to keep the upper levels stable. Forming another side of the square is **Structure XVI**, with a battered monster-mask in its façade. It is dual-fronted, with a second façade on the Main Plaza.

Dzibanché's **Main Plaza**, reached by a climb up from the first square, is one of the largest of all Mayan squares, and standing on it is the tallest of all the city's buildings, the huge pyramid of **Structure II**, another dual-façade building. At the top of its steps there are two levels of galleried chambers. The top one has restored carved stone lintels, while the bottom one consists of three Mayan-arched chambers. In one of them the tomb of a man was discovered, containing exceptionally rich adornments and offerings. He has been dubbed the 'Lord of Dzibanché' and was almost certainly an *ahau* of the city. Opposite this pyramid across the plaza is **Structure XIII** or the **Building of the Captives**, an Early Classic platform with a stucco 'mask' of a spirit-monster on one side of its main staircase, and glyph inscriptions on the steps. Behind Structure II, the third, smaller plaza is much less excavated and more of a scramble, but it has another awe-inspiring pyramid, **Structure I** or **Pirámide del Buho** ('Pyramid of the Owl'), a giant Early Classic tower with an extremely steep staircase. Much more remains to be excavated at Dzibanché, all around the main site in the woods.

Kinichná really consists of just one building, the **Acropolis**, facing a relatively small plaza. This one building, though, is utterly huge, effectively three structures in one, and must have been a ceremonial hub of the multi-centred city. It's a vast temple platform, made up of three complete levels from different eras. Climbing up it makes you think the Maya were a very masochistic culture.

The massive, squat base (**Level A**) was built fairly crudely in the Preclassic, and is in poor condition. More sophisticated masonry and recognizable temples begin at **Level B**, above it. It has all the sense of geometry and symmetry of Mayan architecture, with a dramatic central staircase facing a 'plaza' on the top of Level A, and flanked by twin temples with monster-masks, in poor condition. This staircase in turn leads to **Level C**, another complete pyramid (and giant staircase) on top of B, probably built around 600. At its top there is a temple that contained the tomb of two people who were buried with some of the richest Mayan jade offerings ever found. There was also an effigy of the sun god, the origin of the name *Kinichná*, or 'House of the Sun'.

Kohunlich

Open daily 8–5; adm, Sun adm free.

Kohunlich ruins were discovered in 1967 by a local Maya, Ignacio Ek, whose family were for many years the site caretakers. Kohunlich is one of the grandest of the lesser-known large Mayan cities, and one of the sites where most has been revealed by ongoing excavations, adding continually to its fascination. Like Dzibanché, it was a major city for a long time, from around AD 300 to about AD 900. It's also one of the cities that gives most food for the imagination, with a strong feel of having been a real community, and it is made all the more impressive by an astonishing location. As you reach the end of the road south from Highway 186 you seem to be enclosed by huge palms, an extraordinary jungle vision.

Recent excavations have greatly extended the visitable area, and a path has been created that takes you in a circuit around the site. As you come in you have a choice, between going left into the great main square, the **Plaza de las Estelas**, or beginning the circuit anti-clockwise to the right. Immediately to your left is an interesting, small raised plaza, surrounded by buildings containing many small rooms. Known as the **North-West Residential Complex** and only extensively excavated in the last few years, this gives you first sight of one of the most intriguing 'enigmas' of Kohunlich (also, though less visibly, found at Dzibanché). In most Mayan cities it has been assumed that only royal and élite lineages lived in stone buildings, while the mass of the population lived in wood-and-palm *nas*. Dzibanché, Kohunlich and some of the Río Bec sites, on the other hand, have a high number of solid, stone residential complexes, suggesting an unusually high level of prosperity, or even a more 'democratic' distribution of wealth. There is even evidence that this North-West Complex was lived in by artisans, perhaps highly-regarded master potters and scribes.

At the paths junction is the giant agglomeration of the **Palace Complex** (Structure B2), the temple-residence that forms the western side of the main square. Filling the north side of the plaza is the main pyramid of Kohunlich, the **Acropolis** (B1). It's an untidy structure that was built over many times, and although mainly a temple platform it too has a residential complex on the top, which would have been invisible to crowds in the square below, and gives a vivid idea of the contrast between private intimacy and public grandeur in this city. Part of the pyramid, facing the plaza, had an impossibly steep 'false staircase' in Río Bec style added to it at some point, but this was part-buried under later additions. Across the plaza is the structure known as the **Gradería** (B3) or grandstand, a 100m-long ramp of steps leading up to a much smaller temple. The Plaza de las Estelas takes its name from the *stelae* on a small platform in the middle of the square and near the building on its east side, the **Edificio de las Estelas** (B4). The *stelae* at Kohunlich, though, are in poor condition, so it has not yet been given a dynastic history. The Edificio de las Estelas is one more Mayan hodgepodge, assembled over centuries, with a second façade facing the Masks pyramid.

Kohunlich

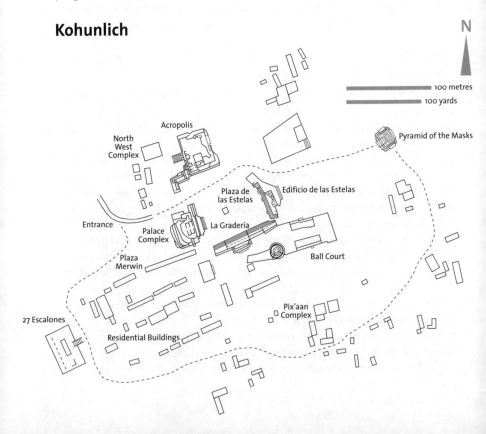

Turn back through the plaza to take the new path around the site. As well as taking you to newly-uncovered areas it's also a fabulous forest walk, between overwhelming waves of green, and a great place to see strange flowers and toucans. You begin in the **Plaza Merwin**, a small square behind the first Palace Complex; from there you skirt the site, through the palms, to come dramatically up to the **27 Escalones** ('27 Steps'), largest of Kohunlich's residential complexes and one of the biggest of all Mayan palaces. Its location alone is hugely grand: reached by the awesome stairway that gives it its name, it was built on to the tallest ridge around the city. This, and its size, means it was almost certainly the main residence of the royal lineage of Kohunlich. You're not aware of quite how big it is until you reach the top, where you find a series of rooms and intimate, atmospheric patios, with a strong sense of exclusivity.

Below the 27 Escalones the path continues around to the **Pix'aan Complex**, a smaller but still impressive residential complex, with unusually large chambers. Beyond it a path cuts left to the main **Ball Court** next to the Edificio de las Estelas. Paths lead finally to the greatest treasure at Kohunlich, the **Pyramid of the Masks** (Pirámide de los Mascarones, Structure A1), facing the east façade of the Estelas building across a broad open space. This is one of the oldest surviving structures in the city, built before 500. Alongside its giant staircase – sheltered beneath an equally giant *palapa*-structure – there are six huge stucco heads, the **Mascarones de Kohunlich**. Now a symbol of the city, they are among the greatest surviving works of Mayan sculpture, staring out through the centuries towards the sunset, with an unnerving stillness. They have been said to be representations of the Sun God, Kinich Ahau, but they also seem to be actual portraits – the faces are all different, and very individual – of the ruling lineage of Kohunlich. Astonishingly, the heads were also partly covered by a later stage of building in the Late Classic, which has been stripped away in modern excavations.

North of the Masks Pyramid a path leads to the largest of Kohunlich's *aguadas*, or reservoirs. Rainfall is heavier here than further north, but the Maya of Kohunlich had the same problems as the rest of the Yucatán in retaining water in dry seasons, and the city did not have a major *cenote*. As in the Petén cities they reinforced natural depressions to catch water in *aguadas*. There are still more structures to be excavated at Kohunlich, away in the woods.

The Río Bec

Highway 186 runs on west past Kohunlich across the bottom of the Yucatán peninsula towards Campeche and the rest of Mexico. In modern times, until this road was built in the 1970s this area was near-uninhabited, a forgotten space on the map. During the Classic era of Mesoamerica, by contrast, this was one of the most heavily populated parts of the Mayan world, a string of cities with a very distinctive architectural style of their own, called Río Bec after one of the largest sites. Not really part of the Río Bec as such, but reached from the same road, is the most exciting of all recent discoveries in the Mayan world, the huge city of Calakmul. It stands within the largest and most wildlife-rich area of untouched rainforest in Mexico, the Calakmul reserve, which has survived precisely because of its remoteness.

Getting to see these sites, if you weren't part of an official expedition, used to be very arduous. When the Mexican government cut the road across the peninsula, the forest on either side was laid open to be settled by landless farmers. 'Villages' grew up of knocked-together huts like improvised squatter camps, and the road also had a tough reputation for robberies. Since the late '90s, though, this has been one more part of Mexico that is changing fast. The villages, especially Xpuhil, still have a feel of the Mexican frontier about them but are much more solid, with proper, permanent buildings. Crime (other than a tendency to try to short-change foreigners) has fallen drastically, and while the atmosphere is not as placidly easygoing as in Yucatán state, it's not threatening. Most of the Mayan sites now have rough but paved access roads.

Above all, the number of visitors has increased as the area's archaeological and natural riches have become more widely known, and so too has the range of facilities. In the early days of Río Bec tourism, there was a strong social and environmental motivation to provide local people with an alternative activity to slash-and-burn, and

Getting Around

By Bus

By bus, you can get to the sites near the road – Xpuhil, Becán, Chicanná and Balamkú – quite easily. Six first- and six second-class buses stop daily at **Xpuhil** village, including services to/from Cancún, Playa del Carmen, Campeche and Mexico City. Three second-class buses turn north to **Zoh-Laguna**, and there's one daily from Zoh-Laguna to **Hopelchén** (from where you can get to Campeche or Mérida). In Xpuhil there are the usual *combis* and taxis. Second-class buses and *combis* drop you at roadside sites on request. Xpuhil cab-drivers will also take you to local sites; for **Calakmul**, you need a taxi for the whole trip (from $30).

By Car

The best way to get to the sites is by car, and all the sites normally open to the public have paved or mostly-paved access roads. The main highway is good, but watch your **fuel**: there are only three *gasolineras* along this road. Going west from Chetumal, the last one is in Ucum (26km); from there it's 95km to Xpuhil, and then 145km to Escárcega. The boys who run the Xpuhil station seem to like short-changing foreigners. From Xpuhil a paved road runs north through Zoh-Laguna to Hopelchén and the Chenes (about 150km), eventually to reach Campeche (230km) or Uxmal and Mérida. There is no fuel on this road between Xpuhil and Hopelchén.

Tourist Information

The Río Bec t (983–)

As well as the trips run by agencies in Chetumal and Campeche, there is a **tourist information** desk in the bus depot at Xpuhil which has very little information but does sell tickets (also available from the Hotel Calakmul) on a daily tour to Calakmul and Balamkú (around $40 per person).

Tours

At the more accessible sites there are nearly always a few men offering to guide you around, although they may know nothing about what they're showing you. The best local guides are those from **Expediciones Aventura Máxima**, a group led by Leticia (Lety) Santiago and Fernando Sastre, who were part of a now-defunct Campeche state ecotourism scheme and have continued working on their own. They provide a fascinating range of ruins visits and forest trips, and are authorized to run camp sites within the Calakmul reserve. Contact: t/f 871 6050 in Zoh-Laguna, t 871 6010, f 871 6011 in Xpuhil or t/f (999) 987 2521 in Mérida. It's advisable to get in touch well in advance; alternatively, if you're in the area they often have someone looking out for interested visitors in the parking area at Calakmul ruins.

At the **site entrances** there may be soft drinks for sale, but very little else. Take water with you.

so lessen deforestation. Most of these projects have fallen by the wayside, but in their place more conventional investors are showing interest, and a wider mix of hotels and tours has begun to appear. Visiting the Río Bec, though, is still a different experience from the convenient world of the Cancún Riviera. Here, tourism and 'service' are recent inventions: many locals are still very unused to foreigners, and may look at you as if you just fell from the moon. Visiting is a learning experience for both parties.

Though the Río Bec is in Campeche, it is included here because it is closer to Chetumal. Xpuhil and Calakmul can also be conveniently visited as a stop-off on a drive through from the Cancún area to Palenque, or vice versa.

History

The Río Bec area was occupied very early, at least from about 300 BC, and there is evidence from Becán that the site was inhabited by 600 BC, before a defined Mayan culture had taken shape. As city-states, though, the Río Bec communities reached

Where to Stay

The Río Bec t (983–)

Due to the cost of bringing services in from Campeche or Chetumal and (probably) the ambitions of local hotel owners, there is not much real budget accommodation, especially not in Xpuhil. Staying in Zoh-Laguna can be both more pleasant and a lot cheaper.

Chicanná Ecovillage, on the Highway near the Chicanná ruins, reservation t (Campeche) (981) 816 2233, t (Mexico City) (55) 5705 3996, *chicanna@campeche.sureste.com* (*expensive*). The most comfortable upscale option in the Río Bec, consisting of attractive rooms with terraces in villas with *palapa* roofs around a garden, with pool and pretty **restaurant**. As an 'ecovillage' it's confused: some electricity is solar-powered, and rooms have a/c, but much of the food you eat is trucked in a great distance. However, it is very comfortable, and it all depends on the value you place on a good shower.

Hotel Mirador Maya, at the top of the hill, Xpuhil (no phone, *inexpensive*). *Cabaña*-style huts with showers that have recently been redecorated and are now quite comfortable (good value), and some larger, pricier rooms.

Hotel-Restaurant Calakmul, Xpuhil, t 871 6029 (*inexpensive*). The main hotel in Xpuhil, this offers simple rooms with showers that are decently airy and have recently been redone (a tad pricey), or simpler *cabañas* with shared showers (borderline-*inexpensive*).

Cabañas Mercedes, Zoh-Laguna, t (village *caseta*) 871 6054 (*cheap*). Just off the grassy plaza in Zoh-Laguna, this is both the best-value place in the Río Bec and one of the most enjoyable. There are five pleasant *cabañas*, with showers and fans, around a yard behind *sra* Mercedes' little restaurant, where she cooks up truly bargain meals of Yucatecan classics to order. She and her husband are also very sweet and friendly, and it's a beautifully peaceful place to stay.

El Viajero, Zoh-Laguna, t (village *caseta*) 871 6054 (*cheap*). A simple *cabaña* operation, also with friendly owners. They have two decent cabins with showers, and even TVs.

Eating Out

The restaurant at the **Chicanná Ecovillage** (*expensive*) is of a different order from everywhere else nearby.

Xpuhil is the only place with a choice of eating: **Hotel-Restaurant Calakmul** is the best, but the **Mirador Maya**, the **Templo Maya** opposite and the **Geminis** closer to the bus depot all offer similar, decent Mexican-Yucatecan food (all *moderate*). Near the bus office there are a few ultra-cheap *loncherías*, and shops with water and picnic food.

In **Zoh-Laguna** *Cabañas* **Mercedes** has great bargain local fare (*cheap*). Further west there is little except a few, very basic roadside *loncherías*, though Puerta Calakmul (*see* p.369) could be handy if it gets more organized.

their peak from about AD 600 onwards. Becán was the dominant centre, but one striking feature of the Río Bec is the concentration of sites so close to each other. They were wealthy communities which, like the Quintana Roo cities to the east, played an important role in the flow of trade that ran west to east across the peninsula and up to Cobá. This was a 'transitional area', with a mixture of cultural influences. Like Dzibanché or Kohunlich, the Río Bec cities seem to have resisted 'Collapse' until after 900, and Becán itself was only finally abandoned after 1300.

The Río Bec is known for the most extravagant and operatic of all Mayan architectural styles. A typical Río Bec temple complex consists of three tall towers in a line, the middle one lower than the ends or vice versa, with a single-storey building linking them. On the tower façades there are 'false staircases', impossibly steep, and created entirely for visual effect (access to the temples at the top was usually via easier sets of steps at the back). Many Río Bec buildings also feature elements of the Chenes style from further north, like monster-mouth temple entrances.

Standing apart from the Río Bec sites is Calakmul, 60 kilometres to the south. Deep in the forest, it is the largest Mayan site to have been only recently explored, and in the 1990s each subsequent excavation upgraded its importance to the point where it has been identified as one of the 'superpowers' of the Classic Maya world. Elsewhere in the forest there are many more ruins, as yet inaccessible.

Xpuhil and Zoh-Laguna

Xpuhil (Xpujil) is the largest village in the region, with shops, restaurants and *loncherías*, a phone office and pharmacies. From the road junction, *combis* and cabs come and go to all the surrounding villages. Once most definitely a part of backwoods Mexico, it has been the main focus of official efforts to give the Highway 186 settlements a less 'provisional' look, and now boasts a market, a shiny bus depot and even proper kerbs. Appearances aside, though, it still has a raggedy feel, helped by its role as a rest stop for truckers who leave their monster vehicles all along the road.

The Mayan site of **Xpuhil** (*open daily 8–5; adm, Sun adm free*) is on the north side of 186 just west of the main village. A small site, it was probably a subordinate community of Becán. Most of its structures were put up between 500 and 750, but some building work went on after 1000; it was only rediscovered in the 1930s. Small though it is it contains one of the most extraordinary Río Bec temples, **Structure I**, with three giant towers, the middle one much bigger than the others, with façades at an angle of 70°. In this case, there was no easier way up at the back, so unless the local priest-lords were especially athletic the temples on top of the towers were entirely for show, while ceremonies went on at a lower level. On the towers there are still many traces of deep-red stucco. The other large buildings (**Structures II–IV**) were aristocratic residences; Structure IV, with intricate decorations and several rooms atop a stepped platform, gives a clear idea of a Río Bec palace building. There are 17 unexcavated structures around the main site, and, like all Río Bec sites, it's great for seeing birds.

Zoh-Laguna is just 10 kilometres north of Xpuhil, but feels quite different. It's more orderly-looking, with a big grass plaza, and although smaller it is an older village than Xpuhil, and has a calmer, friendlier atmosphere, with a likeable feel of rural quiet.

Site Information

Open daily 8–5; adm free.

The ruins of **Hormiguero** are in the savannah 22km south of Xpuhil, down the road south from the main crossroads in Xpuhil village. After 14km, turn right on to a track for the final stretch, which becomes steadily more rutted until the paving gives out completely a short way from the site, although it's still passable (if slow) in a normal car. From the car park there's a sizeable walk to the ruins.

The site of **Río Bec** (*closed to visitors*) is 15km east of Xpuhil and 20km south down a very bad dirt road (4WD only, especially after rain) through the village of **20 de Noviembre**.

Hormiguero

This is another Río Bec community that was at its peak in the Late Classic (650–850), but was partially occupied until around 1200. Only a few of its 84 known structures have been excavated. Not many people come here, so it remains a very atmospheric, remote-feeling ruin, approached through dense woods of brush, *ceibas* and flowering plants.

Straight ahead of you at the end of the entry path is **Structure II**, the most complete excavated building at the site and one of the most wildly theatrical of all Río Bec buildings. It's a rectangular platform, with two soaring, false-staircase towers either side of a massive Chenes monster-portal. Inside this are several outsize chambers, for this is one of many Río Bec-Chenes buildings that seems peculiarly out of scale. From its rooms it appears this was both a temple and a residential building.

Forming a small plaza along with Structure II is the much less excavated platform of **Structure I**, but because so little of the site has been cleared it is difficult to appreciate the layout of Hormiguero, and ruined buildings loom up at you by surprise out of the undergrowth. A path to the right of Structure II leads to the **Central Group**, a complex of large buildings, most of which are unexcavated. In front of you is **Structure V**, a towering, part-excavated pyramid with an awesome Chenes-style temple at its peak.

The site that gave its name to the whole region, **Río Bec** itself, is located some way southeast of Xpuhil down a very poor road, beyond the village of **20 de Noviembre**. The ruins are currently closed to visitors while excavations are in progress; the more enthusiastic ruins-seekers might want to check on the current situation in Xpuhil.

Becán

7km west of Xpuhil; open daily 8–5; adm, Sun adm free.

Becán is a Mayan city unlike any other. The name means 'ditch of water', and it is the only Mayan site ringed by a very recognizable moat. It runs around a very solid wall, which must definitely have been a fortification. Within this tight perimeter, looming Río Bec-style towers around plazas form spaces with a feel of enclosure that adds enormously to their monumental power.

The oldest permanent structures at Becán are dated to about 550 BC, the latest to about 1200. From around AD 650 to 900 this was the dominant centre of the whole Río Bec region, and it is believed other cities nearby were its offshoots or vassals. The site was discovered by the American archaeologist Karl Ruppert in 1934, but was only really uncovered by the INAH in the 1980s, and major excavations are still underway.

The entrance to the city is now through a gap in the east side of the wall, beyond which you enter a small space that gives you a choice of routes into Becán's maze. The giant **Structure IV** forms the north side of the smallest but most dramatic of the city's squares, the **East Plaza**. It's a huge residential platform, with an internal staircase on the north side. Its rooms extend over several levels and into an 'annexe' at the back, and some retain fine geometrical-pattern decoration. From its top levels you get a fine overview over the square, and can appreciate that despite its immense structures this was very much a residential plaza for the élite of Becán, for all the buildings have multi-room complexes above their temple-façades. Several bear traces of red stucco and checkerboard-pattern facings. **Structure II**, on the west side, has the most intact façade, while **Structure III** facing it has the best-preserved rooms, including a *temazcal* or Mayan steam bath. Outdoing Structure IV in size is the vast pile of **Structure I**, with two of the steepest-ever Río Bec staircases on its giant towers. From their positioning it is likely the temples on top of these towers were astronomical observatories. Structure I is dual-fronted, and its principal façade actually faced south, outside the plaza. In the East Plaza there is a small round **altar**, a later addition from around 1200.

One of the most distinctive features of Becán is the way in which it combines immensity with a sense of being a contained whole: a series of interlocking, interconnecting spaces. This also helps to give the ancient city its remarkable feel of human habitation. Instead of continuing round in a circuit from the East Plaza, walk back through the square to the entrance square. To the right is a uniquely intact Mayan 'street', which runs between two buildings for 60 metres and served as a direct

Becán

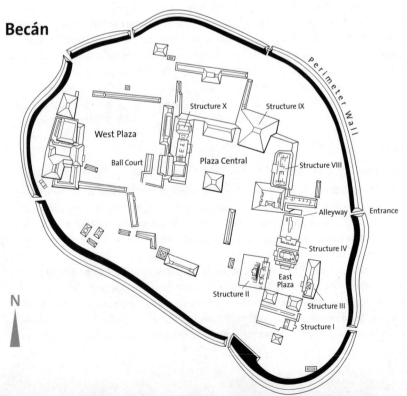

route between the East Plaza area and the **Plaza Central**. Beneath its Mayan arches there are niches where offerings were once left. At the end of this alley you emerge into the light right into the Plaza Central, which is much larger but less of an ordered whole than the other squares of Becán. On your right is the mysterious **Structure VIII**, a massively vertical Río Bec platform, with temples on top. Its strangest feature is inside it, a series of labyrinthine chambers, very tall for Mayan rooms, that are utterly dark and have no openings to the outside beyond an entrance passageway. Their purpose is not clear: a mundane suggestion is that they were storage spaces, but a more common view is that they were built for rituals that required darkness and seclusion, or to represent the underworld, Xibalba.

On the north side of the Plaza Central is the tallest building at Becán, **Structure IX**, a huge pyramid, while forming the west side of the square is **Structure X**. A combined temple and residence, it has 12 rooms over two levels, atop a glowering Río Bec façade with an elaborate frieze in the centre. While excavations are ongoing here it may be closed off, but if you can climb up it, from the top you will see another pyramid almost alongside, and the last and biggest of the squares, the **West Plaza**. The density of large buildings in the city is extraordinary. In the West Plaza is Becán's main **Ball Court**. The residential buildings within walled Becán were obviously used by the city's elite; around the walled city there were other buildings, an extensive network of sacbés, and humbler residential areas and fields.

Chicanná

2km west of Becán; open daily 8–5; adm, Sun adm free.

Only slightly west of Becán, Chicanná was almost certainly an offshoot of the larger city, but is very different. It is the most striking example in the region of the mixing of styles: Río Bec, Chenes, even the Puuc styles from the north. It does not have giant pyramids, but relatively small buildings with an ornateness and quality of decoration that suggest this was a centre only for the region's élite. Relics of jade, obsidian and other fine materials have been found here, imported from Guatemala, Honduras and further south. It was occupied almost as long as Becán, from about 100 BC to around AD 1000, and as with other sites seems to have been part-inhabited until about 1100.

The main path now takes you around in an anti-clockwise circuit from the entrance. The first major building you come to is the tallest at Chicanná, **Structure XX**. It's a large two-tier building, facing south, and one of the latest at the site, from around 850. The main entrance is an impressive Chenes monster-mask of Itzamná, while above, on the second tier, are 'towers' of Chac-heads. Inside, there are 11 rooms at ground level and a T-shaped staircase up to more chambers above. In some rooms there are benches with fascinating stucco decoration, such as rosettes around little human faces. A detour to the right takes you to another large complex, **Structure XI**, which by contrast is one of the oldest and simplest at Chicanná, from around AD 300.

From there it's 100m to Chicanná's central plaza. To the right, approaching on the main path, is the largest building here, **Structure I**, which goes back to Río Bec style with two near-vertical towers, at either end of a six-room building. Interrupting the

Chicanná

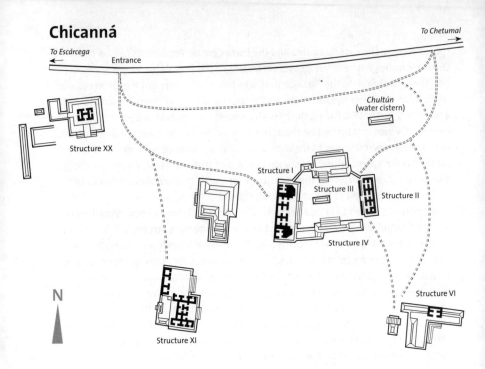

'staircases' of the towers are Chac-faces, but these and the traces of red stucco are in bad condition. **Structure III**, the north side of the plaza, is another Mayan structure built up over centuries; **Structure IV**, opposite, is a residential-temple platform which had rooms on an upper level, but little trace of them remains.

The most famous and most photographed building at Chicanná is **Structure II**, making up the east side of the square. Built around 700, it's relatively small, with eight rooms reached from several doorways, but its awesome main entrance is one of the greatest of all Chenes monster-portals. Above and around the doorway, formed by the gaping mouth of the beast-like god, are its teeth; further above are its eyes with hook-like pupils, while its ears, alongside, are adorned with jewellery. Winding away either side of the mouth are more diagrammatic shapes, perhaps indicating the flow and breath of the spirit. These Chenes portals were representations of an 'Earth Monster', one of the spirits of the Earth of which Itzamná was the most prominent manifestation (though referred to as 'monsters' in English, like most Mayan gods their fearfulness was very ambivalent). Between the eyes above the centre of the doorway there's a niche that probably held an image of a member of the lordly lineage that lived here, making clear his divine status. Elsewhere, there are some carved animals, looking unusually cute among the terrorific style of Chenes sculpture.

From the southeast corner of the square a path leads to another isolated building, **Structure VI**, like others a combination of elements added at different times. The main section dates from around 650, and has a restrained Chenes portal and a large roof-comb; on the east side, there are two rooms with Puuc columns added around 900. From there, the path continues through the woods back to the entrance, passing the remains of one of the *chultún* reservoirs that kept Chicanná supplied with water.

The Calakmul Biosphere Reserve

The largest forest reserve in Mexico, Calakmul covers an area of 7,230 square kilometres. It extends both north and south of Highway 186, but there are few entry routes into the northern area. The main changes in vegetation are from Yucatán scrub in the north to dense rainforest in the south, but within the whole area there is a prodigious range of plant life, including 85 species of orchid. Animal life includes tapirs, monkeys, armadillos, rodents, over 230 species of bird and every one of the region's types of big cat. Animals you can come across quite easily in the early morning are grey foxes, *tepezcuintles*, white-tailed deer and margays (a medium-sized cat, here called *tigrillo*). Jaguars are, as ever, an outside bet. Among those birds that aren't too hard to see are ocellated turkeys, curassows, *chachalacas*, cardinals, Yucatán jays, orioles, hummingbirds, toucans and hawks, while yellow-headed parrots are positively plentiful.

The first 20 kilometres south of the highway is a 'buffer zone', where some farming is still permitted, before you reach the reserve proper, at an empty warden's hut. About seven kilometres further on a small parking area has been cleared on the right side of the road, which should have a sign with the word *sendero*. This indicates a specially-cut nature path, leading in about 200m to a natural *aguada*, a dip in the ground that fills up with water during the rains (June–Sept) and retains it for several months. All the forest animals come here to drink, and this is one of the places where, especially in the rainy season, you have most chance of seeing rarities such as the jaguar (or, with no great effort, a band of monkeys arguing with a coati over some fruit). It is accessible during the rains, but you will get bitten a great deal by bugs and

Getting There and Site Information

Calakmul t (983–)

The entrance to the Calakmul reserve is a turn south 52km west of Xpuhil. From there, it's another 60km, or a bit over an hour's drive, along a paved but bumpy road to the Mayan city of Calakmul. As it's a long drive and the ruins are in the heart of the reserve, it's best to do both in one day-trip. The main Calakmul ruins are now quite well-cleared and a guide is not really necessary, but if you want to see more, especially local wildlife, it's a good idea to have a guide such as those of Aventura Máxima with you. The birds and animals of Calakmul are most active around dawn, so it's necessary to leave Xpuhil at around 5.30–6am to see as much as possible.

At the Calakmul turning off the highway there is a check-in hut where the warden lives and works. Cars are admitted to the reserve daily from 7am–6pm (with no last-exit time),

and there is an adm charge of around $4 per vehicle plus $2 per person; the ruins are open normal INAH hours (8–5), and have a separate adm at the usual rate, around $2.50.

Where to Stay

The old, free camp site at the Calakmul ruins has been closed. Only a few organizations are now allowed to run campsites in the reserve, and so the best way to get this close to the ruins and the forest is with **Aventura Máxima** (*see* p.362) or a similar guide group.

Puerta Calakmul, *puertacalakmul@starmedia .com* (*expensive*). A new investment, with *cabañas* in the woods by the turn on to the Calakmul road off Highway 186 (around 1km down a track that turns left behind the warden's house). The *cabañas* are pretty and nicely laid out, with superior jungle comforts, a pool and a palm-roof **restaurant**, but the weird staff seem to have no idea how to deal with people.

ticks and will need to be careful of scorpions and snakes. From the *sendero* it's a tiring 33 kilometres to the ruins. There are other good places along the road to find birds and animals that a guide will be able to show you.

The Calakmul Ruins

Open daily 8–5; adm, Sun adm free.

The great city of Calakmul is the most important recent discovery in American archaeology. It was actually discovered in 1931, but mapping was only begun in 1985. Already, within an area of over 25 square kilometres over 600 structures have been found, and more are being discovered. Its population at its peak has been estimated at over 60,000. Over 115 carved *stelae* have been uncovered, although the quality of the local stone means that they are far harder to make out than inscriptions from cities to the south such as Palenque and Yaxchilán. The dates deciphered range from the 4th century AD to 810. Many superb artefacts have also been uncovered – such as ceramics and the fabulous jade funeral masks known as the *Máscaras de Calakmul* – the finest of which are in the **Fuerte San Miguel** museum in Campeche (*see* p.389).

History

Ever since the first Mayan name-glyphs were deciphered in the 1950s one of the great questions for Mayanists was the identity of a place known as the *Kaan* or Snake Kingdom, references to which were found in inscriptions all over the Mayan lands, indicating a city-state of enormous power and prestige. As excavations have gone on it has become clear that the Snake Kingdom was Calakmul. With the aid of inscriptions from other cities – given the poor state of its own carvings – the position of Calakmul as one of the 'great powers' of the Classic Maya world has emerged.

The site of Calakmul was occupied very early, from around 600 BC, and the first layers of most of its large structures were already in place in the Preclassic before AD 100. It is believed that its enmity with other cities further south also originated in this era, in particular its rivalry with Tikal. Calakmul's rise to major power status, though, seems to date from the early 6th century, when Tikal had been the dominant force in the Petén for over 100 years. From the 520s to the 550s Calakmul's rulers forged a series of alliances with cities in the southeast Petén (in modern-day Belize and Guatemala), such as Naranjo and Caracol. This culminated in the great defeat of Tikal by Calakmul and Caracol in 562, after which Tikal's ruler was sacrificed and his city fell into a long crisis. For the next 140 years Calakmul was the foremost power in the whole Petén, with a web of alliances and vassal relationships that ran from Yaxchilán to Dzibanché. One indication of its wealth and size is its extraordinary water management system, with five huge reservoirs to retain water in dry seasons, including one, two kilometres north of the main site, that is 51,000 square kilometres in area and the largest such *aguada* in any Mayan city.

Calakmul's greatest ruler was Yuknoom 'the Great' (636–86), a contemporary and enemy of Pakal of Palenque. A constant feature of his reign was warfare against a resurgent Tikal, which was allied with Palenque; in 657 Yuknoom attacked Tikal and was again victorious, forcing its ruler to take refuge in Palenque (*see* p.434), so that Calakmul's pre-eminence was maintained for another 30 years. Yuknoom is not as well known as his son Yuknoom Yich'ak Kak, known as Jaguar-Paw (*Garra de Jaguar*), the first Calakmul ruler to be identified. He reigned for only eight years (686–95), but was easily identified because in 695 he led Calakmul into a disastrous defeat at the hands of Hasaw-Chan-Kawil of Tikal, which turned the scales again and brought the city's 'golden age' to a fairly abrupt end.

It was believed that Jaguar-Paw was captured and sacrificed at Tikal, but the recent discovery of his tomb indicates that he at least survived the actual battle, and one of his successors Yuknoom Took (702–31) fought back against decline by cultivating an alliance with Yaxchilán. However, the prestige and power of Calakmul never fully recovered from the 695 defeat. The vigour of Becán and the Río Bec cities in the following century is probably related to the decline of Calakmul, since Mayan cities often gained energy when they came out from 'under the shadow' of larger states. In the later 8th century Calakmul's main contacts, as reflected in ceramics and architecture, seem to have been with the Río Bec, the Chenes and other cities further north, in place of its earlier interaction with the Petén to the south. From about 790 it appears to have 'collapsed' more rapidly than other cities nearby: the last dated inscription at the site is from 810, although there is evidence that some people inhabited (or at least visited) the city into the 13th century.

The Great Plaza and Structure II

The entrance gate and parking area have lately been moved back from the main site, so you have a forest walk of about a kilometre to the ruins. At the end of the path you come into the north side of Calakmul's giant main square, the **Great Plaza** (Plaza Central). This is one of the great, immense Mayan ceremonial spaces. Around it there are many *stelae* (mostly pretty indistinct), some of which were excavated in other parts of the site and then brought together here. Immediately to their right is the small **Structure VIII**, probably an astronomical observatory, beyond which is the much larger **Structure VII**. At the top of it a tomb was found which contained the most beautiful of the jade *máscaras* now in the Campeche museum. The largest building in this part of the plaza is the residence-platform to your left, **Structure IV**. Its base is extremely ancient, perhaps older than 100 BC, but the last rooms were added above it around 750. In front of it are over a dozen *stelae*, all referring to events from between 750 and 810. **Structure VI**, facing it across the plaza, was one of the ceremonial hearts of the city, an astronomical platform incorporating a Mayan cosmological trick. On the shortest and longest days of the year the sun shines directly through the building to land on the small altar in front.

Next to Structure IV is another small platform, **Structure V**, around which are some of the city's best-preserved *stelae*. The most prominent on the north side, facing the main square and dated to 623, unusually tell the story of a marriage, between the daughter of an *ahau* of Calakmul and a prince from Yaxchilán. In the *stela* on the right the prince is shown making offerings of friendship; to the left the princess is shown

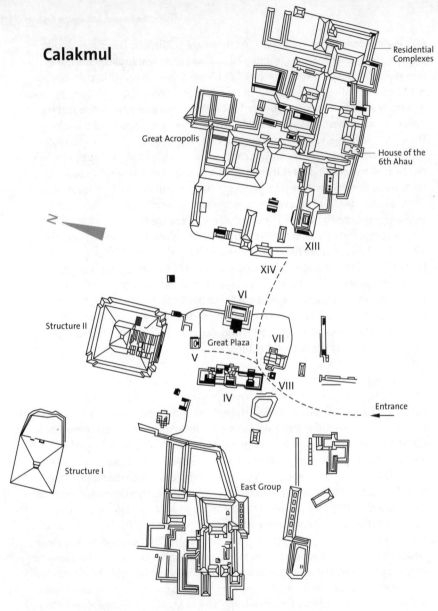

Calakmul

Residential Complexes

Great Acropolis

House of the 6th Ahau

N

XIII

XIV

VI

Structure II

Great Plaza

VII

C

V

VIII

IV

Entrance

Structure I

East Group

in a more belligerent posture above an earth monster, and trampling down a prisoner. On the south side are eight *stelae* erected by Yuknoom the Great around 660–70, including one, **Stela 33**, showing his predecessor (and probably father) Scroll-Serpent, who launched two attacks on Palenque, in 599 and 611.

Beyond here in the south section of the Gran Plaza you come to the true monster of Calakmul, now prosaically known as **Structure II**, the **Great Pyramid** of the city and the hub around which the rest is arranged. This is the largest of all Mayan pyramids. Its base covers several acres; above, there are complete pyramids upon pyramids – from the bottom you cannot see the top – and climbing up is an awesome progression. The role of Mayan architecture in creating a power centre – symbolically and literally – was never clearer. This great pyramid is the ultimate product of the Mayan practice whereby each *ahau* had to add something to the city's buildings to continue the glory of his lineage: as such, it just got bigger and bigger. Curiously, they did so not so much by covering over the existing structure – it had already nearly reached its final height in the Preclassic era – as by building up successive façades, so that it 'grew' north-wards into the plaza. Either side of the central stairway are enormous monster-mask carvings, added in the Early Classic, built over in the 7th or 8th centuries and only recently uncovered. In the main temple on the first large flat level (**Temple 2B**) an exceptionally rich tomb was discovered in 1997, containing a man with a jade funeral mask, and surrounded by lavish offerings of jade, ceramics, obsidian and more. This is very probably the tomb of Jaguar-Paw. He was lying on a unique painted wooden bier, which disastrously disintegrated very shortly after air entered the tomb; the other objects (and a reconstruction of the tomb) are now in Campeche.

From this temple there's a further climb up three more levels to the plain, small platform at the top. Your great reward is the view, towering over everything in the endless green forest. From here, you have a view of another pyramid, **Structure III**, which would count as huge itself were it not seen in comparison, a short distance to the east. Very tall and vertical, and built in a simple Petén style, it has a palace-residence complex with large chambers on its upper levels.

The Great Acropolis and the Muralla

Off to your left as you come down Structure II is the other main excavated area of Calakmul, known as the **Great Acropolis**. The first building you come to, **Structure XIV**, is one of the few dual-fronted buildings in the city, dated to 740. The Acropolis is structured around another large square, within which is Calakmul's main (but surprisingly small) **Ball Court**. Next to this is a *stela* with a remarkably clear carving of a ball player (above all his sandals and toenails). He seems to be holding a kind of tablet, which may have been used to keep scores. **Structure XIII**, on the right, is a temple-residence with a *stela* of a woman.

Much of the Great Acropolis is still overgrown and scarcely excavated, but a path to the right of Structure XIII leads to one of the most atmospheric parts of the site, a line of residential complexes, spread over different levels that are sometimes reached by scrambling down steep steps. Their unusual size is another testimony to the wealth of Calakmul, but they're also very varied, and the one known as the **House of the 6th Ahau** (Casa del 6 Ahau, although it cannot be identified with a specific ruler) has a particularly secluded feel. At the far, western end of the Acropolis they are built against a section of the giant **Muralla** or defensive wall that circled the central area of Calakmul. This too seems to be built on a different scale from most Mayan cities, thick enough to have come from a European castle.

Beyond the walls there are of course more structures still in the woods. Not far away but hard to find without a guide is a round slab often called the **Piedra de los Cautivos** ('Stone of the Captives'). On its flat surface there are four huge, apparently tormented carved figures, and it is suggested prisoners were tortured here. Another school of thought calls it the **Piedra de la Fertilidad**, suggesting people came here if they wanted a child, on the basis that one of the figures seems to have an erection.

Balamkú

Five km west of the turn off to Calakmul, a good road leads off the highway in 2km to the ruins; open daily 8–5; adm, Sun adm free.

This small site is a long way from the main Río Bec area. It was only discovered in 1990, but is one of the most fascinating of the small sites. It has one of the largest surviving stucco friezes in the Mayan world, and nowhere else will you see so much original Mayan colour.

Balamkú is another site that was occupied from about 300 BC, but its most important buildings are from AD 300–600. There are three groups of interlocking plazas, only two of which have so far been excavated. You first reach the **Grupo Sur**, with two broad squares divided by a near-Río Bec-style semi-vertical pyramid. From there, you carry on along the wooded path to the larger **Grupo Central**, announced by a medium-sized square with a platform on one side with a residential patio, and monster-masks on its façade.

Beyond that is the largest of the city's plazas and the great star of Balamkú, the **Templo de los Frisos** ('Temple of the Friezes'). During excavations the removal of a later layer of building uncovered an intact, 20m-long painted stucco frieze from before AD 600, a mass of mythological images and animal figures. This is now sheltered within a strange concrete structure to preserve it, guarded by one of the site warden's children, who will let you in (*for a tip*). Inside, the new 'shed' generates a temperature of around 45°C, but the visit is worth it. Along the bottom level of the frieze there are earth monsters, representing the basic level of existence, the border between this world and the underworld, from which all other things spring. Above them are various animals, including finely modelled monkeys. The most prominent creatures at Balamkú are toads, companions and helpers of the earth spirits. The largest toad's mouth is thrown right open, and a king-like figure, an *ahau*, is shown emerging from it. The frieze thus presents and reaffirms the *ahau*'s sacred origin and his connection to the spirits of the earth.

Leaving Balamkú, if you don't have to go back to Xpuhil, it's 88 kilometres west to **Escárcega**, from where there are roads to the north and south (*see p.402*). Around 40 kilometres along the road at Centenario is the **Laguna Silvituc**, a big jungle lake with a waterside restaurant where locals (and the odd intrepid foreigner) go to cool off.

Campeche State

12

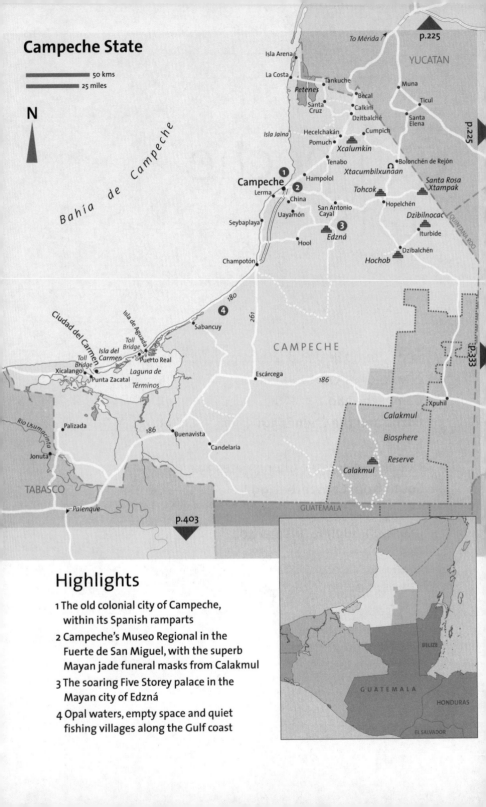

Campeche State

50 kms
25 miles

N

Bahía de Campeche

To Mérida

YUCATAN

p.225

p.225

p.333

Isla Arena
La Costa
Petenes
Tankuche
Santa Cruz
Becal
Calkiní
Dzitbalché
Muna
Ticul
Isla Jaina
Hecelchakán
Pomuch
Cumpich
Santa Elena
Xcalumkin
Tenabo
Bolonchén de Rejón
Campeche
Lerma
Hampolol
Xtacumbilxunaan
Tohcok
Santa Rosa Xtampak
China
San Antonio Cayal
Hopelchén
Seybaplaya
Uayamón
Dzibilnocac
Edzná
Hool
Iturbide
Champotón
Dzibalchén
Hochob

180

261

CAMPECHE

186

Ciudad del Carmen
Isla de Aguada
Sabancuy
Toll Bridge
Isla del Carmen
Toll Bridge
Puerto Real
Xicalango
Punta Zacatal
Laguna de Términos
Escárcega
Xpuhil
Calakmul
Rio Usumacinta
Palizada
Biosphere
Jonuta
186
Buenavista
Candelaria
Reserve
Calakmul
TABASCO
Palenque
GUATEMALA

p.403

BELIZE
GUATEMALA
HONDURAS
EL SALVADOR

Highlights

1 The old colonial city of Campeche,
  within its Spanish ramparts
2 Campeche's Museo Regional in the
  Fuerte de San Miguel, with the superb
  Mayan jade funeral masks from Calakmul
3 The soaring Five Storey palace in the
  Mayan city of Edzná
4 Opal waters, empty space and quiet
  fishing villages along the Gulf coast

The state of Campeche feels hard done by. Until very recently, of the thousands who visit Mérida and Yucatán state each year, or the far larger crowds who fly into Cancún, only a handful took even a look at the third state of the peninsula.

Campeche, though, has plenty of attractions. The state capital is the most complete Spanish colonial fortified city in the whole of Mexico, still ringed by its 17th-century bastions. The city has perhaps the most striking archaeological museum in the whole region – a 'must' for anyone interested in the ancient Maya – with, as its centrepiece, the superb treasures recently excavated at Calakmul. There are rare and fascinating landscapes, and a remarkable range of wildlife. Campeche has Gulf-coast beaches, and the most varied and subtle food in the Yucatán. Inland there is the great city of Edzná, one of the most enigmatic of Mayan sites. In fact, Campeche has the largest number of archaeological sites (excavated and not) of any state in Mexico.

Campeche was the first city founded by the Spaniards in the Yucatán, and until virtually the end of the colonial era was the only port of the peninsula and one of the most important cities of Spain's American empire, one of the few allowed to carry on foreign trade. After independence it squabbled endlessly with Mérida in the semi-independent Yucatán, refusing to accept second-city status, until Campeche finally got its wish with the granting of separate statehood by Juárez in 1863. It's true to say, though, that left to itself Campeche has scarcely ever taken off. The ending of the imperial trading monopoly, and the diversion of Yucatán trade through Sisal and then Progreso, were the beginnings of a prolonged decline. Since the 1970s oil, discovered around the Laguna de Términos, has pumped new wealth into parts of the state, but more than other cities Campeche seems to hark back to old glories. The state is still very thinly populated, and compared to Yucatán state there's noticeably less activity, a more remote feel and a pervasive sense of quietness.

Travelling in rural Campeche therefore has its eccentricities. Since there have been few visitors, there have been few facilities. Things have begun to change a little in the last few years, and the state government is making great efforts to attract more outside attention, polishing up the old city of Campeche and improving access to Mayan sites. The range of places to stay has expanded discreetly but significantly, from luxury *haciendas* to Río Bec *cabañas*. In many areas, though, hotels, signposts and organized tours remain thin on the ground. To appreciate the place you have to be prepared to meet it more than halfway, and explore.

The Camino Real and the Campeche Petenes

The northern part of the state grew up around the *Camino Real*, the old Spanish road to Mérida that is now Highway 180, and all its main towns lie along it. Just inside Campeche is the famous little town of **Becal**, long dedicated to the making of *jipis*, panama hats, woven from the local *jipijapa* palm. Becal hats are found all over the Yucatán, but strangely in Becal itself surprisingly little is done to push them at the passing tourist. Around the plaza there are several shops (*often closed*) with local *artesanía* inside, and on the north side of town there are a few small workshops.

Traditionally hats have been made in caves in the limestone to keep the palm supple, and some workshops towards the Mérida road have backyard caves that customers can visit. One shop that's usually open and has hats, palm bags and other accessories is **Artesanía Becaleña** (C/ 30), off the plaza. Be sure to get the price clear when buying.

Eight kilometres further on is **Calkiní**, the largest town on the road, with a big market and one of the most venerated of Yucatán country churches, **San Luis Obispo**. Built in the 18th century, it has a fine neo-baroque façade, but is known above all for its carving, especially the painted altarpiece. In a chapel left of the altar is the Cristo de Calkiní, a powerfully carved figure of Christ surrounded by flowers and clad in a vivid purple apron. The chapel also retains some of its original wall painting, in a kind-of European neoclassical style, but in Mexican pinks and blues with plenty of flowers.

The Petenes

Calkiní is the point of access into the Petenes region of coastal Campeche. The northern coastal strip of the state consists of a dense network of mangroves, lagoons and *petenes*, a word of Mayan origin for 'islands' of solid land and jungle vegetation that appear within the swamp. Because of their isolation the *petenes* form micro-climates, and are peculiarly rich and fragile ecosystems. The whole area contains a wealth of fish, crustaceans, birds and animals such as flamingos, dwarf falcons, armadillos, deer and (they say) pumas. Above all it is full of water birds such as ibis and blue herons, unused to being disturbed by humans and therefore easy to spot.

Since 1996 this little-known and scarcely inhabited region has been a protected area. From Calkiní a seemingly endless road winds 70 kilometres west across the *petenes* to **Isla Arena**, one of very few communities on this coast. This island fishing village used to be a secret kept by *campechanos*, but since 1999 a causeway from the mainland has made getting to it easier (a relative term). With the aid of island fish-ermen many trips are possible: into the *petenes* and mangroves, up to the flamingo grounds and Celestún, or to 'lost beaches' nearby. Isla Arena is developing a commu-nity ecotourism scheme to offer more regular trips, and there's already a small hotel (*see* facing page). On the way to Isla Arena, in incomprehensible isolation about half-way along the road from Calkiní at **El Remate**, there is a surprisingly neat and pretty little nature park (*official adm charge, but there may be nobody around to collect it*).

Lancheros from Isla Arena can also take you to see and just possibly visit the mysterious **Isla Jaina**, one of the most remarkable but least seen of Mayan sites. For centuries Mayan lords were brought here to be buried, often with exceptionally fine offerings: ceramic pots, jade jewellery and, above all, superbly modelled clay figurines, made in a unique local style. Often in the form of whistles, each one was a completely individual portrait, of the lord, his family and retinue; they are some of the greatest creations of Mayan art, and are among those artefacts that most bring the culture to life before the modern eye. Jaina figurines can be seen in many museums, but until very recently it was all but impossible to visit the island: so in demand are Jaina figures among collectors that there has been heavy looting of the site, and to prevent

Getting Around and Tourist Information

Isla Arena t (996–)

Second-class buses run twice daily from Calkiní to **Isla Arena**, at 8am, 1pm; ask the drivers or in the village about current times of returns. *Combis* run more frequently, especially before noon.

Tours

Tours from Isla Arena: Sociedad Ojo de Agua, t (village *caseta*) 963 6567. The village cooperative in Isla Arena, which can provide boat trips to any part of the area with local guides. Costs are quite high (around $140 per boat for a whole day) so as with most such trips you need to gather a group together (boats take a maximum of six). Arrangements are made through the president and chief guide, José Luis Cupul; the only phone is a village *caseta*, so be ready to explain what you want.

Isla Jaina permits: INAH-Campeche, Casa del Teniente del Rey, C/59 no.36, x 14 & 16, Campeche, t (981) 516 9111; or via INAH central office on *www.inah.gob.mx* (Spanish only). If you obtain your own permit you will have to arrange transport separately; at present, the Isla Arena cooperative can take you there if you have a permit. Agencies and hotels offering trips to Jaina include **Chito Tours** (*see* p.383), and **Hacienda Uayamón** (*see* p.384). Permits are issued at the INAH's discretion: with such trips it's wise to make arrangements as far ahead as possible.

Where to Stay and Eat

Isla Arena t (996–)

Hacienda Blanca Flor, reservations via Mérida t (999) 925 9655, *www.ccecamp.com.mx /blancaflor.htm* (*moderate*). An 18th-century hacienda near the Camino Real north of Hecelchakán converted not into a luxury *hacienda*-hotel but something much more modest, with fittings like those of a mid-range hotel. But, it still has the feel of a crumbling mansion, with rambling gardens, and is very peaceful. Simple meals are provided, and there's a pool, horse riding and other activities. Reservations are essential, as the staff are not ready for casual callers.

Isla Arena, t (village *caseta*) 963 6567 (*cheap*). The village hotel has just three very basic rooms (more are promised) with showers, right by the water's edge, for around $10 per night.

this the island is protected by the Mexican military. However, visits are now occasionally permitted, with a special permit from the archaeological authorities of the INAH. You can apply for one directly, or some tour agencies and hotels have them; the Isla Arena cooperative is also applying to be allowed to take trips (*see* above).

Back on the Camino Real, from Calkiní it's another 24 kilometres to **Hecelchakán**, the last sizeable stop before Campeche. On one side of its plaza there is a small museum, the **Museo Arqueológico del Camino Real** (*open Tues–Sat 10–1 and 4–7, Sun 9–noon; closed Mon; adm free*). Its main attraction is its collection of Jaina figurines, but it has ceramics and stone *stelae*, all unlabelled. A detour of 12 kilometres up the road east towards Bolonchén will lead you to a Mayan site recently opened up at **Xcalumkin** (*open daily 8–4.30; adm*). It's down a dirt track about a kilometre from the road on the south side, indicated by a small blue INAH sign. This is really one of the Puuc sites, but is little known due mainly to its out-of-the-way location in Campeche. It is of considerable historical significance as one of the oldest 'pre-Puuc' communities, established in the early 7th century. Several small pyramids and temple platforms, with instantly recognizable Puuc-style mouldings, are visible today, but one of the site's greatest attractions is its atmospheric location, nestling in a snug, lonely valley.

Returning again to the *Camino Real*, 20 kilometres north of Campeche a sign right indicates the **Hampolol wildlife reserve** (*often closed; officially open Mon–Sat 9–noon; closed Sun; adm*). It's primarily a study centre, but has a small collection of local wildlife on show (and a very tame and greedy spider monkey).

Campeche

The old city of Campeche sits within a ring of seven *baluartes* or bastions, over-looked by fortresses on hills to the north and south, which make it impossible to forget its one-time status as a citadel of the Spanish Main. Within the old walls, there is as great a density of churches as in many a European city, and streets of elegant colonial houses with tropical patios glimpsed behind sober façades and windows faced with very Spanish-looking iron grilles. In the last few years the houses of old Campeche have been beautifully restored and repainted in their original delicate colours of blues, greens and ochre, with details picked out in white.

Campeche's old city is one of the gems of the Yucatán, and thanks in good part to the model way in which its charms have been restored it was declared a UNESCO world heritage site in 1999. This in turn has played its part in putting it a little more 'on the map', and more clusters of foreigners are now visible on the streets. There is,

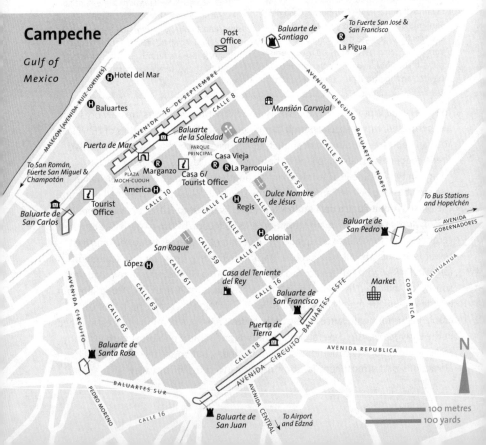

though, something a tad odd about Campeche. To add to its fine architecture it has a romantic history, of pirates, seafarers and sieges. It has a seafront location, and some of the best restaurants and one of the best museums in the Yucatán. Parts of the city are quite prosperous, and there's less visible poverty than in many Mexican towns. The oddness is that the constant street life that is so much a feature of colonial cities like Mérida or San Cristóbal just isn't there in Campeche. It is visibly a city, but on most days it seems to have the movement of a small town. Even the market is relatively quiet. The excitement of pirate days seems long forgotten, and the city's people have a rather quiet reserve. Essential to its charm is an airy, seafront tranquility.

History

There is no real evidence Campeche was an ancient Mayan settlement, but by the end of the Postclassic, about 1500, it was a prosperous small city on the trading route around the Yucatán, the capital of a lordship known as Kin Pech or Ah Kin Pech (translatable as 'Lord Sun Tick', as in cattle tick). Its ruler was a redoubtable leader called Moch-Cuouh. Its people got their first sight of Europeans on 22 March 1517, when the ships of Hernández de Córdoba hove into view. It was the day of Saint Lazarus, and so the Spaniards first called the town San Lázaro. They were desperate for water, having found nowhere to put in all the way round the peninsula. Moch-Cuouh gave them some, but made it clear he wouldn't allow them to stay. Hernández sailed on to the mouth of the river at Champotón, still within the lands of Kin Pech. When they landed Moch-Cuouh attacked the Spaniards, and nearly destroyed the whole expedition.

Grijalva was also driven off in 1518, and although the *Adelantado* Montejo took Campeche in 1531 he was forced to abandon it three years later. It was not until 1540, by which time Moch-Cuouh was dead – almost certainly from disease – that Montejo *el Mozo*, marching up from Champotón, managed definitively to take Campeche. On 4 October that year he made it the first properly established Spanish 'city' in the Yucatán, this time with the name San Francisco de Campeche.

As the essential point of communication between the Yucatán and both the home country and New Spain to the west, Spanish Campeche grew and prospered. In 1545 the Franciscans arrived and began to build the first permanent church in the peninsula, San Francisco. Although the Yucatán produced no precious metals Campeche developed a trade that was almost as valuable in salt and tropical dyewoods, *palo de tinte*, found around the Laguna de Términos and in great demand throughout Europe.

It was the dyewood trade and its profits that attracted the attention of the one group who would have most impact on the history of Campeche: pirates. In the 1550s a band of French maritime roughnecks established a stronghold on the Isla de Tris at the mouth of the Laguna de Términos (now the Isla del Carmen), and the first attack on Campeche followed in 1561. The city was rich, and yet its relative isolation made it a far safer target than a better defended city like Veracruz. For over a century, battered Campeche would be one of the places most raided by the Caribbean buccaneers. Time and again, the Spanish population would take refuge from pirate bands in the convent of San Francisco, closer to God and the most solid building in Campeche.

Getting Around

By Air

Campeche's little **airport**, reached along the avenue that runs east from the Puerta de Tierra, Av. Central, has daily flights to **Mexico City**, and nowhere else, with **Aerocaribe, t** 816 9074. The usual taxi arrangements from airports apply (*see* p.107).

By Bus

The separate bus depots in Campeche are helpfully all in the same place. The main ADO **first-class terminal**, used by several companies, is on the corner of Av. Gobernadores and Av. de Chile, four (quite long) blocks east of the Circuito Baluartes from the Baluarte de San Pedro. The main **second-class station** is behind the ADO. ATG's Elite first-class buses have a depot on the same block, a little further toward the centre. To get to the centre from the bus stations, take a cab or any local bus marked 'Centro', which run to the Parque Principal. Main bus routes from Campeche are as follows; many first-class and all second-class buses south stop at **Champotón**:

Ciudad del Carmen (*3hrs*): one ADO GL, 12 first-class and more *intermedios* and second-class daily. First-class fare about $11.

Chetumal (*7hrs*): one first-class daily (12 noon) via **Escárcega** and **Xpuhil**. Fare about $20.

Cancún (*7hrs*): via Mérida, two first-class and one *intermedio* daily; one first-class bus (11.30pm) continues to **Playa del Carmen**. Fare to Cancún about $27.

Hopelchén: at least 12 second-class daily; six continue to **Dzibalchén** and **Iturbide** (from where one goes on to Xpuhil), and five go on the 'slow route' to **Mérida** passing via **Kabah** and **Uxmal**.

Mérida (*3hrs*): one GL daily and ADO first-class roughly every hour, plus five Elite first-class and second-class buses every half-hour, roughly 6am–11.30pm daily. Fare about $9.50. There are also five second-class buses daily on the 'slow route' to Mérida via Hopelchén and Uxmal.

Mexico City (*21hrs*): one ADO GL and six ordinary first-class daily. Fare about $71.

Palenque (*7hrs*): via **Escárcega**, five first-class daily from the ADO and several more ATG-Elite and second-class. Two of the ADO services (Altos, 10.15pm, Maya de Oro, midnight) also continue to **San Cristóbal de Las Casas** and **Tuxtla Gutiérrez**. Since these buses originate in Mérida timings through Campeche may vary. Fares from about $17 to Palenque, $26 to San Cristóbal.

Villahermosa (*6hrs*): one ADO GL, seven ordinary first-class and at least nine second-class (via Ciudad del Carmen or Escárcega) daily. First-class fare about $22.

Xpuhil: one first-class (Chetumal bus, *5hrs*) and two second-class daily via **Escárcega**, and one second-class via Hopelchén and Zoh-Laguna (*7hrs or more*). First-class fare about $15.

Combis, some second-class routes to nearby villages (including Edzná) and local city buses in Campeche nearly all leave from or pass by the market, near the Baluarte de San Pedro and Av. Costa Rica on Circuito Baluartes. The local buses can be useful for getting out to the fortress museums.

By Car and Taxi

Campeche's lack of traffic means it's extremely easy to drive around, and there's even unrestricted parking in many streets. There are *gasolineras* on Av. Ruíz Cortines north and south of the old city, and further south on the way to Lerma. Campeche is the one Mexican city where you actually have to look around to find a **taxi**, or even call for one. However, they're still cheap.

Car Hire

Car hire is not well developed. The few local agencies are expensive, and if you can you will get a far better deal by going on to Mérida and hiring there.

Auto Rent, Hotel del Paseo, C/ 8 no. 215, **t** 811 0100. About the best of the agencies, a little south of the Baluarte de San Carlos toward San Román church.

Jaina, Av. López Portillo 51, **t** 816 2233. Has a limited stock of cars for hire.

Orientation

The main north–south road forms a wide loop inland around Campeche, making it possible to bypass the city completely, although this is hardly necessary given the low density of traffic. The road into Campeche meets the shoreline and becomes Av. Ruíz Cortines along the waterfront, the Malecón. Most of Campeche's hotels and attractions – except for the two fortress museums – are within the old city, contained inside the Spanish walls, the Circuito Baluartes. Streets parallel to the sea have even numbers, those running away from it have odd ones.

Tourist Information

Campeche t (981–)

Tourist Offices: The **city information desk** is inside the Casa Seis on the Parque Principal (*open Mon–Fri 9–2.30 and 5–9, Sat and Sun 9–1*). The **Campeche state office** (*open Mon–Sat 8–2 and 4–8; closed Sun*) is housed in the government buildings on the Plaza Moch-Cuouh, to the left of the Puerta de Mar looking seawards. Both have similar information on and can make bookings for tours in and around Campeche; the Casa Seis desk will also have information on the city's entertainment programme, and sells tickets for the Sound and Light show (*see below, p.385*).

Banks: Main branches are all near the Parque Principal. All have ATM machines.

Health: There's a **pharmacy** in the arcades on the Parque Principal.

Internet Access: There are plenty of Internet shops, especially along C/ 8 (the apparently nameless one next to the Hotel Reforma has good rates).

Laundry: A good one is Tintorería-Lavandería Campeche, at C/ 55 no. 22, x 12 & 14.

Phone Office: A decent-value office is on C/ 8 near the corner of C/ 59.

Post Office (with Mexpost): Corner of Av. 16 de Septiembre and C/ 53 (*open Mon–Fri 8–7, Sat 9–1; closed Sun*).

Tours and Tour Agencies

A special tourist bus, the **Tranvía de la Ciudad** or 'City Tram' (an open-sided bus) does a circuit of the old city that takes in all the main sights. It starts from the Parque Principal, where there's a ticket booth; there are seven departures daily (*9.30–12.30 and*

6–8) and it costs around $2 (children half-price). Another daily tourist bus known as **El Guapo** continues on to the fortresses of San José (*9am, 5pm*) or San Miguel (*10am, 11am, 6pm, 7pm*).

Several tour agencies run city tours and offer one-day tours to Edzná and the Chenes, and tours of one or more days to Calakmul and the Río Bec (*see p.362, p.369*).

Chito Tours, C/ 51 no. 9, x 8 & 10, t 811 3996, *chitotours@your-house.com*. City tours, Edzná, Calakmul and 'rural routes' north on the Camino Real. Also now offers guided trips to Isla Jaina (*see pp.378–9*), but these need to be arranged well in advance.

Intermar, Av. Miguel Alemán s/n, t 816 9006, *intercan@prodigy.net.mx*. Campeche city tours (by day and night), a smarter than usual tour to Edzná (with the possibility of lunch at Hacienda Uayamón), the Chenes and Calakmul.

Viajes Picazh, t 816 4426. Twice-daily tours to Edzná (*9am, 1.30pm*); with a guide (around $25 per person) or transport-only (around $20). They leave from the Puerta de Tierra, and tickets are sold there, in hotels and from the Tranvía ticket booth. They will also pick up from hotels.

Shopping

Casa de Artesanías Tukulná, C/ 10 no. 333, x 59 & 61. Although privately run this is the official state showcase-store for local handicrafts, occupying a charming old house filled with a wonderful selection of ceramics, basketwork, embroidery and less classifiable things such as handmade deckchairs (which might be a bit hard to transport). There are beautiful traditional Campeche blouses, a variation on the *huípil*, only with sober black on white embroidery instead of the livid colours of Yucatán.

Where to Stay

Campeche t (981–)

With the recent modest tourist 'boom' in the city hotel prices have taken a noticeable hike, and not always with a corresponding improvement in services.

Luxury–Expensive

Hacienda Uayamón, reservations via Mérida
t (019) 944 3637, *www.grupoplan.com
/www.luxurycollection.com* (*luxury*). Upscale
accommodation around Campeche has
been drastically transformed with the
opening of this '*hacienda* hotel', in the 19th-
century buildings of an old *henequen* estate
about 30km from the city, off the Edzná
road. There are 10 rooms and two very chic
suites, with *de rigueur* opulent bathrooms,
in separate pavilions around the main
house, which like all the *haciendas* has a
lovely terrace and fine **restaurant** (*expensive*). The conversion has been done with
great panache, and the pool, in an unre-
stored ruined building, is stunning
(although its sun deck can be a fearsome
sun-trap). The countryside around is very
empty, and it feels still more like a lost rural
retreat than the Yucatán *haciendas*, but a
superior range of excursions is available.
Room prices start from around $300.

Hotel del Mar, Av. Ruiz Cortines 51, t 816 2233,
delmarcp@camp1.telmex.net.mx (*expensive*).
Campeche's established 'top hotel' (formerly
the Ramada), presiding over the Malecón.
A big, white 1970's block, it has all the
comforts you'd expect (superior a/c), but
is fairly characterless. A compensation in
rooms at the front (over $100 a night) is
the fine sea view; those at the back are a
bit cheaper, but the car-park view is drab.

Moderate

Hotel América, C/ 10 no. 252, x 59 & 61, t 816
4588, *www.hotelamericacampeche.com*. A
characterful old-city hotel, very near the
main square, in a renovated colonial house
with a big, light patio. Not all the rooms are
as impressive as the exterior and they're
now pricey for the state of their fittings,
but they are at least spacious and airy.
Most of them have a/c, but some are
fan-only. The service is charming, and a
continental breakfast and free Internet
access are also included.

Hotel Baluartes, Av. 16 de Septiembre 128, t 816
3911, f 816 2410. Alongside the Hotel Del Mar,
in similarly bland style, the Baluartes has
recently undergone substantial renovation,
but remains a lot cheaper. Rooms are big,
light and airy; it also has a pool and a
pleasant **restaurant**, and from the front you
get the same sea view as from the best
rooms at the Del Mar.

Ocean View, Av. Pedro Sainz de Baranda, t 811
99 99, *www.oceanview-hotels.com*. A very
competitive innovation in Campeche, an all-
new hotel with sea view amid the car parks
and open spaces at the north end of the
Malecón near the Convention Centre. The
rooms have every mod con and business
facilities, and it's much better value than the
Del Mar, but don't go looking for character,
as the hotel's corporate style is completely
international-bland.

Inexpensive

Hotel Regis, C/ 12 no. 148, x 55 & 57, t 816 3175. A
pleasant hotel in a well-renovated old house
two blocks from the plaza, with comfortable
rooms all with TV and a/c.

Hotel López, C/ 12 no. 189, x 61 & 63, t 816 3344,
f 816 2488. Along the same street as the
Regis, the López has a pretty patio and
rooms (most of which have a/c) that are
almost overfurnished, to the point of being
somewhat cramped. They are also a little
more expensive.

Posada del Angel, C/ 10 no. 307, x 53 & 55, t 816
7718. A straightforward place right next to
the cathedral. Its rooms (some with a/c) are
a bit dark, but clean and well kept.

Cheap

Hotel Castelmar, C/ 61 no. 2, x 8 & 10, t 816
2886. Campeche has a clutch of very cheap
hotels, all situated near the Parque Principal.
This is about the best of them: the nearby
Reforma and Campeche are pretty dingy.

Hotel Colonial, C/ 14 no. 122, x 55 & 57, t 816
2630. A Campeche institution located in
the one-time home of Miguel de Castro y
Araoz, Lieutenant-Governor of Campeche
and one of the last Spanish governors of
the Yucatán, who died in 1820. The hotel
has a distinctive elderly character, as do
the owners, who have not jacked up their
prices at all since 1999. The rooms are very
well maintained, and actually as good as
most of those in the next price slot up.
Most of them are fan-only, but some have
a/c (*inexpensive*).

Eating Out

One major reason to stop off in Campeche could be to eat. Though apparently unexcited about so many things, this city cares about its food, and *cocina campechana*, based on fish and seafood, is very distinctive and has greater subtlety than many Mexican cuisines. Classic local dishes are *pan de cazón*, young hammerhead shark (*cazón*) chopped up and baked between *tortillas* in a tomato sauce, *camarón al coco* (prawn/shrimp cooked in coconut), *arroz con pulpo* (octopus and rice salad), *manitas de cangrejo* (crab claws, served mixed with other seafood) and fish served many different ways, especially shark, red and black snapper, pompano and prawns.

Expensive

La Pigua, Av. Miguel Alemán 179-A, **t** 811 3365. Generally recognized by Campechanos as the best in town, this pretty but discreet seafood restaurant is just north of the *baluartes* on the avenue that continues from C/ 8, and recognizable by a bright blue entrance. Its variations on traditional dishes are very skilfully done – especially the great *arroz con pulpo* – with superb local ingredients, and it's extremely comfortable; by any international standard it's also still very cheap. Like older-style upscale restaurants in Yucatán it only opens for lunch.

Restaurante Marganzo, C/ 8 no. 265, x 57 & 59, **t** 811 3898. With colourful semi-traditional décor, the Marganzo is just off the Parque Principal. Service is charming. It's better-known than La Pigua (and open at night), but the dishes, on similar themes, are not quite as inventive.

Moderate

Casa Vieja, C/ 10 no. 319 (Parque Principal). This bar-restaurant with refined Campechano dishes stands or falls by its wonderful location, in the elegant first-floor colonnade above the *portales* of the Parque Principal, with a lovely view of the square and the floodlit Cathedral. .

La Iguana Azul, C/ 55 no. 9, x 10 & 12. A vaguely youth-oriented modern restaurant, opposite the traditional La Parroquia, with self-conscious tropical décor but an original menu offering an imaginative, contemporary take on Mexican Gulf Coast cooking.

La Parroquia, C/ 55 no. 8, x 10 & 12. A great, long-running family restaurant with relaxing character, just off the main square. Unfussily friendly and fine value, it offers enjoyable *campechano* fish specialities as well as Mexican standards and bargain breakfasts. *Usually open 24hrs.*

La Principal, Parque Principal. Gains by its bandstand location in the middle of the Parque, and its terrace tables are a fine place for enjoying light meals, pastas, snacks and sandwiches alfresco.

Restaurant Miramar, C/ 8 no. 203-A, corner of C/ 61. Further along the same street as the Marganzo, but simpler and cheaper, the Miramar also offers good seafood dishes (particularly *arroz con mariscos*) served in a charming, old-Campeche setting.

Cheap

Café-Restaurant Campeche, C/ 57 no. 2, x 8 (Parque Principal). For some reason this big, light restaurant is less popular with the backpacking clan than Restaurante del Parque next door, but is no more expensive and has a more interesting menu (and a/c).

Restaurante del Parque, C/ 57, x 8 (Parque Principal). A foreigners' favourite on the corner of the Parque, which gives you an opportunity to sample a few of the local specialities at bargain-basement prices, and also has enjoyable breakfasts.

Entertainment and Nightlife

A recently-upgraded **Sound and Light spectacular** evoking Campeche's pirate history is put on at the **Puerta de Tierra** at 8pm every Tues, Fri and Sat, and daily in holiday seasons (Christmas, Easter). Tickets can be bought on the spot or from the Casa Seis information desk. The city also sponsors a variety of free live entertainment: there are *Serenatas Campechanas* of traditional music in the Casa Seis every Thurs at 8.30pm, and concerts – from chamber music to pop and *boleros* – nearly every Fri and Sat performed from the bandstand in the Parque Principal.

One of the greatest attacks was in 1635, when 500 men, led by Diego *el Mulato* and a Dutchman known as *Pie de Palo*, 'Peg-leg', seized the town and held it to ransom, sending a message into San Francisco that they would only leave for a hefty pay-off in gold. The locals decided not to pay, and launched a break-out. The pirates went back to their ships, but took almost everything movable in Campeche with them. The Spanish governors seemed incapable of eliminating the anarchic haunt of Tris, or of holding on to pirates when they captured them. In 1669 'Rock Brasiliano' (another Dutchman) was caught in an attack on Campeche, but had a letter sent to the city threatening an assault by another (nonexistent) pirate band if he was not released. The governor was suitably duped, and let him go.

When in 1684 another large-scale attack was made on Campeche, led by the Flemish pirate Laurent Graff (or *Lorencillo*), the Spanish governors decided something must be done. A special tax was levied, and work began on building a ring of ramparts and bastions around the city. The city's merchants were able to sleep more peacefully in their beds, especially once the pirate den of Tris was finally overwhelmed in 1718. The walls of Campeche were further supplemented throughout the 18th century, above all with the building of the forts of San José and San Miguel north and south of the town, this time against possible attacks by the British Navy.

As a trading city in contact with the outside world Campeche had great hopes of independence. However, as soon as it lost the commercial privileges of the Spanish imperial system its trade – and with it shipbuilding and many of the town's occupa-tions – fell by almost mathematical progression. The dyewood trade faded away too during the 19th century, the Campeche forests having been over-exploited. Nor were Campeche's politicians ever able to sort out their relationship with Mérida in the new state of Yucatán. The two were briefly able to come together in 1842, when Santa Anna (*see* pp.70–71) tried to reincorporate the Yucatán into Mexico by force, and landed an army and besieged Campeche, using the Fuerte San Miguel as his head-quarters. To the surprise of all concerned, the Yucatecan army was victorious, and the 'Mexicans' were beaten back. The shock of the Caste War, though, undermined the idea of a united Yucatán and made easier the division into two states in 1863. From then on the role played by city and state in Mexican affairs has been discreet. Since the 1960s, revenues from oil – discovered in southern Campeche – have provided the main new element in the state capital's fortunes.

Around the Old City

At the core of old Campeche there is naturally a plaza, the **Parque Principal**, which once opened directly on to the shore and landing-stages for ships. At its centre there is a very Victorian-looking bandstand between magnificently spreading trees, and the inland side is lined by attractive, shady arcades; part of the seaward side is now occu-pied too, by a **library** built with an arcaded façade to harmonize with the rest of the square, but which is actually brand new, completed in 2001. On the left-hand side, looking towards the sea, there is the **Casa Seis** (*open daily 9am–10pm; adm free*), a more than usually gracious old Campeche house which has been very carefully restored. As well as housing the city tourist information desk, exhibitions and cultural events it contains several fascinating rooms where antiques from around the city have been charmingly used to recreate Campeche interiors of the 19th century. Guided tours are sometimes available. The Casa Seis patios and the square's bandstand are also the hub of the city's free music and entertainment programme.

The view across the Parque Principal is dominated, though, by the giant towers of Campeche's **Cathedral**. It was built over a very long time, mostly from the 16th to the 18th centuries, and so is a mixture of several different elements. The central section of the façade is one of the older parts of the building, from the early 17th century, and in a plain Spanish Renaissance style reminiscent of the Escorial near Madrid or other buildings of the reign of Philip II; the towers either side of it were added over the following century, and not entirely finished until after independence.

Behind the new library on the seaward side of the square is one of the largest bastions of the Spanish city wall, the **Baluarte de la Soledad**, and one of the longest remaining sections of rampart. Walled Campeche had two main entrances. Curiously, the **Puerta de Mar** ('Sea Gate') is not on the plaza itself but just to the south of the Soledad at the end of C/ 59, which runs straight through to the other main gate, the Puerta de Tierra. If you walk through the Puerta de Mar you come into another broad plaza, with cannon and other relics of old Campeche and a great view of the Soledad. One of the strange things about Campeche until recently was how little it made of its seafront. In the 1960s, when 'modernization' rather than tourism was seen as the way ahead, the city was the object of a prestige programme called the *Resurgimiento* (Resurgence) *de Campeche*, which included rebuilding the waterfront so that the way to the sea was left dominated by offices, two big hotels, now the Del Mar and the Baluartes, and their car parks. However, the very different policy adopted in the '90s of respecting historic Campeche has led to the **Malecón** or waterfront being rebuilt again, so that it's now a much more attractive waterside promenade that's popular with locals for evening strolling, although it could still do with some cafés, especially for watching the (often wonderful) sunsets. Just south of the Puerta de Mar is the **Plaza Moch-Cuouh**, built during the *Resurgimiento* as a new, 'modern' town centre for official Campeche. Here are the tower-block **Palacio del Gobierno** and the **Palacio del Congreso**, the state Congress; the latter must have looked the height of new-wave modernity back in 1962, and is known as the *platillo volante* ('flying saucer').

An enjoyable way to get an idea of the old city is to walk around the *baluartes*, following the line of the walls. Most of the bastions now contain museums and other cultural institutions. The full circuit is about two kilometres, but can be shortened by cutting corners.

Campeche's walls were major products of the military technology of their time. The initial work, planned by the Spanish engineer Martín de la Torre, was refined and extended by French military engineers – then the greatest fortress-builders in Europe – after the arrival on the Spanish throne of the Bourbon dynasty under Louis XIV's grandson, Philip V, in 1700. The bastions are massive hexagons, with pepper-pot watchtowers at the corners. The **Baluarte de la Soledad**, designed to protect the Puerta de Mar and the sea approach to the city, is a classic example. Inside it there is the **Museo de las Estelas Mayas** (*open Tues–Sat 9–2 and 4–8, Sun 9–1; closed Mon; adm* *free*), with a collection of carved *stelae* from Mayan sites throughout Campeche state. Some of these *stelae* had been looted, but have since been recovered by INAH authorities. The drawback is that it's badly labelled even in Spanish, let alone English.

Taking the circuit in an anticlockwise direction, the next bastion, past the Puerta de Mar and Plaza Moch-Cuouh, is the **Baluarte de San Carlos**. This is one of the oldest parts of the wall, begun in 1686, and houses the **Museo de la Ciudad** (*open Tues–Sat 8–8, Sun 8–1; closed Mon; adm free*), the city history museum, an entertaining, old-fashioned but very detailed collection (in Spanish only) on *conquistadores*, Franciscan church-building, pirates and much else. As well as climbing up to the ramparts visitors can look into the dungeons down below. On the south side of the city there was once another gate, now demolished, which led to the *barrio* of San Román. Near where it stood there remains the **Baluarte de Santa Rosa**, now an exhibition space. It has a very impressive ramp that was used to take cannon up to the battlements, and very solid rooms for storing shot and gunpowder. Next after that is the **Baluarte de San Juan**, the beginning of the longest surviving unbroken stretch of wall, which runs 500 metres or so to the **Puerta de Tierra** ('Land Gate'), and alongside it the **Baluarte de San Francisco**, now an INAH library. Inside the Puerta de Tierra, built in 1732, there is another engaging small **museum** (*open daily 9–8; adm free*), dedicated to 'Maritime Campeche' and pirates. Ask the caretaker to let you up to the ramparts (*they're kept locked, but there's no charge*), where you can walk back along the wall to San Juan, and enjoy fine views over the old city. To tell him to let you back down again you have to ring the bell that once warned travellers that the city gates were about to be shut for the night. The Puerta de Tierra is also the site of the Sound and Light show (*see p.385*).

Just outside the walls by the Puerta de Tierra there is a shady but rather unkempt park dating from the colonial era, the **Alameda**, with a curious little bridge called the **Puente de los Perros** because of the stone dogs guarding it. The next block along is the only place in Campeche where you are ever likely to see a real crowd, since it contains the **market**. Beyond it in the eastern corner of the old city there is the **Baluarte de San Pedro**, which was used as a prison by the Inquisition and so has a Vatican coat-of-arms above its gateway. Next to it there is now a handicrafts market. The last bastion in the northern corner, the **Baluarte de Santiago**, was partly torn down in the 1900s and then restored in the 1950s. It now contains a very unusual and delightful little garden, the **Jardín Botánico Xmuch Haltún** (*open Tues–Sat 9–8, Sun 9–1; adm free*). Occasional free explanatory tours are given, in Spanish and English.

Within the 'walls', the streets of old Campeche have a special, old-world atmosphere enhanced by their very quietness, especially at night. Some of the most distinguished buildings are on C/ 59, between the two main gates. At number 36, between Calles 14 and 16, is the **Casa del Teniente del Rey**, former residence of the Spanish Lieutenant-Governor of Campeche, with plain, ochre-walled patios behind a grander portico, and which now contains the local INAH offices. Old Campeche is also full of churches, more colourfully ornate than those of Mérida and Yucatán proper. On the corner of C/ 59 and C/ 12 is the 18th-century **San Roque**, also known as San Francisquito, a wonderfully lush piece of Mexican Baroque with a vividly ornate altarpiece of ochre columns surrounded by white filigree plasterwork. It also contains a 17th-century painting of the Sacred Heart, by an artist, probably Flemish, called Michael Budesino. Three blocks along C/ 12 at C/ 55 there is the much larger **Dulce Nombre de Jesús**, also 18th-century, with a white interior interrupted by huge gold-on-white side altars.

On the next block on C/ 12 is the city's very imposing neoclassical **theatre**, built in the 19th century and now little used. One block from there towards the sea is one of the most impressive post-colonial residences in Campeche, the **Mansión Carvajal** (*C/ 10 no. 14, x 51 & 53*). It was built around 1900 for Ramón Carvajal y Estrada, a local *henequen hacendado*, in a Hispano-Moorish fantasy-style with patios of blue and white columns vaguely inspired by Córdoba and Granada. Today anyone is free to wander around, as it's an advice and health centre, and usually full of families with small children. At the other end of C/ 10, beyond the Parque by C/ 63, stands one of Campeche's largest churches, **San José**. Originally built as a Jesuit church in 1756, it's used today as an exhibition space. It's often closed, but it's still possible to appreciate its tiled façade, in chequered patterns of blue, white and gold.

Outside the Walls

Early colonial Campeche, like other Spanish American cities, had separate *barrios* outside its walls for other racial groups who were not allowed to live within the purely white city. San Román, south of the Circuito Baluartes and reached by continuing a few blocks along C/ 12, was originally the district for blacks and *mulatos*. At its centre there is a large, pretty and very tranquil plaza, dominated by the early Franciscan church of **San Román**. Inside it's similarly simple but pretty, with fine tiling, but its most distinctive feature is the figure of Christ above the altar, which is black.

North of the *baluartes*, a walk along Av. Miguel Alemán, the continuation of C/ 8, takes you into the *barrio* of Guadalupe, past little houses painted in blues, greens, reds and more of the local ochre. Continue on from there for another 500 metres or so to the very oldest surviving building of Spanish Campeche, **San Francisco**. Founded in 1546, this was the first missionary convent, and so chapel, built by the Franciscans anywhere in the Yucatán, as well as the place where *campechanos* sheltered from pirate attacks. Just outside the church there is the **Pozo de la Conquista**, a well where the expeditions of Hernández de Córdoba and later the Montejos are said to have come for fresh water. The district between San Francisco and the sea is modern Campeche's new 'growth area', with a gleaming new convention centre, and very un-*campechano* looking shopping malls and multiplex movie houses.

The Museo Regional and the Fortresses

For years the **Museo Regional de Campeche** was one of the more modest Mexican local museums, despite the wealth of archaeological sites in the state. It has been transformed by the extraordinary discoveries made at Calakmul and the Río Bec sites (*see* p.361) in the 1990s, including such spectacular artefacts as the jade funeral masks known as the *Máscaras de Calakmul*. Having outgrown its old home in the Casa del Teniente del Rey the museum was split and relocated to the two Spanish forts on hilltops either side of the town: the Mayan collection is in the Fuerte

Getting to the Forts

Fuerte San Miguel is easy to find by car: follow the coastal avenue, and look for a sign left on to a winding road up the hill. The **El Guapo** tourist bus runs there (*see* p.383), but otherwise you can take any normal bus marked 'Lerma' along Av. 16 de Septiembre or Av. Ruíz Cortines to the same road junction, and take on the steep (but not killing) walk up to the fort. If you take a **taxi**, it may be worthwhile to pay the driver to wait to take you back; check whether there are any other cabs waiting outside when you arrive.

Fuerte San José is harder to find: if you're going there by car, follow Av. Miguel Alemán to San Francisco, turn right and look out for signs to the left for San José el Alto. The road takes many twists and turns. As well as *El Guapo* there is a fairly direct bus: from the market, take any marked José el Alto or Bellavista, and ask the driver for the Fuerte San José. Buses return by the same route. **Taxis** are not plentiful.

San Miguel, to the south, while post-Conquest and maritime history is in Fuerte San José to the north. In 2000–2001 the Fuerte San Miguel was made into a striking modern museum space, to show off Campeche's Mayan treasures at their best. In particular, a visit here is now an essential complement to a trip to the Río Bec.

The two forts, built from 1779 to 1801 (San Miguel before San José), were as much at the forefront of military technology as the city's ramparts a century earlier, and are among the best examples in the Americas of the ideas of the French fortress-builder Montalembert. They squat deep into their hilltops, behind mounds of earth and moats, with sunken zigzag driveways to prevent any attacker getting a clear shot at the gates. However, they were only ever used once, during Santa Anna's attack of 1842.

The **Fuerte San Miguel** (*open Tues–Sun 8.30–7.30; adm*) stands atop its hill about three kilometres south of the Parque Principal. Despite the expensive renovation the museum still has its quirks, especially in labelling (*still Spanish only, with many items not fully identified*), but is very well worth the trek, a fascinating demonstration of the sheer range and variety of Mayan art. Most of its rooms are arranged by theme (Time, City Life, etc.) rather than location, which can be confusing, but the most impressive spaces deal with specific places, especially **Room V**, devoted to Calakmul, with the great stars of the museum, the *Máscaras*. With white stucco and black obsidian for their strange, staring eyes, and all with their accompanying necklaces and earrings, they have faces that range from monstrous to highly naturalistic; some have an extraordinarily lifelike beauty, an almost smiling stillness (*note, though, that the masks are also in demand for exhibitions worldwide, so some may be absent at any one time; check ahead if you're hoping to see the full set*). There's also a replica of the tomb of King Yichaak Kak or Jaguar-Paw of Calakmul just as he was discovered in 1997. Another room (**Room IV**) is given over to Isla Jaina, with a dazzling collection of the island's figurines, showing an enormous variety of posture and expression: big-bellied merchants, women quietly weaving, even a man having a very difficult shit, another example of the Mayas' constant ability to surprise. Spread through all the rooms there are superb, intricate ceramics, such as a fabulously beautiful, modern-looking alabaster vase believed to have been made in Honduras, macaw-design painted pots from Balamkú, and stucco reliefs from Xcalumkin. After you've been around the collection, you can go up to the fort's ramparts for a look at the cannon, fresh air and a wonderful view. Down below by the sea there's another small fort, San Luis.

The collection at the **Fuerte San José** (*open Tues–Sun 8–8; closed Mon; adm*), cut off from the Mayan artefacts, is far less spectacular. There's a fair amount of information on early Campeche and pirates (*all in Spanish*), plus muskets, swords, plates, buttons and other nautical relics, and a few oddities that seem to have got here by accident, like an Arab axe. From the top, though, there's an even better view. Not far from the fort, overlooking Campeche, there's a huge and ugly 1940s statue of Juárez, a fine example of the similarities between Mexican Revolutionary and Stalinist art.

Edzná and the Chenes

If Campeche as a whole does not receive many visitors, the centre of the state sees even fewer. The Chenes style of architecture is referred to in every book on the Maya, yet the Chenes sites and even the nearby city of Edzná are little known, too far from the well-publicized Mérida–Cancún routes and at the end of too many winding forest roads to be an easy trip. This area, though, is not really hard to get to, and the very absence of other travellers can make a visit here an enjoyably personal experience.

Edzná

Open 8–5; adm exp, Sun adm free.

Although Edzná is on the western edge of the Chenes region, it is really one of the great Mayan cities that – like Chichén Itzá – stand on its own, with a unique combination of styles and features that reflects its position at a crossroads in the flow of trade and cultural influences. The site was occupied very early, from around 600 BC, but as a city Edzná developed from about AD 200 and reached its greatest extent, like others in the central Yucatán, in the Late Classic. The valley it occupies is slightly isolated from any of the main regions of Mayan civilization. This same location, though, also

Getting There

By Car

There are two ways to drive to Edzná from Campeche. The shortest route (52km) is to take Av. Central south from Circuito Baluartes as far as the main highway around Campeche, turn left, and then look for a right turn signposted to the village of Chiná. From there a rolling country lane carries on for 30km until you meet the Hopelchén–Champotón road, where you turn left, from where Edzná is 10km to the east. A longer alternative route (61km) is to stay on Av. Gobernadores until it becomes Highway 261 to Hopelchén and Mérida, and then, after 40km, turn southwards in San Antonio Cayal.

By Bus

The Edzná area is thinly populated, and there are few buses. *Combis* and *micros* from the market area in Campeche to the village of **Pich** all pass the ruins, but their timings may be inconvenient if you hope to return to the city the same day (most leave midday–2pm, as the market closes). Tours can be useful, especially those run by **Viajes Picazh** (*see* p.383).

Eating Out

La Hechicera, by the entrance to Edzná. Pretty *cabaña* bar-restaurant run by prestigious Campeche restaurant La Pigua, with surprisingly refined food for this remote spot. There is nowhere **to stay** near to Edzná.

gave it an influential position on major trade routes – between the Puuc, the Chenes and the northern Yucatán to the north and east, and the Río Bec, the Petén and the Usumacinta valley to the south – and helped it become a wealthy city.

It also brought Edzná into early contact with the Putún-Itzá traders of Tabasco. It used to be thought the name Edzná came from the Yucatec for 'House of Grimaces', a reference to the faces on the Temple of the Stone Masks, but a more recent theory is that it meant 'House of the Itzá', suggesting the city was influenced by the Itzá long before they arrived in Chichén Itzá. A substantial number of carved *stelae* have been found here, with dates that run from the 4th century to 810, the same year as the last date at Calakmul. The great Mayan crisis reached the city between about 800 and 950, but the site was still occupied on a far smaller scale until after 1300. Despite its relative closeness to Campeche, Edzná was entirely lost in the forest until 1927, when it was found by a local ruins enthusiast, Nazario Quintana Bello.

The Great Plaza and the Great Acropolis

Edzná is one more site where a great deal has recently been opened up. The area normally visited around the Great Plaza is only one part of the city, known as the 'Eastern Group', and there is another group of still virtually unexcavated buildings a kilometre to the west, centred on a large pyramid known as the **Casa de la Vieja**

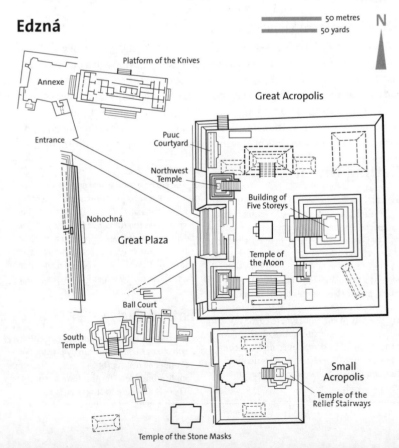

Edzná

50 metres
50 yards

N

Platform of the Knives

Annexe

Great Acropolis

Entrance

Puuc Courtyard

Northwest Temple

Building of Five Storeys

Nohochná

Great Plaza

Temple of the Moon

Ball Court

South Temple

Small Acropolis

Temple of the Relief Stairways

Temple of the Stone Masks

Hechicera ('House of the Old Witch'). Edzná, in a very dry area, also had one of the most sophisticated Mayan systems for channelling and retaining water, with over 13 kilometres of canals and ditches connecting more than 100 *chultunes* and *aguadas*.

Edzná's mixture of styles stands out immediately: the layout of the city – its recurrent 'trios' of pyramids on top of flat platforms – is reminiscent of the Classic cities of the Petén such as Tikal, but among the individual buildings there are several in Puuc, Chenes or Río Bec styles, and others that are entirely original. The path from the main entrance takes you to the northwest corner of the Great Plaza. To the left, forming the north side of the square, there is a long, low platform, the **Platform of the Knives**, so-called because flint ritual knives were discovered buried beneath it. This was a residence for some of the élite of Edzná, with seven large rooms and an **Annexe** at its western end. To the right of the path along the west side of the Great Plaza there is a giant 130m ramp of steps, the **Nohochná** or 'Big House'. At the top of the steps are the remains of four substantial buildings, which may have been the administrative centre of Edzná. It is likely, though, that the abnormally long steps of the Nohochná were also used as 'grandstands' for spectators watching ceremonies in the Great Plaza.

This was only fitting, for the plaza and acropolis of Edzná form one of the most dramatic examples of the Mayan conception of cities as theatrical, ritual stages. As well as systematic geometry the whole ensemble has its cosmological design: a straight line from the steps of the Building of the Five Storeys, through the centre-stones of the main acropolis steps and the Nohochná and across to the partly excavated Structure 501 (west of the plaza) corresponds to the line of the setting sun on 13 August, the Mayan creation day. The Great Plaza also has a very distinctive echo, which was deliberately accentuated by such constructions as the ramps on the back of the South Temple, at the south end of the Nohochná.

The **Great Acropolis** itself is a huge, low platform, measuring 170m by 96m, probably started in about AD 400. It conforms closely to the Petén style of temple platform, with one large pyramid and several smaller ones forming a raised 'sanctuary-plaza', of a higher level of sacredness and exclusivity than the main square below it. The structure that dominates the view, though, is unique to Edzná, the extraordinary **Building of the Five Storeys** (Edificio de los Cinco Pisos). It was built in five different stages, and probably began as an Early Classic pyramid in a simple Petén style (the 'storeys' are built on to the pyramid sides, not on top of each other). Then, from about AD 600, five tiers of rooms were added to the side facing the plaza. This took a long time: an inscription near the bottom has a date from 652, but it was probably finished after 800. Inside are rows of rooms, which were probably both ritual spaces and residences for the *ahau*-lineage of Edzná. A steep ramp of steps runs straight up the middle to the fifth 'storey', a small temple with a Río Bec-like roofcomb. There is also an internal tunnel-staircase to all five levels, though unfortunately this cannot be visited. From the top there is a superb view, across to the 'Old Witch' pyramid to the west. This too aligned with the Five Storeys, along the line of the moon on certain nights of the year.

As you come down the steps you can better appreciate the features of the other buildings on the Acropolis. All face inwards, accentuating the separateness of the Acropolis-plaza. To the left is the **Temple of the Moon**, a large and very steep platform.

Next to it in the corner of the Acropolis is a small pyramid, the **Southwest Temple**, which, it is believed, was only added to maintain the symmetry of the Acropolis after the **Northwest Temple** was begun on the other side of the steps. The latter was added to many times, from around 450 until the last days of the city, and has Puuc columns and Chenes carvings on its basic Petén structure. In around 800 a small platform was added on its north side, which forms one side of the **Puuc Courtyard**. This and other buildings on the north side of the Acropolis were probably residential complexes, possibly for priests or scribes. In one there was a *temazcal* or ritual steam bath.

The Small Acropolis and the Stone Masks

On the south side of the Great Plaza is the main **Ball Court** of Edzná, surrounded by several annexe-buildings which must have had some (unknown) function to do with the game and its ritual. Next to them, at the south end of the Nohochná, is the **South Temple**, which you approach from the back: the main temple faces into another plaza to the south. The main body of this pyramid was built around 500 in a Petén style, but the final temple at the top was added much later, after 700.

Walk round into the south plaza and filling the square to the left are the buildings of the **Small Acropolis**. It is a temple platform very similar to the Great Acropolis, but its earliest buildings are probably some of the oldest at Edzná, from the Preclassic or Early Classic. In the same way that the Maya built pyramids on top of older ones, so the Petén cities built whole new temple platforms to supplant earlier, smaller ones, even though these might only have been in use a relatively short time. Thus, this platform was 'replaced' by the far larger Great Acropolis. It was also considerably altered, since at some point in the very Late Classic – presumably after the great decline in literacy – *stelae* from around Edzná were brought here and used fairly chaotically to make the staircase of the **Temple of the Relief Stairways**, the largest pyramid.

Just next to the Small Acropolis is one of the most fascinating structures at Edzná, the **Temple of the Stone Masks** (Templo de los Mascarones). It's a smallish temple with, either side of its main stairway, two giant stucco faces or *mascarones* representing the sun-god Kinich-Ahau: as dawn, a young face, on the left (eastern) side; as dusk, a wizened old man, on the right (the west). The mythological faces incorporate many features of the Maya of the time – the god's teeth have been filed, and he is shown fashionably cross-eyed – while around them other motifs symbolize the sky and other natural elements. It is believed that there is a similar mask covered by later rebuilding in one of the temples of the Small Acropolis, yet to be unearthed. On the other sides of the south plaza, unexcavated bits of Edzná extend into the woods.

Hopelchén and the Chenes Sites

Chen is Yucatec for well. In the Chenes Hills of central Campeche, as in the Puuc Hills just to the north, the water table is a long way beneath the surface. To obtain water, the Maya – as well as using *chultunes*, *aguadas* and other ingenious techniques – had to search far underground, in 'wells' that were sometimes giant caverns. Nevertheless, in the Late Classic era this apparently unfavourable area contained a large number of small Mayan cities, which flourished at the same time as the Puuc and Río Bec sites to north and south, and were an important conduit in the flow of trade and communications in the Mayan world. The Chenes cities developed a very original style of architecture, in which intricate decoration was used to make whole buildings in the form of gods and mythological creatures, around giant-mouth doorways, presenting more vividly than any other style the Mayan idea of a building as a point of contact with the spirit world. These Chenes characteristics spread all over the Yucatán.

The original Chenes sites have been known about for years, but only very recently has much effort been put into making them properly accessible to visitors. They can be recommended to people who like a sense of solitude with their ruins, and enjoy exploring; one that until 1999 was all but inaccessible, Santa Rosa Xtampak, counts among the most dramatic of Mayan sites. The Mayan villages along the roads, most with names ending in –*chen* because of their wells, are full of remote placidity.

While Edzná is close enough to Campeche to make an easy day trip, visiting the Chenes means staying at least one night in the area. **Hopelchén** is the region's town,

Getting Around

By Bus

There are plenty of second-class buses to Hopelchén and the Chenes: five daily each way taking the 'slow route' which goes between Campeche and Mérida via Uxmal, and two more between Dzibalchén or Hopelchén and Mérida only. From Campeche there are six more services every day to Hopelchén, Dzibalchén or Iturbide, one of which continues on the long drive to Xpuhil. These buses will take you to the villages, but not Mayan sites: to do that, negotiate with local *combi* drivers.

By Car

Hopelchén is on Highway 261, the 'slow route' from Mérida to Campeche via Uxmal, and can therefore be visited easily from the Puuc Route. By car, from Campeche, the 261 road is a continuation of Av. Gobernadores, often signposted Mérida–Via Larga; to get to Hopelchén from Edzná, turn right out of the site to join Highway 261 at San Antonio Cayal (19km), where you turn right again.

From Hopelchén there is also a paved road leading south to Xpuhil in the Río Bec (*see* pp.362–4), through 150km of forest, swamps and lonely farmsteads. Note that there is a **petrol/gas station** at Hopelchén.

Tourist Information

Hopelchén t (996–)

Hopelchén has a **bank** (with ATM), **post office**, **shops** and a **tourist information kiosk** (*officially open Mon–Fri 8–2 and 5–8; closed Sat and Sun*), next to the Hotel Los Arcos in the plaza. Low visitor numbers make for individual service, and the staff can find local guides for you and advise on routes around the area. Just north of the village on Highway 261 (towards Bolonchén) there is a small shop-workshop to promote local handicrafts, the **Centro Artesanal Los Chenes**.

Where to Stay and Eat

Hopelchén t (996–)

Around the plaza there are many *loncherías* and *taco*-houses. As they're all *loncherías*, nowhere seems to serve alcohol with food, which should please the Mennonites.
Hotel Los Arcos, on the plaza, t 812 0123 (*cheap*). Exploring the Chenes still involves coming to terms with Los Arcos. It has two things going for it: a) it's there; b) it doesn't capitalize on this monopoly by pushing up prices. Be prepared for minimal furniture, plain beds and cell-like walls. But it's clean, the rooms are big, and the showers work.

road junction, bus stop, market and centre of everything else, and has the one hotel. It's also an enjoyably quirky piece of the Mexican countryside.

In the middle of Hopelchén there are two interconnecting plazas, a little market, a large, plain Franciscan church and, quite often, signs welcoming you in an old German dialect. This is because Hopelchén was 'chosen' to be the site of Campeche's largest colony of Mennonites, numbering over 4000, who came here since the 1950s from the USA and Canada. The local Maya regard them with exemplary tolerance, sometimes do good business driving them around, and comment only that they work very hard and have a lot of children, which coming from a Maya is saying something. Just west of the town there is a tiny Mayan site, **Tohcok**, with one small, Puuc-style plaza.

The sites described here are those normally accessible to visitors. True ruins devotees can find many more that have never been opened up or scarcely excavated at all, and are reachable only by 4WD trek and/or a hike. At Hopelchén town hall they can help you find guides and maybe even a vehicle, but this may take a day or so to set up.

Santa Rosa Xtampak and Bolonchén

About five kilometres north of Hopelchén on the road toward Uxmal there is a turn-off east for **Santa Rosa Xtampak** (*open daily 8–5; adm, Sun adm free*). The sign says 36km, but the real distance is a little more. The Mayan site at the far end was visited by Stephens and Catherwood and many expeditions since then, but its distance from any road long kept it utterly remote. A paved road was laid in 1998 as one product of the local administration's plan to open up the area, but not much has been done to maintain it. It's now very bumpy, and in a standard car you need to take your time.

Studies have indicated that, despite its apparent isolation, Xtampak was the dominant city in the whole of the Chenes region, enjoying its greatest prosperity in about 650–850. It had 67 *chultunes* for retaining water, which could have supported a population of about 12,000, and had more glyph inscriptions than any other Chenes site, with dates running from 750 to 889. Sadly, all these carvings were looted from the site between the 1920s and the 1980s. Another, very intriguing aspect of Xtampak is the exceptional size of its surviving structures, some of which look as if they were made on a completely different scale from that normally seen in Mayan buildings.

Xtampak stands on some of the tallest and steepest hills in the Yucatán, which were added to by the city's builders. They are still covered in forest and at first, as you trudge off up the very steep path from the caretaker's hut, you don't see any ruins except the remains of a few *chultunes*. After Stephens came to Xtampak, which he knew as Labphak, in 1841 he wrote that '...we saw peering through the trees the white front of a lofty building, which in the imperfect view we had of it, seemed the grandest we had seen in the country...'. You can have virtually the same experience today. As you emerge near the top of the hill into a broad area flattened off as a plaza, there ahead of you is the towering mass of the **Palacio**, rising through three levels. This is the most sophisticated of all Mayan 'multi-storey' buildings, with over 40 rooms and intricate internal staircases; very unusually it must have been planned from the outset as one structure, rather than being built up through 'add-ons' over decades like most large Mayan buildings. At its top is the **Casa del Rey**, a monster-mouth temple with a fabulous view. One of the most striking features of the Palacio is its un-Mayan scale: even the doorways seem made for a different race of people.

Since some of the brush on the hill has been cleared it's easier to appreciate that the Palacio formed the axis of two interconnecting plazas. Facing the palace across the larger one (to your left, from the entrance) there is another fine Chenes monster-mouth, and a temple featuring a **Diving God** carving like those at Tulum or Sayil, the presence of which is unexplained. A path out of this plaza leads to a residential complex called the **Casa Colorada** ('Red House'), because when Teobert Maler came here in 1902 it retained some of its original colour. Further down the same path is the extraordinary **Cuartel** ('Barracks'), so named for its severe appearance, a giant block-house that seems far too big to be Mayan, and which once formed just one side of a huge quadrangle. In the woods are more quadrangles – the **Monjas** (the Nunnery), the **Southeast Quadrangle** – all built on a similar scale. Along the way you pass relics of *chultunes*, a ball court and other buildings part-covered by forest, and the foot of the **Pyramid of the Sun**, one of four pyramids at Xtampak, built on to an existing hill.

As you wander around the site you also find wonderful views, over the empty forest stretching into infinity around you. With its canopy of forest Xtampak is also among the sites with the widest variety of wildlife around, including some of the most exotic the Yucatán has to offer: jaguars supposedly appear here quite frequently, and there are said to be a lot of snakes about, above all whenever it's wet.

Leaving the Xtampak access road, the road north toward Uxmal will take you after 30 kilometres to **Bolonchén de Rejón** or 'Nine Wells', one of the most pleasant of the Chenes villages. About three kilometres before you reach the village a sign left points to the **Grutas de Xtacumbilxunaan**, or Great Well of Bolonchén (*open daily 8–5; adm*), the most spectacular of the cavern-wells in the Chenes and the subject of one of Catherwood's most famous drawings (*see* overleaf). For centuries, this was the only source of water during the dry season for miles around. When Stephens came here he described an extraordinary scene as long lines of Maya clambered down with their water jars, in pitch darkness or by the light of flaming torches, through narrow passages hundreds of feet below ground to whichever level retained water. Once a year, he was told, a *fiesta* was held at the bottom of the great chamber of the cave.

The cavern also has its legends. *Xtacumbilxunaan* means 'the hidden maiden', and refers to Lolbé, a Mayan princess who wished to marry a humble young man called Dzulan. Her father the local king, however, wouldn't hear of it, and in his rage decided to hide Lolbé in the cave. The hero Dzulan, of course, found out and went in after her, and the two wandered the caverns for ever after. What is known for certain about the bottom of the cave is that it leads into seven underground rivers. Today, visitors to Bolonchén are only allowed as far as the first level of the cave, the top of the great pit. The huge wood-and-rope staircase that Catherwood saw survived until a few years ago, and it has been promised that it will be rebuilt, but this is a long time coming.

South of Hopelchén

A narrow road winds south from Hopelchén for about 40 kilometres to the second-largest community in the Chenes, **Dzibalchén**. The road, shrouded in forest, is paved,

The well at Bolonchén, drawn by F. Catherwood (1842)

but it's still useful to have a guide, as many roads and tracks are unsignposted. Also, as often in rural Campeche, village *topes* are not indicated, so you need to watch out.

When you eventually bounce into the grass-patch plaza of Dzibalchén, there's a ramshackle hut grandly marked '*módulo de información turística*'. This can seem wildly optimistic, as there may be no one in the hut and no tourists, but there are many places in this empty region – good for wildlife, lost ruins – that are impossible to find without local help. Eventually, someone will offer their services. Nearby at **Hochchob** (*open daily 8–5; adm, Sun adm free*), four kilometres away and reached by turning southwest from the plaza, there is a small Chenes site of three steep plat-forms around a hilltop plaza, with intricate decoration using typical Chenes imagery.

Returning to Dzibalchén plaza, to the right is the road which after many hours will get you to **Xpuhil** (*see* pp.362–4); alternatively, if you continue through the village to the northeast, you will in 20 kilometres come to **Iturbide**, a village marked forever by the Caste War, with crude blockhouses built to defend against Mayan attacks. Around two kilometres east is another Chenes site, **Dzibilnocac** (*open daily 8–5; adm, Sun adm free*). It's potentially a large site, but only the central plaza has been fully excavated.

South from Campeche

There is only one route towards 'Mexico' from Campeche city. The avenue along the Malecón goes through several changes of name, until it runs south into **Lerma**, now Campeche's main port area and the base for most of its fishing fleet. Beyond Lerma is **Playa Bonita**, traditionally Campeche's favourite beach, although water and sand are often dirty. The coast road meets the *Periférico*, the ring-road around Campeche, where drivers have a choice: for heavy-duty traffic there is a *cuota* motorway that runs inland to Champotón (toll), leaving the winding Highway 180 coast road more tranquil and traffic-free. First-class buses take the *cuota*, second-class the coast road.

The old 180 road also runs a little inland after Lerma, rolling through small valleys just out of sight of the sea. It rejoins the coast 30 kilometres south of Campeche at **Seybaplaya**, a windblown, dusty little fishing town with a long beach lined with fishermen's launches. The Gulf Coast waters are sandy and opal-coloured rather than crystalline, but by this point are pretty clean, and the beaches along this route can be fine for a stop-off. A better place to stop than Seybaplaya is **Sihoplaya**, 10 kilometres further south, with a more attractive strip of sand, and an upscale hotel.

The road continues on past more beaches, and a turning inland for Edzná and the Chenes. Sixteen kilometres on from this junction you reach **Champotón**, at the mouth of the Río Champotón, the most northerly river in the Yucatán. This was where Hernández de Córdoba made the first proper Spanish landfall on the Mexican mainland in 1517, and nearly died shortly afterwards at the hands of Moch-Cuouh and his men, in a struggle so desperate that the Spaniards remembered the place as the *Bahía de la Mala Pelea* or 'Bay of the Bad Battle'. To commemorate its place in history Champotón still has a crumbling Spanish bastion at the mouth of the river, built like the walls of Campeche in the 17th century to guard against the pirates of Tris. It's a

Where to Stay

Hotel Snook-Inn, C/ 30 no. 1, t (982) 818 0018 (*inexpensive*). Champotón has a likeable old hotel in this friendly and wonderfully-named little place, impossible to miss on a bend in the main riverside road in the middle of town. Its 19 rooms are large and airy, and have recently been done up: all have fans, a/c and phones, and there's even a small pool.

Hotel Tucán Sihoplaya, Ctra Campeche–Champotón Km35, t (982) 823 1200, *tucan sihoplaya@yahoo.com.mx* (*expensive*). Distinctive hotel in a much-altered old *hacienda* in a wonderful location atop low cliffs right by the Gulf Coast. The modern rooms and **restaurant** could be more in style with the setting, but they're very comfortable, and its great assets are its tranquil isolation, its beach all to itself (where turtles breed in spring) and its pool above the rocks.

friendly, straightforward little town, with a sizeable fishing fleet. It also has another role as a no-frills beach town, mostly for day-trippers from Campeche. The main pleasure beach, with the essential restaurants, is by the main road north of the river.

Below Champotón the road divides. The heavy traffic takes Highway 201 straight south to Escárcega – the only direct road to Chiapas – but a slightly more scenic alternative is to follow the Gulf Coast round to Villahermosa on Highway 180.

The Gulf Coast Route

The coastal strip along which the 180 road runs is all but uninhabited for 150 kilometres, with on one side a continuous shell beach and opal sea, and on the other mangroves and an endless line of electricity pylons. Towards evening there are superb sunsets, from terracotta at the base to deep purple blue. At distant intervals there are stopping-places – **Playa Varadero**, **Sabancuy** – with beach-bars offering fried fish.

After Sabancuy the road runs along a peninsula called **El Palmar**, the Palm Grove, once lined with coconut palms, although in the 1990s it was severely hit by lethal yellowing (*see* p.88), which transformed long stretches into palisades of ghostly, leafless stumps. There are, though, lush banks of *ceibas*, and sea birds are abundant, with flocks of pelicans and terns running against the wind.

After 105 kilometres from Champotón you reach the end of El Palmar, on the north side of the Laguna de Términos, and come on to the three-kilometre-plus Puente de la Unidad (*toll*) to Isla del Carmen. It's some 40 kilometres along the island to reach Ciudad del Carmen, with beach bars dotted along the way.

Ciudad del Carmen

Ciudad del Carmen is not on anyone's list of must-see Mexican cities today, but it has as romantic and dramatic a history as any in the country. The Isla del Carmen on which it stands was once none other than the Isla de Tris, a legendary pirate stronghold that for decades drove the region's Spanish governors to despair. In the last 25 years two giant bridges have clamped the island into Mexican territory, but in the 17th century its position at the mouth of the Laguna de Términos left it completely isolated, a perfect place to defend. French low-lifes were the first to gather here in 1558, to be joined by others from England, Holland and many other countries. It was from Tris that buccaneers like Diego the Mulatto, 'Peg-Leg' and *Lorencillo* launched their assaults on Campeche, while one Spanish expedition after another was sent against the island without much success. Finally, a more solid attack was mounted, and in 1717 the island was taken. Every last pirate was driven out, and in 1722 a new town was founded, with the suitably Catholic name of Ciudad del Carmen.

After the pirates, the town made its living from fishing and exporting dyewoods, but the biggest thing to hit it lately has been oil. It's a sprawling town, and noticeably busy: it looks, in fact, as if all the bustle and movement of the state of Campeche that's missing from the capital has drained down into Isla del Carmen. It's a major fishing port, and is known to Mexicans as a holiday town, with Gulf Coast beaches.

Getting Around

By Air

Carmen has a busy **airport**, with Mexicana or Aerocaribe (**t** 832 1203) flights to Mexico City, Mérida, Veracruz and Villahermosa.

By Bus

The bus station is on Av. Periférica, out of the centre. There are first- and second-class **buses** almost hourly to Villahermosa or Campeche, eight daily to Mérida, three to Mexico City, three to Cancún and Playa del Carmen via Mérida, and one to Chetumal via Xpuhil.

By Car

From the north, Highway 180 runs apparently endlessly through the town's outskirts before it becomes Av. Periférica. Follow this round to the right and look for signs for Centro on to C/ 31, which leads direct to the main plaza. **Taxis** are more expensive than the norm (about $3).

Car Hire

Agrisa, C/ 40 no.101-B, x 31 & 31-C, **t** 382 7550. From around $45 a day.
Alamo, C/ 31 no.45-A, x 34 & 36, **t** 382 9304. Better-than-average rates, with cars from $40 a day, and good rates for drop-offs.

Orientation

Despite its sprawl and a disconcerting street numbering system (odd numbers east–west, evens roughly north–south, but each street is divided into sections, 42A, 42B, etc.), Ciudad del Carmen is soon easy to find your way around. Once off Av. Periférica, streets converge on the plaza, officially Parque Ignacio Zaragoza, by the waterfront on the western edge of the island. Carmen's two main commercial streets, 31 and 22, meet at the plaza.

Tourist Information

Ciudad del Carmen **t** (938–)

Tourist Office: near the plaza, in the Casa de Cultura, C/ 24, x 27 & 29 (*open Mon–Fri 9–2 and 5–8; closed Sat and Sun*). Ciudad's office is of limited usefulness.

Banks: Main branches are also around the plaza or on C/ 24 alongside.
Internet Access: **CompuNet-Cyberclub**, on C/ 29, just off C/ 24, is cheap.
Post Office (with Mexpost): Corner of Calles 22 and 29.

Where to Stay

Ciudad del Carmen **t** (938–)

Pemex and other oil companies are continually sending people to Ciudad del Carmen, so it can be surprisingly difficult – and more expensive than average – to get a room.
Hotel Acuario, C/ 51 no. 60, x 26 & 28, **t/f** 382 5995 (*moderate*). On the north side of town toward the beach, but with good rooms and other facilities, a pool and a garden.
Hotel del Parque, C/ 33, x 20 & 22, **t/f** 382 3046 (*moderate*). Very popular, comfortable mid-range hotel right on the main plaza. Book well in advance.
Hotel San Rafael, C/ 24 no.73C, x 37 & 39, **t** 382 0979 (*inexpensive* with a/c; *cheap* fan-only). There are no great cheap choices, but this is reasonable and central.

Eating Out

The cheapest places are on the plaza, the two-level line of little *loncherías* along the C/ 33 side (all *cheap*), which are great vantage points for taking in the square's movements.
Cafetería La Fuente, C/ 20 x 29 (*moderate–cheap*). Like Tabasco, Carmen has a coffee culture unknown in the Yucatán. This café on the Malecón is a favourite place for coffee and one of the most attractive cheap restaurants, where gents play dominoes next to two pirate-era cannon. No alcohol, but great for breakfast.
La Ola Marina, C/ 20 x 29 (*moderate–cheap*). By La Fuente: the terrace has the same view and atmosphere, but specializes in larger seafood dishes, opens later and serves beers.
Los Pelícanos, C/ 24 no. 24-A, x 29 (*expensive*). Pretty restaurant-bar in a garden, with Mexican standards and local seafood specialities. The bar is a local meeting point.
Portal del Regis, Parque Ignacio Zaragoza (*moderate*). Pleasant local on the plaza.

Down by the waterfront is **Parque Ignacio Zaragoza**, with the town hall, an 1880s bandstand, restaurants and, around dusk, a stream of people meeting up, talking, looking, eating and just mingling. The slightly Gothic **Cathedral**, built in the 1850s, is plain and white from the outside, but inside its apse is a riot of colour, with pink and grey marble walls and chubby painted cherubs around a gold-clad *Virgen del Carmen*.

Calle 20 leads to the recently tidied-up **Malecón**, with some laid-back waterside bars and cafés. South of the plaza is the remaining part of the little 18th-century town of Carmen, with a few streets of elegant, grille-windowed colonial houses. Five blocks north along C/ 22 from the other side of the plaza is Carmen's **Museo de la Ciudad** (*open Wed–Sun 9–5; closed Mon and Tues; adm*), an attractive small collection that tells you an enormous amount about the town and its island, from Mayan settlement to pirates. Carmen has beaches on both sides of the island: **Playa Caracol** on the south side, and **Playa Norte**, on the ocean side and a much bigger affair.

In the southwest corner of the town the Periférica runs on to the huge **Puente Zacatal**, across the mouth of the Laguna de Términos. A few kilometres beyond its western end is **Xicalango**, famous as the site of a landing by Cortés in 1519 and the place where he acquired *La Malinche* (*see* p.62). The 70-kilometre road to the Tabasco state line is thinly populated and very swampy in parts, lined by lakes full of birds.

Inland through Escárcega

The main route for all traffic out of Yucatán is Highway 201, south from Champotón. After a long while the Yucatán woods begin to fade away, to be replaced by cattle pastures and *ranchos* across southwest Campeche into Chiapas and Tabasco.

Escárcega, 150 kilometres from Campeche and 86 kilometres from Champotón at the junction of Highways 201 and 186, has the reputation of being the ugliest town in Mexico. It's probably a town best seen in the rain. The road is lined with cheap *loncherías*, grubby shops and, above all, trucks, all pulled up wherever they can. Just about every vehicle travelling into or out of the Yucatán peninsula has to stop in Escárcega, at the giant *gasolinera* that is the town's *raison d'être*, but few choose to stay much longer. Beyond Escárcega, the road, now Highway 186, continues southwest for over 140 kilometres of flat, featureless, almost hypnotically green tropical cowboy country to enter Tabasco. About 60 kilometres west is a turn off south to Candelaria, which leads in another 70 kilometres to the ruins of **El Tigre**. This is believed to be the site of **Itzamkanaak**, capital of one of the last of the Mayan kingdoms, which resisted Cortés when he came through here in 1521. Facilities at and near the site are minimal.

Where to Stay and Eat

Escárcega t (982–)

Both these worn but reasonable hotels in Escárcega are positioned along Highway 186, and both have straightforward **restaurants** attached (*moderate*).

Hotel Escárcega, Av. Concordia 36, **t** 814 0186 (*inexpensive*). Plain but decent rooms, with fans only or a/c, they have good light and are lined up around a quite pretty patio.

Hotel María Isabel, Av. Justo Sierra 127, **t** 814 0045 (*inexpensive*). Motel-style, with big rooms (fan or a/c), well-worn carpets and TV.

Tabasco

13

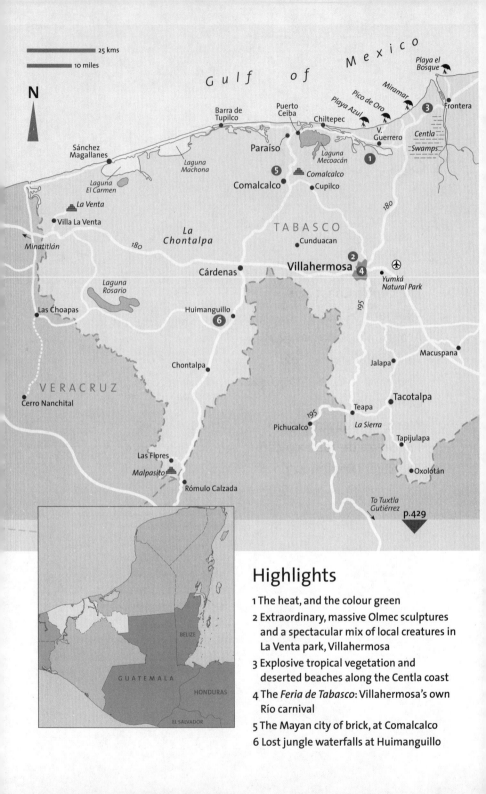

Highlights

1 The heat, and the colour green
2 Extraordinary, massive Olmec sculptures and a spectacular mix of local creatures in La Venta park, Villahermosa
3 Explosive tropical vegetation and deserted beaches along the Centla coast
4 The *Feria de Tabasco*: Villahermosa's own Río carnival
5 The Mayan city of brick, at Comalcalco
6 Lost jungle waterfalls at Huimanguillo

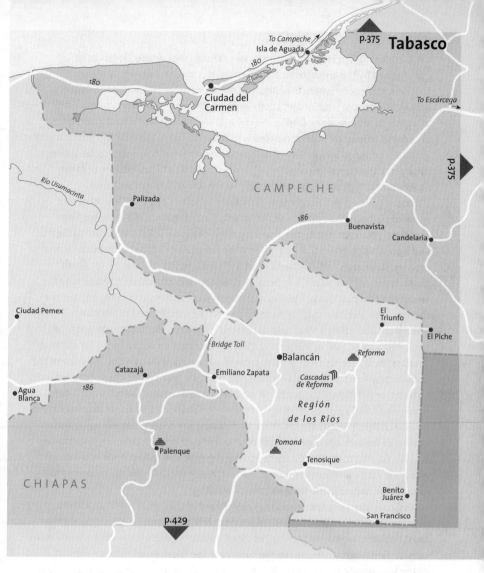

To Campeche
Isla de Aguada

P.375 **Tabasco**

180

180

Ciudad del
Carmen

To Escárcega

P.375

Rio Usumacinta

C A M P E C H E

Palizada

186

Buenavista

Candelaria

Ciudad Pemex

El
Triunfo

El Piche

Bridge Toll

Balancán

Reforma

Catazajá

Emiliano Zapata

Cascadas
de Reforma

Agua
Blanca

186

Región
de los Ríos

Pomoná

Palenque

Tenosique

C H I A P A S

Benito
Juárez

p.429

San Francisco

Tabasco has the distinction of being the only Mexican state subjected to sustained abuse by a major English writer. This was where Graham Greene came in 1938 to investigate the persecution of the Catholic church, on the trip that produced a travel book, *The Lawless Roads* (published as *Another Country* in the USA), and *The Power and the Glory*. Greene loathed Mexico, and he loathed Tabasco most of all. He virtually made the place into a metaphor, an unsullied image of heat, squalor, brutality and hopelessness.

That was then, and this is now. Today, if you're not a morose English Catholic convert looking for things to disapprove of, Tabasco has much to recommend it. Greene did get one thing right, in that it is powerfully hot, a steamy tropical delta where the thermometer sits close to 40°C for much of the time. The state capital

Villahermosa is, like Phoenix, Arizona, one of those cities where life has been transformed by the arrival of air conditioning. It is the least Mayan of Mexico's southern states, one where the culture of the modern Maya – and of the Zoque, a non-Mayan people who inhabit south-western Tabasco – has largely retreated to villages and remote areas. During the colonial era Tabasco was all but ignored for decades at a time, an underpopulated wilderness of rivers, swamps and forest. It was gradually occupied by a variety of independent settlers: dirt farmers, coffee growers, dyewood loggers, even pirates. This diversity is reflected in the mixture of family names that is typical of Tabasco: English, French, Maya, Spanish and more.

Tabasco grew up as a rough-and-ready, frontier sort of place, with much less of a sense of tradition than other parts of Mexico. Since the 1950s the state has been completely transformed by the discovery of oil, the basis of Tabasco's current wealth, and a population boom that has made Villahermosa one of the busiest cities in the country. This rough-and-readiness must be at least partly responsible for a trait characteristic of Tabascans, a noticeable openness and friendliness. People have far less of the ceremonious politeness and reserve so pronounced in many parts of the country, even a certain chippiness compared to the soft stillness of Yucatán.

The state also offers a total contrast in landscape from the Yucatán. Whereas in the peninsula a great part of life seems to have been taken up with looking for water, in Tabasco there's too much of it. Criss-crossed by two giant rivers – the Grijalva and the Usumacinta – and innumerable tributaries, the state seems almost a series of islands between broad lagoons, as roads roll over bridge after bridge. Everything is a deep, lush green. Until 30 or 40 years ago, between the channels and creeks you would also have seen dense forest. Alongside the oil business the other great modern transformation of Tabasco has been the cutting down of over 90 per cent of its forest cover, and the turning over of the state to agriculture: fruit and coffee farms in the south and west, cattle pastures in much of the rest. Along with oil, this new economy has made some people in the state extremely wealthy.

Tabasco is also sexy. Foreigners may have heard of the Olmec relics of La Venta, but one oft-repeated part of modern Mexican folklore is that Tabasqueñas are the most beautiful women in Mexico. Tabascan traditional dress for women – rarely worn outside *fiestas* nowadays, unlike the *huípiles* of the Yucatán or Chiapas – consists of the kind of off-the-shoulder blouses and embroidered skirts once worn by Rita Hayworth in her most sultry Latin-spitfire roles. The beauty of the local womenfolk is a big thing in Tabasco. It is celebrated above all in the election of the *Flor de Tabasco* at the State Fair, an annual *fiesta* of off-the-shoulder-blouses and big hair.

Tabasco has more conventional attractions. Its greatest treasures are relics not of the Maya but of the far older Olmec civilization, the extraordinary sculpted heads in the Parque La Venta in Villahermosa. The city also has one of the region's best archaeological museums, a fine zoo, and the busiest airport close to Palenque, a very good jumping-off point for travel to northern Chiapas. Elsewhere there is a unique Mayan city at Comalcalco, and deserted Gulf beaches. One thing that does not belong to the state is Tabasco sauce, which was invented in Louisiana, but it does have very good food, making great use of types of river fish unique to the Grijalva-Usumacinta delta.

History

Until the building of roads – in living memory – Tabasco's inhabitants have always been river people. It was the rivers, swamps and creeks around the base of the Gulf of Mexico in Tabasco and Veracruz that were home to the **Olmecs**, the first civilization of Mesoamerica, providing them with a food source and a means of communication. From there, Olmec influences spread across the region from northern Mexico down to Guatemala and Honduras. Later cultures avoided the deltas until, centuries later in the middle Classic, eastern Tabasco and southern Campeche saw the emergence of the people known as the **Putún** or **Chontal Maya**, one of whose sub-groups – it is now believed – were the **Itzá**, who were among the rulers of Chichén Itzá.

The Putún are a mysterious people, the object of a great deal of speculation and theorizing. Skilled sailors, they were an illiterate culture, which, given that the glyph writing system was one of the defining elements of Mayan civilization, has led many to doubt whether they were Mayan, although it is now generally accepted that in language and most other aspects they were. Though the more refined Maya of the cities to the east looked down on them, they were important to these Eastern Maya as fetchers, carriers, traders and intermediaries with the cultures of central Mexico. Then, in the Late Classic, they began to raid more aggressively up the Usumacinta and around the coast, taking over whole cities and even founding some of their own, as at Chichén. Nevertheless, many stayed in their home region, and the largest Mayan group in Tabasco today, the Chontal of the Centla region east of Villahermosa, have a language of their own which is believed to be descended from that of the Putún.

When the Spaniards appeared off the coast, after sailing around the Yucatán, the great river that Grijalva named after himself soon attracted their attention. In 1519, after landing at Xicalango on the Laguna de Términos, **Cortés** fought his first battle in Mexico at Centla in northeast Tabasco, before moving on to Veracruz. He passed through Tabasco again in 1521, in pursuit of an unruly subordinate, **Cristóbal de Olid**, who was trying to carve out an independent governorship for himself. Cortés brought with him as a prisoner **Cuauhtémoc**, the last Aztec Emperor (who had rallied resistance after the death of Moctezuma), as he was afraid to leave him in Mexico City. Believing, so he claimed, that Cuauhtémoc was planning a revolt, Cortés had him executed somewhere near Tenosique, a brutal action which, according to chronicler Bernal Díaz, 'seemed bad to all of us', since Cuauhtémoc had been promised he would not be ill-treated, and his dignity had impressed all the ordinary Spanish soldiers.

When Graham Greene came to Tabasco it was shortly after the fall of Governor Tomás Garrido Canabal, who had attempted to eradicate Catholicism in the state. Garrido used to say that this would not do anyone any harm since Tabascans had never been good Catholics anyway. He had a certain point, in that Tabasco was something of an anomaly within the very Catholic Spanish Empire. It was the object of an unbrotherly dispute between the Franciscans of Yucatán and the Dominicans of Chiapas as to whose responsibility it was to evangelize the area, and consequently nobody quite took on the task. In the 'spiritual conquest', Tabasco seemed to fall through a bureaucratic loophole.

In the absence of friars, Tabasco was populated by those seeking dyewoods and cacao, then the area's most valuable commodities. Like Campeche, it was plagued by pirate attacks from the 16th to the 18th centuries. To escape them, people moved further up the rivers, to be joined later on by descendants of the pirates themselves.

After independence Tabasco, as a non-traditional state, was a centre of radical and anti-Church feeling, and strongly resisted the French and Maximilian. This was the background to the rise during the Revolution of the most famous figure in Tabasco's history, **Tomás Garrido Canabal**, absolute boss of the state for 16 years from 1920. With his Partido Socialista Radical and its youth wing, the *Camisas Rojas* ('Red Shirts'), he made Tabasco into a little republic of his own, launching 'antifanaticism campaigns' of anti-religious propaganda, establishing co-ed schools and a feminist movement and generally doing anything that wasn't Catholic. Greene presented Garrido as a kind of totalitarian dictator, but he had a lot in common with a huckster politician like Huey Long of Louisiana, wheeling, dealing and using demagogic appeals to get the vote out. He sums up a lot of the contradictions of Mexican Revolutionary *caudillos*: perhaps genuinely idealistic in some ways, but also full of his own power and up to his neck in deals with foreign oil companies. His fall came after he began to believe too much in his empire-building and tried to keep control of his party outside the official PNR. In 1936 Lázaro Cárdenas had him expelled from office and the country.

The 1950s and 1960s saw the beginning of Tabasco's great transformation, with the arrival of **oil**, **deforestation** and **air conditioning**. The oil boom was at its loudest during the 1970s, when Villahermosa acquired its most prominent modern buildings. This ended with a bump in 1982, and since then the city has got along more modestly. Tabasco has retained a tradition of argumentative politics – and spectacular corruption scandals – and in the 1990s this was one of the states where the old PRI machine met with most opposition. Nevertheless, in 2001, after a no-holds-barred election campaign, the PRI just managed to keep hold of the state governorship, by a whisker.

The Centla Coast

The main route into Tabasco from the Yucatán is Highway 186 from Escárcega, which, after dipping into eastern Tabasco near Emiliano Zapata, cuts across northern Chiapas to re-enter the state and cross pastures and fruit farms to Villahermosa. To the west, the same road, renumbered Highway 180, runs away towards Veracruz. If you have time and are looking for a beach, there is another route from Campeche on the old, eastern 180 road from Ciudad del Carmen. The beaches of this region, Centla, are on weekdays some of the most deserted anywhere on the Mexican coast.

After crossing the Río San Pedro (the state line), the road runs on past swamps, ranches and a few oil-wells to the capital of Centla, **Frontera**. This was where Greene arrived, when the only way to get from here to Villahermosa was by river boat. From the centre of town a road leads north to **El Bosque** at the mouth of the Grijalva, with a long beach, a wonderful view and innumerable pelicans. If, on the other hand, you stay on the main road, you quickly come to the bridge across the Grijalva.

The Centla world of lagoon, creek and causeway begins on the other side. Only theoretically a highway, the road is narrow, winding between exuberant clumps of coconut palms, banana plants, cacao plantations and tropical flowers, with a lushness that's absolutely overwhelming. About 20 kilometres west of the bridge, past Chontal Maya villages and smart ranch-houses, a road north leads to **Miramar** (5km), with a curving beach stretching away for miles. On Sundays food stands are set up and the place may suddenly get noisy; on other days you can have it to yourself.

About five kilometres further on the 180 road bends south toward Villahermosa, and in the tiny village of Santa Cruz a road turns off to continue along the coast. This is even narrower, with some alarming dips at the sides, but passable if you take your time (*combis* from Frontera or Paraíso negotiate it regularly). In Vicente Guerrero there's a turn north to **Pico de Oro** (8km), one of the best Centla beaches, with a restaurant, **Las Huellas del Pescador** (*cheap*), where you can camp or sling a hammock under a *palapa* for free, assuming you eat there (which, as there's nowhere else, you probably will). In Cuauhtémoc, seven kilometres west, there is a turning to another fine beach, **Playa Azul**.

At around this point the channels and lagoons become wider and even more numerous, making it feel as if you're travelling more through water than land. From Chiltepec (more beaches), 13 kilometres from Cuauhtémoc, the road runs along the north edge of the huge **Laguna Mecoacán**. On its west side is **Puerto Ceiba**, from where *lancheros* offer trips to see the mangroves, birds and islands in the lagoon. From there it's only about four kilometres to the town of **Paraíso**, near Villahermosa's favourite Sunday beach, with rather more permanent beach bars and restaurants.

At Paraíso the road turns south for Villahermosa (75km) via Comalcalco (*see* p.422). West of Paraíso a road runs straight for 150 kilometres along the sandbar beside the coastal lagoons, past beaches, palms, a few isolated fishing villages (only **Sánchez Magallanes** approaches town-size), thousands of birds and vast, watery horizons.

Villahermosa

To know how hot the world can be I had to wait for Villahermosa.

Graham Greene, *The Lawless Roads*

Tabasco's state capital is not one of Mexico's colonial cities, nor is it, today, the sweltering, languid tropical river town that Greene would recognize. As you approach the city you pass what appear to be endless miles of suburbs and *colonias*, and big highways that seem to carry as much traffic as the entire state of Campeche. Further in, many areas are taken over by a disorderly mixture of cars, offices, parking lots, billboards and brash shop fronts. Parts of Villahermosa look a bit like downtown Los Angeles (after all, everybody there speaks Spanish too). All this bustle and scrambled modernity (and the heat, which hasn't changed) has led some people who only come to Mexico looking for the traditional and picturesque to dismiss the place outright, and avoid it. But, like the state as a whole, Villahermosa has its positives.

First of all, there are the unique Olmec relics of Parque La Venta, alongside which lie one of the best wildlife collections in the region. Villahermosa's Anthropology Museum gives a more comprehensive overview of all the Mesoamerican cultures – as opposed to the Maya alone – than any other in Mexico outside Mexico City. On a wider level, it's a lively city, with an urban edge in place of the tranquillity of Yucatán cities, so that you need to have your guard up more than you would in Mérida or Chetumal, but there's plenty of Tabascan friendliness too. One feature of Villahermosa is the continual presence of water, in creeks, rivers and entire lakes that turn up in all kinds of places, or the winding, slow-moving River Grijalva. And the city has a living heart: in the centre, the streets of the 19th-century town that Greene knew, renovated as the **Zona Luz**, are full of movement, street life and talk, with cafés – a Tabascan institution – in which to sit out as the heat of the day fades a little, and just watch everybody go by.

Villahermosa began life in another place and under another name. In 1519 Cortés founded a settlement at the mouth of the Grijalva, near present-day Frontera, called Santa María de la Victoria. After the pirates of Tris appeared off the coast in the 1550s, however, life for its inhabitants became increasingly impossible, and in 1596 it was decided to move the whole town upriver and take over a Chontal fishing village as the site of a new 'city', to be called Villahermosa de San Juan Bautista, the 'Beautiful City of Saint John the Baptist', normally known simply as San Juan Bautista. Over the next two centuries the city gradually became the hub of the Tabasco dyewood trade, surpassing in importance older towns such as Tacotalpa. San Juan Bautista covered itself in glory in 1846–7 during the Mexican-American war, when American ships sailed up the river in an attempt to take the town, and the *gringos* were actually forced to withdraw in defeat. Since the Revolution the city's name has been reduced to Villahermosa.

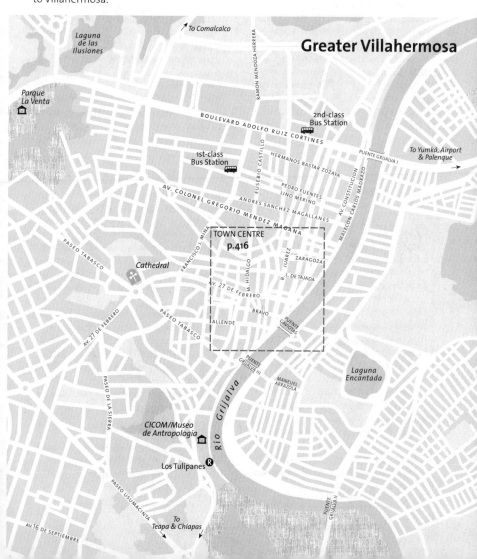

Greater Villahermosa

Laguna de las Ilusiones

To Comalcalco

RAMON MENDOZA HERRERA

Parque La Venta

BOULEVARD ADOLFO RUIZ CORTINES

2nd-class Bus Station

1st-class Bus Station

PUENTE GRIJALVA I

To Yumká, Airport & Palenque

EUSEBIO CASTILLO

HERMANOS BASTAR ZOZAYA

PEDRO FUENTES

LINO MERINO

AV. COLONEL GREGORIO MENDEZ MAGAÑA

ANDRES SANCHEZ MAGALLANES

AV. CONSTITUCION

MALECON CARLOS MADRAZO

PASEO TABASCO

FRANCISCO J. MINA

TOWN CENTRE p.416

Cathedral

M. HIDALGO

JUAREZ

ZARAGOZA

B. L. DE TAJADA

AV. 27 DE FEBRERO

AV. 27 DE FEBRERO

PASEO TABASCO

BRAVO

ALLENDE

PUENTE CAVIOLAS

PUENTE GRIJALVA III

MANEUEL ARRAZOLA

Laguna Encantada

PASEO DE LA SIERRA

Grijalva

Río Grijalva

CICOM/Museo de Antropologia

Los Tulipanes

PASEO USUMACINTA

PUENTE GRIJALVA II

To Teapa & Chiapas

AV. 16 DE SEPTIEMBRE

Getting There and Around

Driving in from the east, immediately after the **Grijalva I bridge** look for an exit marked *Centro*. This takes you on to Av. Francisco Madero, the main route from Ruíz Cortines to the **Zona Luz**, centre of old Villahermosa. First-class **buses** into Villahermosa stay on Ruíz Cortines for a few more streets and turn left down on to Paseo Francisco Javier Mina.

By Air

Villahermosa's airport, 13km east off Highway 186, is one of the busiest in southern Mexico. **Aerocaribe, t** 316 5046, and its parent **Mexicana, t** 316 3132, have flights to Cancún, Ciudad del Carmen, Mérida, Mexico City, Oaxaca, Tuxtla Gutiérrez and Veracruz, with more connections possible via Cancún or Mexico City. Villahermosa is on Aerocaribe's daily Havana–Cancún–Mérida–Villahermosa–Tuxtla–Oaxaca bus flight. **Aeroméxico, t** 312 1528, has frequent flights to Mexico City, **Aviacsa, t** 316 5700, has services to Mexico City, Cancún and Mérida and the small airline **Aerolitoral, t** 312 1528, has direct flights to Veracruz and Tampico.

From the airport, there is an abundance of Transporte Terrestre **airport taxis** to take you into town (about $9); on departure, a normal city cab to the airport will cost $7–8.

By Bus

First- and second-class bus stations are separate, and there are some single-company terminals. Most main companies use the **ADO first-class station**. It is north of the Zona Luz (corner of Paseo F.J. Mina and Av. L. Merino), far enough from the centre to be an uncomfortable walk carrying bags (a taxi is about $1.70). There is a **left-luggage** office. Many buses stop en route to other destinations. Main services from the ADO are listed below; there are more to central Mexico and north on the Gulf Coast.

Campeche (*6hrs*): one ADO GL and around 10 ordinary first-class daily. Fare about $22.

Cancún (*14hrs*): three luxury and 10 ordinary first-class daily, via **Escárcega** and **Chetumal**; four of the ordinary buses also stop in **Xpuhil**, and most stop in **Tulum** and **Playa del Carmen**. Fares about $27 Chetumal, $41 Playa, $45 Cancún.

Ciudad del Carmen (*3hrs*): three luxury buses daily, and hourly ordinary first-class 5.30am–11.30pm, all via **Frontera**. Fare about $10.

Comalcalco (*1hr*) and **Paraíso**: three ordinary first-class and five *intermedio* buses daily. Fare $2–$4.

Huimanguillo (*1½hrs*): one daily (3.30pm). Fare about $4.

Mérida (*10hrs*): two luxury and 10 ordinary first-class daily. Fare about $31.

Mexico City (*14hrs*): 12 luxury and 20 ordinary first-class buses daily. Fares from $48.

Oaxaca (*12hrs*): three daily. Fare about $36.

Palenque (*2½hrs*): 12 daily 6am–7.45pm. Fare about $8.

San Cristóbal de Las Casas (*7½hrs*): one daily (7.35am), via **Palenque** and **Ocosingo**. Fare about $17.

Tapachula (*15hrs*): via **Tuxtla Gutiérrez, Arriaga** and **Tonalá**, one daily (7.15pm). Fare from $40.

Tenosique (*4hrs*): 10 daily 4.15am–6.15pm. Fare about $10.

Tuxtla Gutiérrez (*6½hrs*): via **Teapa**, nine daily with different companies. Fare from $14.

La Venta (*3hrs*): four buses daily. Fare about $7.

Villahermosa's **second-class bus station** is on Blvd Ruíz Cortines (north side between Paseo F.J. Mina and Grijalva I bridge). It has stopping services to every part of Tabasco, and to Palenque, northern Chiapas and places in Campeche, plus gruelling but cheap long-distance routes. Further along the Boulevard is **Servicios Somellera**, offering cheap services to delta towns such as Paraíso and Comalcalco.

Combis and *colectivos* to towns and villages around Villahermosa, including Comalcalco and the coast, mostly leave from streets near the second-class station.

Villahermosa's **local buses** and *combis* aren't hard to use. Any bus north up Paseo Tabasco marked 'Tabasco 2000' or 'La Choca' will take you to the Ruíz Cortines junction and Parque La Venta; from Av. Madero or Av. Constitución, buses south marked CICOM run down the Malecón past the Anthropology Museum. To get back, take any bus marked 'Centro'.

By Car

If you have a car consider staying in a hotel with parking, as parking space in the old centre is at a premium. There are plenty of *gasolineras* around the city.

Car Hire

Villahermosa is a major car hire centre.

Budget, Malecón Carlos A. Madazo 761, **t** 314 3790. Decent local franchise based south of the Grijalva bridge (check the car for lights, strange noises etc., before you drive off).

Dollar, Paseo Tabasco 600, **t** 315 4830. Bearable rates for long-distance drop-offs (ie. Mérida).

Ecorenta, Av. Vicente Guerrero 120, **t** 312 9890, *ecorenta@prodigy.net.mx*. Near to Puente Gaviotas, south of Plaza de Armas. Nothing especially *eco* about its cars, but it has some of the best rates (VWs from $40 a day, all in).

By Taxi

Taxis are abundant (around $1.70 in the city). It's pretty much accepted practice here that, should your taxi driver see any potential passengers going in the same direction, he'll pick them up too, which may lead to irritating detours if you're in a hurry. However, drivers rarely overcharge or cheat the tourist.

Orientation

Post-oil boom Villahermosa is built to car scale, with districts connected by broad avenues and freeways. Chief of the latter is the main road in from the airport, Palenque and the east, Highway 186 – **Blvd Adolfo Ruíz Cortines** inside the city – which rolls in over **Puente Grijalva I** bridge (toll), curving through the city to continue out the other side as Highway 180, towards Veracruz (the three Grijalva bridges are numbered according to when they were built, so the next one south is Puente Grijalva III). In general, wider streets are *avenidas* or *paseos* and smaller ones *calles*.

The main visitor attractions are concentrated in three areas. The Zona Luz runs back from the riverside avenue of the Malecón. South of the old centre is Paseo Tabasco, which runs north–west from the river for 3km to cross Blvd Ruíz Cortines. This crossing is the hub of the second major area of interest, with **Parque-Museo La Venta** and the zoo, the main upscale hotels and the Tabasco 2000 complex. The final focus of attraction is the **CICOM area**, with the Anthropology Museum, which is south of the Zona Luz and Paseo Tabasco along the river, south along the Malecón.

Tourist Information

Villahermosa **t** (993–)

Tabasco State Tourist Office: In Tabasco 2000, signed *Turismo*, in a round building on the main esplanade, **t** 316 1080 (*open Mon Fri 9–3 and 6–9, Sat 9–1; closed Sun*). Quite efficient, with a wide range of literature, but far out. Information desks are also open at the **airport** and (at times) **Parque La Venta**.

Banks: Central branches on or near Av. Madero, between Parque Juárez and Av. Reforma.

Health: 24-hr **emergency medical service**, Clínica AIR Médica 2000, Paseo Tabasco 114, **t** 315 2527. Several **pharmacies** can be found along Av. Madero and C/ Juárez.

Internet Access: There are several around the centre, including **Hardware Net**, C/ Aldama 627-B, near corner of Av. I. Zaragoza (*open all day Mon–Sat*), which has low rates.

Laundry: Super-Lavandería Rex, corner of Av. Madero and Av. Gregorio Méndez Magaña.

Post Office: Corner of C/ Narciso Saenz and Av. Lerdo de Tejada (*open Mon–Fri 8–6, Sat 9–1; closed Sun*). Has a Mexpost desk.

Tours

Viajes Villahermosa, Av. 27 de Febrero 207, Zona Luz, **t** 312 5456. Tours to Comalcalco and other attractions further afield; they also produce a handy free city-and-state map.

Universo Maya, Hotel Maya Tabasco, Blvd Ruíz Cortines 907, **t** 314 3696, *www.amtave.com /univmaya*. Innovative ecotourism-oriented trips to the Centla swamps, Huimanguillo waterfalls and more familiar destinations.

Festivals

Feria de Tabasco: *27 April–May*. Tabasco is a pagan state, so it's only fitting that its great celebration is not some saint's *fiesta* but the State Fair, with its own site in Parque Tabasco northwest of the city. It is preceded all through April by a pre-*feria* of parades, parties and competitions and it's a blast: the parades are the city's mini-Río carnival, while the park is an amazing combination of amusement park, market, free concert, stock fair and rodeo. Here you can buy local produce or motor oil in bulk, watch folk dancing or buy a prize bull, but the highlight is the election of the annual **Flor de Tabasco**, queen of the state's celebratedly pretty girls, and there are shows by the reigning stars of Mexpop, often free.

Shopping

Flor de Tabasco, Av. I. Zaragoza 801, near the Museo de Cultura Popular. It's surprisingly hard to find traditional Tabascan products, but this has interesting local handicrafts.

Where to Stay

Villahermosa t (993–)

The city has a wide range of hotels, from corporate luxury to cheap. Many business hotels sometimes offer weekend discounts.

Expensive

Hotel Cencali, Av. Juárez, corner of Paseo Tabasco, t 315 1999, *www.cencali.com.mx*. Pleasant, locally run and modern with a bit more character than its competitors. It has a pretty pool in a garden, and an impressive lobby with a spectacular mural by local artist Montuy on Mayan themes. It's not on C/ Juárez in the Zona Luz, but in an upscale 'hotel zone' by the Ruíz Cortines/Paseo Tabasco junction near Parque La Venta.

Hyatt Regency Villahermosa, Av. Juárez 106, t 315 1234 and worldwide Hyatt reservation numbers, *www.hyatt.com.mx* (suites *luxury*). Top of the line, this has every comfort, two **restaurants**, a fine pool and a large garden.

Moderate

Casa Inn Olmeca Villahermosa, Av. Madero 418, t 358 0102, freephone in Mexico t 01 800 201 0909, *www.casainn.zl.com.mx*. Recently opened and business-oriented with superior facilities: a/c, bathrooms, TV, **restaurant**. No real character, but undeniably comfortable.

Hotel Plaza Independencia, C/ Independencia 123, south of Plaza de Armas, t 312 1299, *www.hotelesplaza.com.mx*. Long-running, but attractively renovated in traditional style with a very pretty **restaurant**, parking, laundry, spacious rooms and one of few hotel pools in central Villahermosa.

Howard Johnson Villahermosa, C/ Aldama 404, Zona Luz, t/f 314 4645, freephone in Mexico t 01 800 50549, *www.hojo.com.mx*. Reliable range of modern services (and off-street parking), and the staff are very friendly (winning several HJ service awards).

Inexpensive

Hotel Madán, Av. Madero 408, t 312 1650, f 313 5246. Long-running, in the Zona Luz. Rooms are spacious; staff could be more helpful, but it's very popular. Prices near *moderate*.

Hotel Pakaal, C/ Lerdo de Tejada 106, t 314 4648, f 312 4501. Modern place between the Zona Luz and the river that's one of the best-value hotels in the city. Rooms are as good as many in the next range up.

Hotel Provincia Express, C/ Lerdo de Tejada 303, t 314 5376, freephone within Mexico t 01 800 715 3968, *villaop@prodigy.net.mx*. In the Zona Luz, comprehensively renovated, with bright, comfortable, well-fitted rooms. The upper floors have the most light.

Cheap

Hotel del Centro, Av. Pino Suárez 209, t 312 5961. One of the best-kept of the many cheap hotels, northwest of Parque Juárez. It has pleasant, clean rooms (fan-only *cheap*, a/c just-*inexpensive*). The same owners have another **Hotel del Centro** on Av. Madero 411, t 312 2565, with big, plain, double a/c rooms and studios with kitchenettes for 3–4 people (*inexpensive*).

Hotel Madero, Av. Madero 301, t 312 0516. Big, blue and pink, and very central, this is battered but friendly in a slightly dozy way.

Hotel Tabasco, C/ Lerdo de Tejada 317, t 312 0077. Best of the budget bets on this street, with friendly owners and very cheap fan-only rooms (some with a/c are *inexpensive*).

Eating Out

Tabasco has a distinctive cuisine, although local dishes can be hard to find on restaurant menus. Being built on rivers, its chief specialities use river fish, especially the pike-like *pejelagarto*. Sometimes called crocodile-fish, it's unique to the Grijalva-Usumacinta delta, and may have been a staple food of the Olmecs. It has a subtle, almost sweet flavour.

Expensive

Capitán Beuló, t 312 9217. A local institution, this old riverboat features *pejelagarto* and other local specialities. Dinner cruises (about 2hrs) sail from the Malecón near Grijalva I bridge; booking essential. *Lunch and dinner cruises daily except Mon (3 sailings on Sun).*

Los Tulipanes, Av. Carlos Pellicer Cámara 511 (CICOM), **t** 312 9209. Very attractive spot to sample local specialities, by the river and anthropology museum. Enjoy the view from an exceptionally comfortable dining room (with a/c), or braver souls can opt for the heat of the terrace.

Moderate

Café del Portal, C/ Independencia 301, Plaza de Armas. With lofty ceilings and a shady colonnade, this was one of the city's historic cafés Refurbished in 1997, it provides good coffee and breakfasts, and local standards. It has no a/c, just a few rather inadequate roof fans.

Las Jardineras, Hotel Plaza Independencia, C/ Independencia 123. One of the best central hotel-restaurants: pretty, airy and painted in bright Frida Kahlo-ish colours, it serves up superior Mexican and Tabascan dishes.

Restaurante Madán, Hotel Madán, Av. Madero 408. It's simply decorated and the fare is unexceptional, consisting mainly of Mexican standards with a few Tabascan fish dishes, but it has effective a/c and lots of animated sociability, and in the evening many people come to sit and chat in the cool.

SoyAquarius, Av. Zaragoza 513. Villahermosa is oddly well-supplied with vegetarian restaurants. This mini-chain offers a radical change from the usual fare with a varied vegetarian menu; it also offers a cheap ($6) set lunch. Branches are at **Av. F.J. Mina 309**; above **Av. G Méndez Magaña** near the bus station; and at **Av. G Méndez Magaña 403-B**.

Cheap

Villahermosa has any number of cheap eateries, particularly catering to the crowds in the Zona Luz and around the bus stations.

Cocktelería Rock & Roll, Av. Reforma 307, between Madero and Juárez. Big, boisterous and boozy bar-restaurant specializing in good quality *ceviches* and *cocteles*, which are also very cheap. Don't go seeking a quiet

dinner, but for local colour, and the *cantina* atmosphere that spills on to the street.

Noche y Día, Av. F.J. Mina, opposite the ADO. Basic little place providing bargain *tacos* or full meals at any hour. Other similar places lie along the same stretch. *Open 24hrs.*

Restaurante-Cafetería La Zona Luz, C/ Aldama 615. Pleasant little restaurant, more tranquil than some, that has good *tortas* and salads and a bargain lunch menu.

El Torito Valenzuela, Av. Madero, corner of Av. 27 de Febrero. Classic stop for *tortas*, *tacos* and some larger dishes (but no alcohol).

Cafés, Ice Creams and Coolers

Villahermosa is distinguished from the Yucatán by its taste for coffee. Having a coffee is normally an activity in itself, so cafés rarely serve food, but they usually have a few snacks.

Café La Cabaña, C/ Juárez 303. Smart, airy café, opposite Casa de los Azulejos.

Café de la Calle Juárez, C/ Juárez 513. Another attractive, modern café, near Av. Reforma.

La Flor de Michoacán, C/ Lerdo de Tejada, near corner of Av. Aldama. Best traditional ice cream and juice shop in the Zona Luz.

Horchatería La Catedral, Paseo Tabasco. The local speciality is *horchata*, made from rice and cinnamon. And as all Tabascans know, the best *horchata* in Mexico is made at this street-corner booth, opposite the cathedral.

Entertainment and Nightlife

Las Botanas, Hotel Madán, Av. Madero 408. One of the centre's more popular night spots, a pubby bar hosting live bands playing Mex-rock and more international music.

D'Ovidio, Av. Venustiano Carranza 132, north of Parque Juárez. Large bar-restaurant where, most days, from about 3pm, musicians gather to play the music of tropical Mexico: *boleros*, *danzón*, Yucatecan trios... Some have been playing for decades, some are able musicians, some are bawling drunks. Any foreigner who wanders in will be drawn into conversation; women without male companions should perhaps avoid it unless they have a very high banter-tolerance. Sessions usually break up by about 9pm.

The Zona Luz

The streets of 'old' Villahermosa (which dates mostly from the late 19th century) occupy a walkable area between Av. Gregorio Méndez Magaña, the river, Paseo Tabasco and Av. Miguel Hidalgo. At its heart is a clutch of pedestrianized streets, called the Zona Remodelada or Zona Luz. Its hub is the little square of **Parque Juárez**, with the busiest street, **Avenida Francisco Madero**, alongside it and the main pedestrian *paseo*, **Calle Juárez**, running south from it to Av. 27 de Febrero. The name 'Zone of Light' makes it all sound rather grand, but the area is really a more entertaining

combination of a slight elegance and a more basic, very tropical take-it-as-you-find-it quality. Mixed up together on Madero, Juárez and Aldama are some quite smart cafés, cheap hotels, great ice cream stands, the kind of shops typical of Mexican city centres with names like 'Liz Minelli', pile-'em-up-high stocks of shoes, bags or curtain material, and 'domino clubs' where old men sit and play the game for hours beneath slowly whirring roof-fans.

Villahermosa is something of a centre for contemporary art, much of it with a noticeable Tabascan sensuality. Opposite Parque Juárez on Madero is the **Centro Cultural Villahermosa** (*open Tues–Sun 10–8; adm free; closed Mon*), a strikingly sleek modern arts centre, opened in 2000 and designed with great panache by young local architects. It houses exhibitions, theatre, concerts and film screenings, and there's a spectacular roof terrace and a café. A few streets west there is a clutch of smaller galleries in the charming **Calle Narciso Sáenz** (also just called C/ Sáenz), housed in well-restored old Villahermosa townhouses with bright patios that make excellent showcases for the often vividly colourful artwork. **Galería Casa Siempreviva**, opposite the post office at the corner of Av. Lerdo de Tejada, occupies a lovely old house with beautiful stained glass inside; among other galleries are **El Jaguar Despertado** (on C/ Sáenz 117), a semi-official centre that hosts a big range of activities, and **Galería de Arte Tabasco** (no. 122).

On the corner of C/ Juárez and Av. 27 de Febrero is old Villahermosa's most historic building, the **Casa de los Azulejos** ('House of Tiles'), so-named for its façade of bright metal-blue tiles set between ornate windows and white porticoes. It was built in 1889–1915 for the most prosperous merchant in Villahermosa at that time, with the fine Tabascan name of José María Graham McGregor; in style it mixes Hispano-Moorish with French Beaux-Arts opulence. Restored in the 1980s, it now houses the **Museo de Historia de Tabasco** (*open Tues–Sat 10–8, Sun 10–5; closed Mon; adm*). The small but interesting collection (partly labelled in English) covers every period of the state's past, with artefacts from Comalcalco and the time of the Conquest, and plenty from the Garrido Canabal era, including an *Himno Feminista Tabasqueña*. There's a good bookshop on the ground floor. Just as interesting as the collection is the house's part-restored interior. One strange feature is that it has a corrugated iron roof, since in this climate the first parts of a house to go are usually the roof timbers.

From the museum, walk one block up Av. 27 de Febrero, cross it and then walk up the steep Av. Aldama to come up beside the Porfirian-era **Palacio de Gobierno**, Tabasco's state house, into the **Plaza de Armas**, the 'official' main square of the old city. Also renovated recently, it stands on a hilltop, with a view over the river. At the south end of the square is Villahermosa's most historic church, La Concepción, better known as **La Conchita**. Like Tabascan Catholicism in general it has been through torrid times. Begun in 1800, it was bombarded by the US Navy in 1846, rebuilt, demolished by Garrido Canabal in 1931 and rebuilt yet again in the 1940s, but in the same bizarrely ornate, neo-Gothic, wedding-cake style. One corner of the Plaza de Armas leads to the **Puente Gaviotas**, a 1990's footbridge over the Grijalva. Despite the bridge, old passenger ferries alongside it still function (*daily 6am–9.45pm*), so that if you walk down to the Malecón you can enjoy a short but very cheap (*under one peso*) boat trip.

A few blocks uphill west of the Zona Luz, at Av. Ignacio Zaragoza 810, near the corner of C/ López Rayón, is the **Museo de Cultura Popular** (*open Tues–Sat 10–7, Sun 10–5; closed Mon; adm free*). In a few rooms of a little old house, it's an engagingly simple collection of traditional costumes, embroidery, ceramics, and musical instruments (labelling is in Spanish only). Cutting south three blocks from there on C/ Colorado, a hot walk along Av. 27 de Febrero will lead to the junction with Paseo Tabasco and Villahermosa's **Cathedral**, or what there is of it. The city's 19th-century cathedral was knocked down by Garrido Canabal in the 1920s, and the building of a new one did not begin until 1960; construction then fizzled out with it only part-finished in 1963, and one indication of the lack of religious fervour in Tabasco is that not much has been done to complete it.

Parque La Venta, the Zoo and Tabasco 2000

Villahermosa's greatest cultural possessions are matchless, with no equivalent collection anywhere else. They consist of over 30 huge basalt heads and other sculptures from the Olmec city of La Venta, 130 kilometres west of Villahermosa, arranged around a unique open-air 'museum' in a jungle park between Blvd Ruíz Cortines and the Laguna de las Ilusiones, the largest of the city's lakes. As with other cultural institutions in Tabasco the park arose out of an initiative by the poet and writer Carlos Pellicer Cámara. In the 1950s, when oil exploration was accelerating in the state, it seemed that the monuments of La Venta could be threatened, and Pellicer proposed that they be moved to Villahermosa for protection. The result was the creation of **Parque-Museo La Venta** in 1957.

La Venta flourished from about 900 to 400 BC: as the 'mother culture' of Mesoamerica, the Olmecs are seen as precursors in many areas – the building of monumental symbolic cities, the calendar, the central cosmic vision of a 'live' universe divided into three levels of existence – in which their influence was inherited by many later cultures. Olmec sculpture, however, has a special quality that stands out across the centuries. The peculiarities of Olmec carvings – the emphasis on massiveness, the faces that at times seem African, at others vaguely European, only occasionally Native American – have given rise to a great deal of speculation, and fed theories of some kind of early transatlantic contact. However, it appears likely that the Olmec heads may have been given their 'strange' features in an effort to make them similar to the face of the jaguar, an animal with a central place in Olmec religion and mythology.

Site Information

Park open daily 8–5 (last entry 4pm); Zoo (entered on same ticket) open Tues–Sun; closed Mon; adm. Museo de Historia Natural open Tues–Sun 8–5; closed Mon; adm.

You enter the park via a small **museum**, with a model of the original La Venta site. By the entrance there are always guides waiting (*tours $15–$20*) but the park is well-organized and it's easy to find your way on your own.

Past the museum you have a choice of paths, to the zoo or the Zona Arqueológica, although they later run into each other. The sculptures are laid out in a circuit of a little over a kilometre, with 33 'stops' (each monument also has a separate archaeologists' number, which can be confusing). At various points you can cut back if you want a shorter walk. Along the way, despite being within a city, you feel as if you're passing through a real jungle of dense, lush vegetation (*wear insect repellent*).

As well as the Olmec relics another essential draw of Parque La Venta is the **zoo** that is partially intertwined with the monuments. Within the limitations of a zoo, most of the animals, all native to southern Mexico, have a fair amount of space, and the enclosures are quite well landscaped; some of the non-dangerous animals, such as spider monkeys and coatis, scratch about fairly freely around you. Most striking of all are the dazzlingly colourful parrots and toucans, and the astonishing display of the different kinds of cat from the region, from jaguars and pumas to some near-unknown species. By the park entrance, a **Museo de Historia Natural** has some more static displays.

Virtually every one of the sculptures has its own dynamic character. Already striking at stop 3 is **Monument 5** (*la Abuela*), 'the Grandmother', a strange bug-like creature that seems different from any other Mesoamerican monument; similarly, while the giant Olmec heads can sometimes appear African, the next sculpture, **Stela 3** or the 'Bearded Man', could almost be European or Middle-Eastern, although it has been shown that his un-Mesoamerican 'beard' could be a chin-strap to a headdress. At stop 12 is **Altar 5**, the *Altar de los Niños* ('Altar of the Children'), one of several altars to show a male figure with a jaguar-skull headdress semi-seated in an alcove beneath a slab-like stone, also with a carved jaguar-face. They are believed to represent Olmec priests or priest-lords emerging from the Underworld, the origin of gods and kings, an image repeated many times in Olmec carvings. Altar 5 is one of the most intriguing, since the figure is carrying in his arms a child who appears dead, while on either side of the altar are pairs of figures, each of which also carries a strange-looking child.

About halfway round (at stop 15) there is a refreshment stand and craftwork shop. In the second half there is a near-unbroken sequence of powerful sculptures. At 18 is **Monument 56**, the *mono mirando el cielo* ('Monkey looking at the sky'), an eerily modern carving of a remarkably strong monkey-face. Stop 23 is **Altar 4**, the *Altar Triunfal*, the finest of all the Olmec altars showing priest-lords in the entrance to the Underworld. The lord, a tremendous figure of strength, has a rope in each hand attached to the wrists of submissive prisoner-figures on the sides of the altar, and appears to be dragging them towards the netherworld. Three stops further on you come upon the finest of the colossal Olmec heads and the best-known image of La Venta, **Monument 1** or the *Cabeza del Guerrero* ('Warrior's Head'). In spite of its having survived nearly three millennia, it can still seem bizarrely modern in its near-abstract form. Despite the distortions in their faces – flattened noses and thickened lips – some experts think these heads were 'portraits' of Olmec rulers, filtered to appear more jaguar-like, and shown wearing a kind of helmet believed to have been worn for the ball game. Finally, stop 33 is **Stela 1**, the 'Young Goddess', a rare large-scale Olmec sculpture of a woman, although at first sight she may not look especially feminine.

Between Parque La Venta and Paseo Tabasco is the **Parque Tomás Garrido Canabal**, a pleasant, shady park, and if as you leave La Venta you walk to the right around the outer wall you will come to a lovely walkway beside the **Laguna de las Ilusiones**. Parque Garrido leads to the junction of Ruíz Cortines with Paseo Tabasco, on the west side of which is Villahermosa's main upscale hotel zone. A turn north up Paseo Tabasco leads via a short but sweaty walk (this road is designed to be driven, not walked) to a symbol of Villahermosa's oil-boom wealth, the **Tabasco 2000** complex, begun in the 1970s. Within it are the modern city hall, a convention centre, a planetarium and a shopping mall; further out, there's a smart residential area. Like many similar 'prestige' projects around the world, it features a lot of hot, unusable empty space, with esplanades around striking fountains. On the side furthest from the city centre, where Paseo Tabasco meets Villahermosa's second river, the Carrizal, is **Parque La Choca**, another park, this one with a public swimming pool, while a dramatic modern bridge leads over the river to yet another, **Parque Tabasco**, which is mainly taken up by the permanent site for the annual *Feria de Tabasco* (*see* pp.413–14).

CICOM and the Museo de Antropología

South of the city centre is another grouping of modern buildings in a landscaped area beside the Grijalva, known as the CICOM. The **Centro de Investigación de las Culturas Olmeca y Maya** arose out of another initiative of Carlos Pellicer in the 1950s, and since then has expanded to become a general cultural complex: within the CICOM are the state theatre, a public library, an art school, a gallery and a bookshop. There are also restaurants, and a footpath along the river that would be more pleasant if it were better maintained. The centre's prime attraction, though, is the **Museo Regional de Antropología Carlos Pellicer Cámara** (*open Tue–Sun 9–7; adm*).

The great attraction of Villahermosa's museum is that it seeks to cover all the many ancient cultures of Mesoamerica, providing additional context to set around the region's purely Mayan museums. It is labelled in Spanish only, and has suffered from a degree of neglect since it was opened in the 1980s, but the collection is strong enough to outweigh these 'buts'. The museum has three floors, and a normal visit begins by going to the top and working down. The **top floor** presents the history of civilization throughout Mesoamerica more or less in chronological order, beginning with the local Olmecs but going on through Tlatilco, Monte Albán, Huastecs, Mixtecs, the Maya and many more. Unmissable are the pieces from the groups that inhabited the Gulf coast in the Classic era, such as the Totonac *Remojada* culture: their wonderfully individual ceramic *cabezas sonrientes* ('smiling heads') – which are just that – exude a kind of gentle amiability that seems completely at odds with the awesome aspect usually emphasized by the larger cultures such as the Maya or Teotihuacán. In a cabinet on its own is a 1,500-year-old toy of a jaguar mounted on wheels, from Veracruz – a staggering demonstration that the Mesoamerican cultures did know of the principle of the wheel, but didn't use it for anything practical.

On the **first (middle) floor** the museum reverts to more local material with the Olmec and the Maya. From the former there are small figures to compare with the giant sculptures in Parque La Venta, all with the same short, squat physique, especially the images of women, while Mayan artefacts include a finely carved fragment of a *stela* found at Paraíso. The **ground floor** houses monumental pieces, including an Olmec head that could easily be in Parque La Venta, and Mayan *stelae* from Reforma. Finally, not to be missed is the small 'Obras Selectas' section, where some of the museum's finest pieces are kept in a darkened room in order to preserve their colours: a tiny jade 'Olmec Venus' from about 1000 BC, the *Urna de Teapa*, one of the most sophisticated of Mayan funeral urns, and wonderfully vivid Mayan painted vases.

Around Villahermosa

The delta country around Villahermosa is a maze of intersecting lanes, between creeks, palms and banana leaves. Apart from sleepy towns with eccentric churches, its main visitor attractions are the Yumká nature park and one of the strangest of Mayan sites, at Comalcalco.

Yumká Nature Park

The park of Yumká was a private estate, covering 101 hectares, which was taken over by the state government in 1987. The most staggering fact about it is that, because its former owners did not develop it, it became, pretty much by accident, the sole remaining patch of original forest in central Tabasco, which 25 years before had been covered in trees. Since 1993 it has been managed as a park, seeking to preserve examples of the three characteristic natural landscapes of Tabasco: jungle, savanna and lagoon. One surprise of Yumká is that as well as local wildlife it contains 'exotics', such as tigers, elephants, antelopes and zebras. This is because purely native animals were not thought sufficiently interesting for local visitors, although foreigners tend to be far more interested in the Mexican wildlife. Even so, it can be an enjoyable day out.

Getting There

Yumká

Yumka is situated 16km east of Villahermosa near the airport. There is no public transport to the park, except for very infrequent *combis* that leave from C/ Río de la Serra, behind the second-class bus station in Villahermosa. This seems to be due to an alliance between travel agencies, who run trips to the park, and taxi drivers. A **cab** will cost around $8.

Comalcalco

Comalcalco is 60km northwest of Villahermosa near the road to Paraíso. To **drive** there from central Villahermosa, turn north off Blvd Ruíz Cortines on to Av. Universidad. Follow this to Villahermosa's *periférico*, turn left, then turn right on to the Comalcalco road. This is sometimes signposted to Comalcalco, sometimes to Paraíso, Nacajuca or Jalpa, but once out of the city it's easy to follow. The site is off the Paraíso road north of Comalcalco town; the access road to the ruins' entrance is now easy to find, having been 'improved'.

Three first-class and more *intermedio* and second-class **buses** run to Comalcalco daily from Villahermosa. Buses usually leave you in Comalcalco town, 3km from the ruins (second-class may drop you by the access road, from where it's 1km). However, taxis are cheap.

Site Information

Yumká

Open daily 9–5 (last adm 4pm); adm.

Visits are by **guided tour**; a full tour lasts 2hrs, but you can visit one or two out of the three areas for a lower entrance fee. Tours (about every 45mins) are usually in Spanish only, but can be given in English for groups by prior arrangement, call t (993) 356 0107.

Comalcalco

Open daily 10–5 (last entry 4pm); museum open 10–4 only; adm.

Comalcalco is a competitor for the accolade of hottest of all Mayan sites, and is certainly one of the sweatiest; it's wise to get there early. The heat and humidity also results in a high concentration of bugs (and butterflies), so repellent is especially recommended. Next to the **museum** there's also a small **café**, where after scrambling round the Acropolis you can reward yourself with a cold drink.

The Road to Comalcalco

The road to Comalcalco, winding through the Chontal town of **Nacajuca**, is of interest in itself. As soon as you leave Villahermosa you cross rivers and streams, as the road abruptly widens and narrows to cross small bridges, amid an impossible depth of green. After 40 kilometres there is an essential stop at **Cupilco**, which has the most spectacular of Tabascan churches. The neglect of Tabasco by the missionary orders meant that its village churches were built very late, in the 18th century or after independence, so they are 100 per cent Mexican, and decorated in exuberant colours with slight reference to European styles. Closed up in the 1930s, Cupilco's church has been lovingly restored and recoloured.

Comalcalco

Tabasco's great Mayan city of Comalcalco lies northwest of Villahermosa amid a typical Tabascan landscape of water, drained fields and emerald-green vegetation. Conditions here were different from anywhere else in the Mayan world; the rock that formed the base material of Mayan architecture elsewhere was completely missing, and there was only thick, soft alluvial clay. Comalcalco, however, is one of the great demonstrations of Mayan ingenuity, for out of what they had to hand, its builders created the only Mayan city made of brick.

Comalcalco was once considered remote within the Mayan world, but surveys since the 1970s have revealed a large number of smaller settlements around the Grijalva-Usumacinta deltas. The site was occupied from at least the Preclassic, but flourished as a city during the Classic era and reached its greatest extent around 600–900. Though located near the area inhabited by the Putuns, Comalcalco seems to have been more refined than the small Putún settlements. Apart from its construction in brick, another feature of the city was its burial customs: several bodies have been found here buried in a crouching position, together with jade ornaments and other offerings, inside large cone-shaped ceramic jars. Also distinctive was its complex system of drainage channels; if in the northern Yucatán the Mayan builders devoted their energies to conserving water, Comalcalco is a demonstration of what they could do when they had an excess of it. The city has fine mouldings in stucco, similar to many at Palenque, and one theory suggests that Comalcalco was an important point in trade between the Usumacinta valley and areas further west. The deltas were also an important source of cacao. However, because Mayan inscriptions were usually carved in stone, there are relatively few glyph inscriptions at Comalcalco to provide the city with a fuller history. After about 1100 it was completely abandoned.

The North Plaza

From the main entrance and museum (*see* below) you approach the site on a long straight path, with plenty of trees for shade, from which you see the largest group of buildings, the North Plaza, over to your left. Facing precisely east, toward the origin of the sun, is Comalcalco's great pyramid, **Temple I**. Its long rows of thin red bricks and

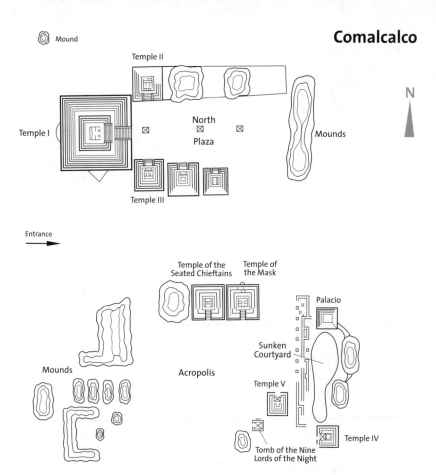

Mound

Temple II

North Plaza

Temple I

Mounds

Temple III

Entrance

Temple of the Seated Chieftains

Temple of the Mask

Palacio

Sunken Courtyard

Mounds

Acropolis

Temple V

Temple IV

Tomb of the Nine Lords of the Night

N

angular lines make it look strangely as if it belongs to another time and place than Classic Mesoamerica, like a Mayan pyramid built as part of some English municipal architecture project of the 1970s. Bricks were, in fact, only used during the second phase of building at Comalcalco. In the first centuries temple platforms were created by massing together huge piles of earth, packing them down and letting them dry out, then cladding them in stucco to give them extra solidity, a method used by the Olmecs. The use of brick, built on to the earth base, developed around 600–700 as the city grew and larger structures were required. In several places, where the brickwork has worn away, the original base can be seen, giant, smooth ramps of stucco baked into a kind of concrete. Even the stucco is unusual: instead of the powdered limestone that formed the main ingredient of Mayan stucco further east, the city's people used ingredients from the coast, especially sand and powdered oyster shells.

Along the southeast corner of Temple I facing the plaza – the first corner you come to if you head straight into the square – there is a tremendous fragment of stucco relief, dated to around 700, showing a reclining figure along with smaller figures and animals. He has especially fine feet. Above him, the pyramid rises in 12 tiers to a flat platform at the top, with a two-room east-facing temple, though the stucco steps have virtually disintegrated so you cannot climb up. The bricks used at Comalcalco, on show at the site museum, also have their own unusual features. Many have modelled shapes of animals (crocodiles), human figures, buildings or symbolic motifs baked into them; stranger still, the bricks were normally placed so that these designs faced inwards, never to be seen again.

The North Plaza is a geometrical, rectangular Mayan plaza, running west–east from the Great Pyramid and built with a tremendous sense of scale. Only two more of its structures have been fully excavated, **Temple II** on the north side and **Temple III** to the south. Both are smaller versions of Temple I, which adds to the impression of the plaza as a coordinated whole. Alongside Temple III two small pyramids have been partly uncovered, while the mounds on the north and east sides remain unexcavated. The square also has a strange echo – almost certainly deliberate – which you can experience if you stand on the mound in front of Temple I and clap your hands.

The Acropolis and the Museum

From the southeast corner of the North Plaza a short walk and a steep climb will take you to the great Acropolis of Comalcalco, atop a huge two-level platform. The only hill for miles in the flat delta, it is entirely man-made, a task that must have taken centuries, and was begun long before the construction of the North Plaza. The Acropolis, and above all the top level, was almost certainly reserved for the élite of the city. Removed from the city below, its Palacio contains unusually intimate spaces.

The Acropolis presumably had smooth sides at one time, but in its semi-excavated state exploring involves some scrambling and stumbling. As you come on to the first level there are two temples to your right, facing into the Acropolis. Immediately right, the **Temple of the Mask** (Temple VI) has, in the middle of its stairway, a stucco mask of the sun god Kinich Ahau, interesting to compare with an image of that god at Edzná. Next to it, the **Temple of the Seated Chieftains** (Temple VII) has a more spectacular relief showing two tiers of seated figures, all superbly individual and in the elaborate regalia of Mayan lords, beneath a vision serpent. In a corner of Temple VII you can also inspect one of Comalcalco's 'crouching burial' funeral jars, still in place under glass.

On two sides of the Acropolis, to the west and east, there are taller, later platforms. That to the west is still to be uncovered, but the eastern platform contains the **Palacio** of Comalcalco, reached after another steep climb. This is one of the most intriguing of Mayan residential buildings, consisting mainly of two north–south, parallel rows of rooms. Several surround a sunken courtyard (*patio hundido*), which must have been the main hub of the domestic life of the lords of Comalcalco. On one side it has a well-head, connected to a drain in the middle of the courtyard, with an intricate network of other drains: this seems to have been an early system of air conditioning, in that water collected in the patio then ran through the building, moderating the heat. From the rear of the Palacio you also get a great view, across the simmering delta.

Beside the Palacio towards the south end there are two more temples, **Temples IV** and **V**, beneath both of which large, vaulted tombs have been found. Temple IV also contained a stucco relief of mythical beasts and spirit-creatures, now in the site museum. One of the most impressive of all structures at Comalcalco, though, is the small temple near Temple V, the **Tomb of the Nine Lords of the Night** (Temple IX). As the name indicates, this is also a tomb, dating from between 720 and 780; inside it there is a magnificent relief of nine figures in discussion. Parts of it are in a poor state, and you are no longer allowed to go inside the tomb, but it's still possible to make out a great deal from outside. The modelling of at least two figures evokes a remarkable vigour and naturalness; they do not carry the sceptres of power which identify Mayan *ahauob* in sculptures, but they may represent the 'Nine Lords of the Night', dominant spirits of the night sky come to accompany the tomb's occupant into the next world.

As you leave the ruins you can visit one of the best of the Mayan site **museums**, even though its labelling is Spanish-only. Among its highlights are funerary urns and burial relics, and some very vivid sculptures of birds and animals of the delta coast.

Western Tabasco

The western part of Tabasco, beyond **Cárdenas**, is economically productive but does not have many attractions for the visitor. On the borders of Veracruz, 130 kilometres west of Villahermosa and eight kilometres from Highway 180, is the original site of **La Venta** (*open daily 10–5; adm*). Contrary to what was said during the 1950s it has not been totally destroyed by oil exploration. Stripped of its main monuments, though, the site is a little denuded, but copies of some of them have been installed, and a few of the originals are still there as well. The greatest attraction is the awesome size and immense age of the Olmec city, parts of which, such as the glowering earth mound of the great pyramid and the ball court of **Complex C**, are 3,000 years old.

From Cárdenas, a turn south leads in 20 kilometres to **Huimanguillo**. South and west of there the land climbs into a range of thickly forested hills, thinly inhabited with Zoque villages and crossed by fast-flowing rivers and streams. Now known as the **Agua Selva** reserve, the whole area contains more than 100 waterfalls, including some over 100 metres high. In the forests near Las Flores in the far southwest corner of Tabasco there is also the very little-known ruined city of **Malpasito** (*open daily 10–5; adm free*), believed to have been built by ancestors of the Zoque in around 700–900. This spectacular landscape has been extremely remote, and is still hard to get to without your own transport. **Universo Maya** in Villahermosa (*see* p.413) offers tours.

Getting Around

Four first-class **buses** daily run from Villahermosa to **Villa La Venta** (3km from the ruins), and more second-class.

There is one first-class bus daily to **Huimanguillo** (at 3.30pm), continuing to **Malpaso** in Chiapas. There are more second-class services, and *combis* from Huimanguillo run to most places in the area. From Las Flores, south of Huimanguillo, you may be able to get *combis* or taxis to nearby waterfalls.

Where to Stay

There is nowhere to stay in **Villa la Venta**, so it's best visited on the way to somewhere else. The nearest regular hotels to the Agua Selva reserve are at Huimanguillo, though *cabañas* are due to open in villages near Malpasito.

Huimanguillo t (917–)

Hotel del Carmen, Av. Morelos 39, t 375 0202 (*inexpensive*). The best of Huimanguillo's four hotels (the others are basic and *cheap*).

The Sierra de Tabasco

South of Villahermosa Highway 195 runs straight down towards Tuxtla Gutiérrez and San Cristóbal de Las Casas, eventually to become one of the most spectacular mountain roads in Mexico (*see* p.465). It already begins to climb before it enters Chiapas, into what is known as the **Sierra de Tabasco**. Some of its mountain valleys are home to one of Mexico's least-known indigenous peoples, the non-Mayan Zoque.

The road south stays fairly flat, lined by banana plants, until you reach **Teapa**, after which it begins to rise very quickly. The valleys of the Tabasco sierra are not high by the standards of Chiapas – under 1,000 metres – but enough to moderate the temperatures a little. Teapa is a pleasant little town, with an attractive plaza and three 18th-century churches. The hills around it are full of caves that were important focuses of pre-Hispanic settlement, and in nearby valleys there are beauty spots – among them **El Azufre** and **Puyacatengo** – that are visited by Tabascans for their river swimming and natural 'spas', some (pretty pungent) sulphur pools in the rocks.

East of Teapa is **Tacotalpa**, a quiet little town that until 1795 was the capital of the colony of Tabasco, long preferred by the Spaniards to anywhere down below. About 20 kilometres south down a mountain road is **Tapijulapa**, largest of the Zoque villages of the Sierra. The Zoque, whose language is one of the Nahua group like the peoples to their west, were a reclusive people, who avoided major conflicts with the Aztecs or the Maya. They did not offer strong resistance to the Spaniars either, but retreated into their mountains. Their religion, even more than others in Mesoamerica, venerated mountains, rivers and natural features as centres of divine energy, and rather than build temples they held their ceremonies in caves. Some are still held today.

The Zoque's unobtrusiveness means that their distinctive culture is less apparent than that of the Maya. You are more likely to notice the idyllic prettiness of Tapijulapa. It comes as a complete surprise: the houses are almost Mediterranean, with white-

Getting Around and Tourist Information

Teapa t (932–)

Teapa, main centre of the Sierra, is 54km south of Villahermosa down Highway 195, and it has a *gasolinera*. A minor road leads east to the area's other major town, **Tacotalpa**, near which is a turn south to **Tapijulapa** and **Oxolotán**. This road is more or less paved all the way, although parts are in bad condition; however, it's still passable in a normal car (watch where the buses go).

First-class **buses** from Villahermosa to Tuxtla (nine daily) stop in Teapa. There are also frequent second-class buses, and local *combis*.

There are two **banks** on Teapa's main street, both with ATMs.

Where to Stay and Eat

Teapa and Tapijulapa t (932–)

Teapa's plaza has several cheap restaurants.

Hotel Quintero, C/ Eduardo R. Bastar 108, Teapa, t 322 0045 (*inexpensive*). The best hotel in the Sierra, a block from the plaza, with modern rooms.

Hotel-Balneario El Azufre, t 322 0522 (*cheap*). By the springs of El Azufre, this is the best of the simple hotels in the riverside *balnearios* near Teapa, with cabin-style rooms.

Hotel Jardín, Plaza Independencia 123, Teapa, t 322 0027 (*cheap*). Basic, sleepily friendly hotel, with décor that's a curious mix of religious images and ceramic dogs.

Restaurant Mariquita, Plaza Mayor, Tapijulapa (*cheap*). A pleasant, simple and friendly *lonchería*, easily located on the main square.

washed walls and red-tile roofs, and climb up mountain sides along winding streets connected by narrow alleyways. At the heart of the village is the chapel of **Santiago Apóstol**, high on a hill with a superb view. Below are more sulphur springs and water-falls at **Villa Luz**. In a house nearby Governor Garrido Canabal entertained his cronies.

South of Tapijulapa the road winds, rises and falls, until finally you see below you a lush valley, with a village around the very medieval-looking monastery of **Oxolotán**. It feels like the middle of nowhere today, and it's extraordinary to think what it must have felt like for the Franciscan friars who began to build here in the 1550s. It was intended as a way-station on a possible land route to the Yucatán. However, the friars found it very hard to sustain, and by the 1640s it had been abandoned. The chapel continued in use as the village church; built with rocks from the nearby river bed, it has a rough-hewn quality almost like a European early Christian church. Still cruder are the monastery buildings which now house the **Museo de la Sierra** (*open daily 9–5; adm. free*), a small collection of Baroque religious images and relics of the colonial era. The building and the sombre friars cells are the most remarkable artefacts of all.

The Rivers Region

On the map of Tabasco there is a separate region stretching to the Guatemalan border in the east, almost an 'annexe', which cannot be reached directly by road from the main part of the state. Known as the *Región de los Ríos* or Rivers Region, it is part of Tabasco because it was settled not by road but by river, up the meandering Usumacinta and its tributaries. It's a classical tropical savanna landscape, now mostly deforested, of great stillness and vast, flat horizons that seem to simmer in the heat. It can make for an interesting detour in between the Yucatán and Palenque, and Emiliano Zapata makes a more attractive stopover on this route than Escárcega.

The name of **Emiliano Zapata** gives it away as a largely post-Revolutionary town, strung out along one main street (Av. Corregidora). It's very much a riverside town, almost on an island between the Usumacinta and a lake. From Zapata a road rolls south until after nearly 40 kilometres there is a sign to the Mayan site of **Pomoná** (*open daily 10–5; adm*), which is about three kilometres up a poor but passable track. Despite its remoteness this was one of the first Mayan cities for which an 'emblem-glyph' was identified, allowing references to it to be traced in inscriptions. Pomoná was first occupied in the Preclassic, but reached its peak after AD 500. The last Long Count date at the site is from 790, suggesting the 'Collapse' reached here very early.

Pomoná was spread over several low hills, and the excavated area, one large plaza, covers only one of six main areas. Its builders faced similar problems to those at Comalcalco, lacking any local building stone, but instead of using brick they brought stone in fragments from mountains to the south, up to 20 kilometres away. Hence, Pomoná's structures have a strangely rubble-like look. It gets few visitors, but has a very attractive **museum**, with exceptional ceramics, carvings and reliefs from the site.

Back on the main road, about 15 kilometres from the Pomoná turn the road crosses the Usumacinta at **Boca del Cerro**, where the river emerges dramatically from a gorge.

Getting Around

Highway 203 turns south off the 186 Escárcega–Villahermosa road inside Chiapas, signposted for Emiliano Zapata (9km). From there it continues to Tenosique (66km). There are **fuel stations** at Emiliano Zapata, Tenosique and Balancán.

There are frequent first-class **buses** that run from Villahermosa to Emiliano Zapata and Tenosique and less frequently to Balancán, and many more second-class. Local *combis* and buses run mostly from Tenosique. With them or second-class buses you can get to Pomoná (3-km walk from the main road), but harder to get to Reforma.

Festivals

Tenosique
Juego del Pochó 'Game of Pochó', *20 Jan*.
Tenosique is famous for a unique *fiesta*, which begins on St Sebastian's day, but continues every Sunday until Shrove Tuesday. It's of pre-Conquest origin, but its history is unrecorded and its meaning is open to interpretation. Men dance through the streets in anonymous painted wooden masks, amid strange sounds made by a kind of drum called a *pochó*, while women dance gracefully around them in near total silence.

Where to Stay and Eat

Tenosique and E. Zapata t (934–)
Hotel Don José, C/ 26 no. 103, x 27, Tenosique, **t** 342 0555 (a/c *inexpensive*, fan-only *cheap*). Decent small-town hotel near the main square in Tenosique, with bright, pleasant rooms and an unfussy, pleasant **restaurant**.
Hotel Maya Usumacinta, Av. Corregidora 49, Emiliano Zapata, **t** 343 0239, **f** 343 0403 (*inexpensive*). Top of the line in the Rivers Region, near the junction of the main street and the plaza. It has well-used but well-kept rooms, and the town's best **restaurant**.

From there it's a short distance to **Tenosique**. A rather ragged town along another long main street, it reveals its river-born origins in its waterside promenade from which to stare into the still horizon, while a few slow-moving launches still pull in.

The best way to go on to the more distant Mayan site of Reforma is to make a 'loop' to the northeast towards El Triunfo. After 45 kilometres a sign left indicates the **Cascadas de Reforma**, waterfalls and rapids where Tenosique residents picnic and swim in big, cooling pools. A couple of kilometres further north, just before the village of La Cuchilla, a signed turning leads to the **Reforma** site (*open daily 8–5; adm*). Like Pomoná it is potentially very rich; it was discovered by Teobert Maler in 1897, and later expeditions found many fine *stelae*. It is estimated that it was occupied from AD 200, and prospered from around 650. Between expeditions it was heavily looted, and in 1961 a local initiative led to some *stelae* being removed to the museum in Balancán (*see* below). Significant excavations began in 1992, and only five of 25 major structures have been uncovered, the most intriguing an unusual, very steep 'stepped pyramid'.

From the ruins the road continues north 10 kilometres to meet the dead-straight road that runs across the Rivers Region. Head west for 30 kilometres to reach the turn for **Balancán**, beside the Usumacinta another eight kilometres south. An archetypally sultry, slow-moving little town by a bend in the river, this has in its plaza the humble **Museo Dr José Gómez Panaco** (*open daily 9–8; adm*), named after the local doctor who suggested that the Reforma *stelae* be rescued. Though some have been taken to Villahermosa, it still has a few fine exhibits, the highlight being Stela I, dated 756 and known as the **Señor de Balancán**, a fearsome image of a king subduing a prisoner.

Chiapas

14

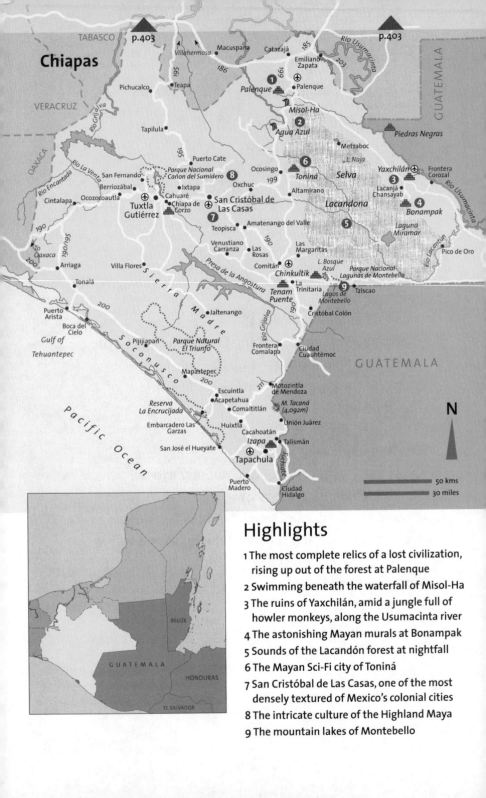

Chiapas

VERACRUZ

OAXACA

GUATEMALA

Villahermosa   Macuspana   Catazajá

Pichucalco   Teapa

Tapilula

Puerto Cate

San Fernando   Parque Nacional   Ocosingo
Cañon del Sumidero

Berriozábal   Ixtapa   Oxchuc   Toniná

Cintalapa   Ocozocoautla   Cahuaré   Chiapa de Corzo   San Cristóbal de Las Casas   Altamirano

Tuxtla Gutiérrez

Teopisca   Amatenango del Valle

Venustiano Carranza   Las Rosas   Las Margaritas

Villa Flores   Comitán

Arriaga

Tonalá

Presa de la Angostura

Chinkultik   L. Bosque Azul   Parque Nacional Lagunas de Montebello

Puerto Arista

Boca del Cielo

Gulf of Tehuantepec

Tenam Puente   La Trinitaria   Tziscao   Lagos de Montebello   Cristóbal Colón

Jaltenango

Parque Natural El Triunfo

Frontera Comalapa   Ciudad Cuauhtémoc

Pijijiapan

Mapastepec

GUATEMALA

Escuintla   Motozintla de Mendoza
Acapetahua

Reserva La Encrucijada   Comaltitlán   M. Tacaná (4,092m)

Embarcadero Las Garzas   Huixtla   Cacahoatán   Unión Juárez

San José el Hueyate   Izapa   Talismán

Tapachula

Pacific Ocean

Puerto Madero   Ciudad Hidalgo

Villahermosa   Emiliano Zapata

Palenque

Misol-Ha

Agua Azul

Metzaboc   L. Naja

Piedras Negras

Selva   Yaxchilán   Frontera Corozal

Lacanjá Chansayab   Bonampak

Lacandona

Laguna Miramar

Pico de Oro

Sierra Madre

Soconusco

Sierra

50 kms
30 miles

N

Highlights

1 The most complete relics of a lost civilization, rising up out of the forest at Palenque

2 Swimming beneath the waterfall of Misol-Ha

3 The ruins of Yaxchilán, amid a jungle full of howler monkeys, along the Usumacinta river

4 The astonishing Mayan murals at Bonampak

5 Sounds of the Lacandón forest at nightfall

6 The Mayan Sci-Fi city of Toniná

7 San Cristóbal de Las Casas, one of the most densely textured of Mexico's colonial cities

8 The intricate culture of the Highland Maya

9 The mountain lakes of Montebello

BELIZE

GUATEMALA

HONDURAS

EL SALVADOR

Each of the four states that make up the north of Mayan Mexico has a certain uniformity: the flat, dry scrub and Yucatec Maya villages of Yucatán and most of Quintana Roo; the forested quietness of Campeche; the sweltering delta of Tabasco. No such generalization can be applied to Chiapas. It feels almost like a continent to itself, with as much variation in landscape as a continent, taking in dense tropical rainforest, near-alpine mountains and valleys of desert-like aridity. The sheer diversity of animals, birds and plant life is staggering, and most of Mexico's rarest species are found only here: quetzals; green macaws; near-extinct types of forest cat.

As late as the 1960s the route from Palenque up to San Cristóbal de Las Casas was only a dirt track. Early explorers searching for Mayan ruins in the 19th century often travelled in a *silla*, a 'chair' on the back of an Indian bearer, since the only paths were impassable even to mules. The different regions of the state developed in isolation from each other, and the state as a whole was almost equally isolated from the rest of Mexico. Under Spain Chiapas was governed as part of Guatemala, and it was joined to Mexico in the 1820s more or less as a result of a political fix.

The many diversities of Chiapas can be broadly divided into four main regions. For the last millennium the hot lowlands to the north and east along the Usumacinta river have been covered in forest and – until very recently – thinly populated, but 1,500 years ago this was one of the greatest areas of Mayan civilization. It contains not only the great city of Palenque, but also the comparably spectacular sites of Bonampak and Yaxchilán. To the south and 2,000 metres up are the Highlands, centred around the Spanish mountain city of San Cristóbal de Las Casas, where the temperature, even the feel of the air, are utterly different. Along the valleys and ridges around San Cristóbal are the Tzotzil- and Tzeltal-speaking communities where a living Mayan culture survives most completely today. Still well above sea level but much lower than San Cristóbal is the Central Valley, stretching southeast from Tuxtla Gutiérrez and closed off to the north by the gorge of the Sumidero. This is the driest part of the state, and the dominant economic region of modern Chiapas. Along the south side of the valley is the massive barrier of the Sierra Madre, the highest and least-populated mountains in Chiapas, home to its rarest wildlife. This separates off the last of the four regions, the hot Pacific plain of the Soconusco, with the city of Tapachula and the oldest Mayan city in Mexico, Izapa.

The isolation of the state from the rest of Mexico and of its regions from each other has long been put forward as one of the causes of the 'problem' of Chiapas. Economic development, political reform, have always arrived here last. Chiapas has also been a wild and backwoods region, the source of some of the most jaw-dropping stories of official corruption and cronyism in Mexico. Most recently, this has become famous as a key region in Mexico's political crises, with the Zapatista rebellion and its long-drawn-out stand-off with the government, the army and other local forces (for more on the political situation, *see* pp.466–70). However, in current circumstances this situation does not seem to create special dangers for foreign travellers (*see* 'Political Violence and Military Checks', pp.119–20). Without dismissing these problems in any way, they need not detract from the immense fascination of Chiapas.

Palenque

There is no other Mayan city about which so much is known as Palenque. It was the first Mayan site to attract exploration in the 18th century, the primary target of Del Río, Waldeck and then Stephens and Catherwood when they made their way into the region. The grandeur and unquestionable sophistication of the architecture of Palenque, the very model of a 'lost city', first brought the attention of the outside world to the existence of a refined ancient culture in the Mayan region, even if its early explorers thought it had been built by stray Greeks or Egyptians. Later, it was here again that the 'Palenque Round Table' meetings of the 1970s first succeeded in deciphering Mayan glyphs. Palenque has the most magical location of the major Mayan cities, its pyramids and temples looming out of valleys between cascading vegetation and fast-flowing rivers. No other Mayan city has such a density of sculpture and of glyph inscriptions, which have given it a vivid living history.

Palenque is also one of the largest of Mayan sites, in its full extent spreading over a huge area well beyond the section normally open to be visited. And, despite all that's known about the city, a vast amount remains to be excavated and major new finds are still being made – so that for the non-archaeologist, too, there are always new things to discover. In particular, after several years during which the big discoveries in the Mayan world came from less well-known cities, the spectacular finds made in Temple XIX and XX in 1998–9 have once again placed Palenque centre-stage, opening up a whole 'new' area of the site (note, also, that thanks in part to the scale of recent discoveries it's even more common at Palenque than elsewhere in the Mayan world to find alternative spellings or whole names for the same person, see p.42).

The town of Palenque is also the main centre for visiting anywhere in the forest lowlands of Chiapas, the jumping-off point for trips into the Lacandón rainforest and to the other great Mayan sites in the Usumacinta valley, Yaxchilán and Bonampak.

History

'Palenque' is a Spanish word for a palisade or fence, and comes only from the name of the Spanish town, which was then extended to the ruins. The original name of the city was almost certainly *Lacamha* ('Big Water'), while the domain over which it ruled was often referred to in inscriptions as *Bak* or the 'Bone Kingdom'. The hills around it were probably sacred spaces long before any pyramids began to be built at the site. Palenque was a growing settlement through the Preclassic era, but is associated above all with the great flourishing of Classic Mayan civilization in the Usumacinta region during the centuries from about AD 300 to 800.

The first *ahau* or ruler of Palenque whose name is known was K'uk-Balam ('Quetzal-Jaguar'), who ascended to the throne in March 431, at the age of 34. From then on we know the names and also the birth, accession and death-dates of ten generations of Palenque's rulers, from the 5th to the 8th centuries. This unique dynastic record is preserved above all in inscriptions on monuments erected by the city's greatest *ahauob*, **Pakal 'the Great'** (more properly known as Janaab Pakal, 'Great Sun-Shield'), who ruled from 615 to 683, dying at the age of 80, and his son **Kan-Balam II** ('Snake-

Jaguar', also known as Chan-Bahlum), who ruled officially from 684 to 702. Pakal's greatest work was the Temple of Inscriptions, which contains his extraordinary tomb; Kan-Balam II completed this giant pyramid and then matched or surpassed his father with the trio of temples called the 'Cross Group', the temples of the Cross, the Sun and the Foliated Cross.

These two recorded their 'family tree' in such detail – Pakal in great 'king-lists' of glyphs on the Temple of Inscriptions – for good reasons. Like all Mayan cities Palenque had its long-running feuds – notably with Toniná and Piedras Negras, now on the Guatemalan side of the Usumacinta. In the intricate politics of the Maya lowlands it also became an ally of Tikal, and therefore attracted the enmity of the other 'super-power', Calakmul. Another, separate issue was that the royal house of Palenque seems to have had a problem in maintaining an unbroken male line: on two occasions, with no male heir, the throne passed to daughters of a previous ruler, and it is clear from the inscriptions that these women were not just consorts or regents but actually rulers themselves. In 583 Lady Kanal-Ikal (also called Yohl Ik'nal) succeeded her father Kan-Balam I. She ruled for 22 years, but during this time, in 599, her kingdom suffered a ferocious attack from Calakmul, recorded as a disaster in the Palenque inscriptions. She was followed by her son Ah-Ne-Ol-Mat, but the city was then sacked by Calakmul a second time, in 611. Ah-Ne-Ol-Mat's exact fate is not recorded, but when he died in 612 the only remaining heir to the royal line was Lady Sak-Kuk, the daughter of a brother (Pakal I) who had never actually ruled. Sak-Kuk and her husband Kan-Mo-Balam were the parents of the great Pakal, born in 603. By this point, however, not only had Palenque suffered two devastating defeats but the succession of the *ahau* contravened all the normal rules of Mayan patriarchal lineage, since Pakal, in terms of the male line, was two removes away from the original ruling house. It seems certain there was a long period of instability in the early years of Pakal's reign, while he was a child, which was dealt with by his mother.

Pakal's great monuments can be seen as fulfilling two propaganda functions: 'confidence-building' as he restored Palenque's power, and simultaneously legitimizing his own status as *ahau*, by presenting very graphically his own connections with all previous rulers. On his tomb, for example, he is shown surrounded and aided by six preceding generations of the ruling house. These carvings also re-emphasized and re-interpreted the divine nature of the *ahau* lineage as a conduit to the Otherworld, beyond mere male and female. On Pakal's tomb, his ancestors are shown emerging god-like from fruit trees in the earth, and far from hiding the shifts in his ancestry these monuments give pride of place to his mother and great-grandmother, associating Sak-Kuk with the First Mother, mother of gods and *ahauob* at the dawn of creation. In the face of any crisis of confidence in the dynasty, its divine source and the ritual passing-on of power, as much as simple details of heredity, are shown as the basis of authority. Kan-Balam II in his temples went further, creating the greatest ever statement in inscriptions and sculpture of the mystical concept of Mayan kingship and the *ahau*'s place in the divine order of the universe. In the Cross group temples his ancestry is traced further and further back in time to a supposed first king of Palenque who ruled from 967 BC, and was in turn descended from three gods known as the 'Palenque Triad', all born in 2360 BC to the First Mother herself.

This grandiose self-image was a reflection of real power, for Pakal rebuilt Palenque's strength and wealth and made it the dominant power in the northern Usumacinta. For many years Pakal, who officially became *ahau* at the age of 12, had to follow the directions of his mother. She was evidently not someone to trifle with; he did not began to commission significant buildings himself until after 640, the year she died, when he was already 37. A significant event, given great importance in Pakal's inscriptions, came in 659 when Palenque welcomed the *ahau* Nun-Bak-Chak of Tikal after he had been driven into exile by Calakmul, and it is likely that Pakal and his son aided Tikal in later campaigns against their old enemy. Pakal also conquered at least six smaller cities, while Kan-Balam II attacked another traditional enemy, Toniná, in 687. At its height Palenque was one of the largest Mayan cities, with a population of as much as 70,000, and its tributary-cities extended from Tortuguero, near Villahermosa, in the west – or possibly Comalcalco – well into the Petén to the east.

This grandeur, however, was still fragile. Kan-Balam II died childless, and was succeeded by his brother, **Kan-Hok-Chitam II** (also called Kan-Xul), who was already 57. He was an energetic builder, adding to the Palacio in particular, but in 711 he launched another war against Toniná. Against the odds, for Palenque was much the larger city, Kan-Hok-Chitam II was defeated, captured, tortured and executed, as was gleefully recorded in monuments at Toniná (*see* p.471). Palenque was again thrown into crisis. Knowledge of what happened next has been transformed by the recent discoveries in Temples XIX and XX, which were built by the next ruler, **Kinich Ahkal Mo Naab III**. He was most probably a grandson of Pakal the Great and so a nephew of the previous two *ahauob*, but did not formally take the throne until 721, ten years after the death of his predecessor, reigning until some time between 736 and 740. He was greatly aided by a general called Chak Suutz, not a member of the royal house but treated with great respect in inscriptions. Until the new discoveries it was believed that Palenque entered into a fairly steady decline after the Toniná war, but it now appears that between them these two succeeded in re-establishing much of its regional influence, and Kinich Ahkal Mo Naab III undertook the last great round of building at Palenque in Temple XIX and the structures around it. Not much is known about his successors, although in general it seems Palenque had to struggle harder against outside threats in the 8th century than it had had to in the 670s. The 'Collapse' came upon the city less than a century after the death of Kan-Balam II, and Palenque's last dated inscription, on the accession of an *ahau* still called Pakal after his ancestor, is from 799. Despite the city's size – or perhaps because of it, given the social crisis that must have ensued – it was abandoned, unusually completely, over the next century.

By the time of the Spanish Conquest the site was completely overgrown, and was not even noticed when a village was established nearby in the 1560s. Some time in the 18th century Indians from the village came upon the ruins, and rumours about them began to filter up to their Spanish overlords. In 1773 Friar Ramón de Ordóñez y Aguiar, a canon at the cathedral in Ciudad Real (San Cristóbal) with antiquarian interests, decided to follow them up. He returned with an enthusiastic account of what he had seen, and was the first to suggest that the city must have been created by some strange alien civilization from across the Atlantic. He wrote a description and sent it to Guatemala, from where it reached Madrid, and in 1787 Captain del Río was duly sent to take a proper look. Following visits by Waldeck, Stephens, Maudslay, Blom and many others, major excavations were undertaken by the INAH from 1946 under the great Cuban-Mexican archaeologist Alberto Ruz Lhuillier. His finest achievement was the discovery of the tomb of Pakal in 1952, and in recognition Ruz himself is buried here, just below the Temple of Inscriptions.

Palenque Town

Originally Santo Domingo de Palenque, the town now 'attached' to the ruins was founded as a colonial way-station on the long trails between Tabasco, the Highlands and Guatemala, one of very few Spanish settlements in a region that was virtually left to itself after the Conquest. Since the time Captain del Río arrived in the 1780s its inhabitants have grown used to the interest shown by the outside world in the nearby relics. When Stephens arrived here in 1840, 'the most dead-and-alive-place I ever saw', the local Prefect offered to sell him the ruins for $1,500. He was eager to go ahead with the deal, but came up against a hitch in the Mexican law – which even in this godforsaken spot had to be observed – that a foreigner could only buy land if he or she was married to a Mexican citizen. Stephens looked into it, but after noting that 'society in Palenque was small; the oldest young lady was not more than fourteen, and the prettiest woman, who already had contributed most to our happiness (she made our cigars), was already married', he had to accept that the deal was off.

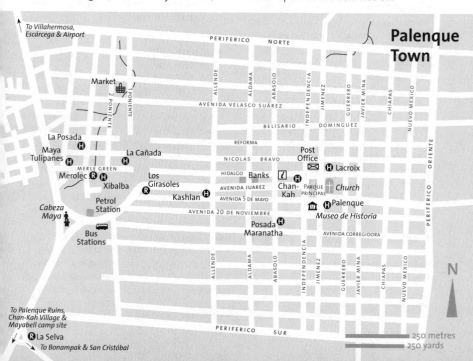

Getting Around

By Air

Palenque's **airport**, 2km north of town, takes turbo-props and light planes. **Aerocaribe, t** 345 0618, has daily flights to/from Mérida and Tuxtla Gutiérrez and twice-weekly flights to/from Cancún via Flores/Tikal in Guatemala. Connecting flights are possible via Mérida.

By Bus

Palenque's various bus companies have not collaborated to set up a joint bus station, but their depots are in the same place, in the lower stretch of Juárez. There are two depots for **first-class buses**: ADO (shared by Cristóbal Colón and Maya de Oro), and the rather unreliable Autotransportes Tuxtla (ATG), which also has second-class services. The main first-class services are listed below; there are many more to northern Mexico via Villahermosa.

Cancún (*12hrs*): via **Escárcega, Chetumal, Tulum** and **Playa del Carmen**, five first-class daily from ADO, with different companies; two daily ATG via Mérida. ADO fares $37–$46.

Emiliano Zapata (*1½hrs*): three first-class daily from ADO. Fare about $4.

Mérida (*10hrs*): via **Escárcega** and **Campeche**, four first-class daily from ADO. Fare $26–30.

Mexico City (*17hrs*): two ADO/Maya de Oro first-class daily, 6pm, 9pm. Fare around $60.

Oaxaca (*17hrs*): one ADO first-class daily at 5.30pm. Fare about $42.

Tuxtla Gutiérrez (*8hrs*) and **San Cristóbal de Las Casas** (*5hrs*) via **Ocosingo**: nine first-class daily from the ADO; six daily, ATG, plus two more to Ocosingo and San Cristóbal only. Fare about $10 San Cristóbal, $13 Tuxtla.

Villahermosa (*2½hrs*): 13 ADO first-class daily 7am–11pm; four ATG first-class. Fare from $8.

Second-class companies are near the first-class depots. ATG has at least seven daily second-class services to San Cristóbal and Tuxtla Gutiérrez, all via Misol-Ha and Agua Azul; more second-class buses, especially for the Ocosingo–San Cristóbal–Tuxtla road and to Villahermosa, are run by TRF, Transportes Lacandonia or Transportes Unidos. Lacandonia has one service daily (12.30pm), which runs into the jungle at **Lacandón** and **Naha**, using their most clanky, rattling bus, which is not intimidated by the very long, rough dirt road.

Combi companies are further into the town. *Colectivos* to Palenque ruins, Frontera Corozal (for Bonampak), Catazajá and other regional destinations run from Av. 5 de Mayo between Juárez and Allende; the more organized but less friendly Colectivos Chambalú (corner of Av. Hidalgo and Av. Allende) serve Misol-Ha and Agua Azul, and run uncomfortable transport-only trips to Lacanjá and Bonampak.

Getting To Palenque Ruins From Town

Frequent *combis* run along Av. Juárez out to the site from early morning until about 6pm. Look for any marked 'Ruinas'. Colectivos Chambalú run *combis* to the ruins from their office, but foreigners must buy a return ticket, which may be useless when you want to leave the site and there's no Chambalú vehicle in sight. It's better to flag down a *combi* on the street, or go to Av. 5 de Mayo. *Combis* drop you anywhere en route, such as the camp site.

By Car and Taxi

The **fuel station** in Palenque is the last one south until Ocosingo (103km). Main highways in the area are good; other roads may be semi-paved or just dirt tracks. There are no car hire agencies; most drivers to Palenque hire in Villahermosa, Mérida or Cancún. **Taxis** are plentiful (basic fare around $1.60); local drivers will go anywhere in the area for the right fare.

Orientation

The Palenque **ruins** are 8km from the town, down a right turn off Highway 199 south. The surrounding area has been made into a nature reserve. An official entrance gate is about 4km down the same road, but traffic is not stopped and there's no charge for entering the reserve.

The modern town is a rectangular grid, running east–west. The *gasolinera* and main bus stations are all in the 'dip' of Av. Juárez, near the **Cabeza Maya** monument (*see* p.440). From the bus stations, head uphill for the town centre. Nearly all main services are on **Av. Juárez** or around the **Parque Principal**. Most of the lanes of La Cañada (*see* p.440) do not connect – except by difficult and unattractive footpaths – with the streets of the main town, even if they are shown as doing so on some maps. The way in to this area is from

Highway 199, by the Cabeza Maya and the Maya Palenque hotels.

Despite Palenque having well-established street names, a curious effort has been made to introduce a fiendishly incomprehensible street-numbering system as found in most Chiapas towns. Hence you can see street-signs like 'Av. 1 Norte Poniente (Av. M. Hidalgo)'. Most people use the names shown in brackets.

Tourist Information

Palenque t (916–)

Tourist Office: By the Mercado de Artesanías, at the junction of Av. Juárez and Abasolo (*open Mon–Sat 9–2 and 5–8; closed Sun*).

Banks: Banamex, on Av. Juárez (corner of Aldama), only changes money at certain times (if at all); Bancomer on the next block is more helpful. Both have ATMs. There is a private *cambio* on Juárez, off the plaza. Most **tour agencies** (*see* below) change dollars.

Health: There is a **24-hr pharmacy** east of the Parque on Av. Hidalgo (corner of C/ F.J. Mina). The same building houses a private **medical clinic**; Palenque's official state **hospital** is on Juárez near the petrol station.

Internet Access: Branches of **T-Net Ciber-Café** are on Av. Independencia by the Parque Principal, and on Av. Juárez near C/ Abasolo.

Phone Office: Av. Juárez, by Hotel Chan-Kah.

Post Office: Av. de la Independencia, just north of the Parque (*open Mon–Fri 9–1 and 3–6, Sat 9–1; closed Sun*).

Tours

Palenque has several agencies that run tours around the region. These are a great help in getting to places that are hard to reach under your own steam, especially **Yaxchilán** and **Bonampak**. All offer guided tours of **Palenque ruins** and trips to **Misol-Ha** and **Agua Azul**, and most offer transport-only trips to **Flores** and **Tikal** in Guatemala, so that you don't need to arrange the border crossing yourself. A few agencies offer visits to the Mayan ruins of **Piedras Negras**, in Guatemala, as an 'extra' in Yaxchilán trips. The best agencies tailor itineraries to your needs, as long as you can make up a group (usual min. 4 people; costs depend on numbers), and can arrange trips to more

remote destinations such as **Naha, Las Guacamayas** in the Lacandón jungle or the ruins of **Seibal**, also in Guatemala and accessible from Benemérito on the frontier highway. For all such 'non-standard' trips, it's best to contact the agency well in advance.

Some agencies offer **horse-riding treks** (around 4hrs; $30) along the River Chacamax. Another option is **rafting trips** on the rapids of the Lacanjá river, near Bonampak.

Tour Agencies

Kichan Bajlum, Av. Juárez, corner of C/ Abasolo, **t** 345 2068. Low-priced agency; it offers Bonampak and Yaxchilán including a forest walk, with the option of going on to Piedras Negras ($160 per person, min. 4 people) and Flores in a 3-day trip. Also Naha, Metzaboc, and rafting.

Na Chan Kan, Av. Hidalgo, corner of C/ Jiménez, **t** 345 0263, *www.palenquemx.com /viajesnachan*. Low-cost, friendly agency, with better-than-average 1-and 2-day tours to Yaxchilán and Bonampak. Also Naha, Metzaboc, Las Guacamayas and other parts of the Lacandón by request.

Viajes Shivalva, C/ Merle Green 9, **t** 345 0411, *www.palenquemx.com/shivalva*. Based at Hotel Xibalba and run by Marco Antonio Morales, this excellent agency has decent prices and flexible itineraries: Yaxchilán and Bonampak with the opton of Piedras Negras, and other remote spots following demand. Mr Morales knows a great deal about the least-explored routes around Chiapas.

Yax-Ha, Av. Juárez 123, **t** 345 0798, *www.geo-cities.com/yaxhatravel*. Well-established agency; good Flores trips, and they use the better camp sites at Lacanjá for visits to Bonampak. They also have a desk at the Maya Bell camp site, near Palenque ruins.

Shopping

At the entrance to the ruins **Lacandón Indians** sell hand-made arrows and their distinctive simple ceramics, but Palenque is not renowned for handicrafts. By the ruins museum is an official **Casa de Artesanías**, with work from around Chiapas, while in town, the **Mercado de Artesanías** (corner of Juárez and Abasolo) has the best range.

Where to Stay

Palenque t (916–)

Palenque accommodation ranges from tour hotels and luxury *cabañas* to comfortable lower–mid-range options and, since it's long been a backpackers' den, a bigger-than-usual budget choice. Hotels tend to be divided between three areas: in the centre around the main square and Av. Juárez; in the wooded lanes of La Cañada – some of the best *inexpensive* hotels – and along the road to the ruins, where there are upscale hotels, several *cabaña*-style operations, and camp sites. All La Cañada hotels have ample parking space.

Expensive

Chan-Kah, Ctra de las Ruinas Km3, t 345 1100, f 345 0820 (*expensive*). Distinctive 'resort village' beside the ruins road, with rooms in comfortable bungalows spread around a forest estate full of flowers and humming-birds; there is a shaded terrace **restaurant**, an extraordinarily lush garden and a fabulous pool that's almost an artificial lagoon.

Moderate

Chan-Kah Centro, Av. Juárez, corner of Av. Independencia, t 345 0318, f 345 0489. Under the same management as the Chan-Kah, but more modest, with a great location right on the plaza and entertaining views from the best rooms, with balconies. Rooms are smallish but well equipped, and prices drop into *inexpensive* outside peak seasons.

Hotel Maya Tulipanes, C/ La Cañada 6, t 345 0201, *mtulipan@tnet.net.mx*. Popular hotel which now has 70 high-standard, recently renovated rooms, a good **restaurant** and an Internet café, a garden and a great new pool. In the lobby are reproductions of the reliefs from Pakal's tomb and the Temple of the Cross, to examine at leisure. Rates drop outside the winter and Easter seasons.

Hotel Palenque, Av. 5 de Mayo 15, t 345 0188, *htipque@tnet.net.mx*. Another 'institution' on the town square, like the Chan-Kah: the comfortable rooms are bigger but a little plainer, and its greatest assets are a tropical garden and nice pool. Prices are eccentric: *inexpensive* most of the year, but going up sharply in the winter season, Easter and July.

Inexpensive

Hotel-Cabañas Safari, Ctra de las Ruinas Km1, t 345 0026, *http://welcome.to/safarihotel*. One of the smarter of the ruins-road *cabaña*-hotels, quite near the town, with pretty palm-roofed cabins with showers, and decorated with traditional textiles.

Hotel La Cañada, C/ Merle Green, t/f 345 0102. A very long-established Cañada hotel, at the end of the street furthest from the main road, and with the prettiest **restaurant** (*see* below). Popular with archaeologists, its five rooms (a/c) are divided between two cabins with terraces in a garden near the ravine. They're a bargain, so it's worth booking.

Hotel Chablis, C/ Merle Green 7, t 345 0870, f 345 0365. Modern Cañada hotel with recently refurbished rooms with a/c and a plusher look than some nearby hotels. Not distinctive, but reliably comfortable; may be *moderate* at peak times.

Hotel Kashlan, Av. 5 de Mayo 117, t 345 0297, *www.palenque.com.mx/kashlan*. Impossible to miss as you walk up Av. Juárez from the bus stations, this big, friendly hotel is one of Palenque's most likeable. All rooms (fans $22, a/c $45) are bright and well looked after, and there's a pleasant breakfast bar and Internet café. The owners are very helpful; they will store luggage, and even offer some vegetarian dishes in the **restaurant**.

Hotel Xibalba, C/ Merle Green 9, t 345 0411, *www.palenquemx.com/shivalva*. Far from resembling the Mayan underworld this La Cañada hotel has big, light rooms, in a main block and in garden châlets, with good bathrooms and a/c. It also houses a **restaurant** and the **Viajes Shivalva** tour agency (*see* above); owner *sr* Morales intends to add a souvenir shop and a museum centred on a precise reproduction of Pakal's tomb.

La Posada, Av. Nicolás Bravo 50, t 345 1756, f 345 0968. Cheapest in La Cañada, with simple, comfortable rooms around a jungle-like patio. Rooms with fans are as well kept as many pricier ones elsewhere; some have a/c. The Gomez family who run it are very friendly and helpful, in a sleepy kind of way.

Cheap/Camping

Camping Maya Bell, Ctra de las Ruinas Km6, t 348 4271, *mayabell82@hotmail.com*. Long the backpackers' hangout of choice, offering space to camp or sling a hammock ($2–$3 per person), or small, comfortable rooms in cabins, some with shared facilities, some with bath and some with a/c (*inexpensive–cheap*). There's a nice **restaurant**, a little pool, a **Yax-Ha tour agency** desk and good toilets and water supply, and it's the best-equipped of the camp sites, with full RV facilities. The location is lovely, with a waterfall nearby and the ruins an easy walk away. It's affiliated to AMAJ (*www.hostels.com.mx*).

Hotel Lacroix, Av. Hidalgo 10, **t** 345 0014. In a quiet street just off the Parque, this is the most characterful budget choice in town, though it's borderline-*inexpensive*. One of the oldest Palenque hotels, it's run by a family of French origin who arrived here, as a painted sign by the entrance informs you, in 1830, even before John Stephens. Further inside there are more home-made murals, a garden patio and rooms that have a bit of personality as well as simple comforts.

El Panchán, Ctra de las Ruinas Km4, *www.el panchan.com*. By the official entrance to the reserve a track turns south into a glade by a stream that's a private little 'nature reserve' set up by a local family. Amid the trees are three *cabaña* outfits offering everything from camping or hammock space through communal *palapas* to quite comfy individual cabins (all *cheap*), and **restaurants** offering food from Mexican to Italian or vegetarian. The layout doesn't allow much privacy, but the mellow atmosphere and the beautiful setting make it very popular with a raft of travellers, not just those on a shoestring.

Posada-Hotel Maranatha, Av. 20 de Noviembre, between C/ Aldama and C/ Abasolo, **t** 345 1007. A recently opened hotel with enthusiastic owners and fan-only rooms that are much brighter and more comfortable than the local cheapo norm.

Eating Out

Expensive

La Selva, Ctra de las Ruinas Km0.5, **t** 345 0363. South of town near the ruins turn-off, this comes as a surprise in a seemingly remote spot. It's positively elegant, with neatly laid tables beneath a giant *palapa* roof or in a delightful garden, smooth service and a wine list that even lists good French and Spanish labels (at a price). The food – mostly delicate variations on traditional Mexican dishes – is less impressive than the setting, but for a treat it's very comfortable.

Moderate

Casa Grande, Av. Hidalgo 116, Parque Principal. Attractive restaurant on a *palapa*-roofed balcony with a good view of the square; it's more stylish and modern than is usual here, with lighter-than-usual dishes on the menu.

Chan-Kah Centro, Av. Juárez, corner of Av. Independencia. Of the hotel-restaurants this usually wins for food and atmosphere, with a dining room at ground level and another on the floor above with a fine view and a restful atmosphere. Great for breakfast.

Merolec, C/ Merle Green. By the Hotel Xibalba, this friendly bar-restaurant has a pretty garden-terrace, a relatively varied menu (great meaty *fajitas*) and an enjoyable feel, helped along by waiters who like their cocktail mixing. Note it's not open for breakfast.

Restaurant La Cañada, C/ Merle Green. Part of the La Cañada Hotel (*see* above), this is one of the most attractive of the town's hotel-restaurants, serving Mexican classics beneath a timber roof or in a garden where hummingbirds flit between the bushes.

Cheap

There are clutches of *taco*-stands on the plaza and Av. Abasolo and cheap *loncherías* along Av. 5 de Mayo on the south side of the square. The plaza is also the place for good *licuados* and juices, while budget restaurants proliferate on Av. Juarez. Towards the ruins, the Mayabell and El Panchán (*see* above) have great bargain (and vegetarian/health) meals.

Artemio's, Av. Hidalgo, corner of C/Jiménez. Likeable café next to Na Chan Kan tour agency, with a suitably lazy-feeling terrace, amiable service, breakfasts and good snacks.

Los Girasoles, Av. Juárez 150, corner of Av. 5 de Mayo. Great for watching the world go by, this big place on a balcony is a long-running favourite. It has enjoyable traditional food, especially breakfasts, and if service can be slow, you're not supposed to be in any hurry.

Since then, as the flow of visitors has increased, Palenque (having lost the 'Santo Domingo') has grown up as a town of hotels, restaurants and other services for archaeologists and tourists. More recently, as commercial farming has expanded in northern Chiapas, it has grown considerably as a regional centre in its own right.

As you approach modern Palenque from the north you come to its main monument, in the middle of a road junction, the **Cabeza Maya** ('Mayan Head'), a giant bust based on a head of Pakal found at the ruins. Ahead, the road continues towards the ruins and San Cristóbal; to the left is the main street, **Avenida Juárez**, which curves down through a marked dip in the ground before winding left and climbing up again to the main square, the **Parque Principal**. Surrounded by snack-stands and box trees, it's a likeable square, usually occupied by a mix of local teenagers, old men, backpackers and Highland women down from the hills to sell handicrafts, all sitting around. On its east side, opposite the Hotel Palenque, there is now a **Museo de Historia** (*open daily 10–4; adm free*), which is dedicated to the (albeit limited) history of the town itself rather than the awesome ruins. It's an engaging little collection, mostly made up of old photographs gathered from local sources.

To the north and west of Av. Juárez the 'dip' becomes quite a steep, forested ravine, which effectively separates off the area running west to Highway 199 from the main part of town. Known as **La Cañada**, this area is made up of unpaved, tranquil wooded lanes centred on C/ Merle Green (named after the American founder of the Palenque Round Tables), and is one of the most attractive areas for hotels and restaurants.

Palenque is not a heavy town by modern urban standards, but in its busier tourist areas, at Agua Azul and on second-class buses, you need to be more aware of the possibility of petty crime than in the innocent calm of the Yucatán (keep bags closed, and don't leave them out of sight in bars). If you have a car, then at the ruins and Agua Azul small boys will appear and offer to *cuidar el carro*. It's best to say you'll pay up when you leave; they know how to flatten tires. Once you've made a deal, you can rest assured that your car will be protected from other ten-year-old terrorists.

The Ruins of Palenque

The path from the entrance leads you up a hill and into Palenque's grand main plaza (for a plan of the whole site, *see* p.444). The first building you pass, on the right, is a relatively small pyramid, called the **Temple of the Skull** for its very clear skull-motif carvings, while on the left, a small stone marks the grave of Alberto Ruz Lhuillier.

Two buildings along from the Temple of the Skull there is another of the remarkable recent discoveries at Palenque, in **Temple XIII**. Inside this temple-pyramid the tomb of a woman has been discovered, with rich grave-offerings, which it has been strongly suggested may be that of Pakal's mother Sak-Kuk, suitably placed next to his own giant tomb. It has already been labelled the **Tumba de la Reina Roja** ('Tomb of the Red Queen'), but so far has not been opened to visitors. However, the eye cannot avoid for long the giant mass of the **Temple of Inscriptions**, soaring up next to Temple XIII and dominating the square.

Site Information

Site and museum open daily 8–5; adm.

The road from Palenque town curls north of the site through the reserve, to approach the ruins from the west. On the way you pass the **museum** (*adm included in site ticket*) which it's best to leave until after you've seen the site. At the site entrance there's a line of Lacandón and Highland Maya selling handicrafts, the car-watching boys, a **restaurant** and drink stands and a **visitor centre**. There is, though, nowhere that sells decent site maps (and the fixed map-boards around the site have not been updated with any recent discoveries), so it's best to have your own.

Guides, as at the major Yucatán sites, will give you a 1–2-hr tour for around $30. This will take you through the main areas – and many guides are very knowledgeable – but Palenque is, more than most, a Mayan site where you can choose between viewing the best-known buildings or exploring further along forest paths. It's naturally very hot and humid, and Pakal and Kan-Balam's constructions provide some of the most exhausting climbs of any Mayan temple-mountains.

The best way to experience Palenque is to give it a full day. Get there as it opens, when the pyramids are often shrouded in a ghostly mist. Plenty of water and insect repellent are also advisable.

The Temple of Inscriptions

Commissioned by Pakal as his tomb and monument, the Temple of Inscriptions is an awesome testimony to his importance in the life of the city. Built against a natural hill, it rises through nine levels, ascended by a narrow, very steep stairway. The nine 'grades' of the pyramid are more visible now than they were for most of its history, for shortly after it was built it was strengthened with buttress-walls either side of the stairway. When these buttresses were removed during Ruz's excavations the core of the pyramid 'slumped' again, and it had to be stabilized. At the top is a temple with a characteristic architectural feature of Palenque, a Mansard-style roof, which once supported a roof-comb. This type of roof was an innovation made by the city's builders, who in place of the conventional Mayan arch with sides of equal length developed a variation with two rows of rooms either side of a central wall thicker than those at front and back, so that the outer sides of the arches 'leant' against the centre. This made it possible to create larger multi-room spaces.

The pyramid was begun many years before Pakal's death. The upper temple has five entrances. Of the pillars between them, the outer ones are covered in inscriptions, while the stucco panels either side of the stairway were taken over by Kan-Balam II to glorify his own position by showing his presentation as heir as a baby in his father's arms, an important occasion which would have taken place in the year 641 (the two central pillars show Pakal and his queen with the child, while the second from the left shows the founder of the dynasty Kuk-Balam and that to the right the 6th-century *ahau* Kan-Balam I, both looking favourably on the succession from the Otherworld). Kan-Balam II seems to have had six toes on each foot, making him recognizable in many carvings. Inside the temple, the two large panels in front of you and the back wall of the middle inner chamber contain Pakal's 'king lists', detailing his divine lineage. They are among the longest of Mayan inscriptions, and were of great importance in the first deciphering of Mayan glyphs. The length of Palenque's inscriptions is perhaps one reason for a peculiarity of the city – that its rulers did not commission standing *stelae*, preferring to place their historical records directly on to buildings.

Also in the central inner chamber there was a flagstone in which, in 1949, Alberto Ruz noticed some holes made by the Maya through which ropes could be passed, in order to move the stone. It was removed to expose a passageway, deliberately closed up with earth. After three more years of digging this was found to lead to the most dramatic of all discoveries at Palenque, the **Tomb of Pakal**. This has been one of the most popular parts of the site, but in order to protect the tomb access to it has been

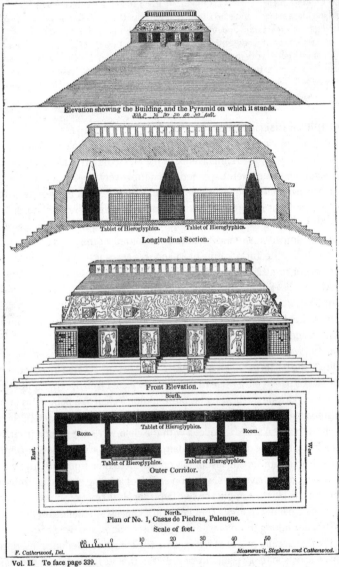

Catherwood's plan of The Temple of Inscriptions at Palenque.

Visiting Pakal's Tomb

Visitors to Palenque are often told that the Tomb of Pakal has been closed completely to all but professional archaeologists, but it can still be seen if you are prepared to take some time over it. To get into it you need a *permiso especial*, obtainable from the site administration office next to the museum. Only a small number are allowed in each day (maximum 20), and to get on to the list of *permisos* for any day you need to go to the office as early as possible after 8am (you may also be allowed to 'book' a day in advance). You must then go to the Temple of Inscriptions at 4pm, the only time when groups are taken into the tomb. There is at present no extra charge for this, nor do you need archaeological credentials. If you can't find the right office, ask the staff at the museum, who are usually helpful.

drastically restricted (*see* box, above). Inside, there's a remarkably steep (and steamy) staircase that was built, in a considerable feat of engineering, as a succession of Mayan-arched vaults in order that the whole pyramid could not collapse on top of it. The tomb itself is at the same level as the very bottom of the pyramid. A small triangular stone door sealed off the Mayan-vault tomb after Pakal was interred. Beyond this door Ruz's team found five skeletons, those of four men and a woman, captives sacrificed to accompany Pakal to the Otherworld; past them, at right-angles to the antechamber, was the great sarcophagus containing the *ahau* himself, dressed in jade jewellery and a jade and obsidian funeral mask. These treasures have been taken off to the national museum in Mexico City, together with two busts of Pakal placed beneath the tomb. However, still in place is the giant sarcophagus lid, one of the most extraordinary images in Mayan sculpture (there is a reproduction of it in the site museum, and another at the Hotel Xibalba). As he dies, Pakal is shown sliding down the *wakah-kan*, the world-tree, which also represents the Milky Way, the path of the heavens, into Xibalba, there to join the gods and be reborn.

The Palacio and the North Group

From the top of the Inscriptions pyramid there is also a superb view over the plains stretching away to the north and over the **Palacio**, just below. Palenque's palace is an astonishing maze of patios, corridors, chambers and – contrary to appearances – entirely separate buildings, interlocking on top of an 80m by 100m artificial platform and reached by two massive banks of steps. It has always been recognized as a palace, and its many spaces served the lords of Palenque both as a residence and as a place for special ceremonies, meetings and state functions. It was built and rebuilt over 400 years, but its surviving form is mainly the work of Pakal, who from the 650s almost completely rebuilt the central sections, building on top of many earlier structures, including entire buried chambers. Within its disorderly structure it has three main patios, the largest, the East Patio, in the northeast corner. The palace's most distinctive feature, its three-storey tower, with a small Mansard-ish roof (and which nowadays you are not normally allowed to climb up) was probably added much later, in the mid-8th century. It is believed it was used as an astronomical observatory.

The use of Mansard-style arches enabled the Palacio's builders to create one of the most refined of Mayan buildings, with a much greater feel of spaciousness and light than most Mayan royal residences. The Palacio was once literally covered in fine stucco reliefs and carvings, and many survive; some have been removed to the site museum. Still in place in House E, near the East Patio, is the 'Oval Tablet', dated to 654, in which Pakal is shown receiving his royal status from his mother, whose costume is that of the Maize Goddess, emphasizing her divine status. Near this tablet there was once a throne on which rulers of Palenque sat during their accession ceremonies; part of it was removed by Del Río in 1787, and is now in the Museo de América in Madrid. In the East Patio there are several very large stone reliefs of male figures, in a massive, powerful style that makes them appear strangely modern, which commemorate captives taken by Pakal during the 660s. Pakal's unfortunate second son Kan-Hok-

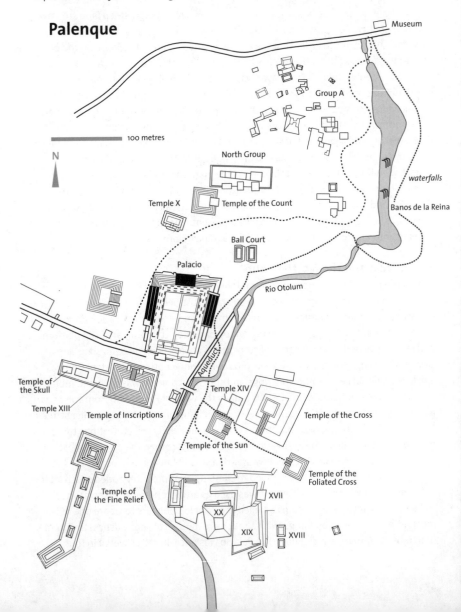

Palenque

Museum

Group A

waterfalls

100 metres

N

Banos de la Reina

North Group

Temple X

Temple of the Count

Ball Court

Palacio

Río Otolum

Temple of
the Skull

Temple XIII

Temple of Inscriptions

Temple XIV

Temple of the Sun

Temple of the Cross

Aqueduct

Temple of
the Fine Relief

Temple of the
Foliated Cross

XVII

XX

XIX

XVIII

Chitam II also took a great interest in the Palacio and added the North Gallery, closing off the East and West Patios. In it he placed a 'Palace Tablet', on which he is shown receiving symbols of authority from his father and mother.

From the Palacio a path leads across a grassy square to **Temple X**, a small, very old temple platform, and next to it the larger **Temple of the Count**, facing east. This was the second major project undertaken by Pakal at Palenque when he began building in the 640s, after the **Templo Olvidado** ('Forgotten Temple'), away in the woods to the west. It is so named because a hut at the foot of this pyramid was where mad Count Waldeck and his Indian mistress lived in 1832–3. Next to it is the **North Group**, a line of several temples atop a platform, some built by Pakal, facing back into the city. Some have fine reliefs, and a very impressive large stucco relief has recently been uncovered in the temple furthest to the right, looking from the square.

Between the North Group and the Palacio is a **Ball Court**. Not far from it, along the east side of the Palacio, there is one of the most ingenious constructions at Palenque. Called the **Aqueduct**, it is really a covered canal, a 100-metre diversion of the Otolum river through a corbel-vaulted, reinforced underground channel. The purpose of channelling the river in this way was to prevent the fast-flowing stream from flooding and undermining the Palacio platform when in full spate during the rainy season.

The Cross Group

A path leads across the Otolum to Kan-Balam II's group of temples, built at the end of the 7th century. This 'Cross Group' faces away from the main ceremonial core of Palenque, which seems strangely disorderly in a Mayan city, but Kan-Balam would have had his reasons for building in this way. Having the group form a partial square open to the south echoed the earliest Mayan plazas, and so emphasized the temples' strength as power points; the use of three temples also mirrored the three centring-stones in the Mayan creation story (see p.47), and the number three continually crops up in the group, in the number of entrances, chambers and so on. In building the Cross temples Kan-Balam II naturally wished to place himself and his lineage centre-stage, but at the same time he created the most comprehensive presentation ever made of Classic Mayan beliefs, of cosmic order and the interconnected universe.

The recently relaid path from the river brings you into the Group around the back of the **Temple of the Sun** (from where the path to the right leads to the Southern Acropolis). The Sun Temple is relatively small, atop a four-level pyramid, with a still-intact roof-comb; also partly preserved is the entablature on the front of the Mansard roof, which was decorated with images of cosmic monsters that, like Chenes temple doorways, made clear the temple's role as portal to the Otherworld. The subject of the relief inside is warfare. Kan-Balam II, the large figure on the right, receives the power to wage war from his father Pakal. As in all the Cross Group reliefs, Pakal is shown as smaller than his son, as he was already dead and in Xibalba, and wrapped in peculiarly thick clothing, perhaps his funeral robes. He is also standing on a kneeling god, and the great war-shield at the centre of the relief is bearing down on the two gods that support it, as if warfare was a burden for gods as much as men. Panels either side refer to the formal accession of Kan-Balam II as *ahau* in January 690.

Opposite is the **Temple of the Foliated Cross**, the façade of which is in much worse condition but which holds a more spectacular and better-preserved relief within. The theme here is more pacific, the sustaining of existence. The 'Foliated Cross' is a flowering variant of the world-tree, representing cultivation and agriculture, the cycle of growth essential for the community. It arises out of a 'water-lily monster', the Mayan god of swamps and drained land, and at the end of the 'arms' of the cross human heads appear out of ears of corn, a reference to the Mayan idea of humans as having been created out of maize. Beside the 'tree' Kan-Balam, this time on the left, waits to receive a blood-letting instrument that Pakal holds in his left hand, in order that he might fulfil his duty of sacrifice. At the top of the tree sits the Celestial Bird, spirit of nature, kept in order by cultivation and the performance of sacrifice by the king.

Drama is heightened in reaching the **Temple of the Cross** itself by a far more intense climb up six banks of steps. It still has its roof-comb, but the façade has deteriorated. The subject of its extraordinary relief is not any one aspect of existence but all of it. The 'cross' at its centre is the great world-tree itself, the axis of existence, topped again by the Celestial Bird; on either side, once again, are Pakal and Kan-Balam, at the time of the latter's accession. The great scheme of the universe and the relationship to it of the lords of Palenque could not be clearer. At the point of his formal accession, the relief indicates, Kan-Balam through vision rituals descended to Xibalba to be reunited with his great father, and there receive from him the attributes of kingship. The side panel to the left, as in the other temples, shows Kan-Balam II on his accession day, 20 January 690, in all his kingly regalia; in the right-hand panel there is the figure of 'God L', one of the wizened old gods of Xibalba, who has helped the new king return from the Otherworld to the land of the living. He is shown with a spectacular cigar. This is the oldest known image of anyone smoking in the world.

In the space between the Temples of the Cross and the Sun there is another, small structure, **Temple XIV**, built slightly later for Kan-Balam's brother Kan-Hok-Chitam II and facing, unlike the Cross Group, towards the main plaza. Inside there is a fine relief showing Pakal dancing with his mother in the Underworld. Further excavations are now underway on the north side of the Temple of the Cross.

The Southern Acropolis

The area that has tentatively been given this name to the south of the main Cross Group represents a remarkable extension to the 'known area' of Palenque, excavated only since 1997. Interpretation of new finds is still very much in progress, but a great deal has already emerged (more of the buildings will also become accessible as work progresses). The core of the 'Acropolis' is a large square, which as the brush and earth has been cleared can be seen to have effectively faced and 'complemented' the Cross plaza to its north. It was built in the 720s and 730s by *ahau* Kinich Ahkal Mo Naab III, a previously fairly obscure ruler who evidently built massively, creating in **Temple XIX** the largest single building yet found at Palenque. A long, thin structure along the south side of the square, it served as a new palace-residence and as a ceremonial temple. As mentioned, he had taken power at a chaotic time in Palenque's affairs following defeat by Toniná, and as was usual in Mayan cities in times of crisis he turned to building, to reassert the cosmic roots of the kingdom and his own authority over it. The most dramatic discovery in Temple XIX has been a stone bench, which probably served as a 'throne', with exceptionally fine carvings. On one side, Kinich Ahkal Mo Naab is shown seated between two men, probably early kings of Palenque, while on the other, he is surrounded by six powerfully carved but still unidentified figures. In the inscriptions on the bench Kinich Ahkal Mo Naab connects himself to an ancestry traced back into mythological time, and to the divine source of the ruling house of Palenque. Other finds from Temple XIX include a superb carved tablet showing Kinich Ahkal Mo Naab and a more delicate stucco relief of a young man, both now in the site museum.

Other structures around the Acropolis are yielding up discoveries of equal worth. In **Temple XVIII** on the east side, three still-unidentified tombs were found, along with further inscriptions on the life of Kinich Ahkal Mo Naab, while **Temple XVII** has an altar with a stucco relief (now in the museum, but the temple has a reproduction) of a woman kneeling before a king, perhaps Kinich Ahkal Mo Naab and his queen. Most intriguing of all is **Temple XX**, the massive pyramid on the west side. In 1996, ground-penetrating radar discovered a space inside it; in 1999, a camera was lowered into it, to reveal a chamber with mural paintings of figures involved in some kind of ceremony, which will almost certainly be the most important Mayan wall paintings after Bonampak. No one has yet been permitted inside the chamber while efforts are made to ensure that opening it does not destroy it, but the prospects are tantalizing (some of the pictures can be viewed on *www.mesoweb.com/palenque*).

Other Buildings at Palenque

From the north side of the main area of Palenque several paths lead down to the access road and the museum, in a walk of about a kilometre. These join up towards the bottom, but note that the path signposted to the museum from beside the North Group is a steep scramble in parts, and the Sendero Ecológico path closer to the river is prettier and easier going. The great attraction of these paths is that they take you through some of the most magical jungle at Palenque, past delicious pools and waterfalls on the Río Otolum and its partner the Arroyo Murciélago ('Bat Creek') where you can cool your feet or even swim. They also give you a feel for the sheer mysterious size of the city, with all kinds of still-unexcavated structures visible in the woods, often gripped by the roots of giant *ceiba* trees. Along the way there are some buildings that have been excavated, known as the **Murciélagos** ('Bats' Group), mostly consisting of 8th-century residential complexes that were probably home to some of the élite families of Palenque. Most striking of all is Group B, for its fabulous location next to the falls known as the **Baños de la Reina** ('Queen's Bath'), clearly chosen so that its wealthy inhabitants could make the most of the natural setting.

The buildings described so far make up the main 'public' area of Palenque, but anyone who enjoys exploring can find many more. Another path leads from behind the **Temple of Inscriptions** uphill to the tiny **Temple of the Fine Relief** (*bello relieve*). Perched on a forest slope, it has inscriptions and reliefs that are in a poor state, but once featured an image of a jaguar (it's now only possible to see one paw clearly).

An alternative for true explorers is to head out of the main site and take the path to the west from the car park, in which direction ruins extend for over a kilometre to Pakal's first building, the **Templo Olvidado**. Many of the professional site guides may be willing to take visitors to the less 'usual' parts of the site, for a negotiable fee.

The Museum

Not to be passed over (in contrast to some site museums) is a visit to Palenque's museum, which has one of the most spectacular of all collections of Mayan artefacts, nearly all from the city itself. Ceramics and modelling in stucco are especially impressive, above all a wonderful female head and some male busts. Of Palenque's kings, there is a large sculpture of Kan-Balam II, a replica of Pakal's sarcophagus-lid and superb reliefs from the Palacio, as well as spectacular recent additions in the reliefs and sculptures discovered in the Southern Acropolis. There is exquisite jade jewellery, and the world's largest collection of Mayan ceramic incense burners, an extraordinary menagerie of creatures of the Otherworld. Most, as is usual, represent the three levels of existence and other aspects of the Mayan cosmos, with monsters of Xibalba at the bottom and the Celestial Bird appearing at the top.

There is a great deal of information to digest, but good English translations are now provided. In the building alongside there's also a café and a traditional crafts' shop.

Misol-Ha and Agua Azul

As Highway 199 winds into the hills south of Palenque it passes two of the most dazzling tropical landscapes in northern Chiapas, the waterfalls of Misol-Ha and Agua Azul. They make easy day-trips from Palenque or stop-offs on the way south.

The entry road to **Misol-Ha** runs out at the crest of a steep valley, near a small restaurant. A path winds down to the waterfall, a 35-metre drop into a huge, deep-blue pool surrounded by mahogany trees, *ceibas* and emerald-green vegetation. A rope slung across indicates where swimming is safe. There's a precipitous path called **La Cortina** ('the curtain') behind the great sheet of water of the falls, where you get suitably drenched (local girls tackle it in high heels, which shows how un-dangerous it is). On weekends and holidays big groups come here to picnic and cool off, but on other days you're likely to share the falls only with a few foreigners.

About another 23 kilometres down the road, by a sharp hairpin, a sign indicates a less well-known point of access to the forest rivers at **Agua Clara**. This *ejido* of Tzeltal-speaking Maya, alongside a beautiful, unusually wide stretch of the Tulijá, is another that has a community ecotourism scheme, with *cabañas* (*see* facing page).

A further eight kilometres along the main road, a sign at another precipitous bend points downhill to **Agua Azul**. After about four kilometres this road ends in a broad green valley floor by the largest of many pools in the Agua Azul river, a tributary of the Tulijá. Above this pool the river bubbles, crashes, divides and redivides through a magnificent water staircase surrounded by thick forest for over seven kilometres, through wide green pools, white-water rapids, whirlpools and quiet streams.

There are several points where it's possible to swim, beginning with the lower pool itself, although the water is often murky. Great care is necessary at all times when swimming at Agua Azul, for as in any white-water river the currents can change in a few metres. Not far above the first pool is a cataract called the *Licuadora* ('Liquidizer'), where crosses in the rocks commemorate people killed here trying their luck too far. Swimming here is absolutely to be avoided. If in doubt, stick to the quietest pools and

Getting There and Tours

Some *combis* from Palenque run direct to both falls, and it's worth enquiring at *combi* stops on Av. 5 de Mayo. Most *combis* and second-class buses along Highway 199 stop on the main road (at Crucero Agua Azul).

The turn-off for **Misol-Ha** is 19 kilometres from Palenque. From there, it's two kilometres to the falls, which isn't too hard a walk if you don't have a car.

The turning for **Agua Azul** is 50km from Palenque, 8km beyond Agua Clara. There may be local *combis* running to and from the Crucero (mostly at weekends), but otherwise, while the walk down is long (4km) but quite easy, getting back involves a wearying, hot climb. Neither place is very good to visit in the rainy season. Insects make camping uncomfortable, and swimming at Agua Azul demands still more caution than usual.

Tours

All Palenque tour agencies run day-trips to Misol-Ha and Agua Azul, usually offering the two together ($9–$10), but this generally gives you only a rather hurried stop at Misol-Ha and then around 4hrs at Agua Azul; if you want any flexibility, you need to make your own way. Some agencies offer **horseback treks** at Agua Azul, and some now include Agua Clara.

Site Information

Misol-Ha
Open daily 7–6; adm.

Travellers sometimes pass these falls by in favour of those at Agua Azul, which are larger and better known. However, they're an easier ride from Palenque (and a shorter hike from the main road), less crowded, less hassled in atmosphere and far better for swimming. There's also a **restaurant** and **souvenir shop**.

Agua Azul
The local ejido charges adm for vehicles and individuals, but there are no fixed times.

Tour buses turn up fairly frequently, and there's a grass airstrip, used by private planes. If you have a vehicle, you'll be approached by kids wanting to watch your car, and by the lower pool the fruit and handicrafts sellers are very insistent. There are plenty of cheap open-air **restaurants**, especially by the bottom pool. Mexicans on family outings bring along half their house to stake out spots for picnics.

Where to Stay

Misol-Ha t (916–)
The area is administered by the local *ejido*, which has a community-run hotel scheme: **Cabañas Misol-Ha, t** 345 1210 (*inexpensive–cheap*). Simple, comfortable two-person cabins (not palm-roofed *cabañas*), with fans and showers, and family-size models with kitchens. The location is superb, nestling in the forest on the valley slopes within view of the falls. The pleasant **restaurant** is open during the falls' official opening times.

Agua Clara
The *ejido* has a **restaurant** and eight basic cabins with shared bathrooms, attached to a *hacienda* above the Tulijá river (**t** 345 0356, *cheap*). Kayaks and forest guides are for rent.

Agua Azul
You can park an RV or camp by the pool right at the bottom, but there are always people wandering around. For some tranquillity, walk up 1½km to the regular sites renting tent- or hammock-space, most of which are called **Camping Agua Azul**. The first also has a cabin-like room (*cheap*). A bit further on, **Hamacas Casa Blanca** also has some small cabins, and its owner, Jerónimo, works as a forest guide.

stay near the 'beaches'. Further along the path the weekend crowds thin out a little. About a kilometre from the parking area is one of the most attractive spots, **La Selva**, with a ravishingly pretty lagoon that's good for swimming, more pleasant restaurants than those lower down and delightful, shady paths. The path goes on, increasingly steep but still quite populated, until at about two kilometres from the bottom it swings over to the right side of the river – by now a stream – via a broken-down but passable metal bridge. This is as far as most people go, but it's possible to carry on for at least three kilometres, past more jungle pools and waterfalls.

Note: in the whole region covered by this book, **thefts** are most frequently reported at Agua Azul. Serious robberies and occasional assaults on women backpackers seem to be most common on the 'empty' stretch of the path, beyond the rickety bridge. If you want to explore this path it's best to go with a guide from one of the camp sites. Wherever there are plenty of people about, the danger of serious incidents is low, but be careful where you leave your things when swimming. This is one place where it can be better to stick with the crowds. Despite these provisos Agua Azul is a popular place to **camp** (*see* above, p.449).

Yaxchilán, Bonampak and the Lacandón Forest

The Usumacinta valley southeast of Palenque is perhaps the part of the Mayan world that shows the greatest contrast between the landscape as seen over the last ten centuries and that of 1,500 years ago. By the time the Spaniards came it was taken over by 'virgin', scarcely inhabited rainforest; yet, up to around AD 800, this was one of the most thickly populated regions of Mayan civilization, with a line of cities trading and warring along the river. The fully excavated sites on the Mexican side of the river are two of the greatest relics of the Maya, **Yaxchilán** and **Bonampak**, with some of the finest of all Mayan art. Bonampak is in the territory of the **Lacandón**, the forest Maya who, until a few decades ago, kept all their non-Christian traditions and had scarcely any contact with the rest of Mexico. This is an area that is changing fast, and one that, partly due to political 'accident', has become vastly more accessible, so that determined travellers can now go ever further into the Lacandón jungle. Above all, though, it is the trip to Yaxchilán and Bonampak that is one of the 'musts' when travelling in the Mayan lands, a journey that still has a great feel of adventure.

Lacanjá and Frontera Corozal

Almost as soon as you leave Palenque the road begins to climb and you enter much denser vegetation, especially after the turn-off for Bonampak eight kilometres south of the town. The road runs for mile after mile over the tops of ridges along the valley of the Usumacinta, like so many misty scales on the earth's surface. Around and above you there is fabulously lush mountain forest, towering masses of high mahogany, palms, vines and creepers like great green waterfalls. This is no longer an unbroken forest, though, for there is plenty of evidence of the settlement that has

The Lords of Palenque: The Lacandón

The Lacandón of the forests of eastern Chiapas were, until about 35 years ago, the most isolated of all the Mayan communities, the one least touched by European civilization. They were the only Maya never conquered by the Spaniards, and so never Christianized by the Catholic friars. According to one theory they are descended from Maya who at the time of the Conquest fled into the forest to preserve their old traditions. Although this is hotly disputed, in their book *The Last Lords of Palenque* the anthropologists Victor Perera and Robert Bruce argued that they are the closest surviving relatives of the inhabitants of the ancient Mayan sites.

The Lacandón survived by retreating into the remotest part of the Chiapas jungles. They lived very simply, relying on hunting and basic agriculture. They have their own language, in which they refer to themselves as *hach winik* or 'true people', and have always kept apart from the more settled Maya. Their beliefs and rituals have many equivalences with older Mayan ideas, sharing a typically Mayan conviction that the whole world is alive around them. They venerated Yaxchilán as a sacred site, the origin of the gods. They make their own distinctive leather drums and simple earthenware pottery; the few who keep up all the old ways still make 'god pots' with faces upon them, regarded as living things in which copal incense is burnt to summon up the gods. They also have – or did have – an enormous knowledge of the forest. Their most instantly recognizable characteristic, though, is their appearance: traditionally the Lacandón do not cut their hair, and wear long white smocks of coarse cotton. The impression can be that of a bunch of hippies wandering round in hospital gowns.

The Lacandón have also attracted a great deal of attention from anthropologists and researchers. They are most associated with Frans and Trudi Blom of Na Bolom in San Cristóbal de Las Casas (*see* pp.489–90), who established a particularly personal relationship with them, and still today Na Bolom acts as a major centre for aid, information and education programmes connected with the Lacandón.

The Lacandón today have many problems. There are only about 600 of them, living in the villages of Naha, Metzaboc, San Javier, Bethel, Lacanjá and a few offshoots. They are extremely inbred, as evidenced by the large number of albino Lacandón. They no longer have the forest to themselves, as since the 1960s more and more other Maya and *mestizo* settlers have moved into the area. This, though, has done less harm than the activities of US Protestant missionaries, who sought them out. The Lacandón had grown used to ignoring the Catholic Church, but, often confused by the modern world, had less resistance to more intensive tactics. This led to a split in the tiny community: the Lacandón of Naha and Metzaboc try to keep to the old ways, and have broken off relations with Lacanjá, where many are now 'Evangelicals'.

In 1996 the great patriarch of Naha, Old Chan Kin, died at Na Bolom, at an age of well over 100. He is often referred to as 'the Last True Lacandón', and it's said that a great deal of the community's traditional ways – in religion and awareness of the forest – died with him. Today, some Lacandón now cut their hair and wear ordinary T-shirts and jeans; some are doing well out of tourists and wear Ray-bans. Others, though, speak no Spanish, and still seem remarkably like people from another world.

flooded this area since the 1970s: slash-and-burn *milpas*, improvised *colonia* villages, empty patches of cleared ground, isolated *ranchos*, great gashes stripped by logging. It is almost as if the forest and deforestation were arm-wrestling before your eyes.

Once you are 70 kilometres from Palenque, the forest seems for now to be winning more than it is losing, becoming ever more dense until you come to the first Lacandón village of San Javier, where the road forks. The **Fronteriza Carretera** continues to the left, while the road to the right runs toward Bonampak via the largest Lacandón

Getting Around and Tours

Tour operators in Palenque are eternally in debt to Subcomandante Marcos and the Zapatistas. In the early 1990s, getting to this area, 150km from Palenque, involved bouncing for hours over a dirt track to Bonampak, or an expensive light-plane flight to Yaxchilán. Then the Zapatistas burst into the headlines in 1994 and it was noticed equally suddenly that one reason why they had been able to train there might have been the lack of communications in the huge stretch of Chiapas that juts east into Guatemala. Long-ignored infrastructure projects were thrown centre-stage: for its own purposes the Mexican army began to build a paved road along the Bonampak track around the frontier to Montebello, the **Carretera Fronteriza**, completed in 1999. As a corollary, the journey time from Palenque to Bonampak has been cut to 3hrs.

Like all trips in this area visiting Yaxchilán and Bonampak is more difficult (but not impossible) in the mid-June–Oct rainy season.

Even if you don't cross the border into Guatemala, you need to have your passport and Mexican tourist card with you and in order, as identity checks are more rigorous than further into Mexico.

By Bus and *Combi*

If you really don't want a tour, or want to stay longer, it is possible to get to this area by **bus** or *combi*. A transport-only return trip to Lacanjá can be booked from *Colectivos Chambalú*, with return dates potentially flexible (around $60, but costs can be shared between several people). There are also a few ordinary *combis* and second-class buses to Lacanjá or Frontera; ask around at the bus stations. In Frontera, you will have to negotiate with *lancheros* to get to Yaxchilán. For points south of there and further into the

Lacandón forest, there is Lacandonia's bus to Naha, and *combis* from Palenque now run to most points on the *Fronteriza* south of Lacanjá and to Pico de Oro (for Las Guacamayas). Finding them is a matter of looking and asking around the second-class bus depots and *combi* stops.

Tours

All Palenque agencies (*see* p.437) offer 2-day trips combining Yaxchilán and Bonampak, (about $100 per person). With the improvement of the road most also offer 1-day tours ($50–$65), and light-plane tours are still available. The **1-day tours** can be very rushed, and having come this far it's better to take at least a **2-day trip** with a night in the Lacanjá area. The usual tour consists of a drive by *combi* to Frontera Corozal on the Usumacinta, a boat downstream to Yaxchilán and back, and a night in one of the camp sites in Lacanjá; on the second day you visit Bonampak before returning to Palenque. Meals, soft drinks and all camping equipment are included, but it's a good idea to take water, sun block, bug repellent (essential) and a torch for the camp site and examining the murals at Bonampak.

Some Palenque tour agencies now arrange trips to **Naha** on request, but the most authoritative tours are those run from Na Bolom in San Cristóbal, who have the best contacts.

From San Cristóbal (*see* p.477–8), local agencies provide 2- or 3-day tours, generally with a stopover in Palenque or nearby. Explora offers longer, more adventurous jungle trips and the Na Bolom centre runs its own trips which may be the most interesting for anyone wishing to learn about the Lacandón Maya.

Guatemalan authorities now allow tours to go on to the much less excavated Mayan city of **Piedras Negras** on the other side of the Usumacinta after visiting Yaxchilán, but only a few agencies will arrange this. This stretch of village, **Lacanjá** (or Lacanjá Chansayab). This is now a curious, disorderly place of huts of planks and corrugated zinc, government subsidies having paid for the replacement of the old ones of stick and palm. An airstrip has been cleared through the middle of the village, there's a basketball court, and a few of the houses have satellite dishes. Look around, though, and you're soon reminded that you're in a remote point in the forest. As you arrive a few of the Lacandón still peek out at you from behind bushes like timid birds, as if they'd never seen a *gringo* before (note that this gentle wonder

the river is more difficult than that near Yaxchilán, and not all the Frontera Corozal *lancheros* are experienced enough to take it on: if you wish to go there this needs to be clearly arranged with an agency in advance.

Selecting a Tour

Prices vary between agencies, sometimes by $20. It's worth comparing before you choose, and not necessarily taking the cheapest. Check what guarantee you will have that the tour will actually leave when you expect it to (most tours require a minimum of 4–6 people, and agencies may take bookings, then cancel at the last minute), whether there will be an English-speaking guide with you throughout, and, especially, whether the *combi* will stay with the group at all times. Some agencies 'double up' at busy times, taking one group to Bonampak, for example, leaving them there and going back to Palenque to pick up another group, which can leave you abandoned for hours if problems arise. Also consider which camp site is used at Lacanjá (*see* below), whether adm charges are included in the tour price (visitors to the Bonampak must pay a community *cuota* on top of the INAH adm), and what 'extras' are provided: to get to Bonampak from Lacanjá, some use one of the Lacandóns' *combis* (the only vehicles allowed in the area), while some give you a forest walk, with Lacandón guides who, with the main guide as interpreter, can open up aspects of the forest that otherwise go unnoticed.

Where to Stay and Eat

Frontera Corozal

Escudo Jaguar, *escudojaguar1@hotmail.com* (*inexpensive*). Palm-roofed *cabaña*-hostel near the Usumacinta with beds in simple rooms or dorms; it has good showers, a

small **restaurant** and a camping area, and the association that runs it has a launch for trips on the river and to Yaxchilán. Most travellers, though, find Lacanjá a more memorable place to stay than Frontera.

Lacanjá

Several **camp sites** in the village are run by Lacandón Maya or in association with them: **Kin Bor**, **Chan Kin** and (the best) **Chan Bor** (all *cheap*). All are used to dealing with agencies, but will also put up individuals; facilities are mostly basic but as well as tents they have sheltered hammock areas, hammocks for rent, and can arrange meals and forest guides. **Campamento Río Lacanjá**. By far the best equipped, set up by the San Cristóbal-based Explora agency, with comfortable cabins (*inexpensive*), camping space and even hot water, in a beautiful location by the Lacanjá river. It's mainly used for **Explora tours** (*see* p.478), but some other agencies use it and it may be open to individuals, though it's best to contact Explora in advance.

Naha

There is a **camp site** at Naha, but an agency reservation is usually necessary.

Pico de Oro

Las Guacamayas (Ara Macaw), **t** 01 520 15979 (*inexpensive*). One of the most impressive ecotourism projects in Chiapas, set up in association with a local cooperative in one of the most remote parts of the Lacandón forest, 223km southeast of Palenque on the Río Lacantún. The centre is self-sufficient, with seven good cabins, a **restaurant** and a landing stage on the river. Reservations are essential, usually for a minimum of 4 to 6 people, so (as the site's cell phone is unreliable) it's best to go through Palenque agencies, who can make up a group.

at outsiders can extend to a fascination with their things: there have been robberies at Lacanjá camp sites, so care is advisable). Streams run through the village, and pigskin is still tanned in pools to make drums, while many women carry on another tradition, the making of Lacandón ceramics. As the sun goes down nature takes over, with the unforgettable, electronic cacophony of the jungle insects at dusk, a matchless demonstration that the world around you really is alive.

Bonampak is now managed as part of an ecotourism scheme centred on Lacanjá. Facilities (such as the camp sites) have been improving and, at the Explora camp site in particular, activities such as kayaking and rafting on the Lacanjá river are available. If you have time, or are with a tour company that is ready to be flexible (as the best are), there are other places that Lacandón guides can lead you to, such as a beautiful lake, **Laguna Lacanjá**, about eight kilometres south. There is also a largely unexcavated Mayan ruin of Lacanjá, one of many yet to be explored in the Chiapas forest.

Back on the main road, the Fronteriza continues for another 25 kilometres from San Javier before reaching a turn off to the left, which will take you in 13 kilometres to the Usumacinta river, the Guatemalan border and **Frontera Corozal**. Despite a few recent improvements it's still a ragged settler village, a sprawling agglomeration of wood, zinc and palm-roof huts around a clearing and a football field. There's no real 'waterfront', just a slippery, sandy slope down to landing-stages by the river's edge. There are, however, police posts on either side of the river, enabling you to cross over into Guatemala if one of the local *lancheros* will take you over, although formalities are generally dealt with more easily if you take an agency bus from Palenque. Along the banks women chat and wash clothes in the river, and kids run in and out of the water; over on the Guatemalan side, more women can be seen doing much the same thing.

Naha, Metzaboc and the Río Lacantún

As the trip to Yaxchilán and Bonampak has got easier, the frontier for adventurous travel has been pushed further back into the forest. **Naha** and **Metzaboc**, home of the 'pure', still-pagan Lacandón, are deep in the woods northwest of Lacanjá, and reached via a long, unpaved turning off the Fronteriza. Both villages are sited near lakes, an important source of food for the Lacandón. Although they dislike missionaries, they have become slightly more used to other travellers. Lacandón guides can take you around the lakes by canoe, or, if you really want to join in village life, you can go fishing or hunting. There are also Mayan ruins nearby.

In the opposite direction, south of Frontera Corozal, the Fronteriza rolls on through more forest into territory that 20 years ago was virtually a blank space on the map. **Benemérito**, about 80 kilometres further on, is another shabby settler village, and another point where you can cross over into Guatemala. The Marqués de Comillas area, the very easternmost corner of Chiapas southeast of the Río Lacantún, is one of fairly heavy recent settlement that is being rapidly deforested. Northwest of the Lacantún, however, remains one of the largest stretches of rainforest in Chiapas, in the **Montes Azules** reserve. A centre of attraction here, making it possible to stay over in the area, is **Las Guacamayas** centre (*see* p.453) near **Pico de Oro**, reached via a part-paved road off the Fronteriza about 10 kilometres south of Benemérito. *Guacamaya* means scarlet macaw, and this part of the Lacandón jungle contains one of the largest populations of wild macaws in Mexico, as well as crocodiles, ocelots, monkeys and other wildlife. From Las Guacamayas you can explore the forest and kayak on the broad, placid river; not far away there are also still more, as yet scarcely identified Mayan ruins. **Explora** (*see* p.478) also offers adventure trips on the Río Lacantún.

The Fronteriza continues round the border to **Montebello** (*see* p.499). It's possible to visit the western Lacandón forest at Laguna Miramar, via **Ocosingo** (*see* p.470).

Yaxchilán

The first recorded monarch of Yaxchilán, venerated in later inscriptions as founder of the dynasty, was called Yat-Balam, and probably became *ahau* in AD 359. His name is often coyly translated as 'Progenitor-Jaguar', but it really means 'Jaguar Penis', a good title for the founder of a Mayan patriarchy. The site had been occupied for centuries before then. Its extraordinary location, dominating a bend in the river, gave it a powerful presence in politics and trade along the Usumacinta. Instead of resting on artificial pyramids, its temples and palace-residences rose up in terraces on steep natural hills above the river. This location also brought it into permanent rivalry with Piedras Negras, downriver, over dominance of the Usumacinta trade route, and the string of wars between them is one of the longest-running feuds in Mayan history.

Yaxchilán has many of the most skilful of all Mayan carvings and inscriptions, and from them a great deal of information has been gleaned. So fine are the Yaxchilán carvings, in fact, that many have been taken away: the lintels of Temples 21 and 23 were removed by Alfred Maudslay in the 1890s and are now in the British Museum, and others are in the National Museum in Mexico City. In their place are casts, which have been carefully done and are not a bad substitute. As well as with Piedras Negras Yaxchilán fought recurrent wars with its neighbours Bonampak and Lacanha, and at different times battled with both Tikal and Calakmul, although later it seems to have become one of Calakmul's allies. For a long period in the 6th and early 7th centuries few monuments were created at Yaxchilán, a phenomenon which in Mayan cities generally indicates a low point in a kingdom's fortunes, perhaps because Piedras

Site Information

Open daily 8–5; adm free

The outboard-driven river *lanchas* that take you to Yaxchilán from Frontera Corozal have palm-leaf canopies to provide some shade, although in the forest the general ambient heat is more noticeable than direct sunlight. The outward journey, with the current, takes about an hour; going back, the *lancheros* have to work harder, and it takes an hour and a half.

Either way they demonstrate a considerable knowledge of the Usumacinta, a powerful, big green flow with eddies and rapids.

After you hop ashore over the rocks you'll be met by the INAH watchmen who stay at the site for a few weeks at a time. Although there is no admission fee, one of the watchmen will lead you across the grass airstrip and take you around the site, and a tip is in order. Few speak English, but they're generally knowledgeable and helpful.

Yaxchilán

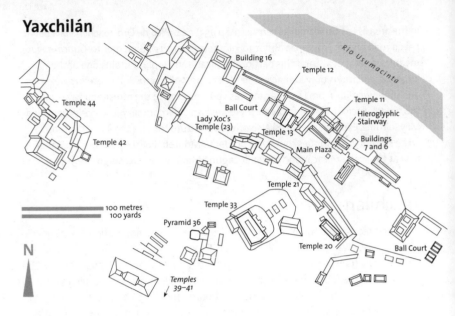

Negras had gained the upper hand. The two Yaxchilán rulers about whom most is known appeared at the end of this time, as the resurgent city entered a 'golden age', **Shield-Jaguar II** (more properly known as Itzamnaaj Balam II) and his son **Bird-Jaguar IV** (Escudo Jaguar and Pájaro Jaguar). Between them they ruled for nearly 90 years. They were the first Mayan kings anywhere to be individually identified, by Tatiana Proskouriakoff in the 1960s. Shield-Jaguar II became *ahau* in 681, apparently at the age of 34. Like his senior neighbour Pakal of Palenque he lived to a great age, 95, and is described as having led his warriors into battle even in his eighties. Even by the standards of Mayan lords he and his son were prolific monument builders. Out of the effort to understand why they built so much, a dramatic story has emerged.

Like other cities Yaxchilán had a favoured style of monument, in this case the downward-facing stone lintels of temple entrances, which were decorated with intricately detailed carvings. They were designed to be 'read' by other members of the city's élite, who would pass beneath them. Although he reigned for over 60 years Shield-Jaguar II did not begin building large-scale monuments until after 720, suggesting he had first had to struggle hard to re-establish the city's strength and his own authority against external and internal enemies. Many of his monuments were accordingly highly militaristic, celebrating victories. The greatest monument of Shield-Jaguar II's reign, though, is Temple 23, built in 723–6. Its three wonderfully carved lintels – two of which are in London and the other in Mexico City – show the king's first wife Lady Xoc (or Kabal Xook) taking part in bloodletting rituals: one to celebrate the birth of the heir Bird-Jaguar in 709, in which she pulls a thorned rope through her tongue; a middle one, in which she summons up Yat-Balam, founder of the lineage, during Shield-Jaguar's accession rites in 681; a third one, in which, after shedding blood, she helps Shield-Jaguar prepare for battle. It was unprecedented for a woman to be given prime position in the portrayal of sacred rituals in this way. More unusual still, Xoc was not the mother of the child whose birth is marked in the first lintel (Shield-Jaguar should then have been 61, and she was probably a similar age). Bird-Jaguar's mother was a younger wife, known as Lady Ik-Skull or Eveningstar.

As at Palenque, monuments were used to reassert the power and legitimacy of the dynasty after a period of weakness, and to overcome political problems. Lady Xoc was a member of one of the most important lineages of Yaxchilán, while Ik-Skull was a princess from Calakmul. In choosing the young Bird-Jaguar as his heir Shield-Jaguar almost certainly passed over other, older sons who probably felt they had a better claim to the throne. It appears he was carrying out a balancing act. By creating a monument to Xoc – in which she herself celebrated the new prince – and paying her (and therefore her family) an unheard-of degree of honour, he could perhaps hope to have his foreign alliance and present his chosen successor without alienating his own aristocracy. This probably involved some practical concessions to Xoc's relatives.

His politicking seems to have worked only to a certain extent. Shield-Jaguar II died in 742, but Bird-Jaguar IV's formal accession did not come until 752, after a murky 'interregnum' during which it seems that another ruler may have been installed, perhaps with the involvement of the eternal enemy Piedras Negras. Bird Jaguar IV's need to assert his authority was thus greater than usual and, even before he was finally declared the city's ruler, he began a massive 'programme' of monument-building. In the great Stela 11, he had himself shown taking part in a 'flapstaff ritual' (a ceremony, the full nature of which is unknown, which involved a kind of banner and was held on the summer solstice) jointly with the old king in 741; he also 'reinserted' his own mother, Ik-Skull, into his father's reign, in carvings that show her taking part in the same kind of rituals as were carried out by Lady Xoc in Temple 23. This suggests that Xoc's family, including his own half-brothers, may have been among his enemies. Bird-Jaguar also needed allies: rather than marry a foreign princess, he took as his principal wife a daughter of another of Yaxchilán's noble lineages, Lady Great-Skull, and in carvings the two of them are shown taking part in rituals together with her brother Great-Skull, with almost equal status. In other temples, such as 21 and 33, different *sahalob* nobles are similarly accorded places of honour. Rather than appear as the all-powerful *ahau*, Bird-Jaguar looks continually to be making deals and appealing for loyalty. All this intrigue was played out, though, within the context of Mayan belief, in which participation in shamanistic ritual and spirit contact was a fundamental element in defining relationships, loyalties and the right to rule.

Bird-Jaguar died in 768 and was succeeded by his 19-year-old son Chel-Te, who ruled as **Shield-Jaguar III**, initially with essential support from his powerful uncle Great-Skull, who seems almost to have acted as 'regent' while the *ahau* was still young. Previously, Bird-Jaguar had created another set of monuments to reinforce Chel-Te's claim to the throne, showing the boy taking part in rituals with his father (Temples 54 and 55). Shield-Jaguar III ruled for nearly 30 years, fought many more wars and added several buildings and monuments to Yaxchilán, and was succeeded by his own son Tatbu-Skull III in 800. By this time, however, Yaxchilán had clearly begun a rapid decline, probably accelerated by internal dissensions. Tatbu-Skull III commissioned only one monument, the last Long Count inscription at Yaxchilán, dated 808.

Like other cities on the Usumacinta Yaxchilán was all-but abandoned within a century. Its temples were visited only by the Lacandón. It was revealed to the outside world in the 1880s by Maudslay and Charnay, after a Dr Livingstonesque encounter when they ran into each other at the ruins, each thinking they had found them first. Maudslay called the place *Menché Tinamit*, a name probably used by the Lacandón, but in 1901 Teobert Maler invented Yaxchilán ('blue-green stones'), which has stuck.

The Labyrinth and the Main Plaza

Its monuments aside, one of the ultimate attractions of Yaxchilán is its superb rainforest location. Above the river, the bluff divides into clefts, ledges and steep hills, reached by paths through thick, high forest; a guide is essential. Although the site has been excavated over many years, there are still a great many buildings half-lost in the undergrowth, and the forest seems ready to reclaim the whole site. In the tops of the trees, toucans and parrots are easy to spot, while in the background there's an extraordinary chorus: the booming of howler monkeys.

The first structure that you come to as you walk up from the airstrip is **Building 19**, also known as the **Laberinto**, a combined residential and ceremonial complex. Beyond it you enter the central plaza of Yaxchilán, which, in place of the usual artificial geometry of Mayan plazas, follows the lie of the land, curving in line with the bluff. In the centre stands a magnificent, tall *ceiba*, the sacred world-tree of the Maya. A line of buildings closes off the plaza on the river side, while on the other more irregularly spaced structures climb up the hills. Unless you've made special arrangements with your guide, you won't have time to see more than a few. On the left, one of the first is a small east-facing temple, **Building 16**, with a finely preserved lintel showing Bird-Jaguar with a vision-serpent summoned up in a bloodletting ritual in July 741. A little further on is the unusually small **Ball Court**. Next to it is **Temple 13**. It was built by Bird-Jaguar, apparently deliberately almost opposite Lady Xoc's monument of **Temple 23**. Its middle lintel shows his mother Ik-Skull taking part in rituals to mark his birth in 709, at the same time as Xoc's spectacular bloodletting (*see* facing page). Behind 13 is **Temple 12**, which has lintels from the 530s that list the first ten rulers of Yaxchilán. First carved for another building, they were probably reset here by Bird-Jaguar IV, as the rest of the temple is 8th-century. Temple 11, a little further along on the left, was built for another of Shield-Jaguar II's wives, known as Lady Sak-Biyaan.

In the middle of the plaza are several *stelae*: the largest is **Stela 1**, showing Bird-Jaguar IV in a bloodletting ritual accompanied by Lady Great-Skull. Beneath them there is the maize god, ready to receive the royal blood. On a platform towards the river is the oldest *stela* at Yaxchilán, **Stela 27**, erected in 514 and showing the city's founder Yat-Balam. The buildings just to the right, **Buildings 6** and **7**, are some of the oldest around the plaza that were not built over by Bird-Jaguar, from 500–550. They still have their roof-combs, as well as masks of the Sun God. Much more imposing is Bird-Jaguar IV's **Hieroglyphic Stairway**, a spectacular glyph text in which he listed all the members of the dynasty of Yaxchilán, culminating, naturally, in himself.

In the next part of the plaza there are still more large *stelae*. The most important is **Stela 11**, erected by Bird-Jaguar IV in 752, and still wonderfully clear. On the main side it shows Bird-Jaguar and the 93-year-old Shield-Jaguar II taking part in the flapstaff ritual in 741; the reverse shows Bird-Jaguar with three soon-to-be sacrificed captives. This is not the original location of Stela 11, which first stood high up on the hill above the city, next to Temple 40. **Stela 3**, also beautifully carved, shows Shield-Jaguar II, Bird-Jaguar IV – standing out with his giant thighs – and Lady Ik-Skull.

The Principal Temples

The temples that contain the most refined carved lintels at Yaxchilán are more or less in a line along the foot of the hill on the landward side of the plaza. If you turn towards them from Stela 3, and so take them from east to west or left to right, you come to them in reverse order. Furthest left is **Temple 20**, built by Shield-Jaguar III. In its three lintels he emphasizes the greatness of his father and his own right to the throne, and pays notable tribute to the lineage of his mother, Bird-Jaguar's queen Lady Great-Skull. The left-hand lintel, now faint, shows Bird-Jaguar subduing captives; the middle one shows him and Lady Great-Skull carrying out a bloodletting rite to mark the birth of Shield-Jaguar III in February 752; the right-hand one shows Lady Great-Skull and her brother Great Skull taking part in Bird-Jaguar's blood rite in July 741 – the same one as on Building 16 – with a vision-serpent between them.

On the platform next to it is **Temple 21**, created by Bird-Jaguar IV himself. The imagery of the lintels – the originals of which were removed by Maudslay – seems deliberately chosen to mirror and match that of Lady Xoc's Temple 23. On the left Lady Wak Tuun, one of Bird-Jaguar's 'junior' wives, is shown summoning up Yat-Balam in a vision rite, as Lady Xoc had done: she holds a bowl with the implements for blood-letting, while the vision arises out of the bowl where the strips of paper used to catch the blood are burnt. In the middle Bird-Jaguar himself and another wife, Lady Mut Balam, 'celebrate' the birth of the future heir Shield-Jaguar III in 752 in typical Mayan fashion, he by preparing to perforate his penis and she by passing a cord through her tongue. On the right-hand lintel Bird-Jaguar is shown standing over an unfortunate captured lord who was needed for sacrifice in his accession rites as king, also in 752.

Lady Xoc's original monument, **Temple 23**, is two buildings west. For all Bird-Jaguar's efforts, his father had better carvers. There is no more graphic image of Mayan blood rituals than the left-hand lintel (*see* overleaf), with Xoc pulling the thorn-spiked cord through her tongue, blood running down her cheek, while Shield-Jaguar II stands over her, and the vision of Yat-Balam on the middle lintel is far more dynamic than the equivalent image in Temple 21. One of the features of these carvings is that Xoc's *huípil* in the bloodletting lintel, like those of Bird-Jaguar's wives in Temple 21, features a diamond design very similar to those still used by Highland Maya weavers today.

From behind Temple 23 a path to the right leads to **Temple 44**, known as Shield-Jaguar II's 'war memorial', completed in 732 and with carvings glorifying a string of campaigns in the 50 years of his reign. To the left a steep path runs up to the 'Great Acropolis' or pyramid of Yaxchilán – a natural hill – topped by Bird-Jaguar IV's largest building, **Temple 33**, still with a towering roof-comb. The carving here is not only on the lintels: some of the most spectacular images are on panels on the base of the temple platform, showing, in the centre, Bird-Jaguar IV playing the ballgame. In the

Lady Xoc perfoming a blood-letting ritual in front of her husband Shield-Jaguar II, in October 709. From Temple 23.

side panels he is accompanied by his dead father Shield-Jaguar II (step 6) and his grandfather Bird-Jaguar III (step 8). Being dead, both play the game from Xibalba. Moreover, this is not meant to represent the ballgame in general, but a specific game in October 744, during the 'Interregnum' before Bird-Jaguar was officially king, when through the game he summoned up his ancestors in his support. This is one of the most graphic images of the ball court as a portal to the Otherworld. The ball is shown as containing the soul of a sacrificial victim; this may be a literal depiction of the facts on certain occasions, when captives were bound as 'balls' for sacrifice in the game.

Temple 33's lintels show scenes around the accession of Bird-Jaguar IV. In the left-hand panel he is preparing for the accession rite in 752, attended by Lady Great-Skull; in the middle, he is with his five-year-old son Chel-Te, in rites to mark the anniversary of his accession in 757; on the right, he presides in a calendar ritual in 756, helped by a *sahal* called Ah-Mac-Kin-Mo. In the temple there is a headless statue, believed to be of Shield-Jaguar II. This is venerated by the Lacandón as an image of their creator-god *Hachakyum*, and around it there is evidence of recent offerings and incense-burning. They have a legend that when its head returns to its body the world will end.

The Southern Acropolis

There are many other areas at Yaxchilán, but after you have spent a while peering at carvings the watchman should suggest that he takes you up to the highest point of the city, the mountain that towers up behind the site. It's a real jungle path, climbing up and down steeply through rocks and forest. Along the way, this is the best place to look for monkeys and birds. When you finally reach the top there are three buildings, **Temples 39, 40** and **41**, thought to have been used as observatories or in astronomical ceremonies. In front of them Bird-Jaguar IV placed more monuments, some of which, such as Stela 11, have been moved lower down. The real attraction, though, is the fabulous view, over the river and the great bed of forest stretching in every direction.

Bonampak

The Mayan city of Bonampak, nine kilometres south of Lacanjá, was a minor burg compared to Yaxchilán. Its unique importance today comes from the fact that it has, in one temple, the only near-complete Mayan mural paintings yet found anywhere (at least until the recent, still-unseen discoveries in Temple XX at Palenque), which justify the journey there in themselves. Considering that nearly all large Mayan buildings were painted in some way, it is perhaps extraordinary that so little has survived. The Bonampak murals portray Classic-era court life with unparalleled vividness, giving a completely new image of Mayan art and of the abilities of Mayan painters.

How the murals were found is part of their mystique. They were discovered by an American, Giles Healy, who in 1944 was sent to Chiapas by the United Fruit Company to make a nature film. He had good relations with the Lacandón, and in 1946 they took him to Bonampak, which was overgrown and unknown to archaeologists. Wandering around the site, he came across a smallish temple. He saw nothing special about it and, when he stuck his head inside, saw only darkness. Then he lit a torch, looked in again and realized, awestruck, that the walls were covered in paintings. The discovery of the murals caused huge controversy among Mayan experts due to their incontrovertible portrayal of war, torture and very bloody rituals, at a time when it was often stated that the Maya were a pacific people.

Beyond the murals, relatively little is known about the history of Bonampak. It seems to have attained a position of power only very late and under only one of its *ahauob*, Chan-Muaan, the same lord shown in the murals, who reigned from 776 until some time after 795. In earlier centuries it was often at war with its larger neighbour Yaxchilán. In 715 Bonampak was a vassal of Toniná, but by Chan-Muaan's time it had become an ally and 'subordinate' of Yaxchilán, and his principal queen, who appears in the murals, was the sister of Shield-Jaguar III. Virtually all the structures that have survived were erected by Chan-Muaan. The murals refer to events from 790 to 792; the last recorded date at Bonampak came only three years later. The murals represent, therefore, a final, dazzling flourish of Classic Mayan civilization.

The Plaza and the Acropolis

The excavated area of Bonampak consists really of just one large plaza, which you enter, at the end of a deep green path, from the north side. In the middle of the grass square are two very fine *stelae* made for Chan-Muaan, one picturing him in a

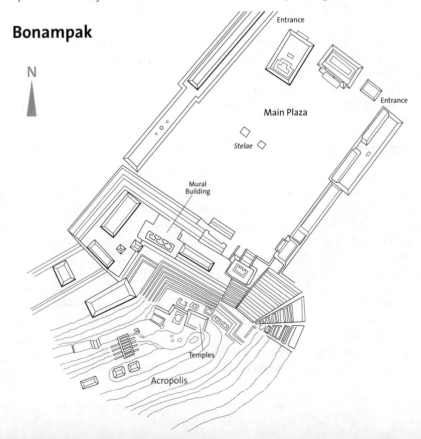

Bonampak

N

Entrance

Entrance

Main Plaza

Stelae

Mural
Building

Temples

Acropolis

Site Information

Open daily 8–5; adm.

To visit Bonampak you must pay an entry fee to the Lacanjá community (around $6) as well as the usual INAH entry charge ($2–3). To get there from Lacanjá, if travelling independently, you can walk, or pay for a lift in a Lacandón *combi*. Only their vehicles are allowed inside the area.

Visiting the Murals

Unlike at Yaxchilán, the watchman at Bonampak doesn't guide you around the ruins, but he does have to accompany you to the murals temple to turn the lights on (it's useful also to have a torch/flashlight, to pick out details). Only three people are allowed in each room at a time. The rooms run in chronological order, left to right.

supremely belligerent posture subduing a captive, and the other presenting him about to puncture his penis in a bloodletting ritual. The sides of the plaza are long, thin platforms, leading up to the **Acropolis of Bonampak**, with temples and banks of steps built up a steep ridge. Several of the temples in a line at the top of the main terrace still have fine stucco decoration. The murals temple, surprisingly small, is to the right, looking from the plaza, now protected from the rain by a modern canopy.

The Murals Temple

The left-hand **Room 1** has in some ways the most fascinating images of all. They portray two separate events, which took place almost a year apart. The upper section of the wall in front of you and the two side walls depict the presentation of Chan-Muaan's heir, on 14 December 790. On the right-hand wall Chan-Muaan himself sits on a dais, with his principal wife to his left and two other children. He appears to be talking to the man holding (pretty clumsily) the son and heir, on the main wall. He stands above a line of 14 nobles stretching round to the left wall, who, however, appear to be paying no attention to him whatsoever and to be far more involved in chatting among themselves. Above it all at the apex of the room are images of the Cosmic Monster, the ultimate spirit of the earth. Immediately apparent is one of the most striking and strangely unsettling features of the Bonampak murals, and of much Mayan art: there seems to be no notion of 'genre', of division of subject matter. The murals portray great state occasions and bloody suffering, and yet at the same time seem to be distracted by everyday details and present some of their characters almost comically, as in the plump, garrulous lords. It as if, rather than being separately reverential, awe-inspiring or comic, the whole of life had to be in the one picture.

The other scenes in this room show a ceremony held 336 days after the first one, on 15 November 791. Above the door behind you, Chan-Muaan and two attendant lords are dressed in elaborate regalia of jaguar skins and green feathers to take part in a ritual dance, performed with Venus in the ascendant, probably to conjure up spirits to ensure that the young prince would be a great king and warrior. The dance itself appears on the lower panels all around the room, with the king and his two followers in the centre opposite the door. To the left are the musicians with their trumpets and maracas and, to the very left, almost by the door, there are dancers in monster costumes, representing the *way* or spirit companions summoned up in their dance.

Room 2 in the middle is the 'battle room'. Its glyphs relate that the battle it shows took place on 2 August 792 and that Chan-Muaan was assisted by Yaxchilán, but do not say who the enemy was. Bonampak was clearly victorious, taking many captives. Although it is in the worst condition of any of the Bonampak murals the battle scene itself, around the facing, left and right walls, is extraordinary, the most horrific and complete image of Mayan warfare. On the left wall, Chan-Muaan's warriors hold up huge, fan-like battle standards. Everything else is a tangle of semi-naked bodies, slashing and slaughtering each other. Pride of place naturally goes to Chan-Muaan, on the far wall, seen grabbing a wretched captive by his hair. The small images in the apex of the roof represent the stars and so the omens for the day of the battle.

The most powerful image of all is on the wall above the door, showing Chan-Muaan disposing of his prisoners. This took place a few days after the battle. The king stands in the centre, attended by *sahalob* all in different regalia, and on his left stands a woman, presumably his queen and the sister of his ally Shield-Jaguar III. Below them is a scene of ferocious cruelty. To the left a bending guard seems to be cutting off a prisoner's fingers, a torment inflicted on captives before final sacrifice. Alongside, prisoners, mutilated and stripped, beg for mercy; in the centre one has already been killed. Yet again, awesome, terrible images are combined with prosaic details, while the figure of the dying captive at Chan-Muaan's feet is astonishing, a demonstration of pictorial skill of a level that would not be seen in Europe for centuries.

Finally, **Room 3** portrays a ritual carried out by Chan-Muaan in his role as great shaman, probably not long after the battle. It is a powerful indication of the role of mystical dancing in Mayan ceremonies. The whole of the far wall is a riot of dancing figures, men in giant feathered back-frames and headdresses, with equally huge banners that stick out on either side of them. At the top dances Chan-Muaan; below him, two men hold another benighted sacrificial victim by the hands and ankles, and seem almost to be throwing him up in the air towards an executioner who stands below the king. On the right-hand wall a strange procession carries a figure standing on a litter, perhaps representing one of Chan-Muaan's ancestors. To the left, Chan-Muaan's queen and other women of the royal house, on a dais, let blood by passing cords through their tongues. Above the door, the king stands in line with his *sahalob*. These ceremonies were almost certainly carried out to give cosmic strength to the king's lineage and ensure continuity for his heir. Obviously, they were not successful.

The Highlands

...at times we had to go up on foot, at times on all fours...
 Dominican friar Tomás de la Torre, travelling from Tabasco to San Cristóbal, 1540s.

The Chiapas Highlands are a giant castle of rock in the middle of the American isthmus, a world of peaks, crags, ridges and valleys abruptly different from the hot, flat plains only a short distance to the north. All the routes into the Highlands involve abrupt, winding climbs. Until the building of modern roads – within the last 40 years – the length and difficulty of this ascent long kept the mountains isolated in space and time from the rest of the world.

There are just two routes into the Highlands from the north. From the point of view of pure scenery, most spectacular is the road from Villahermosa, **Highway 195**, which runs south to meet the Pan-American Highway between San Cristóbal de Las Casas and Tuxtla Gutiérrez. To go along this road is to get a lesson in the immensity of the earth, and to feel very small. Most dramatic of all is the '**Ascent of Tapilula**', *el Ascenso de Tapilula*, up a giant ridge which from the north side is first seen as a line of rock in the sky, and long made this route impassable. It represents just 11 kilometres on the map, but can take a full hour to climb, yawing through giant hairpins. At the end of it in either direction, at **Tapilula** at the bottom and **Rayón** at the top, buses stop so that drivers can have a rest and release their nerves.

The more popular route is the road from Palenque, **Highway 199**, which would itself count as one of the great spectacular roads were it not tame in comparison. You begin to climb a short distance from Palenque, well before Agua Azul, and if you look back on the reverse bends northern Chiapas soon appears spread out flat and green below and behind you. Just over halfway, 103 kilometres from Palenque, is **Ocosingo**, the largest town on this route and the access point to the Mayan ruins at Toniná. From there the road rises up far more steeply, through **Oxchuc**, into a final abrupt climb over a ridge at more than 2,000m before descending through an alpine land-scape of pine woods and mountain grassland into San Cristóbal. This 191-kilometre journey takes at least five hours. Ocosingo is the meeting point of the Highlands,

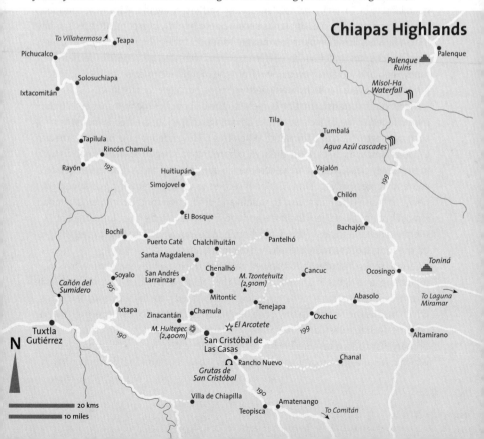

the recently settled, previously forest-covered lower hill country and the western Lacandón jungle. The forests away to the east of the town also contain the original bases of the Zapatista movement, and so this is the place where the political problems of Chiapas come closest, so to speak, to the main highway, but even here on most days whenever you pass through absolutely nothing will be happening.

The Chiapas Crisis

The conflicts of Chiapas are about land, race, poverty and the way in which power is exercised in Mexico. They are also, though, complex and often ambiguous, with fault-lines that are not always clear-cut. They are not simply to do with Chiapas being backward (Chiapas is actually highly productive, the source of 20 per cent of Mexico's electricity, 35 per cent of its coffee, and three million head of cattle). Rather, they are a product of modernity, of economic acceleration in the state as it becomes more and more part of the global economy and the NAFTA area. As is evident as you look around, there are a great many people, mostly Indians, who live by farming with minimal resources on poor land. Ever since the days of Porfirio Díaz, the solution officially recommended for these problems has been modernization: roads, schools, economic dynamism, progress. However, with every step towards an intensification of commercial agriculture, there has been a worsening of rural poverty.

Under Spain and in the first century of independence, it was already customary for good land to be taken by *ladino* planters and settlers, while the Maya were confined to whatever was left. The Highlands became permanently overpopulated, with many Indian families living on plots too meagre to support them. From the 1950s, encouraged by schemes under which 'wilderness' areas were declared open for settlement, many Highland Indians moved down from the mountains to 'colonize' the Lacandón jungles. They were joined by many poor *mestizos*, equally eager for land.

The next great transformation came with the oil boom of the 1970s, when Highland men flooded to the Gulf coast to take advantage of the jobs created in industries such as construction and transport. When this boom ended in 1982 most returned to Chiapas almost as quickly, but the style of farming had begun to change enormously. In the newly cleared forest areas, commercial farmers and cattle ranchers began to contend aggressively for land with poor settlers (*colonos*). A growing gulf appeared between those who had access to capital and production for the commercial market – most but not all of them *ladinos* – and those who had not – most but not all of them *indígenas* (Indians) – many of whom had been pushed into improvised villages on the fringes of the more established communities.

Central to the disputes that followed has been the inoperativeness of law in regulating land rights in Chiapas. Many of the *colonos* and poor *ejido* communities in recently settled 'national lands' have never established clear legal title to their lands, which means their rights to them can be challenged by anybody whenever the land become desirable. Instead of law, the key to land rights has been political power. The primary institutions responsible for deciding on land disputes are the municipalities, which have jurisdiction over scores of villages. However, municipal power in rural

Chiapas has been notoriously corrupt, dominated by farmers and ranchers bound up with the local PRI. Added to this was the unspoken racism of Chiapas, and the way in which the Maya have traditionally been disregarded in questions of legal rights.

Clashes arising out of this situation were already common well before Chiapas exploded into the headlines in 1994, with incidents of Indian peasants being expropriated, terrorized or even murdered by farmers and their men, and of human rights abuses by state and local authorities. During the Carlos Salinas boom years, however, all eyes were fixed on Mexico's soaring GDP, and the government believed in giving productive agriculture its head. Salinas' breakneck liberalization of the Mexican economy also lowered prices for anything poor farmers could produce, and increased those of goods they bought. The PRI élite, however, believed it could keep this kind of problem in check by keeping it out of sight, and in 1993 Salinas expressly denied to US bankers that there were guerrilla groups in Chiapas.

When the Zapatistas took over San Cristóbal de Las Casas and Ocosingo on 1 January 1994, the government appeared paralyzed with shock. Morever, this movement of ignorant Indians seemed far more agile than they could even hope to be – issuing statements on the Internet before many corporations had got the hang of it – with an enigmatic masked spokesman, Subcomandante Marcos, whose sharp, witty denunciations of the Salinas era as one great lie immediately hit home and made him a hero throughout the country. After a brief skirmish, the government was obliged to accept the only intermediary it could find to negotiate a ceasefire, in the shape of Samuel Ruíz, the Catholic bishop of San Cristóbal. A leading exponent of liberation theology, Bishop Ruíz had begun to provide Church assistance for poor peasants in the 1970s, and for many Chiapas farmers was the most despised figure in the whole state, responsible for having stirred up all the trouble in the first place. However, the PRI, which was the party of the Revolution, didn't like to appear as the oppressor, at least in broad daylight. More to the point, the Zapatista rising had caused the foreign investors who had poured into Mexico under Salinas to backtrack, in a movement that became a stampede. At the beginning of 1995 the peso lost half its value, and a complete collapse was only prevented by a US rescue package pushed through by Bill Clinton over Congressional opposition. Mexico's economic project required that the conflict be removed from the evening news as soon as possible.

In the six years following the Zapatistas' emergence they and the PRI governments stared at each other in a strangely immobile ritual dance. The new administration of President Ernesto Zedillo, elected for the PRI in 1994, committed itself to peaceful negotiations as the only means to a solution in Chiapas, while seeming to follow completely contrary policies on the ground. Troops were poured into the state, and a ring of roads and military installations built around the Zapatista areas that would make any repetition of the 1994 events impossible. Another feature in the situation was the growth of right-wing paramilitary groups to oppose Zapatista land claims, and a deal of evidence has emerged to indicate that this was actively encouraged by the army and the state police. At times it seemed there was a deliberate policy of provoking the Zapatistas into violent action that would justify final repression. The

Revolutionary Comedian: Marcos Rides Out

To the Mexican Federal Army, to the Guatemalan Army, to Interpol in Paris, to CISEN [military intelligence] in Polanco:
> *'Gentlemen,*
> *YEPA, YEPA, YEPA, ANDELE ANDELE!, ARRIBA, ARRIBA!, YEPA, YEPA!'*
> > *Subcomandante Marcos, alias 'El Sup Speedy González'.*

Marcos announces his return after several months' silence during which it was rumoured he was dead, July 1998.

No conventional Mexican politicians would compare themselves to Speedy González. Neither do they state their positions through jokes, parables, aphorisms and quotes from an impressive range of world literature (such as the Shakespeare sonnets, in English, on the Zapatista website). Subcomandante Marcos' musings and 'essays', published through the Internet, sometimes maddeningly wandering, sometimes comic routines, have from his first media appearances in 1994 given the Zapatista movement a unique tone and image.

Marcos is *Sub*-comandante because the actual *comandantes* of the Zapatistas are all Maya. In theory he is only the spokesman and adviser of a purely indigenous movement. Inside Chiapas the names and roles of the *comandantes* – David, Tacho, Esther – are well known, even though, like Marcos, they are only ever seen in ski masks. To the media and the outside world, however, Marcos himself has often *been* the Zapatistas. From the first days of the rising in 1994 he has been the ideal frontman: able to speak very well in English, French, Italian, Tzotzil and Tzeltal; witty, quick and able to charm as many news reporters as were put in front of him.

The Mexican government has always preferred to present Marcos as the real leader of the Zapatistas, manipulating his Indian followers. Throughout 1994 they also

Zapatistas, however, didn't take the bait, and adopted an almost Gandhian policy of passive resistance, sometimes being described as a 'moral presence' more than an armed group. For a guerrilla movement which is regularly pictured in full combat gear, in fact, the Zapatistas have scarcely fired a shot since 1994. Violence in Chiapas has come overwhelmingly from paramilitaries.

In February 1995 the Zedillo government sought to take drastic action with raids on supposed Zapatista safe houses around the country, but this backfired when terrorist attacks that the Zapatistas were alleged to be planning in Mexican cities were shown to be a crude police set-up. Looking foolish, the government went back to an earlier tack and not only restated its commitment to negotiations but enshrined them in law, the *Ley de Concordia y Pacificación*, with a cross-party commission, the COCOPA, to see to its implementation. In February 1996, after long negotiations in San Andrés Larraínzar, north of San Cristóbal, a solution seemed to be reached in the *Acuerdos de San Andrés*, the San Andrés Accords, in which government and Zapatistas apparently agreed a system of political and economic autonomy for Indian communities. These Accords have become the touchstone of any subsequent negotiations for the expended a deal of energy in trying to find out who the masked man was. Eventually, they declared him to be Rafael Sebastián Guillén. If this is true (it has not been confirmed or denied), Marcos is a former philosophy student from Tampico who got involved in Marxist groups in Mexico City in the '70s, bummed around Europe for a few years and then disappeared into Chiapas to dedicate himself to political work. The government sought to use this apparent discovery to demonstrate that behind the laughing exterior Marcos was just a hard-line, old-style Marxist-Leninist. This, however, missed the point, in that whatever the ideological past of Marcos and his colleagues might be, since 1994 they have shown a mental agility and an openness to ideas far beyond Cold War stereotypes. Marcos is a very Mexican combination, involved in an historic peasant struggle but with a head full of international mass culture and very aware of his media 'performance' as revolutionary leader. It is in large part due to him that the Zapatistas have appeared not just as a resistance movement of an ancient culture but as very much part of the modern world.

Marcos' open-ended approach has also made him an international figurehead for the anti-globalization movement, and one Mexican commentator has declared sarcastically that his greatest achievement has been in developing 'political tourism', with all the foreign sympathizers (or just the plain curious) who have been drawn to Chiapas. Inside Mexico his appeal has often cooled: behind the easy charm an egomaniac glint emerged that alienated some who worked with him, and his mean-dering website 'statements' can be hugely self-indulgent. Protestations that he is a mere mouthpiece in the Zapatista make-up have also worn thin as it has become clear he wields real (but not exclusive) power. After the 2000 elections, however, he seemed to become less self-absorbed, and at his best he still makes powerful points, and does so with style. For his meditations and Zapatista announcements, take a look at *www.ezln.org*.

Zapatistas, but other than that only started a whole new argument. In November 1996 the COCOPA presented its proposals for the implementation of the agreement. Months followed before the government replied with its own plan, which effectively reduced the *Acuerdos* to an administrative reorganization. The Zapatistas accused the government of never having negotiated in good faith. The Zedillo government seemed ready to sign up to any statement of intent while avoiding giving anything away in practice, hoping maybe to wear its opponent down by the passage of time.

In the absence of an agreement, the situation became increasingly confused. Zapatista sympathizers set up their own autonomous communities in many places, rejecting the authority of local municipalities, and at times violence followed when the military, state police or paramilitaries went in to dismantle them. Elsewhere, local agreements took the edge off some conflicts. In an effort to counteract the poverty of Chiapas the government pumped funding into the state – as seen in its new roads – but this was often distributed selectively, and with the usual chronic corruption. This helped foment tension between pro- and anti-Zapatista communities, visible at its height in the worst incident of the crisis, the massacre at Acteal to the north of San

Cristóbal in 1997, when 45 Zapatista sympathizers were killed by paramilitaries. For their part the Zapatistas also lost support, as, mirroring the immobility of the government, they too refused to negotiate and retreated into silence for months at a time.

In Chiapas, therefore, still more than in the rest of Mexico, the ending of the PRI's 71-year rule with the election of President Fox, in July 2000, seemed to promise a new beginning, despite Fox's right-wing, free-market background. During his campaign Fox had said he could resolve the Chiapas situation 'in 15 minutes' and declared his willingness to negotiate with no preconditions, and as a first sign of goodwill he ordered a reduction in troop levels in the state. Perhaps still more of a shock than the national election was that in December 2000 the PRI also lost the state governorship of Chiapas, to a cross-party alliance headed by Pablo Salazar Mendiguchía, a member of the left-wing PRD with strong liberal credentials. The troop withdrawals produced an immediate reduction in tensions in Chiapas, and the new optimism reached a peak with the Zapatistas' 'March on Mexico City' in March 2001, when the Zapatista *comandantes*, assured safe conduct by Fox, addressed the Federal Congress.

The damp cloth came a month later, when the Fox government presented its own 'Law on Indigenous Rights'. The Zapatistas' central demand, enshrined in the San Andrés accords, has been that indigenous communities should be given inalienable rights to their own territory and decision-making powers, but the new law chipped away at the details to retain an effective veto for conventional authorities. It was rejected by the Zapatistas and other Indian groups across the country, including the semi-official National Indigenous Congress. President Fox, meanwhile, continued to express impeccably liberal sentiments and reiterate his commitment to peace, while (as in several other areas) detailed business was handled by more hard-line members of his party in the Federal Congress. The situation fell back into paralysis yet again, as government hard-liners insisted the law should stand, the Zapatistas broke off negotiations and retreated into one of their enigmatic silences, and time went by. Mexico's new open politics are more complex than the old PRI regime, for the new law was also rejected by Governor Salazar of Chiapas, who stated his intention to continue a 'dialogue' at local level. However, uncertainty has returned to Chiapas, and any final outcome remains unpredictable.

Ocosingo, Toniná and Laguna Miramar

Ocosingo is the main market town for a wide area of the lower Highlands. Its hub is, naturally, the plaza, four blocks downhill from the main highway, with at the western end the town hall and to the east the 17th-century Dominican church of **San Jacinto**. The spectacular **market** is three blocks further east past the church. The Ocosingo valley is known in Chiapas for its cheese, the softish *queso de bola* ('ball cheese'), available in big quantities along with other local produce (fresh-grown coffee, spices, wonderful vegetables), at the market. Around the market and plaza there are always women from nearby Tzeltal-speaking communities in their distinctive blouses, with brilliantly embroidered lace trimmings that reflect Conquest-era Spanish styles.

Toniná

Open Tues–Sun 9–4; closed Mon; adm.

Its inaccessibility long kept Toniná relatively little known, but it is in fact one of the most spectacular of Mayan sites, as well as having been perhaps the last great Classic Mayan city. Built in far more hilly terrain than any city further north, its architecture is almost bizarrely unique. Toniná had a very distinctive monumental style, creating massive statues of its rulers rather than flat *stelae*, and also produced exceptional carvings, reliefs and ceramics, many of which are now in the excellent site **museum**.

Most of the visible structures of Toniná were built in the Late Classic, after 600, but beneath them are unexcavated buildings that are centuries older. The city's location in one of the 'fringe' areas of Mayan civilization meant that it came into frequent conflict with wealthier cities in the Usumacinta region to the east and, above all, Palenque. Toniná's greatest ruler was called Baaknal-Chaak, who became *ahau* in 688 a year after the sacking of the city by Kan-Balam II of Palenque, during which his predecessor and probably father seems to have died. Baaknal-Chaak took revenge

Getting Around

Highway 199 runs along the western side of Ocosingo, and all buses stop along it. **First-class** buses from the ADO in Palenque stop north of the centre on a steep slope, from where you walk uphill and then go left for the plaza. ATG **first-class** and most **second-class** companies stop at the top of the hill near the junction of the Highway and Av. Central. From there, walk down Av. Central or Av. 1 Sur Oriente to reach the square.

Getting to Toniná

The Toniná entry road was paved in 1998, transforming its accessibility. To find it **by car**, coming from north or south, look for signs just outside Ocosingo off Highway 199 on to the *Periférico*, which loops around the town to the east, where the Toniná turn-off is well sign-posted. If you continue into town, turn off 199 down Av. 1 Sur to the plaza, then go right by the church on to C/ 1 Oriente Sur, and follow this road out of town to reach the Toniná road.

Without a car, the way to get to Toniná is by **taxi**, which should cost around $15 (agree price first) if the driver waits while you visit the site. The political situation has led little Ocosingo to have no fewer than five taxi unions, so you have a choice. The old PRI-affiliated union has the main rank in the plaza; others (including the Zapatista OTEZ) are near the bus stops on Av. 1 Norte, one street north of Av. Central.

Getting To Laguna Miramar

It's possible to get to Laguna Miramar independently, but since all visitors must register with the *ejido* (you need to check on what you should take with you) it's best to make contact via their agent in San Cristóbal (who speaks English), **Fernando Ochoa**, C/ Dr Navarro 10, Barrio el Cerrillo, San Cristóbal de Las Casas, **t** (967) 678 0468, *miramar@mundomaya .com.mx*. Miramar can also be contacted through the **Red de Turismo Comunitario** (*see* p.478) and some other San Cristóbal agencies.

Ocosingo has an **airstrip** (on the *Periférico*, near the Toniná road), from which Servicios Aéreos San Cristóbal, **t/f** 673 0188, run light-plane flights to order, to or over Miramar, Montebello and more remote places in the Lacandón region, and more or less daily to Miramar for around $40 one-way (Rancho Esmeralda and tourist offices and agencies in San Cristóbal have information).

Combis and **trucks** run a few times daily from the market area in Ocosingo as far as San Quintín, 1km from Emiliano Zapata. San Quintín also has the airstrip for planes from Ocosingo and San Cristóbal, and a few shops and *loncherías*. This area is the Zapatista heartland, and Emiliano Zapata (unsurprisingly) is a Zapatista community (San Quintín, in a Chiapas disjunction, is more PRI-ista). Most army checkpoints on the Ocosingo road were withdrawn or scaled down in 2001, although they could be 're-activated'; they with a sustained challenge to the larger city, culminating in 711 with Toniná's finest moment when its warriors captured Kan-Hok-Chitam II of Palenque, plunging his kingdom into crisis. A superb relief panel from Toniná, now in the museum in Tuxtla Gutiérrez, exultantly portrays Kan-Hok-Chitam as a bound and humiliated captive. Toniná took full advantage of Palenque's weakness to become a powerful force in the region. Its importance – with that of other Mayan communities in central Chiapas – appears to have increased in the last years of the Classic era, with, it is suggested, a movement of Maya into the lower Highlands as the 'Collapse' developed further down the river valleys. Toniná, in fact, has the last of all inscriptions in the Long Count calendar – and so can be said to represent the 'termination' of Classic Mayan culture – from the year 909, two years after its nearest competitor far away at Uxmal and a full century after cities such as Palenque had fallen silent. A century later, Toniná itself was almost entirely abandoned, but some time after 1000 the site was occupied by a more primitive, non-Mayan people called the Cheneks, who knocked the heads off many of the city's statues perhaps in an attempt to 'terminate' their magical power.

rarely prevent foreigners from travelling down it, although your papers must be in order. There is another road to Miramar via Comitán and Las Margaritas which is actually shorter, but as this goes through the Zapatista 'headquarters' at La Realidad military checkpoints are liable to be more obstructive.

Tourist Information

Ocosingo t (919–)
Tourist Office: The bar-kiosk in the plaza also functions as a very basic information desk.
Banks: Banamex, on the plaza, has an ATM but doesn't change money; Banca Serfín, a block north on C/ Central Norte, changes travellers' cheques.
Internet Access: There are two Internet shops, **Tu Espacio** and **Red Toniná**, almost next to each other near Banca Serfín on the corner of Av. 1 Norte and C/ Central.
Post Office: On C/ 1 Oriente, four blocks north of the plaza.

Where to Stay and Eat

Ocosingo t (919–)
Hotel Central, Av. Central 5, Ocosingo, t 673 0024 (*cheap*). Simple but decently kept hotel on the main plaza. Some rooms, with fans and TV, have views over the square. It

also has an enjoyable if straightforward **restaurant**, La Montura (*cheap*), with a terrace that's a great spot for taking in the local scene.
Rancho Esmeralda, off the Toniná road, f 673 0711, *ranchoes@mundomaya.com.mx* (*inexpensive*). Star accommodation in this area is this 'guest ranch', in a beautiful setting east of Ocosingo, run by Glen Wersch and Ellen Jones. They're very welcoming, and guests stay in pretty cabins with their own porches and fine views, while large-scale meals using garden produce are served. There are good shared showers, RV space, and they also grow their own coffee and macadamia nuts. It's an enjoyable walk from Toniná, and other activities can be arranged, especially 3–4hr trips on horseback through the valley.
El Candil, Av. 1 Norte, corner of C/ 1 Oriente, Ocosingo (*moderate*). Popular restaurant, a block from the plaza, with a friendly feel and generous versions of local dishes.
There are some more *cheap* restaurants and pizzerias around the square.

Laguna Miramar
At Emiliano Zapata, 7km from the lake, a community ecotourism scheme has been set up with *palapas* beneath which you can camp or sling a hammock, as well as some indoor beds. There's also a kitchen that provides simple meals (*cheap*).

You approach Toniná through a very green valley (past a large military command centre) until, 14 kilometres from Ocosingo, you reach the site entrance and museum. From there you see nothing of the ruins, but you walk on down a wooded path that flanks the main hill of Toniná and brings you up into a very unusual **Sunken Ballcourt**, built down into the temple platform. A panel has been found indicating that it was dedicated by Baaknal-Chaak in 699 to commemorate several of his victories. Then, if you turn back on yourself to the right, you will see the great centre of Toniná. It is in effect one vast, pyramid-like structure, facing towards the south, an extraordinary succession of stairways, levels and ledges sweeping up a giant hillside. With massive ramps of stone and steps, some with strange patterns in the stonework, it can look like an enormous abstract sculpture, or a dream-city out of Fritz Lang's *Metropolis*. There is no better example of the cult of awe and height in Mayan building.

The **Great Plaza** of Toniná, beyond the ballcourt at the foot of the mountain-city, has been completely cleared, so that its size can be fully appreciated. There will usually be some men around offering their services as guides, who can be very useful in pointing out parts of the giant structure that might otherwise be hard to find. Right at the lowest level, beyond a well known as the **Cenote Sagrado**, they can show you a mysterious **labyrinth** with a jaguar-mouth entrance, which was probably a tomb. Beyond that you begin the ascent: Toniná is a serious climb, as you zigzag your way up through great walls of steps and stairways, interlocked and incorporated into the natural formation of the hill with enormous ingenuity. On the next level up is a fine stucco frieze of vision serpents and the city's lords. Above that and also to the right is the **Palace** of Toniná. It has some similarities to the Palacio at Palenque, but is a great deal less elegant and open, feeling as much like a bandit's lair as a palace.

After another stiff climb you come to the most important section of Toniná, a broad flat level known as the **Sixth Platform**. To the right there is an enclosure, protected by a tin roof, with some of the most remarkable of all Mayan stucco carvings, discovered in 1992. Known as the ***Mural of the Four Eras***, this combines, making the usual Mayan parallels between this world and the next, images from the history of Toniná with others from the myth of the Hero-Twins. It is split into four sections by a strange X-shaped frame, believed to represent a type of scaffold and portal to the Otherworld on which sacrifices were sometimes put to death; in them are images of the four eras of creation that the Maya believed the world had passed through, the Suns of each cycle represented by human heads. Best-preserved is a tremendous frieze showing a fearsome skeleton figure, the image of one of the Lords of Death with whom the Twins struggled in Xibalba. At the bottom there is a rat in a loincloth standing upright, 'Precious First Rat', thought to be the rat who first showed the Hero Twins their ballgame equipment, and so another creature of the Otherworld.

In front of the frieze are two very large thrones, while behind it lies the huge, monumental **Temple of the Earth Monster**. On the banked front of the next rise there are more stucco carvings. This level, the **Seventh Platform**, is the last, in the middle of which is a small temple with wonderfully natural carved figures of Toniná *ahauob* and nobles around the base. Behind this, however, there are still two more pyramids, the tallest of which really is the summit of Toniná, reached by scrambling up a path at the back, since the main steps are in a poor state. At the very top there's a small inner sanctum, the **Temple of the Smoking Mirror**. The most famous discovery at the city was found near here in 1989, a massive statue-*stela* known as the **Zots-Choj** ('Bat-Tiger'), although it represents a ruler whose name was more like 'Jaguar-Bird-Peccary' and probably became *ahau* in 568. A strange, almost oriental-looking effigy, it has become a symbol of Toniná. The summit is also the last place to look down and take in the whole astonishing structure, and the view for miles over the hills to the south.

Toniná's **museum** (labelled in Spanish only), near the entrance, is in a light, timber-roofed new building and has some superb treasures. As well as the Zots-Choj himself there are *ahau*-statues in the same stocky Toniná style, enormously powerful but very subtly carved. There are remarkable stucco panels, jewellery and a superb collection of painted ceramics showing scenes of court life in the city. Not the least awe-inspiring is a modern relief model of Classic Toniná, bringing out just how strange a fantasy-city this was. As it was a single, interlocking complex rather than a series of separate structures, its builders could extend even further the Mayan liking for connections and cosmic symbolism; in the arrangement of levels and the number of doors, steps and temples, the whole monumental city could be read as one giant representation of the calendar and the Mayan myths.

Laguna Miramar

Some 130 kilometres (but a five-hour drive) southeast of Ocosingo down a long, bumpy dirt track off the Toniná road is Laguna Miramar, the largest of the Lacandón jungle lakes. Marcos cited its beauty as one reason why he has stayed in Chiapas. It's surrounded by scarcely touched forest with some of the rarest Lacandón wildlife – howler monkeys, jaguars, dazzling birds – and the lake itself is full of fish, turtles and other aquatic life. Near the lake, the *ejido* **Emiliano Zapata** operates a community ecotourism scheme where you can stay, though conditions are very simple. Forest guides can be arranged, and canoes hired on the lake (around $10 a day), which is also said to be wonderful for scuba diving.

San Cristóbal de Las Casas

Arrive in San Cristóbal from the sticky north on a morning in April or May and you immediately notice two things: the air and the light. Both are dazzlingly, crystalline clear and fresh. This is only one aspect of the weather in the valley of Jovel. On another day you can wake up amid a cold, damp fog, which turns to soupy humidity for a brief hour as the sun rises and burns off the mist, giving way to superb moun-tain sunshine through the middle of the day, only to be followed by what looks like a wet English afternoon as the sky clouds over before the day ends with icy, spitting rain. It's almost as if San Cristóbal were a volatile world in miniature. Another thing you may notice as you arrive are explosions. This is not because the Zapatistas have reappeared, but because in the Highlands it is traditional for celebrations to be marked with fireworks. There is always something being celebrated in the city.

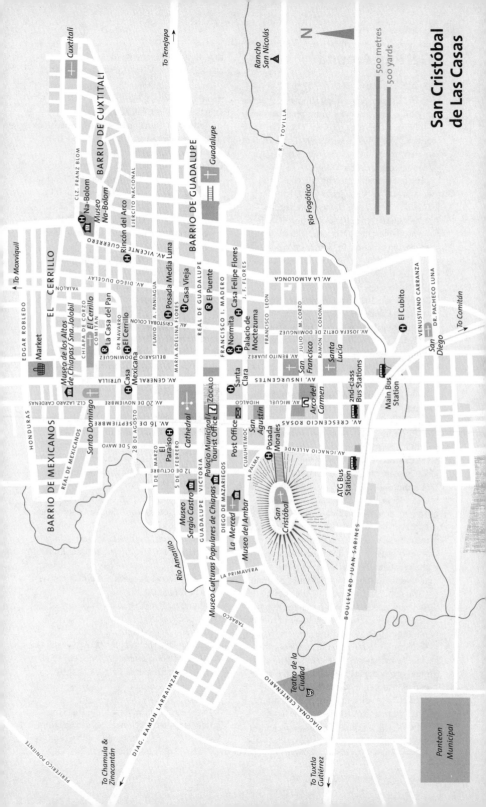

San Cristóbal de Las Casas

N

Rancho
San Nicolás

500 metres
500 yards

To Tenejapa

Cuxtitali

BARRIO DE CUXTITALI

CLZ. FRANZ BLOM

Na-Bolom
Museo Na-Bolom

Rincón del Arco

EJERCITO NACIONAL

AV. VICENTE GUERRERO

AV. DIEGO DUGELAY

YAJALON

To Moxviquil

EL CERRILLO

EDGAR ROBLEDO

Market

Museo de los Altos de Chiapas/ Sna Jolobil

CLZ. LAZARO CARDENAS

Santo Domingo

El Cerrillo
La Casa del Pan
COMITAN
El Cerrillo
CHIAPA DE CORZO
Casa Mexicana
DE NAVARRO

BARRIO DE MEXICANOS

HONDURAS

REAL DE MEXICANOS

28 DE MAYO

AV. 20 DE NOVIEMBRE

AV. GENERAL UTRILLA

BELISARIO DOMINGUEZ

FLAVIO A. PANIAGUA

MARIA ADELINA FLORES

CRISTOBAL COLON

REAL DE GUADALUPE

Posada Media Luna

Casa Vieja

El Puente

BARRIO DE GUADALUPE

Guadalupe

Río Fogótico

R. TOVILLA

Normita
Casa Felipe Flores
Palacio de Moctezuma
J. F. FLORES
FRANCISCO I. MADERO
FRANCISCO LEON
FRANCISCO SARABIA

Santa Clara

AV. INSURGENTES

San Francisco

San Julio M. CORZO
AV. BENITO JUAREZ
RAMON CORONA
RAMON

Santa Lucía

AV. LA ALMOLONGA

El Cubito

VENUSTIANO CARRANZA

AV. JOSEFA ORTIZ DE DOMINGUEZ

San Diego

DR. PACHECO LUNA

To Comitán

Cathedral

Palacio Municipal/ Tourist Office

ZOCALO

Post Office

San Agustín

Arco del Carmen

AV. MIGUEL HIDALGO

AV. CRESCENCIO ROSAS

2nd-class Bus Stations

Main Bus Station

El Paraíso
AV. 16 DE SEPTIEMBRE
5 DE MAYO
1 DE MARZO
12 DE OCTUBRE
5 DE FEBRERO

Museo Sergio Castro

GUADALUPE

VICTORIA

DIEGO DE MAZARIEGOS

Museo Culturas Populares de Chiapas

La Merced
Museo del Ambar

CUAUHTEMOC

LA PALMA

Posada Morales

AV. IGNACIO ALLENDE

ATG Bus Station

San Cristóbal

BOULEVARD JUAN SABINES

Río Amarillo

LA PRIMAVERA

TABASCO

DIAG. RAMON LARRAINZAR

PERIFERICO PONIENTE

To Chamula & Zinacantán

DIAGONAL CENTENARIO

Teatro de la Ciudad

To Tuxtla Gutiérrez

Panteón Municipal

Getting Around

By Air

San Cristóbal has a small **airport** west of the city, big enough only for turbo-props. **Aeromar,** (in Tuxtla Gutiérrez, **t** (961) 615 0552), has the only regular services, with daily flights to and from Mexico City, and also hopes to begin a Mérida–San Cristóbal service.

Fog is a problem, causing diversions and delays. Many people get to San Cristóbal via Tuxtla Gutiérrez, which has more regular services (*see* p.506). Various airport transfers are available, and **Tuxtla airport taxis** will take you to San Cristóbal for a price (around $45).

By Bus

Virtually every bus company has its own depot in San Cristóbal, but most are in more or less the same area, where the Avenidas running south from the centre meet the Highway. The most important **first-class terminus**, normally referred to as the Cristóbal Colón but shared by Altos, Maya de Oro, ADO, Uno and some other companies, is at the corner of the Highway and Av. Insurgentes. Opposite on the south side of the Highway is the depot of Transportes Rodolfo Figueroa (TRF), running **first-** and **second-class** services within Chiapas. Along the Highway west of the Cristóbal Colón (between Insurgentes and Av. Crescencio Rojas) there are the garages of more **second-class** lines, especially Transportes Lacandonia. Off the Highway and three blocks from Insurgentes on Av. Ignacio Allende is Autotransportes Tuxtla (ATG), with **first-** and **second-class** routes. This fragmentation can seem confusing, but it leaves you spoilt for choice: no matter where you're going, there always seems to be a bus about to go there.

The depots do not exhaust the possibilities, for if you walk out along the same stretch of the Highway you will find gaggles of *combis* waiting to fill up a load, their drivers shouting 'Comitán, Comitán', 'Tuxtla, Tuxtla' or other places you may not have heard of. The other great *combi* departure-point is at the other end of Insurgentes/General Utrilla by the market: here you'll find *combis* to Chamula, Zinacantán and other Highland villages.

There is an **international bus service** from San Cristóbal, a three-times-a-week 'shuttle'

to Antigua in Guatemala run by the ATC tour agency (*see* below). Full fare to Antigua is $60.

Between the different bus companies the main services are these:

Cancún (*17hrs*): via **Palenque, Escárcega, Chetumal, Tulum** and **Playa del Carmen,** four first-class daily from Cristóbal Colón; three daily ATG via Mérida. Fare $46–$58.

Comitán (*1½hrs*), **Ciudad Cuauhtémoc** (for Guatemala, *3hrs*) and **Motozintla:** at least 12 first-class daily (Cristóbal Colón, ATG, TRF) and frequent second-class (ATG, TRF) and *combis*. Six Altos buses (from Cristóbal Colón) continue to **Tapachula.** Fare to Ciudad Cuauhtémoc about $5.

Mérida (*16hrs*): via **Palenque, Escárcega** and **Campeche,** two first-class daily from Cristóbal Colón (9.30am, 5.30pm); three daily ATG. Fare $34–$44.

Mexico City (*19hrs*): two luxury and four ordinary first-class daily from Cristóbal Colón, one from ATG. Fare about $58.

Oaxaca (*12hrs*): one luxury and two ordinary first-class daily from Cristóbal Colón. Fare $28–$32.

Palenque (*5hrs*) via Ocosingo: at least 16 first-class (from Cristóbal Colón, ATG, TRF) and frequent second-class (ATG, TRF, Lacandonia) daily. TRF first-class and all second-class stop at **Crucero Agua Azul,** and there are many *combis*. First-class fare around $10.

Tapachula (*8hrs*): via **Tuxtla Gutiérrez** and **Tonalá,** four first-class; several second-class daily, TRF; six Altos first-class from Cristóbal Colón via **Comitán** and **Ciudad Cuauhtémoc.** Fare about $15.

Tuxtla Gutiérrez (*2–3hrs*): 11 first-class daily from Cristóbal Colón, five from ATG, four with TRF; second-class every half-hour with TRF and every hour with ATG via Chiapa de Corzo. Fare $4–$5.

Villahermosa: two first-class daily from Cristóbal Colón and three from ATG via **Palenque** (*7½hrs*), and one Cristóbal Colón first-class via Highway 195 (*8hrs*). Several TRF and Lacandonia *intermedio* and second-class buses on both routes. First-class fare $17.

By Car

To the east and the west there are Pemex *gasolineras* on the Highway. Some trips from San Cristóbal are better made with a tour than your own transport; a car is particularly useful around Comitán and Montebello, especially for Tenam Puente.

Car Hire

Of late there have been only two agencies: **Budget**, Hotel Mansión del Valle, C/ Diego de Mazariegos 39, **t** 678 3100, *acoutinol@info sel.net.mx*. Efficient, friendly and reliable (from around $55 a day). Decent drop-off rates and negotiable longer term rates.

Excellent Rent-a-Car, Turística Chan-Bahlum, Av. Real de Guadalupe 26-G, **t/f** 678 7656, *www.excellent.com.mx*. Can appear cheaper but note that quoted prices may not include tax, full mileage and so on.

By Taxi

San Cristóbal has the usual plentiful supply of **taxis** (most journeys within the city cost about $1.70). Many drivers will take on longer trips if you agree a price.

By Bicycle

San Cristóbal's shortish distances and low level of traffic make it easily cyclable, if you don't mind cobbled hills. Try the following:

Los Pingüinos, Av. 5 de Mayo 10-B, near corner of C/ 5 de Febrero, **t** 678 0202. Rents bikes; offers bike tours to places out of the city.

Cafetería del Centro, C/ Real de Guadalupe 15. Also has bikes for rent, very cheaply.

Orientation

The Pan-American Highway, **Highway 190** (**Blvd Juan Sabines** in the city), runs along the south side of San Cristóbal. To the west it goes towards Tuxtla Gutiérrez and Villahermosa; to the east it bends south toward Comitán and to meet the Palenque road, 199. From the corner on the Highway by the first-class bus station, **Av. Insurgentes** leads up seven blocks to the main square and the centre of town. Central San Cristóbal has a simple colonial grid, with streets with names; north–south are Avenidas, east–west are usually Calles. The only peculiarity is that streets change identity on either side of the main axis from the plaza.

Most of the city is very walkable, but local *combis* can be useful for places such as Na Bolom that are far from the centre.

Tourist Information

San Cristóbal de Las Casas **t** (967–)

Tourist Office: in Palacio Municipal, northwest corner of the plaza (*open Mon–Sat 9–8, Sun 9–2*). Just as interesting as the helpful staff are the racks with leaflets and flyers from virtually every café, bike-hire shop and tour operation in San Cristóbal; there are always new ones starting up, and you can often find ads offering rooms to rent.

Banks: Mostly around the plaza; efficiency is variable (**BITAL** is usually quickest), but all have ATMs (*usually closed afternoons or on Sat*). **Cambio Lacantún**, on C/ Real de Guadalupe 12-A, is a decent private change office (*open Mon–Sat until 7pm; closed Sun*).

Health: There's a **24-hr pharmacy** (corner of Diego de Mazariegos and Crescencio Rojas).

Internet Access: Among the city's positive overdose of these are: **Centro El Puente** (on C/ Real de Guadalupe 55A), which is friendly, and well-equipped with good rates; **Cybercafé** (in Pasaje Mazariegos, the arcade between Real de Guadalupe and Madero, in the next block to the Zócalo), which is more comfortable than most; also try **El Paso** (on Av. Insurgentes 77-A (a block from Cristóbal Colón bus station), a very useful place with left-luggage lockers, Internet access and a long-distance phone office.

Laundries: Two good, cheap ones promising same-day service are **Lavandería La Rapidita** (Av. Insurgentes 9) and **Tintorería Las Américas** (Av. 5 de Mayo 19, by the corner of C/ 5 de Febrero).

Post Office: Corner of C/ Cuauhtémoc and Av. Crescencio Rojas, a block from the plaza. Has Mexpost (*open Mon–Fri 8–7, Sat 9–noon*).

Tours, Tour Agencies and Guides

As in Palenque, there are many agencies in San Cristóbal running tours to the region's attractions. As well as 'well-trodden' routes such as Chamula, day excursions by *combi* to more remote Highland villages are sometimes available, but finding them is a matter of asking around or checking the tourist office flyers; Alex & Raúl (*see* below) and some agencies will also arrange such trips on request. Several other guides and agencies also offer horseback treks.

With variations, the usual itineraries and prices are:

Chamula and **Zinacantán**, with **Tenejapa** sometimes included (around $11 per person).

Chiapa de Corzo and **Sumidero Gorge** ($24).

Comitán and the **Montebello Lakes** ($25).

Toniná, often together with **Agua Azul** and **Misol-Ha** ($24).

Palenque, Misol-Ha and **Agua Azul** (from $35).

Many agencies also offer 2- or 3-day trips to Palenque, Bonampak and Yaxchilán (3 days, from around $140, group discounts available). Organized trips are most useful for getting to Chamula and Zinacantán, and the Sumidero, where tours save the trouble of organizing transport. Palenque and the waterfalls are better visited directly from Palenque. Comitán and Montebello is the key area where you can do more if you travel independently. In choosing a tour similar considerations apply as in Palenque (see p.437). It is worth checking what is included, as this can vary; not all the operators include Amatenango in trips to Comitán, and in Chamula some only take you to the central area, while with the best guides you can walk around the village.

Tour Agencies

ATC, Av. 16 de Septiembre 16, **t** 678 2550, *www.atctours.com.mx*. Organizes rafting, trekking and other adventure tours in Chiapas. Also has its own bus service three days a week to Antigua and Guatemala, the 'Maya Shuttle'.

Explora Ecoturismo y Aventura, C/ 1 de Marzo 45, **t** 678 4295, *www.prodigy.web.com.mx*. Although San Cristóbal-based this doesn't follow the standard local routes, but offers eco- and adventure trips mainly to three destinations: Lacanjá, where it has its own camp site and offers trips to Bonampak and Yaxchilán together with forest exploration and rafting; the forest and kayaking on the Río Lacantún near Pico de Oro and Las Guacamayas (both destinations, six days, $520); and rafting down the Río La Venta gorge west of Tuxtla (four days, $395).

Los Pingüinos (see Getting Around By Bike, above). Organizes bike tours.

Na Bolom Centre (see p.481, p.489). Runs tours to Chamula and Zinacantán, and 4-day trips to the Lacandón jungle.

Pronatura Chiapas, C/ Real de Guadalupe 23 & Av. Benito Juárez 11-B, **t/f** 678 5000, *www.pro natura.org.mx*. Local branch of the Mexican conservation organization, responsible for and running trips to two locations: Huitepec nature reserve, and the recently opened-up reserve and Mayan ruins at Moxviquil (see pp.497–8, p.489). Numbers are small, so enquire ahead; trips may also be organized to more remote places in the mountains, and it's worth checking. Their shop is on Real de Guadalupe, the offices around the corner.

Red de Turismo Comunitario, C/ Real de Mexicanos 16, **t** 678 9601, *turismocomuni tariochiapas@yahoo.com*. Not an agency but the 'Community Tourism Network', an association that brings together low-level and ecologically sustainable projects throughout Chiapas, among them Laguna Miramar (see p.470), a rafters' cooperative in the Montebello lakes, local guides near Ocosingo and Pronatura. So far its main regular activity is 'The Indigenous Face of San Cristóbal', a guided tour through community projects in the city, such as the Maya Ik textile cooperative and the centre for traditional Mayan medicine, but trips in other parts of the state are planned. Tours can be in English.

Viajes Navarra, C/ Real de Guadalupe 15-D, **t** 678 1143, *navarra@mundomaya.com.mx*. Established agency offering all the standard tours but also Chamula and Zinacantán on horseback, a good list of 'nature walk' tours around San Cristóbal (Huitepec, the Arcotete and mountains outside the city), as well as trips to Laguna Miramar or Guatemala.

Zapata Tours, Av. Insurgentes 19, **t/f** 674 5152, *zapatatours@yahoo.com.mx*. This agency, above Madre Tierra vegetarian restaurant, has a friendly, helpful approach, and a book-shop and Internet café. As well as good rates for the usual destinations it has adventure trips to Lacanjá, Bonampak, Montebello, Naha and (on request) remoter places, and will tailor itineraries to customers' needs.

Independent Guides

Some of the very best and most rewarding trips from San Cristóbal are those made with independent guides, especially those to the Highland villages. Guides advertise in the tourist office, but the following operate permanently and come highly recommended:

Alex & Raúl, t 678 3741: these two are in the square daily at 9.30am, by their blue *combi* in front of the Cathedral. Their main route is Chamula-Zinacantán, but they can also organize horseback treks, especially on the beautiful 10-km mountain trail to Chamula, as well as a full range of longer trips around Chiapas on request (with prior notice).

Mercedes Hernández: The 'lady with the umbrella' can be found (you'll recognize her by her big golf umbrella) every day in the Zócalo at 9am, ready to take groups to Chamula and Zinacantán. A one-woman band, she's the daughter of a Zinacanteco father and *mestizo* mother, and her tours, given in individual but very good English, are real performances: they follow no fixed script, but on the way you will learn an enormous amount.

Festivals

San Cristóbal has an intricate calendar of *fiestas* and celebrations. Every *barrio* has its *fiesta*, centred on the saint's day at the local church. Most follow a common pattern. On the eve of the main saint's day the *barrio* is woken up early by a bigger than usual barrage of rockets, an invitation to the *fiesta*, and all day people prepare the church and the image of the saint, leaving it garlanded in flowers, herbs, coloured paper and lace. This work is an event in itself: while it goes on *marimbas* play at the church door, and women bring flowers escorted by *mariachis*. After dark come the *maitines*, when the *barrio* meets up to visit the saint in its completed finery. There's a dance in the plaza outside, amid more fireworks. The morning of the main day is the most religious moment in the *fiesta*, when the saint is carried in procession, giving way to a lighter mood as the music and fairground attractions pick up through the evening. The tourist office has information on *fiestas* that are coming up. The biggest city-wide celebrations are **Semana Santa** (*Easter Week*) and **St Christopher** (*25 July*), when virtually the whole city climbs the Cerrito de San Cristóbal to watch the valley below explode with fireworks.

Among the most important dates in the calendar are the following:

Corpus Christi, *late May*.

Santo Domingo, *8 Aug*.

All Saints' and the **Day of the Dead**, *1–2 Nov*. On these days, as in all Mexico, cemeteries are visited.

Guadalupe, *12 Dec*. Everyone climbs up the hill of Guadalupe.

Christmas and **Epiphany** (Three Kings), *6 Jan*.

Learning Spanish and Mayan Languages

The city's atmosphere and its low prices make San Cristóbal an enjoyable place to learn Spanish. Schools can organize homestays with local families, or you can arrange your own accommodation; most schools offer a range of activities as well as the basic course. Classes in Tzotzil and Tzeltal may also be organized at times by these schools or by Na Bolom. If you fancy a more radical option, it's now possible to study Spanish and Tzotzil in the Zapatista village of **Oventic**, north of San Cristóbal. The pricing policy is based on the minimum wage in a student's country of origin, and it's very cheap; income goes towards providing schools for the community. For full information, look at *www.schoolsforchiapas.org*, or call the support organization (in San Diego, US) on **t** (619) 232 2841.

Centro Bilingüe El Puente, C/ Real de Guadalupe 55, **t** 678 3723, *http://mundo-maya.com.mx/centrob*. Standard courses of 15 hours' tuition a week and homestays from $170 per week, with discounts if two or more people register together. Intensive classes are available, and programmes can be adapted to individual needs. El Puente also gives English classes for locals, including exchanges with the English students, and tours, excursions and activities (e.g. cookery workshops) are available at low cost.

Instituto Jovel, C/ María Adelina Flores 21, **t/f** 678 4069, *www.mexonline.com/jovel.htm*. Courses with homestays from $170 per week, with flexible timetables and small-group classes. Also exchanges with local English students, and activity workshops (cookery, Mayan weaving).

Shopping

With Mérida, San Cristóbal is the region's great centre for **traditional handicrafts**, above all Highland **Maya textiles**. You are offered small pieces of weaving, together with the now-universal Zapatista dolls, all over the city centre, by Indian women and children sitting along the pavement. The largest concentration, though, is in the **Mercado Indígena** around Santo Domingo, where you can find belts and other things (and a fair amount of junk) as well as textiles. These are very varied: tablecloths, waistcoats, scarves and more, all colourful and attractive, although those produced for tourists may not be skilfully worked. Nor are they necessarily made by the people selling them, for textiles from Guatemala are now common in the markets.

The cooperatives like Sna Jolobil (*see* below) are the best places to find traditional **local weaving** of fine quality. Prices are higher than in the market, but one aim of the cooperatives is to ensure that Highland women gain a fair price for their skills and work.

The main market north of Santo Domingo is in general too practical for souvenirs, except maybe **earthenware pots** from Amatenango. An assortment of **chilis and spices** can make a great buy, if you don't mind carrying them over international borders. **Amber** is one of the great specialities of Chiapas, and plenty of shops here sell fine amber jewellery.

Another San Cristóbal feature is its browser-friendly **bookshops**, most of which have stock in English and other languages as well as Spanish, especially on Chiapas and the Maya.

Recommended Shops

El Arbol de la Vida, C/ Real de Guadalupe 27–28A. Largest branch of the city's foremost amber specialist, with fine jewellery at high-ish prices. Several more branches are nearby.

Casa de las Artesanías de Chiapas, Av. Miguel Hidalgo, corner of C/ Niños Héroes. The official state handicrafts showcase covers all Chiapas, with a fascinating variety of work from other areas as well as the Highlands: leather from around Tuxtla, ceramics and basketwork, even some Lacandón crafts, at relatively high prices. An attractive museum is attached, labelled in Spanish and English.

El Encuentro, C/ Real de Guadalupe 63-A. Has a huge stock of superior Chiapas and Guatemalan textiles, leatherwork and toys.

Librería Chilam Balam, Casa Utrilla, Av. General Utrilla 33. Perhaps the most varied, engaging bookshop, with a likeably disorderly stock: particularly good on art and the Maya.

Maya Ik', C/ Real de Guadalupe 69. Mayan women's cooperative, affiliated to the Red de Turismo Comunitario, selling textiles and ceramics from Highland communities.

Sna Jolobil, Convento de Santo Domingo, Calzada Lázaro Cárdenas. 'The House of the Weavers' is the longest established Mayan weavers' cooperative and a superb showcase for the best Highland textiles. It's also a charming 'museum' of weaving, run by women so quiet and contained they (unintentionally) make any *gringo* appear clumsy.

SODAM-J'pas Jovabetik, Casa Utrilla, Av. General Utrilla 33. In the patio of the Casa Utrilla, this cooperative includes men as well as women, and so has traditional wooden toys, baskets and other items as well as textiles.

El Telar, C/ Real de Guadalupe 57. Original, innovative and very attractive textile designs, not traditional, but produced with or based on traditional techniques.

Where to Stay

San Cristóbal de Las Casas t (967–)

San Cristóbal is a city, like Mérida, where the traditional architecture of plant-filled patios makes for wonderfully characterful hotels. For once, a/c and pools are not significant considerations; more important (especially Nov–Feb) is some form of heating. It's worth asking what provision a hotel has: some have rooms with beautiful fireplaces and provide wood. San Cristóbal's hotels are exceptional value, and *moderate* ones are equivalent to *expensive* ones elsewhere. At the budget end, the city offers an exceptional range of rock-bottom accommodation, several offering dorm-style beds for under $5. Budget places are most concentrated in two areas: the streets north of the bus stations, and east of the Zócalo up Real de Guadalupe and Madero. Across the board, prices are lower outside Christmas, the Easter season and July–Aug.

Expensive

Casa Felipe Flores, C/ Dr JF Flores 36, t/f 678 3996, in USA t (616) 469 5824, *www.felipe flores.com*. An 18th-century patio house restored and decorated with antiques to provide truly distinctive accommodation. There are four double rooms with en suite bathrooms; the tower room is especially pretty. Ample meals are served in the equally lovely dining room, there's a lounge with books, and the house is hosted warmly by Nancy and David Orr, who can advise on possible tours, bike rentals etc. The house can also be rented complete ($1,500 a week).

Moderate

Casa Mexicana, C/ 28 de Agosto 1, corner of Av. General Utrilla, t 678 0698, *www.casamexi-cana.com.mx*. Brainchild of artist Gabriel Suárez and his wife Kiki, this venerable mansion has been renovated and then filled with artwork, original photography and traditional crafts. The indoor-garden patio (with Los Magüeyes **restaurant**, *see* below) is wonderfully lush, and the rooms are very pretty, if slightly short of light. Those in the newer annexe are in the same style and a bit larger. Services include a car park, a sauna, massage room and Jacuzzis in the suites.

Casa Vieja, C/ María Adelina Flores 27, t/f 678 6868, *www.casavieja.com.mx*. Elegant hotel in a 1740s mansion, restored in the 1990s. Its rooms combine modern bathrooms, TV, phones and other fittings with traditional wooden furniture and artwork, although some are a bit dark. The suites are excellent, and the distinctly baronial one in an old tower (*luxury*) is spectacular.

El Paraíso, Av. 5 de Febrero 19, t 678 0085, *www.mexonline.com/hparaiso.htm*. Another old, patio-style house, given a chic uplift in powder blue and rag-rolled terracotta. The rooms are as distinctively elegant as the public areas; they're quite small, and those by the street can be noisy, but it's exceptional value, and has a stylish **restaurant** serving Mexican and European dishes.

Rincón del Arco, C/ Ejército Nacional 66, t 678 1313, *www.mundomaya.com.mx/hernanz*. More isolated, in El Cerrillo (a 15-min walk from the centre) this remains one of the star old-house hotels. Rooms are cheaper than others in this bracket, but of equal standard and stamped with antique character; they're also spacious, and most have fireplaces for which wood is provided free. The rambling mansion also has a bar and **restaurant**, but its biggest asset is the magnificent garden; rooms with garden views are exceptional.

Inexpensive

Hotel El Cerrillo, Av. Belisario Domínguez 27, t 678 1283. Bargain patio-hotel in El Cerrillo (a 10-min walk from the centre). Its rooms, decorated with traditional art, are as good as some *moderate* rooms, and there's a pretty **restaurant**. Still more striking are its eccentric 'cabins' on the roof, one with an all-glass wall; all have several beds, working out ultra-economical for groups. An engaging, quirky place, amid peaceful surroundings.

Hotel Palacio de Moctezuma, Av. Benito Juárez 16, t 678 0352. This wins the local patio prize, boasting three of them, each flower-filled. It also has bargain rooms with phones, TV and decent fittings, loads of quirky character, equally pretty bars and a **restaurant**.

Hotel Santa Clara, Av. Insurgentes 1, t/f 678 1140. Pride of place on the Zócalo goes to this venerable hotel, occupying the 16th-century Casa de la Sirena. It's a delightful maze of wooden staircases and balconies, with a pretty **restaurant**, and in one of the patios there's even a small pool. In winter it can be pretty chilly; prices are nearer *moderate*.

Na Bolom, Av. Vicente Guerrero 33, t 678 1418, *www.ecosur.mx/nabolom*. The guest rooms at Na Bolom (*see* p.490), each with bathroom, are individually furnished with Mayan artefacts and local textiles. They're in great demand, especially by study groups, and need to be booked well in advance. The atmosphere is special, and meals, in the Bloms' dining room, are occasions to meet people and talk. The food, featuring southern Mexican specialities and organic produce from the garden, has a high reputation. Rates are at the top of this category.

Cheap

Bungalows El Cubito, Av. Benito Juárez 92, t 678 1963. These brick cabins, set in a huge garden full of pines and lilies up a driveway, are a boon for anyone wanting to stay more than a few nights. The cottages (two units in each building) show their age, but are fully self-contained with kitchens, bathrooms and a living area, and they have fireplaces. They're a bargain (about $110 per week, $270 per month) and are also available by the day. Light, gas and maid service are included.

Hotel Fray Bartolomé de Las Casas, Av. Insurgentes 2, t 678 0932. Perhaps cheapest of the historic-patio hotels, this has shady, atmospheric rooms, a breakfast **café** and friendly staff. Very enjoyable when it's bright, but chilly when the weather turns.

Hotel-Posada Lucella, Av. Insurgentes 55, t 678 0956. Despite an unprepossessing frontage this is the best of the budget hotels near the bus stations. There's a cosy patio, and all rooms have showers and TV. They're simple but bright and clean, and the owners are friendly and helpful.

Posada Doña Rosita, C/ Francisco Madero 35, t 678 1067, *393@correoweb.com*. This is a backpackers' hostel with simple but well-kept, clean rooms, a cosy atmosphere, and a lot of extras: breakfast is included, there's a roof terrace, an open kitchen and even a laundry. There are very cheap dorm beds, or double rooms with or without showers.

Posada Media Luna, C/ María A. Flores 24 and C/ José F. Flores 1, t 678 8814/678 1658, *paint49@hotmail.com*. Very likeable budget option with rooms in two buildings that are simple but spacious and brightly decorated. There are dorm-like rooms (very *cheap*), or single rooms with shared bath or showers (just *inexpensive*). The María A. Flores rooms share showers but the house is more attractive, with a living room with TV (and over 600 videos), Internet access, and an open kitchen. Continental breakfast is very cheap.

Posada Los Morales, Av. Ignacio Allende 17, t 678 1472. Another great find: self-contained 'bungalows' are spread around an eccentric garden overflowing with flowers, in a quiet street on the hill of San Cristóbal. They're available for any period of time and, while simple and well worn, offer all the basic services and plenty of character, and have lots of room, fireplaces and terraces from which to take in the view. The owners are extremely welcoming, and there's a great **restaurant** (*see* below) of the same name.

Camping

Rancho San Nicolás, t 678 0057, *sannicolas-camping@hotmail.com*. Full hook-ups for RVs, good showers and some simple cabins (*cheap*) as well as camping space in a peaceful setting near the Fogótico river. Don't believe the flyers saying it's a 15-min walk from the centre: it's about 2km; head east from Insurgentes up C/ Francisco León.

Eating Out

The traditional cuisine of San Cristóbal, *cocina coleta*, is quite singular. The city has adapted to its American surroundings in some dishes – pumpkin soup (*sopa de flor de calabaza*), *tamales* – but has dug its heels in with others, and continues to eat more Spanish-looking hams and sausages, grilled meats and *estofado de carnero* (lamb stew with chili) than almost any other part of Mexico. Another tradition is wonderful breads. Among local dishes that are more Mexican than Spanish are *chalupas*, the equivalent of the Yucatán's *panuchos* and *salbutes*, small snack-sized *tortillas* with a variety of toppings.

Local specialities do not exhaust the range available, for San Cristóbal's popularity as a multi-national bohemian focus has had a big impact on its restaurants. In particular, it has the best vegetarian restaurants in southern Mexico. Vegetarian dishes are also available at Na Bolom (reservations needed, *see* p.481) where non-residents can eat. The biggest concentration of cheap eating-places is on Av. Insurgentes, especially the *loncherías* and stalls near San Francisco.

Expensive

El Fogón de Jovel, Av. 16 de Septiembre 11, t 678 1153. The city's most prominent showcase for traditional Chiapanecan cooking, including some very enjoyable but rare country dishes. A block from the Cathedral, it's very pretty, not overly kitsch, and popular with locals.

Los Magueyes, Casa Mexicana, C/ 28 de Agosto 1, t 678 0698. The Casa Mexicana's restaurant is very pretty, and has a calm, comfortable atmosphere. Mexican dishes are generally better than the more ambitious-sounding international options.

Moderate

Café-Bar Los Amorosos, C/ Dr. José F. Flores 12A, corner of Av. Benito Juárez. A cultured venue, part of a 'writers' school', which often holds talks and readings (usually in Spanish). The rest of the time it's a snug bar-restaurant.

Café La Selva, C/ Crescencio Rojas 9, corner of Av. Cuauhtémoc. Chiapas complains that its coffee is shipped out and not so much as sniffed here, but San Cristóbal has several cafés. This is quite smart, with light, modern food to go with the main product.

La Casa del Pan, C/ Dr Navarro 10, *www.casadel pan.com*. The most celebrated vegetarian restaurant in town, run by American Kippy Nigh, author of a Mexican vegetarian cook book. It's pretty, mellow, and has a very good organic bakery and a handicrafts shop. *Open all day; closed Mon*.

Centro El Puente, C/ Real de Guadalupe 55. The language school (*see* p.479) café has vegetarian dishes, salads and standard Mexican fare, plus good coffee. *Open lunch and eves*.

Emiliano's Moustache, C/ Crescencio Rojas 7. Very popular *taquería* with all the Mexican classics made with fresh ingredients and served in a buzzy atmosphere.

La Galería, Av. Miguel Hidalgo 3, off the Zócalo. Mellow restaurant, popular with young locals and foreigners, made more attractive for occupying the stately patio and galleries of the house of Diego de Mazariegos, oldest in the city. The *conquistador* wouldn't recognize the food however; it specializes in pizza.

Madre Tierra, Av. Insurgentes 19. The 'other' vegetarian star, also featuring an irresistible organic bakery, the **Panadería Madre Tierra**. As well as in the dining room, imaginative meals may be served in a delightful garden.

Paris-Mexico, C/ Francisco Madero 20. The name reflects its owners' origins, the Left-Bank-meets-Chiapas style, and the menu. Hence, a warming French onion soup makes an alternative to *fajitas*. It's also one place that (sometimes) serves food after 11pm.

La Parrilla, Av. Belisario Domínguez 32, corner of C/ Dr Navarro. Very popular, very Mexican restaurant – in a small chain – renowned for steaks, *coleto* meats and *tacos* with melted cheese. Hefty portions, too. *Closed Mon*.

Posada Los Morales, Av. Ignacio Allende 17. The owners of the unusual hotel (*see* above) have recently opened this equally distinctive restaurant, with enjoyable local dishes charmingly served in a room furnished with a whole collection of antiques.

Cheap

Café Museo Café, C/ María Adelina Flores 10. Set up by a cooperative of small-scale coffee producers (*cmc@mundomaya.com.mx*) to showcase their organic produce. It's smart, cool, comfortable and spacious, and serves alcohol and good snacks as well as great coffee, available in many ways. Attached is an imaginative little **Museo del Café**.

Cafetería del Centro, C/ Real de Guadalupe 15. A backpacker's haven, with ultra-cheap set menus including vegetarian choices. It also has Internet terminals and bikes for rent.

El Gato Gordo, Av. Francisco Madero 28. Hip, cheap little semi-vegetarian café, with breakfasts, pastas and some meat dishes but also a full vegetarian lunch under $2.50.

Restaurante Alameda/Café de los Altos, Casa Utrilla, Av. General Utrilla 33. The patio café has enjoyable Mexican and *coleto* dishes, and is a very pleasant place to sit outside for breakfast or in the middle of the day.

Restaurant Normita, Av. Benito Juárez, corner of C/ Dr José Felipe Flores. For good local dishes in a warm, friendly environment, you can't beat this little *comedor familiar*. Its *platos coletos* – spare ribs or grilled *chorizos* – and Mexican standards are enormously generous, at very low prices There's a second branch at **Normita II**, Av. Insurgentes 5-A.

Entertainment and Nightlife

With so much street entertainment in *fiestas*, nightlife in San Cristóbal often consists of eating, drinking and talking, but the city has organized venues too. Mostly Mexican pop-rock bands share the stage with DJs at **Las Velas**, C/ Francisco Madero 14, and at **Blue**, Av. Crescencio Rojas 2. The Hotel Santa Clara has a pub-style bar on its ground floor, **Cocodrilo's**, with occasional live music. Films are often shown in English at the **Centro El Puente**. Apart from that, you just have to follow the sound of the *marimbas* and *mariachis*…

Nestling in its valley between high peaks, with its arcaded porticoes, time-polished cobbles, Baroque churches, and centuries-old houses with orange-ochre walls and solid gateways giving little away of their interiors, San Cristóbal is a city of deep shadows, patios and glimpses. It is perhaps the most atmospheric of all Mexico's colonial cities. While parts of Mérida can seem transplanted from Andalucía, San Cristóbal more readily recalls a Castilian hill town like Ávila or Toledo, hunkered down against the cold. It also has a very Castilian stateliness.

Simultaneously this is the capital of the Chiapas Highlands, where the Highland Maya – as well as forming a fast-growing proportion of the population of the city itself – come to buy, sell and interact with the outside world. Many men and virtually all the women wear the traditional dress of each community. In some of the city's Spanish churches they worship in their own way, kneeling on the floor surrounded by candles and pine needles. Although San Cristóbal was founded as a colonial island in an Indian sea, the Mayan presence is in every part of the modern city.

All this one might expect, but what is more surprising is that San Cristóbal is the only city in the Mexican south that could be called chic. In the 1960s artists, writers and others of the intellectual fraternity of Mexico City made it a favoured retreat, and they were joined by international bohemians on the famed Gringo Trail. San Cristóbal has trendy coffee shops, small jewellery stores, and shops where designers market their own clothes. It has more good bookshops than the rest of southern Mexico put together. This all adds to the mix. It confirms, perhaps, that this is a power point in the Mayan sense, a place where Mayan shamans, the Spanish Golden Age, backpackers, radicals from around the globe, *mariachis*, experimental infotechnology and Mexican poets can encounter each other, in a rare mountain valley.

History

The first Spaniards to arrive in the valley of Jovel were members of the expedition of Luis Marín in 1524 who, after a hard fight with the Maya of Chamula and Zinacantán, camped by the Río Amarillo, on the western side of the modern city, and commented among themselves that the location would make a fine site for a colony. It was four years later, however, that the real conqueror of Chiapas, Diego de Mazariegos, founded the *Villa* (later *Ciudad*) *Real de Chiapa* on the same site. Capital-to-be of Chiapas within the Spanish Kingdom of Guatemala, it was a classic colonial city as ordained by the *Leyes de Indias*: it had a grid and a plaza with sites marked out for a cathedral and Mazariegos' own residence, and two other main areas: one around the Monastery of Santo Domingo, and one to the south at El Carmen, both linked to the square by the same long, straight street, now Av. Insurgentes and Av. General Utrilla. It was more than usually defensive, since the town was several days' journey from the next Spanish settlement and surrounded by the only-recently subdued Chamulas, Zinacantecos and other Highland communities.

In 1537 the first friars arrived, of the Mercedarian order, and founded the Church of the Merced, to be followed in 1545 by the Dominicans under Bartolomé de Las Casas, who founded Santo Domingo. As the only Spanish town in a region with a large

Conscience of the Conquest: Las Casas

Since the Mexican Revolution San Cristóbal has had included in its name that of its most famous resident (at least before Marcos), Bartolomé de Las Casas, first Bishop of Chiapas. Once called 'the conscience of the Conquest', with a breadth of vision that did not seem to fit his time or place, he remains an inspiration to many today.

Las Casas was born in Sevilla in 1484, and grew up in the years when the city was electrified by the news of Columbus' first discoveries. His father signed up on Columbus' second voyage, and when he was 18 Las Casas himself, just after taking preliminary orders to become a priest, embarked for America as well. In his first years in the colonies he does not seem to have had clear opinions on the way they were run: his revelation, though, came in 1513, when he witnessed a massacre of Indians on Santo Domingo. Like other Spanish churchmen of the time he believed that the American discoveries had come as a trust from providence, and that Spain had an obligation to carry the word of God to the newly found peoples. He proclaimed, though, that the way the colonists were making use of that trust was no more than a cover for theft, murder, greed and savagery. The civilizing mission was a lie and a sin.

He dedicated the rest of his life to making that point. He did so in two ways: one, in practical work in often remote parts of the Americas; the other, by going to the top and buttonholing monarchs and ministers to plead the rightness of his cause. In 1515 he sailed back from Santo Domingo and rushed to get the ear of King Ferdinand on his deathbed, to no avail. In future years he chased many more figures at the court, and in 1542 addressed his most famous work, the *Brief History of the Destruction of the Indies*, to the future King Philip II. Remarkably, he was rarely refused entry, and in 1542 Charles V actually let him revise the *Leyes de Indias* by which Spain's colonies were supposedly run. He even succeeded in getting some reforms implemented, although the real difficulty was in getting them to take effect on the ground.

Shortly afterwards Las Casas was offered the chance to return to America as Bishop of Chiapas. His time in Ciudad Real was actually short: not long after he arrived in 1545 he issued instructions that confession and absolution were only to be given to colonists who released all Indians from slavery, raising howls of *conquistador* protest. By 1547 he was back in Spain to explain himself. In 1550 Las Casas was called to take part in an extraordinary disputation in Valladolid. The subject was none other than the right of Europe to remake the world in its own image. His opponent was a rising star of the Spanish Church called Juan Ginés de Sepúlveda, a prototype of the kind of intellectual who now works in defence industry think-tanks. Sepúlveda's argument was that the world was a kind of divine meritocracy: by their ignorance of true religion the Indians showed themselves to be inferior, and any violence used by Christians was therefore only a measured, justifiable response to the Indians' own violence and barbarism. Las Casas replied with example after example to show that the conquerors' actions were unprovoked and purely brutal with no 'measure' at all, so that any morality in the Conquest was sheer hypocrisy. The texts of this debate were then taken away, to be considered by Church and State. Las Casas continued to argue his case until his death, aged 82, in 1566.

Indian population Ciudad Real was a major centre for the missionary orders, and the 17th century, above all, saw an enormous amount of church building in the city.

In 1712 Ciudad Real received a severe fright when a mass rebellion of Tzeltal Maya marched on the city from Cancuc, northeast of Tenejapa. In the 18th century it acquired many more of its patio houses, and more Baroque churches. From a Spanish city it slowly changed into one of *mestizos* and a tiny, Chiapas-born white élite.

The sudden appearance of politics as the Spanish Empire crumbled caught this closed society almost by surprise. Under Spain Chiapas had always been part of Guatemala but, in 1821, the élite of Ciudad Real – which would become 'San Cristóbal' in 1829 – decided it would be more in their interests to join the new Mexican Empire. They encountered their first opposition from the ranching and trading families of Tuxtla, who objected to not being consulted, and so appeared the first signs of the dispute that would dominate official politics in Chiapas for the next century. In the civil wars of the middle of the century the San Cristóbal élite, Catholic and conservative, supported the anti-Juárez camp and then Maximilian; Tuxtla and the Central Valley supported Juárez against the French. All these contests were utterly irrelevant to the Mayan population, who took no part in politics except in brief outbursts such as the Cuzcat rebellion, a smaller version of Yucatán's Caste War, in Chamula in 1868.

Under Porfirio Díaz – a Juarista before he became dictator – San Cristóbal's pro-Maximilian conservatism led to it being suspected of disloyalty, and the state capital was transferred to Tuxtla in 1892. The Díaz era brought some other changes too: the first electricity arrived in 1908, and a municipal architect called Carlos Flores gave San Cristóbal a number of Victorian-era monuments.

The Revolution looked for a time as if it would bring changes in relationships on the ground, but San Cristóbal remained a very traditional city, its Spanish-speaking people, known as *coletos*, renowned for their insularity and conservatism. Change began to come with the first airstrip in the 1930s, and still more so when the Pan-American Highway in 1947 at last gave San Cristóbal a land-link to the outside world that could be crossed in less than a day. The greatest recent change, though, has been the Mayanization of San Cristóbal. Due to economic pressures or political conflicts in their home communities, Highland Maya have flooded into the city, which has trebled in size since the 1970s. Community relations in the Highlands remain complex, but the situation is now far more fluid than it has been for most of the last 500 years.

The Zócalo

Whichever way you arrive in San Cristóbal, you are almost inevitably led to the gracious main square, the Zócalo, centred on a very Victorian-looking bandstand surrounded by neat rings of shrubs, iron benches and broad, shady trees. In among them are lines of shoeshine men, bunches of Indian women and kids who try to sell you woven belts and bracelets, and news-stands selling a wider range of press than is usual in southern Mexico. Alternatively known as the Plaza Mayor or just '*el Parque*', the Zócalo has a (virtually unused) official title of Plaza 31 de Marzo, the date of the city's foundation.

Contrary to normal Spanish colonial practice, the **Cathedral** does not stand on the east flank of the square but fills its north side. To the main plaza it presents only a giant, blank wall. 'Blank' here is not strictly the right term, for the most remarkable thing about the cathedral is its colour scheme: great bands of yellow and red ochre, with panels in black on the west façade, and details – Baroque columns and capitals, Mayan-looking flowers and Habsburg double-headed eagles – picked out in white. It was begun in 1528 as a simple church, but with the granting of a bishopric to Ciudad Real ten years later its status was elevated to that of cathedral. It was therefore begun well before the cathedral in Mérida, but its construction took much longer, and the façade was only completed in the 1690s. Inside, to contrast with the strong colours of the exterior, the cathedral is lofty and white, with gold trim around its columns. Within the side chapels there is a whole collection of Baroque altarpieces and 17th-century religious paintings by local artists such as Juan Correa and Eusebio de Aguilar.

Behind the cathedral, facing into the Zócalo, there is an entirely separate chapel, the very simple **San Nicolás**, from 1615. This density of religious buildings soon comes as no surprise in San Cristóbal, which is a city of churches, their doors thrown open by day in a way that makes them seem like a series of atmospheric alcoves beside the streets. Moreover, in virtually all of them there will be people quietly coming and going, and observing their devotions. This happens in two ways, especially in certain churches that are highly regarded by the Maya. The *coletos* sit and kneel in pews, in the normal way; the Indians go down on their knees on the marble floors before the altars, surrounded by an untidy circle of candles and pine needles, where they rock rhythmically backwards and forwards while murmuring continuously in Tzotzil or Tzeltal. Suddenly, these very Spanish churches look as if they've been taken over by something very different, with a whole new set of religious references.

The east side of the plaza is filled by **Los Portales**, a deep-shaded arcade which in Ciudad Real was the place where the Spanish gentlemen of the city gathered to find out what was going on. Today it houses a bank, travel agencies, a bakery. Facing the arcade across the plaza is the town hall, the **Palacio Municipal**, built by Carlos Flores in 1885–95 to replace a Spanish one destroyed in the Juárez-era wars in 1863. In a city where for three centuries the standard style of building had been 1550s Spain, Flores did his best to introduce the style of 1840s France.

On the south side of the Zócalo are San Cristóbal's oldest colonial residences. As in Mérida, the first solid building to be completed in the new town was not a church but the house of the chief conqueror, the **Casa de Diego de Mazariegos**, on the corner of C/ Diego de Mazariegos and Av. Miguel Hidalgo, from the 1530s. It has been greatly altered since then, but the main surviving part of the original house – still quite substantial – is the patio occupied by the Galería restaurant, on Miguel Hidalgo. More complete is the **Casa de la Sirena** ('House of the Mermaid'), which is now occupied by the Hotel Santa Clara, on the corner of Av. Insurgentes. It was built a few years later, for another *conquistador* called Andrés de la Tovilla, and its name refers to the carved mermaid on the corner above the square.

Santo Domingo and the Market

From the Zócalo it's possible to head off in any direction, and San Cristóbal is a city that encourages strolling. It also encourages you to take your time, for it's a place of many small details. The doors of its colonial houses are smaller than those in Mérida, offering less of a view inside; a Castilian sense of enclosure, of retreating from the outside world, has long been considered a major element in *coleto* culture. Inside and behind the slab-like outside walls, the patios may be ramshackle, or magnificent.

For an area that contains San Cristóbal's greatest monuments and its most spectacular cultural mixture, head north up Av. General Utrilla. Along the way are some of the grandest patio houses, many of them now hotels. Stay on the pavements and you're remarkably high up, two feet above the street. This partly reflects the sometimes-rainy mountain weather, but also the fact that until the mid-20th century Indians were not actually allowed to mount the pavements within the city. Five blocks from the Zócalo, on the right, is the **Casa Utrilla** (no. 33, by the corner with C/ Dr Navarro), where the patio contains the SODAM crafts centre, likeable cafés and a bookshop.

The eye tends to be distracted, however, across the street to **Santo Domingo**. This is by far the grandest church in the city, more elaborate than the cathedral. It was built as part of a monastery established in 1546 by Las Casas as the main house of the Dominicans in Chiapas, and its construction went on for decades. The main façade on Av. 20 de Noviembre, from the late 17th century, is astonishing, one of the greatest creations of Mexican Baroque: it's completely different from anything the Franciscans created in Yucatán, more Mexican but also more in touch with the late Renaissance. Rising through four tiers of columns, every inch of it is covered in extravagant decoration: fluted columns, flower patterns, bosses, lions, geometrical shapes and figures of saints. Once inside, the sense of the Baroque is even more overwhelming, since much of the interior – the main altarpieces, the giant pulpit – consists of finely carved wood coated in gold leaf. The altarpiece of the *Santíssima Trinidad* (the Holy Trinity), housed in one of the side chapels, is among the finest of all Mexican colonial carvings. Amid this Baroque gilt there will also be the smell of copal incense and the murmur of Tzotzil prayers, for Santo Domingo is also highly venerated by the Maya from the outlying villages.

Outside, the impression of an Indian church is accentuated because the steps and gardens around it are filled with the city's main **handicrafts market**. Forming the south side of the garden-plaza around Santo Domingo, and therefore the market, is yet another church, the **Templo de la Caridad**. This was begun in 1714 to give thanks to the Virgin of Charity for 'delivering' the city from the Indian rebellion of 1712. Ironically, it is now predominantly an Indian church. Its interior is similarly Baroque, but with altarpieces in massive brown and gold wood rather than pure gilt.

The airy cloisters and monastery buildings north of Santo Domingo house cultural institutions, among them the **Sna Jolobil** weavers' cooperative, a must-see even if you don't buy (*see* p.480). Another is the **Museo de los Altos de Chiapas** (*open Tues–Sun 10–5; closed Mon; adm*), with archaeological finds from around the state. It's small (labelled in Spanish only), but has some fine items, especially Late Classic ceramics.

From here it's impossible not to be aware that you are getting close to the **market**, which, from its official location at the junction of General Utrilla and C/ Edgar Robledo, extends over several blocks. The *combi* and pick-up traffic gets much thicker, as do the clusters of Chamulas and Zinacantecas padding by with babies on their backs and great bundles of beans, greens, potatoes or peppers. San Cristóbal's market is perhaps the most extraordinary bazaar in the whole of southern Mexico, one which at times gives the impression it's only changed in piffling details since before the Conquest. On one street you might see heaped from end to end earthenware pots from Amatenango, all looking for a buyer; in the food stalls are the brilliant colours of avocados, lemons, squashes, and countless varieties of chilis, amid live animals, raw wool, and cut flowers. Buying, selling and talking goes on all the time, except when people break off to listen to one of the hucksters pushing magic remedies.

West of the market and Calzada Lázaro Cárdenas the atmosphere changes again very swiftly, as you wander into the **Barrio de Mexicanos**, founded as a district for the loyal 'Mexican' warriors who fought with the Spaniards against the Maya. Now very peaceful and tranquil, it contains the office of the Red de Turismo Comunitario (*see* p.478), and if you go up the continuation of Av. General Utrilla past the market, Av. Salomón González Blanco, you will come to one of its affiliates, the **Centro de Desarrollo de la Medicina Maya** at no. 10 (*open Mon–Fri 9–2 and 3–6, Sat and Sun 10–4; adm free, donations requested*), dedicated to maintaining traditional Mayan medicine and healing, with a small museum.

El Cerrillo and Na Bolom

From Santo Domingo, if you walk east up C/ Comitán you will enter the district of **El Cerrillo** (the little hill), founded in 1549 for freed Indian slaves although, with its low houses and cobbled streets looping over the hill, it looks more than anywhere else in the city like an old Spanish town. C/ Yajalón, which runs north across it, leads out of town for about three kilometres to a curious 16th-century covered bridge, the **Peje de Oro**. The valley nearby is now a nature reserve, within which are the Mayan ruins of **Moxviquil**, first explored by Frans Blom. Tours are run by Pronatura (*see* p.478).

Continue east up and over C/ Comitán or the parallel streets and you will come to the house and museum of **Na Bolom** (*Guided tours in Spanish and English daily at 11.30 and 4.30; times can change, so check, **t** 678 1418, nabolom@sclsc.ecosur.com.mx; adm*), a monument to two of San Cristóbal's most unusual residents, Frans and Trudi Blom. Frans Blom (1893–1963) was born in Denmark, but at an early age gave up on conventional living and began travelling, ending up in Mexico. Drawn to jungles, he worked at many jobs – oil exploration, rubber tapping – before developing an interest in archaeology. He joined Tulane University in New Orleans, and in the 1920s made the first surveys of many Mayan sites. In 1928 he made contact with the Lacandón Maya for the first time, staying with them for long periods. In 1943 he met Gertrude (Trudi) Duby (1901–93), and both recognized in each other the same passions. From Switzerland, she had been a left-wing activist in Germany; arrested by the Nazis in 1940, she had only been spared because of her Swiss nationality. Expelled to Mexico, she became fascinated by her new country, and met Blom on an expedition to the Lacandón jungle. Together, they developed their relationship with the Lacandón, and moved into this house in 1950, intending it to be both their home and a centre for the study of the anthropology, archaeology and environment of the Maya and Chiapas.

Na Bolom is now a cultural centre, staffed by Mexican and international volunteers, supporting a range of development and ecology projects. It still has a close relationship with the Lacandón, and the centre runs its own tours to the Lacandón villages of Naha and Metzaboc (from about $190). There are also rooms available (*see* p.481).

A major attraction is the beautiful old house itself, with some of the most attractive of colonial patios. The garden contains impressive nurseries and seed beds, used in preserving plant species and reforestation schemes. Still very present is the powerful personality of Trudi Blom, from her bedroom with the immaculately elegant clothes she wore for jungle trips to the eccentric objects all around the house, the collection of Baroque religious images or her exquisite photographs of the Lacandón. In other rooms there are Mayan artefacts excavated by Frans Blom, especially from Moxviquil, his archaeological equipment, and mementos of his friendships with such figures as Diego Rivera. The excellent **library** has books on every aspect of Mayan culture (*no fixed opening times, but open to non-residents*).

Guadalupe

Running east from the Zócalo, C/ Real de Guadalupe is perhaps the foreign visitor's favourite street in San Cristóbal, with the biggest concentration of hotels, tour agencies, restaurants, bookshops, cafés and other places in which to enjoy one of the prime attractions of the city – just being here. **Centro El Puente**, at Real de Guadalupe 55, combines a café-restaurant, an Internet shop and a language school, and also hosts film screenings and other activities. Whenever you've had enough of sitting around chatting, head up the hill of Real de Guadalupe to some good handicrafts shops. Walk up in the evening and you'll probably hear music, for several *marimbas* and *mariachis* have little practice-halls along the street. On the parallel C/ Francisco Madero there's a small but colourful fruit market, at the corner of Av. Diego Dugelay, while on C/ María Adelina Flores (at no. 10) there is the **Café Museo Café** (*see* p.483), which contains a 'museum' on the history of Chiapas coffee.

Real de Guadalupe and Madero both end at the hill of Guadalupe, where 79 steps lead up to the **Templo de Guadalupe**. It was built only in 1834, and so in some ways is a lot simpler than the older Spanish churches. As befits a shrine to the Virgin of Guadalupe, though, it's astonishingly colourful, and at the top of the hill you are rewarded with delicious fresh air and a great view back over the city.

Insurgentes and El Carmen

Thanks perhaps to the traffic from the bus stations, the streets south of the Zócalo are quite busy, with cheap hotels, untouristy shops and a small food and Indian market on Av. Insurgentes, between the churches of San Francisco and Santa Lucía. This district was, with the Zócalo and Santo Domingo, one of the three main areas of colonial Ciudad Real. Filling the block between Miguel Hidalgo and Crescencio Rojas is the building that was once Chiapas' Jesuit College, the 1681 **Antiguo Colegio de San Francisco Javier**, now used by the state's Autonomous University. Nearby there is the **Casa de Artesanías**, the official showcase for traditional handicrafts (*see* p.480), which also has a **museum** display (*open Mon–Sat 9–2 and 5–8; closed Sun; adm free*). Two blocks further down Miguel Hidalgo the street is blocked by a large, squat four-storey belltower with a small arch attached to it, the **Arco del Carmen**. Also from the 1680s, this is the only remaining part of the Convento de la Encarnación, once one of the largest closed convents of nuns in the Americas, founded in 1597.

One block east on Av. Insurgentes, and still intact, **San Francisco** was also part of a larger unit, a Franciscan monastery founded in 1577 and demolished in the 19th century. The church is plain, with white walls and a gold altarpiece, but has in one transept an intriguing naive painting of a legend of the life of Saint Francis, with very vivid demon-toads. Next to San Francisco is a big building, surrounded by cheap *loncherías*, called the **Mercado de Dulces y Artesanías**, the 'sweets and handicrafts market'. This curious combination is just what you find inside, although many of its stalls are unused. **Santa Lucía**, two blocks down, is an 1884 wedding-cake church in blue and white; a further walk south and out along the Highway is **San Diego**, built by the Dominicans in 1650 to cater for Indians who were not allowed inside the city.

The Merced and Cerrito de San Cristóbal

The area west of the Zócalo also has its large religious building, **La Merced**, reached by heading straight down C/ Diego de Mazariegos. In front of it there is a delightfully tranquil, park-like square. The Merced was actually the first church in San Cristóbal, begun in 1537 by the Mercedarian friars, but little of the original structure remains. It was rebuilt in the 18th century, and the cloister alongside was made into an army barracks in the 1880s, when it acquired its turret-like sentry boxes and watchtower. Since 1996 it has been under restoration as a multi-purpose cultural centre. Already open is the **Museo del Ambar de Chiapas** (*open Tues–Sun 10–2 and 4–7; closed Mon; adm*), on the first floor, and there's a delightful shop with superb local amber by the entrance below. The museum gives an information overload on what is one of Chiapas' most valued products, from its chemical origins to its worth to the ancient Maya, and there's an eye-opening video on the life of amber miners today. Labelling (and the video) are in Spanish, but the amber on show is fascinating.

Across the street on the corner of Av. 12 de Octubre a former school has been converted into the grandly named **Museo de las Culturas Populares de Chiapas** (*open Tues–Sun 10–2 and 4–6; closed Mon; adm free*), which so far is only an exhibition centre hosting shows on local crafts. More interesting, one block north along Av. 12 de Octubre at C/ Guadalupe Victoria 47, is a very individual museum, the **Museo Sergio Castro** (*open by appointment only, call t 678 4289; adm – a 'contribution' to the costs – seems to be left to each visitor*) The rambling house is the home of Sergio Castro, a remarkable character who has worked for years among the Highland Maya. He has amassed a superb collection of Highland weaving, including some of their very finest work such as wedding shirts from San Andrés Larraínzar, as well as an assortment of musical instruments and other articles from Highland life. He takes you around himself, with explanations in quick-fire but very comprehensible English, and in the process gives you access to a tremendous fund of knowledge.

South of the Merced, Calles Matamoros or Ignacio Allende lead up to the second of the city's two main hills, the **Cerrito de San Cristóbal**. Streets like La Palma that wind around its foot are very tranquil, and surprisingly out of the way. From the end of C/ Niños Héroes, a ramp of steps zigzags up the hill. A prime attraction is the view, across to its 'twin' of Guadalupe. The **chapel of San Cristóbal** is small and intimate, painted in white and pinkish red. Sadly, it no longer has its once-famous cross made of licence plates, donated by local cab drivers, which was stolen in 1996.

To the west of San Cristóbal and back on ground level is something far more bizarre: the **Teatro de la Ciudád**. No one has yet explained why it was that during the Salinas boom of the early 1990s the state government of Chiapas, supposedly short of funds and with a tiny theatre-going public, decided it needed two state-of-the-art public theatres (the other one is in Tuxtla). Whatever the cause, San Cristóbal has its theatre, which still hosts few performances. Its chief claim to fame has been that in January 1994, still unfinished, it provided a very solid strongpoint for the Zapatistas.

Around San Cristóbal: the Highland Villages

After a few days in the Chiapas Highlands, you can feel the place was invented by Jonathan Swift. Gulliver wandered from places where everybody was very small to others where everybody was very large: in and around San Cristóbal there are people who wear blue, black and white and keep sheep (from Chamula), people who wear brilliant reds and purples and grow flowers (Zinacantán), people who make pots (Amatenango), others who are rarer and harder to identify. The Highland Maya communities have an intricate, complex culture, and from one hill to another you can encounter a whole different set of beliefs, legends, customs and traditions: visiting the area is a fascinating, sometimes jarring venture into a world far from the routine ways of the 21st century.

Chamula and Zinacantán gave fierce resistance to the *conquistadors* in the 1520s, and were never totally subdued, settling into co-existence with the Spaniards of San Cristóbal, 10 kilometres away. For two centuries the missionary orders strove to stamp out 'paganism' in the Highlands and establish normal Catholic practice, but the Maya responded with what has been called 'passive resistance', intertwining their old beliefs with the new religion – some say throttling it – in a fascinating amalgam. Maintaining ceremonies and traditions became an essential part of each community's survival. Even so, the Highland peoples have considered themselves Catholics, for the boundaries between orthodox beliefs and others have never been defined.

There are many differences between them – such as language, between Tzotzil and Tzeltal – but despite this a pattern is common to all the Highland communities. All have adapted Catholic saints and images to a very Mayan veneration of the earth and sacred places. In each there is a ladder of social and religious authorities, called *cargos* (literally 'posts' or 'duties'), often referred to by a curious mixture of Spanish names:

Getting Around

It is very advisable to go with a guide when you first visit Chamula and Zinacantán. There is so much that is alien, and so many places to which access is only possible with an introduction, that you will see and understand a great deal more with someone to lead the way. All the San Cristóbal agencies offer tours, but it is most rewarding to go with an **independent guide** (*see* p.478).

If you do want to make your own way, *combis* are easy to find at the market in San Cristóbal (although they tend to head into town in the morning, and head back in the afternoon). **By car**, the road to both villages is also easy to find by following C/ Guadalupe Victoria west out of San Cristóbal. Once you arrive, especially in Chamula and if you don't have a guide, be prepared for kids demanding to *cuidar el carro*, watch your car. Pick one, and make a deal with him.

Amatenango is in a different direction, beside the Highway 190 road toward Comitán. It may be included in some agency tours to Montebello (*see* p.478), but it is also quite easy to reach independently, by car or second-class bus or *combi* on the Comitán route.

Tourist Information

The best day to visit Chamula and Zinacantán is Sunday, which is both market day and the main day when the *autoridades* hold court in their squares. Thursday is market day in Tenejapa, and on that day many guides try to go there as well. Highland markets start early, and clear up by noon.

Photography

In all the villages, but especially Chamula, follow the directions of your guide as to when you may take photographs; in the market it's usually acceptable. The Highland Mayas' resentment of photography is not so much due to a belief that cameras 'steal their souls' as to the simple dislike of being used as decorative objects for no reward, and to their concept of *chu'lel* (vital energy), which is possessed by living creatures and inanimate objects alike. Any contact between people, with animals, or between people and the earth, involves an exchange of *chu'lel*. Picture-taking is rejected because it takes away *chu'lel* without asking and because the Highland Maya dislike all impersonal interactions. There is an absolute ban on taking photos inside Chamula church, and the '**constables**', young *cargos* in white smocks with big sticks, enforce these restrictions. A tale has long gone round that foreigners have been killed at Chamula for taking pictures where they shouldn't. This is a folk myth, repeated by tourist shamans in guide books. The constables will, though, grab your camera, take out the film, and probably give it back to you broken, with a scowl and a lot of aggression.

For a totally different take on the Highland Maya's attitude to photography it's interesting to view the work of the **Chiapas Photography Project**, a scheme that provides Mayan villagers with cameras so that they can take pictures of their world themselves. It is based at **CIESAS**, Carretera a Chamula Km3.5, **t** 678 5670, *www.chiapasphoto.org*, by the road to Chamula (*open to visitors Mon–Fri 8–2, but always call ahead*).

---

pasiones ('passions'), *alfereces* ('lieutenants'), *mayordomos* ('stewards'). Each year's occupants of a post are chosen collectively by the authorities of the previous year, so that the hierarchy is self-perpetuating. Men (rarely ever women) begin by taking junior posts in their twenties and then, if they gain sufficient respect, ascend to the most senior with age. Occupying an important *cargo* and so serving the community wins a man honour and prestige for the rest of his life. It is also very expensive, for the *mayordomo* of a particular saint, for example, is responsible for maintaining the saint's shrine for a year and arranging the annual *fiesta* out of his own pocket, and must contribute to community events like the Carnival. A complex system of debts and loans has built up to allow men to take up a particular position. Other important

Festivals

Given the importance of daily ritual to the Highland Maya, it's no surprise that they keep up an elaborate calendar of celebrations. Easter is important in all the communities, but each has its own schedule of events, and usually one special *fiesta* when religious images, freshly dressed and adorned, are taken out in procession so that the world is 'reborn' for another year, with festivities climaxing on a certain day but building up over preceding days. The villages below hold their special *fiestas* as follows:

Tenejapa: San Ildefonso, *23 Jan.*
Mitontic: San Miguel, *8 May.*
Zinacantán: San Lorenzo, *10 Aug.*

Chamula

This village has the most awesome cycle of celebrations, with over 20 festivals. **San Sebastián** (*20 Jan*), **Easter** and **San Juan** (*24 June*) are all important, but the greatest of all is the **Carnival** (*late Jan or Feb*). It is normally referred to by the Catholic name of Carnival, but its Tzotzil name *K'in Tahimol* translates as 'Festival of Games'. Whole books have been written about the interplay of beliefs within it. It lasts five days, corresponding to the five *uayeb* days at the end of the year in the *Haab* calendar, the unstable time when the world needs to be reborn. For the first three days, officials of the three *barrios* of Chamula, parade around the village with sumptuously coloured banners, representing the Sun and Christ, which in Chamula are amalgamated. Around them, trying to challenge them, dance the *max* or monkeys, representing the men of wood from the previous creation seen in the *Popol Vuh* and as such, symbolizing chaos and disordered nature. The disorder comes over clearly enough, as they look completely mad, in absurd 'uniforms' inspired by those of Maximilian's armies, long ago. Lately they've also taken to wearing shades. Some form bands using a bizarre combination of instruments, which continually play the same meandering tune, the *Bolon Chon*. All this is punctuated by plenty of eating, barrages of fireworks, movement and noise. After three days of challenges to the Sun-Christ by the monkeys, the night of the third day sees the exhausted dancers and banner-carriers run up the hills on the outskirts of the village, as if the forces of chaos have won and banished the Sun-Christ. Then, on the fourth day, the *pasiones* and banners return to the plaza and perform the 'Path of Fire': a path of straw is laid from the church across the square and set alight, and the Sun-Christ banners are run along it through the flames three times. The Sun-Christ is thus reborn, and the universal order, to be celebrated on the last day.

Where to Stay

Rancho La Granada, 1km north of Highway 190 between Teopisca and Amatenango **t** (967) 678 4658, *lagranada@hotmail.com*. Most people only visit the areas around San Cristóbal as day trips, but it's now possible to stay in the countryside southeast of the city at this former *hacienda*. There are simple *cabañas* (*cheap*) and camping and hammock space, and horses can be hired.

figures in the Highlands are the *ilol* or healers, often women as well as men. Another activity throughout the Highlands is the drinking of *posh*, powerful, home-made cane hooch, knocked back in ample quantities to accelerate contact with gods and spirits – as similar brews were used by the Classic Maya – and also used in healing.

Although the Highland communities are often called villages, they actually cover wide areas. Chamula, the largest, has a total population of close to 100,000, of whom only a handful live in the 'ceremonial centre' of San Juan Chamula. The rest are spread across the mountains in tiny clutches of houses and fields called *parajes*. Nor is this world of traditions at all static or cut off from the world. Beginning in the 1940s the governments of the Mexican Revolution established an elaborate bureaucracy to deal with indigenous communities, providing privileged positions for chosen leaders, and in Chamula, especially, many elders have long been closely bound up with the PRI; at the same time, one of the Zapatista *comandantes*, Ramona, is a Chamulan woman. The system of *cargos* creates its own tensions, and is intolerant of those who reject community authority. From the 1970s onwards American Protestant missionaries made many converts in the region with their radical opposition to the old hierarchy (there are also 'autonomous evangelical' churches, who reject the Americans as well), which has led to bitter conflict and the expulsion of several thousand Protestants from Chamula. Many now live in the suburbs of San Cristóbal, or along the Comitán road southeast of the city. These are only some of the complexities of the Highlands.

If you can, it's a wonderful experience to get away from the Highland ceremonial centres and drive a little way up the winding mountain tracks (some of which are paved). On the tops of mountains or at the entrances of villages stand the green-painted crosses that the Catholic Church long sought to present as a sign of the success of orthodox religion in the Highlands, but which are equally if not more symbolic of the world-tree, surrounded by bromeliads and sprigs of pine. They are usually in pairs, representing God the Father and God the Mother.

Chamula

The ceremonial centre of **San Juan Chamula** is a ragged, untidy place, with huts and houses straggling up tracks in no particular order around the church and the market square. Until about 50 years ago, in fact, there were no permanent buildings at Chamula except the church, and the population was dispersed in the *parajes*. The Chamulas are the sheep-herders of the Highlands. On Sundays, especially, many men and boys wear traditional woollen smocks, in black or white, with the now equally 'traditional' addition of a stetson-style straw hat, and Chamulan women virtually always wear traditional dress: black woollen skirts and blue or white blouses with embroidered strips around the edges (now made with synthetics).

The largest buildings around the square at Chamula are the **church**, which is all white but with bands of flowers painted around the portico, and the Coca-Cola and Pepsi distributors. The Mayas' cola-fixation is more peculiar than their dislike of having their picture taken. They believe that burping releases bad energies from the body, and formerly made a kind of natural lemonade to induce burps. Then, when they discovered how well modern gassy drinks can make the tubes gurgle, they took to them with devotion, and now have a consumption per head that must merit an entry to themselves in the annual report. Several of the elders of Chamula have also done very well out of their neighbours by securing cola concessions.

With a good guide you will first be taken to one of the 'shrines' of the different saints. It looks just like another Chamula hut, except that the door is garlanded in bromeliads and dried branches. Inside, the floor is carpeted in pine needles, and the Spanish-looking image of the saint is surrounded by flowers, dried leaves and yet more bromeliads – of special importance because it is an air-feeding plant, and so held to be in close contact with the spirits. The table in front of the image is packed with ceramic incense burners, often in the shape of cows or sheep, pouring out sweet copal incense. The Highland Maya dress their saints in this way because they formerly worshipped in caves, and by reproducing the environment of a mountain cave they create a sacred space. For the same reason they always scatter a layer of pine needles around them when they worship in the ornate churches of San Cristóbal.

After that you go back to the square and into the church, where the 'constables' (*see* Photography, p.493) charge about $1 for entry (*be sure to put your camera in your bag, to avoid misunderstandings*). Once inside, this is naturally the place where you feel most like an intruder, but such considerations quickly fall to the back of the mind, for the little church of San Juan Chamula must be one of the most intense religious spaces anywhere in the world. Everything is dark at first, the windows blocked by hanging plants; the floor is covered in pine needles, and images of saints extend in a line along each side, the main light given by hundreds of candles. There are no 'services' as such; all business is done on the floor. As you shuffle round, trying not to interfere, you trip over rings of empty cola bottles. All of life is there, in a way that recalls the unsettling mixture of tone in the pictures at Bonampak (*see* p.461). In one spot, a man prays alone with agonized intensity before a saint, rocking mesmerically back and forth, while next to him a family sits inside its ring of candles and bottles, chatting or looking bored; elsewhere, two men giggle through a drunken conversation, after taking in a fair amount of *posh*. *Ilol* healers receive patients at points around the floor, holding their wrists and talking quietly in unhurried consultations.

Alongside the church there is a small **museum** (*open daily 9–6; adm*), although it's not as interesting as the village around it. The **market** in the square is primarily for locals, and so most of the stalls have foods, fruit, pots and so on, but there are plenty with local weaving. Around the edges of the square there are a few simple *loncherías*. On a Sunday the raised section of the square will contain, sitting solemnly in line, the senior authorities of Chamula, in the hats that are a symbol of office, with brightly coloured ribbons hanging over their eyes. This is another group who are not to be photographed. On Sunday morning any member of the community may petition them or raise a problem, and a steady flow of men leads their families along the line, kissing the ribbons of the hats as a sign of respect. They can intervene in any dispute. As a final touch, complaints are made and judgements delivered in rhyming couplets.

Zinacantán

San Lorenzo Zinacantán, like Chamula a Tzotzil-speaking community, is only seven kilometres west, but feels remarkably different. The village itself is neater, with orderly streets and whitewashed buildings; the people seem gentler, and it's a less abrasive place to visit without a guide. The **church** (inside which you still mustn't take pictures) is a great deal brighter, exuberantly colourful, and less intense. In pre-Hispanic times Zinacantán was a powerful trading community, and controlled the trade in Chiapas amber, highly valued throughout Mesoamerica. Today the Zinacantecos' love of colour is visible in all kinds of ways. They grow huge quantities of flowers, particularly geraniums, chrysanthemums and carnations, which are distributed to many parts of Mexico. For once the men's costume is as colourful as that of the women, heavy smocks in a strong reddy-pink, embroidered with flower designs. Women, meanwhile, wear their hair bobbed up with flowers and ribbons, and shawls in rich reds, purples and blues laced with gold thread. They are all the brighter nowadays thanks to lurex and other synthetic threads, which have been taken up with enthusiasm by the Zinacantecas, delighted to obtain so much colour with so little effort. During *fiestas* or when they are performing rituals men wear the full regalia of white shorts, red head-scarves, ribboned hats for the authorities, and leather sandals of a type near-identical to those worn by Kan-Balam on the reliefs of the Cross temples at Palenque.

Some textile experts bemoan the domination of synthetics, but the Zinacantecan women are more interesting weavers than those of Chamula, and this is a better place to buy. The little **market** area is next to the church, and the women's textile stalls stay open more or less through the day on Sundays to catch the tourists. A short walk from the church there is also a small folk museum, the **Museo Ik'al Ojov** (*open daily 9–6; adm*), displaying some fine weaving and other relics of Zinacantecan life.

Also on Sundays, around midday, a 'meeting' gathers in front of the church to discuss community business, a less solemn and noisier affair than in Chamula. The authorities of Zinacantán do not sit in the open air to receive petitions but around a table in the chapterhouse beside the church. Even more than the main church, the room is adorned with banners in gold, green, purple and other colours. It's a rather strange experience being led in to stand and watch the community elders sitting in semi-silence through the day, communicating in occasional whispers. At times it is truly unmissable, when they are accompanied by younger men performing the 'Song of the Churchkeeper', the unearthly festival music of Zinacantán.

San Andrés Larraínzar and Mitontic

From Chamula a road – paved most of the way – winds north through fabulous scenery 16 kilometres to **San Andrés Larraínzar**, with a Sunday market that's also used by the people of **Santa Magdalena** (or Magdalenas), almost at the end of the road. A turn-off to the right south of San Andrés curves around to **Mitontic**, a very pretty village winding up a hillside, and eventually **Chenalhó**. From Mitontic a track – difficult but passable in a 4WD or *combi* – climbs and twists up to the summit of **Mount Tzontehuitz**, at 2,910m the highest peak in the Highlands and a sacred spot to the Maya, topped by a television relay station and a sheaf of Mayan crosses. These villages receive only a fraction of the number of visitors that go to Chamula and Zinacantán. However, this is an area that has seen a good deal of conflict, and it's essential to check what current conditions are before making an expedition up there. The better agencies and guides (*see* pp.477–9) are sources of orientation.

Huitepec Nature Reserve

Open Tues–Sun 9–4; closed Mon; regular guided tours in English and Spanish by appt; adm.

The flanks of the volcano of Huitepec, just over three kilometres from San Cristóbal on the Chamula road, have been made into a nature reserve. It covers 135 hectares at a height of 2,400m, rising from grassland and pines into cloudforest. Among the birds that can be seen there are some very scarce forest species. A special nature trail runs through the reserve, which takes about an hour; **Pronatura Chiapas** (*see* p.478) administers the reserve and runs regular tours, as well as supplying full bird lists.

The San Cristóbal Caves

Open daily 7.30–5; adm. Second-class buses and combis on the
San Cristóbal–Comitán route can drop you by the track to the caves.

At **Rancho Nuevo** (10km east of San Cristóbal), the point where Highway 190 meets Highway 199 from Palenque, there is, on the north side of the road, a large and very solid army camp, and on the south side a turn-off into a beautiful pine wood. After less than a kilometre this track runs out at the **Grutas de San Cristóbal**, an extensive cave system. Explored in the 1970s, it is not as meandering as the huge Yucatán caverns, but still impressive, with awesome cathedral-like chambers. A well-kept walkway makes the visit very easy, but it's also very cold, so go prepared.

The woods around the caves are a popular spot for picnics, and horses can be hired (*about $11 per hour*) outside the caves' entrance for rides along the forest trails, which extend for several kilometres. It's also possible to camp.

Amatenango del Valle

The Tzeltal village of Amatenango, 38 kilometres southeast of San Cristóbal off Highway 190, is the *pueblo de alfareros*, the village of potters. For over 1,000 years, at least, its women have been dedicated to making earthenware pots and ornaments, which were a valuable trading commodity in pre-Conquest times. The responsibility of the men, meanwhile, has been to find firewood to keep the open kilns going. They do so, nowadays, by hauling donkey-derby carts up the steep valley sides around the village, and then hurtling back down again with their load of wood at manic speed: if you happen to be driving along the road at the same time, you may have to take frequent evasive action. This only reinforces the impression that it is the women that do the serious work of the community, while the men spend their time playing.

As you approach Amatenango you see ranks of brown pots, jugs and jars for sale, stacked up by the turn-offs from the main road. Then, as soon as you enter the village you will be found by a band of little girls, maybe six years old but already determined, who will ask you if you want to see how ceramics are made ('¿*Quiere ver como se hace la cerámica?*'). Once you have accepted the offer from one, she will take her catch back to the family *jacal* ('enclosure') to meet her mother. You are then sat down to watch while the girl, already practised, models a small figure, perhaps an animal, in about one minute. What you pay is normally up to you. Of more interest to anyone with an interest in ceramics is the firing method, the preserve of the older women, a simple but effective open-fired process. However, to see that you have to be insistent, as the entertaining of tourists seems to be considered kids' business.

The women of Amatenango have another distinctive style of dress, unlike any other in the Highlands: girls and younger women wear Tzeltal-style embroidered blouses and blue skirts; for older women there are heavy red and orange *huípiles*, long wool skirts with muted horizontal stripes, and an almost African-looking headdress.

Around Comitán and the Montebello Lakes

Beyond Amatenango the scenery becomes less grandiose, as the true Highlands descend into a plateau, the *meseta* of Chiapas. Its main centre is the likeable country town of **Comitán**. To the south are two little-known Mayan sites (**Tenam Puente** and **Chinkultik**) and, some 60 kilometres eastwards, the **Lagunas de Montebello**, a string of exquisite mountain lakes. These are very deep and surrounded by almost sheer slopes, which gives their unpolluted waters a superb richness of colour, the origin of their other name: the *Lagunas de Colores*. Most people only visit the area in a one-day trip from San Cristóbal, but to get a real feel of the atmosphere of the lakes it's better to stop over, in Comitán or in one of the few places closer by.

Comitán

Comitán's official name is Comitán de Domínguez, after one of its most famous citizens, Dr Belisario Domínguez. He was the only member of the Mexican senate to denounce Victoriano Huerta as a murderer after the assassination of Madero in 1914.

Getting Around

Comitán's main **first-class bus station** (Cristóbal Colón) is on the Highway south of the centre opposite C/ 8 Sur Poniente (a cab ride from the plaza). The ATG station, which has **second and first-class services**, is also on the Highway but more central, by the junction of C/ 1 Sur Poniente. It has very frequent buses to San Cristóbal and Tuxtla. Many *combis* leave from near the ATG.

Taxis are easy to find and usually cost around $1.70.

Getting to Tenam Puente and Chinkultik

A dedicated *combi* service runs from Comitán to the **Lakes** (*see* p.503 for details). On the way they can drop you close to Chinkultik, but very few *combis* go anywhere near Tenam Puente.

If you have your own transport, **Tenam Puente** is signposted to the right around 10km south of Comitán off Highway 190. A rugged but passable dirt track leads you in 6km to the site itself.

Six km further south of the Tenam Puente turn-off on Highway 190, just before the town of La Trinitaria, a turning east is signposted to Montebello. This road runs fairly straight for about 35km until you come to a turn north for the Mayan site of **Chinkultik**.

Orientation

Comitán has a fiendish street-numbering system. It's spread over steep hills. Highway 190 (**Blvd Dr Belisario Domínguez** in town), runs along the west side, and streets run off it into the grid to the east. North–south streets are Avenidas, east–west are Calles. The grid axis is the junction of C/ Central Benito Juárez and Av. Central Dr Belisario Domínguez (called Av. Central), at the Plaza Central. North of C/ Central are C/ 1 Norte, 2 Norte etc.; south are C/ 1 Sur, 2 Sur, etc. Avenidas west of the Central are Av. 1 Poniente, 2 Poniente; on the other side are Av. 1 Oriente, 2 Oriente. As an additional help the grid is divided into quarters, so Av. 2 Poniente north of C/ Central is Av. 2 Poniente Norte. Walk around for a while and it may start to make a little sense. There is a big *gasolinera* on the Highway opposite C/ 2 Sur.

Tourist Information

Comitán t (963–)
Tourist Office: Palacio Municipal, Plaza Central (*open Mon–Sat 9–1 and 5–8; closed Sun*).
Banks: There are several with ATM machines on the plaza or on Av. 1 Oriente Sur.
Consulates: The Guatemalan consulate is on the corner of Av. 2 Poniente Sur and C/ 1 Sur Poniente, t 632 2669 (*open Mon–Fri 8–4.30*).

This was one of the utterly quixotic gestures that stand out in the murk of so much Mexican politics, as the good doctor was taken off and shot. His house is now the **Museo Belisario Domínguez** (*Av. Central Dr Domínguez 35; open Tues–Sat 10–6.45, Sun 9–12.45; closed Mon; adm*), primarily attractive as a virtually unchanged example of a gentleman's home from the 19th century, with charming, secluded patios.

The other famous figure associated with Comitán was novelist Rosario Castellanos, who depicted the town of her youth in the 1930s in her book *Balún Canán* ('Nine Stars'), the Tzeltal name for Comitán. Somewhere beneath the modern town there are the remains of a Mayan settlement, and a short walk from the Museo Domínguez, in a colonial-style building on the corner of the plaza and C/ 1 Sur Oriente, is the **Casa de Cultura**, which has a small **Museo Arqueológico** (*open Mon–Sat 9–8; closed Sun; adm free*) with some local discoveries. In the same building there's also a great café and the **Museo Rosario Castellanos** (*same hours*), with pictures of pre-1950 Comitán.

The Plaza Central is naturally the centre of activity in Comitán, with cafés from which to watch whatever's going on. In the 19th century the town did well out of coffee and sugar, acquiring some Victorian-era architecture that can seem odd in the

Internet Access: In Pasaje Morales, near Viajes Temam, there is a **Café Internet**; connections are slow, but cheap.

Post Office: On Av. Central Sur between C/ 2 Sur and C/ 3 Sur (*open Mon–Fri 8–7, Sat 9–1*).

Tours

In a little pedestrian passageway that runs off the plaza nearly alongside the town hall is a local agency, **Viajes Tenam** (Pasaje Morales 8-A, t 632 1654, *www.viajestenam.com*) with tours to Tenam Puente, Chinkultik and Montebello, and to the Lagos de Colón.

Where to Stay

Comitán t (963–)

Hotel Posada Delfín, Av. Central Dr Belisario Domínguez 21, t 632 0013 (*inexpensive*). Right on the plaza: well-fitted-out rooms in a recently converted old house around a patio.

Hotel Real Balún Canán, Av. 1 Poniente Sur 7, t 632 1094 (*inexpensive*). Behind the plaza, with functional, decently equipped rooms, and quirky 1960s décor.

Posada del Virrey, Av. Central Norte 13, t 632 1811 (*inexpensive*). A block north of the plaza, the most attractive hotel in town, in a pretty, old house with patio, very well restored with individual touches. Rooms are bright, comfortable and have many extras, there's

an attractive café for breakfast, and the staff are charming.

Hospedaje Montebello, C/ 1 Norte Poniente 10, t 632 3572 (*cheap*). Rooms at this decent budget hotel, opening off an old, open courtyard, are plain and simple, but well-maintained. All showers, shared or en suite, have recently been updated.

Eating Out

El Escocés, Hotel Real Balún Canán, Av. 1 Poniente Sur 7 (*moderate*). Comitán's eccentricity continues in the hotel dining room, a Scottish theme restaurant with prints of stags and tartan tablecloths. They haven't managed to extend the 'theme' to the menu, which features Mexican standards and a few international dishes, but eating here still provides one of those wonderfully incomprehensible Mexican moments.

Helen's Enrique, Av. Central Dr B. Domínguez, Plaza Central (*moderate*). Enjoyable café-restaurant with terrace tables on the west side of the plaza, one of the most likeable places to eat in town. Coffee, snacks or sizeable Mexican and Chiapan dishes.

Café Quiptic, Av. 1 Oriente, Plaza Central (*cheap*). Charming, quite stylish café with a great location, in the porches of the Casa de Cultura by the museum.

middle of Chiapas. In the plaza is a wrought-iron bandstand, where *marimbas* play several nights a week, and to one side is the neoclassical **Teatro de la Ciudad**.

Tenam Puente

Open daily 10–4.30; adm, Sun adm free.

The Tenam Puente site was discovered for archaeology by Frans Blom and Oliver LaFarge in 1925, but it is another that has only been opened up very recently. It is still almost impossible to get to by public transport, and the area around it remains a gaunt and very strange landscape, visibly damaged by deforestation and dotted with a few ramshackle settler villages.

It is believed that it became an important city, like others in this region, mainly in the Late Classic after about 700, as the Highlands gained in prominence during the 'Collapse'. Only one dated *stela* has been found here, now in Tuxtla, from 790. Its architecture shows influences from the Guatemalan Highlands and the Petén, and it is suggested that it may have been a point of trade and contact between those areas and the non-Mayan lands to the west. The city continued to be occupied, unlike those in lowland Chiapas, into the Postclassic, until about 1200.

Tenam Puente's greatest impact is in its hilltop location, and the way this is intertwined with its architecture. As so often, only the central area has been excavated. From the parking area you walk up into a giant central plaza, a broad, grassy heath. At one end is a **Ball Court**, with what almost look to be 'grandstands' at one end. The eye is drawn above all, however, to the vast horizontal ramp of stone that fills the whole east side of the square, the first level of the great **Acropolis**. In its day it would have been brightly coloured, but today it is a mute grey mass of awesome slab-like wall and sweeping banks of steps. At the top of the first series of stairways – very steep – you climb up on to a whole new plaza on top of the first platform, big enough to contain another ball court, more pyramids and temple complexes. Since the whole structure was built on top of one of the tallest ridges in the region, the views from the final pyramid are immense. On the front of **Structure 17**, near the upper ball court, there is a carving of a decapitated captive, very like some at Toniná. At the south end of the great platform is **Structure 7**, which Blom believed was the original site of the *stela* with the date 790.

The site has been known by local people for centuries. At the southern end of the Acropolis there is a small wooden cross. This is visited by processions in local *fiestas* for the day of the Holy Cross (3 May) and the Feast of the Assumption (15 Aug).

Chinkultik

Open daily 8–4; adm, Sun adm free.

Chinkultik is better known than Tenam Puente, with some fine carving, much of which is now in Tuxtla. However, much about the city, in an area once considered very remote within Mayan culture, remains to be discovered. Again, it seems to have developed most in the very Late Classic, after 700. A ball-court marker found here has been dated to 590, but most of its inscriptions are much later (810, 844). In the 9th century its lords still erected monuments when many lowland cities had given up doing so, suggesting this could have been one of the 'last redoubts' of Classic Mayan culture. Like Tenam Puente it was at least partly occupied into the Postclassic.

The site has no very impressive buildings, but it is another with a spectacular location. It is divided between three principal groups. From the caretaker's hut a walk along a path of about 300m will take you through meadows and forest – enhanced by beautiful scents – until you go down a dip to cross a stream, jumping over stones. As you descend the dip, ahead and above you you will see the pyramids known as **El Mirador**, appearing through the trees high up on a lofty crag. Only when you're almost at the foot of the temples do you realize just how extraordinary their location is, since the pyramids – a large one and several smaller ones – stand on a neck of rock between two lakes, with almost sheer drops on either side. As a melodramatic, near-unreal setting for a sacred space it could hardly be bettered.

Heading back toward the entrance you can find another excavated area, **Group B**, off to the left, with two temple platforms forming a plaza. From beside the caretaker's hut, another path leads off to the **Ball Court Group**, or **Group C**. As the name indicates, this consists of a large ball court, surrounded by several exceptional *stelae*.

The Montebello Lakes

There are around 60 Montebello lakes in the **Lagunas de Montebello National Park**, ranging from large to tiny. At weekends and in the holidays families from Tuxtla or Comitán come here to picnic and admire the views, but with so many lakes you can always find a spot to yourself. The landscape appears to be exaggerated for extra effect, as the roads wind through pine forest, mountain and tropical jungle past precipitous slopes, with the fabulous colours of the lakes always in sight.

Just inside the park a road turns off left, to the north, for seven kilometres to **Bosque Azul**. This big lake is the busiest, the one on every tour itinerary, but it's not the most attractive. At the end of the road there is an unexciting restaurant, picnic tables shaded by *palapas*, and a **camp site**, and rowing boats can be hired on the lake.

On the main lakes road, the first you come to is **Laguna de Montebello** itself, after three kilometres. This is another large lake, edged by a wide 'beach' area with picnic *palapas* and, usually, some local cowboys offering horseback rides. Because of its size, though, the water can be murky. Another three kilometres east is the turn-off to the **Cinco Lagunas**, the 'Five Lakes', which meet and interlock through an astonishing landscape of forest ravines. There are well-built paths down to the water at most of them, and there will always be somebody offering to take you around the lakes on log rafts, a traditional form of transport here (*about $11 for two; it's cheaper per head for larger groups, max. six on a raft*). Another kilometre on is **Lago Pojoj**, 60 metres deep, in multiple shades of blue and easy for swimming. There will usually be a boy sitting by the small beach with his raft, waiting to take passing travellers around. Pojoj has an island in the middle, and if you want to have a desert island for the day you can arrange for him to take you across to it and then pick you up.

Getting There

This is an area where there has been a big improvement in access, 'courtesy' of the Zapatistas via the Mexican army, since the once-dirt road is now impressively paved, as it is the southern end of the Carretera Fronteriza around the Guatemalan border from Palenque (*see* p.452). The main road to the Lakes is sign-posted east from Highway 190, some 16km south of Comitán. The road leads in about 38km to the official entrance to the **Lagunas de Montebello National Park**, 3km beyond the turn to the site of Chinkultik.

If you're without a car, a *combi* company in Comitán, **Línea Comitán Montebello**, runs only to the Montebello Lakes, with frequent services from about 5.30am–5pm daily (last return from the lakes 5.30pm). Their garage is at Av. 2 Poniente Sur 21–3, between C/ 2 Sur and 3 Sur about three blocks from the plaza.

Park Information

You're not stopped and there's no entry charge at the park gate, but there will always be some local men around offering to act as guides: however, it's easy to find your way on your own. In 1999–2000 there were reports of robberies around the lakes, but to stop this going any further the main lakes are now watched over by state police and 'wardens' sent by the local *ejido* in Tziscao, which runs its own community development scheme. Visitors to the lakes pay a fee of about $2 per vehicle, which goes toward the community and lake conservation; with the one ticket, you can visit any of the lakes if you show it to the wardens at each one.

At the bigger lakes there will also be people selling handicrafts and the community's own-grown coffee (a great bargain).

Where to Stay and Eat

Montebello Lakes t (963–)

Places to stay in the Montebello area cover the opposite ends of the scale. Most are on or near the road in from Trinitaria, just west of the national park near the Chinkultik turn-off.

In the future, a few more *cabañas* and camp sites are likely to open further east around the *Fronteriza* route.

Parador-Museo Santa María, down a driveway off the Montebello road 22km east of Trinitaria, **t/f** 632 5116/633 1421, *www.santa-maria.chiapas.net.mx* (*moderate*). Strange to report, this remote part of Chiapas contains one of the most characterfully baronial hotels in Mexico. This is an 1830s *hacienda*, restored by brothers José Luis and Mario Uvence, filled with antiques and paintings and even featuring a museum of Baroque religious art in the former chapel. It would be ideal for a Zorro movie: each bedroom has different period furnishings, while facilities such as bathrooms are modern (with some quirks). It's pretty isolated, but excursions can be arranged, and there are horses for hire. It has a garden, a great bar-lounge and a pretty **restaurant** (*expensive*) with home-baked bread. They are also building some simpler cabins (*inexpensive*), and a pool.

Hotel Tziscao, by the lake in Tziscao (follow the road through the village round to the left), **t** 633 5244 (*cheap*). Offers both double- and three-bed rooms and *cabañas* (with showers). They're simple, but have been recently redecorated. The **restaurant** offers dead-cheap local classics (and cold beer), the ladies who run it are sweet, and they also rent boats on the lake.

Las Orquídeas (Doña María), beside the main lakes road a little east of the Chinkultik turning (no phone; *cheap*). Doña María's 10 colourfully painted wooden cabins have been here for nearly 50 years. Recent innovations include improved toilets and hot water in the communal showers. The cabins are quite cosy, and there's camping space and an equally simple **restaurant**.

El Pino Feliz, next to Doña María's (no phone; *cheap*). A more recent set-up than Doña María's, with 14 better-standard cabins, some with their own showers, still at very low prices, and camping space. Owners Rigoberto and Berta are very kind, offering to produce food and drinks almost on request, and have a *combi* with which they can take you to the lakes or the ruins. A very relaxing place.

From there it's five kilometres to the only village in the lakes, **Tziscao**, on **Laguna Tziscao**. It's an untidy but amiable little place, with a basic hotel. The lake – the south shore of which is in Guatemala – is wide and shallow, and turquoise rather than blue. It's also good for swimming, but you need to watch out for quicksand at some points around the edge. Not far beyond Tziscao is a turn to **Dos Lagunas**, the last accessible lakes on this road. Beyond there, the road continues on around towards Bonampak.

Tuxtla Gutiérrez

Tuxtla Gutiérrez is only a big warehouse which stores products from other parts of the state.
            Subcomandante Marcos

The Subcomandante wouldn't really be expected to think much of Tuxtla Gutiérrez, the largest city (population over 450,000) and seat of power and wealth in modern Chiapas. True to say, though, the state capital doesn't have many other fans either. Many Mexican cities seem to be forever marked by a particular time: Mérida has a permanent air of the 18th century; San Cristóbal is set in the 1560s; in Cancún it will always be the 1990s. In Tuxtla's case the period is one of Mexico's earlier booms, under Presidents Ruíz Cortines and López Mateos from the '50s into the '60s. Parts of central Tuxtla look like a showcase of angular 1950s high-rises, modern in their time.

If you travel from San Cristóbal to Tuxtla you descend more than 1,400m over 80 kilometres, along a road that at times seems to turn into a helter-skelter as it hairpins down the side of the Central Valley. Tuxtla Gutiérrez sits in a wide, brown, hilly plain, at the foot of an immense wall of rock to the north cut through by the great gash of the Sumidero. Although the Central Valley of Chiapas is still part of the Highlands, its climate has a dry, Mediterranean heat rather than the chill of the real mountains.

Local authorities in Chiapas are always encouraging people to spend some time in Tuxtla. It's an important transport hub and service centre, especially for people coming into the Mayan region from central Mexico, and many travellers find themselves staying one or two days. It has intriguing restaurants. Unless you have some contacts here, though, its attractions are really threefold: its proximity to the older colonial town of Chiapa de Corzo and the Sumidero gorge; a fine museum, displaying artefacts from all over Chiapas; and an extraordinary zoo, the ZOOMAT.

History

Before the Conquest the Central Valley was inhabited not by Maya but by the Zoque and a now-extinct Nahua-speaking people called the Chiapa. Not much trace of them remains today. The main centre of Spanish settlement in the area was initially Chiapa de Corzo, then known as Chiapa de la Real Corona. At the time of independence San Marcos Tuxtla, founded around a Dominican monastery (long demolished), was less important than San Cristóbal or Comitán. However, the Central Valley was becoming richer, producing cotton, maize, horses and cattle that were traded with Mexico.

Tuxtla Gutiérrez

Teatro de la Ciudad

Museo Regional de Chiapas

CALZADA DE HOMBRES ILUSTRES

Jardín Botánico

Parque Madero

C 6 ORIENTE NORTE

C 5 ORIENTE NORTE

C 4 ORIENTE NORTE

C 3 ORIENTE NORTE

C 2 ORIENTE NORTE

C 1 ORIENTE NORTE

CALLE CENTRAL NORTE

C 1 PONIENTE NORTE

C 2 PONIENTE NORTE

AV. 5 NORTE ORIENTE

C 6 ORIENTE NORTE

C 9 ORIENTE NORTE

C 10 ORIENTE NORTE

C 11 ORIENTE NORTE

C 12 ORIENTE NORTE

BOULEVARD ANGEL A. CORZO

Las Pichanchas

Main 2nd-Class Bus Stations

AV. 2 SUR ORIENTE

AV. 3 SUR ORIENTE

C 7 ORIENTE SUR

AVENIDA CENTRAL OTE

María Eugenia

AVENIDA CENTRAL OTE

San Antonio

AV. 4 SUR ORIENTE

AV. 5 SUR ORIENTE

C 4 ORIENTE SUR

C 3 ORIENTE SUR

C 2 ORIENTE SUR

C 1 ORIENTE SUR

AV. 6 SUR ORIENTE

Buses to Zoo

Buses to Chiapa de Corzo

AV. 4 NORTE ORIENTE

AV. 3 NORTE ORIENTE

AV. 2 NORTE ORIENTE

AV. 1 NORTE ORIENTE

Posada del Rey

Casablanca

La Catedral

Post Office

Ayuntamiento & Tourist Office

PLAZA CIVICA

Palacio de Gobierno

Las Canteras

Cathedral

La Casona

AVENIDA CENTRAL PTE

AVENIDA CENTRAL PTE

CALLE CENTRAL SUR

C 3 PONIENTE SUR

C 4 PONIENTE SUR

C 5 PONIENTE SUR

1st-class Bus Station

C 5 PONIENTE NORTE

C 6 PONIENTE NORTE

C 7 PONIENTE NORTE

C 8 PONIENTE NORTE

C 9 PONIENTE NORTE

AV. 5 NORTE PONIENTE

La Selva

BOULEVARD DR BELISARIO DOMINGUEZ

Parque de la Marimba

AV. 1 SUR PONIENTE

AV. 2 SUR PONIENTE

AV. 3 SUR PONIENTE

To Tourist Office & Bonampak Hotel

N

200 metres

200 yards

Getting Around

By Air

Tuxtla is a busy flight hub, and from most destinations offers the most convenient air route to San Cristóbal. **Aerocaribe** (t 612 5402) and **Aviacsa** (t 611 2000) have most services.

Flying into Tuxtla was once complicated by it having two airports, one 28km west of the city, but except in exceptional weather flights are now more conveniently concentrated at Terán (also known as Francisco Sarabia), about 6km to the southwest. If it is foggy, though, it's worth checking for delays or diversions with your airline before going to the airport.

As normal there are Transporte Terrestre **airport taxis** to take you into town (about $6). Tuxtla airport taxis will also be very happy to take you to San Cristóbal (around $45).

By Bus

Bus companies are dispersed between different stations. The main **first-class** station, Cristóbal Colón (used by most large companies, such as ADO), is two blocks from the Plaza Cívica (corner of Av. 2 Norte Oriente and C/ 2 Poniente Norte). Maya de Oro and Uno luxury services operate from an office across the street, on C/ 2 Poniente. Main services from both are as follows:

Cancún (*21hrs*): via **San Cristóbal**, **Palenque**, **Escárcega**, **Chetumal**, **Tulum** and **Playa del Carmen**, three daily from Cristóbal Colón, one Maya de Oro (2.30pm). Fare $48–$63.

Mérida (*20hrs*): via **San Cristóbal**, **Palenque**, **Escárcega** and **Campeche**, one ordinary first-class and one Maya de Oro daily (7.30am, 3.30pm). Fare $37–$50.

Mexico City (*17hrs*): eight ordinary first-class and five luxury buses daily. Fares from $50.

Palenque (*7hrs*): via **San Cristóbal** and **Ocosingo**, nine ordinary first-class and three luxury buses daily. Fares from $13.

San Cristóbal (*2–3hrs*): at least 18 ordinary first-class and five luxury buses daily, several continuing to **Comitán**. Fares from $4–$5.

Tapachula (*7hrs*): via **Tonalá**, ordinary first-class hourly, and seven luxury services. Fare about $19.

Villahermosa (*6½hrs*): via Highway 195, seven first-class and three luxury daily. Fares from around $14.

The ATG bus station, with second- and a few first-class services, and most **second-class** bus companies are several blocks southeast near the market, around the junction of Av. 3 Sur Oriente and C/ 7 Oriente Sur. Garages are spread around several streets, and it's worth looking around to find the destination you want; *combis* to San Cristóbal leave from the same area. Buses to **Chiapa de Corzo** depart from a separate garage, on the corner of Av. 3 Sur Oriente and C/ 3 Oriente Sur.

Given Tuxtla's sprawling layout **local combis** are more than usually useful. Moreover, they have route numbers. Route 1 (often written 01) runs up and down Av. Central; routes 7, 47, 49 and 72 go by the museum, passing C/ 2 Oriente; and *combis* to the ZOOMAT leave from C/ 1 Oriente Sur, by the corner of Av. 7 Sur Oriente. They normally have the number 60 and are marked 'Cerro Hueco'.

What politics there were in Chiapas were dominated by the fading aristocracy of Ciudad Real, San Cristóbal. When they decided to join Mexico in 1821, the ranchers and traders of the Valley rose against them, not so much because they preferred to stay with Guatemala but because they wanted their opinions to be heard. They were led by Joaquín Miguel Gutiérrez, who allied himself with the 'Federalists' in Mexico's endless civil conflicts and by a combination of war and politics firmly established a powerful role for Tuxtla within Chiapas. He was assassinated in 1838, but so revered was he in his home town that his name was attached to it, in 1849.

His position as leader of the Central Valley was taken up by Angel Albino Corzo, governor and chief supporter of Juárez in Chiapas, who was also victorious over the conservatives and *Maximilianistas* of San Cristóbal. The Valley's growth in influence and wealth was formalized in 1892, when the state capital was transferred to Tuxtla from San Cristóbal by Porfirio Díaz.

By Car and Taxi

Tuxtla is a busy city, and parking space is scarce in the centre during daytime. A **taxi** anywhere in the city should cost $1–$2, and they are always easy to find.

Car Hire

Most car rental agencies are towards the western end of Av. Central, near the larger hotels, and renting here is expensive.
Gabriel Rentacar, Blvd Dr Belisario Domínguez 780, **t** 612 2451, *www.gabriel.tuxtla.net*. Local agency that's cheaper than most in Tuxtla.

Orientation

Tuxtla Gutiérrez is a sprawling city, but its bus stations and most mid- and budget-range hotels are in the central district. It also has the prototype of the Chiapas street-numbering system. The city is a widely spread grid. Streets running roughly east–west are Avenidas, north–south ones are Calles. At its centre is the **Plaza Cívica** (Zócalo), meeting point of the C/ Central and Av. Central, the spine that runs right through the city, also called at different points Blvd Dr Belisario Domínguez or Blvd Angel Albino Corzo. Avenidas north of Central are Av. 1 Norte, Av. 2 Norte and counting; to the south they are Av. 1 Sur, Av. 2 Sur and so on. Calles west of C/ Central are C/ 1 Poniente, 2 Poniente; to the east they are C/ 1 Oriente, 2 Oriente. Each has a further 'locator', so that in the top left you will find Av. 2 Norte Poniente (Av. 2 North, West), and in the bottom right Av. 3 Sur Oriente (Av. 3 South, East).

Tourist Information

Tuxtla Gutiérrez t (961–)

Tuxtla City Tourist Office: In a pedestrian underpass beneath the city hall in the Plaza Cívica (*open daily 8-9*). The helpful young staff have information on other parts of Chiapas as well as Tuxtla, and there is a left-luggage service available.
Chiapas State Tourist Office: Blvd Dr Belisario Domínguez 950 (*open Mon–Sat 9–8; closed Sun*). Also helpful, with a wide range of material, but inconveniently bunched together with other government buildings at the west end of Av. Central, almost opposite the Hotel Bonampak.
Banks: There are several branches along Av. Central Poniente, near the Plaza Cívica or on the plaza itself. Most have ATMs. Staff tend to be unused to tourist transactions, and therefore slow.
Health: There are several large **pharmacies** on Av. Central, especially by C/ Central, which are open 24hrs.
Internet Access: There is a whole clutch in Av. 2 Norte Oriente, but note that Tuxtla seems to be the one place where there are frequent problems with Internet connections.
Post Office: In the civic centre on the eastern side of the plaza (*open Mon–Sat 9–6; closed Sun*). Has Mexpost.

Tours

Tuxtla's relatively limited tourist flow does not breed agencies in force, but those listed offer tours to the Sumidero, the ZOOMAT,

The City Centre

In Mexican style the main square, the **Plaza Cívica**, is the hub of activity in Tuxtla. Dominating the east side is the **Palacio de Gobierno**, the state government, while on the north side is the **Ayuntamiento**. To the south, across Av. Central, is the large, white **Cathedral of San Marcos**, begun in the 16th century but rebuilt in the 1900s and only dedicated in 1982. The Plaza is no colonial square, but a business-like space built and rebuilt between the 1950s and the 1980s. The outdoor restaurants on the colonnaded terrace by the cathedral make a popular meeting place, while Av. Central bustles with traffic by day and is full of animation after dark, for Tuxtla has plenty of nightlife.

In the older streets around the Plaza Cívica there are hotels, restaurants and other things a traveller might need. A few blocks southeast, down Calles 4 or 5 Oriente Sur, is the huge **market**, and eight blocks west of the Plaza Cívica up Av. Central there is a

San Cristóbal, Comitán, Montebello and Palenque. From Tuxtla, though, getting to the Sumidero is easy under your own steam.

Viajes Kali, in Hotel María Eugenia, Av. Central Oriente 507, **t** 611 3175;

Viajes Montalvo, Av. Central Oriente 836, **t** 611 4979, near C/ 7 Oriente.

Shopping

Casa de Artesanías, Blvd Belisario Domínguez 2035, **t** 612 2275. This state-run centre combines a shop with high-quality craftwork from all over Chiapas, a bookshop and an engaging museum (labelled in English), and is bigger than those at San Cristóbal and Palenque. The hitch is that it's rather inconveniently located at the west end of the Avenida, but it's worth a *combi* ride.

Where to Stay

Tuxtla Gutiérrez **t** (961–)

Moderate

Hotel Bonampak, Blvd Dr Belisario Domínguez 180, **t** 613 2050, **f** 612 7737. Long-running upper-scale hotel with some character. It has good facilities, a pool and pleasant rooms, and the added touch of reproductions of the Bonampak murals in the lobby.

Hotel María Eugenia, Av. Central Oriente 507, corner of C/ 4 Oriente Norte, **t** 613 3767, *heugenia@prodigy.net.mx*. Comfortable option in the centre, with functionally pleasant rooms and a good **restaurant**; it's also one of few central hotels with a pool.

Inexpensive

Hotel Catedral, Av. 1 Norte Oriente 367, **t** 613 0824. Pleasant, bargain hotel with spacious, airy rooms with fans and good bathrooms.

Posada del Rey, C/ 1 Oriente Norte 310, a block north of the plaza Cívica, **t** 612 2911, **f** 612 2210. A 1960s hotel, thoroughly done up in 2000, that now has bright, pleasant rooms all with a/c, TV and good bathrooms, making it the best-value mid-range choice. There's also the added touch of a rooftop **bar-restaurant,** La Troje del Rey, on the 7th floor, with panoramic views.

Cheap

Hotel Casablanca, Av. 2 Norte Oriente 251, between the main bus depot and plaza, **t** 611 0305, *amhm_chis@chiapas.net*. Pleasant hotel with rooms in various combinations (singles, doubles, triples, with or without a/c or TV) that are plain but clean and well kept. The owners take trouble with their guests, and it's warmly recommended by travellers.

Hotel Plaza Chiapas, Av. 2 Norte Oriente 299, **t** 613 8365. Near to the Casablanca, the fan-only rooms here are simple but bright, with bathrooms above the norm for this bracket, and very good value.

Hotel San Antonio, Av. 2 Sur Oriente 540, near the second-class bus stations, **t** 612 2713. Another good budget option. Its fan-only rooms have been brightly repainted, but are still very cheap.

smaller, prettier square, the **Parque de la Marimba**. The instrument it's named after is almost a symbol of identity for Chiapanecos, and the best *marimbas* in the state perform here for free, most evenings at around 8pm.

Parque Madero and the Museum

From the Plaza Cívica a longish walk or a *combi* ride will take you to **Parque Madero**, a formal but green park northeast of the city centre. Through it runs a walkway, the **Calzada de Hombres Ilustres** ('Pathway of Illustrious Men'), lined with statues of the major figures of the Mexican Revolution and several cultural institutions, including a **Jardín Botánico** (*open Tues–Sun 9–6; closed Mon; adm free*) with examples of Chiapas' most exotic plants, and Tuxtla's white elephant of a public theatre, the **Teatro de la Ciudad**. The prime attraction, though, is the **Museo Regional de Chiapas** (*open Tues–Sun 9–4; closed Mon; adm*). The museum covers the whole history of human

Eating Out

Expensive

Las Pichanchas, Av. Central Oriente 837, corner of C/ 8 Oriente, t 612 5351. If locals want to show off the best of their region they'll almost certainly bring you here. Showcasing both the food and traditions of (mostly non-Indian) Chiapas, it has become something of a monument. There's a floor show with dinner, mostly a reproduction of the dance of the *Parachicos* from Chiapa de Corzo (*see* p.512). It's a bit kitsch, but performed with great exuberance; the mainly local audience get very much into it as well. The food is really excellent, featuring unusual local specialities such as *tasajo* (dry-cured beef), vegetarian *tamales* with *chipilín* (a spinach-like vegetable, almost unique to Chiapas) and some very alcoholic desserts. Service is friendly and professional; note that '*expensive*' is a very relative term: even a real feast here will not cost much over $20.

Moderate

There are several good outdoor eating options in the arcade beside the cathedral on the Plaza Cívica, with a view of the square. The thing to do is just walk along and pick one.

Las Canteras, Av. 2 Norte Poniente, a block east of the bus station. Pretty restaurant that's also open for breakfast, serving local specialities such as a health-giving *chipilín* soup.

La Casona, Av. 1 Sur Poniente 134, a block from the plaza on the south side. Lovely restaurant near the Cathedral, in a 19th-century house that was restored in 1998 with a classically Mexican Kahlo-influenced colour scheme. The menu consists of Chiapanecan specialities – *tamales, tasajo* – and Mexican favourites, and service is very charming.

Restaurante Flamingo, C/ 1 Poniente Sur 168, hidden in a shopping arcade off Av. Central. With its '50s décor and courteous service, it seems to sum up Tuxtla's curious time-warp side, but its Chiapan and Mexican dishes are of a high standard and great value, and it's much appreciated by locals, many of whom look as if they've been coming here for ever.

Restaurante Vegetariano Nah-Yaxal-Soya, Av. Central Oriente 523, between C/ 4 Oriente and 5 Oriente. Though this is the full name of this bright vegetarian café/health-food shop, most prominent on the sign is 'Soya'. Varied meals use fresh local ingredients. There's a central branch at Av. Central Poniente 668, between C/ 5 and 6 Poniente.

Cheap

Mesón del Quijote, Av. Central Oriente, between C/ 2 and 3 Oriente Norte. Perhaps Tuxtla's star budget choice, with ultra-cheap set menus. A student favourite.

La Selva, Av. Central Poniente 782, between C/ 6 and 7 Poniente. Attractive modern café serving local organic coffee and snacks, with a similar branch in San Cristóbal.

Taquería La Providencia, C/ 1 Poniente Norte 24. Handy cheap eating point near the Cristóbal Colón bus station, offering an enormous choice of *tacos, tostadas, gringas* and other classics.

occupation in Chiapas, from distant prehistory. If you read Spanish and are prepared to take the time, you can assimilate a great deal, although some items are poorly labelled even in Spanish. It's particularly rich in relics from the Preclassic: exhibits begin with Olmec or Olmec-influenced reliefs, and there are several items from Preclassic Izapa. The museum has many treasures: *El Danzante* ('The Dancer'), an extraordinary carved image of a dancing jaguar-man, from Izapa prior to 300 BC; there is also the stone with the very oldest date known in the Long Count calendar, from 9 December 36 BC, discovered, for reasons that are still not fully understood, in non-Mayan Chiapa de Corzo. From the Classic era there are superb Zoque sculptures and a beautifully modelled, Mayan ceramic figure of a man sitting deep in thought. On a different scale is the panel from Toniná showing the hapless Kan-Hok-Chitam II of Palenque in captivity. The ceramics collection also includes great rarities, while another section, the Sala de Historia, deals with post-Conquest history.

The ZOOMAT

Open Tues–Sun 8.30–5.30; closed Mon; adm.

It never sounds good to say of a town that the best thing in it is the zoo, but Tuxtla's is something special. Its location is a delight in itself, on top of a forested hill south of the city, which catches a permanent refreshing breeze. The zoo's full title is Zoológico Miguel Alvarez del Toro, after the pioneer ecologist and naturalist of Chiapas who founded it before his death in 1966. At the entrance there is a small museum dedicated to him. The extraordinary thing about the nature park he created is that every one of the several hundred animals, birds and reptiles inside it is native to Chiapas.

The range is astonishing. Here you can see with ease all the most famous but rarely seen creatures of the region: jaguars, tapirs, exquisitely coloured quetzals. There are also many that are far more obscure: the yellow-necked toucan, or a whole collection of chachalacas. It would, of course, be better to see them in the wild, but since that is unlikely this is the next best thing. There is every kind of forest cat, from big pumas to *leoncillos*, crocodiles, anteaters, giant spiders and a special building housing normally invisible nocturnal creatures. Several animals that are no danger to anyone are allowed to run free, so that as you walk along the paths you may spot, scurrying past you, creatures like the strange rodent-pigs called *guaqueques*, and peccaries. Even people who are blasé about going to zoos find this place a real discovery.

Around Tuxtla

Fifteen kilometres east of Tuxtla Gutiérrez stands the oldest Spanish settlement in Chiapas, **Chiapa de Corzo**. It has the attractive features that Tuxtla lacks: a charming central square, quiet streets, fine colonial architecture and a riverside location on the banks of the Grijalva. The town and the adjacent village of **Cahuaré** are also the departure points for boat trips into the **Sumidero Canyon**, a dramatic, sheer-sided gash in the landscape that extends northwards for over 20 kilometres.

Chiapa de Corzo

Buses and the road from Tuxtla bring you into the **Parque Central**, the main square, a very wide colonial plaza with colonnades down two sides occupied by restaurants and a few souvenir shops. On the side of the square towards the river there is a magnificent *ceiba* tree, with a stone set beside it to say that it grew from a branch of an even larger tree, *La Pochota*, destroyed by fire in 1945. It was at the foot of this tree on 1 March 1528 that Diego de Mazariegos founded *Villa Real de Chiapa*, as the first Spanish town in the region. He had just vanquished the Chiapa, whose capital was nearby. A mixture of legend and historical accounts states that their warriors threw themselves into the Sumidero rather than accept defeat, and today they only survive in the name of the town and the state. It has changed name several times. In 1863 it saw a battle between Maximilian's army and the Juaristas, led by Angel Albino Corzo, the town's most famous son, and in his honour it was given its present name in 1888.

Next to the *ceiba* and dominating the view is Chiapa's most remarkable monument, the great brick **Pila** or well. It looks like something from the European Middle Ages, because it is: in fact, it's the finest example of *mudéjar* or Hispano-Moorish architecture in the Americas. Begun in 1562, it is actually a giant canopy over a well-head, with an inner gallery that's a deliciously shady spot in which to sit around the central pool.

Filling the side of the square between the Pila and the river is the town's other great colonial monument, the church and former monastery of **Santo Domingo**, built by the Dominicans' architect Friar Pedro Barrientos in the late 16th century. The church is huge, but made light and bright by being painted white and pinkish red. Walk around it to the right from the square and you will come to the **cloister**, recently restored. The brickwork is both *mudéjar*-influenced and shows Renaissance touches, and at some points the arches still retain patches of their original delicate paintwork. The cloister now contains the **Centro Cultural ex-Convento de Santo Domingo** (*open Tues–Sun 10–5; closed Mon; adm free*). As well as temporary exhibition spaces it has two permanent sections: one presents the powerful work of local artist and engraver Franco Lázaro Gómez, who drowned aged 27 near Lacanjá in 1949; the other is the **Museo de la Laca**, devoted to the main craft of the women of Chiapa de Corzo, lacquerwork.

Getting Around

Buses to Chiapa de Corzo, which stop at Cahuaré, leave from the corner of Av. 3 Sur Oriente and C/ 3 Oriente Sur in Tuxtla, with services every quarter-hour about 5am–10pm (returns run about the same times, but can vary, so check). Buses stop frequently, so the journey can take 40mins or more; some first-class and most second-class buses along this route also stop in Chiapa, and are quicker. In the opposite direction, many buses on the San Cristóbal–Tuxtla route stop here.

Getting to the Sumidero Canyon

Boats into the Sumidero leave from *embarcaderos* beneath the monastery in Chiapa de Corzo, and in the village of **Cahuaré**, beneath the bridge taking the main road across the river. The fare is the same at both (about $9 per person for a 2-hr trip). The boats are fast launches that hold a maximum of 10 people, and don't usually set off until they have at least eight; at weekends they run back and forth continually, but on weekdays you may have to wait around for people to make up numbers. At both *embarcaderos* there are riverside restaurants and bars to wait in.

You can also get fine views over the canyon from the road that runs along the west of the canyon from the Tuxtla *periférico*. *Combis* make the trip from near the second-class bus stations in Tuxtla, especially at weekends.

All **tour agencies** in Tuxtla and San Cristóbal run trips to the Sumidero. From San Cristóbal, this is an easy way of getting there. When choosing a tour, check what is included.

Getting to El Triunfo

The main entry track runs from **Jaltenango**, 140 kilometres (by dirt road) south of Tuxtla; the track that enters from Mapastepec on the Pacific side is rarely used.

Though there are no official visitor facilities within the reserve, 4–10 day tours are available for groups of 4–10 people. These are real adventure trips, involving hiking, climbing and camping in the forest. For tour details, contact: **Sonja Bartelt**, Reserva El Triunfo, C/ Argentina 389, Colonia El Retiro, Tuxtla Gutiérrez, **t/f** (961) 614 0378/614 0779, *ecotriunfo@ hotmail.com*.

Tourist Information

Chiapa de Corzo t (961–)

Tourist Information: In the monastery of Santo Domingo, but the staff, while very amiable, are often not there.

From the western end of the church you can walk down to the landing stage by the river, with its line of restaurants. Some of the nearby drinks-stands sell two Chiapan specialities, both credited with being very healthy. *Pozol* is a mixture of unfermented maize liquor and cacao, usually drunk from gourds; *tascalate* is a powder of ground maize, cinnamon, cacao, sugar and *achiote* pepper, beaten into water or (better) milk. Of the two, *tascalate* is probably more enjoyable for non-initiates.

From one side of the plaza Av. Julian Grajales leads up a steep crest to the colonial church of the **Calvario** or San Pedro, and eventually to Av. Miguel Hidalgo, where an INAH sign indicates the way to the **Archaeological Zone of Chiapa de Corzo**. If you follow it, though, you will be disappointed, as most of the small pyramid platforms are on private land, and their owner won't usually let anyone in to see them.

The Sumidero Canyon

The Sumidero is an awesome rift in the world's surface, a seismic fault between one and two kilometres wide, 20km long and with walls over 1,000m high. The Grijalva runs through the middle of it, but it did not create it. The river used to consist of some of the most dangerous rapids in the world, but in the 1980s the Chicoasén dam was

Festivals

Chiapa de Corzo is known for its spectacular *fiestas*, especially those that go on for a week around **San Sebastián** (20 Jan). These *mestizo* festivals do not have the mystical background of Highland Maya celebrations, and are more to do just with revelry. The central figures are the *parachicos*, men in bizarre outfits of embroidered capes, *sarapes* and lacquered masks with white faces and staring blue eyes. Thought to represent the Spanish conquerors, they began as a way for lower-class *mestizos* to satirize them. The *parachicos* act as lords of misrule, leaping around in flirtatious dances with the women, who wear dazzling flounced dresses with flowers in blue, red, gold and other colours. The *parachicos* also emerge at other *fiestas* (4 Aug, 17 Sept).

Where to Stay and Eat

Chiapa de Corzo t (961–)

Chiapa de Corzo has an unusually good choice of pretty restaurants, which take full advantage of the town's colonnade-and-patio architecture and make great places to laze for an afternoon. There are long rows of outdoor restaurants at the *embarcaderos* in Cahuaré and Chiapa (*moderate–cheap*), where the food is fairly standard, but made very enjoyable by the riverside location.

El Campanario, Av. Coronel Urbina 5, a block from the plaza on the south side (*moderate*). Fine old house, sharing the same owners as the Hotel La Ceiba, which also has a menu on offer featuring very well-prepared Chiapanecan specialities.

Hotel La Ceiba, Av. Domingo Ruíz 300. t 616 0389, *www.laceiba.chiapas.net.mx* (*inexpensive*). Chiapa has one very attractive hotel, in a quiet street a five-minute walk north of the plaza. The rooms, in an imaginatively converted old house, are decorated with traditional textiles and nearly all have loads of light; at the hotel's centre is a lovely leafy patio with a great pool. There's also a similarly pleasant **restaurant**. Prices are near the top of the *inexpensive* range.

Los Corredores, Av. Francisco Madero (*moderate*). By the slope that leads down to the river from the plaza, a deliciously shady patio with bargain Chiapanecan specialities and Mexican snacks.

Jardines de Chiapa, Av. Francisco Madero (*moderate*). Another exquisite patio near the river and the square, this is just a little more expensive, and as such has rather superior local dishes.

built at the north end of the canyon, transforming it from a river valley of massive rocks to a massive reservoir, and so making the current boat trips possible (*see* p.511).

To go into the Sumidero is to be swallowed up by it, as cliffs, crags and densely forested ledges rise up on either side. In parts the gorge is lined by mangrove-like vegetation, in others there are walls of rock. The canyon is full of wildlife, despite the dam. Among those creatures easiest to see as you go along are storks, herons and especially crocodiles, which seem to have adapted well to the new conditions and are plentiful. Waterfalls run down the cliffs, and favourite stops are the weird rock formations they have left over centuries, such as the **Arbol de Navidad**, which looks just like a Christmas tree as you approach it, but is made up of strange layers of calcified rock.

If you have a car you can get another angle on the gorge, from above. A road runs from the Tuxtla *periférico* along the west side of the canyon, past *mirador* viewpoints with fabulous vistas. There is a restaurant at the end of the road.

El Triunfo Biosphere Reserve

Tuxtla Gutiérrez is also the primary starting point for getting to the Biosphere Reserve of El Triunfo, 200 kilometres to the south in the highest ridges of the Sierra Madre, perhaps the most important of all Mexico's forest reserves. It extends over 120,000 square kilometres of tropical mountain, kept uninhabited by utter remoteness. This is the part of Chiapas where the state's most reclusive species are still found – quetzals, ocelots or guans – and all of 392 bird species have been logged within it. There are no conventional facilities within the reserve, but adventure tours (*see* p.511) are run in association with the US-based RARE organization.

Pacific Chiapas

Chiapas' Pacific rim is separated from the rest of the state by its highest, most uninhabited mountains, the **Sierra Madre**. As a result, its history has often followed a different course from that of areas further north. The Olmecs came down here, and later the area became a place of transit for a great many influences. It was not really a part of Mayan civilization in the Classic era, and this was the only part of Mexico's southern states absorbed into the empire of the Aztecs, who passed through on their way to attack Guatemala; a few years later the Spaniards did the same thing.

Anyone who travels down from Tuxtla or San Cristóbal has a choice of routes, as rugged as the two roads into Chiapas from the north. Most impressive is Highway 190 southeast from San Cristóbal. Beyond Montebello you climb and twist into hot, dry hills, where human population is thin on the ground. The road becomes more leafy, as the Pan-American Highway separates from the Mexican highway to turn towards **Ciudad Cuauhtémoc**, for the crossing into **Guatemala**. This is no one's idea of a city, not much more than a dusty street and a customs post; *combis* and taxis take you across the border to La Mesilla, from where there are buses into Guatemala (for information on entering Guatemala, *see* p.521). Back in Mexico, after **Motozintla** the road begins a staggeringly steep ascent into the clouds until, almost at the Pacific

Getting There

Puerto Arista and Boca del Cielo

Getting a *combi* from Tonalá to **Puerto Arista** can involve a trek. From the Cristóbal Colón bus station, turn left along the main street, Av. Hidalgo, and walk 12 blocks until you see, on the right, C/ 20 de Marzo. The *colectivo* stops are two blocks down on Av. J.M. Gutiérrez, near the market.

The *colectivo* corner for **Boca del Cielo** is down a different turning off Hidalgo, closer to the bus station, at C/ 15 de Septiembre. Taxis are very cheap, and run up and down to the coast frequently.

San José El Hueyate

Turn off Highway 200 on to the road signed for Mazatán, 14km west of Tapachula; from 12km south of the main highway, a dirt road leads another 24km to the coast.

Combis can be found from Tapachula to Mazatán, and from there to San José.

Where to Stay and Eat

Boca del Cielo t (994–)

Boca del Cielo (no phone, *moderate*). A recently opened restaurant, more neat and tidy than the others here, which are rough-and-ready but offer freshly caught grilled fish, especially shark.

Hotel El Paraíso, (no phone, *cheap*). Boca de Cielo's one, pretty simple hotel.

Puerto Arista t (994–)

Hotels are spread along the beach-side road. You're usually spoilt for choice for places to eat, but if everywhere is closed the Hotel Lizeth always seems prepared to cook up fresh fish. Seafood – simple classics such as *ceviches* – can be spectacularly good, as can fruit.

Arista Bugambilias, t 663 0182, f 663 0675 (*moderate*). Puerto Arista surprises you with some quite smartly appointed apartment-style hotels, such as this one near the north end of the beach, with fully equipped apartments with rooms for four, kitchens, TV and a living room, which can be a real bargain if you're travelling in a group.

Hotel Lizeth, t 663 0767, ext 141 (*inexpensive–cheap*). A sleepily friendly hotel where the road from Tonalá meets the beach, with pleasant, clean rooms. Some are fan-only, some have a/c, and most have a sea view.

San José El Hueyate t (918–)

San José El Hueyate, t 625 3940 (*inexpensive*). A recently created ecotourism scheme in a remote coastal village to the south of La Encrucijada reserve (*see left*). There are 10 cabins, a little **restaurant** and even a pool, as well as a giant, empty beach. Trips out to the mangroves and the reserve can be arranged with local boatmen.

Ocean, you cross the Continental Divide with a thump, at over 2,500m. You immediately begin to descend, more precipitously than you came up, as the road switchbacks around jungle valleys. For long stretches down to **Huixtla** it runs through cloudforest. The distinctive thing about this trip is that in seven hours you go through several entirely different climatic zones.

Highway 190, in the other direction southwest from Tuxtla, is the least mountainous of the four routes into Chiapas, and also the busiest, but it still has enough hairpins, inclines and giant ascents to qualify as a mountain road in any other country. About 40 kilometres west of Tuxtla a turning north leads to one of Chiapas' largest waterfalls at **El Aguacero** and the spectacular gorge of the **Río La Venta**, a national park where rafting trips are being started up (by **Explora**, *see* p.478). From **Cintalapa** you climb again, and 23 kilometres further south the road splits: Highway 190 leads west into Oaxaca; Highway 195 remains in Chiapas to twist through desert-like ravines and rocky gorges, until you descend to the busy road junction of **Arriaga**, and a Mediterranean-like coastal plain.

Puerto Arista and Boca del Cielo

Tonalá, 23 kilometres from Arriaga, is a hot market town, the mango capital of Chiapas. The site has an ancient history. It was an Olmec settlement, and in the plaza there is an Aztec *stela* of Tlaloc found nearby. Its biggest attraction, though, is as the access-point to the only beach villages in Chiapas, Puerto Arista and Boca del Cielo.

Ideas of Puerto Arista and Boca del Cielo as sophisticated beach resorts need to be done away with. When you arrive in **Puerto Arista** you find, along the one, straight street by the beach, some surprisingly solid hotels, basic shops, weekend houses and any number of typical Mexican beach restaurants, with big tables on the sand beneath huge *palapa* roofs, which only ever seem to get any customers during the Christmas and Easter holidays. And, while they're waiting for someone to turn up, Puerto Arista can be an ideal beach refuge for travellers looking for somewhere simple and peaceful to flop for a while. It has its downside. The beach is grey volcanic sand, which means it's the opposite of the white sand of Cancún that never gets hot: the sand here can be hot to bare feet even after it's had a night to cool off.

Boca del Cielo is even more basic, a shark-fishing village 15 kilometres to the east. It sits opposite a long, island-like sandspit which forms an oddly still lagoon; the name, 'Heaven's Gate', refers to the point where this meets the Pacific breakers, causing rare effects in the water and bringing together an enormous variety of birds. Fishermen will take you to the *estero*, the sandspit, and bring you back for about $5. This is one for serious sun-worshippers.

La Encrucijada Mangrove Reserve

This reserve is on the coast south of Highway 200 between Tonalá and Tapachula, around a 70-kilometre mangrove lagoon, the **Estero Las Palmas**. The area is rich in birds, deer and forest cats, and crocodiles are numerous. The usual way to get there is through **Acapetahua**, 72 kilometres west of Tapachula, but it's also possible to enter from the southern end via **San José El Hueyate**, which has the only place to stay in this area (*see* facing page). **Crucero Tours** in Tapachula (*see* p.518) is the main agent for the local *lancheros* and arranges tours (a day's tour costs around $50). Tourism is very new here, and conditions are simple. Plenty of bug repellent is essential: this coast is known for a persistent type of mosquito, the *zancudo*, and La Encrucijada is best avoided in the rainy season, from July to September or October.

Tapachula

Graham Greene moaned about the heat in Villahermosa, but then he never got to Tapachula. Chiapas' second-largest city sweats, steams, and sweats again. It makes up for this by being the fruit-juice capital of the world. Towards the end of the dry season in May or June, it looks as if every citizen of the town is in continual need of a cold drink. To answer this need, there are wonderful juice stands on nearly every street, as well as young boys with hand-carts, selling natural *cerveza de raíz* (root beer) in plastic bags with a straw, little fixes of coldness to take on the run.

Its position as a frontier town is essential to the identity of Tapachula. It once had the distinction of being a stateless city. In 1824, when the rest of Chiapas joined Mexico, Tapachula and the Soconusco decided to stay with Guatemala. To avoid a war neither was very interested in, the governments of Mexico and the Central American Confederation decided that neither one should own the town, at least until they felt like discussing it again. Sadly for anarchists everywhere, this 'experiment' was not a success. Stateless Tapachula became a refuge for 'delinquents and destructive elements', while 'industry, agriculture and commerce' went to ruin. Finally, in 1842 General Santa Anna decided to make it part of Mexico, against apathetic protests from Guatemala. Later in the century the Soconusco's heat, rainfall and closeness to a coast made it the first area of Chiapas to be developed for modern agriculture, which brought in a new and varied population. The first coffee plantations were established by Germans, and under Porfirio Díaz Chinese and Japanese farmers were encouraged to settle here. The Chinese and Japanese communities are still very influential in Tapachula today, and a characteristic sight in the city are signs like *Taquería Yu Hang*. Modern Tapachula is Mexico's gateway to Central America, and hosts a major trade fair for the region, *Expo Internacional Tapachula*, in March, when all the hotels fill up.

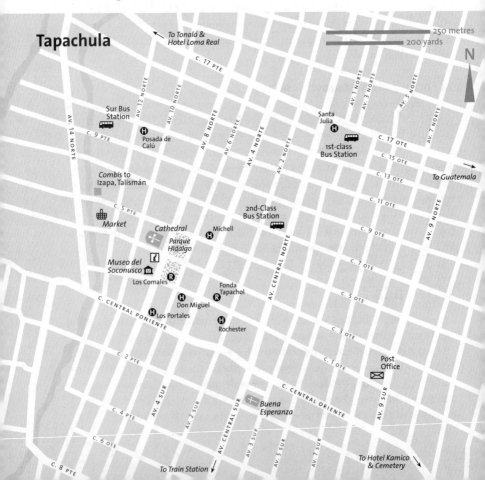

Getting Around

By Air

Tapachula's airport is 17km south of the city near Puerto Madero. **Aviacsa, t** 626 1439, has frequent flights to Mexico City and Tuxtla Gutiérrez; **Aerocaribe, t** 626 9872, flies to Tuxtla, Oaxaca and Veracruz; **Aeroméxico, t** 626 3921, has flights to Mexico City. **Airport taxis**, as usual, are the way in to the city.

By Bus

The **first-class bus station**, Cristóbal Colón, is on the main highway, C/ 17, east of Av. Central by Av. 3 Norte. From there, it's a taxi ride to the centre. Being a border station it has many services, especially to central Mexico, of which some of the most important are these:
Mexico City (*18hrs*): seven ordinary first-class and three luxury buses daily. Fare about $70.
Oaxaca (*14hrs*): two daily. Fare about $30.
Puerto Escondido (*10hrs*) via Huatulco: one daily. Fare about $32.
Veracruz (*19hrs*): two daily. Fare about $40.
San Cristóbal (*8hrs*): six buses daily, via **Ciudad Cuauhtémoc** and **Comitán**. Fare about $15.
Tuxtla Gutiérrez (*7hrs*): via **Tonalá**, ordinary first-class hourly and seven luxury services daily. Fare about $19.
Villahermosa (*15hrs*): one bus daily, via **Tuxtla Gutiérrez**. Fare about $30.

There are also international services: two daily to **Guatemala City** (*6hrs*; fare about $22); for those arriving from Guatemala who don't want to see anything of Mexico there's a bus through to **Brownsville, Texas**, leaving every night at 10pm and getting there in around 48hrs (about $70); for fans of really long trips the Costa Rican Tica Bus company has a daily bus all the way through to **Panama**, calling at all the capitals en route. Full fare is about $90.

Second-class bus companies are spread in several garages. Most important is Rápidos del Sur, near the market area on C/ 11 Poniente, near Av. 12 Norte, with frequent services along the Soconusco, and towards San Cristóbal and Tuxtla. The market streets are the main *combi* centre of Tapachula, and two blocks south on C/ 5 Poniente you'll find *combis* to Talismán, all of which pass **Izapa**. Another useful company is Omnibus de Tapachula, on C/ 7 Poniente just off Av. Central, which has services to the Guatemalan border at Ciudad Hidalgo.

By Car and Taxi

There are two *gasolineras* on C/ 17-Highway 200, either side of the city centre. **Taxis**, not local buses, are the key form of city transport, costing about $1.70 for any journey in town.

Car Hire

Car hire companies are mainly based in hotels, and relatively expensive.
Chiapas RentaCar Hotel Cabildos, Av. 2 Norte 17, t 626 3792. Local company that's slightly cheaper than the bigger companies.

Orientation

Tapachula has a Chiapas street numbering system. Avenidas are north–south, Calles east–west. The city's peculiarities are, firstly, that Calles north of the central axis have odd numbers, while to the south they are even (but still have locators like C/ 6 Poniente, C/ 6 Oriente, etc.); Avenidas west of Av. Central are even, and to the east are odd. Another surprise is that the main square, **Parque Hidalgo**, is not at the axis of the grid but in the northwest quarter. **Calle 17**, on the north side of the city centre, is the local identity of Highway 200, the main east–west road through the city.

Parque Hidalgo and the Museum

Tapachula's main square has a character it owes to the heat, the city's early 20th-century prosperity and its peculiar role in the Mexican-Guatemalan economies. The heat is reflected in the line of terrace restaurants, which specialize in pint-size glasses of blended fruit – pineapple, mango, papaya, melon – over which to sit after the sun goes down. The coffee boom is reflected in the town's tropical Art Deco architecture, especially the smart, former town hall, now the **Casa de Cultura**. The very white **Cathedral** alongside was built in the 18th century, but has been heavily renovated.

Tourist Information

Tapachula t (962–)

Tourist Office: In the Art Deco former town hall, on Parque Hidalgo (*open Mon–Fri 9–3 and 6–9*). Its staff are not always that well informed, but they try hard.

Banks: Near the plaza or on Av. Central. All have ATMs.

Consulates: The Guatemalan consulate is at C/ 2 Oriente 33, t 626 1252, near the corner of Av. 7 Sur (*officially open Mon–Fri 9–5, but often closes for lunch*).

Health: Tapachula has a glut of 24-hr **pharmacies**, as is evident when you arrive.

Internet Access: Katzuaki: Av. 2 Norte 6-D, near the Hotel Rochester in the block north of C/ Central, is a laid-back Internet café with decent rates (and video games).

Mexican Immigration Office: Av. 14 Norte 57, t 626 1263 (*usually open Mon–Fri 9–1*). Tapachula has a special status as a frontier zone: on Highway 200 20km north of the city there are inspection points where bus and vehicle passengers may be checked as thoroughly as at the border itself. If you enter from Guatemala and are given only 15 days in Mexico, it's better to go further into the country and get an extension there (not Tuxtla), rather than in Tapachula.

Post Office: East of the centre at C/ 1 Oriente and Av. 9 Norte (*open Mon–Fri 8–6, Sat 8–noon*). Restrictions apply to parcel mail from Tapachula, and anything bigger than a letter has to be checked by a customs agent.

Tours

Of the local travel and tour agencies, the following is the most interesting:

Crucero Tours, C/ 1 Poniente 10, t 625 2257, *www.crucerotours.com.mx*. As well as conventional travel agency services director *sr* Rodolfo Flores has been developing adventure tours, such as rafting trips in the Sierra Madre, and is the main agent for the ecotourism scheme of the *lancheros* cooperative in the Encrucijada (*see* p.515).

Where to Stay

Tapachula t (962–)

Moderate

Hotel Don Miguel, C/ 1 Poniente 18, t/f 626 1143, *dmiguel@tap.com.mx*. The smartest central option, with recently refurbished rooms, with new bathrooms, and very good a/c; an appreciable factor in Tapachula.

Hotel Kamico, Prolongación C/ Central Oriente, t 626 2640, *www.kamico.com.mx*. East of the city centre (outside walking distance), this modern hotel has large, high-standard, comfortable rooms spread around a tropical garden, and a beautiful pool with a poolside **restaurant**.

Hotel Loma Real, Ctra Costera Km244, t 626 1440, f 626 6520. In a lush garden, just off Highway 200 on the northwest of the city. Spacious rooms with all the trimmings, a gym, and a very good pool and **restaurant**.

Inexpensive

Hotel Colomba, Av. 8 Norte 16, a block from the plaza, t 625 0142. In a recently converted building with pleasant rooms, all with a/c, and has nice details such as bigger-than-usual bathrooms and flowers in the rooms.

Hotel Michell, C/ 5 Poniente 23-A, between Av. 4 and 6 Norte, t 625 2640, f 626 8874. Functional hotel off the north side of Parque Hidalgo, with light, modern rooms, all with TV, a/c and other comforts.

The city's relationship with Guatemala is seen in the tropical bustle of the square – despite the heat – and the multi-assorted, cranky range of shops, discount department stores, and an unfathomable number of huge pharmacies, a hypochondriac's heaven, apparently because pharmaceuticals are overtaxed in Guatemala. Along the top of the square is what may be Mexico's largest single concentration of *taco*-stands and cheap snack places, while in the middle a *marimba* plays every night.

The old town hall also contains the **Museo Regional del Soconusco** (*open Tues–Sun 10–5; closed Mon; adm*), one of the more unusual local archaeological museums, with

Hotel Los Portales, Av. 8 Norte 19, t 625 4050, f 626 3822. South of the plaza past the Museo de Soconusco, this was completely renovated in 2000 and has bright, comfortable rooms with a/c, cable TV and excellent bathrooms, decorated in modish Frida Kahlo-esque colours. Breakfast is served in a similarly pretty patio.

Hotel Rochester, Av. 2 Norte 6, north of C/ Central, t 626 1406. The best near-budget option in the centre. Its fan-only and a/c rooms don't have much furniture (just cable TV), but they're clean, and the upper floors get plenty of light and air.

Hotel Santa Julia, C/ 17 Oriente 8, t 626 3140, f 626 2486. Handy for the bus station, next to the Cristóbal Colón on the main highway. Its rooms are straightforward, but all have a/c, phones and TV; the primary disadvantage is noise from the road.

Cheap

Tapachula has several bargain-basement hotels, especially near the market, but some are real flop-houses; some specialize in rock-bottom rooms for Guatemalans passing through in the hope of moving to the USA.

Posada de Calú, C/ 11 Poniente 34, t 625 1595. Probably the most attractive real cheapie, in the market area. Rooms, with fans and decent showers, open on to a patio giving lots of light, and the owners are friendly.

Eating Out

Moderate

Café Monaco, C/ 1 Poniente, corner of Av. 4 Norte. Pleasant little modern café with light, health-foodish snacks, excellent juices and good coffee. A calming place for breakfast.

Los Comales, Parque Hidalgo, corner of Av. 8 Norte. Claims pride of place among the big, shaded terraces of the plaza. Specialities include huge glasses of juice, but they also have enjoyable local and standard Mexican dishes and excellent breakfasts. *Open 24 hrs.*

Fonda Tapachol, C/ 1 Poniente, between Av. 2 and 4 Norte. Here Tapachula showcases its local cuisine, in this very pretty courtyard adorned with *fiesta* decorations, and even a live *marimba*. Drinks include *tascalate* and *pozol*, with the usual beers. The Soconuscan variations on more common Chiapan dishes include several combining the vegetable *chipilín* with seafood, *fríjoles* or rice – even completely vegetarian dishes – and a range of *tamales*. Meals are interesting, pleasant, and, considering the price, remarkable value.

Cheap

It's never difficult to find a cheap meal in Tapachula, since if you just walk around the plaza, above all along C/ 5 Poniente, you'll be bombarded with cheap food on all sides.

Chun Seak, C/ 1 Poniente, near Av. 4 Norte. A particularity of Tapachula is its many Chinese restaurants, although these only seem to offer fairly standard Cantonese food. This one has enjoyable set menus; the nearby **Meng Sheng** is very similar.

La Flor de Michoacán, Av. 6 Norte, corner of C/ 7 Poniente. More coolers: great ice creams, and also giant tanks of fresh fruit *aguas*.

Refresquería **Los Troncos**, C/ 5 Poniente, just off Av. Central. Any full listing of Tapachula's unmissable *juguerías* would make a whole study in itself, but this is one to recommend, with *tascalate*, *pozol*, a more than usually varied range of juices and even some space to sit down (many juice stands have no seating at all).

two halves. The ground floor contains mainly relics from Izapa, including **Stela 25**, showing a small human figure holding up a giant bird-like standard, while hanging in the air alongside him, pointing snout-downwards, is a crocodile-like dragon. This is one of the most important carvings from Izapa in terms of its mixture of Olmec and later Mayan imagery; the crocodile is thought to be an early symbol of the *wakah-kan*, the Milky Way. The second floor covers the remarkable range of peoples that have inhabited the Soconusco, as a zone of passage. Highlights are an exquisite Mayan carved bottle, and an extraordinary Mixtec skull inlaid with turquoise mosaic.

Izapa

This is far more ancient than any of the Mayan cities described previously. Izapa was occupied from about 1500 BC, and its most important buildings were erected in the Early Preclassic, around 300 BC; by about AD 400 it had been abandoned. It is thus more contemporary with an Olmec city like La Venta than with the Classic Mayan cities. The style of buildings and sculptures at Izapa was strongly influenced by the Olmecs, and the Izapan culture – which extended as far as Kaminaljuyú, on the site of modern Guatemala City – was illiterate and did not use Mayan glyphs. However, many elements of later Mayan culture and mythology are evident – early forms of the god Chac, or of *Vucub-Caquix* or 'Seven Macaws', the Celestial Bird, a symbol of nature challenging the gods, that appears in the *Popol Vuh*. Izapa has been called 'Proto-Mayan', the first stage in the emergence of a recognizably distinct Mayan civilization.

The site is widely dispersed, with 80 structures in three visitable areas. *Combi* drivers will almost certainly drop you at **Group C**, the largest and the closest to the main road. Here there is a large plaza of several temple platforms, rather crude by the standards of later Mayan buildings, but recognizable nonetheless. There are also several badly deteriorated *stelae* and sculptures, with an Olmec-like massiveness. Another feature of Izapan carving similar to Olmec styles are the many anthropomorphic images, particularly the huge toad-heads.

The southern groups of buildings are reached by walking back along the road toward Tapachula for about 700m – a hot trek – to a signposted path south, along which you have a more enjoyable walk for about another kilometre through an overwhelmingly green landscape of giant leaves in which even the trees seem to sweat. At an (unmarked) three-way fork in the path, take the centre path for the ruins. **Group A**, to the right, is a big open plaza, partly planted with corn and surrounded by various unexcavated mounds and *stelae*. The carvings here are in a better state than those in Group C; highlights are Stela 4, a very clear figure of a warrior, and Stela 5, with a bird-image believed to be *Vucub-Caquix*. **Group B**, a little to the east, is similar, with more impressive carving and toad-heads. A feature of Izapa are the 'headstones' in front of several *stelae*, which seem to be a kind of phallic imagery not found in later Mayan styles. After that, retrace your steps to the road, with another steamy walk in deep-tropical Mexico.

Getting There

The ruins of **Izapa** are 12km east of Tapachula on the road towards Talismán, almost in Guatemala. If you don't have your own transport the way to get there is with a *colectivo* to Talismán, which leave about every half an hour from C/ 5 Poniente near the market. Tell the driver you want *Las Ruinas de Izapa*, and he'll let you off there (usually by Group C). On the way back, just flag down any Tapachula-bound *combi*.

Site Information

Open (officially) daily 8–5; adm.

This is one of the most rustic sites you can possibly visit: each section is set on a small *rancho*, and the farmers are the caretakers. There's actually no set adm charge, but each farmer expects a tip, so you end up paying (a little) three times.

Getting between the different sections involves a steamy walk, so it's advisable to have water with you.

In and Out of Guatemala

Visas and Immigration

Citizens of the USA, Canada, Britain and most EU countries, Australia and New Zealand do not need visas to enter Guatemala. However, there can be variations in the amount of time you are given in the country, from 30 to 90 days. Taking a US- or Canadian-registered **vehicle** into Guatemala requires another temporary import permit, which should cost about $30 but is a time-consuming procedure that can include spraying the vehicle against crop plagues.

If you **enter Mexico** from Guatemala, you may be given a tourist card for only 15 days, and may have to pay for it (about $20, *see* p.111); if you need more, try to travel further into the country, to San Cristóbal or into the Yucatán, and apply for an extension there.

Into Guatemala

There are two crossing points across the Suchiate river into Guatemala from Tapachula – at Talismán (20km) to the Guatemalan town of **El Carmen**, and to the south at Ciudad Hidalgo (38km) to **Ciudad Tecún Umán** on the other side. Ciudad Hidalgo is the busier crossing, and recommended to drivers. If you are not on a through bus to Guatemala City, the same *combis* that take you to Izapa will take you to Talismán, and Omnibus de Tapachula run frequently to Ciudad Hidalgo. At each crossing you can walk or take a *combi* across the river bridges, and on the other side there are buses to many points within Guatemala.

Language

Several features of Spanish make it one of the easiest languages to pick up at least a little of from scratch. Firstly, it is phonetic, with very practical spelling that provides an immediate connection between how a phrase is written and the way it is pronounced. Stress is all-important in speaking Spanish in an understandable way. The stress is on the last syllable in words ending with most consonants, or on the penultimate one, in words ending in a vowel, an *s* or an *n*; where this pattern is not followed the 'new' stress is indicated by an accent, as in *Mérida*, *Cancún* (but no accent on *Campeche*). Secondly, basic Spanish grammar is very simple. Questions, in particular, are formed not by any changes in sentence order but by tone of voice: thus, the difference between *tiene mucho dinero* (he has a lot of money, statement) and *¿tiene mucho dinero?* is just in how you say it, which anyone can understand. There are also particular advantages in Mexican Spanish for the absolute beginner. Most Mexicans speak more slowly than most other Spanish speakers, and stresses are very strongly emphasized, making words recognizable and giving plenty of time to think about a response.

Anyone who already knows some Spanish from other countries will find many differences in the language of Mexico, above all if they learnt Spanish in Spain. Beyond individual words or phrases, most important is that Mexicans lay great store on politeness, and use forms of courtesy to an extent that would now be considered quaint in many other countries (Mexicans find Spaniards rude and aggressive, just by the way they speak). Expect to use polite phrases, even a simple *por favor*, a great deal. Also, use the polite form of the second person (*usted*) unless and until the other person makes it clear you've established your relationship sufficiently to call each other *tú*. The second person plural form is always *ustedes*, as a polite or a familiar term.

A useful phrase book is *Mexican Spanish* (Rough Guides). Books on 'Latin American Spanish' are likely to be no more use than a general Spanish phrase book, since there is no such thing as Latin American Spanish.

For vocabulary related to eating out and a menu decoder, *see* **Food and Drink**, pp.98–103.

Pronunciation

Vowels

a	short *a* as in 'pat'
e	short *e* as in 'set'
i	as *e* in 'be'
o	between long *o* of 'note' and short *o* of 'hot'
u	silent after *q* and 'gue-' or 'gui-'; otherwise long *u* as in 'flute'
ü	*w* sound, as in 'dwell'
y	at end of word or meaning and, as *i*

Diphthongs

ai, ay	as *i* in 'side'
au	as *ou* in 'sound'
ei, ey	as *ey* in 'they'
oi, oy	as *oy* of 'boy'

Consonants

c	before *i* or *e*, a soft *s* sound; otherwise as in 'cat'
ch	like *ch* in 'church'
g	before *i* or *e*, pronounced as *j* (*see* below)
h	silent
j	like the *ch* in 'loch', but harder; this sound does not exist in English
ll	*y* or *ly* as in 'million'
ñ	*ny* as in 'canyon'
q	*k*
r	usually rolled, which takes practice
v	harder than in English; closer to *b*
x	between consonants, hard like a *j* (*see* below for *x* in Mayan words)

Pronunciation of Mayan Names and Words

The most widely used spellings of Mayan languages are also fairly phonetic. Yucatec Maya is a language of very strong, throat-breaking consonants, and in a name like Oxcutzcab both *c*-syllables are pronounced with a powerful *k*-sound. *Z* indicates a real *z* sound, especially in the heavily voiced combinations *dz* and *tz* (although non-Mayan Mexicans commonly say them with an *s*). The letter *x* normally indicates a *sh* sound, with a slight vowel sound before it when it comes before a consonant; thus **Xcambó**, **Xcaret**, are *Eesh-cambó*, *Eesh-caret*, and so on.

Chiapas Mayan languages are much softer and more whispering, and in names like *Chenalhó* the *h*-sound is very faint.

Frases Mexicanísimas

There are certain phrases that, within the Spanish language, are marked out as quintessentially Mexican. The following are a few that you will hear all the time, and might need to respond to:

ahorita The diminutive of *ahora* (now), theoretically meaning 'right now' but really referring to an indeterminate period of time, as in *ahorita viene*, 'she's coming right now', although she may be along in a minute, or in five hours, or *ahorita no sé*, 'I don't know at the moment' (but there's no guarantee I'll know in future either).

ándele An expression of encouragement, and/or amazement; also said when leaving, as in *ándele, pues* (let's be going).

bueno Good, but also the first thing Mexicans say when they answer the phone, with the stress almost transferred to the o.

¿cómo no? 'Why not?' or 'How could it be otherwise', roughly equivalent to 'of course', as when you walk into a deserted restaurant and ask if they're open, and the answer comes back *sí, ¿cómo no?*

mande Literally a polite word meaning 'command', but corresponding to 'Pardon me?'; when you ask many people a question they will automatically reply *mande*, so that you will then have to repeat the question, maybe in a more polite form.

órale An expression of amazement. Wow.

Useful Words and Phrases

yes *sí*
no *no*
Hello *Hola*
Goodbye *Adios/hasta luego*
Good morning *Buenos días*
Good afternoon *Buenas tardes*
Good evening, Goodnight *Buenas noches*
I don't understand Spanish *no entiendo español*
Do you speak English? *¿habla usted ingles?*
Speak slowly, please *Hable despacio, por favor*
Can you help me? *¿Puede usted ayudarme?*
I (don't) like... *(No) me gusta...*
Help! *¡Socorro!*
Leave me alone! *¡Déjame en paz!*
please *por favor*
thank you (very much) *(muchas) gracias*
How do you do? *mucho gusto* (when greeting someone for the first time)
Well, and you? *¿Bien, y usted?*
What is your name? *Cómo se llama?*
My name is... *Me llamo.../Soy...*
you're welcome *de nada*
I don't know *no sé*
It doesn't matter *no importa*
All right *está bien*
excuse me, sorry *disculpe*
excuse me (to attract attention) *oiga* (polite)
I'm sorry *Lo siento*
be careful! *¡(tenga) cuidado!*
maybe *quizá(s)*
nothing *nada*
It is urgent *es urgente*
What is that? *¿Qué es eso?*
What...? *¿Qué...?*
Who...? *¿Quién...?*
Where...? *¿Dónde...?*
When...? *¿Cuándo...?*
Why...? *¿Por qué...?*
How...? *¿Cómo...?*
How much...? *¿Cuánto.../cuánta...?*
How many...? *¿Cuántos.../cuántas...?*
What time does it open/close? *¿A qué hora abre/cierra...?*
exit/entrance *salida/entrada*
I am lost *Estoy perdido*
I am hungry/thirsty *Tengo hambre/sed*
I am tired (man/woman) *Estoy cansado/a*
I am sleepy *Tengo sueño*
I am ill *No me siento bien*

here/there *aquí/allí*
close/far *cerca, cercano/lejos*
left/right *izquierda/derecha*
over there, that way *p'allá*
straight on *todo recto*
forwards/backwards *adelante/atrás*
good *bueno/a*
bad *malo/a*
slow *despacio, lento*
fast *rápido/a*
big *grande*
small *pequeño/a*
hot (food, drink) *caliente*
cold *frío/a*
I am hot/cold *tengo calor/frío*
Pull/Push (on a door) *Jale/Empuje*
toilets/toilet *servicios/lavabo*
men *señores/hombres/caballeros*
women *señoras/damas*

Numbers

one *uno/una*
two *dos*
three *tres*
four *cuatro*
five *cinco*
six *seis*
seven *siete*
eight *ocho*
nine *nueve*
ten *diez*
eleven *once*
twelve *doce*
thirteen *trece*
fourteen *catorce*
fifteen *quince*
sixteen *dieciséis*
seventeen *diecisiete*
eighteen *dieciocho*
nineteen *diecinueve*
twenty *veinte*
twenty one *veintiuno*
twenty two *veintidos*
thirty *treinta*
thirty one *trienta y uno*
forty *cuarenta*
fifty *cincuenta*
sixty *sesenta*
seventy *setenta*
eighty *ochenta*
ninety *noventa*

one hundred *cien*
one hundred and one *ciento uno*
two hundred *doscientos*
five hundred *quinientos*
one thousand *mil*
one million *un millón*
first *primero/a*
second *segundo*
third *tercero*

Time

What time is it *es?*
It's 2 o'clock *Son las dos*
...half past 2 *...las dos y media*
...a quarter past 2 *...las dos y cuarto*
...a quarter to 3 *...un cuarto para las tres*
noon *mediodía*
midnight *medianoche*
day *día*
week *semana*
month *mes*
morning *mañana*
afternoon *tarde*
evening/night *noche*
late night (around 1am–dawn) *la madrugada*
today *hoy*
yesterday *ayer*
tomorrow *mañana*
now *ahora*
later, after *después*
it is early *es temprano*
it is late *es tarde*
Monday *lunes*
Tuesday *martes*
Wednesday *miércoles*
Thursday *jueves*
Friday *viernes*
Saturday *sábado*
Sunday *domingo*
January *enero*
February *febrero*
March *marzo*
April *abril*
May *mayo*
June *junio*
July *julio*
August *agosto*
September *septiembre*
October *octubre*
November *noviembre*
December *diciembre*

Shopping and Sightseeing

I want, I would like... *Quiero...*
Where is/are...? *¿Dónde está/están...?*
How much is it? *¿Cuánto es?*
Do you have any change? *¿Tiene cambio?*
open/closed *abierto/cerrado*
cheap/expensive *económico/caro*
shop *tienda*
(super)market *(super)mercado*
bank *banco*
money *dinero/plata*
box office *taquilla*
newspaper (foreign) *periódico (extranjero)*
pharmacy *farmacia*
police/police officer *policía*
police station *comisaría*
post office *correos*
postage stamp *estampilla*
telephone (phone call) *teléfono (llamada)*
phone office *caseta*
hospital *hospital*
church *iglesia*
museum *museo*
theatre *teatro*
beach *playa*
sea *mar*

Accommodation

Where is the... hotel? *¿Dónde está el... hotel...?*
Do you have a (single/double) room? *¿Tiene usted una habitación (sencilla/doble)?*
...with twin beds *...con dos camas*
...with a double bed *...con una cama grande/de matrimonio*
...with a shower/bathroom *...con ducha/baño*
...for one night/one week *...para una noche/una semana*
Can I see the room? *¿Puedo ver la habitación?*
Are there rooms with more light? *Hay habitaciones con más luz?*
How much is the room per night/week? *¿Cuánto es la habitación por noche/semana?*
air conditioning *aire acondicionado, clima*
swimming pool *alberca, piscina*

Driving

to rent, hire *rentar*
car *carro, auto, coche*

motorbike/moped *moto*
bicycle *bicicleta*
petrol/gasoline *gasoline*
garage *garaje*
This doesn't work *Esto no funciona*
road/street *carretera/calle*
dirt road *camino de terracería*
motorway *autopista, cuota*
Is the road good? *¿Es buena la carretera?*
breakdown *avería*
(International) driving licence *carnet de manejar/conducir (internacional)*
tyre *llanta*
driver *conductor, chófer*
speed *velocidad*
danger *peligro*
car park *estacionamiento*
no parking *estacionamiento prohibido*
give way/yield *ceda el paso*
stop *alto*
road works *obras*
army checkpoint *retén militar*
NOTE: most road signs will be in international pictographs.

Transport

aeroplane *avión*
airport *aeropuerto*
customs *aduana*
bus/coach *autobús/camión*
bus station *estación de autobuses/camiones*
bus stop *parada*
seat *asiento*
platform *andén*
port *puerto*
ship *buque/barco/embarcación*
small boat *lancha*
ticket *boleto*
I want to go to... *Quiero ir a...*
How can I get to...? *¿Cómo puedo llegar a...?*
When does the next (bus) leave for...? *¿Cuándo sale el próximo (autobús) para...?*
What time does it leave/arrive? *¿A qué hora sale/llega?*
Where does it leave from? *¿De dónde sale?*
Does it stop at...? *¿Para en...?*
How long does the journey take? *¿Cuánto tiempo dura el viaje?*
I want a (return) ticket to... *Quiero un boleto (de ida y vuelta/redondo) a...*

Glossary

aguada natural depression in the ground that retains water during the rainy season; the Maya reinforced them with masonry to create semi-permanent reservoirs.

ahau (pl. **ahauob**) king and chief shaman of a Classic Mayan city state.

alux Mayan leprechaun-type goblin, benign or hostile according to whether offerings are made to them. In colonial times, they were believed to exact revenge on the Spaniards for the old Mayan gods.

batab (pl. **batabob**) Mayan community headman in colonial Yucatán, descended from the pre-Conquest aristocracy.

cenote a cave or sinkhole giving access to water through the dry rock of the Yucatán, or an underground cavern filled with water.

chultún artificial cistern: in Puuc regions and other very dry areas, large pits dug into the ground and lined with pottery, creating giant vats in which rain water was collected to be retained through the dry months.

criollo in colonial and post-independence times, native-born Mexicans and Spanish-Americans of purely Spanish descent.

cruzob the followers of the rebellion of the 'Talking Cross' after the 1840s Caste War.

ejido rural community that owns lands in common, as recognized in the Mexican Constitution after the 1910 Revolution. *Ejido* land can be worked collectively, or as individual plots; areas such as forests are often managed by the community as a whole. Land can only be sold or redistributed by a vote of the whole community, although amendments to the Constitution associated with the NAFTA agreement have now made it much easier to buy and sell *ejido* lands. An *ejidatario* is a member of an *ejido*.

encomienda under early Spanish rule, system by which areas of land and all the people in them were 'entrusted' (*encomendado*) to individual *Conquistadores*, who were theoretically responsible for ensuring that the areas were pacified and their inhabitants instructed in Christianity. In return they could demand labour or tributes from the local Indians, over whom they had almost absolute power. The system was modified from the 1550s, in case the *encomenderos* (holders of *encomiendas*) became so powerful as to challenge royal authority.

henequen type of *agave* cactus native to the Yucatán which, when stripped and carded, is used to make sisal rope.

ladino(s) in the colonial era and first century of independence, words used throughout the Yucatán, Chiapas and Guatemala to denote the Spanish-speaking community (*criollo* or *mestizo*) as opposed to the pure-Indian population. Now rarely heard in the Yucatán peninsula, as the ethnic divide has become far less marked, but retains some of its original force in Chiapas and Guatemala.

mestizo any person of mixed European-indigenous American descent.

milpa small field cleared for farming by slash-and-burn techniques, used for planting maize, in combination with small quantities of squashes, beans, chilis etc.

multepal system of collective leadership seen in Postclassic Mayan communities, with authority shared or rotated between lords.

sahal (pl. **sahalob**) aristocracy of the Classic Mayan cities, subordinate lords to the *ahau* (*see* above).

stela (pl. **stelae**) large, upright carved stones, installed as monuments in the main plazas or in front of major buildings in most Classic Mayan cities. Commonly erected to mark significant events, they have often been the most important 'public record' found in the city of the community's history.

xibalba the Mayan Underworld, one of the three levels of existence with the Earth and the Heavens. The realm of most of the gods with whom the Maya were in regular contact through shamanistic ritual.

Further Reading

Fewer books on Mexico and the Maya are available in Britain than in North America; US editions are now available via the Internet.

The Maya

Coe, Michael D., *The Maya* (Thames & Hudson, 1966–96). A lively general introduction; also *Breaking the Maya Code* (Penguin, 1992). The fascinating story of the development of knowledge of the Maya.

Drew, David, *The Lost Chronicles of the Maya Kings* (Orion, 2000). A very readable, wide-ranging survey of Mayan history.

Gill, Richardson B., *The Great Maya Droughts* (Univ. of New Mexico, 2000). A challenging theory on what happened to the Maya in the 'Great Collapse'.

Houston, S.D., *Reading Maya Glyphs* (Univ. of California (US), British Museum (UK), 1989). A guide to really get to grips with the ruins.

Landa, Diego de, *Yucatán Before and After the Conquest*, trans. and ed. William Gates (Dover, 1978). A translation of Landa's *Relación*, an enormously detailed account of Mayan life as encountered by the Spaniards.

Martin, Simon, and Grube, Nikolai, *Chronicle of the Maya Kings and Queens* (Thames & Hudson, 2000). Wonderfully clear, incisive summary of the current state of knowledge of Mayan history, told city by city.

Miller, Mary Ellen, and Taube, Karl, *An Illustrated Dictionary of the Gods and Symbols of Ancient Mexico and the Maya* (Thames & Hudson, 1993). Enables you to know your God L from the Lords of Night.

Proskouriakoff, Tatiana, *Album of Maya Architecture* (Univ. of Oklahoma, 1977). Superb, detailed reconstruction-drawings of Mayan buildings.

Schele, Linda. The essential texts in bringing together modern knowledge of the Maya for a non-specialist public: only one has been published in Britain: with Miller, Mary Ellen, *Blood of Kings* (1986; Thames & Hudson, 1992). On Mayan art. In the US: with Freidel, David, *Forest of Kings* (William Morrow, 1990). The first reconstruction of Mayan history. With Freidel, David, and Parker, Joy, *Maya Cosmos* (William Morrow, 1993). On religion and belief. With Mathews, Peter, *The Code of Kings* (Touchstone, 1999). A summary of some of Schele's previous work, with fascinating guides to buildings at Palenque, Chichén Itzá and Uxmal.

Schmidt, Peter, De la Garza, Mercedes, and Nalda, Enrique, ed., *Maya Civilization* (Thames & Hudson, 1998). A very bulky, encyclopaedic, illustrated overview of every aspect of the Maya, by international writers.

Tedlock, Dennis, trans., *Popol Vuh* (Touchstone, 1996). The best English version of the central book of Mayan mythology.

Post-Conquest History and Culture

Benjamin, Thomas, *A Rich Land, A Poor People* (Univ. of New Mexico, 1996). The history of Chiapas since the 19th century.

Clendinnen, Inga, *Maya and Spaniard in Yucatán, 1517–70* (Cambridge UP, 1989). A complete account of the Yucatán Conquest.

Collier, George A., ed., *Basta! Land and the Zapatista Rebellion in Chiapas* (Food First, 1994). Informative collection of essays.

Díaz, Bernal, *The Conquest of New Spain* (Penguin, 1963). The most extraordinary of soldier's tales.

Farriss, Nancy M., *Maya Society under Colonial Rule* (Princeton, 1984). Mayan survival.

Krauze, Enrique, *Mexico: A Biography of Power*, trans. H. Heifetz (Harper Collins, 1997). An acute history of Mexico since independence.

Marcos, *Shadows of Tender Fury: The Letters and Communiqués of Subcomandante Marcos and the Zapatista Army of National Liberation* (Monthly Review Press, 1995). The man speaks.

Oppenheimer, Andrés, *Bordering on Chaos* (Little, Brown & Co., 1996). Mexico's 1990's crisis: unmissable on the realities of power, given to stereotypes on the Zapatistas.

Paz, Octavio, *The Labyrinth of Solitude*, trans. L. Kemp (Grove Press in US; Penguin in UK). The essential book on modern Mexico; read it after you've been there for at least a week.

Reed, Nelson, *The Caste War of Yucatán* (Stanford, 1986). Classic, readable narrative of the Yucatán's extraordinary conflagration.

Thomas, Hugh, *The Conquest of Mexico* (Pimlico, 1996). A complete overview.

Wells, Allen, *Yucatán's Gilded Age* (Univ. of New Mexico, 1985). The extravagant and ambitious Yucatán of the *henequen* boom.

Womack, John, Jr., *Zapata and the Mexican Revolution* (Random House, 1970). Fully informs you just who and what Zapata was.

The Modern Maya

Bruce, Robert D., and Perera, Victor, *The Last Lords of Palenque: The Lacandón Mayas of the Mexican Rain Forest* (Univ. of California, 1982). A detailed report of Lacandón life.

Everton, MacDuff, *The Modern Maya: A Culture in Transition* (Univ. of New Mexico, 1991). Perceptive, quirky account of the Yucatán as it meets tourism, with superb photographs.

Foxx, Jeffrey, *The Maya Textile Tradition* (Harry N. Abrams, 1997). Wonderfully illustrated.

Laughlin, Robert M. and Karasik, Carol, eds., *Mayan Tales from Zinacantán* (Smithsonian Institution, 1996). Delightful collection of mythology, dreams and folk tales.

Morris, Walter F., Jr, *Living Maya* (Harry N. Abrams, 1987). Beautifully illustrated account of the life of the Highland Maya.

Sullivan, Paul, *Unfinished Conversations: Mayas and Foreigners Between Two Wars* (Alfred A. Knopf, 1989). Based on time spent with the Santa Cruz Maya of Quintana Roo.

Travels

Canby, Peter, *The Heart of the Sky: Travels Among the Maya* (Kodansha, 1994). Fine book of encounters with the modern Maya.

Greene, Graham, *The Lawless Roads* (US title: *Another Country*, Penguin). For his fans only, written from a position of near-complete ignorance of the country.

Stephens, John L., with illustrations by Frederick Catherwood, *Incidents of Travel in Central America, Chiapas and Yucatán* and *Incidents of Travel in Yucatán* (Dover, 1969). Always enjoyable and still informative.

Tree, Isabella, *Sliced Iguana: Travels in Unknown Mexico* (Hamish Hamilton, 2001). Captures a lot of the downright crankiness of modern Mexico, with style and humour.

Wright, Ronald, *Time Among the Maya* (Weidenfeld & Nicholson, 1989). A journey through all the Mayan countries, written in the mid-1980s, but still highly perceptive.

Fiction

Castellanos, Rosario, *Nine Guardians* (Readers International, 1992). A translation of *Balún Canán*, by Chiapas' foremost modern writer (1925–74), on the intertwined worlds of *Ladino* and Indian as seen by a child in the 1930s. Also *City of Kings* (Latin American Review Press, 1993); *Ciudad Real*, a collection of stories about San Cristóbal; *Another Way to Be: Selected Works of Rosario Castellanos*, ed. Myralyn Allgood (Univ. of Georgia, 1990).

Greene, Graham, *The Power and the Glory* (Penguin). Some say this book is about Mexico, but it's really about GG's obsessions.

Birds and Wildlife

Useful, well-illustrated field guides include:

Howell, Steven N.G., and Webb, Sophie A., *Guide to the Birds of Mexico and Northern Central America* (Oxford UP, 1996).

Howell, Steven N.G, *A Bird Finding Guide to Mexico* (Cornell University Press, 1999). Focussing on the best spots to see rare birds.

Reid, Fiona A., *A Field Guide to the Mammals of Central America and Southeast Mexico* (Oxford University Press, 1998). Excellent and finely illustrated.

Food and Drink

Coe, Sophie D., *America's First Cuisines* (Univ. of Texas, 1994). Fascinating study into the diet of Pre-Hispanic Mesoamerica; equally good is *The True History of Chocolate* (Thames & Hudson, 1996), with Prof. Michael Coe.

Wisniewski, Ian, *Classic Tequila* (Prion Books, 1998). History, folklore, the best labels....

Martin, Lyman, and Rosario, George, *Yucatán Cookbook: Recipes and Tales* (Red Crane Books, 1996). Bright and usable cookbook.

Nigh, Kippy, *A Taste of Mexico: Vegetarian Cuisine* (Book Publishing Co., 1996). Nigh's vegetarianized Mexican dishes are based on many years of living in the country.

Index

Main page references are in **bold**. Page references to maps are in *italics*.

Acknowledgements

Nick Rider

Putting together a book like this is only possible thanks to the kindness, interest and help along the way of a whole raft of people, and I have to apologize first of all if for reasons purely of space I can only mention some of them here. My warmest thanks and *más sincero agradecimiento* are due to: Manuel Díaz Cebrián and Lupita Ayala at the Mexican Tourist Office in London, Philip Hamilton-Grierson at Cox & Kings Travel, and Cathy Matos and Joanne Matos at Cathy Matos Mexican Tours; in Cancún, to Angélica Delgado of Aerocaribe, the staff of the Quintana Roo state tourism department, Catalina Prince and Gabriela Pardo at Amigos de Sian Ka'an, and Juan Zetina, EasyWay car rental; in Mérida, to Ana Argaez and Lic. Saúl Ancona at the Yucatán state tourist office, Lic. José Antonio Ruíz Silva at the Yucatán state ecology department, Antropólogo Elías Alcocer and Francisco Kantún of the Fundación Cultural Yucatán and the members of the Yaxuná cooperative, Maricela Castro of GHM Hotels, Nelson and Nicole at the Hotel MedioMundo, and Pablo da Costa at Casa San Juan; to Aníbal González and Mónica Hernández at Hacienda Katanchel; Don Jacinto Pool in Tinúm; to all at Rancho Libertad in Puerto Morelos; in Playa del Carmen, to Ricco at Mom's, and Patrick and Catherine; in Akumal, to Nancy de Rosa at Aquatech-Villas de Rosa; and in Tulum, especially, to John Kavanagh at the Weary Traveler. In Xcalak, to Robert Schneider and Margo Reheis at Villas Sin Duda; in Campeche, to CP Ricardo Rodríguez Dives, State Secretary of Tourism, and to Rick Bertram and Diane Lalonde at Chicanná; in Tabasco, to Lic. Claudia Castillo, Instituto de Turismo; and in Chiapas, to Marco Antonio Morales, Viajes Shivalva, Palenque, Glen Wersh and Ellen Jones at Rancho Esmeralda in Ocosingo, Rodulfo Castillejos, Budget Rentacar, Alex and Raúl and Carlota Duarte, Chiapas Photography Project, all in San Cristóbal, and Claudia Vírgen and Sonja Bartelt of the RARE Center for Tropical Conservation and Reserva El Triunfo in Tuxtla Gutiérrez. And very special thanks and *abrazos* go to Denis Lafoy, the Alonzo family at Mexico Rentacar, and Madeline Parmet at Luz en Yucatán in Mérida.

At Cadogan Guides I want to thank most of all Vicki Ingle for all the support she has given to myself and this guide, and Justine Montgomery for editing the book with dedication and great patience, and ploughing on through it despite all interruptions and difficult situations. And thanks of all sorts to Ethel, for putting up with it for months at a time too, and for sharing in appreciating pelicans in Puerto Morelos and the Laguna Bacalar.

Cadogan Guides

We would like to thank Thames & Hudson for permission to reproduce the Mayan glyphs on p.52, taken from Michael D. Coe's *The Maya*.

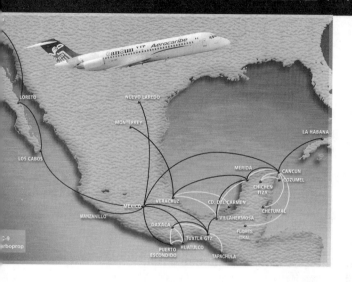